Culturally Alert
COUNSELING

To the survivors of Black 47 and their progeny.
May they remember the work of healing.

Culturally Alert COUNSELING

A Comprehensive Introduction

GARRETT McAULIFFE
& ASSOCIATES

SAGE Publications
Los Angeles • London • New Delhi • Singapore

For information:

Sage Publications, Inc.
2455 Teller Road
Thousand Oaks, California 91320
E-mail: order@sagepub.com

Sage Publications India Pvt. Ltd.
B 1/I 1 Mohan Cooperative Industrial Area
Mathura Road, New Delhi 110 044
India

Sage Publications Ltd.
1 Oliver's Yard
55 City Road
London EC1Y 1SP
United Kingdom

Sage Publications Asia-Pacific Pte. Ltd.
33 Pekin Street #02-01
Far East Square
Singapore 048763

Printed in the United States of America

Library of Congress Cataloging-in-Publication Data

Culturally alert counseling : a comprehensive introduction/[edited by] Garrett McAuliffe.
   p. cm.
Includes bibliographical references and index.
ISBN 978-1-4129-1006-4 (pbk.)
  1. Cross-cultural counseling. I. McAuliffe, Garrett.

BF636.7.C76C853 2008
158'3—dc22   2006103539

This book is printed on acid-free paper.

09 10 11 10 9 8 7 6 5 4 3 2

Acquiring Editors:	Kassie Graves, Art Pomponio
Associate Editor:	Elise Smith
Editorial Assistant:	Veronica K. Novak
Developmental Editor:	Sabra Ledent
Copy Editor:	Diana Breti
Typesetter:	C&M Digitals (P) Ltd.
Proofreader:	Kristin Bergstad
Indexer:	Jeanne Busemeyer
Cover Designer:	Janet Foulger

Contents

PART III. SOCIAL GROUPS

Preface

Culturally alert counseling is a moral enterprise. It is an effort at *tikkun olam,* a Hebrew word that refers to renewing or repairing the world. Culturally alert counseling is an attempt to include all other human beings in the great work of helping and healing, with no exceptions. Counselors cannot, in conscience, leave anyone out. That has not been easy for human beings over the centuries. Class, race, gender, sexual orientation, ability, ethnicity, and religion have been used as dividers. Counselors, above all professionals, are asked to look into those great divides, to see themselves in others, to see others in others, to know the rich differences among mixed-up human beings, and to relish the great similarities. The philosopher Richard Rorty explains this obligation as

> reminding ourselves to keep trying to expand our sense of "us" as far as we can . . . [to include] the family in the next cave, then of the tribe across the river, then of the tribal confederation beyond the mountains, then of the unbelievers beyond the seas (and, perhaps last of all, . . . the menials who, all this time, have been doing our dirty work). This is a process that we should try to keep going. We should stay on the lookout for marginalized people—people who we still instinctively think of as "they" rather than "us."

Rorty asks us to stretch our vision. To know others as they are, by knowing them well, is our obligation as counselors. And that is a central purpose of this book.

Four Guiding Dimensions Behind the Book

This book is a beginning text for emerging counselors and psychotherapists of all kinds. It has been written with four guidelines in mind. The writers hope that these dimensions make this book both useful and moving. They are *depth, breadth, readability,* and *applicability.*

Depth refers to two levels. First is the personal conceptual depth, or framework, that is presented in the notion of constructivism. Constructivism is here defined as the simple idea that each human being makes meanings in her or his own culturally influenced way. Constructivism reminds counselors to be humble, to realize that they are always making sense, and to take responsibility for the sense that they are making. To aid in that sense-making, further conceptual frameworks are provided in this book for the journey. In the first two chapters, the notions of critical consciousness, ethno- or culture-centrism, privilege, social stratification, pluralism, dominance and nondominance, and oppression are examined in hopes that they might guide the reader through the remaining chapters.

The second dimension of depth is found in the content of chapters on ethnic and social groups in this book. Chapter authors who are known experts in each culture or topic were recruited to pen the particulars. Those chapters are, therefore, characterized by accurate and meaningful insights into the human conditions of each cultural group.

Breadth is the second of the four major impulses that led to this book. The notion of culture can be writ large, and it is here. Thus, culture no longer refers only to race or ethnicity. Our worlds are also culturally constructed through the lenses of social class, gender, sexual orientation, and religion. This book, therefore, honors those topics with corresponding chapters.

Readability is the third major impulse that led to the writing of this book. Much textbook and academic writing on culture and counseling suffers from the malady of academic prose: It is overly abstract, insufficiently illustrative, and often wooden. To remedy this problem, the editor selected writers who could bring out the power of this material in vital, rich ways. Thus, the text is littered with vignettes, anecdotes, figures, and exercises that make the concepts come alive. We have tried to make the writing clear and accessible.

Finally, *applicability* guided the writing of the book. The book presents actual skills to be used in culturally alert counseling. Counselors are practical people; they must act. Multicultural counseling skills have not been very fully articulated until now. This book tries to stretch that boundary by presenting explicit sets of counseling skills that might be used with culture in mind. The final chapter, and the accompanying DVD, sum up the current knowledge of multicultural counseling skills so that readers might practice right away in a culturally alert way.

Outline of the Book

The book begins with the more tender topic of you—the cultural being that you, the reader, are. You are asked to know yourself better, in order to know others. At the end of the first chapter, you will perhaps be less likely to project your cultural assumptions onto others; you will be more likely to listen and wait. Then Chapter 2 launches into the topic of human equality, with a description of social stratifications and how to challenge those that are harmful.

The journey then leads in Chapters 3 and 4 to an explanation of ethnicity and race—a topic that includes all readers. No one is left out of this book, whether she or he is in a dominant/majority group or in a less-powerful minority. The following seven chapters (Chapters 5 through 11) describe specific ethnic groupings. In those pages, readers will come to better know both themselves and others. Next, in Chapters 12 through 15, are readings and activities devoted to exploring the wide worlds of social class, gender, sexual orientation, and religion. The book ends with a depiction of the key skills for doing culturally alert counseling. That topic has been scarce in the counseling literature, and Chapter 16 is an attempt to remedy that omission. With exposure to actual counseling skills, readers will be better equipped to apply the understandings that they have learned and try them out in solidarity with those now-familiar others.

The Challenge to Counselors

But why is there a book on culturally alert counseling at all? The work of counseling is like almost no other work. It is difficult. Complex. Personally challenging. Ambiguous. Emotional. Concrete. Abstract. It takes a particular kind of person to encounter other human beings in their uncertainty and pain, to hold them, and to journey with them on the bumpy road to becoming more fully human. As my brother says, "How can you do this work? Isn't it too hard? You have to be so engaged all the time." To each her or his own, said the philosopher. Those of you who have chosen to accompany other human beings through their doubts and discoveries must, therefore, be prepared. There is much to learn and try, and try again, and learn.

It used to be simpler. Counselors worked with the supposedly autonomous individual to "cure" her or him. Now we have acknowledged the inextricable cultural dimension in the life of the individual. Counselors have to acknowledge that, metaphorically speaking, there are hundreds of people in the room with the individual client or family, to paraphrase Paul Pedersen. Clients bring with them ancestors, parents, religious teachers, ethnic models, and neighborhood friends. There are films seen and lyrics heard. There are the aunts and uncles of childhood, the siblings of yesterday and today, the weddings, the memorial services, the dinner table conversation. All are represented in clients' memories, in their strivings, their manners, and in their morals. All sit with the client before you. Thus, the work of counseling is now made larger by our recognition of these "people in the room."

It is not the purpose of the multicultural counseling movement to unnecessarily daunt the novice counselor. The field did slog on for many years without a full appreciation of these silent, and noisy, presences in clients' lives. But there was a cost. Minority group members and poor folks didn't seek counseling, or dropped out early, when the field was seen as a white middle-class endeavor. I know this fact personally—no working-class Irish kid from Queens had access to counseling, or would go for it, even if he were lost, anxious, scared, confused, or addicted. And we were all of those. The community didn't support emotional exploration, or vulnerability. The working-class environment didn't often value probing for personal meanings and seeking right relations with others. But to counseling I did go—only after it seemed acceptable to tell all to a stranger. But we feared that these therapists wouldn't understand our ethnic group, our religion. And sometimes they didn't. Therapists of the time rejected religion as superstition but prayed to the god of analysis and insight. They didn't know that they were engaged in a great privileged enterprise of trying to heal the white upper middle class. Counseling must now be bigger than that. It must embrace the complexity that culture brings. That is the only way to do this good work. With the inclusion of culture in the work of counseling, we extend the possibility of human solidarity that we so long for.

Part I

Introduction

1

What Is Culturally Alert Counseling?

Garrett McAuliffe

Nothing human is alien to me.

—The Roman writer Terence

[My book] celebrates hybridity, impurity, intermingling, the transformation that comes of new and unexpected combinations of human beings, cultures, ideas, politics, movies, songs. It rejoices in mongrelization and fears the absolutism of the Pure. Mélange, hotch-potch, a bit of this and a bit of that is how newness enters the world. It is the great possibility that mass migration gives to the world, and I have tried to embrace it. [My book] is a love-song to our mongrel selves. Throughout human history, the apostles of purity, those who have claimed to possess a total explanation, have wrought havoc among mere mixed-up human beings. Like many millions of people, I am a bastard child of history. Perhaps we all are, black and brown and white, leaking into one another, . . . like flavors when you cook.

—Salman Rushdie on his novel
The Satanic Verses (Rushdie, 1992, p. 394)

The work of counseling is a hopeful, and a moral, enterprise. Through counseling, the disempowered find strength and resources. Counseling is an antidote to cynicism. Counselors embrace a world of possibility, as difficult as that may be at times. Clients come to counselors wounded by the slings and arrows of living. Some of those wounds are created by other humans, humans who find "the other" to be distasteful, foreign, dismissible. Some humans say, "After all, they are 'not like us,' and we cannot understand them because they are . . . gay, black, disabled, Jewish, Christian, poor, white, rich, Asian, Mexican, female, Arab, atheist, or Anglo." And the list goes on. Counselors imagine a world in which there are fewer such wounds. Counselors embrace a moral vision of human solidarity; they commit themselves to principles that go beyond any particular group or place. Counselors cherish the "unexpected combinations of human beings," to quote Salman Rushdie, that is the world and always has been. Those combinations include the Latino migrant worker in Wisconsin, the African American father in Oregon, the gay adolescent in Alabama, the Muslim immigrant in Michigan, the evangelical Christian in Texas, and the white Southerner in South Carolina. And those are but a few descriptors for a kaleidoscope of human diversity. They are not "pure" categories; each individual carries her or his own combinations of cultures with her or him, based on unique experiences and individual temperament. So the reader is welcomed to a world of "mélange" and "hotch-potch," a world in which her or his own point of view must be continually extended as "newness" enters. This book is a "love song to our mongrel selves." The following vignettes will demonstrate the themes and movements of that song. It is a song that the reader must learn to sing, sometimes while improvising, but always with great heart.

The counselor is a middle-aged American white male of second-generation Irish ancestry who was raised Catholic in a working- to lower-middle-class neighborhood in New York City. He is middle class and heterosexual. His client is a 53-year-old New York City fire captain who is also Irish and Catholic.

The counselor and his client probably share many cultural similarities, such as a tendency to suppress negative feelings, especially sadness and pain; appreciation of having fun with groups of people (called "good craic," pronounced "crack" in Irish); an inclination to drink alcohol liberally at social gatherings; enthusiasm for a good song or a sentimental occasion; appreciation of "the talk" as a means of elaborating on experience; a predisposition to indirectness in expressing feelings; and the use of humor, especially sarcasm ("slagging"), as a substitute for intimacy. The counselor may, therefore, make some assumptions about his client without asking. Although the counselor will need to confirm these hunches, they will give him a head start in probing his client's worldview.

Yet the counselor and client, for all their similarities, may not see the world through the same eyes. In each of the following areas, counselor and client differ: When discussing his marital difficulties, the client cannot conceive of divorce. He does not expect his wife to be interested in sex. He does not like to show his feelings or even tell them to anyone. He hides physical discomforts, even from himself. He believes that drinking to excess is an acceptable social practice. He considers his age to be "old," and therefore he engages in no physical exercise. He is uncomfortable with "darker people," as he calls them, and considers immigrants to be ruining the city he loves. He belongs to Irish organizations and trumpets Irish accomplishments whenever he can. Finally, he is very anti-gay and says that homosexuality is unnatural and forbidden by his church. Each of these views contrasts significantly with the counselor's perspectives because the counselor has questioned the inherited norms of his ethnic culture and attempted to construct a more multicultural set of values.

---◆---

A Korean couple and their 15-year-old son come into the public school counseling office unannounced one morning as the children are arriving at school. These recent arrivals to this rural community moved from a major city in another state for a job opportunity. Their son has been in the school for two months and seems morose, commenting that he has no friends among the largely Anglo-American student body.

The school counselor, who is a heterosexual European American, immediately begins making empathic responses to their concerns, mixed with exploratory open questions about their feelings and what the situation means to them. The counselor probes how the parents are feeling about the move and about leaving their homeland. The parents respond with few words and many silences.

The counselor then tells them that she would like to meet with their son alone in order to understand his perspective more clearly. She has been taught to encourage students to think for themselves and to express their views in these situations. After hearing the son describe his hesitance at engaging other students in conversation and banter, or about joining any student organization, the counselor calls the parents back into the room.

She then suggests that the parents teach their son assertive behavior and that the family members practice direct communication of needs and requests at home so that the son will learn how to have his needs met. She teaches them basic assertiveness principles about believing in one's individual rights, making eye contact, having a firm vocal tone, and clearly stating one's needs without necessarily apologizing or empathizing with others' situations. She further directs them to keep a daily record of successful assertive exchanges. The counselor hopes that this will help their son, and them, adjust to life in this new area. She asks them to come back the following week at 9 A.M. to tell her how it has worked. However, the parents do not show up. Furthermore, they take their child out of the public school the week after and send him to a nearby religious private school.

As demonstrated by the first vignette, culture pervades all counseling exchanges. Even though they share the same ethnic culture, gender, social class, sexual orientation, and religion-of-origin in name, the counselor and his client are having a cross-cultural encounter because their experiences of those cultures differ significantly. The counselor and client have been enculturated into the same Irish Catholic ethnic group, but each has a different relationship to that culture. There is clearly more to culturally alert counseling than meets the eye.

The second vignette also demonstrates the complexity of culturally alert counseling because the counselor's presumption of Western communication styles and individualism resulted in the clients not returning. Here the culture clash was more obvious—an individualistic, direct European American style encountering (unsuccessfully) a collectivist Asian tradition. The counselor lost the clients by promoting an individual, rights-oriented, confrontational communication style that is better suited to the European American notion of assertiveness. The Korean clients instead saw their primary allegiance to the group, namely the family and the community. The counselor expressed no knowledge of Korean culture. That is unfortunate because such knowledge might have engendered trust. In addition, the counselor did not acknowledge the family's cultural isolation and failed to connect the clients with Korean persons and resources in the community. Finally, she did not acknowledge the social prejudice that is likely adding to some of the isolation and feelings of displacement.

In these two examples, the themes that will permeate this book emerge. A primary theme is that all counseling encounters are multicultural, in that the cultures of gender, ethnicity, race, sexual orientation, religion, and social class are always present. In the two vignettes, each of the following important counseling-related themes are embedded: attitudes toward health maintenance, sexuality, alcohol use, expectations of intimacy with a life partner, socialized gender roles, the valuing of emotional expressiveness versus emotional control, the level of acculturation to a dominant culture, ethnic identity, and being in a nondominant culture versus a more privileged one. And these are only two vignettes. The contemporary counselor is likely to be confronted with many more culturally saturated situations, for culture is everywhere in each human being's life. Culturally alert counseling is therefore defined as *a consistent readiness to identify the cultural dimensions of clients' lives and a subsequent integration of culture into counseling work.*

This chapter establishes a foundation for culturally alert counseling by responding to two of the three fundamental questions that must be asked of culturally alert counseling. First, the question, "Why are culture and culturally alert counseling important?" is examined. The second question discussed is, "What is culture and culturally alert counseling?" The third and most critical question, namely, "How does one actually do culturally alert counseling?" will be addressed in subsequent chapters, especially in Chapter 16.

This chapter is divided into five major sections. It begins with the aforementioned "Why" and "What" segments, followed by a section on other important concepts for understanding culture. The fourth major section presents factors affecting the relationship between individuals and their cultures. The chapter then ends with a description of the competencies required for becoming a culturally alert counselor and concluding thoughts. Thus this is a stage-setting chapter, one that provides foundational concepts for the rest of the book.

The "Why" of Culturally Alert Counseling

All counseling can be seen as multicultural counseling. Individuals see the world, and are seen, through lenses of ethnicity, race, social class, gender, sexual orientation, and religion. Thus, connecting culture with counseling should be nothing new. Nevertheless, until relatively recently, little attention has been paid to culture by mental health professionals.

One argument for culturally alert counseling is the inevitability of cross-cultural contact. More than ever before, people encounter cultural diversity daily, in their schools and neighborhoods and through media. Robert Kegan (1994) iterates this sea-change in world culture with this statement:

> If indeed we could sustain a life in which we would only meet people from our own culture and never have a thing to do, directly or indirectly, with people from other cultures, we might need to learn only the rules of our own culture and adhere to them. But such a world is rapidly disappearing if not already gone. Diversity of cultural experience may once have been the province of the adventurous, the open-minded, and those too poor to live where they wished. Tomorrow it will be the province of all. (p. 208)

That sea-change in diversity translates into counseling practice. If there were universal solutions for all populations, then culture wouldn't matter. But these words from sociologists Carol Aneshensel and Jo Phelan (1999) belie the universalist position:

> There are pronounced group differences in the course and consequences of mental illness, . . . differences that . . . point to the . . . powerful influence of the social factors that differentiate one group from another. The impact of gender, race, age, and socioeconomic status are apparent at virtually every juncture. (p. xii)

So universalist approaches to counseling are not so universal, it seems.

A second argument for culturally alert counseling concerns equity and inclusiveness. The counseling field is dedicated to equity, that is, access for all people to the things that matter in society, like good education and jobs (see Chapter 2 for a discussion of this topic). And inclusiveness is closely related to equity. In the past, that has not been the case. Counseling theory and practice have been laden with cultural bias, despite their being considered universal. The cultural bias was due to the largely heterosexual, male, middle-class, European, and European American perspectives. The values, and valuing, of those cultures are exemplified by the infusion into counseling of such Western cultural notions as self-actualization, identity, Choice Theory, and autonomy.

While these towering ideas have produced much good for some, reducing human suffering and increasing human potential, they have left others out. Stanley Sue and Amy Lam (2002) note the inequality in mental health assessment and the provision of services:

Women, ethnic minorities, gay/lesbian/bisexuals, and individuals from lower social classes . . . have been subjected to detrimental stereotypes, have not been targeted for much psychological research, and are often underserved or inappropriately served in the mental health system. . . . There is an increasing urgency to provide effective treatment to these groups, as reflected in the "cultural competency" movement, which tries to identify the cultural knowledge, skills, and awareness that permit one to effectively work with clients from diverse populations. (p. 401)

Examples of being "inappropriately served" include the following: Lesbians and gay men were treated as maladjusted. Women were seen as overly dependent and emotional and were encouraged to follow limiting life paths. Many persons of color were ignored; they, in turn, viewed counseling with suspicion. Counseling was always, in fact, "cultured," but it was dominated by one set of cultures.

That dominant-group bias is no longer acceptable. Nondominant groups of people have asserted their rights to be heard and to be dealt with. There is no going back to the previously mentioned "bad old days" of white, male, middle-class hegemony over cultural norms, values, and assumptions. "We are everywhere" is the refrain of formerly silent and voiceless minorities.

Here are some of the facts about diversity and culture in the United States (Sue & Sue, 2003):

- Students of color make up 45 percent of public school students in the United States.

- Seventy-five percent of people entering the United States labor force are women and racial/ethnic minorities.

- Gay, lesbian, and bisexual persons make up at least 7 percent of the population and seek out counselors at high rates.

- Men's and women's roles have become unclear for many, leading to distress over family and career commitments.

- Religion is a central enterprise for 70 percent of the United States population, and 90 percent of the population believes in God.

- Asians are the largest recent immigrant group to the United States and constitute 30 percent of new immigrants.

- Latinos have become the largest "mega-minority" in the United States.

- African Americans continue to experience segregation and bias in housing and jobs, and their poverty rate is double that of European Americans, despite significant economic gains over the past 30 years.

These facts matter for two reasons. The first is *ethical responsibility*. It is the ethical responsibility of counselors to respond to all segments of the larger community, not just to individuals. Therefore, counselors must ask themselves,

"Whom are we serving?" "Are we part of the problem of, or the solution to, social inequity?" "How are we acting to change the conditions that lead some people to have fewer obstacles while others must scramble through the thicket of hidden and overt bias, limited opportunities, and legacies of deficit?"

The second reason for the urgency of culturally alert counseling is *professional self-interest.* If counselors are not convinced of its importance, their credibility will be challenged by both clients and employers (Sue & Sue, 2003). Clients will ask, "Can you be trusted to help me?" A counselor's livelihood may depend on the answer. For example, counselors who adhere to an insight-oriented practice may lose clients from cultural groups who eschew public emotional expression and expect direct problem-solving action for life concerns. Such can be the case for many people from so-called collectivist cultures, such as traditional American Indian and East Asian cultures, where individual emotions are often considered secondary to group welfare.

This section on the "Why" of culturally alert counseling should end with a reminder: All counselors and clients are cultured. Even in a world of cultural equity, people would need to know how they are constructed through their cultures in order to make choices about their lives. Therefore, culturally alert counseling is for all people, not just members of nondominant groups.

The "What" of Culture and Culturally Alert Counseling: Key Notions

In order to present the foundational notions that pervade all chapters in this book, this section explores the key notions of culture and diversity. First, definitions are provided. Then, qualifiers and related concepts are discussed, including such topics as overgeneralizing and stereotyping and the use of various terms for cultural groups.

DEFINING CULTURE

Culture is defined here as the attitudes, habits, norms, beliefs, customs, rituals, styles, and artifacts that express a group's adaptation to its environment— that is, ways that are shared by group members and passed on over time. Especially important for counseling, of course, are the internalized dimensions of culture represented by "attitudes, habits, norms, and beliefs" in the above definition. Those internalized assumptions can drive clients' expectations about relationships, their career aspirations, and their self-esteem, to name just a few impacts of internalized culture.

Culturally saturated situations that counselors might encounter include the following. In each case, the counselor needs to be mindful of culture and bring it into the work.

- A middle-class African American teacher is uncertain about how to be "herself" in the largely European American school in which she teaches.

- A man is so bottled up emotionally that he drinks, broods, and isolates himself because he doesn't feel able, as a male, to ask for help or to show sadness.

- A working-class 20-year-old woman can't imagine pursuing a medical career because she just "doesn't know where to start" and can't imagine delaying paid work for school, plus she doesn't know where the money would come from for her training anyway.

- A Chinese American daughter of immigrants cannot figure out how to combine family loyalty and her desire to move across the country on her own to try an acting career.

- A gay 16-year-old boy is infatuated with another boy in the high school but is terrified of being found out.

- A Southern Anglo American woman would like to express her negative feelings directly but has learned "proper manners" so well that she finds herself being angry at herself for not saying what she feels.

In each of these cases, culture can be both an opportunity and a barrier. Either way, culture is a consistent presence in the counseling room (see Activity 1.1).

Culture: Pervasive and Invisible

Culture is so pervasive in people's lives that it can be likened to the water that surrounds a fish or the air that humans breathe—in other words, an ambient element outside of their consciousness. That pervasive invisibility is a danger to clients' well-being. Much of what individuals assume to be individual "choice" is instead culturally constructed and automatic. This invisibility can lead to ignorance of how saturated culture is in a society. For example, what were once seemingly universal standards in American life are now seen as often culturally white, male, European American, middle-class, Christian, and heterosexual. With cultural awareness, such standards can be seen instead as the adaptations of some groups to their historical environments.

This monolith has been toppled by other communities in U.S. society clamoring to be recognized. However, U.S. society never was monolithic because the nation has always been culturally diverse, to a great extent. Women, gay people, non-Christians, Africans, Asians, American Indians, non-English-speaking people, poor persons, and individuals with disabilities have always been a part of American life (Takaki, 1993; Zinn, 1999). However, they are no longer background to the dominant culture but are, more and more, foreground on the American cultural landscape in numbers and in public voice.

ACTIVITY 1.1

The Personal Experience of Culture

Think of a recent time when your ethnicity, race, social class, gender, sexual orientation, or religion affected any of the following:

A relationship with a parent

A relationship with a partner

A career or work decision or aspiration

Your sense of opportunities or of limitations

Your self-esteem

Now describe the situation and how the cultural dimension affected it:

Culture as Discourse

Another way to describe the pervasiveness of culture and its importance is to understand culture as an expression of a "discourse." *Discourse* is a general term for a system of thought, a network of historically, socially, and institutionally held beliefs, categories, statements, and terms that give meaning to the world. The term *discourse* comes from linguistics, where it refers to the connection between sentences and their social context. To understand discourse as it relates to culture, it may be helpful to keep in mind that every sentence a person utters reflects her or his historical, social, and institutional context, from the words themselves, which are part of a language, to the ideas, which are a product of a time and place. A discourse is like the lenses in a pair of glasses. People actually wear many "discourse lenses." These lenses reflect the various cultural groups to which they belong.

A person is always living within many discourses. That fact limits the meanings that can be made at any one time because any particular discourse differentiates that meaning from other ways of understanding the world. Thus, if a counselor speaks from her own gender discourses, she might be excluding more male ways of knowing and being. "Cultures" are groups of people who share particular discourses. Any one individual is influenced by many discourses. A person's gender, ethnicity, and religious expression, for example, inform or provide a basis for the way she or he views issues, situations, and people; they affect how individuals think and act. Each of these discourses sets the foundation for the argument that one might make about what is important in life.

A person can be aware of the discourses from which she or he is speaking or acting, or not. One of the aims of this book is to help counselors become aware of how their discourses are influenced by the groups to which they belong, that is, to know the discourses through which they are thinking and acting. It might be some combination of their middle-class discourse, their social justice discourse, their conservative discourse, their feminist discourse, and their traditional religion discourse. By being alert to the discourse that is informing their thinking, counselors can see their "truths" as perspectives, not monopolies on the one "true" way that one can view an issue. Discourse alertness will open counselors' eyes to seeing additional perspectives, informed by the cultural affiliations of others who also seek to understand and to share their truths (see Activity 1.2).

History of the Term *Culture*

Culture is an often-used, yet elusive, term. The earliest known use of the word referred to care for the earth (e.g., "culturing the soil") so that it would produce. The extension of the term to human customs is credited to the Roman writer and orator Cicero, who wrote of the "culture of the soul," that is, taking care to live well in general. Thus, culture came to refer to the human creation of ways to live better through establishing social norms, roles, and customs.

Through the years, culture became associated with the notion of "civilization" itself, until in 1871 Edward Tylor, one of the great early anthropologists, offered an inclusive definition of the term: the "capabilities and habits acquired by [a person] as a member of society" (Tylor, 1871/1924, p. 1). For Tylor, "knowledge, belief, arts, morals, law, and customs" were expressions of culture. The definition given earlier in this chapter is parallel to Tylor's concept of culture. Each makes reference to the human creation of ways of living well in community. Those means include rituals, languages, celebrations, and hierarchies in relationships.

Culture Broadly Applied

The notion of culture, in this book, is used broadly. It includes national, regional, generational, and organizational customs, expressions, and values. It also refers to social groups that are identified by race, ethnicity, gender, class, sexual orientation, and religion. Note that the concept of culture here is not restricted to the traditional anthropological usage, in which culture is equivalent only to ethnicity. Culture in this broad sense can be translated into such notions as "youth culture," "disability culture," "school culture," "male culture," "gay culture," "working-class culture," and "agency culture." In each case, culture refers to how a group creates artifacts, behaviors, and values in order to adapt to circumstances, to survive, and to live well. The resulting particular expressions of culture, such as accents, dialects, rituals, expressions, and family structures, are human ways of coping, each deserving consideration and respect.

ACTIVITY 1.2

Introductory Cultural Self-Awareness

Activity 1.2 begins your exploration of the realm of culture by asking you to define your current understanding of your own cultures.

Description of Activity

   This introductory Activity has two Parts. You will respond to each cultural group in terms of two notions: name of group(s) and general status of group(s). After you put your responses in the boxes, write your thoughts about doing each Part on the second page of this Activity, in the spaces provided, or as otherwise directed by your instructor.

   First, complete Part 1 on the following "Cultural Group Memberships Worksheet" by naming the cultural groups that you belong to, across six categories. Then write down your thoughts on doing this Part.

Cultural Group Memberships Worksheet

Directions for Part 1: *Below are five cultural categories. As you consider each of the categories in the far left column, name your own particular group identity in the second column, under "Part 1." Use whatever label makes sense to you. Do Part 1 first and then read the directions for Part 2, below. (Note: You may be asked to share as many of these as you are comfortable with.)*

Cultural Group Categories	Part 1: NAMES	Part 2: STATUS
Ethnicity **Race**	**A name for your current group membership(s)**	**Whether this group is generally dominant or nondominant in many contexts**
Social class or SES (e.g., upper middle class, poor, working class)	**Of origin:** **Current:**	
Gender **Sexual Orientation** **Religion**	**Of origin:** **Current:**	

Comments on Part 1: What thoughts came to you as you tried to name your cultural groups?

Directions for Part 2: *When directed, note in the next column on the Worksheet whether you see each of your groups as "dominant" (e.g., generally in a position of greater power and/or favor at the current time and place) or "nondominant" (a group whose access to significant social power is generally limited or denied) in most contexts (e.g., occupations; standards for language, beauty, power; presence; access to resources). The issue of dominance/nondominance will be taken up more extensively in Chapter 2.*

Comments on Part 2: What thoughts do you have on naming your groups' statuses?

This cultural group membership activity is aimed at stimulating your awareness of your being "culturally constituted," that is, being made up by your cultures. It is meant to begin your movement toward what Paolo Freire called "critical consciousness," which is one of the major aims of this book. That topic is discussed later and in Chapter 2.

This book explores culture as it is expressed through six cultural categories— race, ethnicity, social class, gender, sexual orientation, and religion. These categories are described in Box 1.1.

BOX 1.1   The Six Major Categories of Culture

The six categories of culture defined here are neither exclusive nor final. For example, "age" and "ability/disability" are not explicitly included, despite their importance in counseling. Those two concepts are usually addressed in other areas of counselor education.

Race. "Race" is an especially contested and, indeed, controversial notion. What is uncontestable, however, is its power to affect human relations and individual lives. The most basic definition of race is "*a group of people of common ancestry, distinguished from others by physical characteristics, such as hair type, color of eyes and skin, stature, etc.*" (Sinclair, 2000). Like other cultural categories, it is a social construction—the creation of people in a language, a time, and a place. As such, it takes on many meanings, depending on the era, the society, and the speaker. The notion of race is especially intertwined with power and intergroup conflict.

Ethnicity. Ethnicity, too, carries many definitions. Here it is defined as *the recognition by both the members of a group and by others of common social ties among people due to shared geographic origins, memories of an historical past, cultural heritage, religious affiliation, language and dialect forms, and/or tribal affiliation* (Pinheiro, 1990). As might be seen, it also is an elusive and loose notion. Ethnicity matters for two reasons. First, it is a source people's standards, beliefs, and behaviors, even when they are unaware of its impact. Second, for those people from non-dominant ethnicities, it is an external marker, one that defines their opportunities or lack thereof.

Class/Socioeconomic Status. One powerful factor in a person's aspirations and experiences is socioeconomic status, sometimes also called social class. Socioeconomic status inevitably influences many life roles and choices, including religious affiliation, gender roles, career aspirations, diet habits, entertainment choices, health, housing, self-esteem, dress, and recreation.

Class is defined here as *a person's position in a society's hierarchy based on education, income, and wealth.* As might be seen, this definition is external; here the status is given by others. Yet social class also is an internalized set of assumptions and an identity. Clients will bring internalized expectations and self-images to counseling based on their social class. Counselors also need to know their own class-based assumptions.

(Continued)

(Continued)

Gender. Gender is often conflated with the term *sex.* Anthropologists, however, now reserve "sex" for references to biological categories and reserve "gender" for culturally defined categories. Here the term *gender* refers to *a socially constructed set of roles ostensibly based on the sex of individuals.* Gender stems largely from the division of labor roles in a society, not the physiological differences between men and women. As cultural creations, gender roles can and do shift with social, economic, and technological change. Influences on gender are the formal legal system, which reinforces customary practices; sociocultural attitudes such as ethnic-based obligations; and religious beliefs and practices. Like all cultural constructions, gender is both externally imposed and internalized to a greater or lesser extent by individuals. The culturally alert counselor needs to be aware of both.

Sexual Orientation. The gender(s) for which a person has consistent attachments, longings, and sexual fantasies define her or his sexual orientation. The American Psychological Association defines sexual orientation as *an enduring emotional, romantic, sexual, or affectional attraction to either gender or both genders* (Gonsiorek, Sell, & Weinrich, 1995).

Sexual orientation is a complex notion because it refers to a continuum of affectional attractions, ranging from exclusive homosexuality through various forms of bisexuality to exclusive heterosexuality. Sexual orientation does not imply particular behaviors. Indeed, the exact origin of sexual orientation is uncertain at this time. The American Psychological Association has declared that sexual orientation is shaped in most people at an early age and that biology plays a significant role in it. Being in a sexual minority can be a source of significant stress and self-doubt. Counselors have a particular role in reaching out to sexual minorities in order to provide advocacy and support.

Religion and Spirituality. Religion is also fraught with definitional difficulties. Religion will be defined here as *the organized set of beliefs that encode a person's or group's attitudes toward, and understanding of, the essence or nature of reality.* By this definition, religion does not require belief in a higher power or a deity. Spirituality can be distinguished from religion by its locus in the individual rather than the group. Spirituality refers to *a mindfulness about the existential qualities of life, especially the relationship between self, other, and the world.* Religion and spirituality are powerful sources of meaning, esteem, and social life to many, but not all, individuals. Religion is an especially powerful force in American life, as compared to other industrialized nations. It is part of the culturally alert counselor's task to evoke clients' relevant religious and spiritual beliefs and practices, as well as those of any related communities to which they might belong. Clients can draw strength from religious and spiritual sources. Such sources can also result in maladaptive attitudes.

DEFINING DIVERSITY

Diversity is a word that is heard regularly. Diversity is, most simply, the existence of variety in human expression, especially the multiplicity of mores and customs that are manifested in social and cultural life. When used with words like "celebrate" and "embrace," diversity represents an appreciation of multiple perspectives, a recognition of the contribution that many cultures make to a community.

In contrast to much of the United States today, there are places where diversity is minimal. Members of isolated groups are often unaware of alternative cultural expressions and frequently are surprised by and disapproving of them

(Kegan, 1994). If group members associate only with their group, they might consider their ways to be "the" ways to think, judge, and act. But even within mono-ethnic societies there is diversity by, for example, gender and sexual orientation. When a group encounters other groups, its members become aware of differences between their way of life and those of others. That encounter might be about religious beliefs, culinary customs, communication styles, or sexual behavior, to name a few possible expressions of diversity.

Before reading further, the reader is invited to assess her or his experiences with diversity by completing Activity 1.3. This activity is best done privately, so that a person may be completely honest in her or his responses.

ACTIVITY 1.3

Encounters With Cultural Diversity

By now you have read about how pervasive culture is in the sensitive work of counseling. However, perhaps you are still not sure about the power of culture in human lives.

Review your life, looking for times when you were especially aware of cultural dimensions in a situation, perhaps when you had a nondominant status. Remember, culture includes ethnicity/race, gender, sexual orientation, social class, and religion. List as many occasions as possible. Then list up to three examples of situations in which you were aware of cultural differences:

_____

_____

_____

Perhaps you had trouble coming up with such encounters. That in itself might be a message for you to try more culturally different experiences. If you did remember at least one experience, answer these questions:

Did you notice that it is unsettling to have your automatic assumptions and/or behaviors challenged?

Did you sense that it is especially uncomfortable to be in the nondominant or minority group? Use the feelings you had in these situations to remind yourself of the confusion and discomfort experienced by others when they are in a culturally unfamiliar situation, such as counseling itself.

Can you also see that it is at first unsettling to experience cultural newness? And that it might be exciting, if you open up to it?

Try to turn that confusion into curiosity. This book aims to engender that curiosity and encourage those experiences.

Attitudes Toward Diversity

Proponents of diversity in human communities argue that diversity makes communities stronger. In that vein, novelist Salman Rushdie, in the opening quote in this chapter, refers to "the transformation that comes of new and unexpected combinations of human beings, cultures, ideas, politics, movies, songs." Robert Kegan (1994) connects diversity with healthy organisms and societies in this way:

> Biologists tell us that the ongoing variability of the gene pool is a key to the health of any organism. . . . The more a family intermarries, for example, and succeeds at preserving the "purity" of its line, as has happened throughout history with several dynasties, the greater the likelihood of physical and mental debilities in its issue. Psychologists tell us that the single greatest source of growth and development is the experience of difference, discrepancy, anomaly. So it is for a society—an encounter with some new custom is a challenge for us to accommodate, to see the power of alternate ways of living. . . . These images . . . raise the possibility that diversity is best conceived not as a problem in need of a solution, but as an opportunity or a necessity, to be prized and preserved as a precious resource. (pp. 210–211)

The "precious resource" that is diversity doesn't always feel so appealing on a day-to-day level. Instead, the encounter with difference is seen as a "problem," in Kegan's word, a source of fear and discomfort. The reader is invited to complete Activity 1.4 privately in order to assess the work she or he might need to do on encountering diversity.

Psychological Processes for Encountering Diversity: Assimilation Versus Accommodation

Diversity challenges people's familiar ways. It can surprise an individual as she or he encounters a different religious view, moral position, or child-rearing custom, to name a few examples. Individuals have, in a sense, two ways to encounter diversity. They can assimilate it to their current mode—for example, by deciding that what is different is "bad"—or they can accommodate it by rethinking their assumptions in light of the new information.

These two notions, assimilation and accommodation, come from the work of Jean Piaget (e.g., Piaget & Inhelder, 1969). Of the two, assimilation is easier. Psychological *assimilation* can be defined as *the cognitive process of fitting new information into existing cognitive schemas, perceptions, and understanding* (Psychology Glossary, 2003). In assimilation, when individuals are faced with new information, they make sense of this information by referring to information processed and learned previously. Thus, a child may fit all men into the category "Daddy." She or he is trying to fit the new information into the understanding that she or he already has. Assimilation is the viewing of experience through familiar lenses.

ACTIVITY 1.4

Attitudes Toward Difference

Below are eight possible responses to cultural difference. Read through each and, in the spaces at the bottom, name a cultural group that is not your own. Then respond to the three questions below.

Repulsion:	People who are different in this way are strange and repellent. Anything that will change them to being more normal or part of the mainstream is justifiable.
Pity:	People who are different in this way are to be pitied. One should try to make them "normal."
Tolerance:	Being different in this way is unfortunate, but I can put up with their unfortunate presence.
Acceptance:	I need to make accommodations for this difference because these people's identity is not of the same value as my own.
Support:	I would like to act to safeguard the rights of these people, even if I am occasionally uncomfortable myself. I know about the irrational unfairness toward them.
Admiration:	I realize that it takes strength to be different in this way. I am working hard on changing my bias.
Appreciation:	I value this diversity for what it offers society, and I will confront insensitive attitudes.
Nurturance:	This group is indispensable to our community. I have genuine affection and delight for this group, and I advocate for them.

1. Name a cultural group that is not your own (an ethnic group, a race, a social class, a gender, a sexual orientation, a religious or non-religious group, or a disability).

2. Name your current attitude toward that group, based on the eight attitudes defined above.

3. What does this exercise tell you? Write a comment.

Interpreting the results: This exercise indicates where you and others might have work to do to move toward more positive views of cultural others. The scale is particularly important because it demonstrates that attitudes toward others are not merely "yes-no" matters. There are gradations in attitudes. Note that "Tolerance" is in the bottom half of the levels. While the U.S. Constitution and civil rights laws require mere "tolerance" of some diversities, that is not sufficient for the counselor. The first four of the attitudes imply that there is something inadequate or even wrong with the cultural group. Even the notions of "tolerance" and "acceptance" do not require a counselor to fully understand the other from his or her point of view, to peer inside other cultures with respect, interest, and active engagement. The last four—support, admiration, appreciation, and nurturance—are positive in that they endorse the diversities as important for a well-functioning, growing society, one that is confronted by newness and made stronger for it. The last four imply that you will take active steps to be an ally or activist to oppose prejudice or oppression.

SOURCE: Adapted from Riddle (n.d.).

Assimilation is adaptive. If, in early summer, a hiker comes across a mother bear with her cubs in the woods, it is adaptive to assimilate quickly with a thought such as, "This is dangerous. I should flee." Humans are hardwired to assimilate in this way in order to make life predictable at times, especially when encountering situations that might be dangerous.

However, overassimilation, that is, trying to fit all unfamiliar or uncomfortable phenomena into one's current lenses, is maladaptive. Such overassimilation is exemplified by the person who stereotypes to easily identify "the other." Unexamined prejudice of any kind is a form of overassimilation. Overassimilation may damage relationships; for example, a father may reject his lesbian daughter because his old assimilation of what is good and bad, right and wrong in human sexual expression cannot accommodate the possibility that his daughter's sexual orientation is a positive, natural expression of her attractions. Diversity is, there-fore, dangerous to him. He has only assimilated the data on his daughter's homo-sexuality to his current way of knowing. The result of such overassimilation would likely be a rift in the family, increased emotional distancing, and isolation for both her and him.

By contrast, "appreciation of diversity" might be considered an act of mental *accommodation* to newness. Accommodation can most simply be defined as *the cognitive process of revising existing cognitive schemas, perceptions, and under-standings so that new information can be incorporated.* In order to make sense of new information, a person actually adjusts the mental schema she or he already has in order to make room for the new information. In relation to diversity, accommodation is needed so that individuals can recognize rich differences in human expression and characteristics, even when it is somewhat uncom-fortable to do so. Mary Belenky, Blythe Clinchy, Nancy Goldberger, and Jill Tarule (1986), in their landmark study of ways of knowing, found that those who could accommodate diversity were able to "pause" in their thinking process to weigh the value of a phenomenon before judging it. One aim of the multi-cultural movement, and of this book, is to encourage such pausing before mak-ing assimilations.

QUALIFIERS AND CONTROVERSIES SURROUNDING CULTURE

Now that the definitions and importance of both culture and diversity in U.S. life have been explored, qualifiers about culture and its role in explaining human behavior must be addressed. The next sections are offered in order to address readers' concerns about overgeneralizations and misuses of the notion of culture. For that purpose, the following four topics are discussed next: balancing culture with other explanations of human behavior, acknowledging bias and stereotyp-ing, concerns about exclusive emphasis on "minorities," and recognizing the evolving terms used about cultures. At the end of this section, guidelines for flexi-bility in addressing culture are offered.

Balancing Culture With Other Explanations of Human Behavior

There is often confusion about the relative importance of culture in counseling. Some people think it can be harmful to notice race, ethnicity, and other cultural attributes, as if doing so will automatically lead to prejudice. One graduate student of counseling recently expressed the shift in thinking in terms of race awareness. She declared that she had been taught to see others, without prejudice, as unique individuals. These were her words:

> Here's my dilemma. . . . In the past, thinking about race and ethnicity was a problem, as those ideas were used against people from minority groups. Then the shift was toward "color-blindness," that is, ignoring race and ethnicity in favor of seeing only the individual. Now we're going back to awareness of race and ethnicity. And it is considered to be good, rather than a problem. Whew. It seems like a circle in some ways. It's hard to know whether it is good or bad.

The Legacy of Universalistic Individualism. There are thinkers who advocate de-emphasizing culture in counseling (e.g., Patterson, 1996). Those critics of the cultural dimension have described the multicultural movement as a distraction from the essential work of knowing and helping the individual by applying universal theories of the ways people grow and change. Those authors propose that current individual-oriented counseling models are universally applicable, without reference to culture. That perspective is here called "universalistic individualism."

Historically, the field of counseling ignored culture by assuming that only individual and universal factors mattered. In fact, the great hope of modernist Western psychological science was to reach beyond culture to discover universal laws of behavior. Thus, such universalistic notions as "personality" and "mental disorder" have emerged.

To a great extent, the universalistic endeavor has been positive because a more compassionate understanding of mental distress has replaced moral condemnation of emotional suffering. Depression and other emotional distresses are no longer explained as demonic possession, a lack of will, nor as any other sign of moral inadequacy. For those reasons, counselors might applaud the good that modern applied psychological science has wrought.

Yet, despite its contributions, this universalistic bias is embedded in an oppressive history, one in which the assumption that all human beings are the same was based on the premise and practice that generalizations for all humans could be made from middle-class, Western, generally male culture. Psychologists and counselors talked to each other, studied each other, and theorized about each other and their culturally similar students and then called their theories and findings "universal." Few dared to engage in conversations with cultural "others" about their ways of seeing the world. But work in the fields of anthropology and social work, among others, as well as the political changes after the 1960s, challenged this conspiracy of the dominant group in favor of a declaration that all people are "cultured" and must be included in the conversation.

It is now acknowledged that clients view themselves and others through cultural lenses. And it is recognized that all cultures are valuable human adaptations to their particular environments. Finally, the recognition that some cultures are privileged and some are oppressed has been brought to the forefront of the social sciences.

It might be seen, therefore, that social identities, in the form of race, ethnicity, class, gender, sexual orientation, and religion, drive both clients' emotional lives and their relative social influence, or the lack thereof. Counselors cannot simply address a mythical "individuality" because to do so is to inevitably impose a set of cultural assumptions on clients. Thus, relying only on traditional universalistic-individualistic counseling, such as classic psychoanalysis or "pure" humanism or behaviorism, can be considered inadequate and unethical, for two reasons. First, some dimensions of traditional counseling approaches are not helpful for many members of particular cultural groups. This point will be delineated in later chapters. Second, universalistic individualism often ignores social inequality. It fails to address the institutional and societal arrangements that contribute to human distress.

Toward a Tripartite Model of Human Experience. What might be an alternative to universalistic individualism? Is culture itself a sufficient explanation for human behavior? Of course not. People have both a unique individuality and a common humanity. For example, a woman who is experiencing severe doubts about the viability of her marriage might become sad and depressed (universal emotions). She might be prone to depression (an individual factor) because of her temperament or unique past and present life circumstances. Her Anglo American, evangelical Christian culture might frown on acknowledging and expressing negative feelings, so she hides the sadness and low mood (cultural factor). Thus, humans are always, in a sense, "in" culture. In the case of this woman, the culturally alert counselor might evoke the concerns over the marriage, probe the client's religious perspective, note the proscription against acknowledging negative feelings while also reflecting them back to her, respectfully ask whether she would like to look at those issues, and perhaps collaborate with a selected clergyperson.

It follows from this example that in place of the universalistic model, a more complex, ethical, and accurate view of human behavior is needed. It is not a question of counselors engaging in either universalistic individualist practice or culturally oriented counseling. Instead, it is imperative that counselors acknowledge all dimensions of human influence and meaning-making. Each alone is insufficient. To incorporate all of these dimensions of human experience into counseling, a three-part model of human experience has been proposed by Speight, Myers, Fox, and Highlen (1991). This three-part, or tripartite, model will serve to remind the counselor of the sources of human behavior and meaning-making (see Figure 1.1):

1. The *universal* qualities shared by all humans

2. *Individual* temperament, personality, and history

3. *Culture*

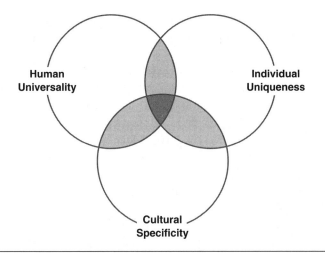

Figure 1.1 The Intersections of Culture, Universality, and Individuality

SOURCE: Reprinted from Speight, Suzette L., Myers, Linda J., Cox, Chikako I., & Highlen, Pamela S. (1991). A Redefinition of Multicultural Counseling. *Journal of Counseling & Development*, 70, 32. © 1991 The American Counseling Association. Reprinted with permission. No further reproduction authorized without written permission from the American Counseling Association.

Universal human qualities include the common human emotions, such as love, sadness, joy, doubt, and anxiety. Individual dimensions include particular persons' learning styles, talents, and career-related personality styles. (Of course, these notions of individual differences are also culture-bound, rooted as they usually are in Western languages and in limited samples.) Finally, and of greatest interest in this book, are cultural group factors, such as styles of communicating, occasions for shame, expressions of celebration, rules for adherence to group norms, and the structure of social and family groupings and gender roles.

Culture can be addressed without it being emphasized to the exclusion of individual and universal explanations for behavior. Here is how one student handles the complexity of including culture in counseling without it becoming another source of stereotyping and without it excluding individual and universal matters:

> I agree that labeling people and stopping there is detrimental. However, one reason that we will probably never be rid of classifying people is that classification is an activity inherent in beings [who are] capable of conceptual thinking. In early times, the ability to classify was vital to survival and it still serves us well today in a number of ways. Ironically, some of the classification activity we perform on other human beings may be the result of earlier classification which resulted in prejudice. For instance, when I was a child in the 1950s, many black people were not admitted to a number of places that white people were. Now when I counsel an African American, I am aware that I *may* be dealing with a person who may

have undergone this kind of exclusion or may have been raised and strongly influenced by people who suffered this kind of experience. As I get to know my client better, I will find out whether or not this is true without putting him or her on the spot about it, but it will be helpful if I am aware that this possibility exists and helps me understand why this individual may not trust white people. My client may not be aware of how this kind of distrust may color his or her actions, but I will be able to work with my client in exploring this avenue of self-awareness. We should [also] not let classifying that person blind us to the factors that make that person unique. Differences exist within categories as well as between them.

This writer asks counselors to engage in a mental "dance" among many possibilities—mainly between the cultural and the individual. Such thinking has been called "dialectical" (Basseches, 1984) because it asks the person to entertain two or more seemingly contradictory notions at once. For example, John Bracey, director of African American Studies at the University of Massachusetts, was once asked, "Should I think of a person as black first or as an individual first?" Bracey responded, "Try doing both at the same time." Counselors, too, might attempt the delicate task of holding at least two notions at once: the client as a cultural being and as an individual.

Acknowledging and Moving Beyond Bias and Stereotyping

The case for counselors being alert to culture has now been introduced, and the place of culture among other explanations of behavior has been discussed. However, there may still be lingering doubt about infusing culture into counseling. The reader might be concerned about the danger of paying so much attention to culture. Doesn't discussion of culture invite bias? Doesn't every individual have bias? How might bias be contained? A related question the reader might ask is, "Isn't generalizing about cultures akin to stereotyping?"

Dealing With Bias. Counselors cannot be expected to have no emotional response, or, alternatively, an immediately positive reaction to all diversities. As has been discussed before, humans notice difference, such as skin color, body type, religious orientation, mannerisms, sex, and dress. A basic psychological activity of being human is to classify. Humans resort to quick categorization so that they can be alert to danger. There is even genetic evidence that "outsiders" are perceived by humans as threats (Cottrell & Neuberg, 2005). As social animals, humans identify with their "tribe" and are wary of members of other groups. Thus, counselors need not condemn themselves and others for these initial, automatic human responses to cultural groups.

It is what an individual does with her or his initial response, how she or he acts on that response, that matters. Kegan (1994) proposes an approach for dealing with the immediate reaction to a difference that might be called the "first five seconds strategy." He suggests that individuals not blame themselves for their immediate perceptions, whether those be fear, distaste, or attraction to a person from a particular cultural group. Instead, individuals should accept that they will have automatic responses, but then they can take responsibility for the sense they are making after the initial response—that is, after the first five seconds. In his words, "We 'make sense,' but we do not always take responsibility for it as made" (p. 206). Then counselors needn't pretend to be color, or gender, or sexual-orientation blind, for example. They can begin to do the work of taking responsibility for the sense that they are making of their and others' cultures, after their initial, somewhat automatic response.

Managing Stereotyping. A stereotype is an oversimplified conception, opinion, or image that one has about groups of people, including one's own group. It can be negative or positive: "The English are unemotional," "Women are nurturing," "The French are sexy," "Gay men are effeminate," "Evangelical Christians are conservative," or "Italians are expressive." The key dimension of stereotyping is oversimplification. A stereotype may be generally, but not universally, true, or it may be totally baseless. Throughout this book, generalizations about cultural groups will be made, based on current knowledge. The reader might ask, "Isn't that an invitation to stereotype?"

Generalizations about cultures are always approximations; they are always inadequate attempts to capture some phenomenon with language. That subtlety must not be lost. It asks counselors to recognize the variations among individuals within groups, the limits of any generalization, and the potential ethnocentrism in stereotypes. Thus, culturally alert counselors would be willing to withhold judgment about groups and individuals within groups in favor of remaining open to alternative information. This cognitive complexity might be seen, for example, in the contrast between the following statements:

Stereotype: Women are _____.

Cognitively Complex Generalization: Many women tend to _____ for _____ reasons under _____ conditions. I must continue to experience the individual who is with me, as well as other group members, in an ongoing tentative fashion.

The ability to refrain from stereotyping while recognizing generalizations is a dimension of the aforementioned dialectical thinking.

Concerns About Exclusive Emphasis on "Minorities"

When culture is addressed, who is being spoken of? Some members of dominant groups, such as European Americans, men, and heterosexuals, have, in the past, felt left out of the conversation about culture due to an understandable emphasis in the field on nondominant groups. This emphasis has been a necessary corrective to the dominant cultural stories that have pervaded all aspects of

U.S. society because the stories of nondominant groups were, historically, left out or minimized (Takaki, 1993).

Therefore, since much is already known about the dominant groups, intentional effort has been made in the field to present the issues of nondominant cultures and to describe the power differentials among groups. As has been discussed, however, everyone has culture and all cultures matter, not just those of so-called minorities. Counselors will deal with culture with every client, in some form.

Acknowledging the Evolving Terms for Cultures

A final proviso about the notion of culture lies in the fuzzy and ever-changing area of labels for cultural groups. Humans constantly name phenomena. However, names are merely social constructions, that is, expressions of a time and place. Names have no direct link to the phenomena that are labeled. Language is a set of conventions that counselors inherit, and those conventions are not neutral. They are rooted in discourses, that is, there are connotations for all terms. Language carries power. Nondominant groups try to claim power by naming their own terms. Thus, terms for groups change regularly, often in response to nondominant groups' objections to the negative connotations of the words used to describe their groups.

Consider the movement away from once seemingly neutral terms such as "mulatto," "colored," "girl" (for an adult woman), "Negro," "Oriental," "queer," "retarded," and "red man." These terms were created by the dominant group to refer to members of nondominant groups. They often were accompanied by connotations of being "other," "exotic," and/or "inferior." Today, terms such as "people of color," "gay," "developmental disability," and "brown" are having their day. These, too, will someday pass.

Instead of becoming frustrated with not knowing supposedly "correct" terms, counselors should be open to the evolving, fluid nature of language. They must recognize that words do hurt, that those who are in greater power often label the less powerful with terms that become negative. In practice, counselors can start by asking a client what she or he prefers to use as a cultural label, when and if the matter comes up. Counselors need to work toward using language that is preferred by the group.

Guidelines for Flexibility in Working With Culture

To close this section on qualifications about culture, three guidelines for avoiding oversimplified, rigid applications of cultural generalizations are offered:

- *Recognize fluidity in culture.* Do not treat cultural concepts as essences. They are changing social constructions. Members of a particular cultural group create norms for thinking and acting, and members of other groups interpret those norms. And those norms change when conditions change and when cultures encounter each other (see Chapter 3 for a related discussion of acculturation). For example, the customs of immigrant groups change when they encounter other cultures, especially the dominant one. Similarly, men's and women's "cultures" have changed in the past 30 years and will continue to change. Terms also change over time. For example, the word *queer* has been reclaimed by many gay and lesbian persons, when once it was a put-down used by many heterosexuals.

- *Make measured, tentative generalizations.* Be wary of treating cultural norms as absolutes. Watch out for tentative generalizations about some people becoming stereotypes about all members of a group, such as, "Asians always include extended family in their lives," "Anglo American Protestants don't care about extended family," and "Men are all competitive and overly autonomous." Instead, make reasonable generalizations. These generalizations can then be treated as "probabilities," not certainties because, in Marger's (2002) words, "we cannot predict the behavior of any single individual or event" (p. 8). For example, men are generally taller than women, but some men are shorter than some women.

- *Adapt traditional counseling theories to cultures, but do so flexibly.* Clemmont Vontress (2003), the noted counselor, educator, and writer, warns about "groupism," that is, the attempt to uniformly match counseling with culture: "Theories of counseling should be about people, not subgroups based on race, gender, etc. Trying to develop a theory for a specific group of people seems like 'groupism,' if not racism. In order to have a people theory, one must agree that people are essentially the same. However, [people] are forced to adapt to their environments. The environmental adaptation necessarily causes cultural differences. As they move from one environment to another, they must readapt, so to speak. Environmental conditions create cultural change." Thus, the culturally alert counselor can utilize traditional counseling theories judiciously, adding elements of indigenous healing and other culturally specific approaches as they seem warranted. There is no culturally specific counseling approach that is absolute at this time, nor is there a universal one. More on the topic of culturally alert counseling intervention will be presented in Chapter 16.

Other Important Concepts for Understanding Culture

Now that some of the potential controversies and qualifiers around working with culture in counseling have been addressed, a number of subtopics that will expand the reader's understanding of culture will be presented: (1) objective and subjective culture, (2) the individualism-collectivism continuum, (3) the invisibility of much culture, (4) cultural relativism, and (5) convergence and intersectionality. The first is a basic distinction between objective and subjective culture.

OBJECTIVE AND SUBJECTIVE CULTURE

A distinction can be made between overt, or external, expressions of culture and the mental, or internal, contents of culture. These two manifestations of culture will be clarified through the notions of "objective" and "subjective" culture.

Culture that is associated only with visible, concrete expressions, such as languages, art forms, dances, and clothing is called "objective culture" (Triandis, 1994). This type of culture might also be called "surface" and "folk" culture (see Figure 1.2). Objective culture can be seen at such events as Caribbean Days, a Gay Pride Parade, or a Greek Festival: parades, costumes, and foods. In the area of gender, objective culture is what is most concretely associated with stereotypical men or women: styles of clothing and sex-typed activities.

Such manifestations are not permanent; they are historically and situationally located. In fact, the visible manifestations of culture are sometimes revitalized versions of former, antiquated customs. Thus it might be with German Oktoberfest events and costumes or with old-time Appalachian handicrafts and music. Objective culture can also be quite vital, such as African American worship services, a Hindu temple for a local Asian Indian community, Cajun *fais do-dos* (parties), or the social clubs of Haitian immigrants.

Of greater interest to counselors is the dimension of culture that is internalized by its members. This "subjective culture" or "deep culture" includes norms, attitudes, beliefs, and values. Subjective culture is often automatic, unarticulated, and may even be beyond the awareness of the members of a culture themselves. Examples of subjective culture include sexual norms (e.g., the relative restrictions of traditional Chinese and Irish cultures) and emotional expressiveness (e.g., in Mediterranean and African American cultures). Subjective culture is especially important in the work of counseling because clients operate out of implicit norms and values that affect such crucial aspects of life as relationships, career behavior, aspirations, and support systems. Much of this book will be devoted to aspects of subjective culture.

INDIVIDUALISM AND COLLECTIVISM
AS A DIMENSION OF SUBJECTIVE CULTURE

One example of a dimension of subjective culture is the much-studied notion of "individualism-collectivism." In some ethnic cultures, the needs and rights of the autonomous self are highly valued (individualism). In others, individual needs are secondary to those of the group (collectivism). The North American, Australian, and Anglo Germanic cultures in general value individualism, with an emphasis on rights, freedom, and independence. By contrast, the Latin American and South Asian cultures are collectivist; the individual defers to the group's needs (Hofstede, 2001). Collectivist cultures emphasize the social networks to which the person belongs and social rules for behavior. Collectivist cultures are often hierarchical; they value adherence to authorities such as elders, husbands, religious figures, and fathers. They are also characterized by "high context"

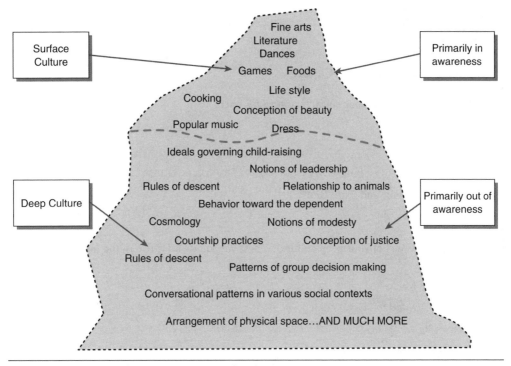

Figure 1.2 The Iceberg Conception of Culture

SOURCE: Adapted from University of Minnesota Extension Service, Office of Diversity and Inclusion (2006).

communication, in which the literal meaning of words is less important than the social message behind them. For example, "Would you like tea?" for some Middle Eastern people is a statement of welcome, one that shouldn't be turned down. In traditional Chinese cultures, an offer of a beverage should first be turned down in order to show humility and then accepted when offered again. In some cultures, bargaining while shopping is another example of a high context communication, in which the named price is not considered the "real" price.

THE INVISIBILITY AND DEPTH OF MUCH CULTURE

A third, and related, concept for understanding culture is its visibility or invisibility—whether it is "surface" or "deep." Because much of culture is not visible or obvious much of the time, elements of it must be inferred from practices and from disclosures by cultural group members. An iceberg metaphor illustrates the levels of awareness that individuals have about their cultures.

Activity 1.5 asks readers to name elements of their surface, or visible, cultures and elements of their deep, or invisible, cultures.

The tip, or conscious, part of the iceberg consists of those dimensions of cultures that are at least partly known and can be named, such as a group's history, language, and customs. Thus, a Cuban American is likely to be aware of some

ACTIVITY 1.5

The Iceberg Conception of Culture

- **Name one aspect of your surface culture for each:**

Music Tastes

Dress

Home Décor

Language Accents and Expressions

Foods Valued and Preferred

- **Name one aspect of your deep culture, as best you know it, for five of the following areas:**

Notions of Modesty

Behavior Toward the Dependent

Gender Roles

Conceptions of Beauty

Ideals Governing Child-Raising

Rules of Descent

Patterns of Superior/Subordinate Relationships

Definitions of Sin

Conceptions of Right and Wrong

Courtship Practices

Incentives to Work

Ideas of Leisure

Ideas of Cleanliness

Attitudes Toward the Dependent

Theories of Disease and Healing

Conceptions of Status Mobility

Eye Behavior

Roles in Relation to Status by Virtue of Age, Sex, Occupation, Class, and Kinship

Preference for Competition or Cooperation

Rites of Passage

Notions of Adolescence

Patterns of Handling Emotions

aspects of the homeland, immigration, and life of her people in the United States. So, too, would a woman know something about common women's roles and history.

The "undersea," or deep culture, portion of the iceberg contains much that people do not know but that nevertheless influences them. They might think of such invisible elements as merely "the way things are" (and must be): communication styles (e.g., direct/indirect, high/low affect, ironic/earnest), role expectations (e.g., children are to be unquestioning, men are to be strong), nonverbal communication (e.g., a sidelong glance indicating disapproval, handshaking as universal), order of priorities (e.g., work preceding rest, relationships mattering over achievement), and formality/informality in relationships (e.g., self-disclosure being desirable with all acquaintances, even elders; compliments being required in all relatively new acquaintances). Other elements of deep culture include notions of modesty; conceptions of beauty; ideals governing child-raising; relationship to animals and nature; patterns of superior/subordinate relationships; definitions of sin; conceptions of right and wrong; courtship practices; incentives to work; ideas of leisure; patterns of group decision making; ideas of cleanliness; attitudes toward the dependent; theories of disease and healing; conceptions of status mobility; eye behavior; roles in relation to status by virtue of age, sex, occupation, class, and kinship; preference for competition or cooperation; body language; notions of adolescence; patterns of handling emotions; facial expressions; and arrangements of physical space (University of Minnesota Extension Service, 2006).

It might be obvious that deep, invisible culture is important for counselors to know if they are to successfully engage with their clients. It is this dimension of culture that will often assist clients to live well or deter them from managing their lives well. Counselors can help clients to seek those aspects of culture that are "below the surface," especially those assumptions that are maladaptive. For example, for a gay client who has internalized messages from society that same-sex attraction is "sick" and/or evil, an uncovering and questioning of dominant cultural assumptions would likely be important. One way to do that is to use a narrative approach to counseling, which is discussed in Chapter 16.

Another advantage of counselors knowing about invisible culture is that such knowledge can deflect any superficial assumptions about others based on appearances. For example, an individual who looks "black" cannot be assumed to have all supposed African American cultural assumptions and characteristics. After all, "black" persons can be Jamaican, Puerto Rican, Haitian, Nigerian, or Ethiopian, to name just a few groups. Culture is often not visible to the eye.

CULTURAL RELATIVISM

A fourth important concept that is related to understanding culture is cultural relativism. Cultural relativism means treating other cultures as equal to one's own and deserving of respect. The idea of cultural relativism emerged in the first half of the twentieth century, especially from the work of anthropologist Franz Boas, who will be discussed in Chapter 4. It supplanted notions of cultural superiority and ethnocentrism that had dominated both popular thinking and intellectual discourse.

Cultural relativism is a controversial topic, with extreme views on either side. Some would have it that certain cultures are superior and even more moral than others, based on some supposedly objective standard. Others would propose that there is no noncultural basis for judging cultures. The full argument will not be engaged here, as that is an issue for other texts.

The idea of cultural relativism is relatively new. In the recent past, a clear hierarchical arrangement of cultures has prevailed. For example, Western society has spent the past two centuries trying to demonstrate the superiority of its culture, applying the very notion of "culture" or "civilization" to certain, usually Western, forms of human expression. Claims of superiority have been made, for example, for male, heterosexual, upper-class, and Judeo-Christian cultures. Dominating national cultures have made similar claims of cultural superiority, from the Nazis in Germany to the English in their Empire era. The notion of superiority has led to a kind of cruelty toward others because many people have been made to feel ashamed of their language, customs, appearance, accents, expressions, and clothing. The notion of cultural hierarchies is still alive, but its power has been declining.

Further questioning of cultural hierarchy has come with the diversity movement because it has opened the fountain of cultural pride for formerly denigrated cultures, such as gay people, people of color, women, and working-class persons. Those groups have claimed their cultures as worthy and as deserving of respect.

Despite its egalitarian appeal, controversy arises over whether some established cultural practices are immoral, demeaning, or cruel. Extreme examples include human and animal sacrifice, female clitorectomy, and women's subservient roles in some cultures. Conversely, some non-Western cultural groups might object to Western norms for the drinking of alcohol, treatment of elders, and explicitness about sexuality.

Cultural relativism challenges counselors to remove their cultural lenses and to empathically imagine how a culture works for its members. Cultural relativism, as presented here, is a call for counselors to "de-center" from their own cultural absolutes and to consider the positive functions of seemingly foreign cultural norms. Perhaps Perry's (1981) notion of relativistic thinking might be a useful framework for considering the value of cultural practices: "I must be wholehearted while tentative, fight for my values yet respect others, believe my deepest values but be ready to learn. I see that I shall be retracing this whole journey over and over" (p. 79). This tolerance of ambiguity, which is part of what Perry calls "relativistic thinking," is a desirable quality in the culturally alert counselor.

INTERSECTIONALITY AND CONVERGENCE

The final topics in this section on important dimensions of culture are those of intersectionality and convergence.

Sometimes multiple cultural group memberships conspire to affect individuals' lives in particularly oppressive ways. This phenomenon is called "intersectionality."

It refers to the multiple, overlapping oppressions, or "compound discrimination," that some persons experience. Oppressions, particularly racism, sexism, classism, and homophobia, are simultaneous and multilayered.

The metaphor of a pedestrian at a large intersection can illustrate the situation of intersectionality. Racially subordinated women and other multiply burdened groups who are located at these intersections by virtue of their specific identities must negotiate the traffic that flows through these intersections in order to obtain the resources for the normal activities of life. This is a particularly dangerous task when the traffic of the dominant social expectations, norms, and opportunities flows simultaneously from many directions. These are the contexts in which intersectional "injuries" occur, when disadvantages or conditions interact with preexisting vulnerabilities to create various forms of disempowerment. A woman of color who is lesbian and who is poor must "fight through" a thicket of social barriers to gain respect and access to the things that matter. Counselors must be empathically supportive of this daily struggle for some clients.

Convergence also refers to multiple and simultaneous cultural identities, but it doesn't specifically refer to intersecting oppressions. Each person is influenced by multiple cultural discourses. Each discourse affects an individual's beliefs, limitations, and opportunities. The notion of convergence helps counselors and clients avoid attributing all client experience to one cultural domain. Instead, they can recognize the multiple cultural dimensions that converge in one person's life.

Individuals' Varying Relationships to Their Cultures

Culture can vary in its importance for any particular client. In a related vein, it can also have more or less impact on that person's life. This section will explore three ways to describe an individual's relationship to her or his cultures: salience, culture-centrism, and cultural identity development.

SALIENCE

The importance of culture varies from person to person, especially in different circumstances and at different times in their lives. In particular, culture is far more important to persons who are in a minority or nondominant group in a community, including immigrants (Jones & McEwen, 2000). For example, recent immigrants are likely to have continuous awareness of their ethnicity in all encounters with the dominant culture, whereas members of the dominant ethnic cultural group commonly pay little attention to the artifacts and expressions of their culture.

Because of their relative obliviousness to their culture, dominant group members are sometimes heard to complain, "Why do _____ [Name a nondominant group] care so much about their identity? We're all just individuals."

Dominant group members are able to focus exclusively on their individuality because their cultural group membership is relatively invisible.

Cultural salience is also high during an early phase of cultural awareness (called "Encountering" and "Immersed" in the Cultural Identity Development Model described below) that many individuals go through. These times of intense awareness about culture can be triggered by encounters with bias, discovery of past cultural self-denigration, or other realizations of the presence of culture in one's life. Sometimes this salience is short-lived, as when a member of a dominant culture spends time with members of other cultures. Thus, an Anglo-American Protestant couple might become aware of their culture when their offspring marries a Greek Orthodox individual (cf. the film *My Big Fat Greek Wedding*).

When working with clients, it is important to assess cultural salience. Clients who demonstrate low "cultural self-esteem" (i.e., a view of their culture as inadequate, inferior, or wrong) might need to discover cultural strengths in order to move toward a more positive perspective. Methods for helping clients with cultural self-esteem are described in Chapter 16. Counselors can also help members of the dominant culture discover the cultural prescriptions they are subject to and discover which ones are and are not working for them.

CULTURE-CENTRISM

A second way to understand individuals' relationships to their cultures is by examining how embedded they are in a monocultural perspective. It should be noted that all people tend to judge members of other groups from the perspective of their own group. Thus, the lens of culture is unavoidable.

However, when such judging is almost total it might be called "culture-centrism." In psychologists Matsumoto and Juang's (2004) words, culture-centrism is "a tendency to judge people of other groups, societies, or lifestyles according to the standards of one's own in-group or culture, often viewing out-groups as inferior" (pp. 62–63). Individuals act in a culture-centric way when they treat their group as the center and all other groups as satellites. Culture-centrism is a broad application of the notion of ethnocentrism, which will be discussed in Chapter 3, in that culture-centrism can be based on the lenses of gender, social class, religion, ability, age, and sexual orientation, as well as ethnicity.

Some level of culture-centrism cannot be avoided because it is a consequence of enculturation. People learn from birth to make sense through culture because parents and others demonstrate or instruct individuals in the norms, manners, beliefs, and other expressions of culture. As they grow toward adulthood, individuals are more and more infused with their cultures. As a consequence, members of all groups share common perceptions about what is good and bad, attractive or unattractive, desirable or undesirable, worth attaining or not. That process helps them adapt to their social and physical environments.

However, such enculturation has a negative dimension. Because cultures communicate what is good and desirable to their members (i.e., the in-group), those members often use their culturally based standards to judge other groups (out-groups). Judgments by in-group members about the ways of out-groups are frequently negative. The particular danger lies in the fact that such judgments are treated as objective fact. People are frequently oblivious to their own cultural filters. They do not recognize their ethnicity, sexual orientation, religion, ability, social class, age group, and gender as the source of a "story" that could be different.

One's culture-centered story can be recognized as one story among many about how to live, or it can be treated as "the way things are." In the latter case, it is called "received knowledge" (Belenky et al., 1986), that is, an accepted set of lenses that a person has inherited without questioning it.

A culturally alert counselor would need to go through a process of de-centering from her or his own cultural assumptions in order to have a more multicultural, and therefore less culture-centric, perspective to help clients. De-centering involves the process of taking one's culture as one perspective among many. The more culturally de-centered individuals are, the more aware they are of experiencing others and themselves through their own cultural lenses. With that awareness, the person can try to "bracket" (mentally set it aside for the moment) her or his cultural filters on the world and consider other perspectives. Matsumoto and Juang (2004) propose a three-step approach to cultural de-centering:

1. Recognize one's own culture and acknowledge that it is likely to be one's default view.

2. Learn about other cultures.

3. Make a constant effort to question one's cultural assumptions.

Activity 1.6 guides readers to examine how they have constructed some of their assumptions—through a culture-centered lens or through a more intentional choice of attitudes, beliefs, values, and behaviors.

CULTURAL IDENTITY DEVELOPMENT

Cultural identity development is a third descriptor of the relationship that a person might have to her or his cultures. Cultural identity development theories plot the stages of the personal experience of culture. Those stages generally show movement from a naïve relationship with one's culture through an "integrated" or multicultural orientation. It should be noted that the stages are not rigid; people inhabit ways of thinking from a number of stages at any one time.

These developmental theories are important tools for counselors because they are both descriptive and prescriptive. As descriptors, they help a counselor understand clients' current attitudes toward themselves, their cultures, and other cultures, including clients' attitudes toward the counselor herself or himself. These theories can reveal the basis for client self-doubt and mistrust of others or cultural pride and openness. Cultural identity theories are also prescriptive; they can point the way to more adaptive cultural identities. Counselors can then intervene to help clients develop their cultural identities, if that seems warranted.

Many kinds of cultural identity models are available, including those for race, ethnicity, women, gay men and lesbians, and minorities in general. Many of those models will be described in the chapters that follow. Because of the sheer quantity of different models of cultural identity development, a general model, called the Cultural Group Orientation Model, is described in Box 1.2. The stages are called "orientations," to avoid the impression that they are fixed, unified states. These orientations should be seen as general tendencies; individuals are affected by situations and also show characteristics of other, proximate orientations. It is recommended that counselors understand the commonalities among the various models of cultural identity, many of which will be presented in subsequent chapters. As practitioners, counselors should know enough about cultural identity development to help themselves and their clients, if warranted, to be challenged toward a more complex cultural identity.

A counselor herself or himself should aim to achieve the most developed orientations in each model. At those statuses, greater appreciation of one's own and others' cultures is possible.

Using the descriptions of the five orientations, the reader is invited to complete Activity 1.7 in order to assess her or his own cultural identity development in a number of areas.

This discussion concludes this section on a person's relationship to her or his culture. What follows is a description of the competencies and the mental capacities that are desirable in a culturally alert counselor.

The Requirements for Becoming a Culturally Alert Counselor

The preceding sections have established some evidence for the importance of culturally alert counseling and have presented some of the issues that surround that work. The reader might ask at this point, "What is required to actually do such counseling?" Those requirements are enumerated in the basic multicultural counseling competencies.

THE MULTICULTURAL COUNSELING COMPETENCIES

The basic competencies required for culturally alert counseling fall into three categories: awareness, knowledge, and skill (Sue, Arredondo, & McDavis, 1992). They are enumerated in detail in Appendix A. While the competencies needn't be memorized by the reader, a counselor should be familiar with them and be able to assess her or his competency in each area.

ACTIVITY 1.6

The Challenge to Culturally Self-Authorize

Walt Whitman, the nineteenth-century American writer, wrote in his poem "Leaves of Grass,"

Re-examine all you have been told at school or church [or at home] or in any book, dismiss what insults your own soul, and your very flesh shall be a great poem.

That poem might be translated as the self that chooses the cultural elements that it wishes to claim for itself, as much as that is possible. Whitman encourages us to have a *self-authorized* (Kegan, 1982) vision of what we believe and value and how we act, a vision based on careful consideration of what matters to us, a vision that is separate from the supposed "givens" of culture. In this vision of the self-authorizing person, all cultural conventions are treated as social constructions, that is, creations of a community at a particular time and place. They are examined for their origins in and usefulness for a particular historical, political, or cultural context. Then we can ask the questions of our assumptions, values, beliefs, and behaviors: Do they still work? Do they help? Whom do they serve? What shall I discard and/or reclaim? What new, more multicultural perspectives might I take?

In order to claim, or reclaim, your culture and perhaps move closer to "self-authorizing" it, try this activity. It may take several months of searching, questioning, and re-examining for you to complete all of the columns. Perhaps you might begin with the first two boxes, and work on the other two columns during the course of a few months. Once you have begun the work on your own capacity to self-authorize, you, as a counselor, will be better able to consistently act in a socially critical fashion with both individuals and organizations.

Column 1. Name some strong, deeply held beliefs or assumptions (e.g., "Gay and lesbian people are somehow odd and unnatural" or "The only courageous existential stance is to be agnostic") that you hold absolutely about how things should be, or about what is true and right. You can also name some "lighter," more superficial customs (e.g., "One must always be pleasant" or "Everyone should have specific table manners, such as _____"). You can use the six cultural group memberships of ethnicity, race, gender, social class, sexual orientation, and religion as stimuli for thinking about beliefs and behaviors you have inherited.

Column 2. In the second column, "Alternative Position," write an alternative behavior, custom, or belief, one that challenges the inherited one ("The gay and lesbian sexual orientation is natural and I support and appreciate the presence of gay and lesbian people in our community" or "Agnosticism is not the only viable or valuable stance; belief in God is important for many people and can be a positive force").

Column 3. Decide how you might examine each inherited belief by talking with people, by reading, by writing, by visits to new places. Write a plan for at least one of your inherited beliefs in Column 3.

Column 4. NOTE: This part of the activity is best done after new experiences (e.g., in a course on culture and counseling) and after a period of time, such as three months, has elapsed. Review each initial inherited belief and each alternative belief. Decide on the one(s) that you might now hold based on the evidence you have gathered for your customs or beliefs. Write it/them in Column 4. What information do you have for the alternative positions? What information do you lack and therefore need to know?

Column 1 Inherited/learned beliefs/customs	Column 2 Alternative position (Name an alternative behavior, custom, or belief that is different from and challenges the inherited one.)	Column 3 What you need to know (What you need to know about alternative perspectives in order to make a decision for yourself. Make a plan to learn about alternative views in each of the areas below.)	Column 4 Self-authorized choice and evidence for it (Your self-authorized position; it can be similar to the original position, but now is chosen based on exploration and weighing of alternative views)
What I was taught at school (e.g., about history, gender, authority, intelligence, career roles, patriotism, hierarchy):			
1.			
2.			
3.			
What I was taught in my religious/ spiritual tradition (e.g., about divinity, sin, morality, afterlife, gender roles, authority, sexuality, extended family):			
1.			
2.			
3.			
What I was taught in my family (e.g., about gender roles, customs, career ambition, authority, use of humor, grieving, celebrating):			

1.			
2.			
3.			

Finally, below or on a blank page, write a paragraph on your reactions to doing this activity—your feelings and thoughts.

The importance of this process of self-defining beliefs is that self-authorized knowing is desirable for counselors. More complex ways of knowing are associated with higher empathy levels, which is a fundamental element of good counseling (Benack, 1988; Bowman & Reeves, 1987; Lovell, 1999; McAuliffe & Lovell, 2006). It is also associated with internal locus of control and open-mindedness in counselors (Neukrug & McAuliffe, 1993), as well as with the abilities to tolerate ambiguity, be reflective, use evidence for choices, and demonstrate insight into clients' issues (McAuliffe & Lovell, 2006). Self-authorized knowing may be important if counselors are to avoid imposing their values on clients and are to help clients to move toward a religion of choice (Brendel, Kolbert, & Foster, 2002).

Broadly speaking, culturally alert counselors must have

- *awareness of their own cultural values and biases.* They must be cognizant of their own cultures' impacts on their choices, values, biases, manners, and privileges; be comfortable with cultural differences; recognize discrimination and stereotyping; acknowledge their culturally based limitations; and be ready to seek further training. The readings and exercises in this book, coupled with other life experiences, can increase counselor competency in this area.

- *knowledge of clients' worldviews.* They should possess "multicultural literacy," which consists of a reasonable knowledge of many groups' and clients' worldviews as seen through the lenses of race, ethnicity, class, gender, sexual orientation, and religion, as well as the counselor's own negative reactions to and stereotypes of other groups. The readings in the subsequent chapters provide a foundation for understanding cultural worldviews.

- *intervention strategies or skills.* Counselors must incorporate cultural knowledge into counseling and advocacy for all members of their populations. They should consider clients' language proficiencies, the use of assessment instruments, their ability to refer to indigenous helpers, their capacity to adapt communication styles, their commitment to doing advocacy, and

BOX 1.2   Cultural Group Orientation Model

Orientation One: Naïve/Accepting

- Accepts the status quo
- ~~Is unaware of own cultural position~~
- Is unaware of power differentials among social groups ("What do you mean? What are the assumptions of my cultural group? I'm just a human, like everyone else! We're all the same. I don't think about it. I'm just me.")
- Often characteristic of those who have had little encounter with other groups
- If in the dominant group, likely to think of oneself as "culture-less" (e.g., having no ethnicity or treating one's gender, social class, sexual orientation, and religion as "the way things are")
- Could have disparaging attitude toward other groups with whom one might have slight contact
- Might have self-depreciating attitude toward own group. (This is likely the most common position for members of dominant groups and for members of minority groups who have had little contact with other groups.)

Orientation Two: Encountering

- Initial meaningful contact with other group(s) through personal or vicarious experience (e.g., media)
- Beginning awareness that personal history can affect one's assumptions and beliefs
- Beginning awareness of power and status disparities among cultural groups in one's society
- Accepts disparities among groups

Orientation Three: Immersed

- Active exploration of one's cultural identity
- Immersion in cultural activities, reading about the culture, celebration of the group's present or past struggles against injustice. Interest in cultural styles and customs (e.g., "I now realize how some assumptions I've made about being a woman are limiting and yet many can be empowering"; "As a male, I realize that I have engaged in many stereotypical behaviors, ones that cause me to miss a lot")
- Often mystification about or denigration of other groups at this stage (Intolerant version: "I don't understand why those people have to talk so loudly. We always keep conversations private," or "I can't believe that they put earrings in children's ears! How weird!" or "Men are so aggressive and self-centered.")
- Individuals can become "stuck" in this phase

Orientation Four: Reflective

- Able to stand back from, or "take a perspective on" one's culture (Kegan, 1982)
- Recognizes the constructed "story" of one's cultural group, therefore is less likely to adhere automatically to cultural prescriptions
- Aware of value and strengths of one's group, as well as the limiting elements in the culture (e.g., "There is an anti-intellectual strain in my religious tradition that I do not value.")
- Can choose cultural attributes that one wishes to claim, reclaim, or discard

- Consistently faces painful history and/or current oppressions
- Beginning commitment to addressing social inequality, but little action

Orientation Five: Multicultural/Critically Conscious

- Seeks out multiple cultural experiences and perspectives
- Firm commitment to creating a multicultural self by engaging in multicultural experiences
- Dedicated to amelioration of oppressive conditions
- Is empathic, compassionate, and willing to act
- Recognizes effects of oppression on all groups
- Can see dilemmas even for dominant group
- Interested in instigating dialogue
- Open to one's own rigidities and biases and seeks feedback

SOURCE: Adapted by Garrett McAuliffe, Old Dominion University, from the racial and cultural identity development models of Helms and Cook (1999) and Ivey (1995). It is partially based on the developmental theories of Belenky, Clinchy, Goldberger, and Tarule (1986), Kegan (1982, 1994), and Perry (1970).

their sensitivity to trust issues with culturally different clients. Chapter 16 outlines the skills needed for culturally alert counseling. Specific strategies are described toward the end of each of the cultural group chapters.

The first competency, cultural self-awareness, is an ongoing task, one that has been initially addressed in the Activities in this chapter. Cultural self-awareness is achieved through personal examination of how one is "cultured" in every aspect of one's life. One aim of this book, especially of the Activities in the first few chapters, is to have the reader discover the cultural discourses that guide her or his thinking and acting. Representative awareness competencies are (1) "Culturally skilled counselors are aware of how their own cultural background and experiences, attitudes, and values and biases influence psychological processes"; and (2) "Culturally skilled counselors are comfortable with differences that exist between themselves and clients in terms of race, ethnicity, culture, and beliefs" (Sue et al., 1992, p. 482).

The second competency, multicultural literacy or "knowledge," will be tackled in each of the subsequent chapters. Two of the knowledge competencies are (1) "Culturally skilled counselors possess specific knowledge and information about the particular group that they are working with"; and (2) "Culturally skilled counselors understand how race, culture, ethnicity, and so forth may affect personality formation, vocational choices, manifestation of psychological disorders, help-seeking behavior, and the appropriateness or inappropriateness of counseling approaches" (Sue et al., 1992, p. 482).

In light of this broad expectation, a counselor might ask, "How many cultural characteristics and groups must I know about in order to be culturally alert

ACTIVITY 1.7

Assessing Your Cultural Group Orientations

Having now read the Cultural Group Orientation Model in Box 1.2, complete the column on the right below by noting your current general cultural awareness. Comment on this Activity and on what your tasks ahead might be.

Cultural Group	Names	Awarness
Categories	A name for your current group membership(s):	Your current level of cultural awareness: (1 = naïve/acceptant; 2 = encountering; 3 = immersed; 4 = reflective; 5 = multicultural/ critically conscious; see descriptions in Box 1.2)
Ethnicity		
Race		
Social Class, or SES (e.g., upper middle class, poor, working class)	Of Origin: Current:	
Gender		
Sexual Orientation		
Religion	Of Origin: Current:	

Comment on

(1) what you noted while doing this activity:

(2) some goals you might set for yourself based on this assessment:

enough?" The question is a legitimate one. Complete knowledge of every important aspect of all cultures is not possible. "Enough," to start, is a solid grasp of the ideas in this book plus some experience in applying them to the groups with whom the counselor is likely to work. In practice, counselors can extend their knowledge and test it in the fire of experience by having an inquisitive and open mind when they are confronted with cultural unknowns.

A reminder of the limits of cultural generalizations is in order at this point. Such generalizations are time-bound because cultures change. Old norms and customs evolve when they encounter each other in an act of mutual acculturation (see Chapter 3). Thus, Anglo American culture has incorporated many African American elements in the past 40 years, leading to an incorporation of language, music, and attitudes about expressing feelings. The same might be said of the Jewish American influence on the dominant American culture through the arts and other public expressions of that culture. And some elements of lesbian and gay culture, as much as one can generalize, have changed since the 1970s in significant ways, while other elements remain stable.

An additional limitation on how much one can know about cultures is the fact that all generalizations must be qualified, as mentioned earlier in this chapter. Even if cultural knowledge were relatively complete and fixed, it would not apply to all individuals at all times. Such overgeneralization would, in fact, be dangerous. Counselors must walk a fine line between assuming that some characteristics are true for members of a cultural group in general and applying them selectively to individual clients.

Thus, instead of questing for perfect cultural know-how, counselors can aim to become relatively multiculturally fluent. They should know basic terms and concepts such as "coming out" (for gay persons), *marianismo* (for some Hispanic people), "the ethic of care/connected knowing" (for many women), and "filial piety" (for some Chinese people). Nevertheless, counselors will inevitably be looking through a glass darkly, in the Christian Apostle Paul's words; that is, they will always have an obscure or imperfect vision of their own and others' cultures.

The third area of multicultural competence, "skills," is still the weakest area of multiculturalism (Rodriguez & Walls, 2000). Nevertheless, counselors must be ready to apply culturally alert practice immediately. Therefore, skills in applying multicultural awareness and knowledge must be generated, communicated, and enacted. Examples of such skills are (1) "Culturally skilled counselors are able to engage in a variety of verbal and nonverbal helping responses. . . . They are not tied down to only one method or approach to helping but recognize that helping styles and approaches may be culture bound" and (2) "Culturally skilled counselors are able to exercise institutional intervention skills on behalf of their clients. They can help clients determine whether a 'problem' stems from racism or bias in others . . . so that clients do not inappropriately blame themselves"(Sue et al., 1992, p. 483). Again, these are general. They must be translated into specific practices. Those practices will be described in all of the upcoming culturally specific chapters as well as in Chapter 16.

Summary

This book represents a challenging, even threatening, excursion into the frontier territory of culture and counseling. Counselors cannot bring all of their old supplies for this expedition into this "new world."

The journey into culturally alert counseling takes counselors through three major territories: cultural self-awareness, knowledge of other cultures, and skill at intervening in a culturally alert way. The book will interweave these three themes throughout.

This chapter has offered some basic provisions for the journey in the form of foundational definitions, opportunities for self-examination, a description of the changing landscape in the field of counseling, and ways of knowing that can fortify counselors when they are seemingly lost. Much of this material will be new to counselors as they discard the legacy of universalistic individualism and incorporate social construction into their thinking.

But much is unknown and unknowable until the journey begins. Counselors must also pack provisions of openness and humility along with cultural knowledge. Openness allows counselors to tolerate ambiguity, to discover exceptions, and to allow surprises to occur with clients. Humility helps counselors avoid the hubris of overgeneralizing and applying pat methods to solve complex human dilemmas.

Counselors cannot look at this landscape from afar: There is no way to know deeply but through experience. Encountering culture is not just an abstract exercise. Personal contact with cultural others will be required, supplemented by reflections on the meaning of those experiences.

And one word of warning for the traveler: The map is not complete. Despite the great progress that has occurred in the field of culture and counseling, all is not settled. As counselors embark on the journey to cultural alertness, they must know that they ought not strive for perfect knowledge of cultures. They can be culturally alert without being completely multiculturally fluent. They must accept that they will always be looking through a glass darkly at their own and others' cultures. Nevertheless, counselors will be well supplied with the basic provisions of an inquiring attitude, great empathy, a "leaning in" to difference, an appreciation of diversity in human expression, and a willingness to examine their own standpoints while inviting those of others. The reader who can begin with those qualities will be capable of beginning the great work of culturally alert counseling.

References

Aneshensel, C., & Phelan, J. (1999). Preface. In C. Aneshensel & C. Phelan (Eds.), *Handbook of the sociology of mental health* (pp. xi–xiii). New York: Springer-Verlag.

Basseches, M. (1984). *Dialectical thinking and adult development.* Norwood, NJ: Ablex.

Belenky, M., Clinchy, B., Goldberger, N., & Tarule, J. (1986). *Women's ways of knowing: The development of self, voice, and mind.* New York: Basic Books.

Benack, S. (1988). Relativistic thought: A cognitive basis for empathy in counseling. *Counselor Education and Supervision, 27,* 216–232.

Bowman, J. T., & Reeves, T. G. (1987). Moral development and empathy in counseling. *Counselor Education and Supervision, 26,* 293–298.

Brendel, J. M., Kolbert, J. B., & Foster, V. A. (2002). Promoting student cognitive development. *Journal of Adult Development, 3,* 217–227.

Cottrell, C. A., & Neuberg, S. L. (2005). Different emotional reactions to different groups: A sociofunctional threat-based approach to "prejudice." *Journal of Personality & Social Psychology, 88,* 770–789.

Gonsiorek, J. C., Sell, R. L., & Weinrich, J. D. (1995). Definition and measurement of sexual orientation. *Suicide and Life Threatening Behavior, 25,* 40–51.

Helms, J. E., & Cook, D. A. (1999). *Using race and culture in counseling and psychotherapy.* Boston: Allyn & Bacon.

Hofstede, G. (2001). *Culture's consequences: Comparing values, behaviors, institutions, and organizations across nations.* Thousand Oaks, CA: Sage.

Ivey, A. (1995). Psychotherapy as liberation: Toward specific skills and strategies in multicultural counseling and therapy. In J. Ponterotto, J. Casas, L. Suzuki, & C. Alexander (Eds.), *Handbook of multicultural counseling* (pp. 53–72). Thousand Oaks, CA: Sage.

Jones, S. R., & McEwen, M. K. (2000). A conceptual model of multiple dimensions of identity. *Journal of College Student Development, 41,* 405–414.

Kegan, R. (1982). *The evolving self: Problem and process in human development.* Cambridge, MA: Harvard University Press.

Kegan, R. (1994). *In over our heads: The mental demands of modern life.* Cambridge, MA: Harvard University Press.

Lovell, C. W. (1999). Empathic-cognitive development in students of counseling. *Journal of Adult Development, 6,* 195–203.

Marger, M. N. (2002). *Social inequality: Patterns and processes.* New York: McGraw-Hill.

Matsumoto, D., & Juang, L. (2004). *Culture and psychology.* Belmont, CA: Thomson/ Wadsworth.

McAuliffe, G. J., & Lovell, C. W. (2006). The influence of counselor epistemology on the helping interview: A qualitative study. *Journal of Counseling and Development, 84,* 308–317.

Neukrug, E. S., & McAuliffe, G. (1993). Cognitive development and human services education. *Human Services Education, 13,* 13–26.

Patterson, C. H. (1996). Multicultural counseling: From diversity to universality. *Journal of Counseling and Development, 74,* 227–231.

Perry, W. G. (1970). *Forms of intellectual and ethical development in the college years.* New York: Holt, Rinehart & Winston.

Perry, W. G. (1981). Today's students and their needs. In A. W. Chickering (Ed.), *The modern American college* (pp. 76–116). San Francisco: Jossey-Bass.

Piaget, J., & Inhelder, B. (1969). *The psychology of the child.* New York: Basic Books.

Pinheiro, V. (1990). What is ethnicity? *Revista Farol, 2,* 7.

Psychology glossary. (2003). Retrieved January 8, 2005, from http://www.alleydog.com/ glossary

Riddle, D. (n.d.). *Attitudes toward differences: The Riddle scale.* Retrieved January 8, 2005, from http://www.glsenco.org/Resources/the_riddle_scale.htm

Rodriguez, R., & Walls, N. (2000). Culturally educated questioning: Toward a skill-based approach in multicultural counselor training. *Applied & Preventive Psychology, 2,* 89–99.

Rushdie, S. (1992). *Imaginary homelands.* London: Granta Books.

Sinclair, J. M. (Ed.). (2000). *Collins English dictionary.* New York: HarperCollins.

Speight, S. L., Myers, J., Fox, D. F., & Highlen, P. S. (1991). A redefinition of multicultural counseling. *Journal of Counseling and Development, 70,* 29–36.

Sue, D., Arredondo, P., & McDavis, R. J. (1992). Multicultural counseling competencies and standards: A call to the profession. *Journal of Counseling and Development, 70,* 481–483.

Sue, D., & Sue, D. W. (2003). *Counseling the culturally diverse: Theory and practice.* New York: Wiley.

Sue, S., & Lam, A. (2002). Cultural and demographic diversity. In J. C. Norcross (Ed.), *Psychotherapy relationships that work: Therapist contributions and responsiveness to patients* (pp. 401–421). New York: Oxford University Press.

Takaki, R. (1993). *A different mirror: A history of multicultural America.* Boston: Little, Brown.

Triandis, H. C. (1994). *Culture and social behavior.* New York: McGraw-Hill.

Tylor, E. B. (1924). *Primitive culture.* New York: Brentano's. (Original work published 1871)

University of Minnesota Extension Service, Office of Diversity and Inclusion. (2006). *The iceberg conception of the nature of culture.* Retrieved April 7, 2006, from http://www.extension.umn.edu/units/diversity/The%20Iceberg%20Conception%20of%20the%20Nature%20of%20Culture.pdf

Vontress, C. (2003, January 19). Matching counseling with culture. Message posted to the Diversity/Multicultural/Cross-Cultural Counseling Listserv diversegrad-l@listserv.american.edu

Zinn, H. (1999). *A people's history of the United States: 1492 to present.* New York: HarperCollins.

Social Inequality and Social Justice

2

Garrett McAuliffe, Mona Danner, Tim Grothaus, and Lynn Doyle

Frank Parsons (1854–1908), often hailed as "creator" of the counseling field, was a tireless innovator and advocate for all people. In 1908, the year of his death, he founded the Vocational Bureau in a poor immigrant section of Boston. There, the youth of the neighborhood and beyond were counseled and mentored by a fleet of undergraduate volunteers from nearby colleges. Parsons' hope was that no person would be denied her or his dreams because of social class or environmental circumstances.

Less well known is Parsons' broader and lifelong role as a social activist, in which he took on the excesses of large corporations, promoted the ballot for women, and worked for the popular vote for legislation. For Parsons, counseling was inextricable from societal activism. He used the lectern, the classroom, and the press all of his life to promote the interests of the disempowered. As a consequence, he was ousted from his teaching post at Kansas State University in 1899, although the entire junior class appealed for his reinstatement.

Parsons went on to write 14 books, and in them he called on his colleagues and others to commit themselves to social progress and to do so in practical ways. In his humorous style, Parsons characterized those who didn't work for social improvement as being "not developed much beyond the oyster stage." One of Frank Parsons' last acts was to establish the work of counseling. Advocacy for social justice was thus knitted into the original fabric of the counseling profession.

Over the years, many voices have challenged counselors to move beyond the provision of remedial services in order to attack the causes that perpetuate mental and social disorder. Frank Parsons was one of those voices. More recently, the American Counseling Association (ACA) developed a set of "Advocacy Competencies" for counselors that further defines the advocacy dimension of the work of counseling (Lewis, Arnold, House, & Toporek, 2002).

This chapter examines the social stratifications that contribute to human inequality and distress and the responsibility of the counselor to contribute to social justice. This responsibility represents a shift in thinking: away from the model of counselor-as-case-by-case-responder to counselor-as-preventer-and-advocate. It moves the conversation from one in which the counselor is to be sealed away in her or his office working with clients in 50-minute increments to one in which the counselor is also in the principal's office, the city council meeting, and the street—that is, anywhere that prevailing social arrangements privilege some and exclude others from having access to the means of leading fulfilling lives.

Counselors commonly ground their commitment to the field in their desire to help others. In many beginning counselors' minds, such helping centers on one-to-one or group emotional exploration and individual behavior change. That commitment is admirable. However, without a complementary dedication to social justice action and advocacy, counselors may find themselves to be unwitting accomplices in the preservation of an unjust status quo. Methods such as client advocacy and organizational intervention are at least equal to the clinical interview as ways of "counseling," in a large sense. While the clinical interview continues to be a powerful means for helping others, socially critical actions that are described throughout this book and in this chapter will be required of counselors in order to ameliorate conditions that lead to client distress. The power of advocacy to create pervasive social change might be best illustrated by the story in Box 2.1.

This chapter is divided into three major sections. The first section explores the notion of social justice itself. The second section describes the pervasive impact of the social context on individual lives, most pointedly through the notion of the sociological imagination. In that second section, the key concepts that explain social inequality are introduced: socialization, social stratification, inequity, oppression, dominance, hegemony, and privilege. The third section addresses counseling for social justice, particularly the notions of socially critical thinking, critical consciousness, and principled thinking and action.

Social Diversity Versus Social Justice

Appreciation of social diversity, which was discussed in Chapter 1, is a revolutionary idea. It requires members of a community to encourage all voices to be heard, especially those that were formerly silenced and marginalized. But social diversity is a limited notion. It refers only to the recognition of differences in customs, styles, and ways of thinking in a community. It does not refer to power differences among groups; therefore, simple appreciation of diversity is inadequate for the broader work of counseling. The notion of social justice must be brought in to address opportunity, power, and inequity.

> **BOX 2.1 A Parable About Advocacy**
>
> A counselor was walking along a riverbank one day when she heard the mournful cries of an infant coming from the river. The infant was placed in a poorly constructed basket that was quickly taking on water, endangering the child. The counselor "alertly" called 911 and then proceeded to wade into the water to rescue the child. No sooner had she bundled the child in warm blankets and checked vital signs than another cry was heard from the river. This time two infants were drifting perilously downstream. Additional personnel were recruited and rescue efforts ensued. As the reader might surmise, soon myriad infants, too numerous to rescue, were seen in the river. The counselor's response was to turn and walk upstream. Some of the other rescuers were distressed by this and asked the counselor why she was doing this. She replied that she needed to head upstream to determine why the babies were landing in the river in the first place, in order to address the problem at its source.

DEFINING SOCIAL JUSTICE

Although social justice is a commonly used term, no single accepted definition exists. It can most simply be described as *a societal-level commitment to equity for all groups of people.* This definition by Davis, Cox, and Adler (2005) captures the key elements of social justice: "Social justice is a . . . goal . . . of democratic societies and includes equitable access to societal institutions, resources, opportunities, rights, goods, [and] services" (p. 1). The definition goes on to describe the guiding principle behind social justice, which is a society's responsibility "for all groups and individuals without arbitrary limitations based on observed differences or interpretations of differences in age, color, culture, physical or mental disability, education, gender, income, language, national origin, race, religion, or sexual orientation" (p. 1). Note the words "responsibility for all groups and individuals." In essence, social justice is a declaration in favor of equitable access to a society's resources. It is a commitment to that purpose. Most religious traditions advocate social justice.

In that vein, counselors are challenged to engage in social justice work. It is their professional responsibility to target the important power differences among cultural and social groups in society. Counselors then must work to eliminate biases and to change attitudes and institutional policies that promote inequity. Promoting social justice can be considered a lifelong and universal effort because dominant groups in society or in an organization tend to maintain and reproduce their power (Domhoff, 2005; Mills, 1957).

The tendency for power to reproduce itself can be seen in such phenomena as middle-class counselors seeking to work with affluent clients; men seeking to replace other men in positions of organizational leadership; affluent families sending children to private schools; financial leaders belonging to exclusive clubs where connections are made and business is conducted; and heterosexual counselor educators teaching "marriage" counseling, thereby leaving out lesbian and gay couples. It is the purpose of this chapter to help counselors challenge power that results in significant inequity for some of their clients.

The next section describes the overall social context of individual lives.

The Presence of the Social Dimension in Individual Lives

The counseling field has traditionally emphasized the individual, outside the social context. By contrast, the field of social work has embraced the social context of people's lives as a focus of intervention, whether the context is the family, institutions, or the community. Counselors must similarly begin to acknowledge the powerful social dimension of clients' lives.

Two related concepts capture this interpenetration of the two spheres: the social-in-the-individual and the sociological imagination.

THE SOCIAL-IN-THE-INDIVIDUAL

As described in Chapter 1, individuals internalize messages from culture, family, and other social institutions. One vivid way to remember the social construction of the individual is to think of an invisible presence in the counseling room—the hundreds of ancestors, relatives, opportunities, institutions, policies and legislation, and all other social influences that pervade clients' thinking and acting. Many people, past and present, sit metaphorically in clients' laps, in the form of memories, cultural norms, and beliefs about bias and opportunity. In addition to internalized messages, individuals are also affected by external opportunities and limitations. That might be called "the social-in-the-individual."

This recognition of the social construction of individual lives is a countercultural notion in the United States in contrast with the American ethic of individualism and the myth of the self-made person. From their earliest days, Americans hear rags-to-riches stories of success and are told that anyone can succeed, that only hard work breeds success, that "You can do it if you only try," and that "People are poor because they don't want to work or are unwilling to sacrifice." As a result, Americans have usually resorted to the individual level of analysis to explain a person's place in life. The power of social context is left out of the formula, despite its impact on individuals' life opportunities.

A way to remind oneself of the social context of lives is to use the "sociological imagination" to understand individual lives. That classic concept is the subject of the next section.

THE SOCIOLOGICAL IMAGINATION

The link between the individual and the social context was most starkly presented by sociologist C. Wright Mills (1959) in his description of what he called the "sociological imagination."

Neither the life of an individual nor the history of a society can be understood without understanding both. Yet [individuals] do not usually define the troubles they endure in terms of historical change and institutional contradiction. (p. 3)

The sociological imagination alerts people to the many ways in which their individual experiences, successes, and failures have much to do with historical and social circumstance. Although individuals are able to shape society to some extent, that influence pales in comparison to the extent to which their society shapes them. Mills' (1959) concept challenges the individualistic tendency of people to be purely self-congratulatory or self-blaming for their life circumstances. The socio-logical imagination allows one to see the pervasive influence of circumstances that are beyond individuals' control. For example, if nearly everyone of a person's age, race, gender, and class goes to college, gets a good job with benefits, and avoids prison, it is tempting to see her or his seemingly individual success at these things as nothing extraordinary. In fact, it is the departure from that norm that would be shocking. Such success is often seen to be solely the result of individual effort. This notion can be troubling for dominant-group Americans to acknowledge because their success or failure does not seem to be quite as special as it would be if purely individual effort were the source. As Cámara (1981) notes, "it is very difficult to create awareness in the privileged" (p. 48). The reader is encouraged to complete Activity 2.1 in order to better understand the sociological imagination.

Counselors need to use the sociological imagination in order to work with the full range of clients, especially those from nondominant groups. Counselors must acknowledge the context in which individuals live. They need to appreciate the power that classism, racism, ableism, sexism, and other oppressions continue to have on life in U.S. society (Grant & Sleeter, 1996).

Two additional concepts from sociology, socialization and social stratifica-tion, will be discussed here in order to give the reader a fuller sense of the power of the social context in people's lives.

SOCIALIZATION

Socialization describes the process of how individuals internalize social norms—how the social context infuses the individual. Socialization is defined by Marger (2005) as a total experience:

The process through which people learn their society's culture . . . not simply learning the rules and beliefs of the society but internalizing them, making them an integral part of one's way of seeing and making judgments about the world. . . . If successfully imparted by socializing agents . . . the correctness of those beliefs is henceforth seldom questioned or even given much conscious thought. (pp. 369–370)

This definition emphasizes internalization of the social (what might be called "the social-in-the-individual") and challenges the illusion that individuals are self-made. It is similar in many ways to the concept of enculturation that will be discussed in Chapter 3. However, socialization doesn't refer only to a culture of

ACTIVITY 2.1

Applying the Sociological Imagination

C. Wright Mills (1959) describes the sociological imagination as enabling *"its possessor to understand the larger historical scene in terms of its meaning for the inner life and the external career of a variety of individuals"* (p. 5). The sociological imagination is a cognitive bridge that links individual concerns to the structure of society.

Describe a personal conflict or difficulty you or someone close to you has experienced in these two ways:

1. Start by describing the personal difficulty.

2. Then explain the ways in which this difficulty is tied to larger social forces, such as the economy, the government, any cultural groupings (such as ethnicity, religion, gender, social class), cultural institutions (such as the media), or the family. This is not an easy activity; it requires one to think beyond the individual and the moment.

SOURCE: Adapted from Bettinger (2003).

origin, but rather to the broad process of incorporating social messages of all kinds throughout life.

Socialization is, in essence, the process by which one becomes a member of human society. Through socialization, people accept and internalize the community's rules and beliefs to such an extent that those rules and beliefs are usually not only not questioned but considered to be unquestionable (Marger, 2005). Those rules and beliefs are not recognized as existing outside a person but simply as the way things are and ought to be.

People are socialized within the institutions of the family, education, religious institutions, cultural institutions, the economy, and the state. Each of these institutions reinforces the societal norms, rules, and beliefs about behavior, the society, and the individual's place in society. It is through social institutions that "reality" is constructed and that individuals come to "know" things about themselves and society. In short, all people are "socially constructed" in that they are socialized to be who they are and to know what they know or what they think they know.

In the past, primary socialization occurred in the family, religious institutions, and schools. However, in Marger's (2005) words, "the media are becoming the chief means through which people construct their versions of social reality" (p. 377). In fact, the television is on nearly eight hours every day in the average U.S. home (TV-Turnoff Network, 2005) and 80 percent of people get their national and international news from television (Project for Excellence in Journalism, 2004). The media increasingly define what is good, true, and beautiful.

Socialization is pervasive but not absolute. Counselors can help clients learn about their socialization and make some choices. Gender role analysis and narrative therapy, which will be discussed in upcoming chapters, ask clients to step back from the socialized stories that they have internalized and to choose the stories they wish to tell about what is important for them.

It should be noted at this point that despite the previous discussion of the social context of individual lives, the social dimension shouldn't be the exclusive emphasis in counseling. Recognition of the social context does not imply that the individual level cannot be addressed, or that personal responsibility is discarded. To consider only the social context could mistakenly become a type of fatalism, a sort of predestination-by-caste. Conversely, to factor in only the individual would be to endorse a total freedom that belies the influence of the larger social context. Instead, the individual and the social context are inextricably linked, living in tension with each other. To avoid overgeneralizing about the influence of the social and cultural dimensions on individual lives, counselors can practice "dynamic sizing" in assessing and working with their clients (Sue, 2006). Such sizing consists of an ongoing (dynamic) assessment (sizing) of how well the client fits into cultural generalizations and how she or he doesn't because of individual variations.

INSTITUTIONALIZED INEQUALITY: SOCIAL STRATIFICATION

A final topic in this overall discussion of the social context in individual lives is social stratification. *Social stratification* refers to the status and benefits that people receive within a society according to their group membership.

In some societies, such stratification is formal and institutionalized. So it was with the pre-Civil Rights Movement South and feudal medieval Europe. Formal stratification exists today in some societies, in which there are official castes, and it has remnants even in Great Britain and other countries where there are aristocracies by birth. But social stratification exists in all societies. Social stratification reveals the stark and often uncomfortable fact that inequality is patterned and institutional in the United States, not simply random or personal. It also reveals that inequalities are established in the everyday fabric of society. The reader is encouraged to complete Activity 2.2 in order to enrich her or his understanding of social stratification.

Illustration of Social Stratification: Access to Things That Count

Social stratification affects the things that count in life, both material things, such as jobs and schools, and symbolic things, such as respect and influence. Material things count because they have major implications for a person's future. Quality education, jobs, health care, and housing all further one's social advancement and individual growth and development. Symbolic things count because they increase one's self-esteem, sense of efficacy in the world, and social success.

Poverty and Stratification. Poverty affects access to both material and symbolic things. Poverty is a good illustration of social stratification at work and an example of how the social context affects individual lives. Many Americans believe that poverty is largely a matter of individual choice. That belief belies the group dimension of poverty. Indeed, poverty rates reveal that the individual level of analysis cannot be used to understand social processes because these processes can have great power over individuals. Poverty rates differ dramatically over time. For example, in 1959, 18.5 percent of U.S. families were poor. That figure dropped to a low of 8.8 percent in 1974, rose thereafter to 9.2 percent in 1979, and continued creeping upward to 12.3 percent in 1983 and again in 1993 before hitting its lowest point of 8.7 percent in 2000 and then rising again to 10 percent in 2003 (U.S. Census Bureau, 2004). It's hard to imagine that hundreds of thousands of individuals simply increased their commitment to work during the course of a decade (1959–1969) and then that a decade later (1979–1983) so many adults just decided to quit work, thereby throwing their families into poverty. It is therefore impossible to explain such shifts in poverty as stemming solely from an individual lack of effort. Rather, public policy and social structural shifts provide the keys to understanding changing poverty rates.

Consequences of Stratification

U. S. society reinforces stratification and the ensuing access to those things that count. For example, most people want an excellent education because it increases the likelihood of landing a high-paying job with benefits, including health care. And with the income from such a job, individuals can purchase a good home in a stable neighborhood with good schools. However, access to those things that count is limited: Even though both entrée to public education for children and emergency health care for all are required by law, some groups are more likely than others to access them successfully.

Education is a prime example of stratification. The allocation of educational resources, both human and material, is disproportional and depends largely on one's neighborhood or zip code. Non-accredited schools and schools with less-qualified teachers are overrepresented in areas with families in the lower socioeconomic strata. Stratification extends to higher education. This can be illustrated by the distribution of the students by socioeconomic strata at the 146 most selective colleges and universities: Seventy-four percent of their student body is from the upper quartile of Americans, as measured by income. The lowest quartile is represented by only 3 percent of their student body ("Top Schools," 2004).

The power of stratification is revealed in the disparity between reading and math levels among racio-ethnic groups. On average, African American and Latino/Latina 12th graders read and do math at the level of white 8th graders. But the power of stratification is revealed in the following facts: Students in more affluent schools, most of whom are white, are more likely to (1) be enrolled in a rigorous curriculum and (2) have adequate educational resources, such as highly qualified teachers. Thus, the stratification creates the disparity. This condition is not irreversible: When the deficits of schools serving students from lower socioeconomic strata are ameliorated, the benchmark indicators show significant increases (Sciarra, 2001).

ACTIVITY 2.2

Social Stratification

I. Think of at least two examples of social stratification in your present or past workplaces or other settings.

Examples:

- Regular education students being transported to the front door of their school while students with disabilities are assigned to another door, typically out of sight
- Office staff being called by first names while managers or faculty are called by titles
- Men in corporations gathering for social or sporting events where business is conducted while female colleagues are not included
- Janitors and housekeeping staff being members of certain ethnic groups while the professionals are of another ethnic group

1.

2.

II. Are/were the reasons cited for the continuation of these practices legitimate; that is, in the spirit of necessary hierarchy? Or do/did these practices serve to reinforce unnecessary hierarchy and privilege?

The consequences of stratification can also be seen on a global level. More than eight million people perish each year due to extreme poverty, a rate of more than 20,000 deaths *daily.* (Imagine the entire student body of a major U.S. university perishing each day.) As a nation, the United States spends 0.15 percent (15 cents out of every $100) of the Gross National Product to address such poverty. In contrast, the United States spends more than 30 times that amount on military efforts (Sachs, 2005). The United States' consumption of the world's resources is also grossly disproportionate to its population. The United States constitutes 5 percent of the global human census but consumes approximately one-third of the world's resources and produces nearly half of the world's waste. While some believe that extreme poverty is eradicable by 2025 (Sachs, 2005), it will take advocacy and a social justice mind-set to effect such a welcome change.

The purpose of this discussion of stratification is to heighten counselors' awareness of the social dimension in individual lives. Counselors are challenged to confront the stratifications that maintain unnecessary and enduring inequities. There is hope that this work can be successful. The picture of the past century is not all bleak. Some attempts at reducing unnecessary stratifications have been effective: the creation of vocational guidance bureaus that were the origins of the counseling field, the social work movement, civil rights legislation, and the women's movement. Box 2.2 explores the nature and impact of affirmative action, which is one of the attempts made in the United States to address stratification.

Thus far, the interplay of the social and the individual dimensions of human life has been explored through the concepts of the sociological imagination, socialization, and social stratification. Armed with those general concepts, the reader will now be introduced to the issues of equality and equity. Counselors play parts in many institutions that affect equity.

SOCIAL EQUALITY AND EQUITY: ACCESS AND OPPORTUNITY

Although the terms sound alike, a practical distinction can be made between equality and equity. Equality means that every person receives the same treatment irrespective of her or his social group membership. Equity, on the other hand, goes a few steps farther. It involves fairness and justice. Equity means providing nondominant groups with genuine access to the things that matter in society. If everyone is treated only equally, then there is no need for civil rights legislation, anti-hate crime laws, affirmative action, women's centers, or disabilities services. If equity is the goal, then differential conditions among groups are acknowledged so that actions can be taken to ensure fair access to society's goods.

The distinction is subtle but important. The terms "access" versus "opportunity" are useful here. The public education system illustrates the distinction between equality (mere access) and equity (genuine opportunity): Despite the fact that everyone in the United States has an equal right (access) to receive a free, public schooling, not everyone has the same opportunities for a good education. Middle- and upper-class white students living in wealthy suburban school districts attend schools with better educational facilities and programs, more highly qualified teachers, and higher per-pupil expenditures than their lower-class black counterparts who live in lower-income districts. Thus, social equality provides persons or groups with mere equal access to institutions and experiences. Higher education provides another example. Simple equality means allowing underprepared college students to be admitted to universities, but not providing supplemental services, such as tutoring and career counseling, to help them succeed. The absence of such services results in student attrition due to the lack of academic skills and attitudes. The community college philosophy illustrates the difference between equality and equity. There, equity for underprepared students is provided through supplemental services such as tutoring, advising, and counseling. Open access, or open admissions, is not considered enough. In the words of a common expression, "The open door (open admissions) should not be a revolving door." Thus, community college counselors are agents of opportunity, not just bystanders for access.

Simple equality does not help people succeed once they have achieved minimal access to an institution. True equity requires that all groups have the opportunity to use their access in order to be successful (Zepeda & Langenbach, 1999).

BOX 2.2   Affirmative Action

The debate about affirmative action in the United States reveals the shifts in stratification that can occur through intentional social action. Affirmative action programs aimed at improving the access to jobs for men of color and for all women came into existence under executive orders issued by President Johnson in 1965 and 1967 as part of civil rights advancements. The fundamental tenet of affirmative action was (and is) that *people of color and women must be sought out and given a fair opportunity at jobs.* It did not require quotas, only justifications for not hiring minorities, with clear criteria for hiring.

Affirmative action became a target of critics. As the pool of job and school applicants widened at a time when the available places either decreased or remained stable, some white men did not gain access to the work or education they wanted and believed they otherwise would have obtained. They blamed "unqualified" or "less qualified" women and minority men for "taking their jobs." This belief was sometimes encouraged by employers who did not relish an integrated workforce or who resisted telling a white man he wasn't as qualified for a job as he thought. Simply put, it was easier to blame affirmative action than to change practices to confront racism and discrimination.

The white male backlash successfully linked affirmative action with reverse discrimination and with denial of the fundamental tenet of equal opportunity in public rhetoric, policy, and legal decisions. However, critics of affirmative action failed to acknowledge that equal opportunity had never existed in U.S. society. In fact, white males had benefited from 300 years of "de facto affirmative action" when men of color and all women were restricted in their educational and employment endeavors. White men had seen themselves as successful due to their superior abilities. However, they did not recognize that they did not have to compete for access with a significant portion of the population. As a result of this backlash, some aspects of affirmative action have been scaled back: The U.S. Supreme Court in its 1978 *Bakke* decision declared some dimensions of affirmative action programs to be supporting "reverse discrimination," that is, discrimination against an individual or group that is traditionally in the majority.

Affirmative action was a bold move for the United States. It is not paralleled in many other nations. Coming on the heels of major civil unrest, it is credited with saving the United States from a major social crisis.

Equality and Extreme Individualism

The ethos of equality, as opposed to the notion of equity, has dominated much of the policy and debate in the United States. Helping people from historically underrepresented groups to gain access to education and jobs, for example, has been the practice. When those people arrive, they often are not given the support to succeed. That practice is based on the extreme version of individualism that is part of U.S. culture. It is often heard that there is an "even playing field," that "anyone can be anything she or he wants if she or he tries," that "the only barrier to success is ambition." The underlying assumption of "the even playing field" is that everyone has equal access to resources, such as jobs and education, as if there were no legacies of oppression and privilege.

This common American myth that all have equal opportunity was born out of the experience of European American people who rejected the Old (European)

World of inherited aristocratic privilege. It spoke meaningfully to white entre-preneurs at a time in history when white skin, male sex, and open lands (origi-nally taken from the indigenous peoples) provided opportunity to succeed. Thus, white Americans often now see individual effort as the only barrier to success. However, that effort is accompanied by social privilege.

It is hard for many Americans to acknowledge the historical, and sometimes continuing, oppression of people of non-European descent, of women, and of gays and lesbians (Takaki, 1993). A racing analogy helps describe inequity. Imagine Americans running a 100-meter dash, without recognition of training, inheritance, or other opportunities. In U.S. culture, those who experience multiple privileged statuses appear to begin that race at the 90-meter mark. The less privileged are con-signed to running the full distance, in a lane that also contains numerous hurdles placed along the path. When the race is run and the victor "righteously" claims the prize associated with victory in the "competition," the inequity of the arrangement is overlooked or denied while the victor claims that only her or his hard work was necessary for success.

Guided by the ethos of American hyper-individualism (Bellah, Madsen, Sullivan, Swidler, & Tipton, 1985), attempts have been made to legislate equal access (e.g., fair housing legislation, education improvement legislation for individuals with disabilities). However, those efforts often fail to provide equal opportunity because inequity is embedded in social practices such as race- and class-exclusive housing and neighborhood practices and discriminatory hiring and promotion. Each of these topics is discussed later in this chapter.

It should be noted, lest inequity is seen as part of an intentional conspiracy, that social inequity is often not a conscious effort on the part of the powerful major-ity. It is largely de facto. People tend to associate with others who look and act like themselves. All groups can practice inequity. Thus, people often live near, social-ize with, and hire those who are similar. Inequity may be a daily fact that is ingrained and promoted in habits, associations, and social institutions. It takes a conscious effort to counter inequity.

OPPRESSION AND THE "ISMS"

Inequity is often a consequence of oppression, in that a group in power uses its advantages to keep other groups from accessing resources. Oppression is the con-dition of being subject to another group's power. The term is sometimes confused with "suppression." To suppress ("to press under") involves an action that pro-hibits something. Suppression is an overt use of power, as when a government closes down a newspaper or suppresses a people's language and customs. Historic actions taken by the U.S. and Canadian governments against the Cajun French, people of African descent, French Canadians, and the American Indians/First Nations of the North American continent are examples of suppression. Further examples include the British suppression of Irish culture and religion and the laws that banned women from working when they were pregnant. More subtle sup-pressions were anti-Jewish hiring practices in many companies and the exclusion of many Jews from Ivy League colleges for a good portion of the twentieth century. Those acts represented active suppression by conscious policy and/or law.

Oppression ("to press against") is generally used in a broader way. Its common meaning is to burden or to keep in subjugation. Oppression can be very obvious, such as having Jews wear stars to identify themselves in Nazi Germany of the 1930s and early 1940s, or it can be subtle, such as telling heterosexist jokes or using slurs for nondominant groups. Those jokes and slurs have power only because they are backed up by a larger societal condition of oppression. By contrast, jokes about the dominant group have less or no impact in the world. The reader might consider the impact of such statements as "Just like a man" (gender), "That's so bourgeois" (social class), "You're acting so white (or WASP)." Although these statements can be hurtful, they lack a pervasive social disparagement of these dominant groups' ways.

A look around one's own environment can reveal subtle and not-so-subtle forms of oppression. Who are the janitors, the housekeepers, the kitchen staff, and the fast-food servers at schools, agencies, colleges, businesses, and hospitals? And who are the faculty, the dentists, the bank presidents? How does a national community justify a 9 percent unemployment rate for African Americans compared with a rate for whites of 4 percent (U.S. Bureau of Labor Statistics, 2006)? That disparity has been consistent over time. The figures have been parallel for at least the past 50 years (Council of Economic Advisors for the President's Initiative on Race, 1998).

Are those circumstances coincidental? They are obviously not due to mere chance, which leads to two possible conclusions. One is that group disparities are due to inferiority. The other is that they are due to oppression. The inferiority explanation posits that there is some kind of inherent deficient characteristic in groups, either genetic inferiority or cultural inferiority. Those arguments were attempted by the eugenics movement of the late nineteenth and early twentieth centuries and by the assimilation movement later in the twentieth century, as will be discussed in Chapter 4. In fact, until recently, leading thinkers considered everyone but Northern European Protestants to be inherently inferior. The genetic explanation has a long history, from pre-nineteenth-century racial classification systems, to the Nazis' theories of racial superiority, to the white supremacy movements of the American twentieth century. The genetic explanation has been thoroughly discredited. The cultural inferiority explanation has also been systematically challenged by the multicultural movement, backed by the evidence of progress made by nondominant groups when oppressions are lessened through civil rights legislation and affirmative action. Oppression, rather than inferiority, explains disparities among groups. It is the subject of the next sections. First, however, the special case of internalized oppression will be discussed.

Examples of External Oppression for Specific Groups

An illustration of oppression across a number of cultural groups is provided in Activity 2.3. Most of the oppressive conditions listed are not the result of legal suppression or explicit police force; instead, they are more subtle manifestations of oppressive attitudes and misuse of power. These oppressions contrast with the official U.S. ethic of equal opportunity. Culturally alert counselors can work to ameliorate each element, especially in the settings in which they work.

Internalized Oppression

Up to this point, external oppression has been described. Internal oppression must also be accounted for because it affects clients' hopes and expectations. Internalized oppression is the assumption by members of a nondominant group that they lack power and/or are inferior in relation to a dominant group in some or all domains. Those domains include academic ability, intelligence, language and accents, physical beauty, certain skills, athletic prowess, and customs. Internalized oppression results in a sense of hopelessness, a belief that trying against the odds is useless. For example, living with racism can take a personal psychological toll on African Americans as they experience the indignities of subtle and overt discrimination in their daily lives in public spaces, schools, and workplaces (Cose, 1993; Feagin & Sikes, 1994). Such experience can be internalized. For example, as early as first grade, non-white children and those in lower socioeconomic strata begin to restrict their occupational aspirations (Jackson & Grant, 2004).

The Cycle of Oppression

Oppression can be seen as a constantly renewing phenomenon in the "cycle" of oppression that is shown in Figure 2.1. The cycle of oppression traces the way that oppression occurs through socialization. Readers might think of a nondominant group, perhaps one to which they belong, as they read through the cycle. The domains listed previously can serve as concrete illustrations of the cycle of oppression.

Consider the example of a woman named Nita whose gender socialization has given her the message that she must be pleasant and cooperative at all times and deny her negative feelings about others. Those family and community messages then might be reinforced by media, schools, and religious institutions. She might experience a verbally abusive relationship but be unable to access the rage, hurt, fear, and confusion she feels about her "default" behavior—that is, being only accommodating and nonassertive. She might pass on this message to her female children, continuing the cycle. Activity 2.4 asks the reader to make a personal reference to oppression.

It should be noted that the cycle of oppression is not necessarily how things *must* be, but how things *might* be if vigilance and social justice actions do not happen. Oppressive conditions persist only when others allow them to (Dovidio & Gaertner, 1999). Vigilant voices that have examined and challenged oppression include the writers Jonathan Kozol, who wrote the book *Savage Inequalities* (1991); Carol Gilligan, who wrote *In a Different Voice* (1982); Paolo

Consequences of Oppression for Selected Nondominant Groups

In the boxes below, read the examples of oppression for six nondominant groups. Then note whether you understand the claim made about oppression and, after that, decide whether you agree or not or are undecided about these claims. At the end of the Activity, write down issues you need to know more about, issues you disagree with, and what you can do to increase your understanding of these specific issues.

Overall Consequence of Oppression	People of Color	Old People	Poor People	Gays and Lesbians	Women	Non-Christians and/or Non-White Christians
Isolation	Housing red-lining. White flight. Understand? Agree? ___	Being shut-ins. Not in traditional workplaces for socialization. Understand? Agree? ___	Gentrification. Housing projects. No transportation. Understand? Agree? ___	Forced to stay closeted. Unsafe in some places. Can't easily adopt children. Understand? Agree? ___	Being out alone is seen as dangerous. Having responsibility for an inordinate proportion of both family and career responsibilities. Understand? Agree? ___	Experiencing "church" as universal term for religion. Hearing only Christian prayers at public events. Understand? Agree? ___

(Continued)

(Continued)

Overall Consequence of Oppression	People of Color	Old People	Poor People	Gays and Lesbians	Women	Non-Christians and/or Non-White Christians
Emotional Abuse	Attributions of lower motivation and intelligence. Culture, language devalued. Understand? ___ Agree? ___	Ignored. Often ridiculed. Talked about in their presence. Understand? ___ Agree? ___	Blamed for poverty. Considered universally lazy, crime-prone. Understand? ___ Agree? ___	Seen as sexually perverted. Publicly taunted. Understand? ___ Agree? ___	Called pejorative names, especially for body parts. Treated as objects. Understand? ___ Agree? ___	Considered heathen and unsaved. Understand? ___ Agree? ___
Sexual Abuse	Not commonly portrayed as sexually desirable. Seen as oversexed. Understand? ___ Agree? ___	Seen as unattractive, not able to express sexuality. Understand? ___ Agree? ___	Considered gross and overly sexed, untamed. Understand? ___ Agree? ___	Accused of child molestation. Ridiculed as not being "real" men and women sexually. Understand? ___ Agree? ___	Rape (including date and marital). Objects in pornography and shows. Incest victims. Understand? ___ Agree? ___	Seen as sinful or exotic. Understand? ___ Agree? ___

Overall Consequence of Oppression	People of Color	Old People	Poor People	Gays and Lesbians	Women	Non-Christians and/or Non-White Christians
Economic Abuse	Overt and covert discrimination in hiring and in layoffs. Have to prove selves in job more than others. Understand? _____ Agree? _____	Fraud schemes target elders. Understand? _____ Agree? _____	Welfare/workfare regulations renew poverty. Low minimum wage = permanent working poor. Understand? _____ Agree? _____	Legal discrimination in employment. No access to partner benefits or retirement benefits. Understand? _____ Agree? _____	Low-paying jobs the norm. Paid less than men for same work. Lack of child care accommodation for career. Understand? _____ Agree? _____	Can be subject to Christian holiday and celebration prayers and practices. Understand? _____ Agree? _____
Privilege/Status	Seen as intellectually and socially inferior. Their culture seen as "low." Understand? _____ Agree? _____	Non-income producing, therefore seen as non-productive. Understand? _____ Agree? _____	Don't live up to middle-class values of dress, manners, etc. Understand? _____ Agree? _____	Gay expression not as valued as heterosexual is. Understand? _____ Agree? _____	Second class to men. Often seen as subservient. Labeled as too emotional, weak. Understand? _____ Agree? _____	Holidays not known or recognized. No models of political leaders (e.g., U.S. president). Few corporate or other leaders. Understand? _____ Agree? _____

(Continued)

Overall Consequence of Oppression	People of Color	Old People	Poor People	Gays and Lesbians	Women	Non-Christians and/or Non-White Christians
Threats/Violence/Intimidation	Racial profiling. Brutality. History of genocide, lynchings. Trail of Tears, etc. Understand? ____ Agree? ____	Threatened by violence. Fear being out at night. Understand? ____ Agree? ____	Government threatens to take away benefits. No health insurance for care. Understand? ____ Agree? ____	Public harassment in schools, by police. Gay bashing. Heterosexism rarely challenged. Understand? ____ Agree? ____	Battering. Physical intimidation. Understand? ____ Agree? ____	Swastikas painted on synagogues, harassment of Sikhs and Muslims, black churches burned. Understand? ____ Agree? ____

After you have completed your responses to each item, answer the following:

1. An issue I need to understand better or know more about: _____

2. An issue I don't understand or don't agree is an example of oppression: _____

3. Specific or general actions I might take to increase my knowledge or understanding of any of these issues: _____

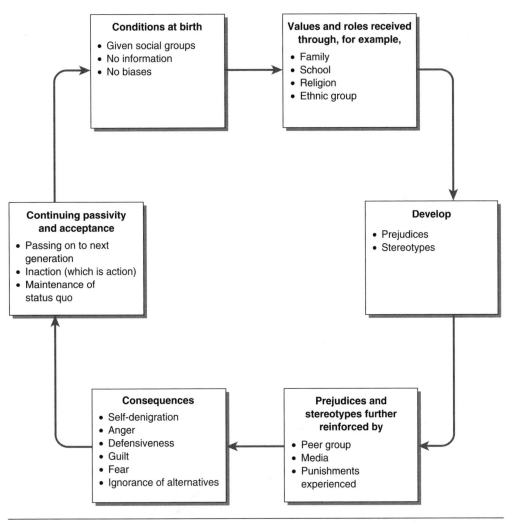

Figure 2.1   The Oppression Cycle

SOURCE: Adapted from Harro, B. (2000). The cycle of socialization. In M. Adams, W. J. Blumenfeld, R. Castaneda, H. W. Hackman, M. L. Peters, & X. Zuniga (Eds.), *Readings for diversity and social justice: An anthology on racism, sexism, anti-Semitism, heterosexism, ableism, and classism* (pp. 15–20). New York: Routledge.

Freire, author of *Pedagogy of the Oppressed* (1970); and bell hooks, who wrote *Teaching to Transgress* (1994). These socially critical writers have examined such phenomena as tracking in schools, everyday language that excludes, and internalized oppressions or beliefs by members of nondominant groups that they are somehow inferior. Their work is in the tradition of people whose lives have been dedicated to fighting oppression, such as Dr. Martin Luther King, Jr.; Dorothy Day (of the Catholic Worker movement); Saul Alinsky (community organizer who formed black-white workers' coalitions); César Chávez (leader of Latino agricultural workers' rights movement); Marion Wright Edelman (advocate for child protection); Archbishop Dom Helder Cámara (Brazilian Catholic archbishop and

---

ACTIVITY 2.4

Name one oppressed group to which you belong and write it up, as in the previous example, for each segment of Figure 2.1. Remember, oppressed groups can include those related to age, disability, and social class as well as gender, race, ethnicity, sexual orientation, and religion. If you cannot think of an oppressed group to which you belong, consider past oppressions against members of your group or a group to which a friend or relative belongs.

Born into the world:

Socialized by:

Learn:

Reinforced by messages from:

Results in:

Forms of conscious and unconscious acceptance:

---

champion of oppressed and indigent persons); and Nelson Mandela and Bishop Desmond Tutu (leaders of the South African liberation movement).

Counselors might wonder what their role can be in reducing oppressions, especially when such powerful figures as those mentioned above are paraded before them. Lest one believe that change efforts can be done only by larger-than-life figures, Kaufman (2003) reminds counselors,

> ordinary people acting together for common goals have accomplished incredible amounts. There is nothing magical about making social change happen. What is required is a sense of hope that it is possible to make a difference and some understanding of the world that helps orient our choices about what kinds of actions to take. (p. 5)

Much of this chapter and subsequent chapters should provide the reader with the understanding and skills for anti-oppression actions. The reader can plot her or his movement toward an anti-oppressive stance through the cultural identity development models that are explored in Chapter 4 and in later chapters. Toward that end, counselors can be guided to assist their clients in breaking the cycle of oppression through the model shown in Figure 2.2. By doing Activity 2.5, the reader can plot anti-oppressive actions that she or he has already taken in her or his life.

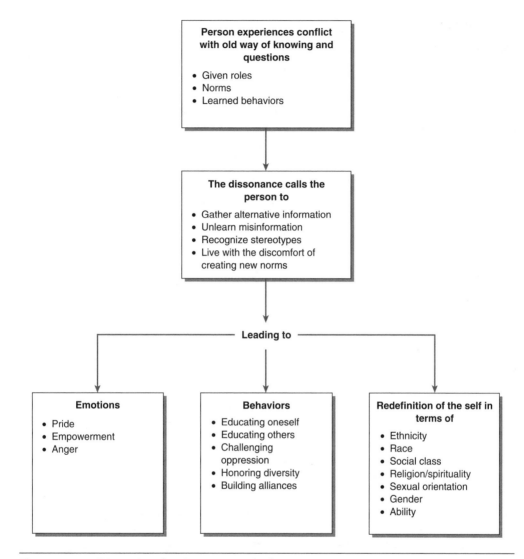

Figure 2.2   Disrupting the Oppression Cycle

SOURCE: Adapted from Harro, B. (2000). The cycle of socialization. In M. Adams, W. J. Blumenfeld, R. Castaneda, H. W. Hackman, M. L. Peters, & X. Zuniga (Eds.), *Readings for diversity and social justice: An anthology on racism, sexism, anti-Semitism, heterosexism, ableism, and classism* (pp. 15–20). New York: Routledge.

   Returning to the case of Nita that was previously mentioned, in order to break the cycle of oppression, counseling can help her to question the roles and rules that have been ingrained as part of her socialization. She might then begin to move out of the comfort zone of family rules by connecting with a support group of other women, or reading, or taking a women's studies course. In the process of learning new information, she might begin to identify her anger, increase her sense of empowerment, act to interrupt her oppression by expressing her negative feelings and acting assertively, and build a supportive community of like-minded women and men.

ACTIVITY 2.5

Using the categories in Figure 2.2, explain how you or someone else has broken or might break the cycle of oppression. (If this is difficult to do at this point, further work on understanding oppression of nondominant groups is in order and can occur partially by working through this book.)

Through dissonance, confrontations, and contradictions we question (e.g., a gender role, an attitude toward disability, an ethnic/racial stereotype)

Which calls us to

Which results in
• **Feelings and actions**

• **Redefining who we are in regard to**

The model of breaking the cycle can serve as a guide for counselors who are working with such clients. Counselors can use some of the following tools to help clients understand their oppressions: the cultural identity model that was mentioned in Chapter 1, the racial and ethnic identity development models that are in Chapters 3 and 4, and the stages in the liberation counseling model that is described in Chapter 16.

DOMINANCE AND NONDOMINANCE

One way to understand oppression is through the lens of dominance and nondominance. All counselors and clients can be members of both dominant and nondominant groups, by any combination of ethnicity, race, class, gender, religion, sexual orientation, ability/disability, and age. In Chapter 1, readers were asked to identify whether they were members of dominant or nondominant cultural groups. The reader might review her or his memberships from Activity 1.2, Introductory Cultural Self-Awareness, as she or he reads the list of the characteristics of dominance and nondominance in Box 2.3 (Baker Miller, 1976). The distinction is important because of the need for counselors to work especially with nondominant groups so that those groups' access to social benefits is not restricted.

BOX 2.3   Characteristics of Dominant and Nondominant Statuses

- Some people or groups are defined as *unequal and nondominant* by "ascription"; that is, by virtue of birth they are ascribed or assigned to a lesser-valued and less powerful social group. Examples of groups assigned a nondominant status by birth include, at some time in U.S. history, African Americans, Chinese, Irish Catholics, American Indians, Italians, the Scots-Irish, Mexicans, Jews, and women.

- Once a group is defined as lesser, the dominant group tends to label it as *defective or substandard.* Thus, at the turn of the twentieth century, people from Mediterranean and Eastern European countries were considered inferior to most groups of Northern Europeans, especially during the great waves of European immigration to North America. See Chapter 4 for further discussion of the eugenics and cultural assimilation movements.

- Dominant groups usually define *acceptable roles* for nondominants. Those roles might consist of providing services that the dominants do not want to perform. For example, some ethnic groups are overrepresented in low-paying housekeeping, agricultural, and janitorial jobs.

- Nondominants are usually said to be *incapable of performing* the preferred roles. For example, African Americans were once deemed unfit for management roles in sports organizations. Catholics in Northern Ireland were considered to be too unreliable and unintelligent to participate in the leadership and the policing of that province.

- Nondominants can come to find it difficult to believe in their own abilities. Nondominants absorb a large part of the story created by the dominants and can feel inferior (i.e., experience "internalized oppression"). For example, American Indians might take on negative stereotypes and feel inadequate within urban Western society; individuals who grow up poor might be embarrassed by their homes, clothing, and tastes. Latinas might want to be taller and thinner, Asians to be rounder-eyed, African American women might want straight hair, and gay men and lesbians might think of their sexual orientation as "wrong" and their erotic attractions as "sick." Similarly, many women might doubt their ability to change an automobile tire, despite there being no evidence for that belief. And some African American adolescent males might have internalized a belief that they are not fit for academic work.

The list of dominance trends in Box 2.3 may imply that dominance and non-dominance are total and unrelenting, but the picture is much muddier than that. Positive social change has, in fact, occurred in U.S. society, resulting in some reduction in the distinctions between dominance and nondominance. However, given the previously stated postulates about dominance, it is easy to imagine increasing dominance by those groups who still have the most resources (e.g., male, Anglo-Protestant, middle class, Christian) unless counselors and others are vigilant about dominance.

These ideas about dominance should also be qualified by social contexts. Every person can be a nondominant in some situations. For example, a white individual might feel nondominant in an all-black religious service. In that setting, the white person might doubt her or his ability to be physically and emotionally expressive and might feel inadequate in relation to the (temporarily) dominant group of African Americans. However, in a broad sense, dominance is consistently the province of some groups in the larger society. When the white person leaves the African American religious service, she or he is again in the dominant racial group where she or he has greater access to the things that count, as discussed previously in this chapter.

HEGEMONY

Hegemony is a special case of dominance. Hegemony describes the condition of a dominant group's all-encompassing influence on a community's (e.g., a nation's) ways of thinking, feeling, and acting. The reader might be familiar with terms like "Roman hegemony" (over the nations Rome colonized). Hegemony leaves no room for a nondominant culture to express its values.

The recent use of the word hegemony to describe total cultural dominance can be traced to the Italian writer Antonio Gramsci. Gramsci was from a poor southern Italian family. He wrote much of his work while imprisoned for eight years in Mussolini's Italy in the 1920s and 1930s (Forgasc, 2000). Gramsci described hegemony as the permeation throughout society of an entire system of values, attitudes, beliefs, and morality that has the effect of supporting the status quo in power relations.

Hegemony, in this sense, might be considered an "organizing principle" that is diffused by the process of socialization into every area of daily life. To the extent that this prevailing consciousness is internalized by the population, it becomes part of what is generally called "common sense" so that the philosophy, culture, and morality of the ruling elite appear to be the natural order of things. It has been hegemonic in the United States to assume that, for example, blond hair and blue eyes are the epitome of female beauty, or that men do science better than women, or that poor persons lack the personal qualities to become educated. It was once hegemonic that all bank presidents were Anglo-Protestant Americans and that Ivy League colleges were for men. Currently, the unquestioned assumption that marriage is only for heterosexuals would be hegemonic.

The following conditions are, or can become, hegemonic, that is, taken for granted as the way things are and must be, either by a whole society or by a particular community. It should be noted that hegemony can occur in specific contexts, such as in a religious community, a gender-exclusive club, or a rigid family system.

- Obliviousness to people with disabilities' needs in public spaces

- Heterosexuality as the only option, resulting in lesbians and gay men being treated as unnatural and having to hide public expressions of affection

- Pre-eminence of male standards of communication, language, and competition, for example, the use of noninclusive language such as "he" and "mankind" to represent women and men

- "Family" being defined only as a husband-wife-children combination

- African American verbal expressiveness being treated as "too loud" and "bad manners"

- One religion's prayers, traditions, or hymns being exclusively offered at public events

- Upper- and middle-class children receiving better educations than poorer children

All of the above examples are often viewed as "just the way things are and must be" by some members of U.S. society. In each of these cases, the dominant group's values permeate the culture so that the nondominants are seen as nonexistent or wrong. What interrupts hegemony is discussion and debate and the recognition that other options are possible in the social construction of norms, values, and institutions. Because hegemony is so pervasive and unquestioned, it is important for counselors to understand the notion so that they can unearth it and challenge it.

PRIVILEGE: INVISIBLE AND UNEARNED

Privilege is the condition of a person having distinct advantages by virtue of her or his membership in a dominant cultural group. Such privilege is not asked for, nor is it obvious. It is not earned through individual effort; it is given by group membership. Privilege is, in a sense, the opposite of oppression.

Privilege, like oppression, is often hidden or "invisible," in Peggy McIntosh's (1998) words. However, it is usually not hidden from the members of nondominant groups, who are often acutely aware of their nonprivileged condition.

A privileged state is often informal and unofficial. Following is an account of the emotional shock that comes from discovery of privilege, written by a journalist who participated in cross-racial dialogues in his city:

> The real eye-opener for me, to which I'd given little thought before these dialogues, was how my life had been shaped by "white privilege." I'd always taken for granted the social opportunities open to me—the neighborhoods where I lived, the schools I attended, the friends I made, the public places I frequented, the activities I freely engaged in, even the dreams I dared dream. It had never occurred to me that these nearly all depended on my being white. . . . I realize now that in accepting white privilege I have benefited from racism in ways for which I can't begin to make restitution. How do [black people] forgive? Or [white people] repent? For both races these are the core questions the dialogues come to, gently but honestly, in an atmosphere of respect. (Delaney, 2004, p. 12)

Delaney (2004) reveals the subtlety of much privilege. In that vein, McIntosh (1998) has conceptualized the notion of "unearned, invisible privilege." This "knapsack" of invisible privilege, as McIntosh calls it, carries assets that the privileged individual can regularly draw on in order to more easily negotiate daily life. Activity 2.6 lists some of the privileges of dominant group members.

ACTIVITY 2.6

Sample Privilege Inventory

I. Following are some of the invisible privileges that members of various dominant groups carry, as delineated by McIntosh (1998). The reader is asked to compare her or his situation with those listed here. Place a check mark next to those that are accurate for you.

___ The day I move into new housing that I have chosen, I can be pretty sure that my new neighbors will be neutral or pleasant to me.

___ When I am told about our national heritage or about "civilization," I am shown that people of my color (or gender) made it what it is.

___ I can do well in a challenging situation without being called a credit to my race (or gender, or sexual orientation).

___ I went to school with my friends and was not humiliated by being labeled and placed in different settings than they were.

___ I can easily buy posters, postcards, picture books, greeting cards, dolls, toys, and children's magazines featuring mostly people of my own race (or sexual orientation).

___ I can go home from most meetings of organizations to which I belong feeling somewhat connected rather than isolated, out of place, outnumbered, unheard, held at a distance, or feared.

___ Most of the time I can arrange to protect my children from people who might not like them.

___ I did not need to teach my children about racism for their own daily protection.

___ In my neighborhood, any police officer who might need to arrest people in my family is likely to be a person of my race.

___ The Constitution that I am subject to was created by people of my ethnic heritage and sex to apply to people of my ethnic heritage and not to apply to people of other races or sex.

___ Those who have been able to afford the high costs of legal and/or medical training have been, for the most part, people of my race.

___ If I stand in line at a bank teller's window, no one looks at me as though he or she has a problem with my being there.

___ If I am laughing with friends on a street at night, or talking loudly in a parking lot, it is not assumed that I am dangerous or a member of a gang.

___ A real estate agent has never discriminated against me to "protect property values."

___ Bad race relations in the United States are not attributed to my race's criminal behavior, despite a history of race-related breaking of laws by whites over the entire span of Anglo European life on this continent.

II. Now comment on what you thought, felt, and noticed as a result of this inventory.

Invisibility

The list from Activity 2.6 is intended to make privilege obvious. However, privilege is often invisible. Invisible privilege is one of the most difficult concepts for members of dominant groups to understand. An apt analogy might be that a smooth road (privilege) is not easily noticed; a bumpy one, however, is vividly experienced. So it is with everyday privilege—it is taken for granted as the privileged person negotiates the challenges of daily life. McIntosh (1998) draws a parallel with left- or right-handedness: "Most right-handed people cannot tell you about right-handed privilege. . . . Left-handed people have a lot to say on the subject of being left-handed, which comes as a surprise to the dominant group" (p. 214). McIntosh further notes that those white persons who do notice race privilege are those "who, through interracial relationships, cross-cultural adoptions, and other 'border crossings,' are positioned . . . to have double or triple perspectives, seeing on both sides of lines of privilege" (p. 214). The lesson is that the privileged must try to walk in the shoes of the nonprivileged by gaining personal knowledge.

Invisible privilege is especially difficult for dominant group members to see because it can be ego-threatening. Recognition of one's privilege challenges one's sense of being a moral and a "nice" person. It is also difficult to recognize simply because it does not stem from explicitly oppressive laws, anti-minority violence, or outright/overt discrimination. McIntosh (1998) proposes that privilege is hidden because those who have privilege have been taught not to see it, in order that the dominant group can maintain a self-serving "feel-good" myth of meritocracy (i.e., that each individual achieves solely on individual merit, without reference to social context) and to confirm that democracy is working as it should. The reader is encouraged to complete Activity 2.7 in order to identify her or his possible invisible privilege.

The more invisible privilege is, the less likely it is privileged group members will challenge the status quo. As has been mentioned, those who have invisible privilege tend to assume that their power has been gained through individual effort, rather than partially by membership in a privileged group. And yet, privilege actively replicates itself. For example, admission to prestigious universities is easier for those with a "legacy," that is, with a family member who attended that institution in the past. In fact, Harvard University admits about 43 percent of legacy applicants, as opposed to 11 percent of the rest of the applicants, despite the fact that legacy admittees score an average of 35 points fewer on the SAT than non-legacy admits (Loverro, 2003; Shapiro, 2006). As a result, European American applicants will be favored at Harvard based on legacy. This type of informal "affirmative action" is in place in many sectors of society, leaving fewer places for those without such legacies. While individuals from any cultural group can and do make great achievements, the subtle external and internal barriers keep a majority of those in oppressed groups from certain kinds of success. One could ask, for example, about the many African American

---

ACTIVITY 2.7

Privilege Awareness Activity

Review the Cultural Group Memberships Worksheet from Chapter 1 (Activity 1.2). In which of your six group memberships do you have invisible privilege? Where that is the case, describe several ways that you have benefited from this privilege while others who do not have such privilege might not.

1. Ethnicity

2. Race

3. Social Class

4. Gender

5. Sexual Orientation

6. Religion

---

singers of the 1950s and earlier whose music was "covered" by white performers and whose original contributions were ignored. Many wound up penniless despite their creative efforts. Was it the white singer's talent alone, or did privilege play a part? Could Elvis Presley have been black? White privilege helped the so-called king of rock and roll.

Responding to Privilege

Counselors should be alert to their own unearned, invisible privilege and to the oppression of groups of which they are not members. That alertness will help them to be sensitive to the "baggage," in the forms of pessimism, low self-esteem, and frustration, that clients from oppressed groups might carry around. Indeed, counselors should keep in mind the comment that can be heard at the end of a long day by some clients who are in oppressed groups: "I'm so tired from being [black, or gay, or female, or a person with a disability] all day. It is a lot of work." What is that weariness about? Being looked at because you are different? Being ignored in a classroom or meeting? Being treated as less able, less bright, less moral than others? Being uncertain whether you were discriminated against in a job, classroom, or housing situation? It could be any of the above for clients from nondominant groups.

Some readers might understandably be thinking, "But privilege and oppression aren't my fault. I didn't scheme to get privilege." Privilege is not necessarily any individual's fault. In McIntosh's (1998) words, "We did not invent [the inherited systems of overadvantage]" (p. 207). Nor can, or should, a person rid herself or himself of all privilege. Randy Cohen (2004) iterates that point in his response to a question about how to avoid participating in oppressive institutions:

> Many who sincerely denounce the inequities of our society inevitably profit from them. If you're a man who works at a job where the lack of flex time or on-site day care disadvantages women who do the bulk of child care, you benefit from sexism. If you're a middle-class white person who attended a decent high school and then applied to college, you had a huge advantage over a poor kid or an African American from an inferior high school. It is impossible to lead an immaculate life in an imperfect world. The task is not merely to insulate yourself from being a beneficiary of injustice—even if that were possible—but to combat injustice. (p. 26)

"To combat injustice" is the task for the counselor. Cohen (2004) suggests that the person with invisible privilege should challenge the inherent rigidity of social arrangements, such as the very existence of whiteness or maleness or heterosexuality as an advantage. Privileged group members can, therefore, act as allies in helping to counter oppressions, instead of participating in continuation of the problem. McIntosh (1998, pp. 213–214) has identified some ways in which she, as a white person, can use her power to weaken unearned racial privilege:

- Choosing to connect with and recruit people of color to all-white organizations in one's life

- Challenging and changing curricula, scholarship, and teaching methods to create more inclusive knowledge and education

- Co-presenting on white skin privilege with persons of color, sharing podium time and honoraria

- Trying to listen and then respond as an ally to participants of color in mostly white organizations

- Understanding how much one has to learn from people whom one was taught to overlook, fear, or avoid

Additional strategies for countering unearned privilege include the following:

- On an individual level, simply making sure that you treat all nonprivileged persons, such as lower-status workers, as equals
- On a career level, countering the easy option to take a job in the more affluent part of town and committing oneself to working in nonprivileged communities
- On an advocacy level, working with clients from nondominant groups in intentional, proactive ways, such as offering free or reduced cost (pro bono) counseling services or challenging the exclusive policies and oppressions in organizations to which you belong

The last suggestion, advocacy, is one of the main tools for challenging privilege in the hands of a social justice–oriented counselor. Advocacy is important because privilege will not disappear of its own accord.

In Bienvenu and Ramsey's (2006) words, "counselors must be advocates. . . . As advocates, counselors are systemic change agents, working to affect social systems in ways that will ultimately benefit the . . . clients with whom they work" (p. 348). Advocacy is discussed in greater detail in Chapter 16 as a type of culturally alert intervention.

McIntosh's (1998) words close this section on privilege with a call to alertness:

I found it is hard to keep alert to myself as white [or as male or heterosexual or middle class]. . . . I myself find that a retreat from the subject of being consciously white [or male, or heterosexual] is tempting. . . . But . . . I would rather be awake. (p. 215)

INDIVIDUAL RESPONSIBILITY AND SOCIAL INEQUALITY

This section has explored the social context of individual lives through the notions of the sociological imagination, socialization, social stratification, social inequality and inequity, oppression, dominance, hegemony, and privilege. It concludes with a qualification. Recognition of the social context in individual lives is not meant to excuse anyone from individual responsibility for working within that context. Culturally alert counselors need not, therefore, discard traditional counseling theories. Counselors can selectively use current counseling theories to help clients take responsibility for aspects of their lives, to see the "choices" that they do have, and to help them build on personal strengths. In other words, counselors can challenge clients to make changes in their lives without denying the power of oppressive conditions.

At the same time, counselors must challenge the subtle and not-so-subtle external conditions that affect clients' lives. To do so, counselors must be armed with a socially critical consciousness, which will be discussed next as a condition for social justice action.

Counseling for Social Justice

Given the fact that their clients will experience various levels of inequity and oppression based on group memberships, counselors are asked to do social justice work every day. Some of that work is, for example, simply helping children from poor families believe in themselves or helping survivors of domestic violence gain power in their lives. But some of the work requires an additional effort. In that vein, Ratts, D'Andrea, and Arredondo (2004) declare,

> Counselors must develop more proactive, value-laden, politically conscious, and advocacy-based counseling interventions. . . . Counseling can, and should, be used as a political and liberatory mechanism for dismantling oppressive systems in society, beginning with the institutions in which we work. (p. 30)

Thus, counseling simply returns to its origins in Frank Parsons's vision of "social improvement" as a major aim of the field.

The rest of this section describes the attitudes required for promoting social justice. Chapter 16 will describe specific actions that counselors can take to increase social equity.

CONSCIOUSNESS NEEDED FOR SOCIAL JUSTICE–ORIENTED COUNSELING

The complexity of social justice work requires intellectual and emotional complexity. That sentiment is echoed by Adams, Bell, and Griffin (1997): "Content [that is] as cognitively complex and socially and emotionally charged as social justice is inevitably challenging at both personal and intellectual levels" (p. 299).

Social justice work requires the ability to understand how systems work, the ability to see through social arrangements, and the ability to question one's own understandings. It also requires an emotional readiness to engage in "difficult dialogues." The counselor must be willing to be uncomfortable as unpleasant stories of oppression are revealed. She or he must approach administrators, colleagues, and clients with unsettling news of inequity. That discomfort has to be embraced because social justice actions will be met with resistance from colleagues, family members, fellow religious believers, and community members, to name some examples.

In Chapter 1, the mental capacity that represents the ability to think autonomously about social inequity was called "self-authorize" (Kegan, 1994). Here, three specific ways of thinking that prepare the counselor for social justice counseling are described. They can give the counselor insight into oppressive conditions. These three "prerequisites" are (1) socially critical thinking, (2) critical consciousness, and (3) recognition of the continuum from oppressive thinking to principled anti-oppressive thinking.

Socially Critical Thinking

Socially critical thinking means engaging in *intense analysis of the effects of social structures on people, especially on marginalized populations.* It derives from the Critical Theory movement, which was born in Germany at the Frankfurt Institute of Social Research in 1923. There, and later after the move of the Institute to the United States, social scientists went beyond mere explanation of society to exploring ways of changing society for the better.

Traditional counselor education has not consistently engaged in the socially critical discourse. Consider the words of a contemporary counselor educator about his own graduate training:

> It seemed like a . . . taboo in the world of graduate training in counseling to discuss issues such as . . . at-risk youth and families, or poverty, social change and multiculturalism. . . . Whenever I would raise questions or comments about my everyday reality in graduate classes, there was a clear message that this could warrant "some" discussion but really wasn't within the mainstream of graduate-level training. Speaking with other graduate students and professors I quickly realized that almost all of them, at best, could "think" and theorize about the issues but didn't really understand the interrelationship of counseling to such realities as poverty, physical and sexual abuse, racism, hopelessness, rage, substance abuse, multicultural differences, or violence. It became apparent that learning would have to come through experience. (Bemak, 1997, p. 86)

Is this situation changing? A major purpose of this book is to ensure that counselors are socially critical. Toward that end, critical consciousness is discussed next. It might be considered the result of socially critical thinking.

Critical Consciousness

The concept of critical consciousness was developed by Brazilian literacy educator Paulo Freire (see Photo 2.1) in his books *Pedagogy of the Oppressed* (1970) and *Education for Critical Consciousness* (1973). Critical consciousness can be defined as the capacity of individuals to consciously re-evaluate and re-interpret their relationships with their culture, their sociopolitical world, and their historical age (Mustakova-Possardt, 2003). As seen in the definition, critical consciousness involves cultural de-centering and self-authorizing of beliefs and behaviors.

Freire first worked to help poor persons overcome illiteracy in reading and writing; however, he expanded the notion of literacy to include social illiteracy. He described social illiteracy as being oblivious to the plight of others and failing to see the hundreds of thousands of people who suffer from homelessness, lack of medical care, and wage slavery (i.e., working full-time but not being able to make a living wage). His original educational efforts were with people who saw themselves as "victims" and who accepted their second-class status in relation to the dominant group of educated, wealthier persons. Freire considered a goal of education to be the development of critical consciousness in those learners. He laid out a model for a "liberatory education" that empowered learners to recognize their own disempowerment in a stratified society and to imagine the possibility of empowerment.

People, according to Freire (1970), can conspire in their own oppression, through social illiteracy, in four ways. The reader might note her or his current level of social literacy in terms of the four criteria.

Photo 2.1   Paulo Freire, 1921–1997

1. Allowing themselves to become individuals who want others to make major decisions for them

2. Failing to keep themselves informed about what's happening in the world

3. Failing to become aware of their own prejudices and blind spots

4. Making themselves believe that they cannot change themselves and their world

Critical consciousness also has a social action dimension. It includes the ability to take steps to diminish the oppressive elements in society.

Critical consciousness is difficult to achieve. It requires an individual to consistently see herself or himself as socially constructed, as "made up" by the gender, ethnic, religious, social class, and sexual orientation discourses that pervade her or his world. It also requires a critical faculty in the form of a restless inquisitiveness about the hidden power relations in a society's everyday discourse. It is especially difficult for Americans, who are accustomed to thinking in individualistic terms. Americans often deny the existence, or the importance, of social stratification, or they attribute stratification purely to individual willpower, instead of connecting it to social policies and attitudes.

Mustakova-Possardt's (2003) research revealed critical consciousness to be a cognitive developmental achievement in the Piagetian sense (Piaget & Inhelder, 1969). Such development can only be attained if a person experiences challenges to her or his received ways of thinking about power and stratification. It requires confronting dilemmas and "stretching" one's thinking. And it requires discomfort, the "irritation" of not letting go of familiar ways of knowing. Thus, to move toward critical consciousness, an individual must have disequilibrating encounters (encounters that upset the equilibrium of a current way of knowing) regarding ethnicity, race, gender, ability, social class, religion, and sexual orientation via personal experiences, reading, and media. Then, she or he must seriously try to understand those phenomena in a new way, especially in terms of power. Finally, she or he must be able to accommodate new learning about power and the construction of cultural identities into her or his old schemas. This book will provide some of those opportunities for disequilibration.

Recognition of the Continuum of
Oppressive to Anti-Oppressive Thinking

A third way to describe the consciousness needed to promote social justice is D'Andrea and Daniels's (1999) continuum of oppressive to anti-oppressive thinking. D'Andrea and Daniels conducted a series of interviews and found there to be five psychological dispositions that persons can have toward oppressed groups.

A person's thinking in this model moves from rigid and simplistic characterizations of cultural "others" to flexibility and complexity in thinking about oppressed groups and oneself. In that sense, it parallels the movement from concrete, dualistic thinking to principled, constructive knowledge of cognitive and ego development theories (e.g., Belenky, Clinchy, Goldberger, & Tarule, 1986; Kohlberg, 1984; Loevinger, 1976; Perry, 1970). (See Box 2.4; some of the language of the original model has been modified.)

One of the most powerful aspects of D'Andrea and Daniels's (1999) model is that it provides counselors with a tool they can use to place their own thinking

---

BOX 2.4   Stages of Oppressive to Anti-Oppressive Thinking

NOTE: The three categories, "cognitive," "affective," and "behavioral," distinguish thinking, feeling, and acting at each stage. The interaction of those three dimensions of human functioning is duly noted.

Stage 1: Impulsive Stage

Cognitive dimensions: Simplistic thinking (e.g., "Women just want a man's money." "The Irish are drunks.")

Affective dimensions: Overt feelings of hostility and aggressiveness toward others from different cultural groups.

Behavioral dimensions: Marginal impulse control. Potential to create a "community of hatred" in which negative views of other cultural groups are condoned. Note: Alcohol/drug misuse often triggers regression to this stage in people who otherwise appear to be functioning at a later stage of prejudice/anti-prejudice.

Stage 2: Dualistic-Rational Stage

Cognitive dimensions: More logical than at the Impulsive Stage, but unable to consistently take the perspectives of "different others." Strong within-group identification and alliance. Rationalizes cultural separatism ("They are different from us, and lesser").

Affective dimensions: Superficial social politeness that masks negative feelings toward different others. Resentment of persons who promote social justice. Fear about persons from different cultural groups (e.g., "They are violence-prone").

Behavioral dimensions: Less overt aggression toward different others than at Stage 1, due to the impulse control of conventional thinking. But hostility is under the surface and can be expressed in stressful conflict situations.

Stage 3: Liberal Stage (The modal position for counselors and counselor educators)

Cognitive dimensions: Abstract reasoning common. Recognizes universal human rights. Aware of legitimacy of different worldviews. Interested in knowing more about cultural differences.

Affective dimensions: "Passionless thoughtfulness." Apathetic disposition about racial/ethnic tensions and injustice in society. Isolated from cultural others, partly through economic stratification.

Behavioral dimensions: Voices liberal views about cultural diversity and social justice but does not take action (doesn't "walk the talk") in professional and personal lives. Minimal risk-taking. Does not initiate discussions on social justice issues.

Stage 4: Principled Stage

Cognitive dimensions: Appreciates the relativism of human views and ideas, including the construction of one's own values and opinions. Aware of the importance of having an open mind to the inaccuracies in one's own thinking.

Affective dimensions: Has greater access to own inner emotional lives. Shows variety of responses to oppression, from continuing apathy to passionate, complex, and more accurate expression of feelings about injustice.

Behavioral dimensions: Range from continuing inaction to sometimes addressing social ills in professional and personal lives. However, lacks ability to act in sustained, effective ways to change unjust or potentially unjust social arrangements.

Stage 5: Principled Activist Stage (Few counselors found at this stage)

Cognitive dimensions: Have expanded understanding of the multiple factors in social injustice, including educational, religious, political, and economic underpinnings. Have clearer ideas on ways to create change to reduce oppression.

Affective dimensions: Non-naïve hopefulness about the capacity of humans to improve conditions based on well-developed ideas for social reform. Passionate about reducing human cruelty, especially as it is extended through social arrangements. Seen by many at other stages as too confrontational.

Behavioral dimensions: Tenacious action in all areas; for example, institutional, one-to-one, outreach, neighborhood, family domains. As counselor, is strengths- versus problem-oriented, empowerment- versus adjustment-oriented.

on the continuum, from consistent hostility toward others of different groups to principled, socially just activism. Counselors can then aim for the more complex way of thinking in later stages in the model. It should be noted that the last stages of the model and critical consciousness are similar, in that the Principled Activist stage is characterized by vigilance about oppression and willingness to act to change it. They will then move to challenge themselves to expand their alertness into action. The reader is encouraged to complete Activity 2.8 in order to personalize the stages of oppressive to anti-oppressive thinking.

ACTIVITY 2.8

Naming Individuals at Stages of Oppressive to Anti-Oppressive Thinking

In order to make the model more vivid, try to name at least one person who might represent each stage, for example, a relative, friend, acquaintance, or public figure. Be sure to also include yourself. This naming is, of course, speculation and not meant to inaccurately label others.

Stage 1: Impulsive

Stage 2: Dualistic-Rational

Stage 3: Liberal

Stage 4: Principled

Stage 5: Principled Activist

Summary

Social justice-oriented counseling is one dimension of culturally alert counseling. By promoting social justice, the counseling field returns to its early twentieth-century roots as an effort to promote equity for underserved and oppressed groups. This work is not easy. Social justice-oriented counseling must be a constant effort because as long as there are human beings, unnecessary stratifications and misuses of power are possible. Each child who experiences school yard taunting, each woman who is sexually harassed by a person in power, each immigrant who is discriminated against in a job application, and each gay person who experiences anti-gay jokes will need counselors, as advocates, to stand up to the more powerful and the victimizers.

The spirit of this chapter can be summed up by the words of counselor educator Reese House (1994). He proposes that socially critical counselors

1. are self-reflective and self-critical;

2. value social interdependence;

3. are compassionate;

4. have a commitment to justice;

5. are opposed to dogma, oppression, manipulation, and control;

6. maintain a systems perspective.

House further proposes that socially critical counselors "have a duty to question the status quo, to examine the morality of power, and to work to make society more just and equitable" (p. 1). If the work of this chapter is done, each reader will be able to respond to that call.

References

Adams, M., Bell, L., & Griffin, P. (Eds.). (1997). *Teaching for diversity and social justice.* New York: Routledge.

Baker Miller, J. (1976). *Toward a new psychology of women.* Boston: Beacon Press.

Belenky, M., Clinchy, B., Goldberger, N. R., & Tarule, J. (1986). *Women's ways of knowing: The development of self, voice, and mind.* New York: Basic Books.

Bellah, R. N., Madsen, R., Sullivan, W. M., Swidler, A., & Tipton, S. M. (1985). *Habits of the heart: Individualism and commitment in American life.* New York: Harper & Row.

Bemak, F. (1997). Counseling at-risk populations: Keeping the faith. In J. Kottler (Ed.), *Finding your way as a counselor* (pp. 85–88). Alexandria, VA: American Counseling Association.

Bettinger, C. (2003). *Sociology 300 reaction paper I.* Retrieved October 20, 2004, from http://bss.sfsu.edu/sociology/bettinger/soc300/paper1.doc

Bienvenu, C., & Ramsey, C. J. (2006). The culture of socioeconomic disadvantage: Practical approaches to counseling. In C. C. Lee (Ed.), *Multicultural issues in counseling: New approaches to diversity* (3rd ed., pp. 703–721). Alexandria, VA: American Counseling Association.

Cámara, H. (1981). *The desert is fertile.* Maryknoll, NY: Orbis Books.

Cohen, R. (2004, April 25). The ethicist. *New York Times Magazine*, p. 26.

Cose, E. (1993). *The rage of a privileged class: Why do prosperous blacks still have the blues?* New York: HarperCollins.

Council of Economic Advisors for the President's Initiative on Race. (1998). *Changing America: Indicators of social and economic well-being by race and Hispanic origin.* Washington, DC: Author.

D'Andrea, M., & Daniels, J. (1999). Exploring the psychology of white racism through naturalistic inquiry. *Journal of Counseling and Development, 77,* 93–101.

Davis, K., Cox, L., & Adler, M. (2005). *Definition of social justice.* Virginia Commonwealth University School of Social Work: Social Justice. Retrieved May 1, 2005, from http://www.vcu.edu/slwweb/aboutus/school/socjustice.html

Delaney, D. D. (2004, January 27). We still have a dream. *PortFolio Weekly, 22,* p. 12.

Domhoff, G. W. (2005). *Who rules America? Power, politics, & social change* (5th ed.). New York: McGraw-Hill.

Dovidio, J. F., & Gaertner, S. L. (1999). Reducing prejudice: Combating intergroup biases. *Current Directions in Psychological Science, 8,* 101–105.

Feagin, J. R., & Sikes, M. P. (1994). *Living with racism: The black middle-class experience.* Boston: Beacon Press.

Forgasc, D. (2000). *Gramsci reader: Selected writings, 1916–1935.* New York: New York University Press.

Freire, P. (1970). *Pedagogy of the oppressed.* New York: Continuum.

Freire, P. (1973). *Education for critical consciousness.* New York: Seabury Press.

Gilligan, C. (1982). *In a different voice: Psychological theory and women's development.* Cambridge, MA: Harvard University Press.

Grant, C., & Sleeter, C. (1996). *After the school bell rings.* Washington, DC: Falmer.

Harro, B. (2000). The cycle of socialization. In M. Adams, W. J. Blumenfeld, R. Castaneda, H. W. Hackman, M. L. Peters, & X. Zuniga (Eds.), *Readings for diversity and social justice: An anthology on racism, sexism, anti-Semitism, heterosexism, ableism, and classism* (pp. 15–20). New York: Routledge.

hooks, b. (1994). *Teaching to transgress.* New York: Routledge.

House, R. (1994). *Characteristics of the socially critical counselor.* Unpublished manuscript, Oregon State University, Corvallis.

Jackson, M., & Grant, D. (2004). Equity, access, and career development: Contextual conflicts. In R. Perusse & G. E. Goodnough (Eds.), *Leadership, advocacy, and direct service strategies for professional school counselors* (pp. 125–153). Belmont, CA: Brooks/Cole.

Kaufman, C. (2003). *Ideas for action: Relevant theory for radical change.* Cambridge, MA: South End.

Kegan, R. (1994). *In over our heads: The mental demands of modern life.* Cambridge, MA: Harvard University Press.

Kohlberg, L. (1984). *The psychology of moral development: The nature and validity of moral stages.* San Francisco: Harper & Row.

Kozol, J. (1991). *Savage inequalities: Children in America's schools.* New York: Crown.

Lewis, J., Arnold, M., House, R., & Toporek, R. (2002). *Advocacy competencies.* American Counseling Association. Retrieved October 23, 2006, from http://www.counseling.org/Publications/

Loevinger, J. (1976). *Ego development.* San Francisco: Jossey-Bass.

Loverro, T. (2003, Spring). A new approach to alumni legacy policies in admissions. *Stanford Undergraduate Research Journal, II,* 48–51.

Marger, M. N. (2005). *Social inequality: Patterns and processes* (3rd ed.). New York: McGraw-Hill.

McIntosh, P. (1998). White privilege, color, and crime: A personal account. In C. R. Mann & M. S. Zatz (Eds.), *Images of color, images of crime* (pp. 207–216). Los Angeles: Roxbury.

Mills, C. W. (1957). *The power elite.* New York: Harper.

Mills, C. W. (1959). *The sociological imagination.* New York: Oxford University Press.

Mustakova-Possardt, E. (2003).*Critical consciousness: A study of morality in global, historical context.* Westport, CT: Praeger/Greenwood.

Perry, W. G. (1970). *Forms of intellectual and ethical development in the college years.* New York: Holt, Rinehart & Winston.

Piaget, J., & Inhelder, B. (1969). *The psychology of the child.* New York: Basic Books.

Project for Excellence in Journalism. (2004). *The state of the news media 2004: An annual report on American journalism.* Washington, DC: Author. Retrieved January 30, 2005, from http://www.stateofthenewsmedia.org/narrative_overview_audience .asp?media=1

Ratts, M., D'Andrea, M., & Arredondo, P. (2004). Social justice counseling: "Fifth Force" in field. *Counseling Today, 47,* 28–30.

Sachs, J. D. (2005). *The end of poverty: Economic possibilities for our time.* New York: Penguin.

Sciarra, D. T. (2001). School counseling in a multicultural society. In J. G. Ponterotto, J. M. Casas, L. A. Suzuki, & C. M. Alexander (Eds.), *Handbook of multicultural counseling* (2nd ed.). Thousand Oaks, CA: Sage.

Shapiro, J. (2006). *A second look: Attacking legacy preference.* Retrieved April 11, 2006, from http://www.digitas.harvard.edu/~perspy/old/issues/1997/nov/second.html

Sue, S. (2006). Cultural competency: From philosophy to research and practice. *Journal of Community Psychology, 34,* 237–245.

Takaki, R. (1993). *A different mirror: A history of multicultural America.* Boston: Little, Brown.

Top schools, rich students. (2004, September 24). *USA Today,* p. 14A.

TV-Turnoff Network. (2005). *Facts and figures about our TV habit.* Washington, DC: Author. Retrieved January 30, 2005, from http://tvturnoff.org/images/facts&figs/ factsheets/FactsFigs.pdf

U.S. Bureau of Labor Statistics. (2006). *Employment situation summary.* Retrieved April 11, 2006, from http://www.bls.gov/news.release/empsit.nr0.htm

U.S. Census Bureau. (2004). *Historical poverty tables, Table 13. Number of families below the poverty level and poverty rate: 1959 to 2003.* Retrieved December 22, 2004, from http://www.census.gov/hhes/poverty/histpov/hstpov13.html

Zepeda, S. J., & Langenbach, M. (1999). *Special programs in regular schools: Historical foundations, standards, and contemporary issues.* Boston: Allyn & Bacon.

3

Ethnicity

Garrett McAuliffe, Bryan S. K. Kim, and Yong S. Park

T he purpose of Chapters 3 and 4 is to provide counselors with a general overview of the notions of ethnicity, race, and related concepts, especially in the United States. These two chapters provide a foundation for the succeeding seven chapters on specific ethnic groupings. First, ethnicity and race will be disentangled from each other. Then ethnicity will be explored for the remainder of the chapter.

Ethnicity and Race: Conflated Concepts

Ethnicity and race are not always clearly distinguished from each other in popular usage. It is common to see the combined notion of "race/ethnicity" on public documents such as job or college applications and government forms. These terms have a tangled history. In the nineteenth century, race, not ethnicity, was the predominant category used to classify groups of people. Race did all the work of categorizing peoples. In fact, the term "ethnic group," as a referent to people who share culture, was not recorded until the 1940s, under the influence of the relatively new field of anthropology.

Race covers many groupings of peoples. It is most commonly based on phenotype, that is, physical features. In the process, distinct ethnic groups, regions, and languages are combined into single racial categories, such as "black" or "white." In fact, racial labels, at best, merely represent convenient demographic categories, not descriptors of unitary biological communities or monolithic cultures.

As mentioned earlier, ethnicity, sometimes merely called "culture," is a more recent addition to the discourse, coming out of the work of anthropologists of the past century or so. Among social scientists, ethnicity is the preferred concept, over race, for describing group membership. It is more easily acknowledged as a socially created notion, rather than as a fixed biological entity. Ethnicity refers to members of a group having a shared history, a history in which customs are passed down.

Among social scientists, there are both opponents and proponents of separating the concepts of ethnicity and race. It should be noted that both proponents and opponents of keeping the concept of race agree that race is an oppressive, nonbiological concept.

Opponents suggest simply discarding the concept of race. Singh (1981) summarizes this perspective: "Distinctions between race and ethnicity . . . are untenable and without empirical support" (p. 2). The opponents recommend that the term "ethnicity" encompasses all aspects of both what has been called "race" and what is called "culture" or ethnicity (Phinney, 1996). From this perspective, race is recognized as a still-important social construct, but one that has much oppressive baggage attached to it. For scientific purposes, it is best discarded. In essence, the opponents of the notion of race hope that ethnicity will replace race in the general discourse and in research.

Proponents of keeping the concept of race in the social science discourse refer to the importance of acknowledging it as a public phenomenon; it carries much social power and, therefore, must be studied.

For practical purposes, it is most important that counselors note the contribution of both ethnicity and race to how people think and act. Counselors must especially recognize that there are power differentials among racial and ethnic groups. They should know the distinction between minority (nondominant) groups and majority (dominant) groups in the United States and the impact of those statuses on whole groups of peoples' opportunities and self-perceptions. First, the notion of ethnicity will be explored.

Conceptualizing Ethnicity

Every person has ethnicity or culture. From the time of their birth, all humans have been enculturated into preferences, manners, behaviors, and values. Everyone has learned how to dress, how and what to eat, and at least some versions of what the good life is. Ethnicity, therefore, matters because a person is never wholly independent of it.

This section of the chapter introduces the notion of ethnicity and explores its importance for counseling work. While ethnicity is often simply called "culture," following anthropological practice, the term "culture" will be used in this book more broadly to include shared social group affiliations such as social class, religion, and sexual orientation. Activity 3.1 introduces the reader to some personal dimensions of her or his ethnicity.

Ethnicity was defined in Chapter 1 as the recognition of common social ties among people due to shared geographic origins, memories of a historical past, cultural heritage, religious affiliation, language and dialect forms, and/or tribal affiliation. Simply put, ethnicity refers to the identity of groups of people who

ACTIVITY 3.1

What's in a Name?

Names are one expression of culture. They are always chosen in a social context. To begin your exploration of your own ethnicity, respond to the following questions as best you can.

What is your full name?

Where do your names come from?

Who gave you your names and why?

What do your names literally mean?

What do they mean to you?

What do they mean to other people? (i.e., What do others think of your names? How do they react to your names? What do you make of those reactions?)

What historical, ethnic, regional, or religious trend(s) do your names represent?

How are they different from those of someone from another region of the world or the country?

Does your name describe your personality, characteristics, or background?

What experiences of negative bias have you had in relation to your names?

acknowledge their shared origins, geographical location, and customs. The origin may be mythical, for example, in the form of the creation stories of many ethnic groups. The geographical location may have been shared in the past, for example, Jews and the Middle East. The customs have perceived commonality, although they can vary from person to person.

There is no "pure" ethnicity. People have migrated and mixed in the past so that all humans are, in a sense, multiethnic. However, over time there emerge groupings of people who are more or less distinct and who name themselves in contrast to others. It is important, therefore, to treat ethnicity as a social construction, as a story told by and about groups of people, rather than to consider it an objective entity. Ethnicity represents a set of assumptions that is transmitted within the family and reinforced by social networks (Giordano & Carini-Giordano, 1997).

The dimensions of living that are affected by ethnicity include family roles and expectations, parenting, gender roles and expectations, attitudes toward sexuality, manners, directness versus indirectness of communication, attitudes toward alcohol or other mind-altering substances/addictions, perceptions of beauty and body image, and the expression of emotion. Ethnicity is expressed in many forms, including in one's sense of self and space (distance, touch, formality), communication and language (directness, gestures, and volume), dress and appearance (rules, status, grooming), food and eating habits (restrictions, use of hands and utensils, location, manners), and time and time consciousness (promptness, pace). Ethnicity is one window that indicates who a person is. Activity 3.2 provides an opportunity to look through that window.

Processes That Affect Ethnicity

This section refers to six processes by which individuals learn about the notion of ethnicity and how important it is to them. The most fundamental of these processes are enculturation and acculturation. From them follow four possible cultural adaptations: integration or bicultural competence, assimilation, separation, and marginalization.

ENCULTURATION AND ACCULTURATION

Enculturation is defined as "the process of learning a culture in all its uniqueness and particularity" (Mead, 1963, p. 187). Through enculturation, a person learns how to live in her or his primary ethnic culture, or cultures, from infancy until death. Everyone is enculturated. The contents of enculturation include learned values, attitudes, and beliefs and corresponding behavior patterns. In the process of learning, a person acquires competence in her or his ethnic culture. It becomes the cognitive map, the term of reference for acting in the world.

While enculturation can occur within one dominant culture, *acculturation*, by contrast, refers to the meeting of at least two different cultures. Acculturation has generally been thought of as the process of an individual's socialization into a different group's ways. It is, therefore, sometimes referred to as second-culture acquisition (Good & Sherrod, 2001). Acculturation has occurred throughout human history as different groups encounter each other. Through acculturation, individuals take on some of the manners, speech patterns, dress, values, and tastes of a culture to which they have been exposed while also maintaining some of their original culture's expressions and norms.

Acculturation is not a one-way process. More than 50 years ago, anthropologists acknowledged the reciprocal exchange that occurs when cultures encounter each other in this classic definition: "Acculturation . . . result[s] when groups of individuals sharing different cultures come into continuous firsthand contact, with subsequent changes in the original culture patterns of either or both groups" (Redfield, Linton, & Herskovits, 1967, p. 182). Thus, for example, European Americans are influenced by Hispanic, African American, American Indian, and Asian American ways, and vice versa. There are mutual

---

ACTIVITY 3.2

Ethnic Self-Awareness

You have already done some work on your cultural group memberships in Chapter 1 in this book. There, you were asked to name your ethnicity as well as your relationship to it. If you were Naïve/Accepting in relation to your ethnicity, the following will be more difficult to complete.

Complete the following questions on your ethnicity. As you do, note areas of uncertainty or confusion on your part. What do they say about your ethnic awareness? The following activity will serve as an alert to work you might do on your ethnicity.

1. What generation(s) in the United States do you represent? (Native Americans can answer "about 11,000 years, or on the continent" if they wish.) Explain.

2. What is your current identification with your ethnic group(s) (i.e., how salient, or important, is it to you)?

3. What is your relationship to your ethnicity; that is, to what degree have you chosen norms and customs to follow? (Note where you placed yourself under Ethnicity in Activity 1.6 of Chapter 1.)

4. Describe one moment or time (specific or general) when you became aware of your ethnic culture (if you have had that opportunity)? for example, when you went to college, a religious event, social event, travel, stayed with other people, or read something.

5. Identify some of the characteristics of your ethnic culture(s), including

   a. any cultural customs that your immediate or extended family practice

   b. social behaviors (e.g., communication style, expression of different emotions)

   c. manners

   d. rituals

   e. traditions

   f. foods

   g. celebrations

   h. other beliefs held by your family

6. What customs do you prize the most?

7. What is the influence of your ethnicity on how you think and act? (Consider elements of your worldview, how that worldview has been shaped, and how your worldview influences your interactions with others.)

8. a. What culturally different groups and behaviors do members of your group commonly share a prejudice against/discriminate against or have commonly done so in the past? (e.g., How are/were issues of race and ethnicity discussed/ addressed in your family?)

   b. What stereotypes, jokes, statements were made about other groups, from your earliest recollection?

   c. Do these sentiments persist today?

9. State something about your ethnic culture that you are

   a. proud of

   b. ambivalent about/unsure of/not attracted to

10. What other influences that might be related to your ethnicity, such as social class, race, and religion, affect your worldview?

11. What might a counselor need to know about your ethnic group in order to be helpful?

influences in language, music, attitudes, mores, and physical mannerisms. A simple example is the pervasiveness of African American music and verbal expression across the United States and much of the world. Thus, both dominant and nondominant groups potentially change each other as a result of consistent encounters (Casas & Pytluk, 1995).

Acculturation for members of nondominant groups can be particularly stressful because in order to function in the dominant society, such individuals must become vigilant about customs and daily practices that they take for granted in their group. Members of nondominant cultures must commonly perform a strenuous balancing act as they simultaneously adjust to the norms of the dominant culture and retain the norms of their indigenous culture. These acculturation issues are especially important for immigrants and refugees. For them, acculturation refers to adjusting or adapting to the new culture while retaining a continuing enculturation in and allegiance to the culture of origin. Those individuals may not know important customs and behaviors that are required for functioning in a new dominant culture (Ponterotto, Utsey, & Pedersen, 2006). Such individuals may experience fear and culture shock in response to the differences that they are not prepared to encounter. That balancing act for immigrants and refugees is called the "acculturation-retaining" tension (Kim & Abreu, 2001).

FOUR EXPRESSIONS OF ENCULTURATION AND ACCULTURATION

Individuals express their enculturation and acculturation in four ways: behavior, values, knowledge, and cultural identity (Kim & Abreu, 2001). Counselors can assess a client's enculturation and acculturation by observing these phenomena.

The *behavior* dimension refers to such actions as friendship choice, preferences for entertainment and reading, participation in cultural activities, contact with the indigenous culture (e.g., time spent in a country of origin), language use, and food choice. For example, an African American may or may not choose African American friends, a European American may or may not listen to country music, and a first-generation Asian Indian may or may not eat more curried foods than a non-Indian.

The *value* dimension of acculturation refers to attitudes and beliefs about social relations, cultural customs, and cultural traditions, along with gender roles and attitudes and ideas about health and illness. For example, an African American might define "family" to include elder friends, aunts, and uncles, as well as cousins and siblings; an Arab American might value the authority of the male figures in a household; and a Scandinavian American might value equal gender roles in a family.

The *knowledge* dimension of enculturation and acculturation refers to culturally specific information, such as the names of historical figures in the culture of origin and/or the dominant culture, and knowledge of the historical significance of culturally specific activities. For example, a Mexican might honor Cinco De Mayo as the commemoration of a great Mexican battle victory, a Southern white might know much about Robert E. Lee and the Confederacy, and an African American might know the significance of Juneteenth as Emancipation Day.

Finally, the *cultural identity* dimension refers to attitudes to one's cultural identification (e.g., a Chinese American having her name in the Mandarin language), attitudes to the indigenous (i.e., one's ethnic group of origin) and dominant groups (e.g., feelings of shame about an indigenous culture and pride in the dominant group), and level of comfort with people of indigenous and dominant groups. The cultural identity dimension is described in the multiethnic identity model in the next section of this chapter.

FOUR TYPES OF ENCULTURATION AND ACCULTURATION

Acculturation and enculturation are not unitary experiences. Instead, four acculturation statuses are possible: integration, assimilation, separation, and marginalization (Berry, Trimble, & Olmeda, 1986). They explain an individual's level of adaptation to a dominant group's norms and the relative maintenance of her or his indigenous (usually meaning original) group's norms.

Integration

Integration occurs when individuals become proficient in the culture of the dominant group (high acculturation) while retaining proficiency in the indigenous culture (high enculturation). A Latino physician who works in California with a multiethnic community might have high acculturation to the dominant culture. She or he might also fully participate in her or his ethnic community through family events, religion, and language, that is, be highly enculturated also. Similarly, an African American who has a strong sense of ethnic identity (enculturation) but who can interact effectively with people from the dominant culture would demonstrate integration.

Another term for such integration of the cultures is *bicultural competence* (LaFromboise, Coleman, & Gerton, 1993). Bicultural competence describes the process of a person's successfully meeting the demands of two distinct cultures. Bicultural individuals often perform a "balancing act" by participating in a dominant culture in one environment (e.g., at work) while fully embracing their original cultural identity in another (e.g., in her or his religious congregation). Thus, an Asian Indian immigrant might adopt the dominant culture's ways while in work situations, but participate in a Hindu community at home or adhere to traditional gender roles. Such might be the case of an Asian Indian woman who is the supervisor in a workplace but who chooses to take a more deferential role in the family (Casas & Pytluk, 1995). Activity 3.3 lists the characteristics of bicultural competence.

Assimilation

Assimilation contrasts with integration. In assimilation, the individual rejects her or his indigenous culture (low enculturation) while absorbing the culture of the dominant group (high acculturation). Such a process has already happened for many European Americans in the United States in their assimilation to the dominant Anglo American Protestant culture. Thus, for example, the so-called Scotch-Irish, those northern Britons who immigrated to North America in large numbers in the eighteenth century (Fischer, 1989), and who were seen as a distinct ethnic group at that time, are now virtually indistinguishable from Anglo Americans. They were similar enough for assimilation to occur.

Sometimes forced assimilation has been attempted in the United States. Many American Indians have ancestral memories of the so-called Indian schools of the

---

ACTIVITY 3.3

Characteristics of Bicultural Competence

Think of a person with whom you have come into contact, even from afar through media, who shows some level of bicultural competence.

Write the name of the person who shows bicultural competence: _____

It should be someone who is from a nondominant culture (People from the dominant culture are not often very bicultural.). Listed below are the capabilities required for bicultural competence. Check off each of the characteristics for her or him and give an example of one.

Knowledge of cultural beliefs and values of both cultures

Positive attitudes toward both groups

Bicultural efficacy, or belief that one can live in a satisfying manner within both cultures without sacrificing one's cultural identity

Communication ability in both cultures

Role repertoire, or the range of culturally appropriate behaviors

A sense of being grounded in both cultures

Which characteristics she or he especially shows: _____

An example of her or his showing one of the characteristics: _____

---

early twentieth century. Native Americans were sent there in order to be assimilated to Christian, European ways. In undergoing the assimilation process, they lost their ethnic customs and their pride in tribal ways.

Assimilation is neither desirable nor safe for many groups. For example, many Jews in Germany during the 1920s had assimilated to dominant German cultural ways. However, they were singled out by the dominant group as "different" (and as undesirable), with catastrophic consequences. As has been mentioned previously, in the United States, people of color cannot assimilate to the dominant European American culture, largely due to racialization; that is, those who don't look white generally remain the "other" in terms of the dominant white society.

In recent years, ethnic pride movements have proclaimed the value of embracing one's ethnic group while also being part of a larger nation, that is, *not* assimilating. A client need not give up her or his cultural identity in order to participate in an increasingly multicultural society. She or he can achieve an integrated status. That notion is the basis for the current ethos of multiculturalism in the United States.

Separation

The third acculturation/enculturation status, *separation,* occurs when an individual is not interested in learning the culture of the dominant group (low acculturation) and wants only to maintain and perpetuate the culture of origin (high enculturation). Individuals with this attitude might reside in ethnic enclaves. For example, an Asian American who works and lives in a Chinatown or a Koreatown in the United States may not have the need to interact with the members of the dominant group. In the past, many first-generation immigrants who arrived in large enough numbers formed relatively separate communities within the dominant U.S. culture. With such separation, a person may not need to learn the cultural customs of the dominant group or learn to speak English.

Marginalization

The final acculturation status, and a problematic one for individuals, is *marginalization.* Marginalization represents the situation of a person who has no interest in maintaining or acquiring proficiency in any culture, neither the indigenous one nor the dominant one (low acculturation and enculturation). Marginalization can occur when a nondominant group is made peripheral by the larger society. A marginalized individual, or group, is excluded, or devalued, in the economy, in the daily social discourse, and in the customs of the dominant culture. Such exclusion results in the marginalized ethnic group seeming to be functionally useless to a society. Members of marginalized groups have not learned the ways of the dominant culture sufficiently to function well within the dominant society and do not feel included in the dominant culture. They also deny their indigenous culture. Thus, they are "persons without a country." The devaluing of the nondominant group's language and customs can occur to such an extent that group members become ashamed of their ethnicity. Marginalization has happened to many ethnic groups throughout history. In the United States, it has occurred to many American Indians. Such marginalization occurred at first through the reduction in population and loss of homelands. It was further spurred by attempted re-socialization of the remaining groups through the aforementioned Indian schools. There, American Indian ways were devalued and replaced with Western language, values, clothing, and other attributes. Another example of marginalization is American Indians who leave a reservation to live in an urban area and who are enculturated into traditional ways that do not help them in their new environment. The difficulty for marginalized peoples is that they then suffer from self-deprecation, unless they can "pass" in the dominant culture. Fortunately, ethnic pride movements have countered such marginalization. Marginalized people need to find ways to connect with their indigenous cultures.

Helping Clients With Acculturation

It is important for counselors who work with clients from nondominant groups, especially immigrants, to assess their clients' levels of acculturation and enculturation. Clients who are living in an unfamiliar culture might have difficulty negotiating the tasks of daily life. In counseling, low-acculturated clients might be unfamiliar with the norms of Western counseling, such as personal disclosure, expression of emotion, and equality between counselor and client. They might also doubt the helpfulness of a counselor who is from another culture.

Acculturation and enculturation are useful concepts, for they move counselors beyond stereotyping of clients (He is _____; therefore, _____.). A counselor cannot know an individual's level of acculturation and enculturation by merely being familiar with her or his ethnic label. One must assess how much meaningful contact the person has had with the dominant culture in order to judge acculturation and enculturation.

Psychological Dimensions of Ethnicity

It might be clear at this point that ethnicity is not a uniform, static experience. Individuals with the same ethnicity can have very different experiences of their culture's meaning in their lives. That fact was illustrated in the first vignette in Chapter 1. The next two sections discuss the psychological experience of ethnicity, in the form of ethnic identity development and salience.

ETHNIC IDENTITY DEVELOPMENT

As has been discussed in Chapter 1 (Box 1.2), an individual's relationship to her or his cultural group can evolve from naïveté and/or shame about her or his culture, through growing awareness and pride, to universal appreciation of all cultures. So it is with ethnicity. The Model of Multiethnic Identity Development (MMID; Harper & McFadden, 2003) was developed in order to describe stages in the evolving relationship that individuals can have to their ethnicity. The MMID, like other cultural identity models, can be useful as a guide for counseling clients in early phases of ethnic identity. Counselors can also use it to discover their own ethnic identity status. The MMID, like many such models, has significant parallels to the general cultural identity model that was presented in Chapter 1 and to the two integrated developmental models of racial identity that are described in the next chapter. The MMID is summarized in Activity 3.4.

It should be noted that a person does not move through these phases in a strict, linear sequence because elements of multiple phases can be present at one time, especially in specific situations.

ACTIVITY 3.4

Ethnic Identity Development

As you review the following five phases, consider your relationship to your own ethnic group or groups.

Note that regional identities can also constitute ethnicity, in the sense that rural German American Midwesterner, Anglo-Protestant Southern Californian, or Puerto Rican New Yorker can be considered ethnicities themselves.

Phase 1: Ethnoentropy. In this phase, individuals automatically find their ethnic group to be distasteful. The word "entropy" itself means a state of disorder and inertness. If individuals' negative attitudes toward their ethnic group are pervasive and they live in denial of their having ethnicity, they might be said to be ethnoentropic. This aversion for their group does not mean, however, that such individuals are "free" of ethnic enculturation. They may still be unconsciously enmeshed in the mores and assumptions of their ethnicity. They avoid other ethnic groups.

ACTIVITY: Name a relative, associate, or yourself at a time in your life who is/was ethnoentropic _____.

INTERVENTION: Here a counselor might help clients identify negative feelings about their own groups. An intervention for increasing positive ethnic feelings might include the guided imagery using positive cultural symbols activity (Ivey et al., 2002). (See Chapter 16 for a fuller description of this intervention.) In this cultural imagery activity, the client creates a visual image of a positive ethnic symbol or figure and uses it as a source of strength. Other activities for the ethnoentropy phase are clients engaging in reading and films about positive figures in the ethnic group, with reflection on the positive meanings.

Phase 2: Ethnocentrism. This term was referred to in Chapter 1 and again in this chapter as a belief that one's ethnic group is superior to others. Ethnocentric individuals use their ethnic group's standards as a basis for judging other groups. Thus, a person in the ethnocentric phase might say about another ethnic group, "Aren't those _____ s loose about their morals?" or "Look at how strangely they wear their hair (or jewelry, or clothing)" or "They are so loud and obnoxious" in reference to a whole group. Key to this phase is a negative judgment about other ethnic groups.

ACTIVITY 1: Name a historical or current event in which ethnocentrism has caused suffering to others. _____

ACTIVITY 2: Name a relative or acquaintance, or yourself at any time, who showed/shows elements of ethnocentrism. _____. Name a price that she or he might have paid for that stance: _____.

INTERVENTION: Here, at least, some pride exists for one's ethnic groups. Now the developmental task involves understanding the "outside" world of other ethnic groups that the client will have to interact with. Multicultural awareness-raising activities, such as reading about and getting to know respected figures from other ethnic groups, are called for if the person is to thrive in a multicultural society.

(Continued)

(Continued)

Phase 3: Ethnosyncretism. "Syncretism" (accent on the first syllable) comes from the Greek root word that means "to combine." At this phase, the person makes an effort to reconcile various seemingly disparate positions or views. Clients who are at the ethnosyncretic phase are open to accepting formerly unknown or rejected notions about their own and other ethnicities. In this phase, the person is beginning to see that each can have positive and negative dimensions. The client is beginning to syncretize these discoveries, seeing both positives and negatives about her or his cultures and doing the same with other cultures.

ACTIVITY: Name a specific dimension of one of your ethnic identities about which you can see both positives and negatives. For example, a person might say, "I like the family-centeredness of my culture, and the love of fun. But I don't like the anti-intellectual strain in my culture, the tendency to bow to authority and dogma. Also, I don't like the mistrust of people who are different from us." _____

_____

INTERVENTION: Allow the client to discover her or his ethnicity through discussions, reading, and other "research." However, counter the remaining ethnocentrism by encouraging intentional cross-cultural experiences and reflections, through such means as travel, conversations with ethnic others, and reading.

Phase 4: Transethnicity. "Trans" means "across." This phase is characterized by an active, intentional moving across multiple cultures, seeking out culturally diverse experiences. In a sense, the person is becoming more bicultural or multicultural. The person has now confronted her or his own ethnic assumptions and habits. She or he is no longer "subject to" them, but can "take them as object" (Kegan, 1982), that is, stand back and consider choices about what ethnic characteristic she or he prefers to embrace. The individual in the transethnicity phase may face rejection by her or his ethnic group of origin, in the form of hearing, "You have left us." That has been the experience of the children of immigrants, children who become more facile with the dominant culture. However, it is important to note that in this phase, the person is not ashamed of or rejecting her or his own ethnicities. Instead, she or he appreciates what they offer and yet seeks to become more multicultural.

ACTIVITY: Consider how "transethnic" you are at this time. Look at how much you seek out diverse ethnic experiences in person, in film, in television, in cultural experiences, in reading, and in friendships, to name some examples. Make a statement on your level of transethnicity and what you might do to increase it:

_____.

INTERVENTION: Help the client in the transethnic phase to find allies who are multicultural themselves, so that possible rejection by one's group of origin is mitigated. As a counselor, be an ally yourself and a model of transethnicity. Your office décor and literature will communicate some of this phase to others.

Phase 5: Panethnicity. "Pan," in its Greek root, means "all." Here individuals are comfortable with all others, regardless of ethnicity. They do not rate their ethnicity as better or worse than that of others. While they appreciate their ethnicity of origin, they can choose specific expressions of it to embrace. They can easily acknowledge limits to and negatives about their ethnic group(s). Individuals in the panethnicity phase know their ethnic origins well. They engage fully with others of differing ethnicities, are aware of ethnic privilege and oppressions, and see the universal humanness in all ethnicities and individuals.

INTERVENTION: There is little or no need for counseling related to ethnic identity or relationships at this phase.

SALIENCE

On an individual level, salience, or the importance of ethnicity to a person, needs to be acknowledged by counselors.

> Some [individuals] are very conscious of their ethnic ties and make efforts to sustain them by choosing co-ethnics as friends, neighbors, and marital partners. Others may de-emphasize ethnicity to the point where it is no longer a significant part of their personal identity and affects little of their social life . . . there is common dilution of ethnicity [i.e., less salience] with each successive generation [that is removed from immigration]. . . . Ethnicity varies from individual to individual. (Marger, 2002, pp. 256–257)

Salience is greater for members of nondominant and minority ethnic groups. By contrast, a very dominant group in any society often does not even consider itself to be "ethnic." Many European Americans do not recognize their ethnicity as a source of the customs, common ancestry, manners, and artifacts that they value because their ethnicity is so pervasive and dominant. Ethnic salience can become high, however, for dominant group members when they are thrust into "foreign" contexts, ones in which they become a minority. Thus, for a European American who attends an African American religious service, ethnic salience is momentarily high. In Waters's (2004) words, "it is not until one comes in close contact with many people who are different from oneself that individuals realize the ways in which their backgrounds may influence their individual personalit[ies]" (p. 422). The Activities of Chapter 1 are meant to increase awareness of ethnicity, as are the following chapters.

Categories and Terms Used for Ethnicity

Common terms for ethnicity include the term "nationality" and expressions used to represent specific ethnic groups. The next two sections explore terms used for ethnicity and their meanings.

NATIONALITY

Nationality has often substituted for the term ethnicity, especially in the past. However, nationality refers merely to a person's citizenship in a particular state. In fact, there can be many ethnicities within a nation. For that reason, nationality is a less useful concept for explaining a person's socialization than is ethnicity (Matsumoto & Juang, 2004). A person's current or former nation of citizenship does not explain her or his values and customs as well as does the notion of ethnicity.

However, nationality can have elements of ethnicity because there are dominant national norms, values, and customs that are shared by most members of a nation across ethnicities. A "national culture" can be spoken of, no matter how elusive and variable it is from person to person. Thus, there is some substance to the notion of "U.S. culture" because people in the United States are generally exposed to shared media, geography, climates, and political institutions. In this book, ethnicities within the overall U.S. nationality will be emphasized.

LABELS FOR ETHNIC GROUPS

When asked, "What are you?" individuals will respond sometimes with a clear ethnic label, a combination of labels, or a confused uncertainty, if they are in the dominant group. There is no official taxonomy of "correct" ethnic terms. As a result, counselors might wonder what terms to use for clients' ethnicity.

Ethnic labels connote different meanings depending on whether the terms have been externally or internally imposed (Comas-Díaz, 2001). In that vein, the term "Hispanic" was created by the U.S. Census Bureau to lump all peoples who are Spanish-speaking or who descend from Spanish-speaking ancestors. Thus, the term "Latino" is preferred by many Latinos, especially those in the Eastern United States. It should be noted, however, that many individuals still do refer to themselves as "Hispanic," especially in the Southwestern United States. Many Latin people prefer the term that refers to their country of origin, such as "Colombian," "Cuban," or "Salvadoran," with Latino or Hispanic being a secondary description.

The term "Oriental" for Asian Americans has a similar, externally imposed origin, as does "Negro" for African Americans. Each was a term imposed by oppressors. Thus, members of those groups have chosen alternate names for themselves, such as "Asian" or "African American." Again, there are cases in which some clients might not mind the so-called colonizers' terms, such as "Hispanic" or "Oriental." Clients may themselves use such terms. That usage might be an indicator of their ethnic identity level and of the possible presence of internalized oppression (Delgado-Romero, 2001). Thus, ethnic terms may vary. Those terms can also have negative, positive, or neutral connotations.

PANETHNIC GROUPINGS

In order to simplify ethnic categories, ethnicity researchers have created the previously mentioned "panethnic" or macro-ethnic groupings for the United States. There are currently five such groupings: Latino/Hispanic, African American, Asian/Pacific Islander American, Native American Indian, and European American (Marger, 1994). In this text, Asian is broken into (a) East and Southeast Asian and (b) South Asian. In addition, there is a separate chapter on Middle Eastern Americans. Those additions reflect broad cultural differences in the subgroups. Such groupings always sacrifice some precision for the sake of simplicity.

It should be noted that those panethnic groupings are slightly different from the U.S. Census Bureau categories for race and ethnicity: American Indian or

Alaska Native, Asian, Black or African American, Native Hawaiian or Other Pacific Islander, and White. The U.S. Census includes a question on Hispanic origin for all respondents—"Hispanic or Latino" or "Not Hispanic or Latino"—and the Census Bureau declares that Hispanics and Latinos can be of any race (U.S. Census Bureau, 2000). The aforementioned conflation of ethnicity and race is illustrated by these categorizations. It should be noted that individuals can select one or more races on the census.

Such large ethnic groupings must be seen as convenient constructions, largely useful for government demographic assessment. Those groupings were created from the popular perception that there is enough shared culture, language, and/or geographical origin within these five sets of peoples to call them groups.

People sometimes ask, "What is the purpose of ethnic categorizing?" Panethnic categories do have a function: They help society, especially the government, to identify residence patterns, social class discrepancies, and discrimination, which do occur on the panethnic level. The limitation of such groupings, however, is that they gloss over distinct ethnic identities. For example, American Indians often want to be associated with their specific tribe. Similarly, the large grouping of Asian American is problematic because, for example, Japanese, Pakistani, and Thai people are culturally quite different from each other and usually wish to be identified by their particular ethnicity. Similarly, European Americans do not commonly see themselves as such. For example, newly arrived Greeks or Russians will see themselves in those national terms, not as European Americans.

Panethnic groupings also do not include all peoples. For example, where do people from the North Africa and the Middle East fit under these panethnic categories? They don't easily fit, although they have been recently included under the general notion of "white," which is defined in the U.S. Census as "a person having origins in any of the original peoples of Europe, the Middle East, or North Africa." It should be clear that the panethnic groupings are demographic categories that may be useful for political purposes. They are not as useful for describing culture, however.

OPTIONAL OR "SYMBOLIC" ETHNICITY

A further complexity in the notion of ethnicity is related to power and status in society. Some ethnic groups have higher status and power. White Anglo-Saxon Protestant has historically been seen as the highest-status ethnicity in the United States. Such is the power of belonging to this group that every U.S. president except for John F. Kennedy has been what is commonly called "white Anglo-Saxon Protestant." By contrast, all other groups have been disparaged at some point, as exemplified by members of those groups often changing their names to Anglo-sounding ones.

In a broader sense, members of European American ethnic groups in general have a certain power that non-European American ethnic groups do not. European Americans can be merely "white" or a hyphenated American, as the situation changes. Thus, ethnicity is mostly "symbolic" or optional for European Americans. By contrast, it is not optional for people of color (Waters, 2004).

Sociologist Herbert Gans (1979) used the term "symbolic ethnicity" in 1979 to describe an ethnic identification that comes without social cost to the person. Gans proposed that as of the last quarter of the twentieth century, European Americans have generally been able to treat ethnicity as a "hobby," that is, as a leisure activity. European Americans, unless they are immigrants, are not generally publicly identified in terms of their ethnicity. However, members of other ethnic groups are publicly identified as non-white. They are racialized ethnic minorities.

The notion of optional ethnicity is important because European Americans sometimes use ethnicity to explain their achievements. They declare their ethnic group's achievements in terms of purely individual accomplishments, ignoring the added value of being white and ignoring the mutual assistance that members of white ethnic groups provide each other. European Americans often claim that their people "made it" despite their ancestors being different from the dominant group. In that vein, European Americans often argue, "Since my ethnic group made it on its own, from poverty and immigration to economic and educational success and acceptance as mainstream Americans, why can't they (people of color) do it too?" Shapiro (2004) describes this phenomenon of laissez faire racism in this way: "[European Americans] view African Americans as individuals just like themselves, . . . rather than as members of a group who were forced to play by rigged rules used historically to ensure their disadvantage and white domination" (p. 101). European American stories of heroic personal effort and family struggle ignore the social benefit that they and their ancestors had, which consisted of being white.

By contrast, racialized ethnic minorities, that is, people of color, cannot choose to have or not have their ethnicity. In Manning Marable's (2000) words, "racialized minorities are fundamentally different from other ethnic groups because they share a common history of oppression, [including] residential segregation, economic subordination, and political disenfranchisement" (p. B34). People of color experience their non-optional group identity on a daily basis—when they are concerned about job hiring and discrimination, when they are not viewed as middle class, when they don't see many people who look or act like them in visible positions, or when they hear of incidents of ethnic bias in the media.

The non-optional dimension of ethnicity for some people is captured by the term "people of color." This is a broad concept that represents all people from non-optional ethnicities, those who cannot assimilate to whiteness. It is, therefore, a useful term for acknowledging racialized minorities, people whose ethnicity is trumped by their "differentness" from white Americans of European descent.

Ethnicity and Counseling

Ethnicity matters in counseling. Ethnic values and customs affect whether clients come to and use counseling at all because of attitudes toward mental health, feelings about health and health care, and views about the use of mental health services. Ethnicity also affects the expression of psychological distress, including the expression of anxiety and depression, somatization, eating disorders, sexual disorders, coping responses, self-esteem, substance abuse, and adolescent behavior problems. Ethnic rules can turn into internalized assumptions about communication, sexuality, or career. Those ethnic rules can get clients into trouble, or, conversely, can help them to live well.

It is important to reiterate, in the spirit of positive psychology and solution-oriented counseling, that ethnicity can also be a source of strength, as has been mentioned. Clients could be asked to do an ethnicity strengths review that highlights people and values that enhance life adjustment. In either case, ethnicity is always with a client, for better and for worse.

ASSESSING AND INCORPORATING ETHNICITY

Counselors are encouraged to assess the place of ethnicity for clients early in the work. Ethnicity is a silent presence in the counseling room, in the form of clients' socially learned attitudes, beliefs, and values. The subtle power of ethnicity is pointed out by family therapists Joe Giordano and Mary Ann Carini-Giordano (1997) in the following description of differences between partners in family counseling.

> When Joe, who is Italian-American, first began working with Jewish families, he found it to be exciting. They not only told him what their problem was, but how to solve it. . . . Some had read more Freud than he. . . . But . . . in [some of the] families, an aptitude for seeking out and expounding underlying meaning was effectively used as a "cultural defense" against changing dysfunctional behavior . . . .
>
> With Irish families, he experienced the opposite. Joe's questions were met with little response and even silence. At other times, these families would be very talkative and humorous, spinning convoluted stories that left him confused as to their meaning. Many [Irish] families had difficulty talking about their feelings or sharing marital conflicts in front of their children.
>
> When working with families that came from Joe's own Italian-American background, he sometimes would over-identify . . . thus totally missing . . . necessary interventions. And then there were other families whose behaviors mirrored back to him his own unresolved negative feelings about his Italian-American identity.
>
> For example, a British [American]-Italian American couple may experience conflict because the British-American takes literally the dramatic expressiveness of the Italian-American, who in turn finds intolerable the British-American's emotional distancing. . . . Thus the British-American husband calls his Italian-American wife "hysterical" and she labels him "unfeeling and rejecting." (p. 4)

These anecdotes illustrate the two-way power of ethnicity in counseling—for client and for counselor. Of course, ethnicity is not the only variable that affects clients' functioning. In that vein, Giordano and Carini-Giordano (1997) reiterate the point made in Chapter 1 about not overgeneralizing across individuals based on ethnicity. In a similar vein, ethnicity might not be as relevant to some clients, although it is always present in every client. Box 3.1 offers guidelines for incorporating ethnicity into counseling. These guidelines might be new for counselors who are used to considering only individual client factors.

BOX 3.1   Guidelines for Incorporating Ethnicity Into Counseling

Consider the extent to which a client identifies with her or his ethnic background (i.e., salience plus ethnic identity development factors).

Determine whether a client's behaviors reflect ethnic norms, even if ethnicity seems to be unimportant to the client.

Determine how much a client's concerns are related to internal and/or external conflicts in values, as opposed to personality factors. In that regard, Giordano and Carini-Giordano (1997) illustrate the danger of ignoring ethnic values. They say that what may appear as a dysfunctional, "enmeshed" relationship in an Italian or Puerto Rican family may be perceived by its own members as "close and loving," that is, normative. By contrast, for Italian and Puerto Rican families, distance among family members may be a more serious problem than for families who value independence.

Consider other contextual factors, such as social class, educational level, degree of acculturation, and gender, in the client's worldview and expectations.

As a counselor, explore your own cultural attitudes, especially if you are ambivalent about your own ethnicity. The latter is common among upwardly mobile professionals who are trying to cast off their ethnicity in favor of "passing" in the dominant professional culture.

Be an "ethnicity educator" who clarifies the meaning of ethnicity-related (and non-ethnicity-related) behaviors for clients and who promotes the idea that ethnic difference exists and must be negotiated in couples and other relationships.

SOURCE: From Ivey, D'Andrea, Ivey, & Simek-Morgan (2002).

CHALLENGING PROBLEMATIC ETHNIC RULES

Counselors must determine whether internalized ethnic norms are harmful or helpful to clients. Often, clients may be married to rigid ethnic rules that cause distress. When clients report such a conflict, counselors can gently probe for the client's allegiances. Such an approach can include such questions as, "How did you come to know that this was the way to be?" These questions address the type of relationship that a person has to her or his ethnicity: Is she or he "subject to it" or can the client have a relationship to her or his ethnicity? In the latter case, the client can make choices about what ethnic norms she or he wishes to adhere to. In Chapter 1, Activity 1.6, The Challenge to Culturally Self-Authorize, asked readers to consider their "received" ethnicity and to consider reclaiming and discarding aspects of it. The narrative approach to counseling, which will be discussed in Chapter 16, is useful for helping clients to separate from problematic allegiances. In that approach, problems are externalized as "stories." New, more effective stories can replace them. Similar work can be done with clients for whom received, rigid ethnic rules are causing conflict. Again, not all clients will wish to challenge their ethnic norms, and their readiness to do so must be respected. In many cases, problem solving for living within ethnic norms will be called for.

Summary

Ethnicity is a pervasive presence in all clients' lives. It is sometimes conflated with race. The distinction made here emphasizes ethnicity as culture and race as a social construction based on phenotype. Individuals internalize the mores of their ethnic groups. These values affect attitudes toward counseling and mental health, career, sexuality, hierarchy, and interpersonal relations, to name a few domains. It should be noted that ethnicity is not equally salient to all individuals. It is especially important to those who are in a minority. Ethnicity has a profound effect on opportunities in society. People of color and immigrants cannot choose whether to pay attention to their ethnicity or not because they are marked in society by their appearance and/or their manners and language. Ethnic groups within the larger European American community can choose whether or not to acknowledge their ethnicity. Guidelines for incorporating ethnicity into counseling include educating clients about the ethnic dimension of their behaviors, clarifying how much clients' concerns are related to internalized ethnic values, and know when counselors' own ethnic assumptions interfere with understanding clients.

References

Berry, J. W., Trimble, J., & Olmeda, E. (1986). *The assessment of acculturation.* In W. J. Lonner & J. W. Berry (Eds.), *Field methods in cross-cultural research* (pp. 291–324). London: Sage.

Casas, J. M., & Pytluk, S. D. (1995). Hispanic identity development: Implications for research and practice. In J. Ponterotto, J. M. Casas, L. A. Suzuki, & C. M. Alexander (Eds.), *Handbook of multicultural counseling* (pp. 155–180). Thousand Oaks, CA: Sage.

Comas-Díaz, L. (2001). Hispanics, Latinos, or Americanos: The evolution of identity. *Cultural Diversity and Ethnic Minority Psychology, 7*(2), 115–120.

Delgado-Romero, E. A. (2001). Counseling a Hispanic/Latino client—Mr. X. *The Journal of Mental Health Counseling* (Special Issue: Counseling Racially Diverse Clients), *23*, 207–221.

Fischer, D. H. (1989). *Albion's seed: Four British folkways in America.* New York: Oxford University Press.

Gans, H. (1979). Symbolic ethnicity: The future of ethnic groups and cultures in America. *Ethnic and Racial Studies, 2,* 1–20.

Giordano, J., & Carini-Giordano, M. (1997). Ethnicity: The hidden dimension in family counseling/therapy. *Family Digest, 10,* 1,4.

Good, G. E., & Sherrod, N. B. (2001). Men's problems and effective treatments. In G. R. Brooks & G. E. Good (Eds.), *The new handbook of psychotherapy and counseling with men: A comprehensive guide to settings, problems, and treatment approaches* (pp. 22–40). San Francisco: Jossey-Bass.

Harper, F. D., & McFadden, J. (2003). *Culture and counseling.* Boston: Allyn & Bacon.

Ivey, A. E., D'Andrea, M., Ivey, M. B., & Simek-Morgan, L. (2002). *Theories of counseling and psychotherapy: A multicultural perspective.* Boston: Allyn & Bacon/Longman.

Kim, B. S. K., & Abreu, J. M. (2001). Acculturation measurement: Theory, current instruments, and future directions. In J. G. Ponterotto, J. M. Casas, L. A. Suzuki, & C. M. Alexander (Eds.), *Handbook of multicultural counseling* (2nd ed., pp. 394–424). Thousand Oaks, CA: Sage.

LaFromboise, T., Coleman, H. L K., & Gerton, J. (1993). Psychological impact of biculturalism: Evidence and theory. *Psychological Bulletin, 114,* 395–412.

Marable, M. (2000, February 25). We need a new and critical study of race and ethnicity. *Chronicle of Higher Education,* p. B34.

Marger, M. N. (1994). *Race and ethnic relations: American and global perspectives.* Belmont, CA: Wadsworth.

Marger, M. N. (2002). *Social inequality: Patterns and processes.* Boston: McGraw-Hill.

Matsumoto, D., & Juang, L. (2004). *Culture and psychology.* Belmont, CA: Thomson/ Wadsworth.

Mead, M. (1963). Socialization and enculturation. *Current Anthropology, 4,* 187–197.

Phinney, J. S. (1996). When we talk about American ethnic groups, what do we mean? *American Psychologist, 51*(9), 918–927.

Ponterotto, J. G., Utsey, S. O., & Pedersen, P. B. (2006). *Preventing prejudice: A guide for counselors, educators, and parents* (2nd ed.). Thousand Oaks, CA: Sage.

Redfield, R., Linton, R., & Herskovits, M. J. (1967). Memorandum for the study of acculturation. In P. Bohannan & F. Plog (Eds.), *Beyond the frontier: Social process and cultural change* (pp.181–186). Garden City, NY: Natural History Press.

Shapiro, T. M. (2004). *The hidden cost of being African American.* New York: Oxford University Press.

Singh, B. (1981). Race, ethnicity and class: Clarifying relationships and continuous muddling through. *Journal of Ethnic Studies, 9*(2), 1–19.

U.S. Census Bureau. (2000, April 12). *Racial and ethnic classifications used in census 2000 and beyond.* Retrieved June 1, 2006, from http://www.census.gov/population/www/ socdemo/race/racefactcb.html

Waters, M. C. (2004). Optional ethnicities. In M. L. Andersen & P. H. Collins (Eds.), *Race, class, and gender* (pp. 418–427). Belmont, CA: Wadsworth/Thompson Learning.

Race

Garrett McAuliffe, Edwin Gómez, and Tim Grothaus

4

Conceptualizing Race and Racism

To the extent that race is even a valid concept . . . it does not come in boxes provided by God or Mother Nature. Race is an undifferentiated continuum of gene frequencies that we break into categories. . . . We place markers at various points on that genetic continuum: cross this one and you are Caucasian, cross that one and you are African, cross another and you are Asian. . . .

The concept called race is an artifact of the way our minds divvy up and simplify an intricate body of information about human beings. The shape of that artifact is not an idle matter—for better and for worse, the way we conceptualize race makes a difference in the world. (Palmer, 1998, pp. 130–131)

In these words, Palmer (1998) captures the difficulty with race. It is a confused and contested social construction. In fact, it is considered to be the most controversial topic in the social sciences (Marger, 2002). And yet, race is an important social phenomenon, even if it cannot be defined in biological terms.

DEFINING A MURKY CONCEPT

Race was defined in Chapter 1 as a group of people of common ancestry, distinguished from others by physical characteristics such as hair type, color of eyes and skin, and stature. The concept of race is "messy," that is, inexact and arbitrary.

AUTHORS' NOTE: Thanks to Dr. Gwen Lee-Thomas of Old Dominion University for ideas on this chapter.

> Race crudely describes people who share a set of similar genetic characteristics. . . . Racial categories, however, [are] highly arbitrary. . . . Physical differences between groups are not clear-cut but instead tend to overlap and blend into one . . . forming a continuum, not a set of clearly demarcated types. Within-group differences are actually much stronger than any across-group differences. (Marger, 2002, pp. 257–258)

There is no "pure" notion of race. Human beings are "mixed up," to quote Salman Rushdie from the beginning of Chapter 1, due to migration, exploration, invasions, intermarriage, and rape from wars and oppression of minorities. Thus, it is not possible to mark out a "race" as a biological group. In fact, humans are remarkably alike, despite superficial differences (King, 1981). Of the small amount of total human variation, 85 percent of the variation in genetics exists within any local population, whether it be Zulu, Sami, Cambodian, Lakota, or residents of a small, isolated community.

In fact, the notion of race is so crude that DNA tests show that the majority of individuals, in one study, shared genetic markers with people of different skin colors. For example, a high percentage of so-called black persons in the United States have some European genetic ancestry (Parra et al., 1998). Informal studies show that many whites also have varied genetic origins in Asia and Africa (Daly, 2005).

It might be clear from these findings that the concept of race is a contested one. It should be contested. In the past, it has been inaccurately constructed as an objective notion by scientists and others who promoted the pseudoscientific notion that there are distinct races. That objectification has been used as justification to divide and rank peoples. Serious harm has resulted from this formulation for many peoples in the United States and elsewhere, including Asians, sub-Saharan Africans, the Irish, Jews, and Mediterranean peoples.

The very notion of seeing physical differences is not, itself, problematic. It is, in fact, automatic for human beings. People tend to classify by appearance. This act of classifying serves a protective function. Using such physical appearance cues allows humans to determine whether individuals are "one of us" or members of another group, tribe, or nation. It is not the classifying itself that is problematic. It is what conclusions are reached from the classifying, conclusions about intellect, sexuality, violence-proneness, and other characteristics that are used to discriminate.

Now complete Activities 4.1 and 4.2 in order to assess your own experience of race.

RACISM

Racism is inevitably tied to the concept of race because race has historically been associated with notions of inferiority and superiority. Racism can most simply be defined as prejudice plus power. David Wellman (1977) captures those two dimensions in this description of racism:

ACTIVITY 4.1

Racial Self-Awareness

Complete the following phrases:

I describe myself as a member of the _____ racial group.

When and how did you first become aware that your race mattered in this society?

The best thing about being _____(insert your racial group) is _____.

The worst thing about being _____(insert your racial group) is _____.

People of my racial group view other racial groups in the following ways.

When I am with members of my racial group, the following issues, feelings, and thoughts are not shared in mixed racial company:

What type of influence might any of these attitudes have on the counseling interaction?

Racism extends considerably beyond prejudiced beliefs. The essential feature of racism is not hostility or misperception, but rather the defense of a system from which advantage is derived on the basis of race. The manner in which the defense is articulated—either with hostility or subtlety—is not nearly as important as the fact that it insures the continuation of a privileged relationship. (p. 34)

In other words, racism consists of (1) the belief that a group of people with characteristics other than those of one's own group is inferior in some way and (2) the ability to act on that belief.

Any person or group can be racist, if they have power to enforce prejudiced beliefs. Thus, racism is possible not only among white people of European descent. However, in U.S. history, so-called white persons have largely had the power to define and enforce the notion of race. For this reason, the term "people of color" has been coined not as a race in itself, but as a description of "racialized minorities" (Marable, 2000; Takaki, 1993), that is, people who have been colonized and dominated by Europeans and European Americans (Martinez, 2004).

The concepts of race and racism are not unique to the United States, however, nor are they limited to recent times. Evidence of racism appears in ancient India, China, Egypt, Greece, and Rome (Gossett, 1997). People have set up hierarchies

---

ACTIVITY 4.2

Cross-Race Contact

Name a "race" other than your own, using whatever term is familiar to you.

Describe your experience with people of this group (including how much contact you have with members of this group and how close that contact is).

Name a time when you had a discussion with a member of this racial group about race itself, if ever.

Think of your most recent racial conflict or situation in your personal or professional life that left you feeling uncomfortable and/or confused.

What did you think?

How did you feel?

How did you react (behave)?

What might your mother think, feel, and say to you about this situation?

What might your father think, feel, and say to you about this situation?

Think of a first session you have had with clients in terms of their race/ethnicity/culture. With what type of client do you have a tendency to feel the greatest level of comfort and confidence?

What type of client raises your anxiety?

What did you discover from responding to these questions?

---

based on various schemes, from skin color to facial features and body types. But these distinctions became especially fixed and universal with European colonial explorations. In the Age of Exploration, Europeans encountered people who looked different from them. Such stark distinctions led Europeans to decide that there were, in fact, distinct races. They failed to acknowledge that there were gradations of peoples who had more-or-less bred together over centuries.

The number of racial categories has varied over the past two centuries from three to more than 20. Until fairly recently, anthropologists placed humans into three supposed racial categories: "Mongoloid," "Caucasoid," and "Negroid."

"Caucasoid" or "Caucasian," like the others, is a problematic term. It is based on the German scientist Johann Friedrich Blumenbach's (1752–1840) assumption that white persons are descended from the original humans in the Caucasus region of the present-day nations of Russia and Georgia. His thesis was based partly on the nearness of the Caucasus to the mythical place where Noah's ark of the Hebrew Bible rested, that is, Mount Ararat in eastern Turkey. Modern anthropologists have thoroughly rejected this notion that the first humans came from that region.

It should be noted that the term Caucasian is used in the United States to represent white persons, but in Europe it represents only people from the Caucasus region of the world. Its inexact usage has led to some racist discomfort. Before 1923, so-called Caucasians in the United States were qualified to become naturalized citizens. However, when several Asian Indians who were, by definition at the time, of the supposed Caucasoid race successfully petitioned for U.S. citizenship in the 1920s, the U.S. Supreme Court reinterpreted the laws to conclude that only those who were deemed "white" were qualified, forcing these Asian Indians to lose their citizenship. This change in the definition of race from a biological base (in supposed skull shape) to a color base further points to the lack of scientific merit for using these concepts. Because of its inaccuracy and racist implications, the term Caucasian is better discarded. Next is a history of the troubled concept of race in the United States.

Origins and History of the Concept of Race in the United States

Regardless of terms used, in the United States, the current conception of "race" was constructed in the nineteenth century. The social construction of racial categories in that era is illustrated by Freeman (1998) in the following description:

> For much of the 19th century . . . the term mulatto was used to indicate a person who had one Black parent and one White parent. This term was essentially abandoned by the end of the century. In the 1900 U.S. Census, the classification quadroon and octoroon were used to denote people who were one-quarter and one-eighth Black, respectively. By the 1920 Census, a Black American was defined as anyone with even one Black ancestor—the "one drop rule." This rule is unique to [the U.S.] and is the current definition of who is Black. During the last half of the 19th century and well into the 20th century, other groups such as Jews and Irish were also classified as separate races. There is still no international agreement on racial classifications. (p. 220)

It might be clear at this point that the U.S. conception of race is a product of the United States' social and political history. The following is a brief overview of the socio-political thought and action in the United States that have led to the current race paradigm.

THEORIES AND MOVEMENTS THAT
REINFORCED THE RACE PARADIGM

Race in the United States is not limited to the black-white distinction. However, that distinction will be discussed most extensively in this section because it has had the greatest impact on American life of any social issue. At least four sets of historical foundations have guided the notion of race in the United States: (1) the law, (2) Evolutionary Theory, (3) Genetic Inheritance Theory, and (4) the assimilationist and melting pot perspectives.

Foundations of Race in Law

The United States was founded on the notion that it was a people held together by common white "blood" and skin color and that only white persons were able to self-govern (Gerstle, 2001). Race theory was not fully articulated at this time. Thomas Jefferson believed that blacks were inferior to whites but declared his uncertainty about the basis for that suspicion (Dain, 2002). Jefferson said, representing the thinking of white writers at the time, "I advance it as a suspicion only, that the blacks, whether originally a distinct race, or made distinct by time and circumstance, are inferior to whites" (cited in Dain, 2002, p. 30). Despite the absence of a clearly articulated theory of race, the notion of a "white republic" was enshrined in the U.S. Constitution. It was further reinforced in the 1790 law that limited naturalization to free white persons. Thus, Africans, Asians, and American Indians were not originally considered to be in the national community (Takaki, 1993).

Foundations of Race in Evolutionary Theory

The notion that blacks and others were inferior to whites was further reinforced by the quasi-sociological view that was called social Darwinism. This perspective was a misapplication of Charles Darwin's concept of evolution, which was published in his *Origin of Species* in 1859. There, Darwin proposed the idea of biological evolution as an explanation of the emergence and persistence of forms of life. In the later 1800s, English scholar Herbert Spencer translated that notion into the social realm. Social Darwinism explained human differences in terms of survival of the fittest, that is, the notion that some races or peoples are more fit for survival than others and are, therefore, designed by nature to dominate inferior races. His ideas led to the notion that white Protestant Europeans had biologically evolved much farther and faster than other "races."

This notion led to an extreme laissez-faire public policy. The social Darwinist political argument went like this: Since the poor are poor because they lack certain genetic characteristics that would fit them for economic survival, society has no obligation to its poor. To help them would be to allow inferior types to survive, and thus interfere with evolution and thereby weaken society. This policy led, for example, to the British non-interference with the Irish potato famine, resulting in millions of deaths in the 1840s.

Social Darwinism was particularly popular in the United States. It led to the overt and sustained subjugation of African Americans even after slavery was declared illegal. The power of Social Darwinism lasted into the 1920s, with its remnants continuing to surface in the present day.

Foundations of Race in Genetic Inheritance Theory

Complementing this application of Evolutionary Theory was the Genetic Inheritance Theory, which arrived with Gregor Mendel's discovery of genes in the 1860s. It gave birth to the eugenics movement at the end of the nineteenth century and beginning of the twentieth century. Eugenics was a wildly popular notion, adhered to by many thinkers of the age. It was coined in 1883 by Sir Francis Galton, who was a cousin of Charles Darwin. Eugenics refers to the study and use of selective breeding to improve a species over generations. Proponents of eugenics advocated sterilizing whole populations to protect against procreation and mixing the biologically inferior "lower races" with the supposed superior races. The lower races were considered to be any groups who were not from Northern and Western Europe and who were not of the Protestant faith. Proof of the racial superiority of Northern European Protestants and their American descendants was seen by its adherents in the U.S. victory over Spain (considered a Catholic and Latin race at the time) in the Spanish-American War in 1898 and in the hegemony of the British Empire on a worldwide scale.

Through Social Darwinism and its cousin, eugenics, race was therefore inextricably connected to biology and tangentially connected to ethnicity and religion. While the massive extermination of peoples based on "race" did not begin until the Nazi era, it had its origins in the "benign" intentions of the U.S. and British elites who wished to use "science" to save human beings from themselves (Black, 2003). Eugenics and "race science" were explicitly taught at major universities throughout the United States from the 1880s through the 1920s. Testimony to the popularity of a biological view of racial superiority was a bestseller in 1911, *Heredity in Relation to Eugenics*. The author, Charles Davenport, warned of the biological inferiority of Southern and Eastern Europeans in these words:

> The population of the United States will, on account of the great influx of blood from South-Eastern Europe, rapidly become darker in pigmentation, smaller in stature, more mercurial [i.e., emotional], more attached to music and art, more given to crimes of larceny, kidnapping, assault, and vagrancy than were the original English settlers. (p. 219)

As a result of this type of pseudoscience, more than 60,000 Americans were actually sterilized and policies were enacted to severely control immigration based on racial and religious attributes (Black, 2003). The influence of eugenics was so pervasive that even Frank Parsons, the social reformer and the founder of the modern notion of counseling, was a proponent of it.

These historical and theoretical developments are important for several reasons. First, through them, non-white persons were legally made subordinate, second-class citizens. Second, the "scientific" evolutionary and genetic arguments justified the hegemonic position of Anglo-Protestants in American society. These arguments also laid the foundation for future theoretical arguments about nature versus nurture in attempts to explain supposed attributes of the races. Biological arguments about race are still put forth (e.g., Herrnstein & Murray, 1994).

Foundations of Race in the Assimilationist and Melting Pot Perspectives

The next major shift that occurred in thinking about race was preceded by the increasing assimilation of European immigrants during the early twentieth century in the United States. Recognition of the fact that the supposedly inferior Jewish and Catholic immigrants were able to assimilate into the American mainstream and achieve in the society in great numbers at the highest levels challenged the arguments that Anglo-Protestants were a biologically superior race.

Further challenges to the biological view were presented from social science. For example, psychologists (e.g., Otto Kleinberg of Columbia University) asserted that earlier psychological testing along racial lines was flawed methodologically. Kleinberg demonstrated that environment was the factor in intelligence in his studies of African American migrants to the North in the 1930s. Anthropologists (e.g., Franz Boas; see Box 4.1) were arguing for a separation between culture and biology (Hannaford, 1996).

The Assimilationist Perspective. During the 1920s, Robert Park and his students from the Chicago School of Sociology proposed the idea that assimilation was the expected end product of inter-race contact (McKee, 1993). The assimilation idea countered the popular view that non-whites and whites were incompatible. It suggested that (in the past) "lesser" racial groups had been assimilated (culturally and physically) into the mainstream civilization of those who had conquered them, as seemed to be the case with the Roman Empire. Parks and his colleagues also noted that assimilation by the dominated group was but one of three possible outcomes to being conquered, the other two being the establishment of a caste system (e.g., India), or having a nation within a nation (e.g., American Indians, Jews). The environment, rather than biology, became the dominant explanation for group differences.

The assimilation notion created a dichotomy between white and "other" in the United States. The common view about assimilation was that the "lesser" peoples (e.g., Catholic and Jewish European white immigrants) would eventually attain equal status with the Anglo-Protestant whites as the former became more like the latter.

But other groups were seen as problematic, as not so easily assimilated. (It should be noted that these distinctions were not made by Parks and his students.) When biological arguments began to wane, sociologists then began to look at blacks and others as culturally, not biologically, inferior: It would take

BOX 4.1   Franz Boas (1858–1942)

Franz Boas is a key figure in turning around the American conception of race. He played a monumental role in eviscerating the racist worldview that prevailed in nineteenth- and early twentieth-century American social sciences. Boas stood out among anthropologists as a proponent of cultural explanations of perceived differences among people.

Boas's own experience as a German Jew made him particularly sensitive to the destructiveness of racial bias. When he arrived in America, he noted that anthropology in this country played a central role as apologist for the notion of racial superiority and inferiority. He challenged the dominant eugenic discourse of the day by careful studies of the Eskimos and the Native Americans of British Columbia.

From these and other analyses, he introduced the notion of cultural relativism. Cultural relativism emphasizes differences in peoples to be the results of historical, social, and geographic conditions and that all populations have complete and equally developed culture. In this vein, Boas warned social scientists and others not to judge cultural practices according to one's own cultural ways. The common practice before this time had been to use one's own culture, usually European and European American, as a standard for "civilization," and to find other "races" wanting in comparison. Boas's predecessors had argued that the evolutionary scale led from savagery to civilization and that Europeans were superior biologically, as evidenced by their version of culture. Boas believed that cultures are too complex to be evaluated according to the broad theorizing characteristic of evolutionary "laws." Instead, Boas sought to understand the development of societies through their particular histories.

Boas worked extensively with black intellectuals, including Booker T. Washington, W. E. B. DuBois, and Zora Neale Hurston. Boas demonstrated that prejudice and racism—not innate inferiority—were black peoples' greatest obstacles in the United States.

Boas's struggle to understand the salience of race in the United States at the beginning of the twentieth century defined the parameters from which we still grapple with racial issues. Just as the work of the early American anthropologists directly influenced the "separate-but-equal" notion in the *Plessy v. Ferguson* case of 1896, resulting in legal segregation, Boas's work led eventually to the 1954 *Brown v. Board of Education* ruling that made segregation illegal.

The Mind of Primitive Man (1911) was perhaps his most influential book; it demonstrated that there was no such thing as a "pure" race or a superior one. In his words, "If we were to select the most intelligent, imaginative, energetic, and emotionally stable third of mankind, all races would be present." Not surprisingly, his books were banned in Hitler's Germany. Boas taught and inspired a generation of anthropologists, notably Margaret Mead and Ruth Benedict, who pioneered the "culture and personality" school of anthropology. Long outspoken against totalitarianism in its many guises, he was a fierce advocate of intellectual freedom, supported many democratic causes, and was the founder of the American Committee for Democracy and Intellectual Freedom. In 1963, the scholar Thomas Gossett wrote, "It is possible that Boas did more to combat race prejudice than any other person in history."

NOTE: Special thanks to Maura McAuliffe and the Anthropology Department of the College of William and Mary.

major re-socialization for them to become more "white," if that were possible at all. Distinctions among non-white groups were made. American Indians were sent to special schools where their "Indianness" was to be expunged and European American ways taken on. Thus, the basic formulation of racial superiority-inferiority remained. Blacks were believed to not be able to assimilate into U.S. society. As a result, whites believed that it was "natural" to have the separate but equal segregation policies that followed the *Plessy v. Ferguson* decision. However, this was not a tenable position. The clamor by black people for full acceptance led to continuing social unrest; for example, the abuses of the Jim Crow system would eventually lead to race riots in the early 1920s.

The notion of racism shifted again, this time to a moral problem, with the publication in 1944 of Gunnar Myrdal's *An American Dilemma*. Myrdal chose this title for his voluminous work because he felt that it captured, in McKee's (1993) words, "his sense of the race problem in the United States: a conflict between the highest of American ideals and lower parochial interests and prejudices" (p. 226). In particular, Myrdal noted that it was not so much a black people's problem as it was a white people's problem. Myrdal, however, still supported the assimilationist perspective that U.S. society was European in its ways and manners and that all others must assimilate to it.

The Melting Pot Perspective. From the 1930s to the 1960s, increased European American assimilation into the mainstream led to the melting pot paradigm. The idea behind the melting pot is that the melding of various cultures makes up one unique America. Unlike assimilation, the Melting Pot Theory, in its ideal formulation, recognized the potential for non-Northern European groups to change the values and customs of the dominant group (Laubeová, 2000) and for a new, mixed culture to be created. It recognized acculturation as a two-way street, with multiple cultures influencing each other to create one amalgam. No longer was the only acceptable model supposed to be Anglo-Protestant in values and ways of living. However, in practice, the melting pot ideal was translated into the same old assimilation model for people of color; it emphasized the European American mix and barely referred to other groups. Laubeová (2000) has noted,

> Ideally the concept of the melting pot should also entail mixing of various "races," not only "cultures." While [nominally] promoting the mixing of cultures, the ultimate result of the American variant of the melting pot happened to be the culture of White Anglo Saxon men, with minimum impact of other minority cultures . . . . The melting pot would [ideally] assume [peoples of all cultures] learning about other cultures in order to enhance understanding, mixing, and mutual enrichment.

The assimilation of non-European cultures into the dominant European American culture could be seen in the continuing valuing of all things European American in the culture, from notions of the "fine" arts, to ideals of beauty, to communication styles, to religious expression. The melting pot hadn't created a new social stew composed of all cultural ingredients.

THE MULTICULTURAL FORMULATION

The current phase in thinking about race is multiculturalism. Multiculturalism is defined as the recognition of the coexistence and mutual contribution of multiple cultures to community life within one nation, without there being one standard cultural norm to which all must assimilate.

Four major occurrences have pushed the race paradigm from the melting pot model toward multiculturalism. The first was the civil rights movement of the 1960s. This movement changed how Americans viewed each other in terms of race, religion, gender, disability, and sexual orientation. The second major occurrence was the arrival in the United States of an ever-growing number of new non-European immigrants in the post–civil rights era. Third, the civil rights movement stimulated many non-whites to "get in touch" with their ancestors (e.g., customs, traditions, histories) and prompted ethnic and racial pride and solidarity movements. A fourth occurrence that prompted the multicultural impulse was the existence of relatively self-sufficient ethnic and racial enclaves in U.S. communities. These enclaves of various Asian, Latino, and African-descended peoples demonstrated the persistence of ethnic group identity after migration and immigration, directly threatening the assimilation and melting pot notions. Glazer and Moynihan (1970) were the first to note the persistence of this ethnic group cohesion. They advocated for movement beyond the melting pot model. They suggested that U.S. society could incorporate multiple ethnic and racial groups in all of their distinctiveness.

Multiculturalism is currently the proposed ethos for the United States. It has replaced the emphasis on assimilation of all other groups to the dominant Anglo American ways. The embracing of multiculturalism as a paradigm has led to an explosion of research and other activity in the area of ethnicity. African Americans, Latinos/Hispanics, American Indians, Asian Americans, and non-Anglo European Americans explored their own histories in the 1970s and 1980s. Despite this trend, some voices still challenge multiculturalism, proclaiming that non–European American cultural groups should assimilate to a standard set of so-called Western values, mores, and other expressions.

The rise of multiculturalism has also been accompanied by a decline in the status of race as a scientifically valid construct. Racial terms like "Mongoloid," "Caucasian," "Red," "Negroid," and "Yellow" are now seen as remnants of an oppressive racist past. Nevertheless, as mentioned at the beginning of Chapter 3, race remains important as long as it is used as a status determiner, as long as bias and social stratification are based on it. The next sections are devoted to the continuing impact of race in U.S. life.

The Contemporary Status of Race and Racism

It should again be noted that a large part of this discussion is devoted to two of the socially constructed "races": blacks and whites. That emphasis is due to the fact that the greatest racial divide in the United States is in the area of black-white relations. However, other forms of racism, such as anti-American Indian, anti-Latino, or anti-Asian attitudes and practices, continue to pervade American life. While there can also be anti-white prejudice, that bias usually lacks the social power to hurt that bias against people of color does. There can also be racism among and between any of the so-called racial groups.

The next sections present the social dimension of contemporary racism, including color-blind racism and racism in organizations. After that discussion, today's racism is discussed in terms of wealth, housing, criminal justice, and jobs.

CONTEMPORARY BLACK-WHITE RELATIONS

The emphasis in the following sections on black-white race issues is due to its particularly thorny role in American history and society, a legacy that Americans live with today because of slavery and massive, officially sanctioned discrimination for almost 400 years. Sociologist Thomas Shapiro's (2004) words iterate the power of the black-white dynamic in the United States: "Recent surveys have shown repeatedly that every social choice that white people make about where they live, what schools their children attend, what careers they pursue, and what policies they endorse is shaped by considerations involving race" (p. 102).

Continuing separation of blacks from other groups is illustrated by speech patterns. Residential segregation and social isolation have caused general black speech patterns, regardless of region in the United States, to differ from Standard American English.

> [Black English] evolved independently from Standard American English because Blacks were historically separated from Whites by caste, class, and region . . . [Black English] has become progressively more uniform across urban areas. Over the past two decades, the Black English vernaculars of Boston, Chicago, Detroit, New York, and Philadelphia have become increasingly similar in their grammatical structure and lexicon, reflecting urban Blacks' common social and economic isolation within urban America. (Massey & Denton, 1993, pp. 162–163)

The ramifications of there being a separate black dialect in the United States are significant. Because black English is uniform and separate, it creates barriers to communication between blacks and whites, thereby decreasing social interaction—even in a racially mixed neighborhood. Furthermore, the language difference impedes blacks' socioeconomic progress because it is more difficult for black-English speakers to find good jobs in the mainstream economy if they do not speak Standard English well. In this regard, Wilson (1996) noted, "Employers frequently [mention] concerns about [black] applicants' language skills" (p. 116). In fact, language code-switching, that is, alternating between two dialects, is often required for many African Americans who enter into mainstream middle-class American society: Massey and Denton (1993) found that successful blacks "who have grown up in the ghetto literally become bilingual, learning to switch back and forth between black and white dialects depending on the social context" (p. 165). This phenomenon resembles similar language fluidity in traditional European and Asian immigrant enclaves, except that within a generation, many non-blacks adopt Standard English, whereas large numbers of black persons continue to learn and pass on black English.

Race is also a status determiner in U.S. society. Sociologists Joe Feagin and Karyn McKinney (2005) point to "the preponderance of data showing that a majority of white Americans, including many who are well-educated, harbor antiblack and other racial stereotypes, and that many whites still discriminate against African Americans in such areas as housing and employment" (p. 13). Feagin and McKinney note further that whites benefit tremendously from racism—from where they live, to with whom they associate, to comfort in public places, to standards for beauty, to inherited wealth, to continuing social connections that assist career development.

More visible, active racism is also present in U.S. society. Feagin and Vera (1995) found that 50 percent of American whites—in essence, 100,000,000 people—are actively racist, that is, at Stages 1 (Impulsive) or 2 (Dualistic-Rational) of D'Andrea and Daniels's (1999) model of oppressive to anti-oppressive thinking (see Chapter 2). In fact, 58 percent of whites attributed at least one of the following characteristics to blacks: "lazy, aggressive or violent, prefer to live on welfare, or complaining" (Bobo, 2001). For a real-life illustration of the power of racism, see Box 4.2.

**BOX 4.2   Racio-Ethnic Categorization and Opportunity:
One Person's Experience**

Consider the following discussion between a high school counselor and a student seeking assistance with choosing a university.

Student: Good morning, thanks for seeing me today.

Counselor: Morning, have a seat.

Student: Thanks.

Counselor: That's "Thank you, sir."

Student: I'm sorry, sir. Thank you, sir.

Counselor: That's better. Now, what brings you here?

Student: Well, sir, I was wondering if you can help me with the application process for three universities I'm looking to get into.

Counselor: Alright, let me see them. [*Counselor looks at the three universities*]. Hmmm. I see you have two public universities and one private university. One university is in-state and two are out of state.

(Continued)

(Continued)

Student: Yes, sir.

Counselor: Have you ever considered vocational school?

Student: Vocational school? What do you mean?

Counselor: Well, vocational school is set up to teach you a trade. I am not so sure that you're university material.

Student: What? Really? Why not?

Counselor: Well, son, it's been shown that people like you are more inclined to do hands-on work. So, perhaps you shouldn't waste your time with trying to get into a full-fledged university. Besides, you have to have pretty high grades to get in.

Student: Well, I got good grades.

Counselor: Yeah, they're good, but they'll need to be even better to get into the universities you want to get into. They'll be looking at extracurricular activities too, and also see how you write. It's a lot of pressure, you know, and a lot of work to get in.

Student: Oh, I see. Okay, thank you for your advice, sir.

Counselor: You're welcome, son.

Answer the questions below, and then read below the background of the counseling session.

Your task is to identify the following:

What is the age, gender, and race/ethnicity of the counselor?

What is the age, gender, and race/ethnicity of the student?

Given the information in this chapter, in what decade would you place a conversation like this?

In the mind of the counselor, what is the student's academic aptitude (A student, B student, etc.)?

In what part of the United States did the conversation take place (North, South, Midwest, West)?

What preconceived notions are impacting the counselor-student relationship?

After you have answered each one of these questions, consider why you gave the answers that you gave.

What clues in the conversation led you to give a particular answer?

What impact do you think the counseling session had on the student?

Background to the Counseling Session

This was an actual interaction that occurred in December 1985 between a student (male, Latino, 17 years old) and his high school guidance counselor (male, white, late 50s). The high school was in Massachusetts. The student was ranked 14th in his class of 136 students; he was vice president of his class, a National Honor Society member, recipient of the state's foreign language award, and had a grade point average of 3.7. In addition, the student was fluent in two languages (without a discernable accent in either language), never participated in bilingual education, ran on the cross-country team, and held a part-time job at a local restaurant. Neither of his parents finished high school, and the language spoken at home was Spanish. Subsequent to this conversation with the school counselor, he was accepted at all three universities to which he had applied and did not pursue vocational schooling. Today, the student has a Ph.D. and is a university professor. He is also a coauthor of this chapter.

This conversation represents the power of race and ethnicity in determining a person's present and future. While the conversation might seem extreme, it is an accurate recollection of the author. Being "sold short" by others, or selling oneself short in terms of aspirations, is the danger of the hierarchical and stereotypical conceptions of race and ethnicity.

Perhaps you might assess your initial response to a person of a different race and, if that response seems negative or stereotypical, you might pause to consider the limits of such a quick assimilation, becoming aware of the damage that such bias has produced in the past. Counselors can be central players in undoing such harm and preventing further inequities.

COLOR-BLIND RACISM

In contrast to "old-fashioned" (overt, legal) racism, modern racism is subtle. It takes the form of the notion that "race no longer matters." This "color-blind racism" consists of people's denying the lingering effects of and continuing presence of racism—for example, in the form of institutionalized racial privilege—in the twenty-first century. It denies the existence of dominant-race members' personal discomfort and aversion concerning members of nondominant races (Dovidio, Gaertner, & Kafati, 2000; McConahay, 1986). That discomfort is expressed in social avoidance rather than intentional aggressiveness, as it often was in the "bad old days." As a result, members of nondominant races do not have access to the mentoring and social connections that play a big part in educational and career opportunities. This type of racial discrimination is, psychologically speaking, traceable to the "similarity effect": tending to associate with, hire, and accept people who look like oneself.

Box 4.3 illustrates a version of color-blind racism in the form of exclusive social networks that sustain the disparities among races. Exclusive social networks, such as the "good ol' boy" network, are not amenable to affirmative action programs. They are related to human socialization patterns and a tendency to associate with and favor people like oneself. They are changeable only through concerted personal effort and advocacy for changed attitudes.

RESPONDING TO SUBTLE AND OVERT RACISM IN ORGANIZATIONS

Given the many forms that racism can take, counselors need to be alert to its power in organizations. One way that counselors might be alert to the subtle and

---

BOX 4.3   The Good Ol' Boy Network

The "good ol' boy" network describes a system of social networking that exists among certain communities and social strata in the United States. Although the term originated in the South, these networks can be found throughout the United States and the rest of the Western world. The term typically refers to informal social, religious, business, and political associations among white males ("good ol' boys"). In some areas, the good ol' boy network is said to still exert considerable influence over many aspects of local government, business, and law enforcement. Usage of the term can often imply a wrongful exclusion of others from the network; however, often the emphasis is on inclusion of a member, as in, "doing a good ol' boy a favor."

A related concept, the "old boy" network in British society, describes a similar social phenomenon, yet the derivation is different: *old boy*, here, refers to alumni, or former students; that is, former classmates from prestigious schools.

The term refers broadly to a highly decentralized social phenomenon rather than to any organized group or groups; there is no central structure or organization. The good ol' boy network is said to manifest in institutions such as white Protestant churches and the local gathering place or tavern.

Alleged effects of the network include ensuring that the leaders of a community can limit business transactions to other elites or to friends or acquaintances within the network, give friends better deals, and generally reinforce traditional power structures over any other elements in the society. The network also functions like any other social network inasmuch as governmental, business, and professional connections and concessions often develop via mutual friendships and introductions established through the network.

SOURCE: Adapted from Wikipedia (http://en.wikipedia.org/wiki/Good_old_boy and http://www.reference.com/browse/wiki/Good_ol'_boy_network).

not-so-subtle racism in organizations is to use the Multicultural Organization Development (MOD) model (Jackson & Holvino, 1988). The model reveals that an overt, legalized form is not the only manner in which racism is expressed. In the MOD, Jackson and Holvino spell out six levels of exclusiveness or inclusiveness (see Box 4.4). Color-blind racism exists on many of these levels. The model is useful for counselors who want to create a more inclusive school, agency, college, or department. Counselors can use it to assess the current multicultural status of organizations and to set goals for helping organizations to become more inclusive (see Activity 4.3).

BOX 4.4   Jackson and Holvino's (1988) Stages of Multicultural Organizational Development

Stage 1. The Exclusionary Organization is devoted to maintaining dominance of one group over other groups based on race, gender, ethnicity, or other social identity characteristics (e.g., the males-only country club, the white supremacist organization).

Stage 2. The Club stops short of explicitly advocating anything like one group's supremacy but does seek to maintain the privilege of those who have traditionally held social power (e.g., the exclusive business club).

Stage 3. The Compliance Organization is committed to removing some of the discrimination inherent in the "club" by providing access to members of nondominant groups. However, it accomplishes this objective without disturbing the structure, mission, and culture of the organization (e.g., some private schools). If a person from a nondominant group is hired, she or he must be a "team player" and not openly challenge the organization's practices, such as admissions or board memberships.

Stage 4. The Affirmative Action Organization is also committed to eliminating the discriminatory practices and inherent "riggedness" of the Stage 2 club by actively recruiting nondominant group members, that is, ones who are typically denied access to organizations. All organization members are encouraged to think in non-oppressive manners. However, members are still required to conform to the norms derived from the dominant group's worldview (e.g., many liberal religious denominations).

Stage 5. The Redefining Organization is a system in transition. It is not satisfied with being just "anti-sexist," for example, but it is committed to examining all of its activities for their impact on all members' ability to participate in the success of the organization (e.g., some universities).

Stage 6. The Multicultural Organization reflects the contributions and interests of diverse cultural groups in its mission, operations, and product or service. It acts on a commitment to eradicate social oppression in all of its forms within the organization. Members of diverse groups are full participants. The organization follows through on broader external social responsibilities to eradicate oppression and educate others in multicultural perspectives (e.g., the Southern Poverty Law Center, Multicultural Student Services Organizations on a campus, the National Council for Community and Justice).

SOURCE: From Jackson and Holvino (1988).

ACTIVITY 4.3

Identifying Multicultural Organizational Stages

Name organizations that you perceive to be at each stage of the model described in Box 4.4:

The Exclusionary Organization:

The Club:

The Compliance Organization:

The Affirmative Action Organization:

The Redefining Organization:

The Multicultural Organization:

Racism can also be expressed within nondominant groups (Telles, 2002). For example, having rounder eyes might be valued in an Asian American community, due to a desire to look more European. Another example is lighter skin being valued more highly than dark skin in the black community (Hunter, 2002). The so-called paper bag test has been used by some blacks to assess the lightness of a black person's skin. The lighter the color (sometimes called the "café au lait" shade), the more status and access to institutions, such as prestigious churches, a black person has in her or his community. Henry Louis Gates, the Harvard historian, quoted the old expression, "If you're black, get back; if you're brown, stick around; if you're white [in this case, "light"], you're alright," to describe that phenomenon (Gates, 2004). Clearly, internalized racism is at work in these examples.

EXTERNAL EVIDENCE OF MODERN RACISM: WEALTH, HOUSING, CRIMINAL JUSTICE, AND JOBS

The legacy of racism is especially evident in wealth, housing, criminal justice, and jobs. Each affects the other, resulting in a continuing disadvantage for people of some racial groups.

Wealth

Wealth is important in any society. It influences access to capital for new businesses, is a source of political and social influence, and provides insurance against fluctuations in labor market income. It affects the quality of housing, neighborhoods, and schools that a family can access, as well as the ability to finance higher education. Wealth is an important "head-start asset," even when it is relatively small. It allows people to borrow from parents to buy new homes, to get by in tough times, to go to college without crushing loans, and to create more wealth through investments (Shapiro, 2004).

Wealth is defined as the total value of things people own minus their debts. Wealth accumulation is different from income. Income is an immediate source of funds, whereas wealth can be inherited and accumulated by generations. However, income is one factor in wealth. Since blacks, on average, earn 59 percent of what whites earn (Menchik & Jianakoplos, 1997; Shapiro, 2004), one would expect blacks to have less savings. Less savings translates into less wealth. Due to these legacies, a high percentage of blacks cannot pass on inherited wealth to their heirs, whereas a high percentage of whites can (Avery & Rendall, 2002; Wolfle, 1987).

The gap in wealth holdings between African Americans and white Americans is far greater than the income gap, with black families having a median net worth of $3,000 compared to a median of $33,500 for white families (Shapiro, 2004). Several studies, including those mentioned here, have found large wealth differences even after controlling for differences between blacks and whites in average income and other factors. This gap is due to the American legacy of racism: Blacks have been kept out of important parts of the U.S. economy for generations. As a result, many blacks lack both the knowledge of finances and the personal contacts that assist wealth accumulation. Such knowledge and contacts affect one's ability to obtain bank loans, one's awareness of investment opportunities, and one's investment knowledge (see Box 4.5).

Demographic variables also play a part in the relative scarcity of black wealth: The fact that blacks are less likely to marry, have less stable marriages, and have more children implies that blacks will have less wealth per household than will whites (U.S. Census Bureau, 2006). The fact that friendships and family ties tend to be within racial groups, such as the previously mentioned "good ol' boy" network, amplifies the race gap in wealth.

Housing

Black Americans continue to face racism when seeking housing (Emerson, Yancey, & Chai, 2001). For example, Feagin (1999) found that 70 percent to 80 percent of white Americans will discriminate against black Americans in housing rentals and loans. In field research, black test renters were found to have faced racial discrimination 61 percent to 80 percent of the time, depending on the city (Feagin & McKinney, 2005). In the area of housing loans, racism, rather than economic factors, accounts for a full 70 percent of the gap between whites and blacks (Tze & Myers, 1995).

Criminal Justice

Bias in the criminal justice system results in a disparity in who gets arrested, convicted, and jailed for the same crimes. A nationwide study prepared by the

BOX 4.5   Wealth Gap Between Races

By IBRAM ROGERS, The Virginian-Pilot

February 25, 2005

Financial consultant Vincent D. Carpenter sees a sharp difference in many of his young clients. "For a 25-year-old white kid, you see the signs of transitional wealth," said Carpenter, the president of Chesapeake Financial Services.

"You see grandmothers or grandfathers giving something to them, giving something to the parents. Whereas 25-year-old black kids are starting from ground zero. It's all coming from them—their first house purchase, the down payment is going to come from them."

That's no accident—it's the result of the major, and often overlooked, racial disparities in wealth, said sociologist Thomas M. Shapiro, who [has written a] book, *The Hidden Cost of Being African American: How Wealth Perpetuates Inequality.*

While the income gap between blacks and whites is getting smaller, there is a dime of wealth in the average black household for every dollar of wealth in every white household, said Shapiro, a professor at Brandeis University.

And that wealth gap has widened in recent years, he said.

"Black and white professionals in the same occupation earning the same salary typically move through life with significantly unequal housing, residential, and education prospects, which means that their children are not really on the same playing field," he writes.

Carpenter knows that from personal experience: He left [college] with $12,000 in student loans.

And at his company, he's welcomed black clients who, at age 50 or 60, are making their first investments in the stock market.

"We have more churches in the African American community that have gross receipts in excess of $30,000 a year than we do businesses, and that's an inverse relationship," Carpenter said.

"You'll see this dynamic throughout the country . . ."

Because Americans believe that equal opportunities lead to equal outcomes, programs like affirmative action were erected. . . .

Carpenter sees the wealth gap as "the final remnants of 300 years of inequality." Only in the past 40 years have black Americans really been able to acquire wealth, he said.

Before then, he said, "we had laws and situations designed to promote ignorance, a spendthrift mentality, and a surviving mode as opposed to a thriving mode, so we're lucky to see these figures."

SOURCE: Reprinted by permission of *The Virginian-Pilot.*

National Council on Crime and Delinquency (2007) found that at every step of the juvenile justice system, African American and Hispanic youths are treated more harshly than their white peers charged with comparable crimes.

In particular, black drug defendants are far more likely to be jailed than white defendants with the same criminal record (Poe-Yamagata & Jones, 2000). In 1996, the National Criminal Justice Commission reported that while blacks account for 13 percent of all regular illegal drug users, they make up 35 percent of those arrested, 55 percent of those convicted, and 74 percent of those imprisoned (Donziger, 1996).

What are the reasons for such disparities? Socioeconomic factors play a part, in that more affluent offenders, who are more likely to be white, can hire better lawyers and work the system through know-how. Also, poorer people who use drugs are less likely to have private places to do so and thus are more likely to actually be seen engaging in drug-related practices, such as distribution and use.

In addition to the socioeconomic factors, there is likely to be bias, whether conscious or unconscious, at work. The media's (news and entertainment) construction of drug use frequently shows people of color engaged in harmful drug-related practices but usually ignores middle-class white persons' drug use, especially the use of alcohol. In addition, bias is expressed through the "similarity effect," in which a person identifies more with someone who is like herself or himself. Thus, white judges and lawyers and black defendants can be an unfortunate mix for the defendants. Regardless of the races of judges, stereotypes of blacks and criminal behavior might be held. And, finally, explicit, intentional bias lingers. Thus, for many reasons, black clients are more likely than white clients to harbor suspicion about the criminal justice system.

Jobs

Job discrimination is also, unfortunately, a continuing fact, as demonstrated in the study described in Box 4.6.

Psychological Dimensions of Race

The psychological impacts of racism for blacks include a tendency to have lower self-esteem (Kwate, Valdimarsdottir, Guevarra, & Bovbjerg, 2003), to hide vulnerable emotions like fear and sadness (White & Parham, 1990), to experience greater stress than whites (Utsey, Chae, Brown, & Kelly, 2002), and to have self-limiting beliefs about opportunities (Auerbach, 2002). Counselors who are from the dominant group need to be especially alert to these psychological possibilities when they work with clients from an oppressed group.

The psychological aspect of race and racism speaks to the internal, personal experience of being a member of a so-called race. That experience is expressed in negative and positive self-perceptions and can be portrayed in stages of racial identity.

RACIAL IDENTITY DEVELOPMENT

Many theories of racial and ethnic identity development have been developed (e.g., Cross, 1995; Helms & Cook, 1999). Some are specifically oriented to people from nondominant racial groups; others are for the dominant racial group.

One of the values of developmental models is that they plot positive movement in individuals' appreciation and understanding of their and others' races.

BOX 4.6   Racial Discrimination: Still at Work in the U.S.

By David Wessel, *Wall Street Journal*

Two young high school graduates with similar job histories and demeanors apply in person for jobs as waiters, warehousemen, or other low-skilled positions advertised in a Milwaukee newspaper. One man is White and admits to having served 18 months in prison for possession of cocaine with intent to sell. The other is Black and hasn't any criminal record. Which man is more likely to get called back? It is surprisingly close. In a carefully crafted experiment in which college students posing as job applicants visited 350 employers, the White ex-con was called back 17% of the time and the crime-free Black applicant 14%. The disadvantage carried by a young Black man applying for a job as a dishwasher or a driver is equivalent to forcing a White man to carry an 18-month prison record on his back.

Many White Americans think racial discrimination is no longer much of a problem. Many Blacks think otherwise. In offices populated with college graduates, White men quietly confide to other White men that affirmative action makes it tough for a White guy to get ahead these days. (If that's so, a Black colleague once asked me, how come there aren't more Blacks in the corporate hierarchy?) A recent Gallup poll asked: "Do you feel that racial minorities in this country have equal job opportunities as Whites, or not?" Among Whites, the answer was 55% yes and 43% no; the rest were undecided. Among Blacks, the answer was 17% yes and 81% no. The Milwaukee and other experiments, though plagued by the shortcomings of research that relies on pretense to explain how people behave, offer evidence that discrimination remains a potent factor in the economic lives of Black Americans. "In these low-wage, entry-level markets, race remains a huge barrier. Affirmative-action pressures aren't operating here," says Devah Pager, the sociologist at Northwestern University in Evanston, Ill., who conducted the Milwaukee experiment and recently won the American Sociological Association's prize for the year's best doctoral dissertation. "Employers don't spend a lot of time screening applicants. They want a quick signal whether the applicant seems suitable. Stereotypes among young Black men remain so prevalent and so strong that race continues to serve as a major signal of characteristics of which employers are wary."

In a similar experiment that got some attention last year, economists Marianne Bertrand of the University of Chicago and Sendhil Mullainathan of the Massachusetts Institute of Technology responded in writing to help-wanted ads in Chicago and Boston, using names likely to be identified by employers as White or African American. Applicants named Greg Kelly or Emily Walsh were 50% more likely to get called for interviews than those named Jamal Jackson or Lakisha Washington, names far more common among African Americans. Putting a White-sounding name on an application, they found, is worth as much as an extra eight years of work experience. These academic experiments gauge the degree of discrimination, not just its existence. Both suggest that a blemish on a Black person's resume does far more harm than it does to a White job seeker and that an embellishment does far less good. In the Milwaukee experiment, Ms. Pager dispatched White and Black men with and without prison records to job interviews. Whites without drug busts on their applications did best; Blacks with drug busts did worst. No surprise there. But this was a surprise: Acknowledging a prison record cut a White man's chances of getting called back by half, while cutting a Black man's already-slimmer chances by a much larger two-thirds. "Employers, already reluctant to hire Blacks, are even more wary of Blacks with proven criminal involvement," Ms. Pager says. "These testers were bright, articulate college students with effective styles of self-presentation. The cursory review of entry-level applicants, however, leaves little room for these qualities to be noticed." This is a big deal given that nearly 17% of all Black American men have served some time, and the government's Bureau of Justice Statistics projects that, at current rates, 30% of Black boys who turn 12 this year will spend time in jail in their lifetimes. In the Boston and Chicago experiment, researchers tweaked some resumes to make them more appealing to employers. They added a year of work experience, some military experience, fewer periods for which no job was listed, computer skills, and the like. This paid off for Whites: Those with better resumes were called back for interviews 30% more than other Whites. It didn't pay off for Blacks: Precisely the same changes yielded only a 9% increase in callbacks. Someday Americans will be able to speak of racial discrimination in hiring in the past tense. Not yet.

SOURCE: From David Wessel, Racial Discrimination: Still at Work in the U.S., *Wall Street Journal Online*. Copyright 2005 by Dow Jones & Company, Inc. Reproduced with permission of Dow Jones & Company, Inc. via Copyright Clearance Center.

Racial identity developmental models describe increasing flexibility, complexity, and openness in an individual's thinking about race. Racial identity can move from denigration of one's own group toward pride in one's own group to a more inclusive perspective about all groups.

Racial identity status affects both clients' and counselors' perceptions of each other. By considering racial identity development factors, counselors can understand a client's mistrust and anger, or, conversely, relative openness to diversity. In that sense, racial identity development provides a nonpathological explanation for clients' negative feelings toward the counselor and counseling.

There are two sets of such developmental models, one for people of color and one for white persons. Two integrated models, one for each group, will be described here.

IDENTITY DEVELOPMENT FOR PEOPLE OF COLOR

"People of color" can be defined as the racialized ethnic minorities in the United States who share a common history of oppression by whites (Takaki, 1993). It does not mean that these groups of people are ethnically similar in terms of values, lifestyles, and behaviors. Instead, the term describes peoples who have not assimilated and cannot assimilate at this time into the dominant white culture because of their physical features (Butler, 2001). As mentioned earlier, people of color contrast to European immigrant groups, who assimilate as "white" (Ignatiev, 1995).

The Racial Identity Development for People of Color (RIDPOC) Model represents a synthesis of Helms's (Helms & Cook, 1999), Cross's (1995), and Atkinson, Morten, and Sue's (1998) minority identity development models, as well as Slattery's (2004) integration of the two. The model has five statuses, each of which represents an individual's overall tendency at any one time. Cross (1995) calls the movement through these stages a "resocializing experience" (p. 97).

The five statuses in the RIDPOC model for people of color are (1) Conformity, (2) Dissonance and Beginning to Appreciate, (3) Resistance and Immersion, (4) Introspection and Internalization, and (5) Universal Awareness. Note that these statuses (sometimes called "stages") are not rigidly sequential nor unitary. They represent the general tendency; one or two statuses will dominate at any one time in any one person (Helms & Cook, 1999).

While this model has general value, the reader should note that not all aspects of an individual's thinking can be neatly fit into any developmental model. For example, a black Haitian who immigrates to the United States may have little direct experience with racial prejudice. She or he will not initially identify as African American or, perhaps, even as "black." But, within the U.S. context, a good part of her or his identity will nevertheless be subsumed as "black." She or he is likely to associate often with African Americans due to U.S. housing and socialization patterns. However, her or his thinking would not fit the RIDPOC model as easily as a U.S.-born person of color.

The RIDPOC model can give counselors an idea of their client's frame of mind. It can also be prescriptive, in that it can suggest directions for individuals who aim for greater complexity in their thinking. In the latter case, liberation counseling, which is described in Chapter 16, can be explicitly applied at each stage to assist with such change.

THE RACIAL IDENTITY DEVELOPMENT FOR PEOPLE OF COLOR MODEL

Status 1: *Conformity.* Here, persons of color consider their race unimportant. They conform to the dominant, negative cultural view of their race and the dominant race.

Individuals in the Conformity status may value the physical characteristics, lifestyles, achievements, and manners of the dominant group and denigrate the qualities of people of color (e.g., valuing European-style classical music and seeing jazz as a lower form of art, valuing the physical features of white people more than those of people of color, assuming that people of color are lacking desirable characteristics in some way). At the negative extreme in this status, they may feel self-hatred because of their race.

That self-denigration is not universal: Research has shown that people of color who are in the Conformity status do not necessarily denigrate their race, nor have low self-esteem (Cross, 1995). Instead, some persons may place little importance on their racial identity (e.g., "I don't know why people make such a fuss about being black"). They are likely to prefer the dominant group's ways while not necessarily feeling negatively about their race.

Counseling Implications: Clients in the Conformity status are likely to prefer a white counselor. They will act to please the white counselor as an authority. The counselor should encourage the client to express her or his negative view of self and her or his group. The counselor should demonstrate positive attitudes toward racial diversity and particularly toward the client's race.

Status 2: *Dissonance and Beginning to Appreciate:* At this status, individuals experience confusion, or "dissonance," about having a negative view of their own group. They begin to consider their race in a positive light. Such changes are triggered by positive experiences around people of color, for example, through reading, seeing an interview, or having a role model who is proud of and immersed in her or his racial group. Initial confusion, or dissonance, from this experience gives way to a dawning awareness that members of one's own group are positive in ways that are unexpected by the client. Box 4.7 illustrates the story of one person's discovery of pride in his race.

BOX 4.7   Learning About Black Achievers Makes Lessons for a Lifetime

February 24, 2005

© 2005—Landmark Communications Inc.

By John Horton

Black History Month is just about over for 2005, but its lessons can reverberate throughout the year—and beyond.

I wasn't aware of the significance of black history until I came of age during the 1960s. Before then, I had spent the first two decades of my life not knowing about the many African American achievers or their achievements.

I was born in 1940 and raised in the colored projects of Chattanooga, Tenn. by a mother who worked as a domestic maid and also received public assistance. My father had deserted my mother and five children when I was 13 years old and in the eighth grade.

During this time, I attended all-black schools in a highly segregated society. My mother taught me to read before I started school. This was quite an accomplishment because she had only two or three years of formal schooling. I became an excellent student, but in the schools of the 1940s and '50s, I learned only about a handful of black heroes and personalities, such as Booker T. Washington, George Washington Carver, Joe Louis, Jesse Owens, and once in a while Harriet Tubman and Sojourner Truth.

But I learned nothing of the likes of more controversial figures such as W.E.B. DuBois, Marcus Garvey, Jack Johnson, or Paul Robeson or of their great dreams and accomplishments.

To boys like me, this lack of information fed into a broader negativity about black people during an era of legal segregation. For example, in the 1940s and '50s in many Southern communities, blacks could not work with whites as policemen, firemen, lawyers, doctors, teachers, pharmacists, contractors, journalists, scientists, economists, and entrepreneurs—no matter how educated or competent they were. As a whole, black people were seen as inferior in terms of abilities and skills.

Meanwhile, things got really tough at home and, in the mid-1950s, I dropped out of 10th grade at age 16. After working at low-paying, go-nowhere jobs, I joined the Marine Corps at 17. It turned out be a good fit because I remained in the Marines for a 30-year career, retiring as a sergeant major in 1988.

I was in the Marines when I read my first textbook about black history. In the early 1960s, one of my white commanding officers had discarded *From Slavery to Freedom,* by John Hope Franklin. The

(Continued)

(Continued)

contents opened my eyes! I realized that I and other black people have been great before and could be great again.

For several months, I read *From Slavery to Freedom* cover to cover, time and time again. To this day, I still use this "Black Bible" for knowledge, reference, inspiration, and teaching.

Inspired, I began to intensely read more black history. During this time, I also pushed on to earn my high school GED. This began my journey to other educational milestones while still in the Marine Corps. I received associate's, bachelor's and master's degrees.

Reading all kinds of black history, especially autobiographies and biographies, I discovered how much black people had done, not only in America and Africa, but around the world. I began writing articles and participating in black history and cultural diversity activities inside and outside the military.

In the 1970s, I began teaching black history for Los Angeles Community College while stationed in Okinawa, Japan. Upon returning stateside, I did the same at Cherry Point, N.C., Memphis, Tenn., and Norfolk [Virginia].

I've also worked with troubled teens for about two decades and I've used black history and African culture to motivate and uplift them. I tell them about the trials and tribulations—and triumphs—of those who've gone before. I explain what Jackie Robinson meant by, "A life is unimportant except for the impact it has upon others."

But I continue to see too many African Americans, especially young males, who have given up hope. They simply don't believe in themselves. They don't think they are worthy or deserving of the good life. I have fathered, befriended, cajoled, pushed, pulled, begged—and yes, even threatened them. Too often, I have not been as successful as I would have liked. There have been successes, but it is the failures and crises that keep me awake at night.

But when I feel dejected, I turn to my black history heroes. I draw on their struggles and victories and their countless contributions. This restores my appreciation of where black people have been, where they are now and hopefully where they'll be one day.

I find the strength to reach out again—not just in February but through the year. So, just as learning about black history never ends, always keep in mind that the lessons from our heritage can carry you through a lifetime. It's worked for me.

John L. Horton, 64, recently retired as a probation officer.

SOURCE: Reprinted by permission of *The Virginian-Pilot*.

John Horton's story reflects the power of heroes as models for people of color. His journey can be a lesson and a guide for other people of color who wish to progress in their racial identity. Counselors can be catalysts for such racial self-discovery at the Dissonance status.

The person of color at this status discovers that whites have privileges that contribute to their success. What emerges is a mixture of the old cultural self-disparagement with a confusing, new cultural self-appreciation. This awareness can be difficult because previous attempts to "fit in" with the dominant culture all of one's life now encounter the reclaiming of one's race (e.g., a Native American Indian might think, "I have taken on the white man's Christianity. We've changed our names to sound Anglo. But my people have many important spiritual traditions that I would like to learn about and honor and a language of our own.").

A natural consequence of this dissonance and cultural self-appreciation is some mistrust of the dominant culture and a sense of having been "had."

Counseling Implications: Counselors should help clients who are at this status move toward a positive identification with their racial group by introducing and discussing positive cultural symbols, persons, and reading materials (Ivey, Ivey, D'Andrea, & Simek-Morgan, 2005). Counselors will first need significant knowledge of related racial and cultural issues for people of color. Counselors can introduce clients here to the Guided Imagery With Positive Cultural Symbols activity (see Chapter 16, Box 16.3) to help clients identify their cultural strengths.

Status 3: *Resistance and Immersion.* At this status, individuals consciously feel consistently negative about the dominant race's hegemony. In the Resistance and Immersion way of thinking, individuals are likely to be angry about past wrongs done to their group. Individuals in this status are immersed in the expressions of their own racial group. They have a beginning sense of pride in their own race for its characteristics and struggles. They tend to see only positive qualities in their own group and attribute all difficulties to whites. From the Resistance and Immersion frame, individuals begin to idealize their race and are unthinkingly loyal to the group; that is, they are "culture-centric," as discussed in Chapter 1. However, positive feelings about one's own race are not monolithic at the Resistance and Immersion status; individuals may continue to have lingering self-deprecating attitudes, especially early in this status.

A type of insularity characterizes Resistance and Immersion. Individuals at this status are now "subject to" the group (Kegan, 1982); they can't step outside of their group's norms and customs to evaluate them. As the word "immersion" implies, awareness of being a person of color here becomes all-consuming.

Late in the experience of this status, individuals of color have a confident identification with people in their own group and a mistrust of whites. They are suspicious of white counselors and see racial slights as pervasive.

Counseling Implications: White counselors who are working with individuals characterized by Resistance and Immersion should expect the client to be suspicious of the counselor as an agent of the oppressive establishment. The client is not as likely to take individual responsibility for choices, but instead will attribute difficulties exclusively to group oppression. The client is likely to prefer a counselor who has knowledge of race-related issues and is well versed in the client's own racial group.

Establishing trust with a white counselor will be difficult. If the counselor is white, she or he should not get defensive about racial issues. The counselor can show knowledge of oppression against people of color and support for efforts to challenge it. If the client is ready, the counselor can help her or him identify her or his autonomous views on issues, rather than the culture-centric view to which she or he is now subject.

Status 4: *Introspection and Internalization.* Here, individuals become more thoughtful and complex about race. They are introspective rather than unquestioningly immersed in their own race. A more complex formulation of racial identity is possible.

The initial challenge to the previous Immersed way of thinking may occur through negative encounters with members of one's own group. Individuals here begin to recognize narrow culture-centric thinking in themselves and in others. Culture-centrism doesn't feel true to their own experiences. These individuals may also have positive encounters with whites in personal or work relationships or through the media, perhaps with white allies who challenge oppression. They thus reconsider their blanket negative assessment of whites.

At Introspection and Internalization, there is a continuing strong sense of pride in and identification with one's own race, its characteristics and struggles. But, from the Introspection and Internalization frame, individuals are better able to step back from automatic assumptions about "us" and "them." They recognize their own ethnocentrism.

There is conflict at the Introspection and Internalization status. Here, individuals experience a dilemma about their strong desire to, on the one hand, attach to their own racial group and, on the other, to discard conformist groupthink. They begin to determine the attractive attributes of their own race, rather than have those attributes be dictated by others.

Inclusion of others is now possible: Due to increasing confidence about internalized racial identity, individuals at the Introspective and Internalization status can associate comfortably with white persons. They can also challenge more immersed members of their own group who criticize their increasing contact with the dominant culture.

Counseling Implications: The counselor might help Introspection and Immersion thinkers to solidify their autonomy. The counselor can help the client connect with other complex ideas and thinkers of all races, especially members of her or his racial group who are able to move comfortably among other racial groups.

Status 5: *Universal Inclusion.* As the term implies, this way of thinking is a multicultural status. Individuals who think from the Universal Inclusion position clearly value their racial identity. However, they also recognize that there can be oppressions for many groups, including whites. They have moved from the absolute black-and-white view of racial groups to recognize the presence of undesirable and desirable dimensions in all cultures. They know the negative legacies of American racism that have led to current attitudes and conditions. They see white racism as unacceptable but as a consequence of a past to be overcome. They can advocate for social justice for all groups. These persons can integrate aspects of European American culture into their own racial-ethnic culture. Further, they are interested in experiencing all cultures.

Counseling Implications: Clients will be interested in working with any counselor who shares a similarly complex worldview and multicultural awareness. From the Universal Inclusion client perspective, the counselor's race co-exists with his or her individuality.

The reader is encouraged to complete Activity 4.4 at this point in order to connect the RIDPOC statuses to her or his experience.

ACTIVITY 4.4

I. Review the description of the racial identity statuses.

Conformity

Dissonance and Beginning to Appreciate

Resistance and Immersion

Introspection and Internalization

Universal Inclusion

II. If you are a person of color, as U.S. society defines it,

1. Comment on where you were in the past in terms of any of these statuses.

2. Comment on your general status now.

3. Write down actions you might take to move toward the next status.

If you are white, think of a person you have encountered or have seen in the media who seemed to characterize each of these statuses. Write down the status she or he seems to represent and why.

WHITE RACIAL IDENTITY DEVELOPMENT

The notion of white racial identity comes as a surprise to some people. For them, it seems like an "empty" notion because whites are generally oblivious to the role of race in their lives. However, because race matters, and because differences in white racial identity have been observed, a number of theorists (Hardiman, 1982; Helms, 1990) have described an evolution in white racial identity. Helms's model has been particularly well researched, accompanied as it is by a measure of white racial identity.

White racial identity development models are particularly important at this time in the field of counseling because the vast majority of counselors are white (Middleton, Erguner-Tekinalp, & Petrova, 2005). White counselors who have poor racial identity development might fail to make a commitment to serving people of color, might underplay inequities, and might fail to challenge racism in clients.

With higher white racial identity development, white counselors can effectively work with clients of color, if trust and credibility are established. White counselors must be prepared to respond nondefensively to the overt or covert challenge from clients of color that can take the form of, "What do you know about being (black, Asian, Hispanic/Latino, American Indian)?" White counselors who are in the early statuses of white racial identity development would be defensive under such scrutiny as well as insensitive to the racial issues that affect clients' lives.

Knowledge of white racial identity development can alert white counselors who are at the early statuses to the work that they need to do on their own racial awareness. Knowledge of the later statuses can cue white counselors to the importance of engaging in advocacy and racial awareness activities.

What follows is an integration of two of the major white racial identity development models, namely those of Hardiman (1982) and of Helms (1990). There are five statuses in this combined model: (1) Acceptance/Conformity, (2) Dissonance/Disintegration, (3) Immersion, (4) Emersion/Redefinition, and (5) Autonomy/Internalization. The student might notice the general similarity between white racial identity stages and the previously discussed racial identity stages for people of color. Like other cultural identity development models, both describe movement from an exclusive and external frame of reference to a more inclusive, self-authorized one. However, the content of the two models necessarily differs, especially at the early positions.

Despite the model being laid out in five stages, movement through them is not strictly linear. Recent research shows that counselors tend to show characteristics of multiple stages at any one time (Middleton et al., 2005). For example, a white individual might show elements of Status 2: Dissonance about her or his former acceptance of the dominant view on race in society (e.g., "I am noticing that being a person of color seems to matter regarding clients' opportunities and self-perceptions") while also wavering between Status 1: Acceptance ("I don't think about it a lot. Color is irrelevant") and Status 3: Immersion (e.g., "I noticed the book *Race Matters* in the bookstore. I browsed through it"). This white person is not likely to show characteristics of the upper stages (e.g., she or he would not intentionally challenge lack of diversity on a staff or go to an event dominated by people of color).

It should be noted that the implications for each status are directed largely at counselors themselves because the majority of counselors are white. For white clients, racial identity can be important in their lives and the lives of other, but it may not necessarily affect their lives in an obvious way because they are in the dominant position in society. Of course, it is the socially critical counselor's role to promote a non-racist society, and she or he can use these stages to instigate challenges to client racism.

Status 1: *Acceptance/Conformity.* At this status, the individual unquestioningly receives the dominant negative views on people of color. She or he is oblivious to the influence of race on others' and one's own life. The acceptant/conformist person sees any social differences as evidence of inferiority (genetically or culturally) of non-white groups. This can be a lifelong status.

Counseling Implications: A white counselor at this status can harm clients of color by rejecting or dismissing those who are demonstrating Resistance and Immersion (Status 3) of RIDPOC. Similarly, the counselor in Acceptance/ Conformity might pathologize mistrust by clients of color instead of probing for the roots of such mistrust in oppression. The Acceptant/Conformist counselor is also likely to avoid clients of color in general and/or to be unaware of their unique issues. She or he will attribute all client struggles to the individual.

Status 2: *Dissonance/Disintegration.* The white individual here experiences a breakdown in the notion that race doesn't matter. Dissonance/Disintegration can be initiated by a person learning about racial inequities, perhaps from a course in social and cultural issues in counseling. Such an awakening can also be triggered by media portrayal of racial issues (e.g., a documentary on the civil rights struggle and/or on high achieving, powerful people of color) or a friendship with a person of color (e.g., one that happens in the workplace) that challenges previous assumptions. The white individual may be moved to Dissonance/Disintegration by observing clear cases of bias that are disturbing. The person is likely to feel some guilt at this point at past participation in racism.

The white person who thinks largely from this framework is still likely to have negative attitudes about some of the lifestyle expressions of people of color and cross-racial romantic relationships. Dissonance/Disintegration thinkers have little meaningful contact with people of color or their ethnic cultures. Such white individuals are unsure whether acting in a non-racist way is worth it, due to the continuing need for approval from peers and others. However, Dissonance/ Disintegration thinkers can achieve some tolerance of people of color if those people meet white standards (e.g., in the arts, fashion, communication styles). If the person at this status continues to be open to this dissonance, she or he might move toward Status 3 (Immersion) and then to Status 4 (Emersion/Redefinition). Conversely, she or he could stay in Dissonance/Disintegration for life, with continuing dissonance, or retreat to the conformity of the Acceptance status. In that case, she or he is likely to retreat to an all-white world and racial biases, to reduce the discomfort.

Counseling Implications: The white counselor at this status is still likely to ignore racism, even to be defensive about it. She or he may avoid working with or reaching out to clients of color. White counselors at the Dissonance/Disintegration stage are likely to associate only with white colleagues in any meaningful way, thereby failing to learn about race.

Status 3: *Immersion.* This status is characterized by a beginning redefinition of "whiteness." At the early point of this journey, the person is very vigilant about racial issues and highly alert to the topic, perhaps reading, discussing, and viewing films and documentaries that evoke race-related themes. Here, the white person actively seeks to understand the nature of racism and of privilege. White individuals in the Immersion status are likely to feel anger at racism. At this status, they are judgmental about their own and other white persons' racism. However, the white person in Immersion continues to have only relatively superficial contact with people of color.

Counseling Implications: The white counselor early in this status might dismiss the non-immersed client of color as not being racially aware enough. Such a white counselor might ignore the non–race-related dimensions of client concerns that are unique to each individual, such as family distress, mood disorders, and career concerns. The Immersed white counselor could also be overbearing with colleagues who do not share her or his awakening and immersion.

Status 4: *Emersion/Redefinition.* As the person integrates this awareness, she or he becomes more secure, even calm, in her or his redefinition of "whiteness." At the Emersion/Redefinition status, white individuals consistently challenge their own racism. They acknowledge that being white brings privilege (see Chapter 2). At this point, individuals feel solidarity with likeminded whites and become more comfortable in and desirous of interacting with people of color.

Counseling Implications: With emersion and the accompanying redefinition of whiteness, the counselor is better able to address race issues in counseling rather than hiding from them or denying their impact on the counseling relationship.

Status 5: *Autonomy/Internalization.* Here, a person has moved toward a nonracist white identity, fully accepting his or her own race without guilt. Race is not a threat to a person in this status. For example, the person can hear people of color speak about racism without experiencing unnecessary personal guilt. At this status, the white person appreciates her or his role in the continuation of racism.

The white person at the Autonomy/Internalization status seeks out cross-racial experiences and personal contacts. In the area of social action, individuals who think from the Autonomy/Internalization perspective make a commitment to take counter-oppression actions. In particular, they attempt to relinquish unearned privilege from being white. They are proactive in promoting actions that increase equity (e.g., in organizational decision making, in inclusion of all people and perspectives, in challenging obvious and subtle dominance).

Autonomy/Internalization can be a difficult stance to sustain in a nonsupportive environment, whether it is societal, organizational, or familial.

Counseling Implications: Here, the white counselor is likely to be comfortable working with all clients and able to integrate race issues into counseling. She or he will be able to invite appropriate discussion of race during sessions, free of guilt and avoidance over the topic.

Activity 4.5 offers an opportunity for the reader to identify white racial identity statuses for herself or himself or for another.

Multiracial Individuals and Families

A simple answer to the common question, "What are you?" is not possible for multiracial persons. This chapter concludes with a discussion of the emerging issue of multiracial identity.

The terms "biracial" and "multiracial" are often used interchangeably. "Multiracial" is broader in scope and is the term preferred by many multicultural

---

ACTIVITY 4.5

I. Review the characteristics of the white identity development statuses.

   Acceptance/Conformity

   Dissonance/Disintegration

   Immersion

   Emersion/Redefinition

   Autonomy/Internalization

II. If you are a white person,

   1. Note where you were in the past in terms of any of these statuses.

   2. Note your general racial identity status now.

   3. Write down actions you might take to move toward the next status.

If you are a person of color, think of an individual whom you have encountered or have seen in the media who seemed to characterize each of these statuses. Write down the status she or he seems to represent and why.

---

researchers and scholars (Ponterotto, Utsey, & Pedersen, 2006). Wehrly (2005) defines multiracial individuals as persons "whose parents are of different racial heritages." She defines multiracial families as "a family grouping that includes members of more than one racial heritage" by marriage, cohabitation, or transcultural adoption (p. 314).

The number of multiracial individuals and families has increased considerably in the past 40 years, ever since the U.S. Supreme Court struck down the anti-miscegenation laws (banning marriage or sexual unions between persons of different races) that still existed in 14 states (Kenney, 2006). The 2000 census was the first to allow individuals to indicate more than one race to describe their heritage (U.S. Census Bureau, 2000). Almost seven million individuals did so, roughly 2.4 percent of the population that was counted. The actual number and percentage of multiracial individuals is probably higher (Paniagua, 2005; Ponterotto et al., 2006; Sue & Sue, 2003). Approximately 93 percent of the multiracial individuals who identified themselves on the census indicated two racial heritages, while the remaining 7 percent chose three or more (Paniagua, 2005).

The issues to which multiracial individuals are subject include many of the stressors and oppressions outlined previously in this book for members of any nondominant group. In addition, individuals with multiracial heritage deal with some unique issues:

- They are often not depicted in U.S. media, including children's books and educational materials. (Sue & Sue, 2003)

- This neglect extends to the counseling and psychology literature, as well as counselor training programs. (Ponterotto et al., 2006; Wehrly, 2005)

- Multiracial individuals may experience a lack of acceptance by segments of their families and/or of the communities in which they live, work, or go to school. (Kenney, 2006; Wehrly, 2005)

- The lack of acceptance by others may lead to feelings of marginalization and isolation. (Sue & Sue, 2003)

- They are subject to unflattering stereotypes and/or myths (e.g., that one or both partners in a interracial couple has suspect motives for the union). (Sue & Sue, 2003; Wehrly, 2005)

- They may endure frequent inquiries about their physical features and/or racial heritage. (Kenney, 2006; Ponterotto et al., 2006)

- Multiracial individuals may be pressured to identify with a single racial referent group and to exclude their other racial heritage(s). (Kenney, 2006; Wehrly, 2005)

In addition to these difficulties, enculturation may be a more complex process when more than one racial or ethnic heritage is involved. While mono-racial or mono-ethnic individuals are socialized in the ways of their racio-ethnic culture and develop their cognitive map for being and acting in the world, multiracial individuals (and families) are not always mentored in both or all of their salient racial or ethnic cultural identities. For example, a person who is both African American and European American may be enculturated in African American culture or in European American culture. Thus, part of her or his heritage and identity are submerged or even dismissed.

MULTIRACIAL IDENTITY

Another area of relative neglect involves multiracial identity development. The development of a positive racial identity is considered vital for individuals with multiracial heritage (Kenney, 2006), yet single-race models of identity development are considered inadequate for use with such individuals (Robinson, 2005; Wehrly, 2005).

Identity development for multiracial individuals is more complex than for single-race persons. In Ponterotto et al.'s (2006) words, it is "a lifelong process that . . . involves continuing efforts to integrate the many facets that make up one's racial identity" (p. 115). Two models for explaining multiracial identity are outlined next.

Root's Multiracial Identity Model

Maria Root's model emphasizes the importance of identity for multiracial individuals (cited in Ponterotto et al., 2006). Hers is not a stage model. Root indicates that there are four choices that a multiracial individual can make to resolve identity status:

- acceptance of the identity that society chooses for the individual (e.g., "Asian" in the case of Asian American and European American),
- identification with the racial reference groups of both parents,
- choosing a racial group identity rather than just accepting the choice "assigned" (e.g., seeking information on American Indian heritage after having been identified as "white"),
- identifying with a different group, other persons of multiracial heritage. (Ponterotto et al., 2006, p. 116)

Each of these choices can both work for individuals and have disadvantages (Ponterotto et al., 2006). Counselors can help clients see which of the choices they have made and which they would like to move toward. Methods include those used to help mono-racial individuals move toward appreciation and pride in their identity.

Choi-Misailidis's Multiracial Heritage Awareness and Personal Affiliation Theory

The Multiracial Heritage Awareness and Personal Affiliation Theory (M-HAPA) was developed by SooJean Choi-Misailidis in 2001. She identifies three identity statuses:

1. *Marginal,* in which individuals lack a sense of connection with any racial group, as is the case with marginalized ethnic status in general (see Chapter 3).

2. *Singular,* which is similar to Root's first choice (acceptance of a given identity), in which an individual accepts the designation of the society in which they live.

3. *Integrated,* which involves two factors, acceptance and integration of all of the aspects of one's racial heritage and an appreciation for the diversity and commonalities among all racial groups. This status is similar to Status 5 of both of the racial identity models previously discussed.

The Integrated identity status was found to be correlated with positive self-esteem and ethnic pride as well as affirmative attitudes toward racial and ethnic diversity. Counselors can help multiracial clients move toward that status.

IMPLICATIONS FOR COUNSELING

When working with multiracial individuals, counselors should broach the topic of culture and identity in the context of a trusting working alliance (Kenney, 2006). Several of the skills discussed in Chapter 16 are also applicable to counseling this population, including counselors being aware of their own biases about multiracial status, having knowledge of each of the individual's racial group cultures, using a strengths-based focus, involving clients' families of choice, exploring possible internalized oppressions, using bibliotherapy, and advocating for and with multiracial clients and families (Kenney, 2006; Sue & Sue, 2003; Wehrly, 2005).

Summary

Race is a socially important but biologically problematic concept. Throughout history, race has been used to divide peoples and to enforce hierarchies. In that sense, it cannot be separated from racism. Counselors must understand the power of race in American life and counter its negative effects. This chapter has traced the history of the American notion of race. The continuing presence of racism in attitudes and social institutions also was explored. Racial identity development was described, as was the emerging importance of multiracial identity.

References

Atkinson, D. R., Morten, G., & Sue, D. W. (1998). *Counseling American minorities* (5th ed.). Boston: McGraw-Hill.

Auerbach, S. (2002). "Why do they give the good classes to some and not to others?" Latino parent narratives of struggle in a college access program. *Teachers College Record, 104,* 1369–1392.

Avery, R. B., & Rendall, M. S. (2002). Lifetime inheritances of three generations of whites and blacks. *American Journal of Sociology, 107,* 1300–1346.

Black, E. (2003). *War against the weak: Eugenics and America's campaign to create a master race.* New York: Four Walls Eight Windows.

Bobo, L. (2001, October). *Inequalities that endure?: Racial ideology, American politics, and the peculiar role of the social scientists.* Paper presented at The Changing Terrain of Race and Ethnicity, Chicago.

Butler, J. (2001). *Color-line to borderlands: The matrix of American ethnic studies.* Seattle: University of Washington Press.

Choi-Misailidis, S. (2001, May). *Mixed race identity: Development of a new measure.* Paper presented at the meeting of the Western Psychological Association, Lahaina, Hawaii.

Cross, W. E., Jr. (1995). The psychology of nigrescence: Revising the Cross model. In J. Ponterotto, J. M. Casas, L. A. Suzuki, & C. M. Alexander (Eds.), *Handbook of multicultural counseling* (pp. 93–122). Thousand Oaks, CA: Sage.

Dain, B. (2002). *A hideous monster of the mind: American race theory in the early republic.* Cambridge, MA: Harvard University Press.

Daly, E. (2005, April 13). DNA tells students they aren't who they thought. *New York Times,* p. B8. Available at http://select.nytimes.com/pages/timesselect/index.html

D'Andrea, M., & Daniels, J. (1999). Exploring the psychology of white racism through naturalistic inquiry. *Journal of Counseling and Development, 77,* 93–101.

Davenport, C. (1911). *Heredity in relation to eugenics.* New York: Holt.

Donziger, S. R. (1996). *The real war on crime: The report of the National Criminal Justice Commission.* New York: HarperCollins.

Dovidio, J. F., Gaertner, S. L., & Kafati, G. (2000). Group identity and intergroup relations: The Common Ingroup Identity Model. In S. R. Thye, E. Lawler, M. Macy, & H. Walker (Eds.), *Advances in group processes* (Vol. 17, pp. 1–35). Stamford, CT: JAI.

Emerson, M. O., Yancey, G., & Chai, K. J. (2001). Does race matter in residential segregation? Exploring the preferences of white Americans. *American Sociological Review, 66,* 922–935.

Feagin, J. R. (1999). Excluding blacks and others from housing: The foundation of white racism. *Cityscape: A Journal of Policy Development and Research, 4*(3), 79–91.

Feagin, J. R., & McKinney, K. D. (2005). *The many costs of racism.* Lanham, MD: Rowman & Littlefield.

Feagin, J. R., & Vera, H. (1995). *White racism.* New York: Routledge.

Freeman, H. P. (1998). The meaning of race in science—considerations for cancer research. *Cancer, 82*(1), 219–225.

Gates, H. L. (2004, February 2). *America beyond the color line* [Television broadcast]. Arlington, VA: Public Broadcasting System.

Gerstle, G. (2001). *American crucible: Race and nation in the twentieth century.* Princeton, NJ: Princeton University Press.

Glazer, N., & Moynihan, D. P. (1970). *Beyond the melting pot: The Negroes, Puerto Ricans, Jews, Italians, and Irish of New York City.* Cambridge: MIT Press.

Gossett, T. F. (1997). *Race: The history of an idea in America* (New ed.). New York: Oxford University Press.

Hannaford, I. (1996). *Race: The history of an idea in the West.* Baltimore, MD: Johns Hopkins University Press.

Hardiman, R. (1982). White identity development: A process oriented model for describing the racial consciousness of White Americans. *Dissertation Abstracts International, 43,* 104A (University Microfilms No. 82-10330).

Helms, J. E. (1990). *Black and white racial identity: Theory, research and practice.* Westport, CT: Greenwood.

Helms, J. E., & Cook, D. A. (1999). *Using race and culture in counseling and psychotherapy.* Boston: Allyn & Bacon.

Herrnstein, R. J., & Murray, C. (1994). *The bell curve.* New York: Free Press.

Hunter, M. L. (2002). If you're light you're alright: Light skin color as social capital for women of color. *Gender & Society, 16,* 175–193.

Ignatiev, N. (1995). *How the Irish became white.* New York: Routledge.

Ivey, A. E., Ivey, M. B., D'Andrea, M., & Simek-Morgan, L. (2005). *Theories of counseling and psychotherapy: A multicultural perspective.* Boston: Allyn & Bacon/Longman.

Jackson, B. W., & Holvino, E. (1988). Developing multicultural organizations. *Journal of Religion and the Applied Behavioral Sciences, 9,* 14–19.

Kegan, R. (1982). *The evolving self.* Cambridge, MA: Harvard University Press.

Kenney, K. R. (2006). Counseling multiracial individuals and families. In C. C. Lee (Ed.), *Multicultural issues in counseling: New approaches to diversity* (3rd ed., pp. 251–266). Alexandria, VA: American Counseling Association.

King, J. C. (1981). *The biology of race.* Berkeley: University of California Press.

Kwate, N. O., Valdimarsdottir, H. B, Guevarra, J. S., & Bovbjerg, D. H. (2003). Experiences of racist events are associated with negative health consequences for African American women. *Journal of the National Medical Association, 95,* 450–460.

Laubeová, L. (2000). *Melting pot vs. ethnic stew.* Retrieved January 21, 2005, from http://www.tolerance.cz/courses/texts/melting.htm

Marable, M. (2000, February 25). We need a new and critical study of race and ethnicity. *The Chronicle of Higher Education,* p. B34.

Marger, M. N. (2002). *Social inequality: Patterns and processes.* Boston: McGraw-Hill.

Martinez, E. (2004). *De Colores means all of us: Latina views for a multi-colored century.* In M. L. Andersen & P. H. Collins (Eds.), *Race, class, and gender* (pp. 111–117). Belmont, CA: Wadsworth/Thomson Learning.

Massey, D. S., & Denton, N. A. (1993). *American apartheid: Segregation and the making of the underclass.* Cambridge, MA: Harvard University Press.

McConahay, J. B. (1986). Modern racism, ambivalence, and the modern racism scale. In J. F. Dovidio & S. L. Gaertner (Eds.), *Prejudice, discrimination, and racism* (pp. 91–125). Orlando, FL: Academic Press.

McKee, J. B. (1993). *Sociology and the race problem: The failure of a perspective.* Urbana: University of Illinois Press.

Menchik, P. L., & Jianakoplos, N. A. (1997). Black-white wealth inequality: Is inheritance the reason? *Economic Inquiry, 35,* 428–442.

Middleton, R. A., Erguner-Tekinalp, B., & Petrova, E. (2005). *Clinical applications of racial identity development: Profile approach to Helms' White Racial Identity Development Model.* Presentation to the meeting of the Association for Counselor Education and Supervision, Pittsburgh, PA.

Myrdal, G. (1944). *An American dilemma: The Negro problem and modern democracy.* New York: Harper & Brothers.

National Council on Crime and Delinquency. (2007). *And justice for some: Differential treatment for youth of color in the justice system.* Retrieved January 16, 2007, from http://www.nccd-crc.org/nccd/pubs/2007jan_justice_for_some.pdf

Palmer, P. J. (1998). *The courage to teach.* San Francisco: Jossey-Bass.

Paniagua, F. A. (2005). *Assessing and treating culturally diverse clients: A practical guide* (3rd ed.). Thousand Oaks, CA: Sage.

Parra, E., Marcini, A., Akey, J., Martinson, J., Batzer, M., Cooper, R., et al. (1998). Estimating African-American admixture proportions by use of population-specific alleles. *American Journal of Human Genetics, 63,* 1839–1851.

Poe-Yamagata, E., & Jones, M. (2000). *And justice for some.* Washington, DC: Building Blocks for Youth.

Ponterotto, J. G., Utsey, S. O., & Pedersen, P. B. (2006). *Preventing prejudice: A guide for counselors, educators, and parents* (2nd ed.). Thousand Oaks, CA: Sage.

Robinson, T. L. (2005). *The convergence of race, ethnicity, and gender: Multiple identities in counseling* (2nd ed.). Upper Saddle River, NJ: Pearson.

Shapiro, T. M. (2004). *The hidden cost of being African American.* New York: Oxford University Press.

Slattery, J. M. (2004). *Counseling diverse clients: Bringing context into therapy.* Belmont, CA: Thomson/Brooks/Cole.

Sue, D. W., & Sue, S. (2003). *Counseling the culturally diverse: Theory and practice* (4th ed.). New York: Wiley.

Takaki, R. (1993). *A different mirror: A history of multicultural America.* Boston: Little, Brown.

Telles, E. E. (2002). Racial ambiguity among the Brazilian population. *Ethnic and Racial Studies, 25,* 415–441.

Tze, C., & Myers, S. L. (1995). Racial discrimination in housing markets: Accounting for credit risk. *Social Science Quarterly, 76*(3), 543–561.

U.S. Census Bureau. (2000). *Racial and ethnic classifications used in Census 2000 and beyond.* Retrieved June 1, 2006, from http://www.census.gov/population/www/socdemo/race/racefactcb.html

U.S. Census Bureau. (2006). *American community survey.* Retrieved January 16, 2007, from http://www.census.gov/acs/www/

Utsey, S. O., Chae, M. H., Brown, C. F., & Kelly, D. (2002). Effect of ethnic group membership on ethnic identity, race-related stress and quality of life. *Cultural Diversity & Ethnic Minority Psychology, 8,* 366–377.

Wehrly, B. (2005). *Breaking barriers for multiracial individuals and families.* In F. D. Harper & J. McFadden (Eds.), *Culture and counseling: New approaches* (pp. 313–323). Boston: Allyn & Bacon.

Wellman, D. (1977). *Portraits of white racism.* New York: Cambridge University Press.

Wessel, D. (2003, September 17). Racial discrimination: Still at work in the U.S. *Wall Street Journal Online.* Retrieved January 13, 2004, from http://www.careerjournal.com/myc/diversity/20030916-wessel.html

Wilson, W. J. (1996). *When work disappears: The world of the new urban poor.* New York: Knopf.

White, J. L., & Parham, T. A. (1990). *The psychology of blacks.* Englewood Cliffs, NJ: Prentice Hall.

Wolfle, L. M. (1987). High school seniors' reports of parental socioeconomic status: Black-white differences. In P. Cuttance & E. Russell (Eds.), *Structural modeling by example: Applications in educational, sociological, and behavioral research* (pp. 51–64). New York: Cambridge University Press.

Part II

Major Ethnic Groupings

5 African Americans

Kathy M. Evans and Rebecca George

Lift every voice and sing
Till earth and heaven ring
Ring with the harmony of liberty
Let our rejoicing rise
High as the listening skies
Let it resound loud as the rolling sea.
Sing a song full of the faith that the dark past has taught us
Sing a song full of the hope that the present has brought us
Facing the rising sun
Of a new day begun
Let us march on till victory is won

—James Weldon Johnson

"Lift Every Voice and Sing," which is quoted throughout this chapter, is also called the Negro National Anthem. It is a powerful evocation of African American strengths and aspirations and of the influence past struggles have had on the present and future of African Americans.

This chapter is devoted to counseling African Americans. It begins by describing terms that refer to African Americans and continues by presenting key notions from the history of the American system of slavery and the evolution of racism and oppression. Following that there is a review of the legacy of slavery and a summary of African American characteristics. The chapter ends with a discussion of counseling practices that build on the strengths of a people. To illustrate these practices, the cases of Tamika and Kendra will be presented. They are two very different African American women who share a common ancestry and problems that have similar sociological and psychological origins.

Tamika is a 20-year-old African American woman who recently gave birth to her second child by a man she has yet to marry. He has been in and out of jail for petty crimes over the past few years, so Tamika lives with her mother and two siblings (ages 16 and 14). After the baby's birth, Tamika started staying in bed longer and longer past her usual rising time and taking to bed during the day. When questioned by her mother about not taking care of her baby, Tamika shared that she just cannot make herself get up. She doesn't know how to make her baby stop crying and doesn't have any energy to take care of herself, let alone her son and daughter. She said she wished everyone would just leave her alone.

Tamika was due to go back to work as a sales associate at a retail store in two weeks. Her mother did not think Tamika was healthy enough to return to work after Tamika was unable to get out of bed for five consecutive days. In fact, her mother became so concerned she took a day off work herself to take Tamika to the hospital in a cab. However, nothing was found to be physically wrong with Tamika, and the doctor suggested counseling.

Kendra is a 20-year-old African American woman. She is a junior at an Ivy League university and an engineering major. She has always excelled in school but is struggling to get C's this semester. Both of Kendra's parents are professionals. Her father is an engineer and her mother is a math teacher in an inner-city high school. Kendra is attending the university on a scholarship. She risks losing it if she does not raise her grades. Her parents are unaware of her academic problems because she is afraid to tell them. She is sure they will blame her white boyfriend for the problems; they have blamed him for every other problem she has reported. After mid-semester grades were posted, Kendra displayed low energy, lack of appetite, and stayed in her room for three days, refusing phone calls and ignoring knocks at her door. Kendra told her boyfriend that she felt stressed out and that there was no way she was going to finish school if she continued in an engineering major. If she continued, she was sure that she would prove to everyone that she was an imposter and a failure and that her life would be over. Kendra's attitude and behavior worried both her boyfriend and her resident director, who referred Kendra to the counselors at the university counseling center.

Labels and Terms

In this chapter, the words "African American" and "black" will be used interchangeably to refer to American-born people of sub-Saharan African descent whose forebears were slaves in the United States. The term "African American" will not apply to other people of the African Diaspora (dispersion), nor will it apply to those who were born in Africa and live in the United States. These latter populations will be referred to by their ancestors' specific countries of origin (e.g., Haitian Americans, Nigerian Americans). The term "African" will be used to describe the native black African (usually sub-Saharan) population on the continent, and "white Africans" will distinguish those who have descended from European immigrants who settled in Africa. Other Africans, such as Moroccans and Egyptians, are referred to by their nationality. Those northern African groups are among the groups discussed in Chapter 9.

There are many words that African Americans have used to identify themselves over the centuries. The terms have changed according to history and popular demand. According to Holloway (2005), slaves and former slaves through the mid-nineteenth century referred to themselves simply as Africans. Evidence of this practice are the names of the first institutions founded by slaves and former slaves, such as the First African Baptist Church and the African Methodist Episcopal Church (Lake, 1997). In the mid-1800s, the term "colored" became more acceptable because it seemed to better describe a population that had both African and European ancestry. "Colored" is a term that was also embraced at that time by black leaders who opposed efforts to return free blacks to Africa. The belief was that a disassociation with Africa would stop the attempts to return them to Africa. In fact, there was a movement at this time to remove the word "African" from the names of black institutions to emphasize this disassociation.

Marcus Garvey's popularity during the 1920s and 1930s caused a resurgence of things African, and the term "Afro-American" became popular among many people. However, Booker T. Washington (who represented those disassociating themselves from Africa) was able to convince the government to adopt the term "Negro," which he thought was a term that better represented all people of sub-Saharan African descent (Holloway, 2005). During the civil rights movement, the term "black" became popular, as African Americans openly embraced their racial heritage. Many people at that time rejected the term "Negro" as one that had been imposed on them by the government. In the late twentieth century, the term "African-American" became popular, with recognition of both the African and the American heritage and cultures rather than race alone.

The current debate is over the hyphen. Many ethnic minority group members resent being referred to as hyphenated Americans. Instead, they prefer to remove the hyphen so that their ancestral homeland is an adjective further describing their Americanness. This may be the rationale used by many writing style guides, including the *Publication Manual of the American Psychological Association*, which recommends no hyphen for ethnic minority populations (American Psychological Association, 2001). Others have suggested that the hyphen should be used for people who are American-born because their association with Africa is so distant, and that it should removed for those who were born in Africa. It seems safe to assume that the name debate will continue as people change and new trends develop.

Derogatory terms used by others (e.g., nigger, darky, spade, spook, coon) have been thoroughly rejected. There has been some controversy of late about the use of the term "nigger" by African Americans themselves. The debate is long and complicated and is beyond the scope of this chapter (see *Nigger: The Strange Career of a Troublesome Word* by Randall Kennedy, 2003, for a discussion of the history and meaning of the term). Suffice it to say that it is a term with a very long history and, as such, it has developed multiple meanings over the centuries when used among African Americans. It is still considered derogatory when used by non-African Americans.

When counseling clients, it is best to find out the terms that they prefer for identifying their race or ethnicity. For example, Tamika's or Kendra's counselor may want to say at some point, "One of the important background areas we need to address is your racial identity. As your counselor, I want you to feel comfortable with me and with any discussions we may have, especially when they involve race. Most people have preferences as to which name they use to refer to their race or ethnicity. What name would you prefer to use for your own racial group?" Whatever name/label clients prefer may very well reflect their racial identity, including their attitudes regarding the history of their people.

Americans of African Descent: The People and Their History

Stormy the road we trod

Bitter the chastening rod

Felt in the days when hope unborn had died

Yet with a steady beat, have not our weary feet

Come to the place for which our fathers sighed

We have come over a way that with tears has been watered,

We have come, treading our path thro' the blood of the slaughtered

Out from the gloomy past, till now we stand at last

Where the white gleam of our bright star is cast.

—James Weldon Johnson

The difficult relationship between African Americans and European Americans has colored most of the social, emotional, and political issues that African American clients bring to counseling. It is a relationship steeped in history. Knowing the history of a people is of great importance for many reasons, the most obvious of which is to keep a society from repeating the mistakes of the past. In 1964, Malcolm X said, "History is a people's memory, and without a memory, man [sic] is demoted to the lower animals" (Spanoudis, 1994). For counselors, understanding the history of a people is important for developing empathy, appreciating the present circumstances, and establishing trust with clients of sub-Saharan African heritage. The stanza quoted above from the Negro National Anthem illustrates the significance of slavery in the lives of today's African Americans.

Avid gardeners know the importance of having soil that is nutrient-rich to enable the roots of a particular plant to grow. The roots provide the foundation for the plant's growth and maturation. Africa was such a rich soil for the growth of the human species and the spread of civilizations. Pre-colonial Africa was a place without strict borders, where African kingdoms shifted with the nutrients of the land. African culture spread also to the Americas, as enslaved Africans created part of the fabric of American society (Cowan, 2004).

The slave trade was a business in which human beings were procured, transported, and sold. It arrived with a vengeance in 1502 when African slaves were brought to the Americas for the first time, although slave trading among Africans themselves had also existed prior to that time. As of 1502, the people of Africa were taken by both force and deception to America by slave traders and others, leaving behind their loved ones, their language, their native land, and their claims to humanity (Phillips, 2004). While this was not the first occurrence of slavery in human history, it was the most extensive and the most widespread based on the color of people's skin.

Millions of Africans were captured and shackled for sale as part of the trans-Atlantic slave trade that first passed through Cape Coast Castle in what is today Ghana, West Africa (Phillips, 2004). The voyages were very profitable (J. J. Connor, 2003). From England, various manufactured products—mainly textiles, metal goods, and liquor—were exported to Africa, where they were exchanged for slaves. The trans-Atlantic slave trade moved the people from Ghana through the "door of no return" to a horrifying journey across the Atlantic Ocean (Phillips, 2004). This journey came to be known as the "middle passage" because it was regarded as the middle leg of the triangular trading route. Over 4,000,000 Africans died in the middle passage on the way to slavery in the Americas (Smallwood, 1998). The English slave owners used the proceeds from the sale of slaves in the West Indies to buy sugar, which was shipped back to England, completing the triangle. By the end of the eighteenth century, this triangular trade route had become a standard feature of the slave traffic (Meier & Rudwick, 1966).

In over four centuries of slave trading, researchers estimate that between 30 and 60 million Africans began the journey (Smallwood, 1998). Millions of enslaved Africans were dispersed throughout the so-called African Diaspora to North America, South America, and the Caribbean as well as to Europe. Table 5.1 summarizes key events and dates in the history of African slavery in America.

Some experts suggest that Western enslavement of Africans is not yet over. Although few traditional forms of colonialism still exist, Blauner (1972) has theorized that a version of slavery exists today, in the form of the post-colonial domination of African peoples that continues around the world and in the United States. The descendants of African slaves continue to exist in a social climate that is associated with inferior treatment, economic subjugation, and

Table 5.1   Key Dates of Slaves and Africans in America

Key Dates	Summary
900–1500	The trans-Saharan (from northern to southern Africa) slave trade
1502–1600	Slave revolts and Maroon communities in the Spanish and Portuguese colonies of the Caribbean and the Americas
1600–1720	The establishment of French, English, Dutch, and Swedish colonies in the Americas and Caribbean
1620–1776	English colonial slavery in the New England colonies, Middle colonies, Southern colonies, and the Caribbean
1650–1755	The Native American slave trade, the legalization of slavery, the rise of Slave Codes, and the growth of the African slave population in the English colonies
1710–1776	The British "Triangle of Trade" with colonial America and the growth of the African American slave population in North America
1770–1783	African Americans participate in the American Revolution
1777–1800	The emancipation of slaves in the North and the expansion of slavery in the Southern states and territories of the new American republic
1800	The combined free black and slave population of the United States reaches one million
1808–1865	Slave smuggling in the United States
1865	Major Southern cities destroyed by the end of the Civil War; Southern economy in ruins
1865–1877	The Freedmen's Bureau and blacks during Reconstruction

sociopolitical inequity. For these reasons, African Americans are still fighting for an acceptable level of freedom. One of the most obvious reasons is continuing racism.

RACISM: THE LEGACY OF SLAVERY

As mentioned previously, a version of slavery continues in a different form, according to some analysts. If a person is denied opportunities to pursue a better quality of life because of color, class, creed, or religion, she or he can be said to be metaphorically enslaved (Osabu-Kle, 2000).

Racism toward African Americans can be directly linked to attitudes that existed at the time of the slave industry. The most powerful misinformation that fueled racist attitudes in the United States was initiated by the Puritans, who identified Africans as inferior on the basis of supposed Christian doctrine (Griffin, 1999). Over the years, Southern slave owners extended that way of thinking, believing that "God had created Black people to be heathen and less than all human beings" (p. 28). The belief in African inferiority grew in popularity over the centuries and persisted in both popular and scientific thinking even after the Civil War ended slavery.

After the Civil War, President Abraham Lincoln's party, the Republicans, strove to ensure that the newly freed slaves had full rights as American citizens. The Fourteenth Amendment to the Constitution in 1868 not only recognized former slaves as citizens but also guaranteed that neither they nor their property could be seized without due process of law. In addition, the Fifteenth Amendment in 1870 guaranteed African Americans the right to vote, resulting in many Reconstruction-era seats for African Americans in state legislatures and in the U.S. House and Senate (Smallwood, 1998).

The backlash from former slave owners and other whites was swift and ugly, however. Whites accused African American legislators of fraud, and the Ku Klux Klan intimidated African American voters and lynched African American men who asserted their rights. These types of terrorist tactics, along with dwindling support from Northern white Republicans, eventually made it possible for whites to garner enough votes to defeat the Reconstruction reforms (Levine, 1996). By 1871, four Southern states were back in the control of white Democrats. Once back in power, the Southern Democrats proceeded to pass a massive number of laws aimed at "putting blacks in their place." Segregation laws (called Jim Crow laws because of a popular black character in minstrel shows of the time) prohibited blacks and whites from being in contact with one another in all public places. To circumvent the Fifteenth amendment, Democratic legislators intentionally excluded blacks from voting by imposing poll taxes and literacy tests on African Americans seeking to vote; whites could get other whites to vouch for them to avoid the poll taxes and literacy tests.

In essence, the Jim Crow laws legalized racism. The Supreme Court condoned those laws. In its 1896 decision, the Supreme Court upheld *Plessy v. Ferguson,* ruling that segregation did not violate the Constitution. For 50 years, that decision maintained the principle of racial segregation. Legal institutional racism made it impossible for African Americans to participate as full citizens in the United States, putting them in a state of limbo, no longer slaves but not really free. In effect, the laws of segregation strengthened the legacy of slavery well into the twentieth century.

Although in 1954 the Supreme Court determined that the Jim Crow Laws were unconstitutional, it was necessary for Congress to pass the Civil Rights Act in 1964 and the Voting Rights Act in 1965 to end legal segregation practices. With the passage of these laws and the attendant policies, executive orders, monies, and military support ensuring their enforcement, the lives of African Americans began to change (Levine, 1996). The biggest changes were in access to public accommodations and in the ability to vote without fear.

Given the subtlety of racism, Activity 5.1 can help the reader determine her or his attitudes.

Contemporary Forms of Racism

Unfortunately, some of the gains that were made during the administrations of Presidents Lyndon Johnson and Richard Nixon were eroded during the 1980s. The 1980s brought an era of so-called color-blindness and white resentment of equal opportunity policies (Levine, 1996), sometimes called a backlash. The political climate during the 1980s fostered a trend in which racism was cloaked in claims of fairness, equality, and "the American Way"—that is, treating individuals purely as individuals, not as connected to social groups. This view was seen as not being racist; it was being American to treat individuals as separate from their opportunity context. This subtler version of racism has been called "aversive racism," "unintentional covert racism," and "color-blind racism" (Dovidio, Kawakami, & Gaertner, 2000; Ridley, 1995). Chapter 4 discussed some of these issues.

The clients in both case scenarios presented earlier—Tamika (the infant's mother) and Kendra (the college student)—would suffer if their counselors held subtly racist beliefs as listed above. Such counselors commonly misdiagnose their racially different clients, either giving them more serious diagnoses than they give a white client with the same symptoms or minimizing the client's symptoms and failing to give the client the treatment he or she needs.

Aversive racism is the phenomenon of individuals simplistically aligning themselves with core American values, such as equality, to denounce affirmative action and other antidiscrimination practices (Dovidio et al., 2000). The mildest form of contemporary racism is what Ridley (1995) describes as unintentional covert racism, in which the person does not intend to be racist, but her or his behavior results in harm to another. For example, a teacher might unintentionally not call on black children in class as often as others. A similar notion is "color-blind racial attitudes" (COBRA; Neville, Worthington, & Spanierman, 2001), in which individuals deny the existence of race as a social issue while also wishing to maintain existing white privilege. They blame people of color themselves for their position in American society, and they resist any political efforts to improve conditions for blacks. People with COBRA claim that their own status of entitlement and achievement is due to their own merit and not related to social placement. This phenomenon is described under Optional or "Symbolic" Ethnicity in Chapter 3; that is, the claim that individual effort is the sole reason for success, and the failure to acknowledge social advantages.

In sum, racism and discrimination have permeated the lives of African Americans—their families, education, employment, and psycho-social development—for generations. Those legacies are still alive. However, African Americans have been neither accepting nor passive about the state of affairs. In fact, protests have occurred quite often, both violent and nonviolent. The next section addresses such responses.

ACTIVITY 5.1

Do You Have Racial Issues With African Americans?

To find out, place a check mark beside each statement below if it resembles one that you have either thought privately or said aloud.

_____ 1. Black people are racists too.

_____ 2. I don't understand what they expect me to do; I can't do anything about racism. I just know I'm not a racist.

_____ 3. I don't know why African Americans are always bringing up slavery when it has been over for 150 years. Other people have been oppressed and they don't keep throwing it in our faces.

_____ 4. I (or my relative) didn't get accepted at my first choice of college because of affirmative action.

_____ 5. I don't see Kathy as black; I see her as a person.

_____ 6. I really don't know what to say when I'm around a lot of black people.

_____ 7. I sometimes feel overwhelmed with all the information I have to learn about minorities.

Reasons why these are racist statements:

1. Implies that black bias and prejudices toward whites have a similar effect on whites as white racism has on blacks. Unfortunately, because of the position of power and privilege that many whites are afforded in U.S. society, this is not the case. Except in the case of physical harm, it is rare that black racism will harm whites as much as white racism hurts blacks. Also, this statement assumes that having racist attitudes is acceptable when the targeted group is also guilty of prejudice.

2. Helplessness gives one an excuse not to change the status quo, whether it is one's own behavior or that of others.

3. Indicates a lack of knowledge about the connection between slavery and racism that still exists today. Also, denies the history of a people, which denies the people themselves.

4. Indicates resentment toward African Americans, with a belief that they have unfair advantage. Shows ignorance of white entitlement, insistence that the playing field is level and that whites do not enjoy privilege merely by virtue of being born white.

5. Although intended to be a statement of inclusion, it can be a statement about how much better it is to be white. The speaker might believe that being black is a handicap and that she or he has been able to ignore this deficit as far as Kathy is concerned by denying her racial identity.

6. Indicates discomfort with African Americans and assumes that the speaker will have nothing in common with them.

7. An expression of helplessness and an excuse not to learn or change.

The African American Response to Racism

We shall overcome, we shall overcome,
We shall overcome, someday,
Deep in my heart, I do believe
We shall overcome someday.

—Civil Rights Anthem

A seminal statement of African American feelings about social conditions was made in 1968 by two African American psychiatrists, William Grier and Price Cobbs, in their book *Black Rage,* when they declared that nothing was more important to know about African Americans than that they were angry. That anger over past and current mistreatment lingers. The scholar Cornel West has been quoted as saying, "We are an unloved people" (Smiley, 2005). If that is the case, non-African American counselors must be especially prepared to gain the trust of their clients and to be alert to such anger and hurt.

Chapter 4 discussed the decades of African American struggle against legalized racism and discrimination, or what has been called "American apartheid." African Americans have chosen to combat racism with education, protest, and sometimes violence. Whatever the choice, African Americans have expressed their unhappiness with their treatment as subhumans with limited citizenship. "We Shall Overcome" was the battle cry of the nonviolent civil rights movement of the 1950s and 1960s. It expressed the hope for a brighter future for African Americans.

The most brutal, visible, effective, and largest civil rights movement by African Americans to date occurred in the 10-year period following the 1954 *Brown v. Board of Education* Supreme Court decision that ruled Jim Crow laws unconstitutional. Thurgood Marshall led the NAACP legal team in the Supreme Court case. He argued that the separate-but-equal policy adopted after the 1896 *Plessy v. Ferguson* decision was a violation of the Fourteenth Amendment, and that education of African American schoolchildren was being hurt by this separatist policy. The Court's decision was in favor of the plaintiffs, thus rendering Jim Crow laws in the United States unconstitutional.

Unfortunately, this Supreme Court decision did not result in states putting aside their Jim Crow laws. As a result of white resistance to equity, the growing anger of African Americans and their supporters led to protests against these laws. They, and many white allies, were hosed down, jailed, and killed, yet they were relentless (C. J. Robinson, 1997). Most of the protests during the 1960s were nonviolent on the part of African Americans, especially those that were under the leadership of the Reverend Dr. Martin Luther King, Jr., who was a strong advocate for nonviolence. In 1963, King and the Southern Christian Leadership Conference (SCLC) led over 200,000 people to march peacefully on Washington D.C., to raise awareness in the national government of legal oppression in the Southern states.

However, there also were many violent protests during the 1960s in the form of deadly riots, fueled by some leaders who stated that African Americans must gain their freedom "by any means necessary," as Malcolm X said, including violence. While the race riots of the 1960s are most memorable, race riots have, in fact, occurred throughout the twentieth century (Robinson, 1997). For example, in 1919, riots broke out in New York, Charleston, Chicago, Knoxville, Omaha, and 21 other cities, triggered by the competition between blacks and whites for the few jobs that existed after World War I. In the 1940s, there were riots near military bases across the country because of the discrimination and violence against black soldiers during World War II. At least twice after the enactment of Civil Rights legislation, there have been race riots. The 1989 riot in Virginia Beach, Virginia, occurred after white police officers confronted African American college students who were vacationing there. In 1991, riots erupted in several cities throughout the country over the acquittal of the police officers who were videotaped beating a black man, Rodney King (Levine, 1996; Smallwood, 1998).

Other reactions in the past to the oppressive Jim Crow laws included migration back to Africa and movement from the southern states to the northern states. In the latter case, African Americans moved north because racism was not as institutionally legalized in the North as it had been in the South, and jobs were more plentiful. However, there was pervasive racism in the North as well. The various responses to racism and oppression are ongoing and have become part of the fabric of the African American subculture.

In conclusion, understanding the history of slavery and its legacy is the foundation for understanding African Americans. In addition to African heritage, this history of oppression has had a direct effect on the culture of African American people. African American survival of oppression is a strength that counselors can call upon when working with African American clients. Using the legacy of the strength of African Americans to fight for their rights can be quite motivating to clients. However, counselors may want to use this tool judiciously because it can easily be rendered ineffective through overuse. Four of these strengths are "flexibility, forgiveness, resilience, and persistence" (Exum, Moore, & Watt, 1999, p. 194). They are some of the values that will be discussed next.

African American Values and Characteristics

God of our weary years, God of our silent tears,
Thou who hast brought us thus far on the way
Thou who hast by Thy might
Led us into the light
Keep us forever in the path we pray.
Lest our feet stray from the places, our God, where we met Thee,

Lest our hearts, drunk with the wine of the world we forget Thee
Shadowed beneath Thy hand, May we forever stand
True to our God, True to our native land.

—James Weldon Johnson

The last stanza of the Negro National Anthem cited above is most revealing of African American culture because it indicates the importance of spiritual values to African Americans and their commitment to the United States. In this section, the predominant attributes of the African American people will be addressed.

African American characteristics cannot be disentangled from the history of oppression. Thus, that history will be called on to explain many African American traits in the following discussion. However, such characteristics can also be traced to West Africa. The following sections describe 10 sets of values and characteristics in African American culture:

1. Time

2. Relationships with others

3. Relationship to nature

4. Religion and spirituality

5. Family and parenting

6. Communication

7. Career

8. Gender

9. Physical and mental health

10. Social class

These topics reveal particular differences between traditional African American and European American cultures.

TIME

African Americans share with many other non-Western cultures the tendency to be "in time" versus "on time." African American culture tends to place less urgency and importance on time and more value on involvement in a specific activity. For example, on a Saturday morning, a middle-class African American professional woman who is a stickler for starting meetings on time at work may wait comfortably in a black beauty parlor for an hour or more for what was supposed to be a 9:00 A.M. hair appointment.

RELATIONSHIPS WITH OTHERS

African Americans also differ from some European Americans in that they value interdependence over independence, especially in regard to kinship relations. For example, a family counselor who focuses on the nuclear family will clash with the African American view of family, which includes extended family and even close family friends (T. L. Robinson, 2005; Sue & Sue, 2003).

RELATIONSHIP TO NATURE

African Americans and other non-European ethnic groups tend to function in harmony with nature rather than be oriented to developing mastery over nature. In other words, they tend to entrust natural phenomena to a higher power rather than to human power.

RELIGION AND SPIRITUALITY

One of the values held dear in African American culture, regardless of socioeconomic status, is spirituality. Spirituality is, in Cook and Wiley's (2000) words, a "foundation of personal and communal life" for African Americans (p. 370). The notion of religion is often synonymous with the Black Church, although there are other religious expressions. This section will explore the Black Church because of its power in African American life. "The Black Church" is a collective term and encompasses African American churches of all Christian denominations. It is considered to be the first truly American (non-Native American Indian) institution (Sanders, 2002) in that it (a) was founded on U.S. soil, (b) is inclusive of several different racial and cultural groups, and (c) has existed in some form since the first Africans were brought to the United States in the 1600s.

African American worship incorporates African heritage with its rituals, such as ancestor worship, ecstatic ceremonies, dancing, drumming, and call-and-response preaching. It also adds Islamic, Judaic, and European American Christian elements (Cook & Wiley, 2000; Sanders, 2002). The Black Church "is a mixture of Africanism, emotionalism, legalism, ritualism, and theological intellectualism" (Sanders, 2002, p. 77).

Functions of the Black Church

The Black Church provides opportunities for support, leadership, social status, education, cultural affirmation, and political action. After a week of experiencing hundreds of microaggressions as members of an oppressed nondominant cultural group, African Americans experience the Church as a safe harbor. It is a safe space, a sanctuary, where at least once per week African Americans can feel empowered. For African American men, the Church offers a way to validate their manhood because those who are relegated to a menial job in the white world may have a high status position in the Church (i.e., deacon, trustee). The Black

Church is also where African Americans learn their history, understand their political power, and gain not only spiritual but also financial support (Cook & Wiley, 2000).

Churches also teach many African and Christian values. For example, collectivism is not only preached but practiced in the Black Church, where all adults are responsible for training and disciplining the children of the congregation. Children learn responsibility, oral communication, and respect for their elders. It is not uncommon for children to participate monthly in church services—reading scriptures, saying prayers, and serving as ushers. Because of its importance in raising children, the Black Church has been an integral part of African American family life.

The Black Church had a critical role in initiating and sustaining the civil rights movement in the 1960s and is still very politically influential today. Once they were freed, many Southern African Americans immediately joined Lincoln's party (the Republican Party), and many more continued to do so in reaction to the rule of the white Southern Democrats, who were called "Dixiecrats." However, during the civil rights movement and afterwards, African Americans found more friends among the Northern Democrats than they did among the Republicans. Consequently, churches were inclined to connect strongly with the Democratic Party and have continued to do so.

Just as the Dixiecrats slowly turned Republican, beginning with the Eisenhower administration and the civil rights movement, party loyalties continue to change (Levine, 1996). The conservative Christianity found in many Black Churches today reflects some conservative Republican beliefs. In fact, some of the credit for recent African American support for U.S. Republican candidates is due to the Black Church's stands against abortion and gay marriage (M. C. Evans, 2004).

The Black Church and Mental Health

The Black Church can be a source of healthy and cathartic experience (Richards & Bergin, 1997). A strong faith was able to sustain African Americans throughout the bitter history of slavery and American apartheid. It may well be a tonic for the challenges of today's African Americans as well. On the other hand, a few individuals may develop an overdependence on the Church, resulting in a reliance on external solutions to problems, dismissing their inner experiences and avoiding conflict.

Historically speaking, the Black Church has eschewed counseling and psychotherapy in favor of prayer and faith. However, in recent years, many denominations have become more receptive to culturally competent counseling (Cook & Wiley, 2000). Counselors would do well to develop their competence in using spirituality in counseling if they work with African Americans (K. M. Evans, 2003; Fukuyama & Sevig, 1999). Chapter 15 of this book expands on that topic. Studies have overwhelmingly found that religion, spirituality, and/or religiosity are so important and so effective in helping African American clients (including adolescent girls) to "get better" that it should be an essential element in counseling most

African Americans (Ball, Armistead, & Austin, 2003; Jang & Johnson, 2004). In particular, establishing ties with the pastors of Black Churches would create a referral network and complementary resources for clients. Box 5.1 provides some resources that counselors might use to learn about the Black Church.

Counselors should always explore an African American client's spirituality because it can be a great resource in treatment. If, for example, Kendra has abandoned her religious upbringing during her college years and she and her family were active in the Black Church during her childhood, she may still find comfort in reclaiming some aspects of her spirituality, as would Tamika.

FAMILY AND PARENTING

The African American family is an institution that has been often misunderstood by the dominant European American society. Prior to the widespread popularity of *The Cosby Show* in the 1980s, the stereotype of an African American family was a single female parent, usually on welfare, living in public housing with several children under the age of 10. The only variation on that theme was the notion of a hard-working single mother whose children must look after one another while she works at menial labor to feed her family.

BOX 5.1   Resources on the Black Church

Books:

Battle, M. (2006). *The Black Church in America: African American Christian spirituality.* Malden, MA: Blackwell.

Pinn, A. B. (2002). *The Black Church in the post-civil rights era.* Maryknoll, NY: Orbis Books.

Internet Links to the Largest Denominations of Black Churches:

National Baptist Convention of America: http://www.nbcamerica.net/

National Baptist Convention USA: http://www.nationalbaptist.com/

African Methodist Episcopal Zion Church: http://www.archaeolink.com/african_methodist_episcopal_zion.htm

African American Episcopal Church: http://www.ame-church.com/

Christian Methodist Episcopal Church: http://www.c-m-e.org/

Progressive National Baptist Convention: http://pnbc.org/index.php

Other Helpful Reading:

Evans, K. M. (2003). Including spirituality in multicultural counseling: Overcoming counselor resistance. In G. Roysircar, D. S. Sandhu, & V. E. Bibbins (Eds.), *Multicultural competencies: A guidebook of practices* (pp. 161–172). Alexandria, VA: Association for Multicultural Counseling and Development.

Those stereotypes have been harmful. Researchers have used poor, single female-headed households to generalize their findings to all African American families (Hill, 1999). Certainly the 30 percent poverty rate among African Americans is higher than that of almost any other ethnic group, and poverty brings with it a multitude of concerns (Arnold, 2002). However, generalizing the results from this subpopulation to the whole group is erroneous and misleading.

The Cosby Show gave the United States sustained exposure to a large, two-parent, middle-class African American family and planted the idea that African American families are very diverse. In fact, low-income, single-parent, female-headed households comprise only 16 percent of all African American families, and fully 38 percent of all African American families have two married parents (U.S. Census Bureau, 2004).

Extended Family

As with some aspects of gender roles, African American family traits have been carried over from their roots in West Africa. Today, there continues to be strong consanguineal (blood related) extended family networks, following the African tradition, primarily among low-income African American families (Sudarkasa, 1988). However, extended family networks also include close friends when family members are not available. Over time, Western influences on African American family structure have become more prominent in middle-class families, with the nuclear family being treated as primary. Regardless of the familial configuration, all African American families assist children in coping with oppression through racial socialization. Getting support from family, especially extended family, is an important part of effective counseling with African Americans (Chadiha, Rafferty, & Pickard, 2003).

Racial Socialization in the Family

To raise a child who has a positive self-concept and high self-esteem, African American parents engage in racial socialization (Greene, 1994; Sanders, 2002; Stevenson, 1994). Racial socialization is the "process of communicating messages and behaviors to children to bolster their sense of identity, given the possibility and reality that their life experiences may include racially hostile encounters" (Stevenson, 1995, p. 51). Many African American parents have their children actively engage in learning about their heritage (Bradley, 2002; Peters, 1976). To begin the socialization process, parents often tell their children about the proud history of their people, starting in Africa and continuing with African American leadership and success stories. African American parents also typically teach their children about the realities of racism and bigotry, preparing them for the unfair treatment that they are likely to receive in the larger society and arming them with coping mechanisms for the times that they will be discriminated against. Children are taught the importance of family and spirituality when coping with racism, as well as other forms of coping (Lipford-Sanders, 2002). Stevenson (1995) called these "proactive messages."

Children also need to hear "corrective messages" that inform them of the untruthful nature of the negative stereotypes about African Americans (Stevenson, 1995). African American children grow up in a society where some of the strongest and most negative stereotypes are about their own people. In the United States, there is the continued belief that African Americans are intellectually inferior and incapable of achieving on their own merits in anything other than athletics and entertainment. Children who do not receive proactive racial socialization are likely to internalize negative stereotypes about being African American and consequently develop low self-esteem and negative self-concepts (Greene, 1990; Stevenson, 1994). Indeed, such individuals might stay in the pre-encounter stage of racial identity development, which will be discussed later in this section. By contrast, children who receive proactive and corrective messages about their race tend to develop a positive sense of self and, in fact, achieve well academically (Bowman & Howard, 1985; Greene, 1990; Hale, 1991). To help children prepare for the rest of their lives in an environment that is likely to be hostile toward them, parenting practices of African Americans may differ from those of other cultures. Box 5.2 lists some of the racial socialization practices of African American families.

It would be important for a counselor to explore the messages that Tamika and Kendra received in terms of racial socialization. If middle-class children are better able to access African American role models who defy stereotypes, then Kendra would be more likely than Tamika to have rejected the stereotypes. Counselors should explore each client's racial identity and consequent ability to withstand racism. Counselors can inquire about the client's level of socialization and should consider how such upbringing can be called upon to help the client in her current depression.

Parenting Practices

Within the family, African American parents utilize a number of disciplinary actions that prepare children to live in a racist environment where unfairness and discrimination are common. The purpose of such practices is to give children the means to survive in that environment (Denby & Alford, 1996). In that vein, respect for authority is typically nonnegotiable in African American families; children who are disrespectful receive the most severe forms of punishment—usually physical (Bradley, 2002).

African American parents have been criticized by some as being overly severe and rigid in their disciplinary practices—especially regarding corporal punishment (Lassiter, 1987; Straus, 1991). This criticism reflects the current democratic, sometimes called "authoritative," disciplinary practices common in the dominant American society. In fact, the overrepresentation of black children among those who have been reported as abused and neglected seems to support this criticism. However, some researchers (Bradley, 2002; Comer & Poussaint, 1992; Peters, 1985) suggest that there are cultural misunderstandings about discipline on the part of social welfare workers, misunderstandings that contribute to the high numbers of

> **BOX 5.2   Racial Socialization Practices of African American Families**
>
> 1. Teaching children about their African and African American ancestors
>
> 2. Reinforcing cultural pride
>
> 3. Teaching children to be aware of racism and social injustice
>
> 4. Using the extended family for emotional support and understanding, especially in instances of racial injustice
>
> 5. Providing a spiritual and religious foundation that can be used to cope with adverse racial experiences
>
> 6. Using corrective messages that de-personalize racial stereotypes
>
> 7. Teaching children how to cope with racism, which includes developing "tough skin"
>
> 8. Disciplining children to reduce behaviors that may get them into trouble later with racist law enforcement officers

child abuse reports. These authors suggest that the strong disciplinary practices of African American parents are preferable to democratic discussion when parents are preparing children to function within the "constraints of oppression" (Bradley, 2002, pp. 32–33). More often than not, democratic discussion is not an option for African Americans in the real world. African American children need to realize that fact early in their lives (Bradley, 2002).

It should be noted that middle-class African American parents are more likely to use explanation of reasons for discipline with their children than are parents from lower socioeconomic classes (Trosper, 2002). However, middle-class African American parents are still more likely than their European American counterparts to use physical discipline where moral misbehavior, such as lying or stealing, is concerned (Pinderhughes, Dodge, & Bates, 2000). Interestingly, Bradley (1998) found that African American parents who applied physical discipline generally did so judiciously, rather than wantonly, with their young children.

Today's African American parents may be conflicted about childrearing practices—especially those who live with extended family members who do not see the need to change from the "old ways" (Arnold, 2002). Regardless of whether physical discipline is appropriate for racial socialization, the fact that the social welfare system has little tolerance for it has had an impact on childrearing practices in the African American community.

In the case of Tamika, the counselor should explore parenting practices because she is currently living with her mother and siblings. It appears that how her children are parented, and by whom, might play into her current issues of depression. For Kendra, exploring her own current and past experiences of being parented, from the adult child's perspective, is appropriate. Her parents' views are important because she is worried about her parents' disapproval, not only of her academic performance but also of her choice of a boyfriend.

RACIAL IDENTITY DEVELOPMENT/NIGRESCENCE

Racial identity development was described in Chapter 4 as a way of plotting positive movement in individuals' appreciation and understanding of their and others' races. The Racial Identity Development for People of Color model was outlined. A more specific model that refers to African Americans is William Cross's (1991) Stages of Nigrescence. Cross describes nigrescence as "the process of becoming black" (p. 157). Cross also called this model the Negro-to-Black Conversion Experience.

The origins of the model lie in Cross's 1971 publication, "The Negro to Black Conversion Experience," in which he articulated the differences among African Americans based on individuals' differential inclinations to identify with their racial reference group (racial identity). Cross proposed that African Americans develop a positive racial identity by going through specific stages. Since 1971, Racial Identity Theory has evolved. Cross's ideas, as well as those of others, set off an explosion of research and the creation of subsequent models of within-group developmental differences, not only for African Americans but within other groups as well.

As noted in previous chapters of this book, an awareness of racial identity development can be important for counselors because it helps them develop empathy for and understanding of their culturally diverse client populations. Also, when they identify their own racial identity attitudes, counselors discover areas of racism and bias that they still need to work on. Since Cross's model is one of the earliest, most researched, and most influential of the development models, it will be the focus here.

The original five stages of the Cross model have been updated and refined over the past 30 years. Recent adjustments were also made in the stages as a result of efforts to develop an instrument to measure racial identity (Vandiver, Fhagen-Smith, Cokley, Cross, & Worrell, 2001). The current stages are as follows:

Pre-encounter attitudes consist of treating the racial dimension of one's life as insignificant. Cross has three categories of Pre-Encounter: Assimilation, Miseducation, and Self-Hatred. The *Pre-Encounter-Assimilated* person is accepting and appreciative of everything about the dominant European American culture. Her or his primary reference group is simply "American" and race is not important. African American individuals with *Pre-Encounter-Miseducation* attitudes believe in the negative stereotypes about African Americans. *Pre-Encounter-Self-Hatred* attitudes are held by those who identify as being African American, but who believe that being black is an intrinsic deficit that is responsible for their negative experiences. Originally, Cross (1971) thought that any black person in the Pre-Encounter stage would have problems with self-hatred. However, after more than a decade of research on the theory, Cross revised his assessment and proposed that "race salience" (i.e., the importance one places on race, in general) has a greater impact on self-concept than racial identity attitudes alone. An individual who places little importance on race may have a high self-concept even if she or he has Pre-Encounter attitudes. The more important race becomes to an individual, the more Pre-Encounter attitudes will negatively affect self-concept (Cross, 1991; Sue & Sue, 2003).

Immersion-Emersion attitudes are divided into two categories—Intense Black Involvement and Anti-White. *Immersion—Intense Black Involvement* attitudes occur when the individual begins the journey into his or her blackness and revels in all things black. The *Immersion—Anti-White* attitudes consist of rejecting and denigrating all things European American (Vandiver et al., 2001).

Internalization attitudes are divided into *Internalization—Afrocentricity,* where individuals develop a long-term commitment to their racial group to the exclusion of all others, and the *Internalization—Multiculturalist Inclusive* view that incorporates both an identity as an African American and an acceptance of other identities (cultures) as well.

The first set of attitudes, that is, Pre-Encounter, are more likely to occur early in a person's life, whereas Internalization occurs, if at all, later in adulthood (Parham, 1993, 1999). Even after one has completed his or her racial identity developmental stages, life circumstances (e.g., a new encounter with racism) may cause the individual to recycle through the stages. For example, a person at the Internalization stage may become so discouraged after years of fighting institutional racism that she or he retreats to the Immersion—Intense Black Involvement stage. A line by an African American lawyer on a popular television show, *Law and Order,* illustrates this cycle perfectly: "Stone once asked me if I was a lawyer who just happened to be black or was I a black who just happened to be a lawyer. I thought I was the former and discovered that I was the latter."

The Nigrescence Theory continues to evolve. Most recently, Cross and Fhagen-Smith (2001) integrated the notion of ego identity development (Loevinger, 1976)—that is, overall ways of knowing, such as authoritarianism, conformism, and autonomous thinking—with nigrescence to further explain Cross's idea of race salience (Sue & Sue, 2003). Activity 5.2 offers an opportunity to assess racial identity.

Racial identity seems to be an issue for Kendra, who is dating a European American man. It is likely that she is not only being rejected by her family but by her friends as well. She may feel a combination of guilt, anger, and hurt. She may also be confused about who she is as a racial and cultural being. A counselor would need to help Kendra identify her stage of racial identity and to understand her attitudes about race and her racial identity. The counselor would then help Kendra move toward a greater acceptance of herself by helping Kendra come to her own definition of what it means to be black.

Ascertaining Tamika's racial identity stage will help explain how she is coping with her world. If, for example, part of Tamika's depression is due to a belief that she must be the stereotypical "strong black woman," the counselor would need to work on the cognitive distortions regarding that ideal and encourage her to learn

---

ACTIVITY 5.2

Assessing Racial Identity Statements

The statements listed below represent various stages of racial identity development (as described by Cross's new model). Read each one and identify under which stage that particular statement falls and why you have classified it as such. Discuss your answers with your classmates.

NOTE: It is not possible to precisely locate an individual in any one stage; therefore, it would be simplistic to provide an answer key here. These items are meant to provoke discussion and understanding of some elements of racial identity.

_____ 1. Affirmative Action is needed only by people who couldn't get the job in the first place.

_____ 2. You can never trust white people so it is better not to tell them anything about your business and minimize your contact with them.

_____ 3. That counselor just tried to sign me up for the African dance class and I think she did it just because I'm black. I wonder how many white kids she tried to put in that class. I don't see why they always have to treat us like we're so different. I'm a regular kid just like everyone else.

_____ 4. I live and work in the black community and I think it is the perfect way for me to give back to my community and to ensure the future of African Americans in this country.

_____ 5. It makes me angry when black folks use race as an excuse for their own failures.

_____ 6. I get a lot of grief for marrying outside my race but I spend a lot of my time with African American adolescents, helping them prepare for their future and support my spouse's efforts in the Latino/Latina community as well.

---

more about African American female stereotypes. If, on the other hand, Tamika were in the Immersion—Anti-White stage, the counselor might work on helping Tamika explore her stereotypes about whites and encourage Tamika to advocate for herself and others to overcome institutional racism.

COMMUNICATION

African Americans have specific styles of communicating that may easily be misinterpreted. The most widely known communication style is the African American Vernacular English (AAVE), also known as Black English or Ebonics. Ebonics, a term coined by Robert Williams in 1975, has been debated over the years. However, there is a consensus today that AAVE is a legitimate language with grammatical rules, semantics, and phonetics (Burling, 1973; Chambers, 1983; Koch, Gross, & Kolts, 2001). An example of AAVE is "There go Susie brother." This statement is grammatically correct in the AAVE. However, in Standard English, it would be incorrect because of the omission of an "es" to "go" to indicate the third person simple present tense and the absence of the possessive "'s" on Susie.

Even though AAVE is considered a legitimate language by many, others consider it to be simply an incorrect form of communication. Those who speak AAVE exclusively are perceived by many African Americans and whites to be uneducated (Doss & Gross, 1994; Garner & Rubin, 1986). While at least one study has shown that African American college students tend to prefer individuals who speak Standard English, other writers contend that speaking AAVE provides African Americans with a method of bonding with each other and a way of identifying as African American (Garner & Rubin, 1986; Larimer, Beatty, & Broadus, 1988; Naremore, 1980). AAVE distinguishes African Americans and can even intentionally exclude others from the communication. For these reasons, AAVE is accepted and, perhaps, revered by many African Americans.

The existence of AAVE does not mean that African Americans must exclusively use this dialect. AAVE can be honored as a legitimate but not exclusive form of communication. AAVE speakers would do well to "code switch," that is, to use Standard English in some contexts while speaking AAVE among fellow AAVE speakers.

It is very likely that both Kendra and Tamika can code switch (change from AAVE to Standard English, based on their audience). In fact, non-black counselors should not be surprised if clients do not use AAVE in their sessions.

Another aspect of African American communication style that can be problematic for non-African American counselors is that in social conversation, African Americans are generally animated and speak loudly. They are expressive and emotional in their speech. Among African Americans, language is fluid and colorful. They often use language creatively to tease, assign nicknames, and add new words that become staples in popular vocabulary. Examples of African American words that have made it to general usage over the years include "cool," "jazz," "chill," "dis," "rap," "bad" (to mean excellent), "hip," "yam," "gumbo," and "bogus." African Americans often engage in a good-natured exchange of insults known as "playing the dozens"—an expression whose roots are in slavery. Playing the dozens has a practical purpose in thickening the skins of African Americans, to prepare them to fight more serious social battles in their lives rather than react to name-calling. Some non-African Americans may interpret such behavior as being aggressive and angry and may be intimidated by it (Sue & Sue, 2003).

CAREER

Career progress has been slow for African Americans because of the realities of discrimination in U.S. society and because of the legacies of exclusion from jobs (James, 2002). The unemployment rate of African Americans is more than twice that of white Americans (U.S. Census Bureau, 2001).

Factors in the career life of African Americans include continuing discrimination, affirmative action, and the existence of protected occupations. Each will be discussed next.

Continuing Discrimination

As discussed in Chapter 2, job discrimination continues to exist in the United States. Because racial discrimination is so intertwined with the structure of U.S. society, African Americans will continue to find occupational achievement difficult (Carter & Cook, 1992). According to Carter and Cook, overcoming discrimination will be a challenge for African Americans because (a) the rules and boundaries of U.S. society continue to control the participation of minority groups in occupations (e.g., in what is possible and appropriate for various ethnic groups, based on career networks and role models or lack of role models); (b) these rules are communicated to African Americans both verbally and nonverbally (i.e., "This career isn't for people like you" might be perceived); (c) these rules and limits are set early in children's lives (e.g., in the overrepresentation of African Americans in special education); and (d) discriminatory practices, such as inadequate funding for urban schools and other services to poor African Americans, result in a continuing restriction of access to higher level careers. Although Carter and Cook's observations were made in 1992, they are, unfortunately, still relevant today.

Affirmative Action

Another factor in career development for African Americans is affirmative action—the practice of proactively ensuring access to employment and education. Affirmative action was briefly presented in Chapter 2. It has been attacked by dominant-group members and others who deny white male privilege and claim that affirmative action is reverse discrimination. This kind of thinking is based on the current popular assumption that affirmative action consists of the arbitrary application of preferential treatment based on race and gender alone, regardless of an individual's qualifications. However, according to Truax, Cordova, and Wood (1998), affirmative action remedies "usually involve goals for hiring and promotion according to sensible timetables. Never are strict quotas allowed, and never should the remedies involve the hiring or retention of unqualified people" (Truax et al., 1998, p. 173). Despite its success in providing access, affirmative action can also hurt African Americans: Some people still see affirmative action as a basis for hiring and admitting underqualified people for jobs. Consequently, African Americans and others can be stigmatized once they are on the job or in colleges, thus continuing a perception of inferiority.

Protected Occupations

Affirmative action is not the only route African Americans have used to avoid racial discrimination in the workplace. Another strategy is for African Americans to participate in traditional or "protected" occupations (Evans & Herr, 1991; Peterson & Gonzalez, 2000). These occupations are referred to as protected because there is either a critical mass of African Americans already employed in them (e.g., social work, service occupations) or they are professions that depend on the African American consumers for survival (e.g., law, medicine, clergy, funeral services).

The Seduction of Athletics and Entertainment

Today, some see these protected occupations as extending to professional sports and entertainment (especially for African American males). Careers in football, basketball, and hip-hop music are high profile and high paying. Many African American boys gravitate to these occupations because they see primarily African American men achieving wealth and status in these professions. In fact, many boys are encouraged to pursue these athletic endeavors if they show even the smallest amount of talent in early childhood. This encouragement can be a trap. Sociologist Harry Edwards (1986) states that although their athletic abilities have been honed, many of these boys are still educationally challenged, as 25 percent to 35 percent of African American high school athletes do not meet the academic requirements to play at the college level. Professional sports organizations have gotten around that problem by drafting athletes right out of high school. The larger concern in this situation is that the emphasis on athletics gives young people permission to disregard other, probably more realistic careers, especially those that require lengthy educational programs (Witherspoon, 2005). Because careers in professional athletics are male-dominated, the rejection of college-based careers in favor of an athletic career is more of an issue for African American boys and men than it is for girls and women. Other ethnic groups have entered sports in large numbers before moving on to other professional careers. Counselors must encourage African American boys to look at other career options.

GENDER

Gender roles in the African American community are rooted in the conditions of slavery. Slaves were treated as property (or stock); therefore, they were valued for their generic capacity as labor, not as women or as men. After the failures of Reconstruction and the subsequent oppression, including terrorist lynchings, any African American man in the South who dared behave like a "(white) man" was shown his place. This process went on well into the twentieth century. Black men were stereotyped in white people's views as angry, dangerous, and so highly sexed that white women had to be protected from them. African Americans, therefore, had to create their own definitions of manhood.

Black women, who were routinely raped by white men during the 250 years of slavery and who bore the children of such violence, were thought of in U.S. society as fitting one of three stereotypes:

Jezebel. Jezebel is a biblical character known as the bad girl, or wicked woman, or prostitute. A Jezebel is a promiscuous woman who uses her sexuality to get what she wants no matter whom she hurts.

Mammy. The mammy is one who is "obese, pitch black, . . . and sexually neutered" (Greene, 1994, p.16). She is seen as motherly, especially in regard to white families.

Sapphire. The Sapphire stereotype depicts a woman who is emasculating to the African American male. She has a big mouth and tells, and tells off, all she knows. She is also laughed at and discounted by black men and is sexually neutered.

With these kinds of stereotypes, an African American woman had no concept of herself as a woman with dignity and pride. That image she has had to create for herself.

Gender Equality in African American Families

African American families have historically promoted egalitarian gender-role socialization. Boys and girls are trained to be assertive and are required to learn all household tasks rather than the tasks being split according to gender (e.g., girls wash dishes, boys take out garbage) (Lewis, 1975). Interestingly, these non-specific gender roles may be a throwback to African roots (Hill, 1999). In West Africa, "women were expected to be economically productive and had some power and authority in sociopolitical matters" (p. 109). This socialization is said to account for the leadership roles of black females, in that they have benefited from developing traditionally "masculine" traits of assertiveness and independence while keeping traditional female traits of nurturing and relationship building. Black males are hurt more for the feminine traits that they acquire, in that U.S. society already values masculine traits more than feminine ones (Carr & Mednick, 1988).

The Dilemmas for Women and Men

Both women and men suffer from the gender consequences of oppression. Those consequences include multiple demands on girls, negative expectations of boys, imbalance in marriage opportunities for women, and dominance of white-based standards of beauty.

According to Chapman (1988), African Americans develop their gender identity at a very early age. There is an old saying, "Black mothers raise their daughters and love [or enable!] their sons." In other words, girls tend to get a strict upbringing and specific information about how to be a good, empowered black woman. For African American boys, on the other hand, independence is not stressed as strongly and they are not as severely disciplined for doing wrong as are girls (Hill, 1999; Staples, 1984). African American girls are taught to be self-sufficient, proud, and strong but caring. They are encouraged to achieve academically, to get a good job, and to be able to take care of their family on their own, if necessary.

Education and Gender

For African American girls and women, education always has been embraced. For example, the fact that Kendra is pursuing higher education puts her in good company; African American women are attending college in greater and greater numbers. However, because she is getting her degree in a nontraditional career, she may still feel separate not only from her African American friends but also from women of other racial groups. Her parents may have high expectations for her success in college, and she may be feeling that pressure. Her counselor should be careful to have Kendra talk about her family's expectation and the isolation she may be feeling. By contrast, Tamika may or may not have completed high school; she was only 15 years old when her first child was born. It would be worthwhile to explore Tamika's attitudes about education and whether or not she connects it to her racial identity and how her socioeconomic status has affected her educational and occupational aspirations.

Negative Expectations for Boys

Boys continuously hear negative statements about black men from a variety of sources—from whites, black women, and other black men. They learn that black men are inferior, that they are unable to obtain and maintain adequate employment or head their households, and that they are unduly hampered by racial attitudes and institutional structures. They and others note that to an alarming degree, African American men are overrepresented among those incarcerated. In fact, almost half the men in jail today are of African descent (Robinson, 2005). In essence, African American males learn that a traditional definition of a "man" is not attainable. However, when questioned, black men still report socially desirable answers regarding manhood. They publicly define manhood as requiring responsibility, humanism, and self-determination (M. Connor, 2002).

Imbalance in Marriage Opportunities

In contradiction to the simultaneous expectation that they be independent, African American women are also taught that the mark of success is to have a husband and family. That is not realistic for a high percentage of African American women. In the United States, women outnumber men. In the African American population, this discrepancy is even more pronounced. The number of marriage-eligible, young African American males is alarmingly inadequate. The scarcity of eligible men is due to several factors: (a) the high number of African American men who are incarcerated, (b) the excessive number of deaths of young African American men due to homicide, and (c) African American men marrying outside of their race. Although it should be noted that, today, more and more African American women are open to interracial dating, they are not likely to find partners among European American men (Moore, 2002).

Standards of Beauty

The shortage of marriageable African American men is an issue that is closely related to the question of beauty among African American women. For all women in the United States, beauty has been a source of social power and privilege. The standard of beauty is based on the Northern European American woman (usu-ally thin, blond, and blue-eyed). Whatever the woman's race, the more closely she resembles the Northern European American standard, the more she is consid-ered beautiful and desirable and the higher is her status. For African American women, meeting that standard is more difficult if their physical attributes resem-ble those known to be more typical of West Africans—attributes that are deval-ued and considered unattractive.

African American women differ in terms of skin color, hair texture, eye color, body type, and facial features. Both skin color and hair have been sources of emotional pain for African American women. Light-skinned women with "good hair" (needing little or no straightening) often feel rejected by their racial group. Conversely, dark-skinned women with "bad hair" (tightly curled) feel resent-ment toward the light-skinned women. The tragedy of this situation is that both African Americans and European Americans value light-skinned women more highly than those who are dark-skinned because of their resemblance to the Northern European American standard (Russell, Wilson, & Hall, 1992; Wade & Bielitz, 2005). In fact, research has shown that lighter-skinned women have more education, earn higher salaries, and have husbands with more prestige than do darker-skinned women (Hunter, 2002). While progress was made in the 1960s and 1970s to raise black standards of beauty to the mainstream, the Eurocentric definition still prevails. It is the counselor's job to counter these one-sided images of beauty that are socially constructed.

PHYSICAL HEALTH AND MENTAL HEALTH

The final issue in this section on characteristics and values of African American culture is physical and mental health. These issues have a social and political connection for African Americans that needs to be understood by counseling professionals. For example, although research has found that the mortality rates of African Americans, like other groups, decrease as their socio-economic status increases, even middle- and upper-class African Americans have higher mortality rates than whites in the same socioeconomic class (Ostrove, Feldman, & Adler, 1999).

While the health of African Americans today is much improved over previ-ous years, they are still more likely than European Americans to be diagnosed with life-threatening diseases such as hypertension, diabetes, obesity, high cho-lesterol, and cancer (Atkinson, 2004). The infant mortality rate is 2.5 times greater for African Americans than for European Americans; the maternal mor-tality rate is 4.2 times greater.

The overall death rate for African Americans was 31 percent higher than it was for whites in 2002. Black males live, on average, 68.8 years compared with white males, who live 75.1 years. Black women live 75.6 years, compared to 80.3 years for white females (Arias, 2004). The causes of death are also reason for con-cern: African Americans die more often from homicide, hypertensive kidney dis-ease, diabetes, and septicemia or "blood poisoning" (a life-threatening infection characterized by bacteria in the blood) than do European Americans. In general, African American males between the ages of 25 and 55 have double the death rate of white males in the same age group, primarily because they are eight times as likely to be victims of homicide.

As for their mental health, African Americans are diagnosed with mental illnesses less often than European Americans. However, they are more likely to have severe diagnoses when they do occur, and they are more likely to be hospitalized for their mental illness (Snowden & Hu, 1997; Wicker & Brodie, 2003). The prevalence of poverty, low educational levels, and high levels of incarceration may account for the diagnosis of severe mental illness for many African Americans (Atkinson, 2004).

African Americans are diagnosed more frequently with certain illnesses than they are with others. For example, they are more likely to be diagnosed with phobias, somatization complaints (Parham, 2002a; Zhang & Snowden, 1999), and schizophrenia (Adebimpe, 1981; Baker & Bell, 1999; Cornelius, Fabrega, Cornelius, Mezzich, & Maher, 1996; Neighbors & Jackson, 1996). African Americans are also more likely to be underdiagnosed for depression (Cornelius et al., 1996).

According to Parham and Brown (2003), the U.S. Department of Health and Human Services suggests that "African Americans may be underrepresented in outpatient services but overrepresented in accessing hospital emergency rooms for mental health concerns" (Parham, 2002c, p. 42). As such, African Americans may be less likely to receive counseling assistance when problems are not severe enough to warrant a complete collapse.

Some of these phenomena can be explained by social class access to outpatient services and some by cultural bias within the African American community. African Americans are inclined to view mental illness negatively and stigmatize those who are in need of such services (Nickerson, Helms, & Terrell, 1994). In fact, in their study, Leong, Wagner, and Tata (1995) discovered that African Americans preferred to seek assistance from family and friends rather than from mental health professionals. Those professionals are typically white and, therefore, suspect. It seems that this distrust might be warranted because research continues to report bias in diagnosis and treatment by white therapists (Trierweiler et al., 2000). Considering the history of discrimination, psychological abuse, and continued racism in the United States, African Americans have a healthy distrust of European Americans, the government, and its institutions (Atkinson, 2004).

THE EFFECT OF SOCIAL CLASS ON VALUES

This major section on the characteristics and values of African Americans concludes with a discussion of the influence of social class. The topic of social class is presented fully in Chapter 12. Class and race intertwine to create values. The two are also conflated by many, with race often totally substituting for class as an explanation of ethnic groups' behaviors.

Social class is the dividing line for a great many characteristics within the African American community. Within-group value differences among African Americans tend to be related to social class status. African Americans are alarmingly overrepresented among the poor in the United States, although, as seen in Chapter 2, there are twice as many middle-class blacks now as there were in 1960. Many of the previously discussed values are more likely to be seen in those from the lower economic status groups, as the middle classes of all cultures tend to have values in common with the dominant European American culture (Sue & Sue, 2003). However, core African American values are likely to be similar across social classes—especially those that are associated with growing up black in the United States. Those include spirituality, interdependence in family and relationships, emotional expressiveness, and ethnic pride.

The Black Middle Class

Middle-class African Americans must often function in both the dominant culture and in their own African American communities. As such, their values may be on a continuum of whiteness to blackness and be applied situationally when they are in those respective settings.

The black middle class is not really parallel to the white middle class, for two reasons. The first is that more often than not, African Americans would not qualify for middle-class status if it weren't for the presence of two incomes in the household (which is more true than ever for all families, but especially so for African Americans due to lower median household salaries). The second way that the African American middle class can be distinguished from the white middle class in general is that most African Americans do not have the accumulated wealth of whites, as discussed in Chapter 2. In fact, Neville and Walters (2003) state that African Americans' net worth is 1 percent of the net worth of their European American counterparts.

Black Poverty

Poverty has its own set of behaviors, beliefs, and values (see Chapter 12 for discussions of the culture of poverty). The aforementioned attitude toward time and timeliness is often class related. For example, many poor people (regardless of race) tend to have a casual view of appointment times with professionals, sometimes due to their time not being treated as valuable by the social agencies that serve the poor (Sue & Sue, 2003). It is not uncommon for an agency serving low-income clients to schedule an appointment for one time and not get to the client until many hours later. Also, living in the present is common among poor people. For poor persons, just getting food on the table today is a chore, and planning for some unseen future seems frivolous.

Many poor people, regardless of race, believe in fate more than they do in their own ability to overcome obstacles. Thus, poor people are ambivalent about their own power to affect their lives. However, that tendency should not cause further stereotyping. For example, the stereotype of poor African Americans is the "unwed" mother, living on public assistance with several small children. However, many poor African Americans, like Tamika, work every day, barely making a living wage and living in fear of becoming unemployed.

Other Differences Between the Black Middle and Lower Classes

While they share a common heritage as well as experiences with racism and prejudice, middle-class and lower-class African Americans differ a great deal in how they live. At this time, the biggest chasm between the socioeconomic groups of African Americans is education. Education was traditionally highly valued in the African American community, in part because education was denied to them in slavery and partly because education seemed to be the best way to overcome oppression. Since the civil rights movement and integration, many African Americans have used their educations for upward mobility and as an exit from poverty-ridden neighborhoods. They often have moved to predominantly white suburbs or, more recently, to "all-black middle-class suburban enclaves" (Cashin, 2000). African Americans who live in the new, predominantly "black suburbs" are cut off from their lower-income counterparts because they do not have to return to the neighborhood to fulfill their needs for goods or services.

The lack of interaction between the socioeconomic classes may be attributed to the fact that education has lost its appeal to African Americans in lower-income areas (Cole & Omari, 2003). Low-income adolescents now see education as a way of abandoning one's culture and becoming an "Oreo" (i.e., perceived to be black on the outside and white on the inside). This seems to be an idea that even some middle-class African American adolescents tend to believe. As discussed in the "Career" section above, rather than perceiving education as the key to escaping poverty, many African American young people, especially males, gravitate toward careers in sports and entertainment that can maximize their income and minimize their need for education (Hughes, 2005; Witherspoon, 2005).

Note that in the vignettes of Tamika and Kendra, there will be a difference in the values of Tamika and Kendra based on their socioeconomic backgrounds. However, many of their core values are similar—especially those associated with growing up black in the United States. For example, a counselor working with Tamika, the 20-year-old mother, or Kendra, the 20-year-old Ivy League college student, would need to ascertain each woman's specific values regarding kinship. It is important to understand the ties that each of them has with her parent(s) and/or other relatives. Care must be taken not to sever these relationships in the name of increasing autonomy. Rather, the counselor may need to call on these relationships as a source of client strength. For Tamika, it may mean actually working with her mother and siblings to help her with her depression. For Kendra, it may mean exploring her commitment to her family and the consequences of disappointing them because of her boyfriend and academic struggles.

Culturally Alert Counseling Interventions

Although this section of the chapter discusses counseling interventions with African Americans, the limits of such generalizations must be addressed. African Americans may share a powerfully influential history in the United States, but there is no stereotypical African American; there is no single African American culture. Similarly, there is no single intervention that works for all African Americans. Therefore, this section of the chapter is not a how-to manual. Instead, particular concerns of African Americans are summarized, guidelines for working with African Americans are presented, and two Africentric counseling models are discussed.

PARTICULAR CONCERNS OF AFRICAN AMERICAN CLIENTS

Some writers in the counseling field have suggested that a unique paradigm is needed for counseling African Americans because of their distinct history and current status in the United States (e.g., Parham, 1999). These writers look to the following five unique issues of African Americans as a basis for the need for a culture-specific model of counseling.

- Why do African American women see skin color and hair texture as so important?

- Why do impoverished, government-assisted African Americans fail to plan for the future?

- Why are many African Americans, when endowed with authority by an institution (e.g., a school), harsher on their own racial group members?

- Why would African American children rather fail than be perceived as acting white and getting good grades?

- Why is it of great importance to African American men to own property and cars?

Other culture-related mental health issues include African American adolescent girls and young women fighting over men and distrust of white teachers, counselors, doctors, social workers, and educational institutions. With an Africentric model, which is described in the following sections, these concerns may be most easily addressed.

Counselors using an Africentric approach should have a solid awareness of their spiritual selves and their ethnic consciousness. To be successful in counseling African Americans, especially using an Africentric approach, counselors need to develop skills for bonding with their clients, participating in rituals, and assisting a client with reaching his or her goals in an African-centered way. What Africentric counseling approaches have in common is a devotion to spirituality, history, kinship and community, and overcoming oppression.

GUIDELINES FOR COUNSELING AFRICAN AMERICANS

In Chapter 16, counseling skills that the culturally alert counselor must be competent to perform will be described. Seven guidelines have been adapted from that chapter as they apply to work with African Americans. They are presented in Table 5.2.

Table 5.2   Seven Guidelines

1. *Be genuine in verbal and nonverbal communications.* African Americans are high-context communicators, meaning that they are likely to depend less on what a person says than on how it was said and the circumstances surrounding the verbal exchange (Sue & Sue, 2003). Therefore, to be effective with African American clients, it is really important that there be no contradiction between what the counselor says and how she or he feels. Genuineness is important.
2. *Engage in advocacy.* Counselors should probe for any bias that the client may experience or perceive to be related to her or his problem. The counselor should be prepared to intervene on the organizational level as well as the community level. Counselors should also empower clients to work toward eliminating institutional racism by supporting client efforts to document incidents and address them.
3. *Utilize nonpsychological methods.* Work with clients' spirituality. Encourage the client to speak with her or his pastor.
4. *Have language flexibility.* Not only should counselors understand AAVE, but they should not have any negative reaction to its use. Rather than responding to the client in AAVE, however, the counselor may want to borrow a word or two as a key phrase when talking with clients.
5. *Judiciously apply assessment methods.* Standardized testing has been criticized as regards African Americans. It is important for counselors to be knowledgeable and confident about the use of such instruments with the African American population. It may be necessary for the counselor to collect her or his own local data on African Americans if data for this population are not available in the test manual.
6. *Proactively acknowledge societal bias.* Rather than keeping the history of African Americans as interesting information to be stored in the recesses of one's mind, the counselor should use that information to understand the feelings and behaviors of the African American client.
7. *Practice culturally informed consent.* Because of the mistrust that African Americans have for health and mental health institutions, it is imperative that counselors explain their roles, client roles, the process of counseling, and techniques to be used.

Lee's Guidelines for Counseling African Americans

Courtland Lee (1995) offers three guiding ideas for working effectively with African American clients. He first suggests that counselors always inquire about all of the influences in their clients' lives—not only that part of the client's life that she or he spends in African American culture, but also the time spent in majority culture. Lee also suggests that counselors explore the client's reaction to oppression. Finally, he iterates that counselors should learn about an African American client's family relationships. Lee cautions that none of these areas is mutually exclusive; when a counselor explores one area, she or he is likely to discover information from another area.

AFRICENTRIC COUNSELING

An Africentric counseling model is one that is consistent with African values and its people. Such a model would also address the impact of oppression (Parham, 2002b). The two Africentric approaches discussed here are African Centered Psychology and the TRIOS model.

African Centered Psychology

African Centered Psychology (ACP) applies African and African American values such as "ancestor veneration, social collectivity, and the spiritual basis of existence" to counseling (Grills, 2002, p. 15). Counselors who utilize ACP must have the ability to make the necessary shift from a Western to an African worldview to accommodate the cultural differences that are present when working with African American clients. ACP represents a way of knowing, viewing, and understanding the whole person, particularly the African American client. ACP is considered a spiritual journey of moving toward optimal living.

ACP uses an African perspective to make meaning of life and the world and to define relationships with others and with one's self (Grills, 2002). Before the colonization of Africa, Africans maneuvered through life within an organized system of knowledge that offered a lens through which to understand reality, values, logic, and historical experiences. This system is organized into five fundamental features in ACP: (1) self-definition, (2) spirit, (3) nature, (4) metaphysical interconnectedness, and (5) communal order and self-knowledge.

Self-definition is the ability to define one's self in one's own terms. This is an empowering act. Becoming empowered enough to use your own frame of reference is considered essential in life. Such a stance parallels the self-authorized way of knowing that is presented in Chapter 1. The second fundamental feature of ACP is *spirit.* Spirit is the energy that pervades the essence of all matter (Grills, 2002). *Nature* is the third fundamental feature. Nature sets forth the conventions by which humans function, the rhythms of life, and the natural order of things (Grills, 2002). The fourth feature of ACP is *metaphysical interconnectedness,* which is the acknowledgment of higher beings and powers greater than oneself. Finally, there is *communal order and self-knowledge*. People of African descent are relational beings and work from the "we" or community paradigm. Grills (2002) emphasizes knowing oneself through relationships with others.

The TRIOS Model

Another Africentric approach is called TRIOS (Jones, 2003). It is a psychological theory of the African legacy in American culture. It describes African American ways of being that occur automatically. The five themes that counselors who work with African Americans should be aware of are time, rhythm, improvisation, orality, and spirituality (thus "TRIOS"). The model describes how the current, residual influences of African culture and the harsh experiences of slavery surface in some African Americans' conceptions of those themes. Following is a brief introduction to the five themes. The reader would need to study the TRIOS model in greater depth in order to fully understand it.

Time can be seen in at least two ways, depending on culture: In time-oriented societies, time may be saved, wasted, or invested much as any valued resource. That conception represents the general perspective of people of European descent, who have a more linear and rigid relationship with the clock than do people of African descent. By contrast, in some cultures, including African American culture, time has no independent status or value and therefore does not dictate behavior and choice. Instead, activities and relationships do. African Americans are caught between these two conceptions of time.

Rhythm defines a recurring pattern of behavior within specified time frames. Racism often causes disharmonious connections between internal and external states. As a result, African Americans may not live in rhythm if they must deny aspects of themselves when in oppressive or Eurocentric situations. They may find the rhythms more consistent in an African American setting. Such would be the case in the use of African American dialect (AAVE) and in expressive communication styles, where the rhythm is different depending on context.

Improvisation is an African-based style of living that emphasizes expressiveness and invention in language, relationships, and action, as opposed to structured, emotionally controlled ways of being. African Americans must play back and forth between these two styles, depending on the environments that they are in. The European American environment values improvisation less than does the African and African American one.

Orality is a theme that captures the traditions of vocality, drumming, storytelling, praise singing, and naming that are part of African and African American cultures. Orality emphasizes context in expression. Counselors should know that in African American culture, language is a means of control through the use of privileged meanings and neologisms, such as "bad" meaning "good" and "stupid" meaning "smart." Hip-hop is a brilliant illustration of orality. It is more than a style of singing and rhyming; it is an assertion of self that is not filtered through the mainstream European American power structure.

Spirituality is defined as the belief in nonmaterial power in human life. African Americans tend to believe that what happens to people is determined, in some measure, by forces that are beyond human control. In African American life, spirituality liberates a person from the dominance of European American cultural expectations and constraints. Instead, the person can make reference to a power greater than the European American norms and rules.

Table 5.3   TRIOS Domains and Assessment

Dimension Name	Description
Time	Present orientation; living in the now
Rhythm	Interconnection with nature, time, and space; environmental flow
Improvisation	Adaptability; ability to withstand external barriers to success
Orality	Narrative expression of meaning; handing down culture through stories and styles of speech or song
Spirituality	Divine intervention; higher power in daily life

ACTIVITY 5.3

Follow-Up to the Cases of Tamika and Kendra

1. Please read the cases that were presented at the beginning of this chapter and, based on the information in this chapter, discuss your original impressions and assumptions about each one.

Tamika:

Kendra:

2. List some questions that you now would have for both of these clients and why you believe it is important to gather this information.

Tamika:

Kendra:

In developing the TRIOS model, Jones (2003) emphasized the importance of passing down family history and African history. The TRIOS model proposes that culture gives credence to the evolution, adaptation, and transformation of people of African descent. Drawing on the human tendency for both self-protection and self-motivation, Jones contends that the TRIOS design assists individuals in coping with racism. As is evident in the summary of the history and characteristics of African Americans in this chapter, many people of African descent employ elements of TRIOS without realizing the legacy on which they are building. See Table 5.3 for a summary of TRIOS domains.

Return to the cases of Tamika and Kendra that introduced this chapter, and using the knowledge that you have gained by reading this chapter, complete Activity 5.3.

Summary

Often, African Americans are asked why they focus so much on slavery when it is "ancient history." The reference to slavery and its legacy is not something African Americans do to garner pity or to make excuses for themselves. Quite the contrary, the fact that their ancestors have survived horrific conditions and many were able to thrive is a testament to their strength and tenacity. The discussion of this history in this chapter was meant to emphasize to the reader the enormity of the influence of slavery on all Americans and its being a necessary element in any discussion of African American culture. The pervasive nature and legacy of racism, which is the lingering byproduct of slavery, should therefore not be taken lightly. African Americans today are still feeling the effects of slavery and its attendant oppressions in the twenty-first century. As Cross (2003) stated, "blacks exited slavery with the type of social capital, family attitudes, and positive achievement motivation that could have readily facilitated their rapid acculturation into the mainstream society, had society wanted them" (p. 80). Counselors need to help African Americans to discover and build on the strengths of their culture and to counter negative models in order to reach their potential as full citizens and human beings.

References

Adebimpe, V. R. (1981). White norms and psychiatric diagnosis of black patients. *American Journal of Psychiatry, 138,* 279–285.

American Psychological Association. (2001). *Publication manual of the American Psychological Association* (5th ed.). Washington, DC: Author.

Arias, E. (2004, November 10). *Table 12: Estimated life expectancy at birth in years, by race and sex. United States life tables, 2002.* (National Vital Statistics Report Vol. 53, No. 6). Retrieved December 1, 2005, from http://www.cdc.gov/nchs/data/dvs/nvsr 53_06t12.pdf

Arnold, M. S. (2002). African American families in the postmodern era. In J. L. Sanders & C. Bradley (Eds.), *Counseling African American families* (pp. 3–16). Alexandria, VA: American Counseling Association.

Atkinson, D. R. (2004). *Counseling American minorities.* Boston: McGraw-Hill.

Baker, F. M., & Bell, C. C. (1999). Issues in the psychiatric treatment of African Americans. *Psychiatric Services, 50,* 362–368.

Ball, J., Armistead, L., & Austin, B. (2003). The relationship between religiosity and adjustment among African-American, female, urban adolescents. *Journal of Adolescence, 26,* 431–446.

Blauner, R. (1972). *Racial oppressions in America.* New York: Harper & Row.

Bowman, P., & Howard, C. (1985). Race-related socialization, motivation, and academic achievement: A study of black youth in three-generation families. *Journal of the American Academy of Child Psychiatry, 24,* 134–141.

Bradley, C. (1998). Child rearing in African American families: A study of disciplinary methods used by African American parents. *Journal of Multicultural Counseling and Development, 26,* 273–281.

Bradley, C. (2002). Parenting: A community responsibility. In J. L. Sanders & C. Bradley (Eds.), *Counseling African American families* (pp. 29–40). Alexandria, VA: American Counseling Association.

Burling, R. (1973). *English in black and white.* New York: Holt, Rinehart & Winston.

Carr, P. G., & Mednick, M. T. (1988). Sex role socialization and the development of achievement motivation in black preschool children. *Sex Roles, 18,* 169–180.

Carter, R. T., & Cook, D. A. (1992). A culturally relevant perspective for understanding the career paths of visible racial/ethnic group people. In H. D. Lea & B. Leibowitz (Eds.), *Adult career development: Concepts, issues and practices* (pp. 192–217). Alexandria, VA: National Career Development Association.

Cashin, S. D. (2000, September). *Middle-class suburbs and the state of integration: A post-integrationist vision for metropolitan America.* Georgetown Law and Economics Research Paper No. 241245, Georgetown University.

Chadiha, L. A., Rafferty, J., & Pickard, J. (2003). The influence of caregiving stressors, social support, and caregiving appraisal on marital functioning among African American wife caregivers. *Journal of Marital and Family Therapy, 29,* 479–490.

Chambers, J. W., Jr. (1983). *Black English: Educational equity and the law.* Ann Arbor, MI: Karoma.

Chapman, A. B. (1988). Male-female relations: How the past affects the present. In H. P. McAdoo (Ed.), *Black families* (pp. 190–200). Newbury Park, CA: Sage.

Cole, E. R., & Omari, S. R. (2003). Race, class and the dilemmas of upward mobility for African Americans. *Journal of Social Issues, 59,* 785–802.

Comer, J. P., & Poussaint, A. F. (1992). *Raising black children.* New York: Penguin.

Connor, J. J. (2003). "The textbooks never said anything about . . ." Adolescents respond to The Middle Passage: White ships/black cargo. *Journal of Adolescent & Adult Literacy, 47,* 240–246.

Connor, M. (2002). Counseling African American fathers. In T. A. Parham (Ed.), *Counseling persons of African descent: Raising the bar of practitioner competence* (pp. 119–140). Thousand Oaks, CA: Sage.

Cook, D. A., & Wiley, C. Y. (2000). *Psychotherapy with members of African American churches and spiritual traditions.* In P. S. Richards & A. E. Bergin (Eds.), *Handbook of psychotherapy and religious diversity* (pp. 369–396). Washington, DC: American Psychological Association.

Cornelius, J. R., Fabrega, H., Cornelius, M. D., Mezzich, J., & Maher, P. J. (1996). Racial effects on the clinical presentation of alcoholics at a psychiatric hospital. *Comprehensive Psychiatry, 37,* 102–108.

Cowan, B. A. (2004). African roots/American cultures: Africa in the creation of the Americas. *Journal of African American History, 89,* 82–84.

Cross, W. E. (1971). The Negro to black conversion experience: Toward the psychology of black liberation. *Black World, 209,* 13–27.

Cross, W. E. (1991). *Shades of black.* Philadelphia: Temple University Press.

Cross, W. E. (2003). Tracing the historical origins of youth delinquency & violence: Myths & realities about black culture. *Journal of Social Issues, 59,* 67–82.

Cross, W. E., & Fhagen-Smith, P. E. (2001). Patterns of African American identity development: A life span perspective. In C. Wijeysinghe & B. Jackson (Eds.), *New perspectives on racial identity development* (pp. 243–270). New York: New York University Press.

Denby, R., & Alford, K. (1996). Understanding African American disciplinary styles: Suggestions for effective social work intervention. *Journal of Multicultural Social Work, 4,* 81–98.

Doss, R. C., & Gross, A. M. (1994). The effects of black English and code-switching on intraracial perceptions. *Journal of Black Psychology, 20,* 282–293.

Dovidio, J. F., Kawakami, K., & Gaertner, S. L. (2000). Reducing contemporary prejudice: Combating explicit and implicit bias at the individual and intergroup level. In S. Oskamp (Ed.), *Reducing prejudice and discrimination* (pp. 137–164). Mahwah, NJ: Erlbaum.

Edwards, H. (1986). The black "dumb jock": An American sports tragedy. *College Board Review, 131,* 8–13.

Evans, K. M. (2003). Including spirituality in multicultural counseling: Overcoming counselor resistance. In G. Roysircar, S. D. Sandhu, & V. E. Bibbins, Sr. (Eds.), *Multicultural competencies: A guidebook of practices* (pp. 161–171). Alexandria, VA: Association for Multicultural Counseling & Development.

Evans, K. M., & Herr, E. L. (1991). The influence of racism and sexism in the career development of African American women. *Journal of Multicultural Counseling and Development, 19,* 173–184.

Evans, M. C. (2004). Gay marriage gained Bush black votes. *Newsday.com.* Retrieved December 1, 2005, from http://www.edisonresearch.com/home/archives/Newsday 11-14-2004.pdf

Exum, H. A., Moore, Q. L., & Watt, S. K. (1999). Transcultural counseling for African Americans revisited. In J. McFadden (Ed.), *Transcultural counseling* (pp. 171–219). Alexandria, VA: American Counseling Association.

Fukuyama, M. A., & Sevig, T. D. (1999). *Integrating spirituality into multicultural counseling.* Thousand Oaks, CA: Sage.

Garner, T., & Rubin, D. L. (1986). Middle class blacks' perceptions of dialect and style shifting: The case of southern attorneys. *Journal of Language & Social Psychology, 5,* 33–48.

Greene, B. A. (1990). Sturdy bridges: The role of African American mothers in the socialization of African American children. *Women & Therapy, 10,* 205–225.

Greene, B. A. (1994). African American women. In L. Comas-Díaz & B. A. Green (Eds.), *Women of color* (pp. 10–29). New York: Guilford Press.

Grier, W. H., & Cobbs, P. M. (1968). *Black rage.* New York: Basic Books.

Griffin, P. R. (1999). *Seeds of racism in the soul of America.* Cleveland, OH: Pilgrim Press.

Grills, C. (2002). African-centered psychology. In T. A. Parham (Ed.), *Counseling persons of African descent: Raising the bar of practitioner competence* (pp. 10–24). Thousand Oaks, CA: Sage.

Hale, J. (1991). The transmission of cultural values to young African American children. *Young Children, 46,* 7–15.

Hill, S. A. (1999). *African American children: Socialization and development in families.* Thousand Oaks, CA: Sage.

Holloway, J. E. (2005). *Africanisms in American culture.* Bloomington: Indiana University Press.

Hughes, T. J. (2005). *Factors that influence the career maturity of African American athletes.* Unpublished doctoral dissertation, University of South Carolina.

Hunter, M. L. (2002). "If you're light you're alright": Light skin color as social capital for women of color. *Gender & Society, 16,* 175–193.

James, E. H. (2002). Race-related differences in promotions and support: Underlying effects of human and social capital. *Organization Science, 11,* 493–508.

Jang, S. J., & Johnson, B. R. (2004). Explaining religious effects on distress among African Americans. *Journal for the Scientific Study of Religion, 43,* 239–260.

Jones, J. M. (2003). TRIOS: A psychological theory of the African legacy in American culture. *Journal of Social Issues, 59,* 217–242.

Kennedy, R. (2003). *Nigger: The strange career of a troublesome word.* New York: Vintage.

Koch, L. M., Gross, A. M., & Kolts, R. (2001). Attitudes toward black English and code switching. *Journal of Black Psychology, 27,* 29–42.

Lake, O. (1997). Cultural hierarchy and the renaming of African people. *Western Journal of Black Studies, 21,* 261–271.

Larimer, G. S., Beatty, E. D., & Broadus, A. C. (1988). Indirect assessment of interracial prejudices. *Journal of Black Psychology, 14,* 47–56.

Lassiter, R. J. (1987). Child rearing in black families: Child-abusing discipline. In R. L. Hampton (Ed.), *Violence in the black family: Correlates and consequences* (pp. 39–53). Lexington, MA: Lexington Books.

Lee, C. C. (1995). *Counseling for diversity: A guide for school counselors and related professionals.* Needham Heights, MA: Allyn & Bacon.

Leong, F. T. L., Wagner, N. S., & Tata, S. P. (1995). Racial and ethnic variations in help-seeking attitudes. In J. G. Ponterotto, J. M. Casas, L. A. Suzuki, & C. M. Alexander (Eds.), *Handbook of multicultural counseling* (pp. 415–438). Thousand Oaks, CA: Sage.

Levine, M. L. (1996). *African Americans and civil rights: From 1619 to the present.* Phoenix, AZ: Oryx Press.

Lewis, D. K. (1975). The black family: Socialization and sex roles. *Phylon, 36,* 221–238.

Lipford-Sanders, J. (2002). Racial socialization. In J. L. Sanders & C. Bradley (Eds.), *Counseling African American families* (pp. 41–57). Alexandria, VA: American Counseling Association.

Loevinger, J. (1976). *Ego development.* San Francisco: Jossey-Bass.

Meier, A., & Rudwick, E. M. (1966). *From plantation to ghetto: An interpretive history of American Negroes.* New York: American Century Series.

Moore, R. M., III. (2002). *The quality and quantity of contact: African Americans and whites on college campuses.* Lanham, MD: University Press of America.

Naremore, R. C. (1980). Language variation in a multicultural society. In T. J. Hixon, L. D. Shrieberg, & J. H. Saxmon (Eds.), *Introduction to communication disorders* (pp. 176–212). Englewood Cliffs, NJ: Prentice Hall.

Neighbors, H. W., & Jackson, J. S. (1996). *Mental health in black America.* Thousand Oaks, CA: Sage.

Neville, H. A., & Walters, J. M. (2003). Contextualizing black Americans' health. In D. Atkinson (Ed.), *Counseling American minorities* (pp. 83–103). Boston: McGraw-Hill.

Neville, H. A., Worthington, R. L., & Spanierman, L. B. (2001). Race, power, and multicultural counseling psychology: Understanding white privilege and color-blind racial attitudes. In J. Ponterotto, J. M. Casas, L. A. Suzuki, & C. M. Alexander (Eds.), *Handbook of multicultural counseling* (pp. 257–288). Thousand Oaks, CA: Sage.

Nickerson, K. J., Helms, J. E., & Terrell, F. (1994). Cultural mistrust, opinions about mental illness, and black students' attitudes toward seeking psychological help from counselors. *Journal of Counseling Psychology, 441,* 59–70.

Osabu-Kle, D. T. (2000). The African reparation cry: Rationale, estimate, prospects, and strategies. *Journal of Black Studies, 30,* 331–350.

Ostrove, J. M., Feldman, P., & Adler, N. E. (1999). Relations among socioeconomic status indicators and health for African-Americans and whites. *Journal of Health Psychology, 4,* 451–463.

Parham, T. A. (1993). *Psychological storms: The African American struggle for identity.* Chicago: African American Images.

Parham, T. A. (1999). African-centered cultural competencies. In T. A. Parham, J. L. White, & A. Ajamu (Eds.), *The psychology of blacks: An African-centered perspective.* Upper Saddle River, NJ: Prentice Hall.

Parham, T. A. (2002a). Counseling African Americans: The current state of affairs. In T. A. Parham (Ed.), *Counseling persons of African descent: Raising the bar of practitioner competence* (pp. 1–9). Thousand Oaks, CA: Sage.

Parham, T. A. (2002b). Raising the bar for what passes as competence. In T. A. Parham (Ed.), *Counseling persons of African descent: Raising the bar of practitioner competence* (pp. 141–148). Thousand Oaks, CA: Sage.

Parham, T. A. (2002c). Understanding personality and how to measure it. In T. A. Parham (Ed.), *Counseling persons of African descent: Raising the bar of practitioner competence* (pp. 38–51). Thousand Oaks, CA: Sage.

Parham, T. A., & Brown, S. (2003) Therapeutic approaches with African American populations. In F. D. Harper & J. McFadden (Eds.), *Culture and counseling: New approaches* (pp. 81–98). Needham Heights, MA: Allyn & Bacon.

Peters, M. F. (1976). *Nine black families: A study of household management and child rearing in black families with working mothers.* Unpublished doctoral dissertation, Harvard University, Cambridge, MA.

Peters, M. F. (1985). Parenting in black families with young children: A historical perspective. In H. P. McAdoo (Ed.), *Black families* (pp. 228–241). Beverly Hills, CA: Sage.

Peterson, N., & Gonzalez, R. C. (2000). *The role of work in people's lives: Applied career counseling and vocational psychology.* Belmont, CA: Brooks/Cole.

Phillips, C. (2004). Restoring a ruptured relationship. *Black Issues in Higher Education, 21,* 31–33.

Pinderhughes, E. E., Dodge, K. A., & Bates, J. E. (2000). Discipline responses: Influences of parents' socioeconomic status, ethnicity, beliefs about parenting, stress, and cognitive-emotional processes. *Journal of Family Psychology, 14,* 380–400.

Richards, P. S., & Bergin, A. E. (1997). *A spiritual strategy for counseling and psychotherapy.* Washington, DC: American Psychological Association.

Ridley, C. R. (1995). *Overcoming unintentional racism in counseling and therapy: A practitioner's guide to intentional intervention.* Thousand Oaks, CA: Sage.

Robinson, C. J. (1997). *Black movements in America.* New York: Routledge.

Robinson, T. L. (2005). *The convergence of race, ethnicity, and gender: Multiple identities in counseling.* Upper Saddle River, NJ: Pearson.

Russell, K., Wilson, M., & Hall, R. (1992). *The politics of skin color among African Americans.* New York: Harcourt Brace Jovanovich.

Sanders, R. G. (2002). The Black Church: Bridge over troubled water. In J. L. Sanders & C. Bradley (Eds.), *Counseling African American families* (pp. 73–84). Alexandria, VA: American Counseling Association.

Smallwood, A. D. (1998). *The atlas of African-American history and politics: From the slave trade to modern times.* Boston: McGraw-Hill.

Smiley, T. (Producer). (2005, February 26). Smiley presents: State of the black union. [Television broadcast]. Washington, DC: C-SPAN.

Snowden, L. R., & Hu, T. W. (1997). Ethnic differences in mental health services use among the severely mentally ill. *Journal of Community Psychology, 25,* 235–247.

Spanoudis, S. L. (1994). *Quotations: African American expression.* Retrieved July 24, 2006, from http://www.theotherpages.org/quotes/q-27-06.html

Staples, R. (1984, October). The mother-son relationship in the black family. *Ebony, 39,* 76–78.

Stevenson, H. C. (1994). Racial socialization in African American families: The act of balancing intolerance and survival. *Family Journal: Counseling and Therapy for Couples and Families, 2,* 190–198.

Stevenson, H. C. (1995). Relationship of adolescent perceptions of racial socialization to racial identity. *Journal of Black Psychology, 21,* 49–70.

Straus, M. A. (1991). Discipline and deviance: Physical punishment of children and violence and other crime in adulthood. *Social Problems, 38,* 133–153.

Sudarkasa, N. (1988). Interpreting the African heritage in Afro-American family organization. In H. P. McAdoo (Ed.), *Black families* (pp. 27–43). Newbury Park, CA: Sage.

Sue, D. W., & Sue, D. (2003). *Counseling the culturally diverse.* New York: Wiley.

Trierweiler, S. J., Neighbors, H. W. Munday, C., Thompson, S. E., Binion, V. J., & Gomez, J. P. (2000). Clinician attributions associated with diagnosis of schizophrenia in African Americans and non-American patients. *Journal of Consulting and Clinical Psychology, 68,* 171–175.

Trosper, T. B. (2002). Parenting strategies in the middle class African-American family. *Dissertation Abstracts International Section A: Humanities and Social Sciences, 63(3-A),* 864.

Truax, K., Cordova, D I., & Wood, A. (1998). Undermined? Affirmative action from the target's point of view. In J. K Swim & C. Stangor (Eds.), *Prejudice: The target's perspective* (pp. 171–188). San Diego, CA: Academic Press.

U.S. Census Bureau. (2001). *The black population: 2000.* Retrieved December 15, 2005, from http://www.census.gov/prod/2001pubs/c2kbr01-5.pdf

U.S. Census Bureau. (2004). *America's families and living arrangements: 2003.* Retrieved December 15, 2005, from http://www.census.gov/prod/2004pubs/p20-553.pdf

Vandiver, B. J., Fhagen-Smith, P. E., Cokley, K. O., Cross, W. E., Jr., & Worrell, F. C. (2001). Cross's nigrescence model: From theory to scale to theory. *Journal of Multicultural Counseling and Development, 29,* 174–200.

Wade, T. J., & Bielitz, S. (2005). The differential effect of skin color on attractiveness, personality evaluations, and perceived life success of African Americans. *Journal of Black Psychology, 31,* 215–236.

Wicker, L. R., & Brodie, R. E. (2003). The physical and mental health needs of African Americans. In D. Atkinson (Ed.), *Counseling American minorities* (pp. 105–113). Boston: McGraw-Hill.

Witherspoon, S. (2005). *The impact of environmental influences on the career choices of African American males: Aspirations of becoming professional athletes.* Unpublished doctoral dissertation, University of South Carolina.

Zhang, A., & Snowden, L. (1999). Ethnic characteristics of mental disorders. *Cultural Diversity and Ethnic Minority Psychology, 5,* 134–146.

6

East and Southeast Asian Americans

Bryan S. K. Kim and Yong S. Park

Jacob, a 20-year-old fifth-generation Japanese American, is attending a private university, but he's finding the year difficult. He is anxious about completing his master's in electrical engineering because he does not like his classes. Yet he knows that this field of study is practical and will land him a high-paying job after college. He is afraid to speak to his parents about this dilemma because they have repeatedly told him that he should become an engineer. Lately, he has had trouble sleeping and does not feel like eating much.

Tuyen is a 50-year-old Vietnamese American immigrant who works as a clerk in a grocery store at a local shopping mall. Recently, Tuyen has noticed that little things irritate her, but she doesn't know why. She says that she doesn't enjoy going to work; she feels lonely without having co-workers who are of the same ethnicity and age range. Tuyen has been to her doctor's office because of recurring headaches and stomach pains, but the doctor can't find anything physically wrong with her. She was advised to take over-the-counter painkillers and antacid medication for her symptoms.

What kinds of questions might face the counselor of these clients? Jacob is a fifth-generation American. What might this mean in terms of his sense of identity as a Japanese American? Jacob is struggling with issues concerning his university major and career and is unable to talk to his parents about it. How might a counselor work with him on this issue? As for Tuyen, she is an immigrant. How does this differentiate her from Jacob? What about Tuyen's Vietnamese ethnicity? Does this characteristic suggest some unique historical, social, and political experiences that differentiate her from Jacob and other East and Southeast Asian Americans? Tuyen seems to be suffering from loneliness, in addition to some physical ailments. How might a counselor try to help her?

The purpose of this chapter is to describe ways in which counselors can become more culturally competent and effective with East and Southeast Asian

American clients. Sometimes the simple term "Asian Americans" will be used to refer to East and Southeast Asian Americans. "East Asians" will refer to Chinese, Koreans, and Japanese. "Southeast Asians" will refer to the peoples of the region between Vietnam and Pakistan. Filipinos will also be included in this chapter, although their geographical and cultural status might easily put them in the category of Pacific Islanders. It should be noted that this chapter is not about South Asians, such as Indians, Pakistanis, and Sri Lankans; Chapter 11 will address the cluster of South Asian cultures.

This chapter begins with a self-assessment of the counselor's current knowledge about Asian Americans. This exercise is followed by descriptions of demographic characteristics, the sociopolitical history, cultural systems, and mental health issues specific to East and Southeast Asian Americans. The chapter concludes with a description of intervention strategies that may be useful with these clients. Throughout the chapter, the cases of Jacob and Tuyen are revisited to illustrate how these descriptions apply to two very different Asian Americans.

To begin, below is a self-assessment about your knowledge of East and Southeast Asian Americans (see Box 6.1). Please complete it before you read the rest of the chapter and return to it at the end to see whether your scores have improved. It is our hope that your final score will be 40 points.

Demographic Characteristics

The East and Southeast Asian American population represents one of the fastest growing groups in the United States. As of 2000, the number of East and Southeast Asian Americans (i.e., not counting Asian Indian and Pakistani Americans) stood at nearly 10 million, or 3.5 percent of the total U.S. population (Barnes & Bennett, 2002; see Table 6.1). These numbers represent an increase of about 67 percent since the previous census in 1990, when the number of East and Southeast Asian Americans stood at six million (U.S. Department of Commerce, 1993). It is estimated that by 2050, one out of 10 people living in the United States will be able to trace her or his ancestry in part or full to Asian countries (U.S. Census Bureau, 2004). This dramatic increase in the number of East and Southeast Asian Americans is largely a result of the huge influx of immigrants from Asia; nearly seven out of 10 Asian Americans were actually born in Asia.

East and Southeast Asian Americans represent a very heterogeneous group that is composed of many ethnic backgrounds, each with distinct cultural norms. Although they are often classified as a single group because of their common geographic origins in the Asian continent, the group includes no fewer than 25 individual ethnic groups, including Cambodians, Chinese, Filipinos, Hmong, Indonesians, Japanese, Laotians, and Vietnamese. These ethnic groups vary significantly in their language, traditions, customs, societal norms, and immigration history.

As for education and socioeconomic status, the proportion of Asian Americans who have a bachelor's or an advanced degree is higher than in any

BOX 6.1   East and Southeast Asian American Knowledge Scale

Instructions: Please indicate the extent to which you agree with each statement.

Strongly Disagree	Disagree	Agree	Strongly Agree
1	2	3	4

_____ 1. I have extensive knowledge about the history of East and Southeast Asian Americans in the United States.

_____ 2. I am knowledgeable about the large diversity among East and Southeast Asian Americans in regard to culture, language, and immigration experiences.

_____ 3. I have good knowledge of the cultural norms that may be generalizable to all East and Southeast Asian Americans.

_____ 4. I can provide specific examples of how East and Southeast Asian Americans have been victims of racism in the United States.

_____ 5. East and Southeast Asian Americans represent a wide range in terms of their adaptation to American cultural norms and the retention of traditional Asian cultural norms.

_____ 6. I am familiar with the terms "acculturation" and "enculturation" as they relate to East and Southeast Asian Americans.

_____ 7. I can give examples of cultural values that are salient to East and Southeast Asian Americans.

_____ 8. I am familiar with the model minority myth and how it has negatively affected East and Southeast Asian Americans.

_____ 9. I can offer possible reasons East and Southeast Asian Americans tend to underutilize mental health services.

_____ 10. I can think of specific ways in which counselors can become more culturally relevant and competent with East and Southeast Asian American clients.

Total Score Out of 40:

---

other ethnic group. However, paradoxically, the proportion of Asian Americans (and Pacific Islanders) who have less than a ninth-grade education is also almost twice that for European Americans (Reeves & Bennett, 2003). This contradiction is explained by the fact that although groups such as Chinese and Japanese Americans tend to have higher rates of educational attainment than European Americans, other Asian Americans groups, such as Cambodians, Hmong, and Vietnamese, have significantly lower educational achievement than European Americans (Hsia & Peng, 1998).

Similarly, there is a significant variation in the amount of earned income for Asian American families. In 2002, 44.2 percent of Asian American (and Pacific Islander) families earned $75,000 or more per year, whereas 40.1 percent of European Americans earned this amount (Reeves & Bennett, 2003). However, 14.3 percent of Asian Americans earned less than $25,000 in the same year,

Table 6.1 Population of the 10 Largest East and Southeast Asian Groups in the United States

Asian Ethnic Group	Number	% of Total
1. Chinese	2,314,537	23
2. Filipino	1,850,314	18
3. Vietnamese	1,122,528	11
4. Korean	1,076,872	11
5. Japanese	796,700	8
6. Cambodian	171,937	2
7. Hmong	169,428	2
8. Laotian	168,707	2
9. Taiwanese	118,048	1
10. Thai	112,989	1

SOURCE: U.S. Census Bureau (2002).

NOTE: Population values reflect respondents who reported only one Asian group.

whereas 11.8 percent of European Americans earned this amount. The figures at the high end of the spectrum must be considered within the context of family size: Family sizes are larger for Asian Americans. In 2002, 19.9 percent of Asian Americans lived in families with five or more members, compared to 12.1 percent for European Americans. Thus, Asian families may have a higher-than-average family income because there are more family members working and contributing to the family's earnings. There is also a significant discrepancy in the percentage of Asian Americans living in poverty, in comparison to European Americans. At least 10 percent of Asian Americans, or 1.3 million, live in poverty, whereas the parallel is 8 percent for European Americans (Reeves & Bennett, 2003). This group includes a high percentage of the Asian elderly population and Southeast Asians (e.g., Cambodians and Vietnamese) in general.

Sociopolitical History

The presence of East and Southeast Asian Americans in the United States can be traced back to the mid-1800s and the arrival of migrants from China, Japan, Korea, and the Philippines. The first group of Chinese arrived in San Francisco in 1848 to work in the gold fields of California. Twenty years later, in 1868, the Chinese were followed by Japanese migrants. Koreans arrived still later, in 1903, followed by the Filipinos in 1906. Most of the Japanese, Korean, and Filipino migrants initially entered Hawaii to work on sugar plantations in the hopes of improving their economic situation (Chan, 1991).

ANTI-ASIAN SENTIMENT

These migrants faced economic exploitation, prejudice, and outright racism. Asian Americans were harassed, beaten, and murdered by other Americans for being Asian (Chan, 1991). This violence against Asian Americans was not limited to individuals or groups, but existed at the structural level as well. Various legislative bodies passed laws forbidding Asian Americans to become citizens, own land, and intermarry. Calling Asians "the Yellow Peril," the media soon labeled Asian Americans as "inassimilable aliens" and pushed for legislation banning further Asian immigration into the United States. In fact, exclusion laws such as the Immigration Act of 1924 were passed to bar Asians from even entering the United States. Thus, the number of U.S. Asian individuals was kept to about one million for many years.

Although immigration from Asia was severely curtailed by these laws, a small number of Asians (several thousand) nevertheless entered the United States between 1924 and 1965. Most of these individuals were wives of American soldiers stationed in various Asian countries during World War II (1941–1945) and the Korean War (1950–1953) (Chan, 1991). These women tended to fall into two categories: those who married persons from the same ethnic group and those who married European Americans. In the first category, approximately 9,000 Chinese women entered the United States after marrying Chinese American soldiers. By contrast, Japanese, Korean, and Filipina women tended to marry European American soldiers.

However, anti-Asian racism triumphed in a significant way during World War II. Soon after the December 7, 1941, Japanese attack on Pearl Harbor, General John L. DeWitt, commander of the Western Defense Command, under the authority granted him by Executive Order 9066, forcefully interned 112,000 Japanese people who were living on the Pacific Coast, including thousands of U.S.-born citizens, into 10 "relocation centers" (also referred to as concentration camps) in desolate areas of the western and southern United States (Chan, 1991). U.S. political leaders believed that Japanese Americans would be forever loyal to the Emperor of Japan, would support the Japanese war effort by sabotaging important infrastructures on the West Coast, and could not be trusted to be loyal to the United States. None of these beliefs was based on tangible evidence.

The recent dramatic rise in the number of Asian Americans in the United States can be attributed to the following two events: (1) the passing of the Immigration Act of 1965 and (2) the ending of the war in Southeast Asia in 1975. These two events served to precipitate a large wave of migrants from various Asian countries, especially Cambodia, China, Laos, South Korea, South Vietnam, and Taiwan.

THE IMMIGRATION ACT OF 1965

The 1960s were a tumultuous time in U.S. history. The social and political landscape was experiencing a major upheaval as many Americans, and racial minorities in particular, engaged in a fight for equality and justice. One of the significant outcomes of the civil rights movement was the Immigration Act of 1965. This Act represented an attempt to improve the international image of the United States as a country committed to freedom, equality, and justice. The severe immigration restrictions imposed by the 1924 Immigration Act had damaged this image.

The 1965 Act (and the 1990 extension of that Act) had the following two intentions: (1) family reunification and (2) the importation of skilled workers (Ong & Liu, 1994). The goal of reunifying family members was expressed by giving immigration priority to persons who were joining their families already residing in the United States. The goal of importing skilled workers arose out of the United States's economic needs. This intention was expressed by giving immigration priority to persons with special skills judged to be in short supply in this country. Using a preference system based on these principles, the 1965 Act allowed a total of 170,000 migrants from the Eastern hemisphere (including Asia) to enter the United States per year. By contrast, 170,000 migrants from the Western hemisphere (including Europe) were allowed to enter the United States. Despite this quota imbalance, between 1978 and 1995 Asian countries were still the leading source of new immigrants to the United States (U.S. Census Bureau, 1997).

THE END OF THE WAR IN SOUTHEAST ASIA

The end of the U.S. involvement in Southeast Asia created a different situation for another group of Asian migrants who began to enter the United States after 1975. Beginning in the mid-1950s, the U.S. government provided military and political aid to the governments in South Vietnam, Laos, and Cambodia in an attempt to prevent the spread of Communism to Southeast Asia. When the United States decided to terminate its involvement in this region in 1975, thousands of Southeast Asians who had worked for, or were otherwise associated with, the U.S. government became fearful of the political persecutions that might be carried by the Communist forces who were on the verge of victory. As a result, these individuals fled their homelands by boat or on foot. Countless people perished during this escape. In response, the United States, out of moral and humanitarian obligation, agreed to receive these refugees and help them settle in the United States. Between 1975 and 1992, more than 650,000 Vietnamese refugees, 230,000 Laotian and Hmong refugees, and 147,000 Cambodian refugees entered the United States (Rumbaut, 1995). In addition, 173,000 Vietnamese immigrated, most of them after the establishment of the Orderly Departure Program in 1989 (Rumbaut, 1995). As of 2000, a total of 1.8 million Southeast Asian Americans lived in the United States (Barnes & Bennett, 2002).

Box 6.2 is a timeline of significant events in the history of Asian Americans.

BOX 6.2   Timeline of Asian American Immigration

1848   California Gold Rush.

1882   Chinese Exclusion Act: Chinese migrants were no longer allowed to enter the United States.

1907   Gentlemen's Agreement Act: Immigration of Japanese was restricted to only wives and family members.

1913   Alien Land Act: It became illegal for non-U.S. citizens, including foreign-born Asian Americans, to own land in California.

1924   National Origins Act: All Asian immigration was barred except for Filipinos, who were considered U.S. nationals.

1934   Tydings-McDuffie Act: A timetable for the independence of the Philippines was established. The Act also restricted Filipino immigration to 50 persons a year.

1942   Executive Order 9066: President Franklin D. Roosevelt authorized the placement of 110,000 Japanese into 10 internment camps during World War II.

1945   War Brides Act: Spouses and adopted children of U.S. military personnel were allowed to enter the United States.

1965   Immigration and Naturalization Act: Abolished the 1924 National Origins Act and increased the quota to 20,000 immigrants per country, with the total not exceeding 170,000 from the Eastern hemisphere.

1975   Fall of Saigon: U.S. military troops pulled out of Vietnam. Southeast Asian refugees begin entering the United States.

1979   Orderly Departure Program. A system for processing and settling refugees to the United States was founded by the United Nations and the Vietnamese government.

SOURCE: Lee (1998).

Jacob is a descendent of the pre-1924 immigrant group. His great-great-grandparents emigrated from Japan in 1890 to work in the sugar plantations in Hawaii. After five years on the plantation, they moved to California to work in agriculture. Soon, they made enough money to purchase their own small farm, which they did in the name of their U.S.-born six-year-old eldest son because the 1913 California Alien Land Law prevented them from owning property permanently in their name. The farm business was successful until 1941, when Jacob's family was forced to leave the farm for an internment camp in Colorado. Jacob has not had much interest in his Japanese heritage and prefers to consider himself an American. However, Jacob recently learned about Japanese American internment while taking a history course in Asian American studies.

Tuyen entered the United States as a 20-year-old refugee in 1975, a few weeks after the fall of Saigon to the Communist forces. Her father was a military official, so on the day Saigon fell she and her family were able to flee via a military helicopter to a U.S. warship. Tuyen remembers the exodus vividly: screaming masses of people trying *to leave Saigon, killings that occurred in the days prior to the Communist takeover of the city, and the chaos and fear that reigned across the country. Even to this day, she sometimes has nightmares about being stranded in the streets of Saigon without her family. Since arriving in the United States, Tuyen has had difficulty adjusting to the life here. Because she has not been able to completely grasp the English language, she has not been able to obtain a college education. Tuyen has worked at various jobs, the latest one being a sales clerk at a grocery store. Although she strongly identifies as a Vietnamese American, Tuyen seldom has contact with other Vietnamese Americans because very few live in her city.*

East and Southeast Asian Cultures

Effective counseling of East and Southeast Asian American clients requires an understanding of the diverse cultural systems in which these persons have been socialized or enculturated. The student must draw on her or his understanding of the notions of acculturation and enculturation and racial and ethnic identity development from Chapters 3 and 4 in order to avoid treating all Asian American clients the same. The following sections review these notions as they apply to Asian Americans. After that, cultural values and communication patterns that are salient across East and Southeast Asian cultures are described.

ACCULTURATION AND ENCULTURATION

As described above, the grouping that is here called East and Southeast Asian Americans comprises individuals with diverse immigration histories in the United States. This diversity, particularly in terms of length of residence, represents a dramatic range in the degree to which different Asian Americans have adapted to the norms of the mainstream U.S. culture, as well as the extent to which they have retained the norms of the Asian culture. To understand this type of diversity related to differential levels of adaptation, the student might recall or review the notions of acculturation and enculturation that were described in Chapter 3.

It makes sense that Asian Americans who are further removed from immigration will adhere to the mainstream U.S. cultural norms more strongly—that is, be more acculturated—than Asian Americans who are recent immigrants (Kim, Atkinson, & Umemoto, 2001). For example, Jacob's behaviors, values, knowledge, and cultural identity may be no different from those of other Americans, given that he is several generations removed from immigration. On the other hand, Asian Americans who are closer to immigration will adhere to Asian cultural norms more strongly—that is, they will be more enculturated to those norms—than their counterparts who are many generations removed from immigration. Such is the case with Tuyen, whose behaviors, values, knowledge, and cultural identity would be similar to Vietnamese persons who are living in Vietnam but significantly different from those of other Americans.

The four acculturation statuses, integration, assimilation, separation, and marginalization, help explain an individual client's adjustment to U.S. culture and her or his mental health (see Chapter 3). For Asian Americans, marginalization is perhaps the most problematic of the four acculturation statuses. Marginalized people adhere to neither their original nor the dominant cultural systems and tend to reject both sets of norms.

By contrast, the integration, or bicultural competence, status may be the healthiest status for East and Southeast Asian Americans (LaFromboise, Coleman, & Gerton, 1993). While European Americans generally have assimilated to the dominant U.S. culture, that option is not desirable, or available, to people of color, including Asian Americans. Biculturality is desirable because Asian traditions and values are distinct from the dominant U.S. culture and because Asians are physically "marked" by visual cues as "not white." Asians do not have the "optional ethnicity" that European Americans have (see Chapter 3). An Asian American with bicultural competence is fluent in the differing cultural norms of both the U.S. and Asian cultures and feels good about being a member of both groups. This person may also be fluent in both an Asian language and English. Furthermore, this person is eager to learn the cultural nuances of both cultures as a way to gain expertise in crossing the cultural bridge. LaFromboise et al. noted that individuals may experience difficulties adjusting to the different and sometimes opposing demands of two cultures, but when they are able to obtain skills in biculturality they are likely to increase their social and academic functioning as a result of their multicultural fluency.

RACIAL AND ETHNIC IDENTITY DEVELOPMENT

Racial and ethnic identity can vary from time to time in a person's life. The Racial Identity Development for People of Color (RIDPOC) model that was mentioned in Chapter 4 might be a useful tool to illustrate the variation in how Asian American individuals see themselves and others. It should be reiterated here that Asian Americans are grouped as "people of color" because, by appearance, they cannot assimilate into the dominant U.S. culture. To remind the student, the five stages of the RIDPOC model are as follows: (1) Conformity, (2) Dissonance and Beginning to Appreciate, (3) Resistance and Immersion, (4) Introspection and Internalization, and (5) Universal Awareness.

Conformity

Asian Americans who are in the Conformity stage will have preference for the dominant European American U.S. cultural values over Asian values. They will have self- and group-deprecating attitudes, while viewing the European American group positively. In addition, because they reject their own status as members of a minority group, Asian Americans at this stage will have discriminatory attitudes toward other people of color, such as Latinos/Latinas and African Americans.

Dissonance and Beginning to Appreciate

Asian Americans who are in the Dissonance stage experience a form of cognitive upheaval that shakes their beliefs and attitudes about their and other people's ethnicities. They may have reached this stage gradually or as a result of a monumental event. An example of a critical event for a Filipino American, for instance, might be learning that thousands of Filipinos served in the U.S. Navy but were not eligible for U.S. citizenship in the past. A Chinese person might learn of the Chinese Exclusion Act and the acts of violence committed against Chinese people in the United States. Asian Americans in this stage will also begin to recognize positive dimensions of their Asian American group (e.g., Confucian wisdom, Asian art forms) as well as negative dimensions of the European American group (e.g., colonialism). As a result of these types of experiences, individuals at the Dissonance stage are now forced to re-evaluate their attitudes toward both the Asian and European American groups and to reconcile these dissonant pieces of information. Asian Americans in this stage waver in a state of conflict between depreciating and appreciating themselves and their group. Similarly, they are in a state of conflict over their positive and negative attitudes toward the dominant European American group and toward other minority groups.

Resistance and Immersion

Asian Americans may next move to the Resistance and Immersion stage, which is characterized by a complete endorsement of the Asian group's cultural values and a complete rejection of the mainstream U.S. values. In addition, Asian Americans at this stage experience a growing sense of camaraderie with members of other minority groups as "fellow outsiders." An illustration of an individual in the Resistance and Immersion stage might be the "activist" person who views all European Americans as racists and fights for equal rights for Asian Americans.

Introspection and Internalization

In the next stage, called Introspection and Internalization, Asian Americans experience feelings of discontent and discomfort with the strong views that they previously held in the Resistance and Immersion stage. They may begin to have concerns about their overwhelmingly positive view of their Asian American groups and their ethnocentric bias in judging others. They also may begin to recognize the value of many mainstream U.S. cultural elements, such as artistic expressions, but be uncertain about whether to incorporate such elements into their own cultural norms. An example of a person in the Introspection stage is someone who seeks to learn about the positive contributions that many European Americans made to the civil rights movement in the 1960s. This person may also question the ethnocentric views of some Asian Americans.

Universal Awareness

Finally, Asian Americans in the Universal Awareness stage experience a sense of self-fulfillment with regard to their identity. According to Atkinson, Kim, and Caldwell (1998), the conflict and discomfort that were experienced during the Introspection stage have been reconciled, allowing for greater individual control and flexibility. For example, a person at this stage has more realistic and balanced views about the positive and negative aspects of the dominant European American group and the Asian American group.

Box 6.3 is an illustration of acculturation and ethnic identity in the cases of Jacob and Tuyen.

ASIAN CULTURAL VALUES

Whatever their level of acculturation and enculturation or their stage of minority identity development, East and Southeast Asian Americans will usually share particular cultural values (Kitano & Matsushima, 1981; Sue & Sue, 2003). Fourteen value dimensions of Asian Americans (Kim, Atkinson, & Yang, 1999) have been identified through focus groups and a nationwide survey. They are listed in Box 6.4. The first 12 values reflect four related themes from Confucianism

---

**BOX 6.3   Illustration of Acculturation and Ethnic Identity in the
               Cases of Jacob and Tuyen**

Jacob feels that he is highly acculturated to the dominant U.S. culture and has low enculturation in his ethnicity of origin, hence placing himself in the "assimilation" category of the acculturation levels. He does not consciously endorse any traditional Asian values, particularly values specific to the Japanese culture. He mainly adheres to the mainstream U.S. values, such as individualism, independence, autonomy, and future orientation. Jacob feels that because he is so far removed from immigration, he does not have any ties to his Japanese ancestry. In terms of his identity, Jacob feels that he is in the Dissonance stage as a result of recently learning about how thousands of Japanese Americans, including his family, were unjustly placed in internment camps during World War II, while many Japanese Americans also fought courageously for the United States in Europe with the 442nd Regimental Combat Team. He is beginning to have an appreciation for being a Japanese American and wants learn more about his heritage.

Tuyen feels that she is highly enculturated but very low in acculturation, hence placing herself in the "separation" category. Because she entered the United States as an adult, Tuyen retained her proficiency in Vietnamese and maintains her traditional values, including collectivism, deference to authority figures, filial piety, and humility. Unfortunately, she has had difficulty fully grasping the English language and adapting to U.S. cultural norms. In terms of her identity, Tuyen feels that she is in the Resistance and Immersion stage; she completely endorses her traditional Vietnamese values while rejecting the mainstream U.S. values. Tuyen admits that a part of the reason she rejects the mainstream U.S. culture is due to racist incidents that she has had to endure in her work setting.

BOX 6.4   Common Asian Cultural Values

Avoidance of family shame. Family reputation is a primary social concern. The worst thing an individual can do is to disgrace her or his family.

Collectivism. Individuals should feel a strong sense of attachment to the group to which they belong and should think about the welfare of the group before their own welfare. Group interests and goals should be promoted over individual interests and goals.

Conformity to family and social norms and expectations. Conforming to familial and societal norms is important; one should not deviate from these norms. It is important to follow and conform to the expectations that one's family and the society have for one.

Deference to authority figures. Authority figures are deserving of respect. Individuals should not question a person who is in a position of authority.

Filial piety. Children are expected to manifest unquestioning obedience to their parents. Children should never talk back to their parents, go against their parents' wishes, or question the authority of their parents.

Importance of family. Individual family members feel a strong sense of obligation to the family as a whole and a commitment to maintaining family well-being. Honor and duty to one's family are very important, more important than one's own fame and power; personal accomplishment is interpreted as a family achievement.

Maintenance of interpersonal harmony. One should always try to be accommodating and conciliatory and never directly confrontational. One should not say things that may offend another person or that would cause the other person to lose face.

Placing others' needs ahead of one's own. An individual should consider the needs of others before considering her or his own. One should anticipate and be aware of the needs of others and not inconvenience them. Over-asserting one's own needs is a sign of immaturity.

Reciprocity. An individual should repay another person's favor, that is, repay those people who have helped or provided assistance to the individual. When one does favors for others, he or she should accept favors in return.

Respect for elders and ancestors. Ancestors and elders should be viewed with reverence and respect; children should honor their elders and ancestors. Elders have more wisdom and deserve more respect than young people.

Self-control and restraint. One should exercise restraint when experiencing strong emotions. The ability to control emotions is a sign of strength.

Self-effacement. It is important to minimize or depreciate one's own achievements. One should be humble, modest, and not boastful. It is inappropriate to draw attention to oneself.

Educational and occupational achievement. Educational and occupational achievement should be an individual's top priorities. Success in life is defined in terms of one's academic and career accomplishments.

Ability to resolve psychological problems. One should overcome distress by oneself. Asking others for psychological help is a sign of weakness. One should use one's inner resources and willpower to resolve psychological problems.

and Buddhism: (1) interpersonal harmony, (2) acceptance of one's place in society and the family, (3) obedience, and (4) orientation toward the group (Uba, 1994). Those emphases contrast with current Western values of competition, challenge to norms, and autonomy. The last two are about achievement and achieving inner peace by oneself.

With any particular client, counselors need to weigh the influence of these values in the context of the client's acculturation, enculturation, and minority identity developmental level. Box 6.5 illustrates how Asian values might influence Jacob and Tuyen. The counselor can inquire, using culturally educated questioning, about the importance of any of these values for particular clients. (See Chapter 16 for more on culturally educated questioning.)

The reader is invited to do Activity 6.1 in order to personalize her or his understanding of Asian values.

Variations in Values Among Asian Cultures

The cultural values in Box 6.4 are commonly observed across a number of Asian American ethnic groups, namely Chinese, Filipino, Japanese, and Korean Americans (Kim, Yang, Atkinson, Wolfe, & Hong, 2001). Generally speaking, the members of these groups perceive and define the values in a similar manner. However, there are also significant differences among the groups on the level of adherence to some of these values (collectivism, conformity to norms, emotional self-control, family recognition through achievement, filial piety, and humility). In particular, Filipino Americans stand out from the other groups, showing (a) less adherence to emotional self-control than the other three Asian American groups, (b) less family recognition of achievement and adherence to filial piety than Japanese and Korean Americans, (c) less adherence to conformity to norms than Chinese and Japanese Americans, and (d) less adherence to collectivism than Japanese Americans. It is clear that Filipino culture has important differences from the other three cultures.

In addition, research revealed that Japanese Americans had higher adherence to conformity to norms than did Chinese Americans, and Japanese and Korean Americans had higher adherence to family recognition through achievement than did Chinese Americans. These findings are important because they suggest that although these value dimensions are present across the four groups, members of these groups endorse the values to different degrees.

COMMUNICATION PATTERNS

In addition to an understanding of cultural values, effective counseling with East and Southeast Asian American clients requires an understanding of communication norms and behaviors among these clients.

BOX 6.5   Values in the Cases of Tuyen and Jacob

Traditional Asian values can be illustrated in the case of Tuyen. Since she is an immigrant and is psychologically closer to the Asian cultural norms, Tuyen strongly adheres to many of the values in Box 6.4. For example, when she interacts with other people, she has a strong tendency to not disagree with what others say, as a way of maintaining interpersonal harmony. She has learned to place the needs of others before her own. She is always respectful, especially to individuals who are older or more educated than she. When someone gives her a gift, regardless of how small, Tuyen always reciprocates with a gift of her own. When others praise Tuyen for such kindness, she attributes it to her parents for raising her properly. Tuyen feels that to behave otherwise would bring shame and dishonor to her family.

It should be noted that Jacob also is likely to share many of these values. However, given that he is many generations removed from immigration, he does not adhere to them as strongly as does Tuyen.

ACTIVITY 6.1

Values Clarification Exercise Using Asian Values

Reflect for a moment about which of the 14 values in Box 6.4 you find most meaningful. Imagine that you have a relationship with a person whose values are different from yours. You are happy in the relationship and your partner has been able to tolerate the value differences thus far in the relationship. Around the time of your one-year anniversary, your partner requests that you give up one of these 14 values or else the relationship is over. You can choose to give up one value so that the relationship can continue. Or, you can deny the request and end the relationship.

What would you choose regarding the relationship?

Which value would you give up and why?

Which value(s) are too important for you to give up and why?

How do you feel about your partner's request?

Pretend that you have decided to give up one value and continued the relationship. After four months, your partner again asks you to give up one of the remaining 13 values. Ask yourself again the questions listed above. After answering a second time, imagine that another four months has passed and the same request is made again to you. Repeat this exercise until you have either ended the relationship or exhausted all 14 of the Asian cultural values. Reflect on what motivated you to either stay in the relationship or end the relationship by keeping your values.

The purpose of this exercise was to help you clarify your own personal values, ones that shape your feelings, thoughts, and behaviors. First, you had to consider which Asian values you shared. Then, being forced to determine which value dimensions are more important than others probably was not an easy task. It is hoped that engaging in this activity helped you to better understand yourself as a person and as a counselor. You might use this exercise to help your Asian American clients better understand themselves as persons whose feelings, thoughts, and behaviors are influenced by these 14 cultural value dimensions.

Language

A first consideration is language itself. Given the high number of foreign-born Asian Americans, low levels of English language proficiency are prevalent among many East and Southeast Asian Americans. This English language difficulty obviously serves as a significant barrier when counselors work with Asian American clients. Language difficulties can contribute to inaccurate exchanges of information, even in the presence of an interpreter. As is the case with other clients for whom English is not a first language, counselors must take care to minimize misunderstandings when they work with clients who have low English proficiency. Chapter 16 has some recommendations in this area.

Context

Beyond literal language are the subtle cues with which people communicate. Every culture uses context to understand messages. For example, in some cultures, vendors initially demand a high price, knowing that the context requires bargaining. Asian Americans tend to participate in "high-context" as opposed to "low-context" communication. In high-context communication, individuals expect the other person to infer information primarily from the context and knowledge of the communicator. Thus, high-context communication tends to be indirect and implicit. For example, "no" may mean "yes" in some cultures, but be the norm for an initial response to an offer. High-context communicators may accurately understand a message among each other without having all of the details spelled out. In contrast, individuals who employ low-context communication assume that the necessary information can be obtained from the explicit transmitted message. Thus, low-context communication tends to be direct and clear (Gudykunst, 2001). Within the purview of the hierarchical social structure predominating in traditional Asian cultures, high-context communication is pervasive.

Consistent with that standard, Asian Americans communicate according to "face." Face, for Asians, consists of having a high status in the eyes of one's peers. It is not culturally appropriate to make fun of another, even in a good-natured way, as it is in other cultures. High-context communication serves the purpose of maintaining and building face. For example, Asians would honor their parent's face by referring to her or him by role, such as "father," rather than "you." Unlike European Americans, who tend to emphasize self-enhancement as a means of building face, Asian Americans are self-effacing and modest. For example, a European American might be encouraged in career counseling to declare her strengths. This would be culturally incongruent for Asian Americans. In addition, while European Americans typically use humor to save face, Asian Americans are usually apologetic.

Pauses and Silence

The importance of face may translate into particular communication patterns when counselors work with East and Southeast Asian American clients. In terms of sequences of vocalizations and pauses, Asian Americans, compared to European

Americans, may talk less at any one time (i.e., use fewer words) and have longer silences between vocalizations when communicating with other Asian Americans. On the other hand, when speaking with non-Asians, Asian Americans might feel uncomfortable with silences because they are anxious about the uncertainty of the norms and rules for communicating based on the stranger's cultural background.

Politeness and Emotional Expression

Asian Americans also tend to be polite in communication because they are considerate of others' feelings, foster mutual comfort, and build rapport. The degree to which Asian Americans are polite depends on the relative social position of the communicators. Individuals with higher social statuses are regarded with more politeness (Gudykunst, 2001). Finally, Asian Americans are less likely to express emotion in communication due to the culturally high value placed on stoicism (Gudykunst, 2001).

In sum, the following characterize Asian American communication: being indirect, making inferences about meanings, using apology to maintain and build "face," acknowledging hierarchy in social situations, being modest, allowing more silence and fewer words, politeness, and controlling emotional expression (see Table 6.2).

Table 6.2 Significant Differences in Communication Styles Between Asian and European Americans

Communication Style	Definition
European Americans:	
Dramatic	picturesque speech; physically or vocally acting out what one communicates
Open	readily revealing personal information about oneself; expressive of one's thoughts and feelings
Precise	communicating accurate information; trying to cover all possible issues in a discussion
Asian Americans:	
Indirect	communicating ambiguously; expecting others to guess the meaning of one's communication

SOURCES: Gudykunst et al. (1996) and Gudykunst (2001).

Mental Health Issues for Asian Americans

In addition to having a good understanding of the cultural systems that have influenced East and Southeast Asian Americans' psychological functioning, it is important to consider the social factors that are related to their mental health. What follows are descriptions of some of these factors that cause East and Southeast Asian Americans to be more vulnerable to mental health problems. Those factors are racism, the model minority stereotype, and acculturative stress. This section on mental health issues will conclude with a description of cultural expressions of mental distress, called culture-bound syndromes.

RACISM

From the time of their first arrival in the United States to the present, Asian Americans have experienced and persevered through racism. As defined in Chapter 4, racism refers to (1) the belief that a group of people with characteristics other than those of one's own group are inferior in some way and (2) the ability to act on that belief. Chan (1991) argued that Asian Americans have faced racism in many forms: through prejudice, economic discrimination, political disenfranchisement, physical violence, immigration exclusion, social segregation, and incarceration. The earliest accounts of racism against Asian Americans go as far back as the 1850s, when Chinese immigrants were denigrated and attacked during the Gold Rush. Anti-Asian sentiment increased, illustrated by the events of 1871, when 15 Chinese Americans were hanged, four shot, and two wounded by a white mob in Los Angeles. Such discrimination and violence continued into modern times, exemplified by the 1982 case of Vincent Chin, a Chinese American who was intentionally run down by a car and hit with a baseball bat by an unemployed autoworker who was frustrated by the competition from Japanese auto makers.

Anti-Asian racism is still present. In 1992, while 4 percent of the Philadelphia population comprised Asians, 20 percent of the hate crimes involved Asian American victims (Uba, 1994). From 1986 to 1989 in Los Angeles, where 10 percent of the population comprises Asians, 15.2 percent of hate crimes involved Asian American victims. Currently, 20 percent of Chinese Americans report that they have been discriminated against in their lifetime, and 43 percent said that the discrimination happened in the past year (Goto, Gee, & Takeuchi, 2002).

In addition to individual acts of racism, institutional racism exists in the current U.S. social structure. For example, the admission rates for Asian Americans who have the same qualifications as their white counterparts are lower at large, prestigious universities in the United States (Uba, 1994; Young & Takeuchi, 1998). Discrimination occurs in the occupational setting as well. With similar education and work experience, Asian Americans are less likely than whites to be promoted to managerial positions (Young & Takeuchi, 1998). They also have lower salaries at the same level of work.

Racism can lead to low self-esteem, learned helplessness, and depression (Fernando, 1984). Counselors should be attentive to these effects on their East and Southeast Asian American clients' mental health. However, counselors should also be reminded that it will be difficult to find out about such effects from many Asian American clients because they tend to underreport racial discrimination (Umemoto, 2000). Thus, it may well be difficult to pinpoint this cause for mental distress in many Asian American clients. Again, culturally educated questioning (see Chapter 16) can be used to uncover these experiences.

THE MODEL MINORITY STEREOTYPE

One stereotype that has long affected Asian Americans is that of the "model minority." First coined by sociologist William Peterson (1966), this notion suggests that Asian Americans embody the modern-day American success story: They are functioning well in society, are somehow immune to cultural conflicts and discrimination, and experience few adjustment difficulties. There is some truth to this general conception, from the perspective that this stereotype represents a central tendency of a number of groups of Asian Americans. Asian cultural values, such as diligence, frugality, emphasis on educational and occupational achievement, ability to hide psychological problems, and maintenance of face, reinforce the stereotype (Crystal, 1989; Kim et al., 1999).

However, the model minority stereotype has other, more troubling implications when these statistics are examined more closely. Two qualifiers are important. First, the model minority notion doesn't apply to all Asian groups. Second, the notion itself creates some mental health difficulties for Asian Americans.

Model Minority and Diversity Among Asian Americans

The characteristics of the model minority notion are not accurate for all Asian groups. As mentioned at the beginning of this chapter, "Asian American" is a broad and heterogeneous ethno-racial category. It includes numerous ethnic groups with different educational, economic, and social characteristics. For example, as mentioned earlier, although Chinese and Japanese Americans tend to have higher rates of educational attainment than European Americans, Cambodian, Hmong, and Vietnamese have significantly lower educational achievement than do European Americans (Hsia & Peng, 1998). Thus, generalization to all Asian American ethnic groups is inaccurate.

Another inaccuracy about the model minority is actual income. As mentioned previously, Asian Americans earn significantly less income compared to white people with the same educational level (Bell, Harrison, & McLaughlin, 1997). A final counter to the universality of the model minority notion is the poverty statistics concerning Asian Americans. As noted above, at least 10 percent of Asian Americans, or 1.3 million, live in poverty, whereas the figure is 8 percent for European Americans (Reeves & Bennett, 2003).

Model Minority as Stressor

The second major difficulty with the model minority stereotype is that it, in itself, adds to mental health difficulties for East and Southeast Asian Americans in at least three ways. First, the model minority stereotype serves to alienate Asian Americans from other ethnic minority groups because of the inherent message, "If Asian Americans can succeed, why can't other minority groups?" In one study, Rosenbloom and Way (2004) found that a high number of black and Latino/Latina students in an urban high school consistently physically and verbally harassed Asian American students, due to Asian Americans being seen as favored by teachers.

Another negative mental health consequence of the model minority notion is that it places extreme pressure on Asian Americans to conform to high educational, economic, and occupational expectations. Failure to meet the expectations of the stereotype may lead to feelings of failure, underachievement, and inadequacy. In turn, these pressures and stresses may be related to psychological problems and suicide among Asian Americans (Hurh & Kim, 1989). Counselors are to be especially alert to this expectation-related distress.

A final mental health consequence of the model minority notion is that the stereotype hinders the allocation of counseling and research resources for Asian American mental health concerns because the common wisdom erroneously assumes that they tend not to suffer from psychological difficulties.

ACCULTURATIVE STRESS

A final major factor, in addition to racism and the model minority myth, that causes East and Southeast Asian Americans to be more vulnerable to mental health problems is acculturative stress. When individuals make contact with the norms of a cultural environment that conflicts with the internalized norms of their indigenous culture, they are likely to experience significant stress. Members of immigrant ethnic minority groups, including Asian Americans, are particularly vulnerable to acculturative stress (Berry & Annis, 1974). For East and Southeast Asian Americans, acculturative stress is particularly pervasive because the dominant European American norms tend to make traditional Asian values and behaviors ineffective in U.S. society. Those norms include cultural differences in the following: the treatment of parents, assertive behavior, independence, communication, emotional expression, and the meanings of body language. Such acculturative stress is related to depression (e.g., Constantine, Okazaki, & Utsey, 2004). Hence, it is important for counselors to be attentive to the presence of acculturative stress among East and Southeast Asian Americans.

Box 6.6 illustrates various culture-related stresses in the cases of Jacob and Tuyen.

The counselor is invited to try Activity 6.2 in order to increase her or his empathy in the area of acculturative stress.

BOX 6.6   Mental Distress and the Cases of Jacob and Tuyen

Jacob feels that his current difficulties regarding career choice may have a lot to do with the model minority myth that he has internalized. Although he realizes that part of the pressure to obtain a degree in electrical engineering comes from his parents and their values of academic and career achievement, he also feels that he can't see himself changing his major to one that might be perceived by others as less prestigious. In addition, his difficulties with mathematics makes him feel ashamed that he is a less-than-good student; he feels that he should be good in math regardless of whether he likes it or not. As a result, he is struggling to stay in a major that he does not enjoy and is trying to cope with its psychological consequences.

Tuyen reports that her ailments could be related mainly to the stresses from her job. Tuyen describes acts of prejudice and racism from her co-workers and customers that she has had to endure. For instance, Tuyen recalls several incidents in which she was called a name (e.g., "dumb Jap") by customers who were angry because Tuyen couldn't understand what they wanted. In addition, most recently, Tuyen was bypassed for a night manager position in favor of a European American worker who had less experience than she. When Tuyen inquired about why she was not selected, the general manager told her that she may have difficulties managing the other workers because she is so "different." Even when Tuyen is not working, she feels like an "outsider," although she has been in the United States for 30 years. Because she is in a predominantly European American community with very few Vietnamese Americans, she has no sources of ethnic support (e.g., Vietnamese Mutual Association). The nearest Vietnamese enclave ("Little Saigon") is in a city 200 miles away, and it is not easy for her to go there. She notes that she has tried to not to think about these problems as a way of coping with them.

ACTIVITY 6.2

Visualization Exercise

A Virtual Trip

Close your eyes and imagine. Imagine traveling to a foreign country named Detinu Setats. Your intention is to spend the rest of your life there. You are traveling alone and you have no relatives in this country. You do not speak the language of the country and virtually no one in the country understands English. You also are ignorant of the cultural norms of the country, although you have heard that the cultural norms there are very different from those of the United States. Although you have a college degree, you are not sure what kind of work you will find there. Finally, you have heard that the people in this country are not very welcoming to foreigners and have, in the past, mistreated them.

How do you feel?

What concerns come to your mind?

What dangers do you foresee?

How long will you be able to survive in such a setting?

What would be some characteristics of your typical day in this country?

CULTURE-BOUND SYNDROMES

The final segment of this discussion of mental health issues for Asian Americans consists of a description of some of the most prominent culture-bound emotional syndromes. Such syndromes are further explored in Chapter 16.

The cultural background of clients influences how they experience, interpret, and manifest their psychological distress. The American Psychiatric Association (2000) developed a list of psychological disorders that are unique to various cultural groups and have labeled them "culture-bound syndromes." Below are examples of syndromes specific to East and Southeast Asian cultures.

Hwa-byung's literal translation in Korean is "anger syndrome." It is a rather broadly inclusive category for the experience of long-term and suppressed anger. Symptoms include insomnia, fatigue, panic attacks, fear of impending death, dysphoria (a state of feeling unwell or unhappy), indigestion, anorexia, dyspnea (breathing discomfort or significant breathlessness), palpitations, generalized aches and pains, and a feeling of a mass in the epigastrium (the part of the abdominal wall above the belly button) due to anger suppression.

Koro is an episode of sudden and intense anxiety over the belief that the penis in males, and the vulva and nipples in females, will recede into the abdomen and cause them to die. This anxiety is based on the folk tale that ghosts who have no penis will steal the penis from the living. Cases of *koro* have been reported mainly in China and Thailand.

Taijin Kyofusho is a culture-bound syndrome in Japan that refers to an intense fear that one's body may displease, embarrass, or be offensive to another person. Within the Japanese nosology for mental disorders, *Taijin Kyofusho* refers to the fears of blushing, a deformed body, eye contact, and having foul body odor.

Shenjing shauriruo consists of the following symptoms: physical and mental fatigue, dizziness, headaches, other pains, concentration difficulties, sleep disturbance, memory loss, gastrointestinal problems, sexual dysfunction, irritability, excitability, and disturbance of the autonomic nervous system. This syndrome has been documented in China and it is highly similar to a mood or an anxiety disorder.

Intervention Issues and Strategies

The previous sections presented the historical, sociopolitical, and cultural characteristics of East and Southeast Asian Americans and described issues related to their mental health. Attention is now turned to culturally relevant, effective counseling with this population. The following section describes treatment issues to be aware of when working with East and Southeast Asian Americans and offers strategies that may be effective with these individuals.

The following topics will be addressed: (a) attitudes toward seeking mental health services, (b) psychological assessment, (c) indigenous healing methods,

(d) conventional approaches to psychological treatment, (e) modification of conventional counseling for Asian Americans, (f) five factors for working with Asian Americans, and (g) additional sources of mental health support.

ATTITUDES TOWARD SEEKING MENTAL HEALTH SERVICES

Client attitudes toward counseling are primary because these attitudes will influence whether or not individuals even seek counseling services and how long they will persist in counseling. In that vein, Asian attitudes are important. Asian Americans tend not to seek psychological services, and even if they enter treatment, they tend to terminate prematurely (e.g., Snowden & Cheung, 1990). More recently, a qualitative interview study found that Asian Americans would see a counselor only as the last resort; friends and family would be their first sources of help (Kim, Brenner, Liang, & Asay, 2003). At first glance, one might interpret these findings as showing that Asian Americans experience mental health problems at a lower rate than other racial groups. In addition, they may suggest that when Asian Americans seek psychological services, the problems tend to be minor, thereby causing clients to not return for subsequent sessions. However, these possibilities have been challenged by thinkers who argue that there are no particular reasons why Asian Americans, in comparison to other cultural groups, should have a lower rate of incidence for psychological problems (e.g., Atkinson et al., 1998). In fact, given the experiences of oppression that Asian Americans face, as described above, it seems reasonable to expect that the need for mental health services among this group would be greater than it is for European Americans.

A number of factors within and outside the Asian American group limit Asian Americans' uses of psychological services. First, within Asian American communities, there may be pre-existing and readily available therapeutic systems. These systems may include a network of family members, respected elders, and practitioners of indigenous healing methods, which may be perceived as more credible sources of help than Western-based psychological services (Atkinson et al., 1998; Sue & Sue, 2003).

In terms of the outside factors, mainstream psychological service providers may be seen as lacking cultural relevance and competency, which may discourage Asian Americans from seeking help (Atkinson et al., 1998; Sue & Sue, 2003). Asian Americans who are not acculturated to the dominant U.S. culture might perceive conventional psychological services to be "foreign" or even threatening (Atkinson et al., 1998; Sue & Sue, 2003). Less acculturated Asian Americans are most likely to exhibit this uncertainty (Atkinson & Gim, 1989). This finding supports the idea that Asian Americans' underutilization of psychological services is related to their lack of familiarity with Western norms and lack of belief that counseling can be helpful.

Even if they are familiar with counseling norms, Asian Americans who are strongly enculturated to their Asian culture may feel ashamed about having mental health problems and hesitant to reveal their problems to individuals outside their family, such as a professional counselor (Atkinson et al., 1998). High adherence to Asian cultural values is associated with both less positive attitudes toward seeking psychological help and less willingness to see a counselor (Kim & Omizo, 2003). Hence, underutilization of psychological services among Asian Americans is related to Asian cultural norms.

Based on these findings, several counseling implications can be offered. First, counselors should consider conducting more Asian American outreach in their schools, colleges, agencies, and private practices. It may be helpful to disseminate educational materials describing the potential benefits of psychological services. Second, mental health agencies should consider hiring Asian American counselors to attract Asian American clients. This suggestion is especially appropriate if the agencies are located in communities with a large proportion of East and Southeast Asian Americans. Third, when working with Asian American clients who are strongly enculturated, low acculturated, or both, counselors can use culturally educated questioning to evoke the issues of shame and embarrassment about seeking help (see Chapter 16). If the clients are embarrassed about their need for counseling, counselors can help them strategize effective ways to cope with these feelings. Fourth, a useful strategy might be to assign clients to an ethnically similar counselor. Having a counselor with a similar ethnic background may lead the client to have a greater appreciation for the normality and the benefits of the help-seeking endeavor. However, it should be noted that some Asian American clients who are assigned to an ethnically similar counselor might feel an increased sense of shame and embarrassment because they may be sensitive to the fact that an "in-group" person will be learning about their mental health problems.

PSYCHOLOGICAL ASSESSMENT

Despite the general reluctance among many East and Southeast Asian Americans to seek mental health services, some of them do enter counseling. However, even then they may have a great deal of skepticism and culture-related concerns. If those uncertainties about counseling are unattended, the client might prematurely terminate counseling. Hence, it is important for counselors to broach the question of clients' attitudes and concerns about counseling itself at the beginning of the counseling relationship.

As with any clients, counselors should assess the nature, severity, and duration of the presenting issue and the ways in which the problem has been addressed in the past. In addition, it is very important for counselors to obtain information about the factors in the concern that are related to clients' cultural background, which could lead to more relevant and helpful counseling relationships and interventions. Finally, counselors should explicitly assess culture-related factors, including (a) acculturation, enculturation, and racial and ethnic identity statuses; (b) attitudes about counseling; (c) experiences with oppression; (d) possible presence of culture-specific psychological disorders; and (e) availability of other sources of support.

INDIGENOUS HEALING METHODS

Based on the results of a psychological assessment, counselors might consider taking one of two routes of treatment: (a) conventional counseling that integrates culturally relevant and sensitive interventions or (b) referral to practitioners of indigenous healing methods.

One type of indigenous healing method for many East and Southeast Asians, especially Chinese persons, is *ta'i chi ch'uan*. Ta'i chi ch'uan is an exercise that induces relaxation and meditation (Sandlund & Norlander, 2000). It involves a complex pattern of slow movements of the arms and legs. Research suggests that ta'i chi ch'uan enhances overall psychological well-being and mood (Sandlund & Norlander, 2000).

Another type of indigenous healing method is acupuncture. Acupuncture treatments are based on principles of Chinese medicine in which health and illness are viewed in terms of a balance between the *yin* and the *yang* forces (Meng, Luo, & Halbreich, 2002). Acupuncture involves inserting small pins in specific points on the body to improve the proper circulation of energy, which may be associated with psychological difficulties. Acupuncture has been used successfully to treat depression, anxiety disorders, alcoholism, and substance abuse (Meng et al., 2002).

CONVENTIONAL APPROACHES TO PSYCHOLOGICAL TREATMENT AND ASIAN AMERICANS

It is paradoxical that Asian American clients who have high adherence to Asian cultural values tend to perceive counselors more positively than do clients who are low in adherence to Asian values (Kim, Li, & Liang, 2002; Kim, Ng, & Ahn, 2005). This phenomenon may be due to Asian respect for professionals and authorities. A counselor may be seen as a physician. Thus, with highly enculturated East and Southeast Asian American clients, counselors may be able to quickly gain the necessary credibility as helpers and then move on to addressing the presenting problems, especially if the counselors are also Asian Americans. However, with low-enculturated East and Southeast Asian American clients, a counselor may need to spend as much time as she or he would with other clients to gain the necessary credibility as a helper.

However, some Western counseling approaches are likely to be problematic with many Asian American clients. A match or mismatch among a client's cultural values, a counselor's cultural values, and the values inherent in the counseling interventions can influence the counseling process and, ultimately, counseling outcome (Atkinson et al., 1998; Sue & Sue, 2003).

In particular, problems can occur when counselors encourage emotional expression, do depth exploration, evoke self-affirmation activities, and promote an egalitarian relationship. For example, Gestalt Theory posits the notion that emotional expression is beneficial and even curative for clients' problems. However, for Asian American clients who adhere to traditional Asian values and believe that stoicism and reticence are signs of psychological strength, being forced to express their emotions might leave them feeling embarrassed and out of control. Regarding depth exploration, psychodynamic theories posit the importance of exploring the underlying unconscious dynamics causing clients' problems, which often include unresolved issues with family members or other significant figures in one's early life. For traditional Asian Americans who value avoiding family shame, such exploration may be threatening and leave them feeling disloyal to their family.

In the area of self-affirmation, as mentioned before, for clients who adhere to Asian values of self-effacement, the cognitive and career counseling interventions of having clients openly describe their achievements and accomplishments, perhaps as a way to dispute their negative self-concepts, may be counterproductive and leave clients feeling arrogant.

Finally, egalitarian approaches to counseling, such as person-centered approaches, may also run counter to traditional Asian American deference to authority figures. Such clients may look to counselors to provide guidance and possible solutions to the problems. Being forced to treat the counselor in an egalitarian manner may lead clients to feel uncomfortable in the relationship.

There may also be positive potentials for combining conventional counseling approaches and traditional Asian cultural values. For example, the value of interpersonal harmony may lead clients to work just as hard as counselors to form a good working alliance, a key ingredient in humanistic counseling theories.

MODIFICATION OF CONVENTIONAL COUNSELING FOR ASIAN AMERICANS

If assessment shows that clients can benefit from conventional forms of counseling, care must be taken to augment the treatment with culturally relevant and sensitive strategies. There have been a number of research studies on counselor types and counseling interventions that may be effective with Asian American clients (see Kim et al., 2005, for a review).

Five Factors for Working With Asian Americans

Five factors have been found to be important for working with Asian American clients: (1) the person of the counselor, (2) counselor cultural sensitivity, (3) counselor self-disclosure, (4) counseling style, and (5) solution focus. The notion of "gift giving" is also potentially important in working with Asian American clients. These generalizations must, of course, be made tentatively, keeping acculturation/enculturation and other individual differences in mind. Box 6.7 summarizes these factors.

BOX 6.7 Five Factors for Working With Asian Americans

Counselor/Session Factors	Counseling Process
Person of the Counselor	Clients prefer counselors who are ethnically similar, have similar attitudes, are more educated, are older, and have a similar personality.
Counselor Cultural Sensitivity	Clients view culturally knowledgeable counselors as being more credible and culturally competent.
Counselor Self-Disclosure	Clients prefer counselors who disclose personal information about successful strategies.
Counseling Style	Clients favor a logical, rational, directive, and authoritative counseling style.
Solution Focus	Clients prefer the goal of looking for immediate resolution of the problem.

Person of the Counselor. Research results suggest that Asian American clients favor ethnically similar counselors over ethnically dissimilar counselors. They also favor counselors who are older than they are, with similar attitudes, more education, and similar personality. For example, research has shown that Asian American clients prefer counselors who try to match the client's worldview in terms of a possible cause of the client's problem than counselors who do not match their worldview (Kim et al., 2005). In this study, match in worldview was simulated by having counselors agree with the client's belief about the cause of the problem. Other examples of worldview match are having similar beliefs about values, religion, and human nature, as well as levels of gender identity and maturity. Also, research suggests that bicultural Asian Americans, in comparison to their Western-identified counterparts, perceive counselors as being more attractive (Atkinson & Matsushita, 1991). To illustrate with the case of Tuyen, she may feel threatened by a non-Asian counselor because of her experiences with racism. She may, instead, connect better with an Asian American counselor because she may perceive her or him to have had similar experiences. Also, Tuyen may find an older counselor to be more credible than a younger one, given the cultural emphasis on age.

Counselor Cultural Sensitivity. Research findings also suggest that Asian American clients view culturally sensitive counselors as being more credible and culturally competent than less sensitive counselors (Gim, Atkinson, &

Kim, 1991; Zhang & Dixon, 2001). Jacob, who is entering the Resistance and Immersion stage, may be more open to a counselor who is sensitive and knowledgeable about Asian-related issues because Jacob's attention is becoming more focused on his Asian ethnicity and culture.

Counselor Self-Disclosure. Asian American clients perceive counselors who disclose personal information about successful strategies they used in similar situations to be more helpful than counselors who disclosed other types of personal information (Kim, Hill, et al., 2003). To illustrate, in many Asian American families, parent-child conflict regarding career choice is not an uncommon occurrence. Thus, a counselor may do well to disclose how she resolved conflicts, if any, with her parents in regard to entering the counseling profession.

Counseling Style. Asian American clients also favor a logical, rational, and directive counseling style to a reflective, affective, and nondirective one (Atkinson, Maruyama, & Matsui, 1978; Li & Kim, 2004), especially if the counselor is an Asian American (Atkinson & Matsushita, 1991). Further research suggests that acculturated Asian international student clients view authoritative peer counselors as being more credible than collaborative peer counselors (Merta, Ponterotto, & Brown, 1992). In the case of Tuyen, for example, an Asian American counselor may teach and direct Tuyen to create a plan for negotiating a promotion at her current job as a way of offering more logical, rational, and directive counseling.

Solution Focus. In general, Asian American clients, especially those who are less acculturated to the dominant American culture, favor looking for immediate resolution of the problem rather than exploring the problem to gain insight about its source (Kim et al., 2002). For example, a counselor can conceptualize the anxiety that an Asian American client suffers as a "problem" that can be "fixed." The counselor would then immediately prescribe relaxation and desensitization techniques to reduce the anxiety before or in lieu of further exploration of related issues.

Immediate Benefit as "Gift Giving"

An additional notion that might be helpful in working with Asian American clients is the metaphorical use of "gift giving." Sue and Zane (1987) propose that counselors focus on clients gaining some immediate benefits from counseling; that is, a "gift." Sue and Zane theorized that for counselors to be perceived as culturally responsive and to reduce clients' premature termination, counselors should help clients experience immediate and concrete benefits of counseling in the initial sessions. Sue and Zane pointed out that ethnic minorities in general, and Asian Americans in particular, have the need to attain some type of meaningful gains early in counseling because they tend to be more skeptical of the long-term benefits of talk therapy; "gift giving demonstrates to clients the direct relationship between working in therapy and alleviation of problems" (p. 42).

Examples of gifts include resolution of a presenting problem, anxiety reduction, depression relief, clarity about a concern, normalization of the distress, and coping skills acquisition. Such gifts can be expressed through such counseling skills as information giving, advice, directives, pointing out logical consequences, interpretation, positive reframing, role playing, and making a complementary referral to a physician or psychiatrist.

ADDITIONAL SOURCES OF MENTAL HEALTH SUPPORT

Counselors might consider referring Asian American clients to organizations serving Asian Americans for adjunctive support services. One inherent benefit of utilizing existing sources of support found within any ethnic community is that service providers may be able to speak the native languages of the clients. Another is familiarity and trust. Such additional resources include religious and fraternal associations. For example, it has been well-documented that Korean Americans and Filipino Americans are highly represented in Christian churches in comparison to other Asian ethnic groups. They therefore tend to seek support from clergy and other parishioners (Park, 1989). Hence, when working with a traditional Korean American client who is Christian, counselors may do well to help establish a connection between the client and a Korean church in the community. Similarly, counselors might refer traditional Vietnamese American Buddhist clients to temples in which priests can provide supportive services. As for Asian American college students, there are Asian organizations that may offer support for culturally related concerns, such as the Chinese Association for Chinese students, Kababayan for Filipino students, and HAPA for interracial Asian students. Also, Asian Americans from the community can be connected to other co-ethnics for support through such organizations such as the Japanese American Citizens League and Korean American Coalition. There also may be more specific Asian American organizations in communities across the United States.

A warning needs to be given at this point on counselors' using culture-based sources of support: Care should be taken that the clients will not experience shame and embarrassment when they seek help from members of their own ethnic group. As mentioned previously, when Asian Americans experience psychological problems, it is readily seen as a source of embarrassment and shame not only for the individuals but their families. Hence, if other members of the community learn that these individuals suffer from psychological difficulties, it could lead to a great deal of discomfort. To avoid such situations, counselors should work closely with their clients to identify support sources with which the clients feel comfortable.

The scenarios in Box 6.8 illustrate the use of culturally alert counseling skills in the cases of Tuyen and Jacob.

BOX 6.8   Applying Culturally Alert Interventions With Jacob and Tuyen

What follows are descriptions of counseling work with Jacob and Tuyen. They describe different counseling approaches that attend to their unique situations, both of which are based on culturally alert conceptualizations. As you read these vignettes, please consider what other culturally alert approaches you might use with these clients.

The Case of Jacob: During the first session with Jacob, you learn that he has no qualms about coming in for counseling. In fact, Jacob reports to you that this is his second time seeing a counselor. As you further assess Jacob, you discover that he is highly acculturated to U.S. culture but low enculturated in his ethnic group of origin, which then allows you to turn to conventional counseling methods. In addition, because you are aware of the beneficial effects of gift-giving, even for a highly acculturated Asian American, you work with Jacob during this session to come up with some concrete ideas on how he might be able to communicate with his parents about his career uncertainty. At the end of the session, Jacob has a number of strategies in mind to help him communicate effectively with his parents, including pointing out to his parents that other majors could still lead Jacob to a well-paying job and prestige. For future sessions, Jacob agrees to work with you to further explore his other problem regarding his internalized view of himself as "model minority."

The Case of Tuyen: During the first session with Tuyen, you learn that she is quite nervous about coming in for counseling and feels ashamed that she couldn't resolve her problems by herself. Hence, you spend time in the beginning addressing this issue and helping Tuyen cope with these feelings of embarrassment. As you further assess Tuyen, you learn that she is highly enculturated but low acculturated, which then allows you to determine that you could either refer her to an indigenous healer or modify conventional counseling methods to address the fact that Tuyen operates largely on traditional Asian norms. Because there are no Vietnamese healers nearby, you decide to modify your service. After further assessment, you determine that Tuyen's problem has a more external origin (i.e., racism). The goal, therefore, becomes to remediate her current problem (i.e., being bypassed for the managerial position). Hence, you decide to use the advocate role, in which you contact (with Tuyen's permission) officials in the local Civil Rights office to see how the racism that Tuyen experienced can be most effectively confronted. In addition, you contact the nearest Vietnamese Mutual Association to find out how Tuyen might be able to access their support network. Furthermore, you work to provide support to Tuyen as she engages in this process of healing.

Summary

From their first immigration phase of the mid-1800s to the large influx that came after the passing of the 1965 Immigration Act, Asian Americans have become visible members of U.S. society. Moreover, it is projected that by 2050, approximately 10 percent of the U.S. population will comprise Asian Americans. In the adaptation, adjustment, and maintenance of their communities, Asian Americans face challenges in common with other racial and ethnic groups such as acculturative stress (Uba, 1994), discrimination and racism (Young & Takeuchi, 1998), and identity issues (Atkinson et al., 1998), all of which are related to mental health problems. However, despite these mental health risk factors, Asian Americans tend not to use counseling services because counseling itself may be culturally incongruent. Thus, it is important for the mental health community to gain appropriate knowledge of Asian American cultural systems in order to provide culturally congruent services to this population. When working with Asian American clients, it is important to first assess their acculturation/enculturation levels, strength of ethnic identity, experiences with racism, as well as other concerns discussed in this chapter before implementing interventions. Through the discussion of Asian culture and counseling strategies, counselors are encouraged to begin reflecting on how they can infuse these cultural considerations into their current therapeutic approach in order to craft a culturally alert way of effectively helping Asian American clients.

References

American Psychiatric Association. (2000). *Diagnostic and statistical manual of mental disorders* (4th ed., Text rev.). Washington, DC: Author.

Atkinson, D. R., & Gim, R. H. (1989). Asian-American cultural identity and attitudes toward mental health services. *Journal of Counseling Psychology, 36,* 209–212.

Atkinson, D. R., Kim, B. S. K., & Caldwell, R. (1998). Ratings of helper roles by multicultural psychologists and Asian American students: Initial support for the three-dimensional model of multicultural counseling. *Journal of Counseling Psychology, 45,* 414–423.

Atkinson, D. R., Maruyama, M., & Matsui, S. (1978). The effects of counselor race and counseling approach on Asian Americans' perceptions of counselor credibility and utility. *Journal of Counseling Psychology, 25,* 76–83.

Atkinson, D. R., & Matsushita, Y. J. (1991). Japanese-American acculturation, counseling style, counselor ethnicity, and perceived counselor credibility. *Journal of Counseling Psychology, 38,* 473–478.

Barnes, J. S., & Bennett, C. E. (2002). *The Asian population: 2000.* Retrieved October 28, 2004, from http://www.census.gov/prod/2002pubs/c2kbr01-16.pdf

Bell, M. P., Harrison, D. A., & McLaughlin, M. E. (1997). Asian American attitudes toward affirmative action in employment: Implications for the model minority myth. *Journal of Applied Behavioral Science, 33,* 356–377.

Berry, J. W., & Annis, R. C. (1974). Acculturative stress: The role of ecology, culture and differentiation. *Journal of Cross-Cultural Psychology, 5,* 382–406.

Chan, S. (1991). *Asian Americans: An interpretative history.* Boston: Twayne.

Constantine, M. G., Okazaki, S., & Utsey, S. O. (2004). Self-concealment, social self-efficacy, acculturative stress, and depression in African, Asian, and Latin American international college students. *American Journal of Orthopsychiatry, 74,* 230–241.

Crystal, D. (1989). Asian Americans and the myth of the model minority. *Social Casework, 70,* 405–413.

Fernando, S. (1984). Racism as a cause of depression. *International Journal of Social Psychiatry, 30*(1–2), 41–49.

Gim, R. H., Atkinson, D. R., & Kim, S. J. (1991). Asian-American acculturation, counselor ethnicity and cultural sensitivity, and ratings of counselors. *Journal of Counseling Psychology, 38,* 57–62.

Goto, S. G., Gee G. C., & Takeuchi, D. T. (2002). Strangers still? The experiences of discrimination among Chinese Americans. *Journal of Community Psychology, 30,* 211–224.

Gudykunst, W. B. (2001). *Asian American ethnicity and communication.* Thousand Oaks, CA: Sage.

Gudykunst, W. B., Matsumoto, Y., Ting-Toomey, S., Nishida, T., Kim, K., & Heyman, S. (1996). The influence of cultural individualism-collectivism, self-construals, and individual values on communication styles across cultures. *Human Communication Research, 22*(4), 510–543.

Hsia, J., & Peng, S. S. (1998). Academic achievement and performance. In L. C. Lee & N. W. S. Zane (Eds.), *Handbook of Asian American psychology* (pp. 325–358). Thousand Oaks, CA: Sage.

Hurh, W. M., & Kim, K. C. (1989). The "success" image of Asian Americans: Its validity, and its practical and theoretical implications. *Ethnic and Racial Studies, 12,* 512–538.

Kim, B. S. K., Atkinson, D. R., & Umemoto, D. (2001). Asian cultural values and the counseling process: Current knowledge and directions for future research. *The Counseling Psychologist, 29,* 570–603.

Kim, B. S. K., Atkinson, D. R., & Yang, P. H. (1999). The Asian Values Scale: Development, factor analysis, validation, and reliability. *Journal of Counseling Psychology, 46,* 342–352.

Kim, B. S. K., Brenner, B. R., Liang, C. T. H., & Asay, P. A. (2003). A qualitative study of adaptation experiences of 1.5-generation Asian Americans. *Cultural Diversity and Ethnic Minority Psychology, 9,* 156–170.

Kim, B. S. K., Hill, C. E., Gelso, C. J., Goates, M. K., Asay, P. A., & Harbin, J. M. (2003). Counselor self-disclosure, east Asian American client adherence to Asian cultural values, and counseling process. *Journal of Counseling Psychology, 50,* 324–332.

Kim, B. S. K., Li, L. C., & Liang, C. T. H. (2002). Effects of Asian American client adherence to Asian cultural values, session goal, and counselor emphasis of client expression on career counseling process. *Journal of Counseling Psychology, 49,* 342–354.

Kim, B. S. K., Ng, G. F., & Ahn, A. J. (2005). Effects of client expectation for counseling success, client-counselor worldview match, and client adherence to Asian and European American cultural values on counseling process with Asian Americans. *Journal of Counseling Psychology, 52,* 67–76.

Kim, B. S. K., & Omizo, M. M. (2003). Asian cultural values, attitudes toward seeking professional psychological help, and willingness to see a counselor. *The Counseling Psychologist, 31,* 343–361.

Kim, B. S. K., Yang, P. H., Atkinson, D. R., Wolfe, M. M., & Hong, S. (2001). Cultural value similarities and differences among Asian American ethnic groups. *Cultural Diversity and Ethnic Minority Psychology, 7,* 343–361.

Kitano, H. H. L., & Matsushima, N. (1981). Counseling Asian Americans. In P. B. Pedersen, J. G. Draguns, W. J. Lonner, & J. E. Trimble (Eds.), *Counseling across cultures* (2nd ed., pp. 163–180). Honolulu: University of Hawaii Press.

LaFromboise, T., Coleman, H. L. K., & Gerton, J. (1993). Psychological impact of biculturalism: Evidence and theory. *Psychological Bulletin, 114,* 395–412.

Lee, L. C. (1998). An overview. In L. C. Lee & N. W. S. Zane (Eds.), *Handbook of Asian American psychology* (pp. 1–19). Thousand Oaks, CA: Sage.

Li, L. C., & Kim, B. S. K. (2004). Effects of counseling style and client adherence to Asian cultural values on counseling process with Asian American college students. *Journal of Counseling Psychology, 51,* 158–167.

Meng, F., Luo, H., & Halbreich, U. (2002). Concepts, techniques, and clinical applications of acupuncture. *Psychiatric Annals, 32,* 45–49.

Merta, R. J., Ponterotto, J. G., & Brown, R. D. (1992). Comparing the effectiveness of two directive styles in the academic counseling of foreign students. *Journal of Counseling Psychology, 39,* 214–218.

Ong, P., & Liu, J. M. (1994). U.S. immigration policies and Asian migration. In P. Ong, E. Bonacich, & Cheng, L. (Eds.), *The new Asian immigration in Los Angeles and global restructuring* (pp. 45–73). Philadelphia: Temple University Press.

Park, K. (1989). "Born again": What does it mean to Korean-Americans in New York City? *Journal of Ritual Studies, 3/2,* 287–301.

Peterson, W. (1966, January 9). Success story: Japanese American style. *New York Times,* p. VI20.

Reeves, T., & Bennett, C. (2003). *The Asian and Pacific Islander population in the United States: March 2002.* Retrieved October 28, 2004, from http://www.census.gov/prod/2003pubs/p20-540.pdf

Rosenbloom, S. R., & Way, N. (2004). Experiences of discrimination among African American, Asian American, and Latino adolescents in an urban high school. *Youth & Society, 35,* 420–451.

Rumbaut, R. G. (1995). Vietnamese, Laotian, and Cambodian Americans. In P. G. Min (Ed.), *Asian Americans: Contemporary trends and issues* (pp. 232–270). Thousand Oaks, CA: Sage.

Sandlund, E. S., & Norlander, T. (2000). The effects of tai chi chuan relaxation and exercise on stress responses and well-being: An overview of research. *International Journal of Stress Management, 17,* 139–149.

Snowden, L. R., & Cheung, F. H. (1990). Use of inpatient mental health services by members of ethnic minority groups. *American Psychologist, 45,* 347–355.

Sue, D. W., & Sue, D. (2003). *Counseling the culturally different: Theory and practice* (4th ed.). New York: Wiley.

Sue, S., & Zane, N. (1987). The role of culture and cultural techniques in psychotherapy: A critique and reformulation. *American Psychologist, 42,* 37–45.

Uba, L. (1994). *Asian Americans: Personality patterns, identity and mental health.* New York: Guilford Press.

Umemoto, K. (2000). From Vincent Chin to Joseph Ileto: Asian Pacific Americans and hate crime policy. In P. M. Ong (Ed.), *The state of Asian Pacific America: Transforming race relations* (pp. 243–278). Los Angeles: LEAP Asian Pacific American Public Policy Institute and the UCLA Asian American Studies Center.

U.S. Census Bureau. (1997). *Statistical abstract of the United States: 1997* (117th ed.). Washington, DC: U.S. Government Printing Office.

U.S. Census Bureau. (2002). *Census brief: Current population survey.* Retrieved September 28, 2006, from http://www.census.gov/prod/2002pubs/c2kbr01-16.pdf

U.S. Census Bureau. (2004). *U.S. interim projections by age, sex, race, and Hispanic origin.* Retrieved October 28, 2004, from http://www.census.gov/ipc/www/usinterimproj/

U.S. Department of Commerce. (1993). *We the Americans: Asians.* Retrieved May 5, 2005, from http://www.census.gov/apsd/wepeople/we-3.pdf

Young, K., & Takeuchi, D. T. (1998). Racism. In L. C. Lee & N. W. S. Zane (Eds.), *Handbook of Asian American psychology* (pp. 401–432). Thousand Oaks, CA: Sage.

Zhang, N., & Dixon, D. N. (2001). Multiculturally responsive counseling: Effects on Asian students' ratings of counselors. *Journal of Multicultural Counseling and Development, 29,* 253–262.

7 Native Americans

Michael Tlanusta Garrett

Old Indian Trick

> hide your thoughts with words
> like white girls
> so blood, crushed bone, burned flesh
> terrify only as ghosts
> of brown women's lives
> Indian silence
> leaves no room to hide
> except in dreams
> visions of light and spirit
> to wipe terror away.

—Rayna Green, Cherokee*

Native peoples have existed on this continent since long before the arrival of any other peoples. The history and stories of the lives of an ancient people are often portrayed in the media, playing on age-old stereotypes about this population. But beyond what is portrayed in books and movies, there are untold stories of pain and persistence that have carried over from generation to generation as the people continue to survive. The poem that opens this chapter evokes that pain and the continuing clash of cultures that is the American Indian experience on the North American continent.

The real lives of real people are what counselors must understand in order to best assist Native clients who may come to them with words, ghosts, dreams,

---

*Rayna Green, Cherokee (excerpt from "Old Indian Trick," in Velie, 1991). Printed with permission.

and visions of their own. The purpose of this chapter is not to offer information about many of the expected problems and issues of particular concern for this population, such as poverty and unemployment, alcoholism and substance abuse, teenage pregnancy, suicide rates, delinquency, and diabetes, or even whether or not casinos and the gaming industry have beneficial or destructive consequences for tribes. Instead, this chapter will offer a comprehensive overview and understanding of this population, one that can be incorporated into culturally alert counseling with Native Americans.

Specific sections of this chapter will address (a) terms and definitions of what group membership means for Native Americans; (b) an overview of the people, with particular discussion of demographics, acculturation, tribal and cultural identity, and the meaning of family; (c) historical context of social, political, and spiritual influences; (d) current social and political issues involved with identity, tribal resources, treaty rights, religion and sacred sites, mascot issues, gaming, and issues of cultural preservation; (e) Native American cultural values and worldview; (f) various elements of Native American communication style; (g) implications for practice with Native American clients using contemporary counseling interventions and treatment modalities; and (h) discussion of practical, tribe-specific interventions. First, a few case scenarios are presented to help guide the counselor's thinking in applying the concepts to be discussed throughout this chapter.

Case Scenarios

The following case scenarios are based on actual cases and are offered to stimulate thoughtful consideration of how to best work with Native clients with a variety of presenting issues and from a variety of backgrounds.

Cheryl is a Navajo woman in her mid-fifties who lives in an urban setting. She is divorced and has two children from her marriage. She has raised them as a single mom while pursuing a career in finance. Cheryl is very talkative and doesn't hesitate to describe her experience in Indian boarding school until age 11 or her participation in Indian activist groups during the 1970s. She proudly expresses that she has been sober now for over nine years and recently has begun to work closely with Native youth as a mentor in the local urban Indian center where her two children are active participants. Although Cheryl says that she was not involved much in cultural matters when she was young, she has found that her talent and involvement as a respected shawl dancer on the local powwow circuit has helped her maintain her sobriety. Since the recent death of her mother, however, with whom she was very close, she has been questioning what she should do next.

Activity 7.1 asks the reader to consider important factors in the case of Cheryl.

ACTIVITY 7.1

Thinking About Cheryl

How would you earn Cheryl's trust?

Furthermore, what would you choose to address first with Cheryl, and how would you approach it in a way that would be culturally responsive to her?

Where does Cheryl seem to be on the acculturation continuum, and how might that affect your approach to counseling her?

How are you similar to or different from Cheryl based on your life experiences and worldview, given what you know about her right now?

Rodney is a Seminole ninth grader who attends public school just off the reservation. He is very bright but reserved, and he frequently gets either shunned or made fun of by other kids because he is overweight. Recently, his grades have begun to drop significantly, and he has been getting into fights with other kids. His family has expressed concern over Rodney's lack of friends in the school and they are thinking about pulling him out of the school to enroll him instead in the reservation school system. Prior to now, Rodney had talked about his hopes of being the first in his family to attend college, and he wanted to study either fine art or business. Lately, he has said that he just wants to "go home."

The reader is encouraged to consider the implications of Rodney's culture by completing Activity 7.2.

Defining Group Membership and Terms

The case scenarios provided above are based on real people and thus are designed to stimulate deeper consideration of what the Native American experience is, particularly as it relates to developing further awareness, knowledge, and skills for dealing with issues that may be pertinent to counseling practice. Before proceeding further, a brief look at how Native American group membership is

ACTIVITY 7.2

Thinking About Rodney

How would you develop rapport with Rodney in order to provide an effective counseling intervention?

How might you include and draw upon Rodney's family as both a personal and a cultural resource for him?

Would you consider conducting a suicide assessment with Rodney, and if so, how might you go about doing that in a way that would be culturally responsive?

How would you characterize Rodney's cultural identity and level of acculturation at this point?

What could you do to help him develop a positive cultural identity that would help him meet his goals?

defined in North America and the terms that are used to describe the Native people of North America will be presented.

It is not uncommon for a Native person to be asked the question by non-Natives, "How much are you?" This question refers to "blood quantum." That is the universally accepted sign of what it means to be Indian. As such, it is critical that the discussion of what it means to be Native American begins by clarifying some definitions and concepts around group membership.

The term "Native American" is often used to describe indigenous peoples of the Western hemisphere in an effort to provide recognition—viewed by many as long overdue—of the unique history and status of these people as the first human inhabitants of the American continents. The U.S. Bureau of Indian Affairs (1988) legally defines a Native American as a person who is an enrolled or registered member of a tribe or whose "blood quantum," or ancestry, is one-fourth or more genealogically derived from Native American ancestry. Native nations across the country set different criteria for membership, from the Cherokee Nation of Oklahoma, which enrolls members with blood quantum as little as 1/512, to the Ute Nation of Utah, which requires a minimum blood quantum of 5/8 for tribal membership. Blood quantum refers to the percentage of ancestry that can be traced to people from that tribe; it is not literally a measure of blood. Most tribes or nations require 1/4 blood quantum (Russell, 1997). The

U.S. Census Bureau, meanwhile, relies on self-identification to determine who is a Native person. Oswalt (1988) points out, however, that

> if a person is considered an Indian by other individuals in the community, he or she is legally an Indian . . . [in other words], if an individual is on the roll of a federally recognized Indian group, then he or she is an Indian; the degree of Indian blood is of no real consequence, although usually he or she has at least some Indian blood. (p. 5)

Some of the terms used historically or currently to refer to Native people are American Indian, Alaskan Native, Native people, Indian, First American, Amerindian, Amerind, First Nations people, Aboriginal people, and Indigenous people. The terms "Native American" or "Native people" (and sometimes, "Indian") will be used here to refer generally to those people who are indigenous to the United States, who self-identify as Native American, and who maintain cultural identification as so-called Native persons through membership in a Native American tribe recognized by the state or federal government or through other tribal affiliation and community recognition. Now that the reader has a better understanding of some of the definitions and terms involved with group membership among Native Americans, it is necessary to discuss in depth what it means to be a part of "the people."

Understanding the People

Native Americans comprise approximately 2.4 million self-identified people, with a population that is steadily growing. Although this number represents only 1 percent of the total population of the United States (U.S. Census Bureau, 2001), Native people have been described as representing "fifty percent of the diversity" of ethnic groups in the United States (Hodgkinson, 1990, p. 1). Across the United States, there are more than 557 federally recognized and several hundred state-recognized Native American nations (Russell, 1997). Given the wide-ranging diversity within this population, it is important to understand that the term "Native American" encompasses multiple individual tribal traditions that are represented by hundreds of Indian nations. Navajo, Catawba, Shoshone, Lumbee, Cheyenne, Cherokee, Apache, Lakota, Seminole, Comanche, Pequot, Cree, Tuscarora, Paiute, Creek, Pueblo, Shawnee, Hopi, Osage, Mohawk, Nez Perce, Seneca—these are but a handful of the hundreds of Indian nations that exist across the United States.

The wide-ranging diversity of Native Americans is illustrated by their approximately 252 different languages (Thomason, 1991). Yet, at the same time, a prevailing sense of "Indianness" based on shared worldview and common history seems to bind Native Americans together as one people among many peoples (Herring, 1999; Thomason, 1991). Although acculturation to the dominant American culture plays a major role in Native American worldview, there tends to be a high degree of psychological homogeneity, a certain degree of shared cultural standards and meanings that are based on common core values that exist for traditional Native Americans across tribal groups (M. T. Garrett, 1999b). For example, Cherokees and Navajos are both Native Americans, but their regional cultures, climatic adaptations, and languages differ greatly. Nevertheless they share a strong sense of traditionalism based on basic cultural values and worldview. However, worldview and degree of commitment to traditional culture varies within groups among Native people.

VARIATIONS IN NATIVE EXPERIENCE OF ETHNICITY

Like other groups, Native people's relationships with their ethnicity can vary. Indeed, Native Americans differ greatly in their individual levels of acceptance of and commitment to specific tribal values, beliefs, and practices (Garrett & Garrett, 1996). Those differences are related to variations in (1) level of acculturation, (2) geographic setting (urban, rural, or reservation), and (3) socioeconomic status (Choney, Berryhill-Paapke, & Robbins, 1995; Garrett & Pichette, 2000; Herring, 1999). Each will be discussed in turn.

Acculturation is defined in Chapter 3 as the process of an individual's socialization into a different group's ways. Garcia and Ahler (1992) add a two-way dimension to acculturation in their definition: Acculturation is "the cultural change that occurs when two or more cultures are in persistent contact" (p. 24). Five levels of acculturation have been identified for Native Americans:

1. *Traditional*—They may or may not speak English, but generally speak and think in their native language; they hold only traditional values and beliefs and practice only traditional tribal customs and methods of worship.

2. *Marginal*—They may speak both the native language and English; they may not, however, fully accept the cultural heritage and practices of their tribal group nor fully identify with mainstream cultural values and behaviors.

3. *Bicultural*—They are generally accepted by the dominant society and their tribal society/nation and are simultaneously able to know, accept, and practice both mainstream values/behaviors and the traditional values and beliefs of their cultural heritage.

4. *Assimilated*—They are accepted by the dominant society; they embrace only mainstream cultural values, behaviors, and expectations.

5. *Pantraditional*—Assimilated Native Americans who have made a conscious choice to return to the "old ways." They are generally accepted by dominant society, but seek to embrace previously lost traditional cultural values, beliefs, and practices of their tribal heritage. Therefore, they may speak both English and their native tribal language. (Garrett & Pichette, 2000)

These five levels represent a continuum along which a Native American individual may fall.

Besides acculturation, and sometimes related to it, is the second factor in Indian acceptance of ethnicity, namely *geographic setting*. Native Americans live in a variety of settings—rural, urban, or reservation (Garrett & Garrett, 1994). It might be surprising to realize that approximately 50 percent of the Native American population resides in urban areas. Thus, the degree of traditionalism versus the degree of acculturation to mainstream American values and cultural standards for behavior is not universal because urban living can reduce traditionalism (Garrett & Garrett, 1994; Heinrich, Corbine, & Thomas, 1990; Thomason, 1991).

Finally, the *socioeconomic* dimension affects a Native person's experience of her or his ethnicity. Native Americans have been described as a group of persons facing enormous social problems. Only 52 percent of Native youth finish high school and only 4 percent graduate from college. The unemployment rates of Native Americans are three to 11 times greater than that of the general population. Seventy-five percent of the Native work force earns less than $7,000 per year. Forty-five percent of Native people live below the poverty level. Their arrest rates are three times those for African Americans, and their rate of alcoholism is double that of the general population (Heinrich et al., 1990). One in six Native adolescents has attempted suicide, a rate four times that of all other groups.

When compared with the rates for non-Native people, the fetal alcohol syndrome rates for Native people are 33 times higher, the incidence of tuberculosis is 7.4 times greater, and the incidence of diabetes is 6.8 times greater (Russell, 1997). Alcohol mortality is six times the rate for all other ethnic groups. Some of the possible challenges that Native people bring with them to the counseling process are evident (Russell, 1997).

THE TRIBAL NATION AND CULTURAL IDENTITY

Traditional Native people experience a special relationship with their tribe. In a very real sense, Native American individuals are extensions of their tribal nation—socially, emotionally, historically, and politically. For many Indian people, cultural identity is rooted in tribal membership, community, and heritage rather than in personal achievements, social or financial status, or acquired possessions. Many Native nations, such as the Cherokee, for example, are matriarchal/matrilineal or matriarchal/patrilineal, which means that children trace their heritage through the mother or grandmother, and the social structure of the tribe may place more emphasis on power held by women. However, there are those who follow patriarchal/patrilineal ways too (or other variations of gender dominance and tracing of family heritage). This pattern of heritage and social/political power, in turn, affects not only the social structure and functioning of the community, but also the structure and functioning of the family/clan. The extended family (at least three generations) and tribal group take precedence over all other affiliations.

The tribe is an interdependent system of people who perceive themselves to be part of the greater whole (i.e., the tribe) rather than to be a whole consisting of individual parts. This principle is expressed in traditional Native people judging themselves and their actions according to whether or not they are benefiting the tribal community and its continued harmonious functioning.

In mainstream American society, worth and status are based on "what you do" or "what you have achieved." For Native Americans, "Who you are is where you come from." Native Americans essentially believe that "If you know my family, clan, or tribe, then you know me." As a result, traditional Native people might be likely to describe some aspect of their family or tribal heritage when asked to talk about themselves.

FAMILY

It has been said that "about the most unfavorable moral judgment an Indian can pass on another person is to say, 'He acts as if he didn't have any relatives'" (DuBray, 1985, p. 36). In the majority culture, when two people meet for the first time, the popular conversational question is "What do you do?" In contrast, many Native people may ask, "Where do you come from? Who's your family? To whom do you belong? Who are your people?" The speaker's intent is to find out where she or he stands in relation to this new person and what commonality exists. In fact, this is a simple way of building bridges—or recognizing bridges that already exist but that are, as yet, unknown. Family may or may not consist of blood relatives. It is common practice in the Indian way, for instance, to claim a non-blood-related person as a relative, thereby welcoming him or her as a real family member. From that point on, that person *is* a relative, and that is that. After all, family can be a matter of both blood and spirit.

In the traditional way, the prevalence of cooperation and sharing in the spirit of community is essential for harmony and balance. It is not unusual for a Native child to be raised in several different households over time. This sharing of childrearing is generally not due to a lack of caring or responsibility, but is due to a Native value that it is both an obligation and a pleasure to share in raising and caring for the children in one's family. Grandparents, aunts, uncles, and other members of the community are all responsible for raising children, and they take this responsibility very seriously.

Native elders are the keepers of the sacred ways. They are protectors, mentors, teachers, and support-givers. Native communities honor their Indian elders, the "Keepers of the Wisdom," for their lifetime's worth of knowledge and experience. Elders have always played an important part in the continuance of the tribal community by functioning in the role of parent, teacher, community leader, and spiritual guide (Garrett & Garrett, 1997). To refer to an elder as Grandmother, Grandfather, Uncle, Aunt, "Old Woman," or "Old Man" is to refer to a very special relationship that exists with that elder, characterized by deep respect and admiration.

There is a very special kind of relationship between Indian elders and Indian children, based on mutual respect and caring as one moves through the Circle of Life, from birth to old age, from "being cared for" to "caring for," as Red Horse (1997) puts it. With increase in age comes an increase in the sacred obligation to family, clan, and tribe. Native American elders pass on to the children the notion that their own life force carries the spirits of their ancestors. With such an emphasis on connectedness, Native traditions revere children, not only as ones who will carry on the wisdom and traditions, but also as "little people" who are still very close to the spirit world and from whom there is much to learn. The following anecdote from Brendtro, Brokenleg, and Van Bockern (1990) illustrates the importance of being a caretaker within Native culture as a manifestation of family:

> In a conversation with his aging grandfather, a young Indian man asked, "Grandfather, what is the purpose of life?" After a long time in thought, the old man looked up and said, "Grandson, children are the purpose of life. We were once children and someone cared for us, and now it is our time to care." (p. 45)

Activity 7.3 invites readers to compare their cultural customs with those of Native peoples.

Surviving "History": A Story of Intergenerational Grief and Trauma

What does it mean to be Native in this day and age? The answer to this question begins with the influence of the historical context from which Native individuals and their families come. As such, it is important to consider the powerful influence of what many Native people refer to as "generational grief and trauma" and the effect it has had on Native worldview.

The story of the past 500 years is a story of loss for Native peoples. Deloria (1988) recounts, "When questioned by an anthropologist about what the Indians called America before the White man came, an Indian said simply, 'Ours'" (p. 166). Throughout U.S. history, mainstream American institutions such as government agencies, schools, and churches have made deliberate attempts to destroy the Native American institutions of family, clan, and tribal structure, religious belief systems and practices, customs, and traditional way of life (Deloria, 1988; Heinrich et al., 1990; Locust, 1988; Reyhner & Eder, 1992). Characterized by institutional racism and discrimination, the dominant culture's long history of opposition to Native cultures and attempts to assimilate Native people has had a long-lasting effect on Native peoples' cultures and ways of life (Deloria, 1988; Locust, 1988).

It was not until 1924 that the U.S. government recognized the citizenship of Native Americans—when they were no longer a threat to national expansion—in the Citizenship Act (Deloria, 1988). Native Americans were not granted religious

---

ACTIVITY 7.3

Comparing Your Assumptions

After reading the sections on Native cultural identity and on family, respond to the following questions:

What is your culture's common way of getting to know people when you meet them? (e.g., Do you ask about what they do or are interested in first, or about who their people are and their origins?)

What was your experience of being raised as a child? Was it largely with a nuclear group or with an extended community?

What is your and your culture's assumption about care for elders? Is it that it is a sacred obligation to be intimately involved in their welfare?

What is your culture's assumption about the connection with offspring? Is it that it is an intimate lifelong interdependence or that they are largely on their own once they reach adulthood?

How do you think your assumptions are similar to or different from traditional Native American ones?

---

freedom until 1978, when the American Indian Religious Freedom Act was passed. This act overturned the Indian Religious Crimes Code of 1889 and guaranteed Native people the Constitutional right to exercise their traditional religious practices for the first time in a century (Deloria, 1988; Loftin, 1989). Even today, the depiction of President Andrew Jackson on the U.S. $20 bill reminds many Native Americans of the betrayal by the government in 1838, when Jackson defied the Supreme Court by signing off on an Act that forced the removal of over 16,000 Cherokees from parts of North Carolina, South Carolina, Tennessee, and Georgia to the Oklahoma territory (M. T. Garrett, 1998). This movement of people has been called the Trail of Tears. In more recent times, massive efforts to "civilize" Native people through government-supported Christian boarding schools and the Relocation Programs of the 1950s added to their generational trauma and cultural discontinuity (Hirschfelder & Kriepe de Montano, 1993). These events have affected Native Americans psychologically, economically, and socially for generations. From both a historical and contemporary perspective, oppression is and continues to be a very real experience for Native people.

In the following quotation, a Navajo elder describes her first experience in boarding school at age seven, over 40 years ago. She was unable to speak any

English and had always lived on the reservation. Her narrative represents a vivid illustration of cultural genocide and a reminder of the soul wound that many Native clients might carry.

It was the first time I'd seen a brick building that was not a trading post. The ceilings were so high and the rooms so big and empty. It was so cold. There was no warmth. Not as far as "Brrr, I'm cold," but in a sense of emotional cold. Kind of an emptiness, when you're hanging onto your mom's skirt and trying hard not to cry. Then when you get up to your turn, she [the teacher] thumbprints the paper and she leaves and you watch her go out the big metal doors. The whole thing was cold. The doors were metal and they even had this big window with wires running through it. You watch your mama go down the sidewalk, actually it's the first time I seen a sidewalk, and you see her get into the truck and the truck starts moving and all the home smell goes with it. You see it all leaving.

Then the woman takes you by the hand and takes you inside and the first thing they do is take down your bun. The first thing they do is cut off your hair, and you been told your whole life that you never cut your hair recklessly because that is your life. And that's the first thing them women does is cut off your hair. And you see that long, black hair drop, and it's like they take out your heart and they give you this cold thing that beats inside. And now you're gonna be just like them. You're gonna be cold. You're never gonna be happy or have that warm feeling and attitude towards life anymore. That's what it feels like, like taking your heart out and putting in a cold river pebble.

When you go into the shower, you leave your squaw skirt and blouse right there at the shower door. When you come out, it's gone. You don't see it again. They cut your hair, now they take your squaw skirt. They take from the beginning. When you first walk in there, they take everything that you're about. They jerk it away from you. They don't ask how you feel about it. They never tell you anything. They never say what they're gonna do, why they're doing it. They barely speak to you. They take everything away from you. Then you think, mama must be whackers. She wants me to be like them? Every time you don't know what they're doing, they laugh at you. They yell at you. They jerk you around. It was never what I wanted to be. I never wanted to be like them. But my mom wanted me to be like them. As I got older, I found out that you don't have to be like them. You can have a nice world and have everything that mama wanted, but you don't have to be cold. (McLaughlin, 1994, pp. 47–48)

Current Social and Political Issues

Native people deal with a number of current social and political issues that create both problems and opportunities. This section examines matters of identity, tribal resources, treaty rights, religious freedom, mascots, gaming, and cultural preservation that provide a context for many of the struggles of Native people as a group.

IDENTITY

Indian people have mixed intertribally for countless generations. They have also mixed interracially, especially with European Americans and African Americans, for at least the last 500 years, resulting in many generations of mixed-blood Indian people (Russell, 1997). According to Russell, it has been estimated that at least 98 percent of the Native population is tribally mixed, while approximately 75 percent are also racially mixed. These days, the term "full blood" is used to refer to those Native people who consider themselves to be 100 percent descended from one tribe. However, more often than not, "full blood" probably has more to do with spiritual and traditional lifestyle than physiological heritage, per se. The continuing dilution of blood quantum and the survival of urban Indians are ongoing identity issues for Native people. Blood quantum causes much division and controversy in Indian communities, and in some cases, leads to social and economic inequities. Although some tribes have modified their enrollment criteria to incorporate members who possess heritage from more than one tribe, no tribe allows enrollment in more than one tribe (see Box 7.1). The reality is that some people are going to be excluded who should be included, and some people will be included who should be excluded.

Like some other ethnic groups, an indicator of Native identity and traditionalism can be the degree to which one is fluent in a Native language. For some, English may have been learned as a second language. That fact itself can tell a great deal about a person's process of enculturation, including the number of concepts he or she may think of or express differently in the first language.

Names may also say something about a Native person's identity. Native people often have Anglo names, due to attempts to be more mainstream or due to marriage. Some may have two names, one mainstream, often Anglo, and one traditional, often based on a traditional tribal family surname or ceremonial rite of passage, depending on the nation. For many Native people of an older generation, both adoption and/or the boarding school experience may have had

---

BOX 7.1   The Indian Card

As a result of the treaty history and laws of the federal government, Native people are the only ethnic minority group in the U.S. that actually have to prove their cultural identity through blood quantum and carry an "Indian card" to prove that they are what they say they are. For some Native people this is yet another form of oppression, while for others it is just a normal part of everyday life and, for some, a source of pride in tribal membership.

long-lasting effects on identity; among many things, their original tribal name may have been changed at an early age.

TRIBAL RESOURCES

When considering tribal resources, it is first important to understand that from a Native perspective, the land is the most important environmental and spiritual resource. Although most of the Native population resides in urban areas, reservations, which are lands set aside by the federal government because of treaty agreements, continue to be the primary center of Native traditionalism and cultural preservation. There are over 311 federally recognized reservations in the United States, totaling approximately 55 million acres. However, it should be noted that 11 million acres (20 percent) within reservation boundaries are owned by non-Indians.

The land base provides many Native nations with an array of resources for the benefit of the people, and also with a number of challenges about how to maintain, protect, or expand that land base. According to Russell (1997), there are 44 million acres in range and grazing, 5.3 million acres of commercial forest, and 2.5 million acres of crop area. Native lands make up 4 percent of the U.S. oil and gas reserves, 40 percent of the U.S. uranium deposits, and 30 percent of western coal reserves. Finally, the land is worth $2 billion in trust royalty payments. It is ironic that some of the most seemingly desolate reservations have become valuable resources because of minerals, other environmental assets, and locale. Many tribes are locked in heated legal battles with the government and private interests to maintain and protect treaty rights to their homelands and sacred sites that are continually being encroached upon by outside interests.

TREATY RIGHTS

As mentioned previously, another issue currently faced by many tribes/nations is that of protecting treaty rights. Two controversial examples are the fishing rights of Native people in the Pacific Northwest and in the Great Lakes area of Michigan, Minnesota, and Wisconsin. In both instances, tribes have resorted to "fish-ins" that defy state law, but that are in accordance with Indian treaty rights with the U.S. government. One of the most controversial topics to hit the media in recent times is the whaling rights of tribes in the Pacific Northwest. Strong opposition has come from state agencies, non-Native fishers, conservationists, and environmentalists and has only added to the strain already placed upon tribes by an increased influx of people, increased industry, and increased recreation in many of those areas.

RELIGION AND SACRED SITES

One of the unique features of traditional Native American religions is the emphasis on place rather than on time. What this denotes is the importance of the land and existing environment as a source of spiritual power and truths.

In that vein, it is important to discuss the social and political issues Native people currently face concerning spiritual matters.

Religious Freedom

As mentioned in an earlier section, passage of the American Indian Religious Freedom Act of 1978 guaranteed religious freedom for Native people in the United States for the first time in a century. However, two U.S. Supreme Court rulings have severely limited the religious rights that the law was enacted to protect. First, in the 1988 *Lying, Secretary of Agriculture, et al. v. Northwest Indian Cemetery Protective Association, et al.* decision, the Supreme Court ruled in favor of allowing the U.S. Forest Service to pave a stretch of road through an area that was held sacred by the Karok, Yurok, and Tolowa tribes of northern California. This decision was made in spite of the testimony of the U.S. Forest Service's expert witness, who concluded that the road would destroy the religion of those three tribes because it would desecrate sacred ground and construction would disturb the natural balance of the ecosystem in that area.

Second, in *Employment Division of Oregon v. Smith* (1990), the Supreme Court denied Alfred Smith, a Native drug rehabilitation counselor, unemployment benefits because he had been discharged from his position for "misconduct." Alfred had attended a meeting of the Native American Church where he used peyote during prayer. Peyote, a sacred hallucinogenic cactus "button," is used in the Native American Church as a sacrament in much the same way that the Catholic Church uses wine during holy communion. The Court failed to recognize and uphold the use of peyote as an integral part of that Native spiritual tradition. So alarmed were both the Native and Judeo-Christian communities that coalitions were formed to restore religious freedoms through legislative means, and those efforts are continuing to this day.

Sacred Sites

Traditional Native practices are inseparably bound to the land and natural formations that exist in whatever geographic location that tribe occupies. Native people have sacred places and go to these sacred places to pray, fast, seek visions, conduct ceremonies, receive guidance from spirit guides, and teach youth the traditional ways. Acts such as spraying and logging trees, damming rivers, fencing, building roads, mining, operating hydroelectric plants, constructing urban housing, tourism, and vandalism violate sacred sites. Unfortunately, many of the sacred sites revered by Native people are not under their control; instead, they are under the control of federal agencies intent on using the land for tourism development, clear-cutting, and uranium mining. Many of the sites that are under government control are cornerstones of Native religious traditions and cannot be replaced. Therefore, tribes across the country are pursuing legal efforts to protect and preserve not only the sacred sites on which their culture is based, but also their very ways of life from generations past.

Repatriation and Reburial

The ancient graves of Native people are among the many sacred sites disturbed or destroyed by erosion and flooding, plowing, urban development, road building, land clearing, logging, and vandalism. Perhaps worst of all has been the desecration of Native graves by pothunters and vandals seeking to loot those graves for objects that are valued in national and international markets. It has been estimated that grave desecration and looting of Native graves reached its peak in the 1980s. Outraged by such disregard for and violations of sacred areas, Native American nations demanded the immediate return of all that was rightfully theirs, including skeletal remains, burial goods, and sacred objects. In the end, Native people have persevered by facilitating the passage of critical legislation that now protects Native gravesites from looting and provides Native people with legal means for reclaiming both remains and sacred objects. Many of these remains and objects have been ceremonially returned to their original sites, when possible, under the careful guidance and blessing of tribal elders and medicine people.

MASCOT ISSUES

As many tribes and nations continue to move toward increased sovereignty and consequent pride in their ethnicity, land and natural resources are only part of the concern. The mascot issue has been a constant source of controversy between Natives and non-Natives. Sports teams and schools across the country have been challenged to do away with stereotypical, racist images of Native people as mascots. A few examples include the Atlanta Braves, the Washington Redskins, and the Cleveland Indians. For the most part, these images tend to fall into one of two categories: the hostile, warlike Indian or the dopey, clown-like figure with headdress, big nose, red skin, big lips, and other stereotypical features. Native people in many places demand the same respect, both socially and legally, that is paid to other cultural groups in the United States.

GAMING

These days, perceptions of Native people are largely dominated by the issue of gaming. Casinos and bingo halls have sprung up like wildfire in Indian country. In most cases, what that means for Native nations is increased capital in a short period of time and the challenges that accompany it. The popular perception by non-Native people is that Indians are becoming wealthy from the per capita checks—the varying amounts of money that are distributed to tribal members as corporate partners, more or less, in tribally owned casinos and bingo halls. In fact, for many tribes, the per capita amounts are small, are usually distributed once or twice per year, and in most cases, have done little to alleviate already high rates of unemployment for Native people across the country. In true form to Native humor, Northrup (1997) reports that when asked, "What is the unemployment rate on the reservation?" he replies, "I don't know, that's not my job" (p. 215). He goes on to comment, "Gambling has done a lot for us in the last decade . . . it has brought our Rez unemployment rate from 80 percent all the way down to 50 percent" (p. 215). Although the gaming industry has become a major source of income and economic development for many Native nations, the challenge at this point is how to maintain that investment and plan for the future so that the growth continues and continues to benefit the people who, in many cases, have started to pull themselves out of decades of having nothing at all.

CULTURAL PRESERVATION

Increased sovereignty for many Native nations also means increased control over the way that cultural resources are maintained and preserved. In many Native nations and communities across the country, huge efforts are being made to preserve culture by developing programs both in and outside the schools to teach Native youth such things as traditional arts and crafts, the language, ceremonies and prayers, songs and chants, and dance. Many of these programs began as remedial efforts in residential youth treatment centers and sobriety programs for all ages. As the efficacy of such programs has become evident, their popularity has grown.

This cultural appreciation impulse lies in distinct contrast to the previously accepted mainstream notion of only one or two generations ago that "civilizing" Indians (to become more European American) was essential. That "civilizing" was done through mandated, largely Christian, government-supported Indian boarding schools whose primary objective was to strip Native youth of their cultural Indian foundation.

Although it is evident that Native people still face many difficulties whose origins lie in the cultural genocide of the past and the resulting cycle of oppression and poverty for hundreds of years, winds of cultural change are crossing the land. With the surge in cultural pride, one of the biggest challenges for Native people today is to eliminate in-fighting among various social or political entities both within and between nations and to find a common vision that will carry the people safely and successfully into the future generations.

Values: Native Ways

Several authors have described common core values that characterize Native traditionalism across tribal nations. Some of these Native traditional values are the importance of community contribution, sharing, acceptance, cooperation, harmony and balance, noninterference, extended family, attention to nature, immediacy of time, awareness of the relationship, and a deep respect for elders

(Dufrene, 1990; J. T. Garrett, 2001; M. T. Garrett, 1996, 1998, 1999b; Garrett & Garrett, 1996, 2003; Heinrich et al., 1990; Herring, 1999; Plank, 1994; Red Horse, 1997). Taken together, these traditional values represent the importance of honoring, through harmony and balance, what Native people believe to be a very sacred connection with the energy of life. This is the basis for the traditional Native worldview and spirituality that crosses tribal nations. Most of these values contrast significantly with those of the dominant American culture, making culture clash inevitable. Table 7.1 compares these two sets of values. A few of the dominant Native values, namely humility, generosity, patience, time, being, spirituality, harmony, purpose, relation, and the sacredness of the eagle feather, are highlighted in the following sections.

HUMILITY

Boasting of one's accomplishments and loud behavior that attracts attention to oneself are discouraged in the traditional way. Self-absorption and self-importance are seen as bringing disharmony upon oneself and one's family. In the Circle of Life, the group must take precedence over the individual. And, as discussed earlier, the wisdom of age takes precedence over youth, although age does not make anyone better or more worthy than anyone else. Many times, a traditional Native person may drop his or her head and eyes, or at least be careful not to look into the eyes of another, as a sign of respect for any elder or other honored person. No one is worthy of staring into the eyes of an elder or looking into the spirit of that honored person. This deferential behavior is also an act signifying that a person does not view himself or herself as better than anyone else.

Table 7.1 Comparison of Cultural Values and Expectations

Traditional Native American	Contemporary Mainstream American
Harmony with nature	Power over nature
Cooperation	Competition
Group needs more important than individual needs	Personal goals considered important
Privacy and noninterference; try to control self, not others	Need to control and affect others
Self-discipline both in body and mind	Self-expression and self-disclosure
Participation after observation (only when certain of ability)	Trial-and-error learning, new skills practiced until they are mastered

Traditional Native American	Contemporary Mainstream American
Explanation according to nature	Scientific explanation for everything
Reliance on extended family	Reliance on experts
Emotional relationships valued	Concerned mostly with facts
Patience encouraged (allow others to go first)	Aggressive and competitive
Humility	Fame and recognition; winning
Win once, let others win also	Win first prize all of the time
Follow the old ways	Climb the ladder of success; importance of progress and change
Discipline distributed among many; no one person takes blame	Blame one person at cost to others
Physical punishment rare	Physical punishment accepted
Present-time focus	Future-time focus
Time is always with us	Clock-watching
Present goals considered important; future accepted as it comes	Plan for future and how to get ahead
Encourage sharing freely and keeping only enough to satisfy present needs	Private property; encourage acquisition of material comfort and saving for the future
Speak softly, at a slower rate	Speak louder and faster
Avoid singling out the listener	Address listener directly (by name)
Interject less	Interrupt frequently
Use fewer "encouraging signs" (uh-huh, head nodding)	Use verbal encouragement
Delayed response to auditory messages	Use immediate response
Nonverbal communication	Verbal skills highly prized

GENEROSITY

Traditional Native views concerning property accentuate the underlying belief that whatever belongs to the individual also belongs to the group, and vice versa. It should come as no surprise to see Indian people sharing and/or giving their "possessions" away to others in certain circumstances, such as during Giveaway ceremonies practiced by many nations. Generosity is considered a sign of wisdom and humility.

PATIENCE

In the Native worldview, everything has its place. Very often, it is simply a matter of time before one recognizes where and how things fit together. In Native traditions, there is a sacred design to the world in which humans live, a design to the process of life itself. And, very often, it is not a matter of whether or not "things" fall into place, but whether or not humans' capacity for *awareness and understanding of "things"* falls into place. It is, therefore, important to be able to learn through careful observation, listening, and patience, as well as by asking questions or thinking things through. Everything offers humans a valuable lesson, from all of their surroundings to each of their experiences. It takes time and a special kind of willingness or openness to receive all of the lessons that are offered throughout life. Many Native elders will share with younger people how important it is to talk less so you can hear more, for example.

TIME

In the traditional Indian view, humans do not always have to live by the clock. Mother Earth has her own unique rhythms that signal the beginnings and endings of things. One need only observe and listen quietly to know when it is time. So-called Indian time says that things begin when they are ready, and things end when they are finished. For example, a ceremony or gathering might be set to begin at sunrise, rather than a specific "clock time," and end whenever sufficient time has been spent to complete what needs to be done. In that sense, the American Indian view of time is similar to that of rural people all over the world, where tasks and natural rhythms dictate time.

BEING

Native tradition ("the Medicine Way") emphasizes a unique sense of "being" that allows one to live in accord with the natural flow of life energy. *Being* says, "It's enough just to be; our purpose in life is to develop the inner self in relation to everything around us." Being receives much of its power from connectedness. Belonging and connectedness lie at the very heart of where Indian people came from, who they are, and to whom they belong. True "being" requires that individuals know and experience their connections, and that they honor their relations with all their heart. So, for many traditional Native people, the relationship with someone is much more important than any personal accomplishment. Consequently, the strength of a person's inner peace and presence in the here-and-now would say more to a traditional Native person than anything else.

SPIRITUALITY

As a result of the historical context in which Western religions have so influenced Native communities and nations, it should come as no surprise that Native people may ascribe to and practice any number of religious belief systems in place of, or even along with, traditional tribal systems. Overall, however, it is important to understand traditional Native spirituality as a basic frame of reference.

Different tribal languages have different words or ways of referring to the idea of honoring one's sense of connection. However, the meaning of honoring connection is similar across nations. It refers to the belief that human beings exist on Mother Earth to be helpers and protectors of life. In Native communities, it is not uncommon, for example, to hear people use the term "caretaking" to refer to that which is a desired way of life. Therefore, from the perspective of a traditionalist, to see oneself as a caretaker is to accept responsibility for the gift of life by taking good care of that gift, the gift of life that others have received, and the surrounding beauty of the world in which one lives (J. T. Garrett, 2001).

The spiritual beliefs of any individual Native American depend on a number of factors, including her or his level of acculturation (traditional, marginal, bicultural, assimilated, pan-traditional), geographic region, family structure, religious influences, and tribal traditions (Garrett & Pichette, 2000; LaFromboise, Coleman, & Gerton, 1993). However, it is possible to generalize, to some extent, about a number of basic beliefs characterizing Native American traditionalism and spirituality across tribal nations. Box 7.2 lists a number of basic Native American spiritual and traditional beliefs. This list of beliefs from Native American spirituality crosses tribal boundaries. It is, by no means, a comprehensive list. It does, however, provide insight into some of the assumptions that may be held by a "traditional" Native client.

In order to better understand what it means to "walk in step" according to Native American spirituality, it is important to discuss four basic cultural elements: medicine, harmony, relation, and vision (Garrett & Wilbur, 1999).

Medicine: Everything Is Alive

In many Native American tribal languages, there is no word for religion. Spiritual practices are an integral part of every aspect of daily life, which is necessary for the harmony and balance, or wellness, of individual, family, clan, and community (Garrett & Garrett, 2002; Garrett, Garrett, & Brotherton, 2001). Healing and worship are considered to be one and the same. For Native American people, the concept of health and wellness is not only a physical state

> **BOX 7.2   Native American Beliefs**
>
> 1. There is a single higher power known as Creator, Great Creator, Great Spirit, or Great One, among other names. (This Being is sometimes referred to in gendered form but does not necessarily exist as one particular gender or another.) There are also lesser beings known as "spirit beings" or "spirit helpers."
>
> 2. Plants and animals, like humans, are part of the spirit world. The spirit world exists side by side with, and intermingles with, the physical world. Moreover, the spirit existed in the spirit world before it came into a physical body and will exist after the body dies.
>
> 3. Human beings are made up of a spirit, mind, and body. The mind, body, and spirit are all interconnected; therefore, illness affects the mind and spirit as well as the body.
>
> 4. Wellness is harmony in body, mind, and spirit; unwellness is disharmony in mind, body, and spirit.
>
> 5. Natural unwellness is caused by the violation of a sacred social or natural law of Creation (e.g., participating in a sacred ceremony while under the influence of alcohol, drugs, or having had sex within four days of the ceremony).
>
> 6. Unnatural unwellness is caused by conjuring (witchcraft) by those with destructive intentions.
>
> 7. Each of us is responsible for our own wellness by keeping ourselves attuned to self, relations, environment, and universe.
>
> SOURCE: From Locust (1988, pp. 317–318).

but a spiritual one as well. "Medicine," as a Native concept, exists as part of the very essence of our being, or life force, that exists in all creatures on Mother Earth (Garrett & Garrett, 1996). In the traditional way, medicine can consist of physical remedies, such as herbs, teas, and poultices for physical ailments, but medicine is simultaneously something much more than a pill taken to cure illness, get rid of pain, or correct a physiological malfunction. Medicine is everywhere. It is that which gives inner power.

Harmony: Everything Has Purpose

The second cultural element of Native American spirituality is harmony. Every living organism has a reason for being. Traditional Native Americans look upon life as a gift from the Creator. As such, it is to be treated with the utmost care, out of respect for the giver. This means living in a humble way and giving thanks for all of the gifts that one receives every day, no matter how big or small. Harmony is also represented by numbers. Native American spirituality often places great emphasis on the numbers four and seven. The number four represents the spirit of each of the directions—east, south, west, and north—usually depicted in a circle. The number seven represents the same four directions as well as the upper world (sky), lower world (Earth), and center (often referring to the heart, or sacred fire) to symbolize universal harmony and balance (visualized as a sphere). In the traditional way, Native people seek to understand the lessons offered to them by giving thanks to each of the four directions for the wisdom, guidance, strength, and clarity that they receive. Not every tribe practices the directions in this way, but almost all tribes have some representation of the four directions as a circular symbol of the harmony and balance of mind, body, and spirit with the natural environment (and spirit world; see Figure 7.1).

Relation: All Things Are Connected

Central to Native American spiritual traditions is the third cultural element of Native American spirituality: the importance of "relation" as a total way of existing in the world. The concept of family extends to brothers and sisters in the animal world, the plant world, and the mineral world, in addition to Mother Earth and Father Sky, to name some examples. Respect for medicine also means practicing respect for the interconnection that humans share. Across tribal nations, certain natural or social laws must be observed, out of respect for relation. These often restrict personal conduct in relation to such things as death, incest, the female menstrual cycle, witchcraft, certain animals, certain natural phenomena, certain foods, marrying into one's own clan, and strict observance of ceremonial protocol (Locust, 1988). A general rule of thumb in Native tradition is that you

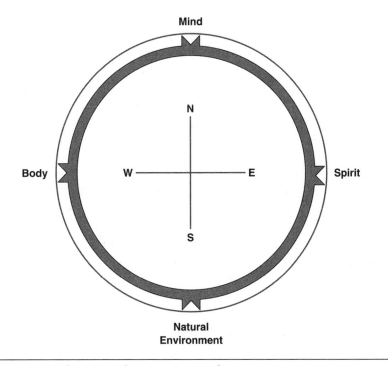

Figure 7.1   Medicine Circle Representing the Four Directions

(a) never take more than you need, (b) give thanks for what you have or what you receive, (c) take great care to use all of what you do have, and (d) give away what you do not need (or what someone else may need more than you). An example of this tradition is put into practice when a spiritual person searches for particular herbs or medicines in the natural environment and must do so following these basic tenets and with the right intent in order to be successful.

Vision: Embrace the Medicine of Every Living Being

The fourth element of Native American spirituality is vision. Understanding one's vision is understanding the direction of one's path as a caretaker moving to the rhythm of the sacred heartbeat. One of the functions of ceremonial practice is to reaffirm one's sense of connection with that which is sacred. By contrast, a major tenet of American mainstream ideology is "life, liberty, and the pursuit of happiness." From a traditional Native perspective, a corollary would be "life, love, and the pursuit of harmony." As Black Elk, Oglala Lakota Medicine Man, referred to the many trials and tribulations of his life journey, "The good road and the road of difficulties, you have made me cross; and where they cross, the place is holy" (cited in M. T. Garrett, 1998, p. 85).

Across tribal nations, many different ceremonies represent this vision of the sacred. Among the various ceremonies are the sweat lodge, vision quest, clearing-way ceremony, blessing-way ceremony, pipe ceremony, sunrise ceremony, and Sun dance (Heinrich et al., 1990; Lake, 1991). Those ceremonies are used for healing, giving thanks, celebrating, clearing the way, and blessing (Lake, 1991).

EAGLE FEATHERS AND EAGLE MEDICINE

The eagle feather represents the fourth major value shared among Native people. Eagle feathers are considered to be infinitely sacred among Native Americans. The eagle feather represents duality in existence. It tells the story of life by symbolizing harmony and balance through which life has been able to persist. It tells of the many dualities or opposites that exist in the Circle of Life, such as light and dark, male and female, substance and shadow, summer and winter, life and death, peace and war (Garrett & Myers, 1996). The eagle feather has both light and dark colors, dualities and opposites. Though one can argue which of the colors is most beautiful or most valuable, the truth is that both colors come from the same feather, both are true, both are connected, and it takes both to fly (Garrett & Garrett, 1996). The colors are opposite, but they are part of the same truth. The importance of the feather lies not in which color is most beautiful, but in finding out and accepting what the purpose of the feather as a whole may be. In other words, there is no such thing as keeping the mountains and getting rid of the valleys; they are one and the same, and they exist because of one another.

The eagle feather teaches about the Rule of Opposites, about everything being divided into two ways. The more one is caught up in the physical, represented by the direction of the West, the more one has to go in the opposite direction, the East or the spiritual, to achieve balance. And it works the other way too—you can't just focus on the spiritual to the exclusion of the physical. You need harmony in all four directions.

Native traditionalists refer to "Eagle Medicine," which represents a state of being that is achieved through diligence, understanding, awareness, and completion of "tests of initiation" such as the vision quest or other demanding life experiences (Garrett & Osborne, 1995). Highly respected elder status is associated with Eagle Medicine and the power of connectedness and truth. It is through experience and patience that this medicine is earned over a lifetime. And, it is through understanding and choice that it is honored. There is an old anecdote that probably best illustrates the lessons of the eagle feather by reminding us about the power of a balanced perspective: Once, while acting as a guide for a hunting expedition, an Indian had lost the way home. One of the men with him said, "You're lost, chief." The Indian guide replied, "I'm not lost; my tipi is lost."

Communication Style

Native interaction style especially emphasizes nonverbal communication over verbal communication. Moderation in speech and avoidance of direct eye contact are nonverbal communicators of respect for the listener. They are used especially if one is communicating with a respected elder or anyone in a position of authority (M. T. Garrett, 1996). Careful listening and observation are used to understand more of what is meant and less of what is actually said. Storytelling is commonly used to express feelings, beliefs, and the importance of experience (Garrett & Garrett, 1997). Oral recitation is common, and listeners are expected to be silent, patient, and reflective.

In an attempt to be respectful of interpersonal harmony, traditional Indian people practice self-discipline through silence, modesty, and patience. Direct confrontation is avoided because it disrupts the harmony and balance that are essential to keeping good relations. It is believed that there are more effective ways to deal with conflict and dissatisfaction. Cooperation and sharing, as a reflection of harmony, are important parts of interacting with others.

By contrast, individuals in the dominant American culture are rewarded for being outgoing and "assertive." Such behaviors as asking questions, interrupting, speaking for others, telling others what to do, or arguing are fairly common in mainstream Western society. These behaviors severely contradict what traditional Native people have been taught are respectful and appropriate ways of interacting with others (M. T. Garrett, 1995). As such, they parallel some of the East and Southeast Asian norms that are discussed in Chapter 6.

INDIAN HUMOR

One element of Native communication that is worth mentioning is the use of humor. Contrary to the stereotypical belief that Indian people are solemn, stoic figures, Indian people love to laugh (Garrett & Garrett, 1994; Maples et al., 2001). Indeed, humor is a critical part of the culture, especially around mealtime. A transformation occurs when Native Americans come together around food—everyone is laughing, cutting up, sharing side-splitting stories, and teasing each other. Many tribal oral traditions emphasize important life lessons through the subtle humor expressed in the stories. Often in the stories, the arrogant, manipulative, vain, clown-like figure of Rabbit, Possum, Coyote, or Raven learns a hard lesson in humility, much to the amusement of others (M. T. Garrett, 1998; Garrett & Garrett, 1996; Herring, 1994). Laughter plays a very important role in the continued survival of the tribal communities. After all, laughter relieves stress and creates an atmosphere of sharing and connect- edness. As George Good Striker, Blackfoot elder, puts it, "Humor is the WD-40 of healing" (cited in M. T. Garrett, 1998, p. 137).

Now that the nature of traditional forms of everyday Native communication and interaction have been explored, this chapter turns to a discussion of con- temporary interventions and treatment modalities involved in culturally alert counseling with this population.

Assessment and Intervention With Native Peoples

The tension that is described in Chapter 1, namely playing back and forth between a cultural and individual understanding of clients, must be reiterated here. In order to work most effectively with Native Americans, it is important to understand the nature of the cultural experience from which they come, but also to remember how important it is to see the uniqueness of each and every client. The cultural dimension, which is emphasized here, allows the counselor to better conceptualize current issues in a cultural context and select methods of approaching that client and issue(s) so that cultural values, beliefs, practices, and experiences are used as strengths and valuable resources for the client.

When working with most Native American clients, counselors should attend to two early assessment factors: (1) assessing the extent to which the process of acculturation has affected the client's cultural identity, and (2) understanding the influence of oppression on her or his experience and presenting issues (Lee, 2001, 2002; Robinson & Howard-Hamilton, 2000). These two factors are impor- tant when working with all nondominant cultures. This section, therefore, begins with a discussion of issues of acculturation and oppression. Then it pre- sents the counseling implications of cultural traditions, spirituality, values about opposites and balance, communication style, and humor.

ASSESSING IDENTITY, FAMILY, AND ACCULTURATION

A first step in the counseling relationship, and a sign of respect, is to find out from which tribe the client comes and whether she or he is directly affiliated with that tribe (federal, state, and/or community recognition). It is not the job of a counselor to pass judgment on who is Indian and who is not. Thus, a counselor should not ask a Native client "how much Indian" she or he is, or relate personal stories of Indian heritage in his or her family as a way of connecting with that client. That is often a quick way to lose a Native person's receptivity and trust. If a client says that he or she is Native, then a counselor must assume that it is so. This acceptance of client self-report is a way to understand that client without having to get into the painful (and sometimes irrelevant) politics of categorization. More important, it gives the counselor insight into that person's perception of her experience and place in the world.

When working with a Native client, it is important to get a sense of that person's level of acculturation. This sense can be gotten by the counselor informally assessing the client's (a) values (traditional, marginal, bicultural, assimilated, pan-traditional), (b) geographic origin/residence (reservation, rural, urban), and (c) tribal affiliation (tribal structure, customs, beliefs). For further discussion of formal and informal assessment of Native American acculturation, see Garrett and Pichette (2000).

Both verbal and nonverbal cues will give counselors a good sense of a Native American client's level of acculturation (Garrett & Garrett, 1994). If questions remain, it is important to pose them in a respectful, unobtrusive way. Box 7.3 provides some examples of general leads intended to respectfully elicit important culturally relevant information.

To further determine acculturation and subsequent worldview, the counselor should gather information on the family history and structure, as well as on community of origin versus community of choice. Counselors must avoid making assumptions about the cultural identity of Native American clients without gathering further information about both the internal and external experience of that person. As mentioned earlier, one cannot assume because a person "looks Indian" that he or she is traditional in his or her cultural and spiritual ways, or

---

BOX 7.3   Counselor Leads for Assessing Native Identity and Acculturation

Where do you come from?

Tell me about your family.

What tribe/nation are you? Tell me a little bit about that.

Tell me about you as a person, culturally and spiritually.

Tell me how you identify yourself culturally.

Tell me how your culture/spirituality plays into how you live your life.

Tell me about your life as you see it, past, present, or future.

that because a person "does not look Indian," he or she is not traditional. Instead, it is important to explore the meaning of the core values and beliefs that characterize what it means to be Native for any given client.

RECOGNIZING THE INFLUENCE OF OPPRESSION

Given both the historical and current social and political issues facing Native people, an ongoing issue in counseling most Native clients is trust versus mistrust, as it is with many oppressed peoples. The counselor must therefore ask herself or himself, "What can I do to create and maintain trust with a Native client?"

It may be time well spent to bring up the topic of oppression with the client, asking her or him to relate experiences that have had an impact on her or his life for better or for worse. Counselors can ask where the client is from, and likewise, where his or her family is from as well. Counselors might further ask what are some of the experiences across generations that have affected the client and helped to shape how she or he sees the world. Counselors should specifically inquire about the ways family and intergenerational history might be playing into what has brought the client in for services. By educating themselves about the history of tribes from which Native clients come, counselors can better understand the impact of institutional racism and acculturation, as well as the meaning of the Native American experience for any given client.

EXAMINING CULTURE CLASH AND USING TRADITIONS

Cultural traditions can be addressed as part of counseling. For Native people, there is great potential for cultural conflicts due to a clash of their values with those of the larger society. Native traditions contrast with the mainstream American values of self-promotion, saving for the future, domination of others, accomplishment, competition and aggression, individualism and the nuclear family, mastery over nature, a time orientation toward living for the future, a preference for scientific explanations, time-consciousness, winning, and reverence for youth (M. T. Garrett, 1995, 1999a, 1999b). Therefore, exploration of cultural conflicts itself may be an important goal for counseling.

Native clients can be encouraged to talk about the meaning of family, clan, or tribe as a way of exploring worldview, especially in light of intergenerational differences or the effects of oppression or presenting issues. Once again, as mentioned above, counselors must ask themselves, "What can I do to create and maintain trust with a Native client and create a deeper understanding of his or her individual needs?" Counselors should think about some of the traditional Native values, beliefs, experiences, and traditions related so far in this chapter. They should ask themselves which of these their client holds and in what ways they are played out in his or her life. Further, counselors should consider how to build on their knowledge of these values, beliefs, experiences, and traditions to show understanding, develop rapport, and matching interventions. Finally,

Native clients can be helped to use their traditions as a source of strength for working on life issues. Methods for helping clients use cultural traditions as a source of strength are presented in Chapter 16.

ACKNOWLEDGING SPIRITUALITY

Spirituality can have implications for counseling intervention. A counselor must first remind herself or himself that there are a variety of spiritual traditions and customs that Natives can be allied with. Native spirituality manifests itself in many different forms, such as traditional tribal ways, Christian traditions, or the Native American Church.

It may be important to let the client tell you what she or he needs in terms of spiritual support or ceremony and how that might be best achieved within the context of counseling. With a client who seems to have more traditional values and beliefs, it may be particularly helpful to suggest that the family or a medicine person participate in the process to support the client as she or he moves through important personal transitions and subsequent personal cleansing. It should be noted that a general understanding of Native American spirituality does not prepare counselors to participate in or conduct Native ceremonies as part of the counseling process (Matheson, 1996). That is the responsibility of those who are trained as Native medicine persons and who also can serve as an important resource to counselors working with Native clients.

USING THE RULE OF OPPOSITES AND BALANCE

Another counseling implication lies in the Rule of Opposites. An understanding of the Rule of Opposites is essential for working with Native American clients who may be experiencing dissonance in their lives. They might perceive such dissonance in a much different way than might majority culture clients. Given the understanding that from the Native worldview, everything has meaning and purpose, a goal of counseling can be to help Native clients discover their purpose, examine their assumptions, seek an awareness of universal and personal truths, and make choices that allow them to exist in a state of harmony and balance within the Circle of Life. Talking with the client about his or her powerful cultural symbols, such as the eagle feather, and what they represent to that particular client may open a dialogue that will provide much insight into current issues, internal and external resources, and necessary approaches. Such cultural symbols provide insight into potential therapeutic goals for achieving harmony and balance among the four directions—mind, body, spirit, and natural environment.

COMMUNICATION

Once the counselor has some general information concerning the client's cultural identity, spiritual ways, and specific needs, he or she has a better understanding of what may or may not be appropriate with and for the client. Table 7.2 provides culturally alert communication recommendations for working with a traditional Native client (M. T. Garrett, 1999b; Garrett & Pichette, 2000).

Table 7.2   Communication Guidelines for Working With Traditional Native Americans

1.	**Greeting.** For traditional Native Americans, a gentle handshake is the proper greeting. Sometimes, just a word of greeting or head nod is sufficient. To use a firm handshake can be interpreted as an aggressive show of power and a personal insult. It may be important to follow, rather than lead, the client in manner of greeting.
2.	**Hospitality.** Given the traditional emphasis on generosity, kindness, and "gifting" as a way of honoring the relationship, hospitality is an important part of Native American life. Therefore, it is helpful to be able to offer the Native client a beverage or snack as a sign of good relation. In the traditional way, to not offer hospitality to a visitor or guest is to bring shame on oneself and one's family.
3.	**Silence.** In the traditional way, when two people meet, very little may be said between them during the initial moments of the encounter. Quiet time at the beginning of a session is an appropriate way to transition into the therapeutic process by giving both counselor and client a chance to orient themselves to the situation, get in touch with themselves, and experience the presence of the other person. This brief time (perhaps a couple of minutes or so) can be nonverbal, non-interactive time that allows the client to be at ease. This is an important show of respect, understanding, and patience.
4.	**Space.** Taking care to respect physical space is an extension of the principle that one need not always fill relational space with words. In Native tradition, both the physical form and the space between the physical is sacred. In counseling, it is important to respect the physical space of the client by not sitting too close and not sitting directly across from the client, which allows scrutiny of the other. A more comfortable arrangement, traditionally, is sitting together side-by-side in two different chairs. The burning of sage, cedar, or sweet grass (a method of spatial cleansing known as "smudging") is customary but should only be done at the request or with permission of the Native client.
5.	**Eye Contact.** Native American clients with traditional values (and possibly those who are marginal or bicultural) may tend to avert their eyes as a sign of respect. To subtly match this level of eye contact is respectful and shows an understanding of the client's way of being. The eyes are considered to be the pathway to the spirit; therefore, to consistently look someone in the eye is to show a level of entitlement or aggression. It is good to glance at someone every once in a while, but listening, in the traditional way, is something that happens with the ears and the heart.

6.	**Intention.** Trust is one of the biggest issues in the counseling relationship for many Native clients. This should come as no surprise given the history of broken promises and exploitation experienced by all tribal nations. Typically, a Native client will "read" the counselor's nonverbals fairly quickly in order to determine whether the counselor is someone to be trusted or not. Therefore, counselors can focus on honoring the mental space between counselor and client by seeking to offer respect and humility in the counseling process. Acceptance by the counselor means not trying to control or influence the client. This is considered "bad medicine."
7.	**Collaboration.** In counseling, more traditional Native clients may welcome (or even expect) the counselor to offer helpful suggestions or alternatives. From a traditional perspective, respect for choice is important, but healing is a collaborative process. Therefore, offer suggestions without offering directions. There is a difference between encouraging and pushing. With traditional Native American clients, actions will always speak louder than words.

HUMOR

While humor is one of the important Native coping mechanisms, it should be used only if the client invites it, meaning that the client trusts the counselor enough to connect on that level. What, in one situation, can be humor between two people, in another can be interpreted as ridicule or wearing a mask. Counselors, therefore, have to be sensitive to using humor in a way that doesn't reinforce various means of oppression that the client has endured probably for all of her or his life.

However, in the positive direction, humor provides the opportunity to connect with the client on her or his ground and share a powerful trust. In sum, although counselors working with Native clients should exercise caution when using humor, they definitely should not overlook it as a powerful therapeutic technique. Indian humor serves the purpose of reaffirming and enhancing the sense of connectedness as part of family, clan, and tribe. To the extent that it can serve that purpose in the counseling relationship, it is all the better.

At this point, general assessment and intervention issues have been discussed. Table 7.3 describes specific interventions that might be used with Native clients and can serve as a summary of some of the themes described previously. The counselor is reminded that individual factors, including acculturation, must guide intervention so that simplistic application to all Native clients does not occur.

Table 7.3   Summary of Practical Interventions for Counseling Native Americans

Foster cultural connections: Native clients can reconnect with a sense of purpose by participating in community programs and cultural activities intended to combat high rates of unemployment, inadequate housing, low educational levels, poverty-level incomes, and isolated living conditions. Participation in community-wide volunteer programs to help those in need has proved to be a successful part of healing for many Indian people. Also, in the past 10 years or so, powwows and other pan-traditional events have become more and more popular in Native communities for whom that event is not indigenous as well as those for whom it is.

Encourage physical health: Native people should be encouraged to get regular physical checkups and blood tests (e.g., blood sugar) as a preventive measure in dealing with high incidence of diabetes and other conditions prevalent among Native populations.

Examine/teach the historical context: A critical component of counseling could include facilitating a psychoeducational experience or dialogue about Native experience in the United States. The counselor can discuss or lead the Native client to resources about the exploitation of Native people through discrimination, assimilation through boarding schools and relocation programs, as well as disruption of traditional cultural and familial patterns. Discussions of this nature might help Native clients to explore their own levels of cultural identity development.

Promote positive cultural identity: Native clients can be assisted with exploration of personal cultural identity and career issues by focusing on the positive cultural themes of belonging, mastery, independence, and generosity identified as culturally appropriate ways of developing positive cultural identity for Native people (Brendtro et al., 1990). Counselors can utilize the following general questions to generate strengths and positive dimensions of clients' lives:

Belonging. Where do you belong?

Mastery. What are you good at; what do you enjoy doing?

Independence. What are your sources of strength; what limits you?

Generosity. What do you have to offer/contribute?

These questions provide an entry into a potentially useful dialogue and any number of therapeutic interventions. In addition, counselors can subsequently help the client learn about the expectations and ways of the dominant culture, so that the client is prepared to engage in mainstream activities, if she or he wishes.

Reduce isolation/enhance social connections: Participation in social events allows Native clients to experience social cohesion and social interaction in their communities. Some Native clients can benefit thereby from a sense of reconnection with community and traditional roles. This has been accomplished through the revival of tribal ceremonies and practices (e.g., talking circles, sweat lodges, powwows, peyote meetings). These revivals can re-establish a sense of belonging and communal meaningfulness for Native people "returning to the old ways" as an integral part of modern life.

Reduce generational splits: Native clients of all ages can benefit from acting as or learning from elders who can serve as role models and teachers for young people. This, too, has become more commonly practiced by tribal nations across the country in therapeutic programs and schools.

Enhance coping mechanisms: Native clients can learn better methods of dealing with stress, boredom, powerlessness, and the sense of emptiness associated with acculturation and identity confusion. Consultation with or participation of a medicine person (i.e., traditional Native healer) may prove very helpful.

Work judiciously with the noninterference principle: The principle of noninterference has been identified as a value of traditional Native culture and is based on a common cultural practice of showing respect among one's relations (Garrett, 1999b). Noninterference means that a person is not to interfere with the choices of another because it would be considered disrespectful and insulting. It should be noted that in certain situations, noninterference can also be seen as avoidance of family and community members who may be in need of help. This avoidance behavior can be challenged with Native clients, as well as with family and community members, to the extent that it may be destructive. Carol Attneave's (1969, 1985) network therapy has been very effective with Native clients as a way of working with an individual in a family and community context where family and community members are included in the counseling process, often through the use of group interventions that complement the cultural context.

SOURCE: Reprinted from Garrett, Michael Tlanusta. (1999). Understanding the "Medicine" of Native American Traditional Values. *Counseling and Values, 43*, 84–98. © 1999 The American Counseling Association. Reprinted with permission. No further reproduction authorized without written permission from the American Counseling Association.

Summary

Through culturally alert counseling, counselors can practice in a way that is more congruent with traditional Native worldviews, experiences, and needs. With the knowledge, awareness, and skills that have been discussed in this chapter, counselors discover a better sense of where Native people have come from and where they are going. Counselors might see the powerful influences of history, social and political issues, acculturation, values and beliefs, spirituality, cultural symbolism and practices, and communication style on individuals, families, and communities. Counselors see the continuity of the Circle in stories of images and experiences that flow from the heart, and they begin to arrive at a better understanding of where they stand in relation to everything around them and in relation to their clients. They also begin to understand the importance of attending to the stories—the meanings, language, experiences, images, and themes—of Native clients. And they begin to learn, as it has traditionally been taught by so many Native elders, that learning is a lifelong process, just as a story unfolds and offers the gift of its life to us.

References

Attneave, C. L. (1969). Therapy in tribal settings and urban network intervention. *Family Process, 8,* 192–210.

Attneave, C. L. (1985). Practical counseling with American Indian and Alaska Native clients. In P. Pedersen (Ed.), *Handbook of cross-cultural counseling and therapy* (pp. 135–140). Westport, CT: Greenwood.

Brendtro, L. K., Brokenleg, M., & Van Bockern, S. (1990). *Reclaiming youth at risk: Our hope for the future.* Bloomington, IN: National Education Service.

Choney, S. K., Berryhill-Paapke, E., & Robbins, R. R. (1995). The acculturation of American Indians: Developing frameworks for research and practice. In J. G. Ponterotto, J. M. Casas, L. A. Suzuki, & C. M. Alexander (Eds.), *Handbook of multicultural counseling* (pp. 73–92). Thousand Oaks, CA: Sage.

Deloria, V., Jr. (1988). *Custer died for your sins: An Indian manifesto.* Norman: University of Oklahoma Press.

DuBray, W. H. (1985). American Indian values: Critical factor in casework. *Social Casework: The Journal of Contemporary Social Work, 66,* 30–37.

Dufrene, P. M. (1990). Exploring Native American symbolism. *Journal of Multicultural and Cross-Cultural Research in Art Education, 8,* 38–50.

Garcia, R. L., & Ahler, J. G. (1992). Indian education: Assumptions, ideologies, strategies. In J. Reyhner (Ed.), *Teaching American Indian students* (pp. 13–32). Norman: University of Oklahoma Press.

Garrett, J. T. (2001). *Meditations with the Cherokee: Prayers, songs, and stories of healing and harmony.* Rochester, VT: Bear & Company.

Garrett, J. T., & Garrett, M. T. (1994). The path of good medicine: Understanding and counseling Native Americans. *Journal of Multicultural Counseling and Development, 22,* 134–144.

Garrett, J. T., & Garrett, M. T. (1996). *Medicine of the Cherokee: The way of right relationship.* Santa Fe, NM: Bear & Company.

Garrett, M. T. (1995). Between two worlds: Cultural discontinuity in the dropout of Native American youth. *The School Counselor, 42,* 186–195.

Garrett, M. T. (1996). Reflection by the riverside: The traditional education of Native American children. *Journal of Humanistic Education and Development, 35,* 12–28.

Garrett, M. T. (1998). *Walking on the wind: Cherokee teachings for harmony and balance.* Santa Fe, NM: Bear & Company.

Garrett, M. T. (1999a). Soaring on the wings of the eagle: Wellness of Native American high school students. *Professional School Counseling, 3,* 57–64.

Garrett, M. T. (1999b). Understanding the "medicine" of Native American traditional values: An integrative review. *Counseling and Values, 43,* 84–98.

Garrett, M. T., & Carroll, J. (2000). Mending the broken circle: Treatment and prevention of substance abuse among Native Americans. *Journal of Counseling and Development, 78,* 379–388.

Garrett, M. T., & Garrett, J. T. (1997). Counseling Native American elders. *Directions in Rehabilitation Counseling: Therapeutic Strategies With the Older Adult, 3,* 3–18.

Garrett, M. T., & Garrett, J. T. (2002). Ayeli: Centering technique based on Cherokee spiritual traditions. *Counseling and Values, 46,* 149–158.

Garrett, M. T., & Garrett, J. T. (2003). *Native American faith in America.* New York: Facts on File.

Garrett, M. T., Garrett, J. T., & Brotherton, D. (2001). Inner circle/outer circle: Native American group technique. *Journal for Specialists in Group Work, 26,* 17–30.

Garrett, M. T., & Myers, J. E. (1996). The rule of opposites: A paradigm for counseling Native Americans. *Journal of Multicultural Counseling and Development, 24,* 89–104.

Garrett, M. T., & Osborne, W. L. (1995). The Native American sweat lodge as metaphor for group work. *Journal for Specialists in Group Work, 20,* 33–39.

Garrett, M. T., & Pichette, E. F. (2000). Red as an apple: Native American acculturation and counseling with or without reservation. *Journal of Counseling and Development, 78,* 3–13.

Garrett, M. T., & Wilbur, M. P. (1999). Does the worm live in the ground? Reflections on Native American spirituality. *Journal of Multicultural Counseling and Development, 27,* 193–206.

Heinrich, R. K., Corbine, J. L., & Thomas, K. R. (1990). Counseling Native Americans. *Journal of Counseling and Development, 69,* 128–133.

Herring, R. D. (1994). The clown or contrary figure as a counseling intervention strategy with Native American Indian clients. *Journal of Multicultural Counseling and Development, 22,* 153–164.

Herring, R. D. (1999). *Counseling with Native American Indians and Alaska Natives: Strategies for helping professionals.* Thousand Oaks, CA: Sage.

Hirschfelder, A., & Kreipe de Montano, M. (1993). *The Native American almanac: A portrait of Native America today.* New York: Macmillan.

Hodgkinson, H. L. (1990). *The demographics of American Indians: One percent of the people; fifty percent of the diversity.* Washington, DC: Institute for Educational Leadership.

LaFromboise, T. D., Coleman, H. L. K., & Gerton, J. (1993). Psychological impact of biculturalism: Evidence and theory. *Psychological Bulletin, 114,* 395–412.

Lake, M. G. (1991). *Native healer: Initiation into an ancient art.* Wheaton, IL: Quest Books.

Lee, C. C. (2001). Defining and responding to racial and ethnic diversity. In D. C. Locke, J. E. Myers, & E. L. Herr (Eds.), *The handbook of counseling* (pp. 581–588). Thousand Oaks, CA: Sage.

Lee, C. C. (Ed.). (2002). *Multicultural issues in counseling: New approaches to diversity* (3rd ed.). Alexandria, VA: American Counseling Association.

Locust, C. (1988). Wounding the spirit: Discrimination and traditional American Indian belief systems. *Harvard Educational Review, 58,* 315–330.

Loftin, J. D. (1989). Anglo-American jurisprudence and the Native American tribal quest for religious freedom. *American Indian Culture and Research Journal, 13,* 1–52.

Maples, M. F., Dupey, P., Torres-Rivera, E., Phan, L. T., Vereen, L., & Garrett, M. T. (2001). Ethnic diversity and the use of humor in counseling: Appropriate or inappropriate? *Journal of Counseling and Development, 79,* 53–60.

Matheson, L. (1996). Valuing spirituality among Native American populations. *Counseling and Values, 41,* 51–58.

McLaughlin, D. (1994). Critical literacy for Navajo and other American Indian learners. *Journal of American Indian Education, 33,* 47–59.

Northrup, J. (1997). *The Rez Road Follies: Canoes, casinos, computers, and birch bark baskets.* New York: Kodansha International.

Oswalt, W. H. (1988). *This land was theirs: A study of North American Indians* (4th ed.). Mountain View, CA: Mayfield.

Plank, G. A. (1994). What silence means for educators of American Indian children. *Journal of American Indian Education, 34,* 3–19.

Red Horse, J. G. (1997). Traditional American Indian family systems. *Families, Systems, & Health, 15,* 243–250.

Reyhner, J., & Eder, J. (1992). A history of Indian education. In J. Reyhner (Ed.), *Teaching American Indian students* (pp. 33–58). Norman: University of Oklahoma Press.

Robinson, T. L., & Howard-Hamilton, M. F. (2000). *The convergence of race, ethnicity, and gender: Multiple identities in counseling.* Upper Saddle River, NJ: Merrill.

Russell, G. (1997). *American Indian facts of life: A profile of today's tribes and reservations.* Phoenix, AZ: Russell.

Thomason, T. C. (1991). Counseling Native Americans: An introduction for non-Native American counselors. *Journal of Counseling and Development, 69,* 321–327.

U.S. Bureau of Indian Affairs. (1988). *American Indians today.* Washington, DC: Author.

U.S. Census Bureau. (2001). *2000 census counts of American Indians, Eskimos or Aleuts, and American Indian and Alaska Native areas.* Washington, DC: Author.

Velie, A. R. (Ed.). (1991). *American Indian literature: An anthology.* Norman: University of Oklahoma Press.

European Americans

Lee J. Richmond and
Mary H. Guindon

8

Most cross-cultural counseling texts do not include a chapter on counseling European Americans. Instead, it is commonly assumed that all a counselor needs to know in order to work with European Americans is Western Counseling Theory and some familiarity with the specific issues that caused them to seek help. Yet culture for European Americans, as for all other humans, is a mediating factor in how life concerns are both perceived and resolved.

In the vignettes that follow, Ellen, Tom, and Tony are all European Americans. However, they not only have different emotional and interpersonal concerns; they also come from different ethnic and socioeconomic groups. Their backgrounds have influenced what they do and how they see the world, as is the case for all human beings.

In this chapter, European Americans are defined as the so-called white people who reside in the United States and whose families originated anywhere on the continent of Europe. They may have immigrated to America at any time from the colonial period to the present day and may vary in native language, religion, education, occupation, and socioeconomic status. Regardless of when they immigrated, they share cultural characteristics. They also share dominance as an overall group in American society.

It should be noted that European Americans may not call themselves by that label because dominant groups usually do not have ethnic labels for themselves. Nevertheless, white Americans of European descent share values and customs as a group, with many variations based on subgroup and regional identity. And, as with all statements about ethnic characteristics, the statements here are generalizations, to be modified by individual differences, enculturation, and acculturation.

Ellen, a 35-year-old vice president of a paint manufacturing company, earns $240,000 year and has stock options. For this, she is expected to work long hours and travel *frequently to several different locations. In addition to her job, Ellen, a Ph.D.-level chemist, has two children—a boy, three years old, and a girl, six. Steve, Ellen's husband, is also a Ph.D. chemist, but unlike his wife, he has not risen rapidly to management. He remains a bench chemist. Steve, Ellen, and their children are Reform Jews who practice their religion. The children attend Hebrew school one afternoon a week and on Sunday. During the week, they attend both private school and day care after school until one of the parents can pick them up.*

There are several problems in the household. Although Steve is proud of Ellen's success at work, his salary is only a third of hers. He also sometimes resents the amount of housework and childcare that he has to do when she travels. Furthermore, Ellen's mother, an Orthodox Jew, disliked the fact that Ellen became Reform, which is a liberal movement in Judaism, when she married. Becoming Reform was a compromise for the couple because Steve had little contact with religious Judaism in his life. His mother was a nonpractising Jew by birth, and his father was not Jewish. By contrast, Ellen grew up in a household where the Sabbath and the Jewish dietary laws were strictly observed. Her grandmother and grandfather used to converse in Yiddish, a language that her mother had learned but Ellen did not learn. There are times when her grandparents still speak Yiddish around Ellen. She thinks that they do so only when they are talking about their displeasure with her marriage to Steve. It annoys her.

Ellen thought she would please her mother by becoming a respected professional and a good homemaker. Instead, her mother seemed to always be criticizing her. In retrospect, it seemed to Ellen that where her mother was concerned, she was never able to do enough. She didn't really know what her mother expected of her. Furthermore, when her mother really seemed riled about something, she involved the kids, especially the six-year-old. Ellen would hear her say things to the children like, "You should come to my house, and have a REAL shabbos [Sabbath] dinner with candles and wine, not like your other grandmother who would serve you bacon if she could."

Ellen's mother often remarks directly to Ellen that if Steve were a better provider, as she thinks he should be, Ellen wouldn't have to work so hard and be away from the children so much. Ellen loves her work, but every now and then she thinks that life would be much simpler if she would return to being a bench chemist, earn what Steve earns, and place the children in public school. Recently, the live-in maid quit working for Ellen and Steve. Feeling overwhelmed, Ellen decided to seek counseling.

Tom, a 52-year-old computer analyst, manages a department of 10 employees responsible for computer training in a large state government agency. He has a college degree that he earned on the G.I. Bill after serving six years in the Navy. He received his initial computer training as a young seaman and has since acquired on-the-job training through the government agency where he has worked ever since. Originally from northeast Pennsylvania, of Scotch-Irish and German parents, Tom grew up in an economically depressed area. Some Polish and Italian families lived in the area, but Tom's parents looked down on "those Catholics" and didn't want him to

associate too much with them. His family, as Protestants and older white Americans sometimes do, thought of themselves as "the real Americans" and considered themselves to be better than more recent arrivals. Originally the family worked on a small farm and were "dirt poor," like the soil they tilled, but in two generations they had saved enough money to buy a small general store, where they sold clothing and notions to the miners. However, they lost what money they had made in the store during the Great Depression of the 1930s. That's when Tom's family started working in the coal mines.

Tom could have been a miner too, but the military took him away from that difficult occupation. He joined the Navy right after graduating from high school. Then there was college and the corporate life. He is the father of three college-age daughters. He has been separated from his stay-at-home wife for six months and has temporarily moved in with his older sister and her husband. This living arrangement is not common in his culture and is a source of tension. Tom considers himself to be a self-made man. He has always been proud of his independence, a trait that he acquired from his Scotch-Irish father's side. He is emotionally restrained, although he sees himself as pleasant and friendly. These qualities, he feels certain, come from his mother's side. His mother called this calm cheerfulness "gemütlichkeit." She herself had the gentility that comes with this warm, yet restrained style. Tom admired those traits in her.

Tom has been turned down for two promotions in the last three years, although he was fully qualified for both jobs and has had outstanding performance evaluations. In each case, Tom believes that the individuals chosen—a 40-year-old African American female and a 34-year-old Dominican male with "a strong accent"—were less qualified in years of service and amount of training. He expresses anger and resentment toward them and toward the government policies that he feels gave them preferential treatment.

He has been referred to the Employee Assistance Program (EAP) for counseling because he has been experiencing symptoms of anxiety and stress. He is both angry and depressed and has been drinking nightly at the roadside tavern.

Tony, a high school senior, is expected upon graduation to work in his father's Italian delicatessen and grocery store, where he has worked afternoons after school since he was in the eighth grade. His father told Tony that upon graduation, he could earn a real salary in the business and soon start doing some of the buying. It is obvious to Tony that his father is very proud to be the owner of a store that started as his immigrant great-grandfather's pushcart and has been passed down from generation to generation. It is also obvious to Tony that his father intends for him to own the business in the future. The problem is that he is not interested in doing so and does not know how to tell his dad.

Although Tony plays on the school football team and enjoys it, sports are not his main interest either. Ever since Mrs. Garner, his English teacher, praised him for his latest composition, Tony has toyed with his real love: writing. He has always secretly enjoyed writing, not only stories but poetry, which he keeps hidden in a secret place *under the loose floorboards in his room. He never expected to go to college, but when Mrs. Garner told him that he should consider attending the state university and that he might even qualify for a scholarship, the thought of college began to take concrete form. The problem is that he could only imagine how disappointed his father would be. His father considers college impractical. What seems really strange to him is that his sister, Mary Louise, has a real head for business and his father doesn't even see it. She could run the store, but if his father has his way, that will never happen.*

Tony feels stuck. Mrs. Garner thinks he should begin to apply to colleges. Dad thinks he should go to work. When he told his teacher that he will have to go into the family business even though he doesn't want to, she suggested that he talk to his school counselor. No one in his family has ever talked to a counselor, as far as he knows. Every now and then, his mother goes to talk to Father Leo, the local parish priest, but Tony does not know what she talks about. And if his dad had problems, he would never let anyone know it. Tony does not know what to do. Perhaps he will speak with Mrs. Garner again. Maybe seeing the school counselor will help, but Tony sure doesn't know how.

Tom, Ellen, and Tony are all European Americans, although their worldviews are quite different. Activity 8.1 requires you to think about how you would counsel each of these clients. The next section of this chapter reviews the key events in the European domination of the United States. Before reading this section, the reader is encouraged to complete Activity 8.2, which asks the reader to assess how much she or he knows about the history of Europeans in America and about their worldviews.

Historical Origins of European America

Modern North America has roots in the worldwide European search for wealth in late fifteenth-century Europe. England, Holland, Spain, and France each explored and seized parts of what came to be called America from its native inhabitants (Gutman, 1989). Many immigrants followed, seeking adventure, release from indenture, and freedom to practice their religion.

It was only logical that each European nation would settle in the geographic areas of America in which its early explorers traveled (see Table 8.1). Permanent English colonies were first established in Jamestown, Virginia, and Plymouth, Massachusetts. These colonies were followed by other English settlements up and down the east coast. During the early seventeenth century, the Dutch paid an Englishman, Henry Hudson, to explore the area around what is now known as the Hudson River, and he claimed that territory for Holland. The Dutch named it "New Amsterdam" and held it until the second Anglo-Dutch war in 1664. It was then claimed by England and was renamed "New York."

ACTIVITY 8.1

Responding to the Vignettes

Imagine that Ellen, Tom, and Tony are your clients.

What do you see as the important issues for each of them?

Ellen:

Tom:

Tony:

What counseling approach would you use in working with each of them?

Ellen:

Tom:

Tony:

What do you think you need to know about European American cultures and history to work effectively with Ellen, Tom, and Tony?

Ellen:

Tom:

Tony

After reading this chapter, the answers to these questions may be fairly obvious to the reader.

The first successful French settlement in the Americas was in what is now Canada and was named Quebec. By the end of the seventeenth century, three-fourths of North America was actually claimed as New France. However, France was not as successful at settling its territories as was England. Over the years and after several wars, almost all French lands were lost to England. Most of the rest of the lands in the Americas were Spanish. Following Christopher Columbus's lead, Ponce de Leon, Hernando de Soto, and Francesco Vasquez de Coronado continued Spanish exploration of the New World. St. Augustine, Florida, was actually the first permanent European settlement in what is now the United States; it was a Spanish fort in 1565. However, most Spanish settlements north of Mexico were in the American West, in places such as Santa Fe (1609) and Taos (1615). What are

ACTIVITY 8.2

Knowledge About European Americans

This knowledge assessment might serve as a guide, and a motivation, for what is contained in this chapter. When you have finished reading the chapter, you may come back to these questions and answer them again. See whether you are more confident in your answers the second time.

In the blanks after the statements below, place a T if you think the statement is true, F if you think that it is false, DN if you do not know. The answers appear at the end of the activity.

1. People of English, Dutch, French, and Spanish origin were the only Europeans in the original 13 colonies.____

2. Georgia was the only English settlement established as a Catholic colony.____

3. Reason and nature, rather than revelation from the Bible, demonstrated the existence of God in the articulated philosophy of the people who shaped America as a nation.____

4. After the French and Indian War, it was clear that Britain stood triumphant in America.____

5. The founders of the U.S. nation strove for liberty and justice for all people who lived there.____

6. The wave of immigration that brought Eastern and Mediterranean European immigrants to America occurred largely in the late nineteenth century.____

7. Like the explorers who originally "discovered" America, the Eastern Europeans came in order to send new wealth back to the countries that they had left.____

8. There is little difference between the cultures of Mediterranean people and Northern Europeans.____

9. The accomplishments that European Americans made during the nineteenth and early twentieth centuries gave them a feeling of superiority, even though other peoples had assisted in these achievements.____

10. White females have historically shared in the achievements accorded to white males.____

11. By the end of the twenty-first century, European Americans will not make up the majority of the American population.____

12. Racism affects those who hold racist views as well as those who are targets of those views.____

13. Diversity pertains to European Americans as well as to other groups of people.____

14. It was not until after the Civil War that Jewish men, like black men, were considered citizens and allowed to vote.____

15. The "Old Irish," or Scotch Irish, Protestants welcomed Irish Catholics to America because they knew that many had suffered greatly from the potato famine in Ireland.____

Answers: Statements 3, 6, 9, 11, 12, and 13 are true. The rest are false.

If you scored 15 or 14 correct, you know some basic facts about European American history and characteristics.

If you scored 12 or 13, you are on the right track. If you scored less than 12, you have much to learn about how Americans, whatever their race or ethnic culture, became who they are today.

Table 8.1   European American Nationality/Ethnic Groups and Immigration Patterns

Historical Origins	Nationality/Ethnic Group	Major Geographic Settlement Areas
1. Early Settlers/Old Europeans (Late 16th c.–mid-18th c.) Original Settlers	English	Virginia Massachusetts Other 13 colonies
	Dutch	New York Delaware River Valley*
	French	(Canada) New England
	Spanish	Florida American West
	Jews	Delaware River Valley* New Mexico
	German	Delaware River Valley* Virginia
	Swedish	Delaware River Valley*
Second Wave: North Britons	"Scotch Irish": Northern Irish Northern English Lowland Scots	13 colonies Appalachians
2. First Wave of "Hyphenated Americans" (Mid 18th c.)	Irish Catholics	Cities/slums in New England, New York, and other
	German Lutherans German Catholics German Jews	Small towns in Delaware Valley, plus Midwest, American West
	Scandinavians: Swedish, Norwegian	Minnesota Upper Midwest
3. Mediterranean and Eastern Europeans (Late 19th c.)	Italian Greek	Industrialized cities: Northern/middle east coast Chicago, St. Louis, San Francisco, New Orleans
	Non-Jews Polish Hungarian Lithuanian Czech Russian	East coast portal cities, then throughout northern half of the U.S.
	Jews Polish Russian	East coast portal cities, then throughout U.S.

* Eastern Pennsylvania, Delaware, southern New Jersey

now Southern California, Texas, and parts of Oklahoma were also explored and settled as part of New Spain.

The English, Dutch, French, and Spanish were not the only European peoples to settle in the Americas during this period. Some Swedes, along with Dutch and English, came to settle in the Delaware River Valley. Many Germans, the so-called Old Germans, came to the colonies in the 1700s. They soon mixed with the Anglo inhabitants, due to their being predominantly Protestant and culturally similar to those groups in some ways. *Tom proudly traces some of his paternal ancestors back to these original Old German settlers in Northeast Pennsylvania.* Jewish families, fleeing the Spanish Inquisition, migrated to Holland and from there to New Amsterdam. Other Jews journeyed to Mexico in the 1600s and from there to Santa Fe and Taos, where their descendants still live (Tobias, 1990). *Ellen's husband, Steve, counts these immigrants among his earliest American ancestors, and he still has cousins in that area.*

Over a hundred years after the original English settlers, Northern Irish, Northern English, and Lowland Scottish Protestants—the so-called North Britons (Fischer, 1989), who later called themselves the Scotch Irish—came in waves in the 1700s to the English colonies. With the fertile flat lands already taken, the Scotch Irish settled in the mountainous country west of the coast. *Tom's maternal ancestors, who settled in the mountains of western Pennsylvania and northern West Virginia, were among these immigrants.* They experienced significant bias, being seen as uneducated and violent people, in contrast to the more pastoral and mercantile English and Germans. The Scotch Irish were a very individualistic and pioneering people, and they settled the backwoods. Many of them, like Daniel Boone, crossed the Appalachians into what is today Kentucky and Tennessee and points farther west. These Scotch Irish produced many American writers (e.g., Poe and Irving), military leaders (e.g., Grant and McClellan), captains of American business (e.g., Rockefeller), and no fewer than 13 presidents of the United States, including Jackson, Wilson, Buchanan, and Clinton (Leyburn, 1962; Webb, 2004).

THE NATION'S FOUNDERS: THEIR PRINCIPLES AND PRACTICES

The people who are thought of as the founders of the United States were, for the most part, of English descent and lived throughout the original 13 colonies. In a literal sense, every person who had a part in the formation of the United States might be called a founder (Cousins, 1958), including African American, American Indian, and European American men and women. However, in time, the term "founder" has come to be used more selectively. It is applied to the largely Anglo American men who drew up the Declaration of Independence, instigated the war against England, created the Constitution, and, with some struggle, united the states.

The early Americans of English ancestry lived throughout the 13 colonies. There were different regions in these colonies, which affected their cultures. In the flatter lands of the Southern colonies, many people lived on farms, tobacco plantations, and, farther south, on cotton plantations. In the more mercantile North, many European Americans lived in cities or on small farms that the family worked. It is ironic that the founding fathers, who spoke so glowingly of freedom and equality, applied neither concept to African American slaves, nor to American Indian peoples, nor to white women, who were literally owned by their husbands.

Much of America's vitality lay in the articulated Enlightenment philosophy of Western Europe. One notion that the European American founders stressed was freedom of religion, which also included freedom from religion. Many of the early settlers came to America in order to find freedom to practice their faith (e.g., the Pilgrims in Plymouth, the Quakers in Pennsylvania, the Catholics in Maryland, and the Congregationalists in Connecticut and Rhode Island). While many colonists called themselves Christians and were versed in scripture, others among the founders were naturalists, rationalists, or Unitarians who believed in divine creation but not a divine trinity nor revelation nor the power of a deity to influence human affairs (Church, 1989; Cousins, 1958). For example, Thomas Jefferson revised the Christian Bible, taking out all miracles, including those surrounding the birth and resurrection of Jesus; his version, *The Life and Morals of Jesus of Nazareth,* is commonly known as The Jefferson Bible. It is Jefferson's Bible that is used when those elected are sworn into office as United States senators (Church, 1989). Reason and nature, rather than scripture, demonstrated the existence of a God for the founders. The "brotherhood of man" and the belief in his ability to govern himself in a just society free from domination by any religion was their creed, and it remains an important belief of the American people to this day.

OLD AND NEW EUROPEAN AMERICANS AND A NEW KIND OF STRUGGLE

The so-called New World was seen as an opportunity to get away from the old world of class issues, religious strife, and the violent competition among European nations. This impulse, coupled with the common cause of liberty and justice for all white men, inspired the new republic and bound together the European American peoples who lived in the former British colonies. The philosophy of the day was amalgamation. Just as various metals can combine to make one amalgam, stronger than any of the metals alone, so the pervasive ethic was that the various groups of European people who lived in America could combine and make one strong American people. Differences were glossed over, and all were one people. Thus, a Jew named Chiam Soloman, friend of George Washington and financier of the Revolutionary War; Alexander Hamilton, Caribbean-born son of a French Huguenot woman and a Scotsman, and first secretary of the Treasury; and John Carroll, a Catholic from Maryland, signer of the Declaration of Independence, all became part of the amalgam that was America. Many of these Americans, however, were not prepared to incorporate the influx of immigrants that was yet to come in the next century. These immigrants would bring worldviews that differed significantly from those of the early citizens of the United States and from each other. It would be up to them to acclimate themselves to a nation whose inhabitants were not entirely open to accepting them.

THE SECOND WAVE OF IMMIGRATION

The most recent large wave of European immigration began in the mid-1800s, long after the settlements of the eastern seaboard had become colonies and after the colonies had become states (Boorstin, 1974). The Western Europeans who came to America in the mid-1800s formed the vanguard of what came to be known as the "Hyphenated Americans" (Boorstin, 1974), that is, German-Americans, Irish-Americans, Scandinavian-Americans, and so forth. These immigrant groups left their countries of origin because those places could no longer economically support them (Boorstin, 1974).

This group of immigrants had some similarities to the earlier dominant European immigrant groups because they were also largely from Western Europe. But they experienced significant bias from the so-called "native" Americans, that is, the earlier European groups. Some of them followed a different religion and others spoke a different language. The Irish Catholics constituted the largest group, followed by the new Germans. After the potato famine of 1847, people left Ireland in order to survive. They generally settled in cities, in slums, and in shanty towns. These "Low Irish," as they were called, were not welcomed by the "Old Irish" Anglo-Protestants who had long before settled with the English in Boston and other cities. Nor were they welcomed by the Scotch Irish, who immediately identified themselves as separate by assuming that new name. But the Irish Catholics huddled together and did the hard labor that was needed in a country building railroads, bridges, canals, and buildings. Women worked as maids in houses and hotels. Many of the men served as soldiers in the Civil War. In time, St. Patrick's Day parades served as a declaration of the Irish presence and growing power, as the Irish worked their way through politics into the life of the nation.

Great waves of German immigration also occurred in the nineteenth century. They followed an earlier influx of Germans who had fled Germany in the 1700s for political and religious reasons. Those early Germans were already living in New York state, Pennsylvania, and the Shenandoah Valley in Virginia. By the 1800s, most of these earlier German immigrants were English-speaking, even in their Lutheran churches. At first, the old Germans did not welcome the influx of new Germans, who set up little German towns in cities like Cincinnati and Milwaukee, where German was spoken in churches and schools. In a short while, the new immigrants became bankers, brewers, machinists, and tailors. *Tom counts many of his paternal ancestors among this group.* Most of the mid-nineteenth-century immigrants from Germany were Lutherans or Catholics. However, with them during this era came 250,000 German-speaking Jews, who were, by and large, Reform Jews, meaning that they had progressive and secular ideas on politics, religion, and social behavior (Richmond, 1999, 2003). As will be discussed later, being Jewish can be both an ethnicity and a religious commitment. They spoke

German in their temples and behaved in other ways very much like their Christian countrymen. *It was from this group of immigrants that Steve's immediate family descended, although the German language was replaced by English by the time of his grandfather's generation. In fact, his mother was not reared in the religion at all. Thus, marrying a non-Jew was not an issue in her family.*

Another major group of peoples who immigrated to the United States throughout the 1800s were the Scandinavians, primarily Norwegians and Swedes. By the middle of the 1800s, a population increase in both countries had led to a squeeze on the land. In addition, oppression drove them out. In 1858, in Sweden, the State Lutheran Church became the official religion, and people who practiced otherwise were fined, jailed, or exiled. Military training also became mandatory. America looked like a place of escape for many. In Minnesota, government treaties with the American Indians made much inexpensive land available, and the Homestead Act of 1862 offered land to settlers who promised to live on it for five years (Zinn, 2003). Minnesota, which had become a state in 1858, had a climate similar to that of Norway and Sweden. Swedes and Norwegians saw both freedom and opportunity in the American Midwest, and they settled it.

THE LATE NINETEENTH-CENTURY WAVES OF EUROPEAN IMMIGRATION

The immigrants thus far discussed were all Northern and Western Europeans. More difficult to assimilate were the Mediterranean and Eastern European peoples who came during the latter half of the nineteenth century. Italians constituted the largest group of Mediterranean immigrants, although Greeks and Lebanese also came in significant numbers. During the latter half of the nineteenth century, many Italians migrated to America with the intent to earn money and return to their homeland. Heavy taxes, antiquated agricultural methods, and lack of industrial opportunities caused men to leave Italy to seek their fortunes in the United States. For the most part, the Italian immigrants were poorly educated, unskilled, and illiterate. They found low-paying jobs in a burgeoning industrial America. Instead of returning home, however, most eventually brought their families over to the new country. *Both Tony's paternal and maternal ancestors were among this immigrant group. His great-grandfather immigrated first, then worked and saved his money to bring over his soon-to-be bride.* The largely Catholic Italian immigrants, like the Irish Catholics before them, were not easily socially integrated into American society. They met with much negative prejudice, even from fellow Catholics. The Italian immigrants built their own small communities, often managed grocery stores, and developed a community life of their own. *This was the case with Tony's family. His parents expected him to continue the family tradition.* The Italian population grew fast and spread rapidly throughout east coast cities and in other urban areas such as Chicago, St. Louis, San Francisco, and New Orleans. By the year 1900, there were over 20,000 Italians living in Philadelphia alone.

Greeks came to America at approximately the same time as Italians, and, like Italians, the Greek immigrants intended to make some money and go back to Greece (Killian & Agathangelou, 2005). However, most stayed and brought their families to America. Despite the fact that Greeks and Italians differed in religion and language, many Anglo Americans, who were not very familiar with either group, lumped Italians and Greeks together as Mediterranean people hitherto unknown and, at first, unwelcome.

Yet another wave of European peoples also immigrated to the United States in the late nineteenth century from Eastern Europe. The Irish, Germans, Scandinavians, Italians, and Greeks continued to arrive through the turn of the century. In turn, from Eastern Europe the "tired and tempest tossed," in the words of Emma Lazarus, also began to appear on America's shores. Half of the Eastern European immigrants were Jews from Russia and Poland. Other new immigrants were non-Jewish Poles, Hungarians, Lithuanians, Czechs, and Russians. Each had different reasons for leaving his or her country of origin. Most came to escape conscription in their country's army or to avoid starvation at home. Almost all were poor. Most of these people had great difficulty with the English language. It was hard for the nation to assimilate them, and many did not wish to be assimilated.

A particularly interesting European American population is the Jewish group. They did not share the dominant religion of most Americans, yet they were culturally European in many ways. Some were Orthodox. *Ellen's mother descended from this group.* Others, whose families had once been Orthodox, were secular. These new Jewish immigrants had experienced only totalitarianism. To the assimilated Reform Jews who had come to America in the early to mid-1800s from Berlin and its suburbs, the Orthodox Jews from tiny towns and ghettoes, *like Ellen's grandparents,* were backward strangers engaging in religious practices that had been abandoned by Reform Jews who liked to call themselves Americanized Jews (Shapiro, 1992). Also strange and sometimes an embarrassment to Americanized Jewry were the secular Eastern European immigrants who were tired of waiting for God or a Messiah to redeem them from the oppression that they had suffered under the Czars, and who became political radicals, particularly Marxists. Because Marx believed that people and societies produced their own material lives and were responsible for their own betterment and that of society (Nerlich, 1989), some secular Jews who espoused that philosophy became part of the workers movement. *The Jewish Daily Forward,* a Yiddish-language newspaper, was founded in 1897 by the Jewish Socialist Press. It helped immigrant Jews define what it meant to be a Jew in America, fostered the American labor movement, and became the most widely read foreign language newspaper in the nation. *Ellen's grandparents and her mother continued to read Yiddish, occasionally spoke it in their home, and identified closely with their Eastern European origins.*

However, Jews were not the only late-nineteenth-century immigrants who struggled to adapt to the dominant American culture. Language was a problem for most of them. It was an immediate identifier of difference for Italians, Greeks, Lithuanians, Poles, and Hungarians. These immigrants were unfamiliar with the grammar, syntax, and intonation of the English language. With little help coming from the dominant society, each new ethnic group had to struggle to adapt to the culture of the Anglo American majority and be accepted by them. Further stress was added by the fact that the various immigrant groups were not always friendly to each other.

FROM EUROPEAN IMMIGRANTS TO EUROPEAN AMERICANS

Each new European group that came to America became the brunt of stereotype and suspicion. Cartoons and vaudeville shows caricatured the Germans, Irish, and Italians who had recently arrived. Gradually, however, each was absorbed into twentieth-century America. By the end of the first quarter of the twentieth century, European immigration had slowed. Eventually, as described in Chapter 3, European Americans of all ethnicities were lumped as so-called Caucasians and came to be regarded as a monolithic majority culture, different from so-called Negro, Hispanic, Native, and Asian American minorities.

In truth, however, European Americans have not become such an amalgam. Customs and religions continue to distinguish groups of European Americans from each other in important ways. The most basic distinction among the groups has been between Northern European Protestant Americans and other European Americans. They often have attended separate schools, social clubs, and, of course, religious institutions.

Despite this diversity, instead of being viewed as a multiplicity of groups with distinct ethnic origins, all whites have tended to be perceived and treated as a monolithic majority in the United States and are thought to share common culture and social privilege. The notion of "white" has trumped other distinctions. However, one group, Anglo American Protestants, has dominated the U.S. political, economic, and cultural scene, electing presidents and becoming board chairmen. As a result, other European Americans have had to try to assimilate to the Anglo standard, for example, by masking their identities through Anglicizing their names in order to have opportunities (Reed, 1997).

The Traditional European American Worldview: Its Benefits and Limitations

A description of the roots of Western thought and philosophy from which the dominant European American culture sprang is beyond the scope of this chapter, but the general worldview that has emerged from these roots is well known to American school children. A worldview is a set of principles that determines how life is lived and how people think, feel, and act. It addresses the issues of identity, meaning, morality, and mission.

EUROPEAN AMERICAN VALUES

From the European American worldview came values such as an emphasis on individualism and autonomy, faith in problem solving that is action-oriented, the desirability of competitiveness and achievement, and materialism. These, along with an orientation toward the future, the maintenance of rigid time schedules, and a strict work ethic in which hard work results in both monetary and intrinsic worth, were all used to build a nation. Trust in rationalism and empiricism (i.e., the belief that reality is knowable and measurable through reason and observation), the imperative of self-discipline and self-monitoring, a belief in utilitarianism (i.e., what is useful is good and is morally superior), and the importance of thoughts and actions over feelings were all a part of the making of America.

The political and commercial accomplishments that were achieved during the nineteenth and early twentieth century in the United States were accompanied by European American feelings of superiority. In some sense, white Anglo American males saw themselves as masters of a universe that their own ingenuity had created. They wrote about it, sang songs about it, sculpted it, and painted pictures of it. Then, by means of a new art form called "movies" (an industry that was largely run by Jewish men, but which nevertheless produced films that portrayed the values of the dominant Anglo American Protestant culture), they mythologized it and eventually worshipped it to such a degree that their version of the dominant worldview became the only one acceptable for many. This myth shaped the belief that to be an Anglo American white male was better than to be anything else.

The white Northern European Protestant American culture held the worldview that was responsible for scientific experimentation and led to many accomplishments. Freedom, individual rights, geographic mobility, the nuclear family, individual achievement, and free market competition became the dominant ethos in America. This worldview was seen in both Western Europe and in America as the only possible "civilized" view. Other worldviews tended to be unfamiliar to, ignored by, or discounted by European-descended males.

LIMITATIONS AND OPPRESSIONS
OF THE EUROPEAN AMERICAN WORLDVIEW

There are many positive elements inherent in the European American worldview, but there are also limitations to it. However much women and minority Americans may have played a part in the achievements of the age, there was little mention of it. European Americans generally saw the white male as the sole creator of this world of invention, of goods, and of the marvels of mass communication. The European American male, who had just recently freed his black slaves and still held power over his wife, convinced himself and all children who read his textbooks that he was rightfully the privileged of the earth, and he continued to instigate and uphold laws that reinforced that view.

Non-whites, whether they were Native peoples, Asians, Latinos/Latinas, or African Americans, were seen as racially inferior (Gutman, 1989). Black Americans were excluded from the front seats of trolleys and trains, forced to use separate lavatories, and forced to drink from separate water fountains. In most American cities, they could not try on clothing in department stores, nor sleep in hotels that were not designated for them alone. Black children could not eat in the very restaurants where their mothers might work as cooks or cleaners. Minorities, for the most part, could acquire only menial jobs that whites either did not want or could not do. Non-whites were seen as people to be used for the good of the dominant culture, not as valuable human beings in their own right. The privilege that is gifted only to white Americans was legally protected throughout the first half of the twentieth century. Thus, contradictions to the Western European values of freedom and equality caused much injustice to large groups of people. This injustice included the sexism that limited the social and political freedom of women and the racism that restricted the freedom of black people. There was also the aforementioned denigration of non-Anglo Americans.

RECENT SHIFTS IN ATTITUDE

In the last half of the twentieth century, Americans have re-thought the messages of Anglo American and European American superiority that they may have learned from earlier, less tolerant generations at home and in school. As mentioned in Chapters 3 and 4, cultural pluralism, rather than amalgamation or assimilation, is emerging as the American model, as European Americans reclaim pride in their ethnic heritages and as America becomes the home of increasing numbers of non-European descendants and immigrants (Portes & Rimbaut, 2001; Reed, 1997). Nevertheless, significant elements of a European American worldview and the values that coincide with this view predominate in the nation's values, customs, and norms. That is especially true of the chief assumption of the dominant European worldview that success is within the control of the individual, indeed, that people have a right, a duty, to act in their own interests and thereby determine their own futures. In fact, that belief and an opportunity to enact it remains one of the main reasons that people from all nations continue to this day to immigrate to the United States.

ROOTS OF THE COUNSELING PROFESSION
IN THE EUROPEAN AMERICAN WORLDVIEW

What has evolved to be the contemporary counseling profession was founded on the premise of this Western worldview. Western thinking incorporates the scientific orientation of psychology and psychiatry through the influences of seminal European thinkers such as Sigmund Freud and Anton Pavlov, the testing movement through the works of European Americans such as G. Stanley Hall and James Cattell, and the pragmatism of the social reform and vocational guidance movements of the late nineteenth and early twentieth century United States through the work of people such as Jane Addams and Frank Parsons. Later, the work of Carl Rogers and others melded these influences into the profession of counseling. Inherent in the practice of counseling is the view that people can change, realize who they are, actualize the highest levels of self, and find meaning and mission in life.

The counseling profession was further founded on the Western scientific assumption that all phenomena are knowable and that all problems are solvable through observation, analysis, and reason. The founding European American researchers and thinkers had no thought of questioning that worldview. They also did not think beyond the world as it existed in their time. They would have assumed that their worldview was superior to others and that it applied to all people regardless of race, gender, country of origin, religion, or ethnicity. They did not know, nor could they have known, how the sociocultural, socioeconomic, and linguistic differences among the diverse groups that settled in the United States would need to be factored into meeting each group's educational and mental health needs.

Mental Health Issues for European Americans

Four of the significant contributors to mental health problems for European Americans are (1) social privilege or entitlement, (2) individualism and isolation, (3) the consequences of intolerance, and (4) gender issues. Each will be addressed in turn.

SOCIAL PRIVILEGE/ENTITLEMENT

The idea of privilege, sometimes called entitlement, may sound attractive, but in reality it creates problems, not only for those who lack it, but also for those to whom it is given. European Americans generally have invisible privileges, as described in Chapter 2. They do not experience the kinds of barriers in work, housing, and other aspects life that are routinely encountered by others.

European Americans are also not aware of the psychological dangers of their "privileged" status. Because of the high expectancy for success, coupled with a lack of social support, setbacks such as loss of an expected promotion or being denied access to a professional or social club might cause difficulties that would be hard for less-privileged people to comprehend. Less-privileged people are more ready for disappointment, and they recognize that environmental barriers are likely to present themselves.

The vignette that describes Tom's feelings when he is twice not promoted illustrates this concept. Tom is distraught about being turned down for two jobs. He belongs to a group of Anglo Americans who believe that they are entitled to get what they want. He is particularly upset because members of groups who were not as qualified, as he sees it, were given the opportunities that he thought he deserved. While it is natural to feel disappointed when one does not get what one wants, Tom adds bitterness and resentment to his anger and depression. He was not only upset because of losing two job opportunities; he was also resentful because those opportunities were given to people whom he believed were inherently not as capable (see Activity 8.3).

By contrast, members of nondominant groups often expect to experience denial of opportunity. That expectation does not make disappointment easy, but such individuals do not always attribute lack of success to personal failure. And, for members of nondominant groups, the experience of bias may itself cause depression and anger. In that sense, privilege causes anger and sadness in both the "haves" and "have nots."

ACTIVITY 8.3

Factors in Tom's Disappointment

In the vignette at the beginning of this chapter, Tom expects to succeed at work and feels anger and resentment that this has not happened. He suggests that the African American female and the Dominican male who were successful were less qualified than himself. He assumed that he deserved the job and that those who received it did so only because they were minorities. European Americans are often unprepared to deal with disappointment because they ascribe success to individual effort. When faced with unexpected barriers to goals, some European Americans, like Tom, react in emotionally unhealthy ways, using denial, resentment, and anger as coping mechanisms. As Tom's counselor, answer the following:

What part do you think privilege plays in Tom's thinking?

If you were Tom's counselor, how would you deal with Tom's notion of privilege?

If you were Tom's counselor, how would you work with his anger?

INDIVIDUALISM AND ISOLATION

The individualism of the mythic American hero can be a mental health hazard. The American hero is frequently thought of as one who leaves family and friends to go forth to bring about some good as a result of his or, in very few cases, her journey (Fiedler, 1966).

It has been suggested that Northern European Americans frequently live more isolated lives than do most Mediterraneans and Eastern Europeans, Hispanic/ Latinos, African Americans, or Asian Americans (McGill & Pearce, 2005). In the vignette that opened this chapter, Ellen follows an individualistic pattern that brings gain and loss to her. She leaves the Orthodox religion of her childhood. When she does this, she loses some connection to her family of origin. She feels fragmented because she does much work with very little help and few people to turn to. She seeks a counselor to assist her with her concerns partly in order to connect with someone whom she believes will be helpful.

The simple fact that most European Americans live in nuclear rather than extended families keeps them from having the kind of supportive group that is typical of multigenerational households. Because courage and lonely individualism are characteristics of the American hero, some young people may be attracted to an "ideal of aloneness rather than togetherness" (Bellah, Madsen, Sullivan, Swindler, & Tipton, 1985, p. 146). Despite this romantic notion of freedom, there is a danger in becoming hyper-individualistic with little regard for community. According to Bellah et al., radical individualism prevents European Americans from understanding their connectedness to each other. Bellah et al. propose that European Americans especially seek community in religion because of this isolation.

INTOLERANCE

Intolerance can be described as "the state of being unwilling or unable to endure or accept the beliefs, perspectives, or practices of others. It also involves a lack of recognition and respect for the fundamental rights and choices of others" (Guindon, Green, & Hanna, 2003, p. 168). Many writers have described the social and psychological problems that result from intolerance, such as racism, sexism, or homophobia (Davidson, 1999; DuBois, 1903/1961; Fanon, 1969; Hanna, Talley, & Guindon, 2000; Kleg, 1993; Miller, 1986; Robinson & Ginter, 1999; Sue, 1981).

European Americans are, of course, not alone in being intolerant toward others who are not like themselves. However, because they are members of the dominant culture in the United States and, de facto, have been in a position of power, they are more able to be oppressors than oppressed.

As a part of their social privilege, some European Americans learn to maintain social distance from those whom they perceive to be different from themselves. Many are fearful and less trusting of ethnic or racial "others"—strangers who are not like them in race, ethnicity, or social class. Some of this discomfort is due to lack of contact. European Americans, unlike members of other ethnic groups, generally do not have to spend a lot of time with ethnic others, due to housing and social patterns. Especially with regard to African Americans, some European Americans experience fear when they are not in the majority. As a result, European Americans are denied the richness of contact with the cultures of people of color.

GENDER ISSUES

The fourth and final mental health-related issue for European Americans is gender. Prior to the women's movement, white women seeking career roles outside the home were looked upon as having psychological problems. In the 1960s and 1970s, as a result of federal grants and initiatives, many married women were able to go college with less social stigma, after having experienced a break in their education. Richmond (1972) studied these so-called returning women and the special programs that community colleges, colleges, and universities provided to ease their way. She found that returning women would frequently tell college counselors that their private therapists urged them not to come to school. Instead, those therapists encouraged them to focus on their intrapsychic conflicts as a means of quelling their needs for achievement outside the home (Richmond, 1972).

Although this view may sound extreme in the present day, Blustein (2006) found that women still "face various forms of sexism in their schooling, preparation for careers, and in the occupational context" (p. 168). Power, according to Blustein, remains at the root of many gender inequities. Such power includes financial advantage, physical strength, and social influence. It is important that counselors, both male and female, be aware of the gender issues that continue to face women. (See Chapter 13 for a fuller treatment of gender.)

In the area of family roles, there is great conflict due to gender differences. Men, rich and poor, black or white, have problems adapting to the changing roles of males within the family (Waite & Nielsen, 2002). The revolution in the roles of today's dual-earner family has caused many men to seek counseling for their confusion about the way they might act as husbands and fathers, compared to the roles that they grew up expecting to play. That confusion includes what is viewed as acceptable sexual behavior and other couple issues such as who diapers, cooks the dinner, and earns the higher salary. In the case of Ellen, from the vignette at the start of this chapter, there is a reversal of traditional sex roles (see Activity 8.4). Ellen earns more; she travels for work. And Steve, her husband, resents being left with childcare and housework. The next sections will further explore the European American gender dilemmas.

European American Men

Problems with intimacy and with achievement are two issues for European American men. It is commonly held that European American men have been taught to show only limited emotional expression. For example, they are taught not to cry when hurt. Because of this emphasis on autonomy and control, many European American men have a difficult time turning to counselors for help in resolving their problems. They may feel isolated or alienated during difficult times. Counselors can expect them to be guarded about revealing family problems and acknowledging personal problems. Sports and alcohol may substitute for intimacy.

With respect to achievement, European American men expect themselves to succeed in their career. Stress reactions associated with lack of achievement are a common result of the dominant-culture worldview that emphasizes performance and achievement over affiliation and relationships.

ACTIVITY 8.4

Gender in the Case of Ellen and Steve

The role reversal between Ellen and Steve is becoming more common among European Americans.

As a counselor, how might you help Steve?

Think about all of the gender issues in the story. List them.

How would you address each of them?

In what ways is the gender gap between white women and white men narrowing?

Widening?

European American Women

Because the dominant culture favors the European American male, European American women are in a paradoxical social situation: They are both members and nonmembers of the dominant culture. Their struggle for gender equality was long fought and gains were hard won. For example, women's right to vote was not granted until 1920. Another 52 years went by before the U.S. Congress passed the Equal Rights Amendment that granted women legal rights to equal education and equal pay for equal work. Although the major legal battles are now over, the "war" is not yet won. Three major issues present conflict: balancing home and work, beauty and sex appeal dilemmas, and status.

Since many European American men "live to work," many men still expect women to keep a home and care for children while those women are also working outside the home to help support the family. As a result, European American women (and some men) experience a major struggle to balance work and family responsibilities (as do Ellen and Steve in the earlier vignette). Whether she is a secretary to the boss or the boss herself, today's woman, regardless of race or ethnicity, is still less privileged than men in a largely male-dominated American workplace. Needed are more family-friendly, relational, and employee-driven workplaces to replace the traditional, individual- and employer-driven ones in which work and family are completely separate (Moen & Han, 2001).

Women particularly struggle with issues of beauty and sex appeal. Many popular magazines publish photographic advertisements showing European American women that esteem and influence often depend more on body build than on character and intelligence and more on youth than on wisdom. Women tend to introject this cultural view. European American women are especially prone to believing that perfection in body, especially as defined by an unrealistic thinness, is an achievable and desirable goal. Hence, a large number of European American women and teens suffer from eating disorders in their attempt to copy the fashion industry's model of beauty.

Social class intersects with gender also. As discussed in Chapter 12, many upper middle-class and upper-class European American women frequently feel inferior to men and dependent on men for status. It is in these areas that counselors can be of great help, not only by listening to client stories, but also by challenging women's maladaptive beliefs about body shape, family duties, and care for self.

Characteristics of Specific European American Ethnic Groups

Lumping European Americans into one large grouping belies the important differences among ethnic subgroups. What follows is a description of some characteristics of particular European American ethnic groups. Included in this discussion are counseling issues and adaptations of counseling strategies that might match members of each of these groups.

These generalizations are inevitably inaccurate for many individuals. As iterated in Chapter 3, the related issues of generation from immigration, enculturation, acculturation, the desire to maintain ethnic practices, and multiethnicity (e.g., due to ethnic intermarriage) all affect any individual's relationship to culture.

Another proviso that the reader should remember is that all European American groups, to varying degrees, have been acculturated into the dominant Anglo American culture (and, conversely, they have, to a lesser extent, affected that culture). Whether the group is Catholic, Jewish, or Protestant is particularly salient because those groups have intermixed to a lesser extent (Shapiro, 1992).

Table 8.2 provides a quick overview of counseling-related matters for eight groupings of European Americans. Again, the reader should be wary of the inaccuracy of all generalizations and should, therefore, take this information as a mere approximation of each group's characteristics.

The sections that follow are focused on five somewhat arbitrary groupings of European Americans: (1) Northern European Protestants, (2) Irish Catholics, (3) Mediterranean peoples, (4) Jews (as an ethnic group), and (5) non-Jewish Eastern Europeans. Not every European American ethnic group is included, not because some do not deserve to be discussed, but because they are relatively small in number in the context of the entire population of the United States. For example, French Canadian Americans, Portuguese Americans, German Catholics, and Cajuns are not explicitly included in this section, although all are deeply rooted in American history and important to its culture. Readers are encouraged to supplement this review with other readings for those groups.

Table 8.2   Counseling Considerations for Specific European American Ethnic Groups

Ethnic Group	Characteristics	Counseling Considerations
Northern European Protestants	Prototype-dominant U.S. culture "Privileged" Respect for work Well-defined nuclear family Values: autonomy; achievement; punctuality; emotional restraint	Traditional counseling techniques useful Employ empathy and genuineness Structure sessions Begin with formal then move toward informal relationships
Regional Variation: **Southern Whites**	Values: hierarchy; religiosity; indirect communication; gentility and good manners	Begin with formality and show of manners Address conformance and perfectionistic tendencies Be aware of rules of behavior and sensitive issues of religion and sexuality
Scotch Irish	Values: independence; religiosity (including evangelism and individual salvation); arguing; discipline and strength; pride in self and community	Difficulty in opening up and guarded emotionality Requires counselor patience Understand and be prepared to discuss sin and salvation Consider family in addition to individual counseling
Scandinavians	Values: independence; heartiness; tolerance for isolation; peace and nonviolence; emotional control; democracy; egalitarianism; orderliness; nonexhibitionism	Counseling undertaken only for critical issues Use client-centered approach to build trust Avoid appearance of leading or authoritarian session structure Work toward helping clients with emotional expression without shame

Ethnic Group	Characteristics	Counseling Considerations
Mediterranean Peoples: Greeks	Sense of alienation from and stigmatization by dominant cultural groups Values: extended family; Greek Orthodox Church; Greek language; Greek neighborhoods; arranged marriages; rigidly defined gender roles; men's male social life; strict child-rearing practice in which sons exceed, fathers and daughters remain submissive	Recognize key cultural importance of family including dominance of familial over individual needs Develop relationship of acceptance and understanding of client's needs and culture Normalize counseling and minimize idea of pathology Restructure client problem as health/stress related Use psychoeducational behavioral approach
Mediterranean Peoples: Italians	Few commonalities across Italian subcultures, locations, generations Most are Roman Catholic Values: celebrations; Catholic Church including pageantry; family interests over education (first and second generation); education and upward mobility (later generation); authoritarian male head of household; revered, powerful mother; sanctity of marriage (no divorce); sexual fidelity in women; infidelity in men expected; large families	Issues vary by generation. Many cause intergenerational conflict Counseling viewed with suspicion; believe problems are kept within family Family enmeshment can cause problems Understand individual's need to stay connected yet separate from family of origin Younger generations present with issues such as interfaith marriage and birth control Older Italians may be dealing with effects of early anti-Italianism and discrimination

(Continued)

Table 8.2 (Continued)

Ethnic Group	Characteristics	Counseling Considerations
Ethnic Jews	Common bond despite lack of homogeneity in religion, social group, or European national roots Commonality of history of oppression and persecution and Diaspora Values: communal life; intellectual pursuit; liberal causes; equality; high achievement; discussion/debate of ideas; direct communication; children's welfare and expression of opinion	Familiarity with and acceptance of counseling and psychotherapy Will seek counseling readily Permeable boundaries between parent and child may be problematic Be aware of easy expression of feelings including negative affect (anger) Inquire about influence of Jewish religion on life and level of client's religious observances
Non-Jewish Eastern Europeans (Polish, Hungarian, Lithuanian, Czech, Romanian, etc.)	Characteristics vary widely. Individual ethnic groups formed own communities, including use of ethnic language and traditions. Some remain so; others are fully integrated into the dominant American culture Values: traditional roles in extended families; ethnic music, food, language; religion (Catholicism); obedience in children; stoicism; conservatism about sex and marriage	Experience shame when seeking counseling Be aware of experience of perpetuated bigotry Alcoholism can be a problem Need for relationship not easily expressed Reticence in discussing nontraditional views of sex and marriage or less traditional gender roles Intergenerational conflict may be an issue

NORTHERN EUROPEAN PROTESTANTS

Northern European Protestants, variously called Anglo Americans, white Anglo Saxon Protestants, and British Americans, make up the Northern European group that is the prototype for the dominant U.S. culture. Their culture is often neglected in the multicultural discourse because it is so pervasive and therefore less visible as an ethnicity. In counterpoint to that neglect, McGoldrick (2005) makes the point that Anglo Americans, like all other people, are "ethnic," in that they are shaped by the culture from which they come.

For the sake of this discussion, Northern European Protestant culture will incorporate the Protestant Dutch, German, Scotch Irish, Southern white, and Scandinavian cultures because they share many characteristics.

Northern European Protestant culture is characterized by restraint, thoroughness, respect for work and a job well done, and a well-defined nuclear family. Such values as autonomy, achievement, and punctuality also characterize Anglo American culture.

General Counseling Considerations

Anglo Americans tend to be responsible about counseling and take it seriously. Materials found in general counseling texts will probably be useful with this population. Overall, Anglo Americans react positively to empathic responding and genuineness. Structure is important to Northern European Protestants, although after the beginning sessions the relationship generally can become less formal. Sessions, whether group or individual, should be well-structured and begin and end on time.

Subgroups of Northern European Protestants

At least three subgroups in this ethnicity have maintained particularly distinct characteristics and ethnic identities. The following groups do also share the general characteristics of Northern European Protestants that were described above.

Southern Whites. A regional variation within the Northern European Protestant group can be seen most notably in the American South. This culture is particularly characterized by hierarchy, indirectness in communication, and religiosity (Batson, 1993; O'Connor, 1953). A way of life that honors the appearance of gentility and the practice of good manners is traditional in the South. Being humble, courteous, well-behaved, friendly, and modest; never forgetting to say "Please" and "Thank you"; referring to women as "ladies"; addressing them as "Ma'am" and calling men "Sir" are all Southern traditions (Cardwell, 2005). Along with courtesy, graciousness, and manners, church attendance has always been particularly important to many Southern whites. Religion in general, religious fundamentalism, and revivalism are more common there than in other regions of the United States. These tendencies have significant mental health implications.

Counseling Considerations

A counselor working with Southern whites, especially those from the middle class, should expect an outward show of manners and formality and be prepared to respond in kind. Counselors should recognize and be prepared to discuss any perfectionist tendencies that their clients may harbor about being socially proper and conforming to social codes. It is wise and appropriate for the counselor to ask the client about those Southern traditions that may seem different from those of the counselor. Counselors should be aware that there are particular counseling implications for many Southern manners, including those related to both religion and sexuality. Both are sensitive issues, and are related, because both are often guided by strict rules for behavior.

Scotch Irish. This group has been discussed in some detail earlier in the chapter. The Scotch Irish have often mixed over the past 200 years with other Northern European Protestant groups. However, there are places, like in the Southern Appalachian region, where their culture is distinct and dominant. Independence is a traditional characteristic of the Scotch Irish, who are also known as proud, strong, disciplined, and notoriously argumentative (Webb, 2004). The strictness in behavioral codes that marked the Scotch Irish Presbyterian Church in early America has continued (Leyburn, 1962). They are a marked element in the evangelistic Christian tradition in the United States, where individual salvation rather than communal social action is emphasized.

Counseling Considerations

Counselors should be aware that in spite of the stalwart appearance and genuine fortitude of the Scotch Irish client, a need for help may be present. It may be difficult for the Scotch Irish client to be open and receive counseling assistance. This is particularly true of males, but women are also likely to be emotionally guarded; therefore, the counselor should be patient and wait for client disclosure and emotional expression. The counselor should also be prepared to converse about sin and salvation if the client chooses to do so. The counselor should also be aware that Scotch Irish parents may not be demonstrative in expressing caring to their offspring. Family counseling as well as individual counseling may be important.

Tom, in the vignette at the start of this chapter, is partially of Scotch Irish descent. Significantly, little is said about the nature of Tom's relationships with others. Tom's tale illustrates the hyper-individualism and aloneness that can be problematic for people of Scotch Irish descent. The reader is encouraged to complete Activity 8.5 in order to apply some of these characteristics to the case of Tom.

Scandinavians. Like the Scotch Irish, Scandinavians are Northern Europeans and most are Protestant. The Scandinavian population in the United States is primarily composed of Norwegians and Swedes, with a strong Danish presence.

ACTIVITY 8.5

Northern European Protestant Culture and the Case of Tom

The case of Tom from the vignette at the beginning of this chapter illustrates aspects of Northern European culture.

What Northern European traits do you see in Tom?

How do you think Tom's inherited family characteristics will affect the counseling process?

How would you respond to Tom's resentment and anger?

How might what you know about the phases of white racial identity (from Chapter 4) help in understanding and helping Tom?

Would you or would you not introduce the concept of white privilege with him?

Finns, while technically not Scandinavians, also arrived in large numbers in the last century and settled in the upper Midwest.

Because of the harshness of the winter climate in their countries of origin, most Scandinavians are independent and share a tolerance for isolation (Christianson, 1992). According to Erickson (2005), Scandinavians also tend to be reflective, honest, and very practical. Not pushy, they tend to value peace and nonviolence. Scandinavians tend to keep emotions inside, emphasizing positive feelings over hurt and sadness. Emotional control extends to affection. An old joke has the Scandinavian husband saying to his wife on their wedding day, "I'll say I love you now. If anything changes, I'll tell you."

Scandinavians have high regard for democracy and egalitarianism, prefer orderliness, and downplay exhibitionism. As a rule, they do not call attention to themselves and they try not to display emotion in public.

Counseling Considerations

The counselor should know that when a Scandinavian client comes for counseling the issues must be critical, due to the independence that characterizes the culture. Because Scandinavians are reserved and suspicious of authority, the counselor should not pose as an authority who has power over the client or over the client's situation. Erickson (2005) suggests that counselors who work with Scandinavians must know how to lead without being obvious and must keep order in sessions without being authoritarian. Client-centered counseling is consistent with Scandinavian culture. He also suggests that counselors should know how to help clients express appropriate emotions without shame and "gently help families speak the unspeakable" (pp. 650–651).

IRISH CATHOLICS

Many Irish Catholics are the descendants of the poor peasants who came to America between the mid-nineteenth and early twentieth centuries, directly or indirectly as a result of the massive potato famine of the late 1840s and British oppression. Although they were Northern European and largely English-speaking, the Catholic Irish nevertheless have been seen as distinct from other Northern Europeans.

They were maligned by the so-called natives. Thus, life in America frequently was difficult for the Catholic Irish. As a result, they used a mixture of humor and pessimism in their culture. McGoldrick (2005) put it this way:

> The Irish are a people of many paradoxes. While having a tremendous flair for bravado, they may inwardly assume that anything that goes wrong is the result of their sins. . . . They love a good time, . . . yet are drawn to tragedy. (p. 595)

Among the distinctive characteristics that counselors might see in Irish Americans is a resiliency and the ability to enjoy life even when circumstances are difficult. Humor is used to mask conflict and pain. They are inclined to celebrate even loss expressively and heartily. They value large gatherings and raucous behavior, which may occur even in times of mourning. However, this hearty gregariousness can mask denial of negative emotions. Drinking alcohol is common, and the bar, like the church, has been a communal meeting place for Irish Americans. Irish social events are almost inevitably accompanied by alcohol.

In Irish Catholic families, fathers have historically been "shadowy or absent figures" (McGoldrick, 2005, p. 602) who deal with their wives and with their family problems by distancing from them rather than confronting them. The Irish mother is legendary, in the sense that she is sentimentalized as strong and all-powerful. However, she is also a very vulnerable person.

The Catholic Church has been a dominant force in Irish American life, and it has traditionally maintained very strict rules of sexual behavior. The straightness of Irish step dancers is analogous to the rigidity of traditional Irish American views toward sex, which is considered a sin outside of marriage. Hence, expressing their sexuality remains a thorny issue for many Irish Catholics.

Counseling Considerations

Counselors should be aware that the Irish have a high tolerance for nonrealistic thinking. They value fantasy. They have difficulty in dealing directly with conflicts and frequently use sarcasm, outbursts of anger, and interpersonal cutoffs in order to avoid them (McGoldrick, 2005). Not inclined to share deep emotions, the family as a whole suffers from the inability of its members to communicate feelings.

Prone to denial, the Irish are also disinclined to acknowledge health problems. Counselors must, therefore, be alert to the possibility that their Irish Catholic clients are concealing physical as well as social and family problems.

When Irish Catholics seek counseling, they are likely to see it as "similar to confession" (McGoldrick, 2005, p. 608). The Catholic Irish endure suffering as for long as possible, then turn to their priest in the secrecy of the confessional and recite that which is believed to be a wrong thought or deed. McGoldrick suggests that when working with Catholic Irish, counselors should keep a friendly distance, not unlike the curtain on the confessional, so as to avoid embarrassing the client. It is important to be serious and businesslike while maintaining a sense of humor. Because the client may use humor to disguise a problem, or fantasize in order to deny it, the counselor will have to read between the lines to determine what is really at the root of the client's issues. It is important that the counselor not use techniques that will increase the anxiety that normally runs high in this population. McGoldrick suggests that a good strategy with which to help Irish Catholic clients is to limit guilt and suffering by restricting them to particular time intervals. Because of the traditional nature of Irish Catholic culture, it may be important for counselors to help males learn to be emotional supports to their mates. In sum, alcoholism, repressed sexuality, and lack of emotional expression disguised as humor are factors that might be present in Irish Catholic clients.

MEDITERRANEAN PEOPLES (GREEKS AND ITALIANS)

Greeks and Italians, while distinct ethnic groups, share some general characteristics. Both traditionally have strong paternal authority in families, allow for much expression of emotion, and value practical and hands-on work.

Greeks

Greeks immigrated to the United States in two major waves. The "old immigrants" came between 1890 and 1920, and "new immigrants" arrived after the Immigration Act of 1965 (Killian & Agathangelou, 2005). The "old immigrant" Greeks came to America for economic reasons. Many were men who made money and later brought their families. The "new immigrant" Greeks came for economic reasons but also left their country because it was devastated by civil war, poverty, and political upheaval. They came as families, and most had the skills required for business or trades. Many intended to educate their children in America and then return to Greece.

The Anglo American culture was quite strange to them. They were also, in turn, strange to non-Greek Americans. The Greek language used a different alphabet; Greek foods were largely unknown; and the Greek Orthodox religion, although Christian, was unfamiliar to non-Greeks. The Greek immigrants who endured alienation from the dominant culture and remained in America took two different paths. Some gave up their Greek ways as quickly as possible, learned English, and identified as Americans rather than as Greek Americans. Those who did not adopt Anglo ways used both the Greek Orthodox Church and Greek language publications to help them very gradually adjust to their new land. These Greek immigrants remained in "Greek towns" and found solace in their neighborhoods and in their families.

Counseling Considerations. Counselors should recognize that family is a very important element of Greek culture. The family's needs are put before the needs of the individual. It is typical of Greeks who are in need to turn to the extended family for support. In traditional Greek family life, marriages are arranged, and husband and wife roles are rigidly defined (Killian & Agathangelou, 2005). Child rearing is strict: Sons are expected to exceed their fathers; daughters are supposed to be well educated but submissive. The Greek Orthodox Church reinforces this structure. Fathers often maintain a distance from their children and their wives, spending much of their social life with male friends. Children often go to parochial school where they learn English and therefore often serve as interpreters for their parents. Counselors need to be sensitive to the English capabilities of Greek clients.

In times of crisis, Greeks will often turn to the priest as a resource for support before they will consider seeking the help of a counselor. If counseling is needed, it is likely that the Greek mother, not the father, will seek it.

Because Greeks have been stigmatized by Anglo culture, it is important that the counselor develop a relationship in which the client feels well regarded and understood. Because counseling carries a negative connotation to many Greeks, who assume that it is primarily for persons who have severe psychological problems, a counselor can reduce her or his client's discomfort by restructuring or reframing the client's presenting problem as health or stress related. A counselor might also use a psychoeducational behavioral approach to trigger client change. This will serve to minimize the notion of pathology and normalize the counseling experience.

Italians

What Americans consider typically Italian is largely Southern Italian. Many Southern Italians, like Greeks, came to America with the intention of making money and then going home. Those who stayed in America brought their families over as soon as they could. Most Italian immigrants came to America as peasants and settled in a "Little Italy," from which the first two generations rarely ventured forth (Giordano, McGoldrick, & Klages, 2005).

Like most ethnic groups, Italians value religion and family. Italians are, for the most part, Roman Catholic by religion and tradition. They are celebratory and enjoy the familiarity and pageantry of the church. To first- and second-generation Italians, family interests are primary, even over education. It is not unusual for the children of first- and second-generation Italian immigrants to have been asked by their parents to stop going to school and to work in the family business or trade. The present generation, however, values education more, and many children are upwardly mobile.

The traditional head of the Italian household is the father, and he can be quite authoritarian. The Italian mother is the heart of the family. She is honored, frequently revered, and as such, is powerful. Italians love their families, which are generally quite large. Women traditionally stayed at home and cared for their children. They were expected to be sexually faithful to their husbands. However, the Italian male was given far greater latitude in sexual and career matters (Giordano et al., 2005).

Counseling Concerns. Italians, like Greeks, have regarded counseling with suspicion. It is assumed that all problems are to be handled within the family. It is considered shameful if a family can't handle its problems. A priest might be consulted because he is supposed to be learned and is also bound to secrecy.

Separation from family can be traumatic and can cause major disruptions in life. On the other hand, enmeshment is typical of many Italian families, and it can also cause serious problems. This is particularly true for Italian young people who may love their families but want to avoid becoming swallowed up by them. Counselors should understand a client's need to be both close to family and to get away from it. This situation was seen in the case of Tony, who wanted to be his own person. However, he did not want to displease his parents, particularly his father.

Counseling issues vary with the generations. Some older Italians may enjoy the strong role the Catholic Church has played in helping them feel at home here, while their offspring may resent the restrictions that it imposes. Young adults may seek counseling concerning interfaith marriage, abortion, or the use of birth control, all of which are inconsistent with traditional religious beliefs. In the area of sexuality and gender, many Italian women dislike the double standard for sexual behavior; younger people are most likely to disregard it or seek counseling with regard to it. Many of these issues of generational conflict are present in the vignette of Tony (see Activity 8.6).

JEWS

Nearly half of world Jewry lives in the United States (Rosen & Weltman, 2005). Over time, many changes have taken place in the Jewish community as Jews from everywhere in the Diaspora (the dispersion of Jewish peoples from Israel over the past 2,000 years) migrated to America.

Being Jewish can be both a religious and an ethnic identity. It may be one and not the other; for example, a Jew may be agnostic or atheist and still identify as Jewish. The common experience of Jews, according to Rosen and Weltman (2005), is the experience or historical memory of oppression found at one time or another in many Jewish settlements throughout the world. The tenuousness of their lives in lands in which they were strangers and the persecution that took place in many communities is one important explanation for the unity of the Jewish people. The United States has been one of the safest places for Jews, although serious anti-Semitism has scarred American history and culture also.

ACTIVITY 8.6

Italian American Culture and the Case of Tony

Review the case of Tony from the vignette at the beginning of the chapter.

Why do you think Tony is so confused?

What class-related work ethic does Tony's father represent?

Why do you think Tony feels that his father does not see Mary Louise as a potential store owner?

What role does Tony's mother possibly play in this vignette and in life?

What is the role of Father Leo and the Church within the community?

What might/should Tony do?

Jewish communal life in America has always been strong. However, the majority of the descendants of turn-of-the-twentieth-century Jewish immigrants are today assimilated into American culture. It was not always that way. Prior to World War II, there was so much prejudice against Jews in this country that Jewish communities built their own hospitals and educational institutions. For example, the existence of Brandeis University is testimony to the exclusionary practices of prestigious universities toward the admission of talented Jewish youth.

Although most Jewish immigrants from Eastern Europe were poor and lacked citizenship in the countries they left behind, many became affluent citizens in their new home. They sponsored progressive social causes and excelled in intellectual pursuits. Jews, a tiny minority (less than 1 percent of the American population), are seen in every walk of American life. Since their beginnings in America, Jews have distinguished themselves in many fields, including medicine (e.g., Jonas Salk), law (e.g., Lewis Brandeis and Alan Dershowitz), music (e.g., Irving Berlin and Leonard Bernstein), and communications (e.g., Louis B. Meyer, Jack Warner, and David Sarnoff) (Lipset & Raab, 1995; Shapiro, 1992).

Counseling Considerations

Most American Jews are familiar with counseling and psychotherapy and are quite amenable to it. Freud, Adler, Frankl, Ellis, Beck, and many other notable counseling theorists and practitioners were of Jewish ethnicity. Jewish culture values high achievement (Rosen & Weltman, 2005). Jewish parents place high value on their children's welfare and are likely to seek help for them whenever and wherever help is needed. Children are generally encouraged to speak their mind. Boundaries between parents and children are permeable. Equality is valued and authority is questioned in Jewish culture. Among both young people and adults, there exists a tradition of discussing and debating ideas. Even religious and ethical issues are seen as not settled and in need of discussion and debate.

Most Jews express their feelings readily. What may be taken by outsiders as anger might simply be disagreement and may well be understood within the group as an expression of affection. Communication is generally quite direct and can seem even aggressive to those from other cultures. Jews are likely to seek counseling for just about any problem when they think that counseling will benefit them. Counselors of Jewish clients should not feel shy about asking their clients about the relative influence of Jewish religious observances on their lives. The case of Ellen illustrates these themes. Note the reference to dietary laws and Sabbath practice in the vignette and in Activity 8.7.

EASTERN EUROPEANS

Many people from Eastern European countries such as Poland, Lithuania, Czechoslovakia (now two countries, the Czech Republic and Slovakia), Hungary, and Romania came to America at the turn of the last century as peasants and unskilled workers. Each group banded together in its own community and worshipped mainly in Catholic churches that were frequently flavored with the language and traditions of the lands that they had left behind. The immigrants often found work as laborers and brought with them ethnic music, food, and language. Many lived out traditional roles in extended families, which were their major source of psychological support. In time, many of their children became educated; intermarried, usually with Catholic European American spouses of other ethnicities (sometimes not with the blessing of parents on either side); and became fully integrated into the mainstream of European American life.

Eastern Europeans are aware of the bigotry that has been applied to them, for example, in the form of the jokes that call them "dumb." Counselors need to know that while many Eastern European immigrants were poor, some were political refugees, professionals and intellectuals, and even former nobility (Folwarski & Smolinski, 2005).

Counseling Considerations

First, it should be noted that traditional Eastern Europeans are likely to experience shame if and when they need counseling. Among Poles and other Eastern Europeans, stoicism is valued, and a need for relationship and connectedness is not easily expressed. The goal in child rearing is obedience. Conservative in

ACTIVITY 8.7

Jewish Culture and the Case of Ellen

Review the case of Ellen from the beginning of this chapter. Respond to the following questions:

What do you think is behind the conflict between Ellen's mother and Ellen?

Are such conflicts universal?

Do you see any ethnic characteristics in the family relationships in this vignette?

Do you think family therapy or couples counseling is warranted?

In what ways does religion play into Ellen's life script?

What do you think Ellen's mother means when she says, "serve you bacon if she could"? Is it about only religious practices and food, or is something else going on here?

How much does Ellen's counselor need to understand about Jewish dietary laws and Sabbath practices to work with Ellen?

How much do you now know about religious difference among Jewish groups?

matters of marriage and sex, many Eastern Europeans are likely to avoid discussions that negate traditional gender roles. However, in younger generations, Eastern European Americans, like other European American ethnic groups, are relaxing the rules, and counselors need to be aware of generational conflicts that may arise as a result. Finally, it is important to recognize that alcoholism is a problem that affects many Eastern European Americans and causes interruptions in smooth family relations.

Box 8.1 outlines counseling strategies that might be used with the clients from the vignettes that opened this chapter. Finally, now that you have read about some European American ethnic groups, answer the questions in Activity 8.8.

BOX 8.1   Counseling Strategies in the Vignette Cases

At the beginning of this chapter, three very different European American clients were presented. Each came into counseling without an awareness that his or her issues might be culture-specific.

Ellen's counselor worked with her individually, but was nevertheless well versed in family therapy. She helped Ellen decide that her allegiance needed to be primarily to her husband, rather than to her mother. Eventually, Ellen and Steve entered couples counseling where they were able to resolve their problems and learned to live in greater harmony, each realizing how their different understandings of "being Jewish" had contributed to their discord. They vowed to raise their children in a different way than either of them had been raised.

Tom's EAP counselor addressed his frustrations and anger using cognitive behavioral processes and techniques. He worked with him on his inappropriate use of alcohol to relieve his anxiety and stress. Tom learned to channel his stress into the healthier outlets of running and family activities. Although Tom did not gain appreciable insight into his prejudice or an understanding of his position of "white privilege," he was able to come to terms with how his use of alcohol might have contributed to his lack of promotions. He learned to live life with less anger.

Tony's school counselor initially empathized with Tony, using Rogerian client-centered processes, then moved to using techniques from solution-focused therapy and assertiveness training. These approaches helped Tony gain insight into his family situation. He was able to articulate to his counselor what his own desires and goals were. He rehearsed how he might express his desires to his father while still honoring his father's traditional Italian values. When he finally did so, his father was more accepting than he had anticipated. Tony's prior talk with Mom and Mom's subsequent talk with Father Leo had added to his father's understanding. Tony also talked to his sister about her telling their parents her business interests. Tony planned to attend community college for his first year of college so that he could continue to work in the family store and train his sister to take his place. He applied for a scholarship to the state university under a delayed entry program.

┌───┐

ACTIVITY 8.8

Post-Chapter Questions on European Americans

1. Describe the changes that have occurred in the European American population from the country's inception to the present day.

2. With which of the European American groups described in this chapter would it be easiest for you to work?

   Most difficult for you to work with?

   Explain.

3. What topic covered in this chapter would you like to know more about in order to be a culturally alert practitioner?

4. Now, after having read this chapter, go back to Activity 8.2 and answer the questions once more.

└───┘

Summary

The Europeans who immigrated to the United States are not a homogeneous group. They formerly lived in different national and social environments. They came to America from European countries at different times and for different reasons. They settled in various parts of America and, by so doing, changed both themselves and the United States.

Professionals who counsel European Americans need to understand each of their unique cultural worldviews in order to be helpful in ways that clients can understand and accept. Counselors need to decide what framework can best be applied when working with individual clients from any of the European American groups. Interventions should not be limited to a "one style fits all" model.

It is also important to know that privilege is not equally distributed among all European Americans. Ethnic origin, gender, social class, and sexual orientation have much to do with privilege and with worldview. Counselors need to be further reminded that European Americans are not all Anglo, and all are not privileged in the same way. Of course, those who have enjoyed social privilege often have struggles and issues, nevertheless.

Finally, it is important that the counselor not overgeneralize. European Americans, along with all other Americans, will continue to change and be changed by this multicultural nation.

References

Batson, A. B. (1993). *Having it, y'all.* Nashville, TN: Rutledge Hill Press.

Bellah, R. N., Madsen, R., Sullivan, W. M., Swindler, A., & Tipton, S. M.(1985). *Habits of the heart.* Berkeley: University of California Press.

Blustein, D. L. (2006). *The psychology of working.* Mahwah, NJ: Erlbaum.

Boorstin, D. J. (1974). *The Americans: The democratic experience.* New York: Vantage Press.

Cardwell, T. C. (2005). *Proper southern manners.* Retrieved November 23, 2005, from http://members.tripod.com/~tcc230/SManners.htm

Christianson, J. R. (1992). Scandinavian Americans. In J. D. Buenker & L. A. Ratner (Eds.), *Multiculturalism in the United States* (pp. 103–129). New York: Greenwood.

Church, E. F. (1989). *The Jefferson bible.* Boston: Beacon Press.

Cousins, N. (1958). *In God we trust.* New York: Harper & Brothers.

Davidson, M. G. (1999). Religion and spirituality. In R. M. Perez & K. A. DeBord (Eds.), *Handbook of counseling and psychotherapy with lesbian, gay, and bisexual clients* (pp. 409–433). Washington, DC: American Psychological Association.

DuBois, W. E. B. (1961). *The souls of black folks.* Greenwich, CT: Fawcett. (Original work published 1903)

Erickson, B. M. (2005). Scandinavian families: Plain and simple. In M. McGoldrick, J. Giordano, & N. Garcia-Preto (Eds.), *Ethnicity and family therapy* (3rd ed., pp. 641–653). New York: Guilford Press.

Fanon, F. (1969). *The wretched of the earth.* (C. Farrington, Trans.). New York: Grove Press.

Fiedler, L. A. (1966). *Love and death in the American novel.* New York: Stein & Day.

Fischer, D. H. (1989). *Albion's seed: Four British folkways in America.* New York: Oxford University Press.

Folwarski, J., & Smolinski, J. (2005). Polish families. In M. McGoldrick, J. Giordano, & N. Garcia-Preto (Eds.), *Ethnicity and family therapy* (3rd ed., pp. 711–723). New York: Guilford Press.

Giordano, J., McGoldrick, M., & Klages, J. G. (2005). Italian families. In M. McGoldrick, J. Giordano, & N. Garcia-Preto (Eds.), *Ethnicity and family therapy* (3rd ed., pp. 616–628). New York: Guilford Press.

Guindon, M. H., Green, A., & Hanna, F. J. (2003). Intolerance and psychopathology: Toward a general diagnosis for racism, sexism, and homophobia. *American Journal of Orthopsychiatry, 73,* 167–173.

Gutman, H. G. (1989). *Who built America?* New York: Pantheon Books.

Hanna, F. J., Talley, W. B., & Guindon, M. H. (2000). The power of perception: Toward a model of cultural oppression and liberation. *Journal of Counseling & Development, 78,* 430–441.

Killian, K. D., & Agathangelou, A. M. (2005). Greek families. In M. McGoldrick, J. Giordano, & N. Garcia-Preto (Eds.), *Ethnicity and family therapy* (3rd ed., pp. 573–585). New York: Guilford Press.

Kleg, M. (1993). *Hate, prejudice, and racism*. Albany: State University of New York Press.

Leyburn, J. G. (1962). *The Scotch Irish*. Chapel Hill: University of North Carolina Press.

Lipset, S. M., & Raab, E. (1995). *Jews and the new American scene*. Cambridge, MA: Harvard University Press.

McGill, D. W., & Pearce, J. K. (2005). American families with English ancestors from the colonial era: Anglo Americans. In M. McGoldrick, J. Giordano, & N. Garcia-Preto (Eds.), *Ethnicity and family therapy* (3rd ed., pp. 520–533). New York: Guilford Press.

McGoldrick, M. (2005). Irish families. In M. McGoldrick, J. Giordano, & N. Garcia-Preto (Eds.), *Ethnicity and family therapy* (3rd ed., pp. 595–615). New York: Guilford Press.

Miller, J. B. (1986). *Toward a new psychology of women*. Boston: Beacon Press.

Moen, P., & Han, S. K. (2001). Gendered careers: A life-course perspective. In A. Hertz & N. Marshall (Eds.), *Working families* (pp. 42–57). Berkeley: University of California Press.

Nerlich, G. (1989). *Values and valuing*. New York: Oxford University Press.

O'Connor, F. (1953). *A good man is hard to find*. Retrieved June 23, 2006, from http://xroads.Virginia.edu/~DRBR/Goodman.html

Portes, A., & Rimbaut, R.G. (2001). *Legacies: The story of the immigrant second generation*. Berkeley: University of California Press.

Reed, I. (1997). *A multi America*. New York: Viking.

Richmond, L. J. (1972). A comparison of returning women and regular college age women at a community college (Doctoral dissertation, University of Maryland, College Park,1972). *Dissertation Abstracts International, 33*(03),1028.

Richmond, L. J. (1999). Transcultural counseling and European Americans. In J. McFadden (Ed.), *Transcultural counseling* (2nd ed., pp. 297–314). Alexandria, VA: American Counseling Association Press.

Richmond, L. J. (2003). Counseling European Americans. In F. Harper & J. McFadden (Eds.), *Culture and counseling: New approaches* (pp. 133–146). Boston: Allyn & Bacon.

Robinson, T. L., & Ginter, E. J. (Eds.). (1999). Racism: Healing its effects. [Special Issue]. *Journal of Counseling & Development, 77*, 3.

Rosen, E. J., & Weltman, S. F. (2005). Jewish families: An overview. In M. McGoldrick, J. Giordano., & N. Garcia-Preto (Eds.), *Ethnicity and family therapy* (3rd ed., pp. 667–679). New York: Guilford Press.

Shapiro, E. (1992). Jewish Americans. In J. Buenker & L. Ratner (Eds.), *Multiculturalism in the United States*. New York: Greenwood.

Sue, D. W. (1981). *Counseling the culturally different: Theory and practice*. New York: Wiley.

Tobias, H. J. (1990). *A history of the Jews in New Mexico*. Albuquerque: University of New Mexico Press.

Waite, L. J., & Nielsen, M. (2002). The rise of the dual earner family, 1963–1997. In F. R. Herts & N. L. Marshall (Eds.), *Working families* (pp. 23–41). Berkeley: University of California Press.

Webb, J. H. (2004). *Born fighting: How the Scots-Irish shaped America*. New York: Broadway Books.

Zinn, H. (2003). *A people's history of the United States*. New York: HarperCollins.

Middle Eastern Americans

9

Julie Hakim-Larson and
Sylvia Nassar-McMillan

Sadie (a pseudonym) is a 49-year-old first generation female Middle Eastern refugee in the United States. Her symptoms of depression and anxiety began in her country of origin shortly after the dramatic arrest and execution of her husband. She began to experience profound sadness, violent suicidal thoughts and dreams, loss of interest in life, an inability to cope with the requirements of daily life, and social embarrassment. For years she struggled to manage the symptoms on her own. She withdrew from social situations due to the fear that her symptoms might embarrass her. However, her symptoms were continually aggravated because her family frequently moved from one place to another, which was very unsettling to her. Finally, she decided to ask for professional help, realizing how important it was for her to be helpful to her children. Treatment focused on helping her to overcome her symptoms and the stigma attached to feeling depressed (adapted from Simman, 2004).

❖

Youssef was born in the United States. He is the 18-year-old son of immigrants from the Middle East. He is in his senior year of high school and was recently arrested for drug possession. Only his family's native language is spoken at home; thus, his parents rely on him to interpret and explain any communication that occurs in English. As a child, he was overindulged and was raised permissively, with few rules and restrictions placed on his behavior. He learned English as a second language and performed poorly throughout school, although he managed to pass. His teachers told his parents that they thought he had attention deficit hyperactivity disorder and that he should see a psychologist for testing and a psychiatrist for evaluation because he might need medication. In high school, he belonged to one of a number of competing local gangs. After his court appearance for the drug possession, he minimized the severity of his situation by mistranslating the proceedings to his parents.

This chapter provides some ways counselors can increase their understanding of people like Sadie, Youssef, and others. It explores the varied cultures and peoples of the Middle East and offers counselors a framework for enhancing their delivery of mental health services to Middle Eastern Americans.

In spite of the differences in age, ethnic background, and life experiences, Sadie and Youssef each have family histories that involve immigration to North America from a country located in the Middle East. Sadie, her husband, and the members of their family experienced the horror and atrocities of torture, extreme wartime trauma, and serious violation of their human rights. The social stigma and shame associated with her family's ordeals contributed to Sadie's sense of despair and despondency. Youssef's symptoms of poor attention, impulsivity, and hyperactivity have been further exacerbated by already difficult acculturation problems and have affected his life at school and in the community.

Counselors must consider both their attitudes and their knowledge about Middle Easterners. Counselors might note their reactions to Sadie, who may be seen as a victim or survivor of extreme trauma, and to Youssef, who fits the pattern of a rebellious teen with a possible disability. It is especially important for counselors to consider whether or not ethnicity plays a dominant role in their own initial reactions and thoughts. Counselors might also examine their current state of knowledge about this population.

Popular Views of Middle Easterners

The reader might ponder at this point what images the terms "Middle Easterner" and "Arab" conjure up. For many people brought up in the West, at least some of their perceptions come from Hollywood and the television news. The Hollywood version, going back to the early days of film, has produced pervasive and stereotypically negative visual images of Middle Easterners as camel-riding villains, ill-mannered and ill-meaning powerful sheikhs, enslaved maidens or harem girls, and terrorists (Shaheen, 2001). Comic strips (Shaheen, 1991) and even computer games (e.g., Wingfield & Karaman, 1995) have also portrayed Middle Easterners negatively.

In fact, Shaheen (2001) discovered that over 900 Hollywood feature films project Arabs as villains:

> When you come across rigid and repetitive movies brandishing stereotypical slurs and images, keep in mind not all negative images are alike: There are distinctions and nuances. Some Arab portraits are dangerous and detestable and should be taken seriously; others are less offensive. And pay special attention to those Arabs you *do not see* on movie screens. Missing from the vast majority of scenarios are images of ordinary Arab men, women, and children living ordinary lives. Movies fail to project exchanges between friends, social and family events. (p. 13)

Because of the recent wars and sociopolitical instability in the region, images of the people of the Middle East pervade the media—papers and magazines, television, radio, and the Internet—as well as the movies. The information on and interpretations of world events that people receive help to shape their attitudes, and ultimately their biases, toward people from the Middle East (see Activity 9.1). Increasingly, however, mental health researchers have challenged the pervasive stereotypes of Middle Easterners (e.g., Nassar-McMillan, 2003b). Counselors need to use empirical data on the nature of Middle Eastern peoples in order to address the mental health needs of Americans of Middle Eastern ancestry with the same compassion and empathy afforded other ethnic groups.

Research has begun on the mental health issues of people from the Middle East. What has emerged are beginning frameworks for the assessment, diagnosis, and treatment of these people, many of whom have settled in North America in search of a better life (e.g., Abudabbeh, 1996; Erickson & Al-Timimi, 2001; Nassar-McMillan & Hakim-Larson, 2003; Nobles & Sciarra, 2000).

ACTIVITY 9.1

Media Coverage of Middle Eastern Issues

Select a recent political issue or conflict between the United States and some region or country in the Middle East (e.g., Afghanistan, Iraq, Iran, Syria, Sunni-Shiite, Kurdish people, Palestinian-Israeli conflict).

Analyze media coverage of the issue/conflict/event, with different students or subgroups studying different media sources.

NOTE: Several Web sites can be used to access Middle Eastern perspectives. They include the Arab American Institute (www.aaiusa.org) and the Arab Community Center for Economic and Social Services-ACCESS (www.accesscommunity.org). International resources, such as Al Jazeera in English (http://english.aljazeera.net/HomePage), may also be referenced for this activity. To test your current knowledge about Arab Americans, take the quiz at www.aaiusa .org/resources/421/test-your-knowledge.

Respond to the following questions:

1. How have the media influenced your views of conflicts in the Middle East and its countries?

2. Has your view changed as a result of this Activity (as researcher/participant, as moderator, as observer)? If so, how?

The first major section of this chapter puts into context the complexities of Middle Eastern ethnic identity. Then the chapter presents an overview of the characteristics of peoples from the Middle East. By now the reader might realize that such a task is complicated by enculturation and acculturation. It is safe to say that first-, second-, and third-generation Americans with a Middle Eastern ethnic background have complex identity issues based on their gender, country of origin (e.g., Afghanistan, Egypt, Iraq, Jordan, Kuwait, Lebanon, Morocco, Palestine), religion (e.g., Melkite, Greek Orthodox, Sunni Muslim, Druze, Shiite Muslim, Jewish, Maronite Catholic), level of education, and socioeconomic status.

The second part of the chapter summarizes the mental health literature on diagnoses and the treatment strategies and techniques that have been used with Americans of Middle Eastern descent. The activities that appear in this chapter will help counselors learn more about the people of the Middle East and how they can best promote the mental health of those who seek their services.

Defining the Identity of Middle Easterners

The peoples of the Middle East are those who generally have inhabited certain portions of northern Africa, southwestern Asia, and Europe.[1] They include the peoples of the 22 Arab League states as well as some of the non-Arab peoples from the surrounding geographical region, such as Afghanis, Kurds, Persians (from Iran), Turks, and Israelis (Farag, 2000; United Nations, 2004). Those people of Middle Eastern descent who reside in the United States are primarily Arab American. In certain regions of the United States, there are also sizable populations of other non-Arabic speaking Middle Eastern groups, such as Iranians, Afghanis, and Turks. To complicate the matter, even within the Arab American population, significant subcultural differences exist, for example, among descendants of the Gulf States (Saudi Arabia, Kuwait, Qatar, Bahrain, United Arab Emirates, and Oman) versus those from Greater Syria (which includes both modern-day Syria and Lebanon), versus those from the Maghreb, or North African countries.

If Americans were asked to explicitly define "Middle Eastern," they might be hard-pressed to articulate their conceptualizations. Nonetheless, and in spite of this geographic expanse, Middle Easterners are often viewed by mainstream Americans as one homogenous group. For example, in the aftermath of the September 11, 2001, attacks on the United States, the image of "Middle Eastern" spanned Arab Americans, Muslim Americans, and Sikhs, as well as non-Arab Middle Easterners such as Afghanis and Iranians, and even further, those who might not fall into any typical definitions of Middle Eastern, such as Pakistanis and Bangladeshis. For example, one study on immigration conducted on behalf of the U.S. Census Bureau defined Middle Eastern immigration to the United States as representing countries ranging from "Pakistan to Morocco" (Camarota, 2002). The author of that study created the perception of immigration problems, including those related to national security, caused by peoples from a region of origin far more vast than the common definition of the Middle East. Given this lack of clarity among mainstream North Americans about exactly how to define "Middle Eastern," it comes as no surprise that individuals of Arab descent may themselves suffer from a confused self-identity (Nassar-McMillan, 2003b).

Over the course of U.S. immigration history, the definition of "Middle Easterner" has been fluid. In the last 100 years or so, Middle Easterners have been variously defined by the federal government as being "from Turkey in Asia," "Colored," "Asiatic," and "white" (Samhan, 1999a). In contemporary U.S. society, individuals of Middle Eastern descent may not themselves have a clear or well-defined ethnic identity. Like their counterparts from other ethnic groups, they may identify as more or less American, depending upon their levels of acculturation and ethnic identity development (Jackson & Nassar-McMillan, 2005). In an age of heightened threats to civil liberties, discrimination and profiling may particularly inhibit the identity development of many Middle Eastern Americans, especially those who fit Middle Eastern-looking or sounding demographic profiles; indeed, these Middle Eastern Americans may be inclined to hide or minimize their ethnic identities. On the other hand, Arab American and other Middle Eastern ethnic groups in the United States have increased ethnic pride and awareness in recent years by organizing to establish a unified voice for advocacy, cultural preservation, and education about Middle Easterners. This collective ethnic pride may well serve to foster improved ethnic identity development and pride in younger generations.

The terms "Arab American," "Muslim," and "Middle Eastern" are often used indiscriminately and interchangeably. Although some people may belong to all three groups, most, in fact, do not. Some people belong to only one or two of the categories (Salari, 2002). For example, a Persian (Iranian) Christian would fit only the Middle Eastern grouping. All Arab Americans can be thought of as being of Middle Eastern descent, but not all Arab Americans are Muslim. In fact, today most Arab Americans are Christian. And many Muslim Americans are neither Arabic-speaking nor Middle Eastern in their heritage (e.g., they may have ancestors from Indonesia or Bosnia). Finally, some people from the Middle East do not speak Arabic (e.g., Turks speak Turkish, Iraqi Chaldeans speak Aramaic, Israeli Jews speak Hebrew, and Iranians speak Farsi).

This complex identity of Middle Easterners underscores the necessity for counselors to think of each person who seeks mental health services as having a unique history, based on her or his family's country of origin, native language(s) and dialect, religion, socioeconomic status, and history of immigration (e.g., Nassar-McMillan, 2003a; Samhan,1999b). However, given that most information available today on Americans from the Middle East concerns Arab Americans, this group will be emphasized in this chapter; where relevant literature is available on other groups, that too will be reviewed.

Immigration From the Middle East

Immigration from the Middle East has occurred in several waves since the late 1800s. Most Arab Americans today actually represent the third or fourth generation in North America. That fact is due to a large immigration around the turn of the twentieth century. At that time, many poor, predominantly Christian uneducated laborers and merchants joined other Mediterranean immigrants. They left Greater Syria in search of better economic opportunities and to escape the Ottoman Empire. Many Arab American Christians (e.g., Orthodox, Eastern Rite, Maronite Catholic), in particular, are descendants of this group.

The later waves of immigration occurred in the mid- to late twentieth century. They included more educated people, more Muslims, and a greater diversity of ethnic backgrounds (e.g., Palestinians, Egyptians, Jordanians, Yemeni, and Iraqis). Of great significance is the fact that many of the more recent immigrants from the Middle East are refugees, and many have histories of direct or vicarious exposure to wars, including the civil war in Lebanon, the Palestinian-Israeli conflict, the Iran-Iraq war, the war in Afghanistan with the Soviet Union, and the Persian Gulf War in Iraq (e.g., U.S. Committee for Refugees, 2000).

Based on the 2000 U.S. Census statistics on Arab Americans in all 50 states, experts estimate that approximately 3.5 million Americans are of Arab descent, with the top five concentrations being in the Los Angeles, Detroit, New York/New Jersey, Chicago, and Washington, D.C., areas. In descending order of frequency reported, Census respondents identified themselves as having the following ancestries: Lebanese, Assyrian/Chaldean/Syriac, Arab/Arabic, Syrian, Egyptian, Other Arab, Palestinian, Iraqi, Jordanian, and Moroccan (Arab American Institute, 2004).

Characteristics of Middle Eastern Cultures

As discussed in Chapter 3, culture is transmitted from one generation to the next and is internalized by all people. Culture serves as a source of memory of the customs, the linguistic categories for everyday experiences, the norms for appropriate behavior, the roles enacted within the social structure, and the values that guide individuals (Triandis, 1994).

As is the case for other major cultural groups, Middle Eastern cultures can best be understood by first considering the core values embedded in the customs, language, and roles that older generations attempt to transfer to younger ones. This section begins with a discussion of the all-important issue of acculturation. In that context, the following characteristics of Middle Eastern culture are then presented: core values, family and parenting roles, gender roles, religion and social support, communication styles, school and career aspirations, traditional clothing, the cultural arts, and general community health.

ACCULTURATION

As introduced in Chapter 3, acculturation explains much about an individual's values and adjustment. Acculturation varies for Middle Easterners based on region, religion, and generation from immigration.

Because most early, turn-of-the-twentieth-century immigrants from the Middle East (largely Syria and Lebanon) were Christian, they acculturated more easily than other groups. They shared a version of the dominant faith in American society (Samhan, 1999b). The similarity of these early immigrants to other immigrants of the time, along with their Christian background, facilitated their acculturation and absorption into American society through intermarriage, a process that has taken place over the last few generations (Abudabbeh, 1996; Samhan, 1999b).

Later waves of immigrants from the Middle East have generally been better educated than the earlier ones. Later immigrants have come from all over the Arab world (e.g., Palestine, Iraq, Egypt, Syria; Abudabbeh, 1996). They have included a greater number of Muslims, whose religious traditions and customs are distinct from those of the dominant American culture, thereby increasing the potential for a clash of norms and values with the predominantly Christian American society. As a result, the normal difficulties associated with the acculturation process are often exacerbated for Middle Eastern Muslims. Samhan (1999b) illustrates these differences:

> The beliefs of Islam place importance on modesty, spurn interfaith marriage, and disapprove of American standards of dating and gender integration. Religious practices that direct personal behavior—including the five-times-daily prayers, the month-long fast at Ramadan, beards for men, and the wearing of the hijab (headcover) for women—require special accommodations in such places as work, school, and the military, thereby making Muslims more visible than most religious minorities and thus often vulnerable to bigotry. (p. 1)

Sociopolitical factors and ongoing tensions in the Middle East are likely to continue to play a significant role in the adaptation of more recent immigrants. After the tragic events of September 11, 2001, Arab Americans, who historically had been considered "white" and not people of color, were looked at differently. In the United States, they were subjected to levels of discrimination, hate, and intolerance unparalleled in the 100 years during which they had participated in and contributed to American economic, political, and popular entertainment domains (Cainkar, 2002). Coping with the backlash in the post-9/11 era may be especially difficult for elderly Arab Americans, Muslims, and other immigrants from the Middle East who may be worried about their safety in public and the future of their children and grandchildren as potential targets of discrimination (Salari, 2002).

It should be noted that merely being Muslim is not a predictor of difficulty in adapting to the dominant U.S. culture. Instead, an individual's level of religious involvement and level of education are likely to be significant in that process (Jackson & Nassar-McMillan, 2005).

CORE VALUES

Two core values for traditional Middle Easterners are *collectivism*, as particularly expressed in strong family cohesion and loyalty, and *paternalism*, as represented in dominant male authority (Nassar-McMillan, 2003a; Nassar-McMillan & Hakim-Larson, 2003). Paternalism is described later in this section within the broader discussion of "Family Roles and Parenting."

Regarding collectivism, individuals from Middle Eastern cultures, particularly those of Arab and/or Muslim background, value interdependence among members of their specific family, nationality, tribal, and/or religious group (Sayed, Collins, & Takahashi, 1998; Triandis, 1994). There is an expectation that the goals of the individual will reflect those of the group. The following Arab proverb demonstrates the importance of collective responsibility for others: "The believer is for his brother—like connecting building blocks supporting each other; if one part falls ill, the whole body crumbles of fever and sleeplessness." Another proverb similarly emphasizes group validation and belonging: "We rise together, we fall together" (Sayed et al., 1998, p. 444). By contrast, in individualistic cultures, the identity of the individual is often linked with an autonomous sense of self and the self's needs and achievements. Table 9.1 summarizes the differences between individualism and collectivism.

Collectivism is often associated with Eastern cultures in general, such as those in Asia or the Arab world, and individualism is often associated with Western cultures, such as those in Europe and the United States. However, the intermixing of cultural values is occurring in much of the world, including the Middle East. Judeo-Christian and Western influences on Middle Eastern culture have been pervasive throughout history and are continuing to influence the peoples from that region.

Regardless of ethnic background, many individuals are likely to now have both collectivistic and individualistic views, to varying degrees. Thus, Middle Eastern

Table 9.1   Definitions of Individualism and Collectivism

Individualism (e.g., Europe and the U.S.)	Collectivism (e.g., most of Asia)
• Views, needs, goals of self are most important	• Views, needs, goals of the collective group are most important
• The pleasure principle and personal profit-loss form the basis of behavior	• The norms and duties determined by the collective form the basis of behavior
• Individual beliefs are autonomous and viewed as independent of the group	• Shared beliefs emphasize what the individual and collective have in common
• Emotional detachment from the collective group and independent social behaviors	• Cooperative, dependent, self-sacrificing in-group social behaviors; indifferent or hostile out-group social behaviors

SOURCE: Triandis (1994).

Americans may vary widely in whether they favor the dominant traditional collectivistic stance or a more Western individualistic one.

FAMILY ROLES AND PARENTING

Because such a large percentage of the Arab world and the Middle East practices Islam, Muslim traditions and values historically have influenced both Christian and Muslim Arab family roles and parenting (Abudabbeh, 1996). For example, many Middle Easterners share the collectivistic emphasis on placing the family's needs before the wishes of the individual.

Extended Family

Collectivism plays out in multiple ways within Middle Eastern communities and families. In typical Middle Eastern families, it is not uncommon for several generations of family members to reside in the same household and play active roles in the structure and dynamics of the family household. It is more common for elderly and aging parents to reside with younger generations than to be in retirement or nursing home communities, even if additional health and physical care is needed. Extended family members are likely to live near each other.

Collectivism extends to the community. Dating back to initial immigration patterns, many families have settled into close-knit Middle Eastern enclaves, by specific country. Within these communities, there is a collective altruistic perspective for taking care of those who are less fortunate. These communities consist of large kinship networks that are connected by blood and origin (i.e., specific city or village in the old country). However, in addition to the sense of connectedness and well-being that results, clannish factions may also develop that compete with each other (e.g., Nassar-McMillan & Hakim-Larson, 2003; Shryock, 2000).

Authority

Fathers and other male members of the family exert the greatest authority (e.g., Shryock, 2000); that phenomenon is called paternalism. Paternalism refers to family power and identity being passed intergenerationally through the males of the family unit. Paternalism does not grant males all authority in the family; rather, it demarcates the decision-making voice for affairs external to the family as being the male elder's responsibility.

In contemporary Middle Eastern American societies, internal family decisions are typically made within the marital partnership, even though the father or male elder might still serve as the family spokesperson. In the absence of a father figure, an elder uncle or even elder son may fill such a role. In refugee populations, this "typical" family structure can be upset, in that there may be no elder male to fill the role. In such cases, the role might fall to the mother or a female elder. Thus, the family dynamics and structure may need to be renegotiated within refugee families (Nassar-McMillan & Hakim-Larson, 2003). Table 9.2 provides definitions of paternalism.

Table 9.2   Definitions of Paternalism

Paternalism
• Men should have more power than women.
• Men should protect and provide for women who are dependent on them.
• Chivalrous protection of and affection for women who hold conventional roles coexists with hostility toward women who try to gain power.

SOURCES: Feather (2004); Glick & Fiske (2001).

Now that two major sets of Middle Eastern values have been introduced, the reader is invited to complete Activity 9.2, which offers her or him an opportunity to analyze her or his own values as compared to traditional Middle Eastern values.

Marriage

Norms and traditions involving marriage and the spousal relationship vary considerably by religion and nationality. Some subgroups of Muslim immigrants may come from countries where practices such as endogamy (marriage between cousins) is the norm or where polygamy or divorce are permitted, subject to certain restrictions (Abudabbeh, 1996; Jalali, 1996), whereas this may not be the case for other specific subgroups.

The nuclear family, like the extended family, is also of utmost importance in Middle Eastern cultures, and the divorce rate is lower than that of average Americans (Abraham, 1995). For Arab Americans, in particular, this familial and marital satisfaction can be attributed to the role of both nuclear and extended family members in collectively meeting the needs of individual spouses. Thus, the pressure that exists in mainstream U.S. society for spouses to solely meet their partners' needs is lessened in the traditional Middle Eastern family model.

Because Middle Eastern families are primarily patriarchal in structure, male heads of household are seen as the primary wage earners. While women often pursue higher education as well as careers, especially in later-generation Middle Eastern American populations, men are still typically relied upon to provide financially for the family

Child Rearing

Children have a subservient role in the family (e.g., Abudabbeh, 1996). Children are expected to respect their parents and other elders. Parental authority is enforced via expressed parental anger and punishment. In a Canadian sample, Egyptian Canadian parents reported greater anger in hypothetical parental discipline situations and higher authoritarianism than did their Anglo Canadian counterparts (Rudy & Grusec, 2001).

ACTIVITY 9.2

Clarifying Values—Individualism, Collectivism, and Paternalism

Consider these terms, as discussed in this chapter:

individualistic and collectivistic

paternalistic

Examine your own value systems according to those values, identifying the ways in which you subscribe to each of the terms (e.g., Who makes the decisions in your family?)

What is the communication pattern in your family or support network, more paternalistic or egalitarian?

What are some examples of collectivistic approaches you take in your life?

Individualistic ones?

Examine your thoughts, emotions, and behaviors (verbal and nonverbal) with respect to the three terms. How might you increase your empathy for clients with differing worldviews on individualism-collectivism and paternalism, based on your increased self-awareness in this arena?

What challenges can you foresee for yourself in such situations?

Consistent with these findings, Arab American teens have been found to complain about the lack of privacy in their ethnic community. Because everyone seems to know everyone, community gossip is prevalent, and parents can thus use this threat of stigma and potential shame as a means of socially controlling their children (e.g., Ajrouch, 2000). Such social constraints are often heightened for girls and young women of Middle Eastern backgrounds due to traditional gender roles.

At the onset of early adolescence, children are taught to conform to traditional gender roles (Meleis, 1991). According to convention, when children, particularly boys, came of age within the family, they would join with the mother and help to maintain her power position in the family. However, intergenerational conflicts, particularly for newer, nonimmigrant generations, pose a challenge to the status quo of the family structure within Middle Eastern communities. As children jockey for increased power and autonomy within the context of contemporary North American culture, this family power structure has been somewhat derailed (Meleis, 1991). Moreover, in recent immigrant families, the children often take on the role of English translator for parents who may be lacking in English language skills, thus resulting in a role reversal within the family structure. The reader is invited to complete Activity 9.3 in order to compare her or his assumptions about family with contrasting perspectives.

GENDER ROLES

In Middle Eastern cultures, gender roles are expressed through gender segregation, in sexual standards, and in differential socialization of sons and daughters. Each of these is addressed in this section.

Gender segregation in the public domain is the norm throughout much of the Middle East. This custom clashes with the dominant American practice. Thus, newly arrived immigrants from the Middle East must contend with the extensive American cross-sex socializing and other gender role flexibilities that are permitted and even encouraged in the United States as normal and healthy in American schools and other settings (Shryock, 2000).

In traditional Middle Eastern cultures, the gender double standard is upheld, with virginity, modesty, and fidelity emphasized for girls and women. Although premarital and extramarital sex is taboo for females, it is criticized but tolerated for males (e.g., Jalali, 1996; Simon, 1996). In traditional families, dating is taboo and, if it occurs, it is expected that a marriage proposal will follow. Family conflicts and even violence can result when parents, who are trying to maintain old-country traditions, discover that their daughters are secretly dating boys and are out in public in mixed company. Traditional Middle Eastern families may also arrange marriages.

Early socialization processes within the family structure reflect the roles of males and females: males are responsible for the family finances, and females are responsible for family relationships. Upon reaching adolescence, boys are given more social autonomy, which is seen as fostering the skills and connections that they will need to pursue financially lucrative careers. Because girls are not expected to have those same skills, there is often not a compelling need for them to socialize outside the family and community structure (Ajrouch, 2000).

First-generation immigrant parents from the Middle East try to hold on to their ethnic identity through their daughters, by attempting to put anti-assimilation pressure on them and carefully monitoring their social activities (Ajrouch, 1999). By contrast, sons will be given more freedom. Parents may attempt to attain the American dream through their sons, who are afforded more opportunities for assimilation into mainstream American life. The resulting permissiveness for boys can potentially be problematic (as in the case of Youssef, which was introduced at the beginning of the chapter) when a child's individual needs require more structured adult monitoring. When such problems do arise in the family, recent immigrants are more likely to go to their religious institution for help than to a public agency.

It should be noted that the Arab American daughter, or "bint Arab," as she is called, doesn't completely fit the stereotype of the oppressed and degraded female, as has been historically depicted in the media. Shakir (1997) notes that while Arab American women have had their share of difficulties in negotiating

ACTIVITY 9.3

Evaluation of Family Characteristics

To gain an appreciation for the family roles and parenting issues that are important to clients, it helps if counselors understand these issues in their own family networks. This Activity asks you to examine your family characteristics and their implications for working with others.

1. a. Generate a list of adjectives that describe your family network (e.g., permissive, controlling, secretive, warm, autonomous, disengaged, sarcastic, ironic, expressive).

   _____

   _____

   _____

   _____

   _____

   b. Evaluate each of these characteristics on a scale of 1–10, based on how much (or how little) you like each one.

2. a. Generate a list of characteristics with which you are less familiar (perhaps some that you have observed but that are not commonly practiced in your own family network).

   _____

   _____

   _____

   _____

   _____

   b. Where do you fall on a scale of 1–10 for each of the adjectives? Write your rating above.

3. Describe the differences in the adjectives and self-evaluations between the first two questions.

Also describe whether your self-evaluations are comparable to where you would like to be.

Finally, assess/discuss what it would be like for you to work with clients who exhibit the noted characteristics that are different from your own.

How might those characteristics serve as facilitative or as inhibitive factors in developing relationships with clients or in working toward client goals?

between American values and those of their Middle Eastern heritage, they have been resilient and resourceful in developing individualized solutions to conflicts about issues such as modesty in clothing, dating, chastity, and rebellion against husband or spousal authority. For example, some Middle Eastern women have developed strategies to flexibly adapt their clothing and social behavior according to the situation. Some also maintain a high motivation to assimilate to North American life by adopting American cultural traditions. They perceive fewer restrictions on their freedom if they are successful in doing so.

RELIGION AND SOCIAL SUPPORT

Muslim Middle Eastern families and communities gain much strength from their religious institutions. Mosques provide avenues for fellowship, education, and cultural events (Council on Islamic Education, 1995). For example, many Islamic centers within Arab American enclaves have begun teaching Arabic language classes to the community's youth. Their imams, or clerics, often provide counseling for marriage and family decisions.

Based on U.S. Census 2000 data, the Arab American Institute (2004) reports that only 24 percent of Arab Americans declare themselves to be Muslim (Sunni, Shi'a, and Druze). Thus, it is important to note that the majority of American Arabs are non-Muslim, and most are Christian. Of Arab Christians, 35 percent are Catholic (Roman Catholic, Maronite, Melkite/Greek Catholic), 20 percent Orthodox (Antiochian, Syrian, Greek, and Egyptian Coptic), 11 percent Protestant, and the rest are other denominations or have no affiliation.

The religion and ethnicity picture is even more complex. For example, some Iraqi Chaldeans and Assyrians are Christians from northern Iraq and do not consider themselves to be Arabs because their language is Aramaic (Schopmeyer, 2000). Lebanese Maronite Christians are Catholics who have maintained some early Christian traditions and are under the jurisdiction of the Pope in Rome. Their religious norms and values appear quite similar to those of typically Catholic European ethnic groups in the United States (e.g., Irish, Polish, Italian).

Both Muslims and Christian Middle Easterners utilize their mosques or churches as centers for community support and fellowship. For both groups, religious traditions are highly salient and valued (Arab American Institute, 2004). Church or mosque attendance and adherence to holiday and other religious traditions are typical behaviors within Middle Eastern communities. Despite this tendency toward religiosity, however, counselors should not automatically assume that a client maintains her or his family's religious beliefs and traditions or even assume that she or he believes in God (Nassar-McMillan & Hakim-Larson, 2003).

COMMUNICATION STYLES

Individuals of Middle Eastern descent, like many individuals of non-Western ancestry, often use nonverbal behaviors to express how they feel (Jackson & Nassar-McMillan, 2005). Nonverbal behaviors characterizing Middle Easterners may include a high volume during intense emotion and gesticulation while speaking. In addition, to make a point, individuals will often repeat the same phrase several times, each time increasing the volume (Via, Callahan, Barry, Jackson, & Gerber, 1997).

Power dynamics within relationships may influence both verbal and nonverbal communication as well as interaction styles between individuals. For example, based on the familial hierarchies addressed previously, a husband or father would express anger to a spouse or child. A mother would, in turn, express anger to a child. However, she would express anger to her spouse only in private.

In terms of physical space, same-gender individuals often speak to one another while standing very close together and often use touch, such as holding hands or kissing one another on the cheek—once, twice, or even three times, depending on country or subculture of origin—for greeting or parting.

Love and attachment are communicated through Arabic metaphors and terms of endearment, passed down from one generation to the next. The word *yahabooboo* expresses the idea of "darling." Love is also commonly communicated through physical gestures of affection and endearment toward loved ones, especially children (Simon, 1996).

Sociability, hospitality, and frequent connectedness to significant others are highly valued in Middle Eastern culture (Shryock, 2000). Shryock and his colleagues found that visits from the extended kinship network of family and friends are frequent. At those times, loud, animated conversations may occur over the noise of TV and stereos, which typically remain on even with guests in the home. Shryock notes that this pattern of frequent contact (e.g., by telephone) within Arab American kinship networks may extend into the workplace as well, and that local employers within large Arab American enclaves might make accommodations for that practice.

SCHOOL AND CAREER

Academic achievement for both males and females is highly valued in many Middle Eastern cultures. Both girls and boys are expected to excel in school, as well as in their later career endeavors. For Arab Americans, in particular, both educational and income levels tend to be higher than the norm for Americans in general (Arab American Institute, 2004). Career paths mirror those of mainstream North American cultures, with the exceptions that Middle Easterners tend to choose more entrepreneurial and fewer governmental careers.

Collectivism may affect the school and career aspirations of Middle Easterners, although further research is needed to clarify how that is playing out at this time in the United States. For example, in a study carried out in Israel, Palestinian Arab high school students had high scores on collectivistic test items that emphasized their own social group. They tended to value such items as "solidarity with the poor in my country" more so than did Jewish Israeli high school students, who scored higher on more individualistic items. For example, Israelis tended to value such items as "freedom of opinion" (Sagy, Orr, Bar-On, & Awwad, 2001).

For Arab Americans, such collectivistic in-group values may also affect the social life of the school-age child. Children in American schools are often taught more individualistic values. This contrast places emotional stress on less acculturated parents (e.g., first-generation immigrants), who may fear losing control over their children (Laffrey, Meleis, Lipson, Solomon, & Omidian, 1989). As a result, some Arab Muslims in the United States prefer to send their children to private Islamic schools because parents want their children to retain the customs, learn Arabic, and read the Qur'an (Samhan, 1999b).

TRADITIONAL CLOTHING

Another characteristic of Middle Eastern culture is the Muslim convention of modesty for both men and women. For devout Muslims, such modesty means wearing opaque, loose-fitting clothing. Some Muslim women may wear a veil, or *hijab*, over their heads; in addition, some women may wear the black *abaya*, which is a traditional robelike cloak (e.g., Abraham, 2000; Walbridge & Aziz, 2000). The cultural meaning of the *hijab* and *abaya* varies. Muslim women who are proponents of wearing traditional clothing believe that veiling protects them from sexual advances and affords them greater respect from men in the public domain (e.g., while at school or work). By contrast, Muslim women who oppose traditional clothing view the veil as an outdated way to socially control women. They feel that they can be good Muslim believers without it (Read & Bartkowski, 2000).

For non-Muslim Middle Eastern Americans, dress is almost as varied as it is in Western, North American cultures, although for those who immigrated more recently, the Muslim emphasis on modesty in clothing may still represent the norm.

COMMUNITY ORGANIZATIONS, CULTURAL ARTS, AND CONTRIBUTIONS TO AMERICAN LIFE

National agencies such as the Naim Foundation and the Arab American Institute in Washington, D.C. (www.aaiusa.com) currently exist to facilitate the dissemination of cultural information and to provide social services (Abudabbeh, 1996). Another agency, called TAMKEEN: The Center for Arab American Empowerment, Inc. (www.tamkeen-us.org) is located in Brooklyn, New York. It was founded to address the needs of Arab American New Yorkers in the post-9/11 era.

One of the highest concentrations of people from the Middle East is in the Metropolitan Detroit area in southeastern Michigan, where early immigrants settled at the turn of the twentieth century and made a living as shopkeepers and peddlers, until the auto industry boom afforded the opportunity for factory work (Shryock & Abraham, 2000). To serve their needs, the Arab American and Chaldean Council (ACC; www.myacc.org) and the Arab Community Center for Economic and Social Services (ACCESS; www.accesscommunity.org) were developed in that area (e.g., Abudabbeh, 1996).

As more immigrants were drawn from the Middle East into the Detroit area during the twentieth century, more Arab/Chaldean-owned businesses emerged, including Middle Eastern bakeries and restaurants, grocery stores, and specialty clothing stores, many of which are adorned with bilingual neon signs in Arabic script and English. Cultural products such as food, music, clothing, and artwork are produced locally or imported from the Middle East and sold in these stores and represent one way that Middle Easterners attempt to preserve their heritage. Some Middle Eastern dishes (e.g., chickpea dip or hummus, parsley salad or taboulee, lamb or beef shish kebab) have now been assimilated into many grocery stores and restaurant menus in parts of North America.

Arab Americans have a rich history of playing musical instruments (e.g., *nay* or flute, *oud* or round-bellied lute, violin, *darabukkah* or vase-shaped drum, *riqq* or tambourine) at their parties, which are called *haflah* or *hafle; v*ariations of line dancing (*dabkah* or *dubke*) and informal individual, couple, or group "belly" dancing commonly occur at weddings and other formal and informal celebrations (Rasmussen, 2000). Traditional folk arts include embroidery, Arabic calligraphy, making musical instruments, making dolls, and henna design applications to the hands and feet of young women (Howell, 2000).

An annual Arab ethnic festival is held in Dearborn, Michigan, every year, and the first Arab American National Museum sponsored by ACCESS has recently opened (see www.theaanm.org). The museum documents the cultural contributions of many Arab Americans to literature (e.g., the poet Kahlil Gibran; the White House journalist Helen Thomas), medicine and science (e.g., renowned surgeon Dr. Michael DeBakey; NASA scientist Dr. Farouk el-Baz; Antarctic explorer Dr. George Doumani), politics (e.g., presidential candidate Ralph Nader), sports (e.g., automobile racer Bobby Rahal), music, and the visual arts, including television and movie actors.

COMMUNITY HEALTH ISSUES

The literature on the health of Arab Americans indicates that they suffer disproportionately from cardiovascular problems, such as hypertension and high cholesterol, and from diabetes (Hassoun, 1999). While the traditional Middle Eastern diet is thought to be healthy (e.g., high in vegetables, fruits, grains), the ready availability of foods in the United States that historically were eaten only occasionally, such as red meat and sugar-laden desserts, has contributed to obesity in Arab Americans, consistent with the general American trend. Diet and obesity are also predisposing factors for Type 2 diabetes, which has been found to be extremely high in Arab Americans (Jaber et al., 2003). Smoking (cigarettes, cigars, or the traditional Turkish water pipe or *nargile*) is a predisposing factor for cancer and for cardiovascular disease. A high incidence of smoking has been found in studies of both Arab American adults (Hammad & Kysia, 1996; Jamil, Hammad, Jamil, Stevens, & Pass, 2001; Rice & Kulwicki, 1992) and teenagers (Kulwicki & Rice, 2003; Rice, Templin, & Kulwicki, 2003).

ACCESS conducted a health needs assessment survey in 1996 on a randomly selected sample of their mostly Lebanese, Iraqi, and Yemeni low-income clients in Michigan (Hammad & Kysia, 1996). This survey identified the main barriers to primary health care. These obstacles were lack of transportation to doctors' offices, language, cultural practices, and lack of insurance or financial limitations. To help address these needs, ACCESS sponsored Biennial National Conferences on Health Issues in the Arab American Community in 1999, 2001, 2003, and 2006. At these conferences, mental health issues such as post-traumatic stress disorder in refugees have figured prominently in presentations, in addition to presentations addressing cardiovascular disease, cancer, diabetes, and maternal and child care, and researchers are currently implementing many of the recommendations for further research.

Mental Health Issues for Arab Americans and Middle Eastern Immigrants

The following sections cover the various mental health issues and diagnostic disorders that particularly affect the lives of those Arab Americans who seek or are referred for counseling. First, diagnosed mental disorders will be discussed. Then ethnic identity and adjustment issues will be presented.

The focus here is on immigrant families, who have special risk factors that are associated with their pre- and post-migration experiences and adaptation to their new culture. They and all Middle Eastern Americans also confront the psychosocial risks and stresses that are common for most Americans in daily life (e.g., family conflicts). Learning and applying the language, laws, and traditions of their new culture, as well as learning about practical resources, such as transportation, add to the emotional burden of the transition for those who are recent immigrants. It is important for counseling interventions to focus on both client struggles and strengths.

PSYCHOSOCIAL RISKS AND DIAGNOSED MENTAL DISORDERS

Immigrants from the Middle East are particularly at risk for anxiety, depression, and trauma-related disorders. These problems can be attributed to four factors: (1) immigration-related traumas, (2) cultural differences with North American life, (3) the loss of the extended family support system if only part of the family has immigrated, and (4) limited knowledge of American legal and health care systems (e.g., Laffrey et al., 1989). It should be noted that for many Middle Easterners, emotional distress might be somaticized, with the client citing medical complaints rather than emotional ones.

One study of a sample of female immigrants illustrated the everyday stresses they encountered and their means of coping. Hattar-Pollara and Meleis (1995) found that Jordanian women who had settled in the greater Los Angeles area had to balance feelings of isolation and unease with the practical requirements of daily life, which included ensuring that the family had a steady income, getting the children enrolled in school, and setting up their home. These women attempted to accomplish all of this while trying to overcome the language barrier and feelings of loneliness due to the loss of social support and status in the community that they had left behind (Hattar-Pollara & Meleis, 1995). Adding to acculturative stress, many of these women also felt a need to protect their ethnic identity and preserve the values of their culture. Conforming to those traditions was seen as bringing honor on the family, whereas violating them by taking on American ways brought shame. One method of coping was to re-create familiar religious and social activities in their Eastern Rite Melkite church parish. Each of these experiences are typical of immigrants' lives, namely isolation, unfamiliarity with customs, the urgency of establishing a home and job, language barriers, attempts at cultural preservation, and the use of the ethnic community for support.

Four specific mental health-related phenomena that are present in Middle Eastern communities are domestic violence, trauma, somatization, and addictions. They will be discussed next.

Domestic Violence

Paternalism, protecting family honor, and avoiding shame, combined with inadequate knowledge of Western legal standards, may contribute to the risk of domestic violence in some Middle Eastern immigrant families (Kulwicki & Miller, 1999). Among the indicators of particular risk for domestic violence are family history of physical abuse, use of corporal punishment, poverty, and social isolation. These phenomena have been the focus of education, prevention, and intervention efforts by community social service agencies.

Trauma

In addition to the stresses that occur once an immigrant has resettled in a new environment, extreme pre-migration stressors such as war trauma, torture, and persecution in the country of origin add to the risk of adjustment disorders or more serious forms of psychopathology for Middle Easterners (e.g., Keyes, 2000). For instance, the people of Afghanistan have suffered more than two decades of war and conflict and years of drought, and many have experienced a series of displacements as refugees. It is thus not surprising that a recent national survey in Afghanistan found high rates of depression, anxiety, and post-traumatic stress disorder in adolescents and adults (Cardoza et al., 2004).

Wartime trauma is perhaps the most extreme psychosocial risk factor affecting those Middle Eastern Americans who entered the United States as refugees. In contrast to the early Middle Eastern immigrants, who left their country of origin voluntarily in the early twentieth century under relatively stable conditions, many recent immigrants left as refugees during or after wars. For example, Bagheri (1992) found that most Iranian immigrants with psychiatric disorders who moved to Canada in the 1980s after the Iranian Revolution and the war with Iraq met the criteria for adjustment disorder with depressed or anxious mood. The adjustment disorders were related to the stresses of adapting to Western life and learning a new language. However, many who had experienced severe trauma and torture in their homeland further met the criteria for post-traumatic stress disorder. Similarly, many refugees from Iraq who immigrated to the United States after the Persian Gulf War of the early 1990s had serious symptoms of depression and anxiety. Those disorders can be traced to broken family ties, shame, and fears related to their history of trauma and torture.

Most recently, refugees from Iraq, who represent a large proportion of recent immigrants from the Middle East, show all of the above disorders. Some Iraqi refugees have witnessed the death and torture of loved ones or have personally experienced torture. Some have experienced malnutrition and inadequate water supplies, multiple relocations, and temporary settlement in refugee camps. Such multiple traumas and serious losses accumulate over time and thus lead to "complex trauma" (Kira, 1999). As with the case of Sadie, described at the beginning of the chapter, many Middle Eastern refugees have suffered years of extreme trauma and emotional suffering before finally receiving treatment.

Somatization

Somatization of symptoms, such as headaches and stomachaches, occurs often in Middle Easterners and others with ethnic origins in the Arabic-speaking world, due to the cultural stigma associated with mental illness (e.g., Nassar-McMillan & Hakim-Larson, 2003). Because mental health problems are often somaticized, many Middle Easterners may initially visit a physician or take their complaints to a medical facility before they are referred for mental health treatment (e.g., Kamoo, Hakim-Larson, Nassar-McMillan, & Porcerelli, 2004). The medical personnel and counselors who work with Arab American clients frequently need to proactively address acculturation difficulties, marital and family conflicts, and school and educational problems in family members.

Addictions: Substance Abuse and Gambling

Another arena of mental health concern for Middle Eastern Americans is that of addictions, such as substance abuse and gambling. Substance use is prohibited for Muslims. Alcohol abuse has been rare in traditional Middle Eastern American communities (Abudabbeh & Hamid, 2001). However, substance abuse is emerging as enough of a problem since 1992 for the first bilingual Arabic and English-language Alcoholics Anonymous program to be formed. It is a response to increasing drunk driving arrests, domestic violence, and illicit drug abuse (Berry, 2003a, 2003b; Jamil, Ajo, & Jamil, 2000). Middle Eastern clients who present with alcohol or drug abuse are typically English-speaking, educated, and Westernized (Abudabbeh & Hamid, 2001).

Some counselors who work within the Arab American community have also been concerned about the cultural practice of use of the stimulant *khat* (also spelled "kat" or "qat") by pregnant women and children (Hakim-Larson, 2001). Khat is a shrub cultivated by Arabs and is the source of a habituating stimulant when chewed or used as a tea.

Counselors who work with Middle Eastern clients have recently expressed their concern about the potential consequences of pathological gambling in this community (Hakim-Larson, 2001). Fortunately, awareness of the potentially devastating consequences of untreated addictions has led to the creation of culturally sensitive treatment programs (e.g., Berry, 2003a, 2003b).

ETHNIC IDENTITY AND ADJUSTMENT ISSUES

The second major mental health concern for Middle Easterners, especially immigrants, is conflict about ethnic identity. Middle Eastern Americans must balance their ethnic identity derived from the heritage culture with their civic identity in the host culture and country of residence. Middle Eastern ethnic identity issues are important across the spectrum of age, gender, and background, but are especially conflictual for youth because identity development is a critical developmental task. The challenge for the adolescent or adult of Middle Eastern heritage is to successfully achieve an integrated identity (e.g., Hakim-Larson & Nassar-McMillan, 2006).

The relative balance or imbalance in degree of assimilation to the dominant culture and degree of ethnic preservation appears to have implications for identity development. In research with Arab American teens (Ajrouch, 2000; Shryock & Abraham, 2000), recent immigrants are sometimes labeled "boaters" (i.e., just off the boat), while very acculturated Middle Eastern Americans are known as "white." Both positive and negative characteristics are attributed to each group (Ajrouch, 2000).

A boater is not yet acculturated and has not assimilated to the dominant culture, as evidenced by her or his speech and dress. Among teens, she or he is generally considered inferior to those who are somewhat more Americanized. The more acculturated or "white" person was seen to have greater status and prestige and better access to education, power, and wealth. Still, there is peril for those who assume an American identity too quickly. The white person was viewed as being too free and lacking in a sense of responsibility or obligation to family and friends. The teens in Ajrouch's (2000) study clearly appreciated the benefits of living in a close, ethnic community with shared values and close family relations, a community where everyone helps each other out. Thus, there is also "assimilation bias" among Middle Easterners, that is, negatively evaluating others in their group who assimilate too completely and too quickly to the dominant host culture (Nassar-McMillan & Hakim-Larson, 2003).

Counseling Interventions

In contrast to the sense of control that exists in much Western culture, Middle Easterners have a certain fatalism about life. The concept of a God-determined "fate" has been traditionally used by people from the Middle East to explain life crises and problems (Nobles & Sciarra, 2000). Thus, many of the functions of mental health professionals have, in the past, been performed by physicians, priests, or imams (Loza, 2001) or by fortune tellers, magicians, or healers (Al-Krenawi & Graham, 2000). However, with outreach efforts by community mental health centers and increased media advertisement of mental health services, many more Middle Eastern individuals in need of treatment are getting appropriate interventions.

This section includes a description of the positive cultural protective factors and resources that are useful in supporting intervention efforts and the various counseling modalities and clinical issues that can arise during interventions.

PROTECTIVE FACTORS FOR MIDDLE EASTERN AMERICANS

Two salient positive mental health factors for Middle Eastern Americans are the family and the ethnic community. Counselors can incorporate those two elements in their work. For example, when an Arab woman is depressed, her female friends and family members may encourage her to dance with them, with the exercise and camaraderie thus helping to alleviate and lift her depressed mood (Hakim-Larson, 2001).

Community centers also provide arts and crafts programs, social programs, and legal, medical, and career advice. Such social support is often viewed as a critical part of a treatment plan for those with compromised mental health. Since the 1990s, Arab American community agencies such as ACCESS have had outreach programs via radio, television, and the Internet to help Arab Americans find and utilize mental health intervention programs and to join support groups in their community (e.g., Abudabbeh, 1996). This effort has helped individuals to overcome the stigma associated with mental health diagnoses and treatment.

INCORPORATING FAMILY AND COMMUNITY IN CLIENTS' LIVES

Counselors should incorporate family and community treatment in plans for Middle Eastern American clients (Nassar-McMillan & Hakim-Larson, 2003). For some clients, family members will get involved at some point in the treatment process. This may occur even when the counselor does not see it as therapeutically indicated. For instance, a woman who needs individual counseling may want her husband and children to be present in sessions. That is especially likely due to the patriarchal tradition: A husband may want to attend some sessions with his wife before feeling he can trust the counselor enough so that she might participate on her own. In line with that tradition, a husband or father may resent perceived challenges to his role as the authority figure in a family, may engage in denial about a family problem, and might then refuse to cooperate in the treatment of his wife or child when his participation is needed (e.g., Abudabbeh & Aseel, 1999).

If the counselor belongs to the same ethnic community as the client and speaks the same language and dialect, issues of privacy, confidentiality, and trust may arise. If the counselor is not from the same ethnic community, the client who is accustomed to the open dissemination of information in her or his own community (i.e., gossip) may have difficulty trusting that the counselor will keep the information confidential. Shame may also play a role because less-educated clients may be particularly reluctant to disclose shameful behaviors that would reflect upon the whole family (Abudabbeh & Aseel, 1999).

RECOMMENDED COUNSELING MODALITIES

Middle Eastern clients are usually oriented more toward survival and solving their immediate, concrete problems than they are toward gaining insight into their past or their family history. They are generally passive in the counselor-client relationship and view the counselor as the benevolent authority who will tell them what to do so that they can be cured (e.g., Al-Krenawi & Graham, 2000). Thus, mental health professionals who have worked with Middle Easterners recommend the use of clear, direct instructions and behavioral or cognitive-behavioral interventions rather than psychodynamic ones (Nassar-McMillan, 2003a). Counseling approaches that are more structured, short-term, and directive in nature have been cited as being more useful in working with recent Middle Eastern immigrants (e.g., Abudabbeh & Aseel, 1999; Al-Krenawi & Graham, 2000).

Choice of treatment techniques and modalities are likely to be influenced by the degree of acculturation and the educational level of the client as well: More educated and acculturated individuals may be better able to complete and follow through with outside homework assignments that involve self-monitoring and documentation for the next session. For those who have experienced extreme trauma as a result of their pre-migration experiences, a comprehensive multidisciplinary and multimodal wraparound approach has been found to be helpful (Kira, 2002).

Box 9.1 provides a series of suggestions that can guide work with Middle Eastern clients.

APPLICATION OF CULTURALLY ALERT COUNSELING STRATEGIES IN THE CASES OF SADIE AND YOUSSEF

In the case of Sadie that was described at the beginning of the chapter, an effective counseling intervention might involve two particular dimensions: (1) focusing on developing the counselor-client relationship and (2) exploring

BOX 9.1   Twelve Suggestions for Counseling Middle Eastern Clients

Erickson and Al-Timimi (2001) have listed 12 questions and suggested counselor actions for working with Middle Eastern clients:

1. *Does the client's cultural background have any relation to her or his current problems or her or his expectations for treatment?* It is important to make sure to ask about ethnicity on intake forms so that cultural background can be addressed if needed and if appropriate to the presenting problem.

2. *What are the client's expectations for treatment? Does the client fully understand the role of the counselor, her or his right to confidentiality, and the limits of confidentiality?* Erickson and Al-Timimi (2001) highlight the need to take as much time as needed to properly orient the client to the counseling experience.

3. *What are the similarities and differences in the cultural backgrounds, values, attitudes, and beliefs of the client and the counselor? Does the gender of the counselor make a difference to the client?* Explicit discussion of these trust-related issues is recommended as the need arises, and will be discussed in Chapter 16.

4. *Since establishing rapport may take extra time, how can trust best be facilitated in the client and patience be practiced by the counselor?* Taking it slowly and not expecting clients to be readily open and forthcoming in discussing emotional issues will help the therapeutic process.

5. *Is the counselor careful to clarify statements made by the client and does the counselor avoid using jargon and colloquialisms with the client?* Erickson and Al-Timimi (2001) cite a case in which a young Arab American woman spoke of a traumatic "sexual assault" in describing an incident where a man asked permission to kiss her but did not persist when she said no. By clarifying what clients mean by the terms they use, or what professional terms mean as used by the counselor, miscommunication and misunderstandings can be avoided.

6. *What are the expectations of the client's family for counseling, and how does the family react to the client's problems?* Given the collectivistic nature of Middle Eastern families, it is quite important to clarify the roles of various family members (i.e., who decides what) and what types of social support are afforded the client. It is also important to note what obligations the client feels toward the various family members and how this sense of loyalty may relate to the presenting problems.

7. *In what ways might the family members be involved as part of the solution?* A counseling goal of individuation and autonomy from the family may conflict with feelings of family loyalty. One resolution of this internal conflict, according to Erickson and Al-Timimi (2001), is for the client to view the family as a supportive foundation and for the client to work with family members in generating potential solutions to problems.

8. *Does the client give evidence of somatization behaviors that are consistent with his or her emotional experiences?* If so, consider whether these behaviors (when no medical basis has been found) can be understood as relatively benign symptoms within the cultural context rather than as indicators of a more severe psychopathology.

9. *Are religious beliefs or practices implicated in the presenting problems and their potential solutions?* If so, Erickson and Al-Timimi (2001) suggest consulting with the client's religious leader.

10. *Does the client perceive a social stigma around receiving mental health services?* Consider ways to counter the stigma and portray the benefits of counseling to the client and his or her family through psychoeducation.

11. *Has the client experienced distress around interpersonal biases related to her or his ethnicity?* If so, how has this affected his or her self-image and identity? Erickson and Al-Timimi (2001) recommend using a feminist therapeutic approach (see Chapter 13), such as instruction in oppression, as a model for helping clients develop healthy coping strategies and identities.

12. *Has the client experienced ethnic discrimination?* Even though Arab Americans are not recognized in the United States as an ethnic minority group under affirmative action and racial discrimination policies, counselors need to explore whether or not they think Arab Americans should be viewed as an ethnic minority and thus be covered under antidiscrimination policies (Erickson & Al-Timimi, 2001).

the specific ways in which her profound sadness affects her everyday interactions, relationships, and functioning.

Regarding the relationship-building component, asking her to tell the stories of her pre-, during-, and post-migration experiences from her own perspective can help the counselor to develop empathy for Sadie, as well as to create opportunities to validate her "normal" adaptive reactions to extreme stressors. In that process of listening to her story, the counselor can "normalize" her grief and loss reactions before making cognitive-behavioral interventions. Shame should be addressed as well, without unnecessarily probing for deeper insights.

The ensuing interventions would then include asking Sadie to describe specific situations when she feels more suicidal, happy, or somewhere in between, as well as her corresponding physical responses. Concrete, behavioral homework could be assigned and should ideally include appropriate traditional Arabic interventions (in consultation with Arabic health or mental health professionals), such as exploring and perhaps using her belief in the evil eye or holy incense.

In the case of Youssef, a psychological evaluation should include exploration of both his drug use history and his attention-deficit-oriented behaviors. This examination should include both parent and teacher input. If Youssef and his parents are to support the diagnostic results of the evaluation and possible medication, they will need to be convinced, from an authoritative and concrete perspective, of the symptoms that have been observed and how the medication can counteract those symptoms when supplemented by behavioral approaches.

After trust is established, the counselor should explore the meaning and power of Youssef's drug use and gang membership by asking him what concrete benefits he gets from those two activities. It may be that he has difficulty being optimistic about the future, given that his parents are not economically successful. The gang membership could provide a place to "fit in" because, like some of his second-generation counterparts residing in ethnic enclaves, he is caught between two cultures and their corresponding values.

At some point, he is likely to need concrete alternatives, such as involvement in teen activities in the local community center or through his family's religious institution. The school counselor can also provide support in this process by asking Youssef about the specific challenges he has in school, both overall and in specific courses. The school counselor can work in consultation with the therapist, as well as with the parents, to provide feedback or monitor problematic or improved behaviors. Both counselors can also support the medication process, if necessary.

Summary

Middle Eastern Americans have a rich and varied history that spans over a century of experiences in the United States. Country of origin, religion, socioeconomic status, and length of time in the United States since immigration are all likely to influence a Middle Eastern client's overall adaptation and adjustment. Particular risks for immigrant Middle Eastern Americans include anxiety, depression, and trauma-related disorders, especially for those who have pre-migration war experiences. Of particular concern are the refugees from the Middle East who have experienced cumulative complex trauma and who may require a multidisciplinary comprehensive approach to address their mental health needs. Family and community social support for Middle Eastern Americans can serve as protection and as resources for treatment planning. Recommended treatments for Middle Eastern Americans include the use of structured cognitive-behavioral interventions and relationship-oriented approaches.

Note

1. *Middle East* is a Western European term designating the lands to the east that were a moderate distance from Western Europe; China and other lands even farther east were termed the Far East. The term Near East was applied to Eastern Europe.

References

Abraham, N. (1995). Arab Americans. In R. J. Vecoli, J. Galens, A. Sheets, & R. V. Young (Eds.), *Gale encyclopedia of multicultural America* (Vol. 1, pp. 84–98). New York: Gale Research.

Abraham, N. (2000). Arab Detroit's "American" mosque. In N. Abraham & A. Shryock (Eds.), *Arab Detroit: From margin to mainstream* (pp. 279–309). Detroit, MI: Wayne State University Press.

Abudabbeh, N. (1996). Arab families. In M. McGoldrick, J. Giordano, & J. K. Pearce (Eds.), *Ethnicity and family therapy* (pp. 333–346). New York: Guilford Press.

Abudabbeh, N., & Aseel, H. A. (1999). Transcultural counseling and Arab Americans. In J. McFadden (Ed.), *Transcultural counseling* (pp. 283–296). Alexandria, VA: American Counseling Association.

Abudabbeh, N., & Hamid, A. (2001). Substance use among Arabs and Arab Americans. In S. L. A. Straussner (Ed.), *Ethnocultural factors in substance abuse treatment* (pp. 275–290). New York: Guilford Press.

Ajrouch, K. J. (1999). Family and ethnic identity in an Arab-American community. In M. Suleiman (Ed.), *Arabs in America: Building a new future* (pp. 129–139). Philadelphia, PA: Temple University Press.

Ajrouch, K. J. (2000). Place, age, and culture: Community living and ethnic identity among Lebanese American adolescents. *Small Group Research, 31,* 447–469.

Al-Krenawi, A., & Graham, J. R. (2000). Culturally sensitive social work practice with Arab clients in mental health settings. *Health and Social Work, 25,* 9–22.

Arab American Institute. (2004). *Arab American demographics.* Retrieved October 26, 2004, from http://www.aaiusa.org/demographics.htm

Bagheri, A. (1992). Psychiatric problems among Iranian immigrants in Canada. *Canadian Journal of Psychiatry, 37,* 7–11.

Berry, A. (2003a, October). *The dynamics of addiction.* Paper presented at the Third Biennial National Conference on Health Issues in the Arab American Community, Dearborn, MI.

Berry, A. (2003b, October). *The dynamics of recovery from alcoholism/addiction.* Paper presented at the Third Biennial National Conference on Health Issues in the Arab American Community, Dearborn, MI.

Cainkar, L. (2002). *Arabs, Muslims, and race in America.* Middle East Report 224. Retrieved October 14, 2004, from http://www.merip.org/mer224/224_cainkar.html

Camarota, S. A. (2002). *Immigrants from the Middle East: A profile of the foreign-born population from Pakistan to Morocco.* Washington, DC: Center for Immigration Studies.

Cardoza, B. L., Bilukha, O. O., Crawford, C. A. G., Shaikh, I., Wolfe, M. J., Gerber, M. L., et al. (2004). Mental health, social functioning, and disability in postwar Afghanistan. *Journal of the American Medical Association, 292,* 575–584.

Council on Islamic Education. (1995). *Teaching about Islam and Muslims in the public school classroom* (3rd ed.). Fountain Valley, CA: Author.

Erickson, C. D., & Al-Timimi, N. R. (2001). Providing mental health services to Arab Americans: Recommendations and considerations. *Cultural Diversity and Ethnic Minority Psychology, 7,* 306–327.

Farag, S. (2000). Arab states: Egypt and the Arab states. In A. E. Kazdin (Ed.), *Encyclopedia of psychology* (Vol. 1, pp. 224–228). Washington, DC: American Psychological Association.

Feather, N. T. (2004). Value correlates of ambivalent attitudes toward gender relations. *Personality and Social Psychology Bulletin, 30,* 3–12.

Glick, P., & Fiske, S. T. (2001). An ambivalent alliance: Hostile and benevolent sexism as complementary justifications for gender inequality. *American Psychologist, 56,* 109–118.

Hakim-Larson, J. (Ed.). (2001, May). *Summary of conference proceedings: Mental health and behavioral issues session.* The Second Biennial National Conference on Health Issues in the Arab American Community, Dearborn, MI.

Hakim-Larson, J., & Nassar-McMillan, S. (2006, April). *Identity development in Arab American youth: Implications for practice and research.* Education session presented at American Counseling Association meeting, Montreal, Canada.

Hammad, A., & Kysia, R. (1996, October). *ACCESS Arab American primary care and health needs assessment survey.* Unpublished manuscript.

Hassoun, R. (1999). Arab-American health and the process of coming to America: Lessons from the Metropolitan Detroit area. In M. Suleiman (Ed.), *Arabs in America: Building a new future* (pp. 157–176). Philadelphia, PA: Temple University Press.

Hattar-Pollara, M., & Meleis, A. I. (1995). The stress of immigration and the daily lived experiences of Jordanian immigrant women in the United States. *Western Journal of Nursing Research, 17,* 521–539.

Howell, S. (2000). The art and artistry of Arab Detroit. In N. Abraham & A. Shryock (Eds.), *Arab Detroit: From margin to mainstream* (pp. 487–513). Detroit, MI: Wayne State University Press.

Jaber, L. A., Brown, M. B., Hammad, A., Nowak, S., Zhu, Q., Ghafoor, A., et al. (2003). Epidemiology of diabetes among Arab Americans. *Diabetes Care, 26,* 308–313.

Jackson, M. L., & Nassar-McMillan, S. (2005). Counseling Arab Americans. In C. C. Lee (Ed.), *Multicultural issues in counseling: New approaches to diversity* (3rd ed., pp. 235–248). Alexandria, VA: American Counseling Association.

Jalali, B. (1996). Iranian families. In M. McGoldrick, J. Giordano, & J. K. Pearce (Eds.), *Ethnicity and family therapy* (pp. 347–363). New York: Guilford Press.

Jamil, H., Ajo, S. M., & Jamil, L. H. (2000, October/November). *Cultural differences in substance abuse between Iraqi and Caucasians in a mental health clinic, USA.* Paper presented at the International Congress on Environmental Health Issues in Primary Health Care, Cairo, Egypt.

Jamil, H., Hammad, A., Jamil, L., Stevens, T., & Pass, H. (2001, May). *Characteristics of Arab and Chaldean smokers residing in south-east Michigan 1999–2000.* Paper presented at The Second Biennial Conference on Health Issues in the Arab American Community, Dearborn, MI.

Kamoo, R., Hakim-Larson, J., Nassar-McMillan, A. C., & Porcerelli, J. H. (2004). *Mental health and Arabs and Chaldeans.* Unpublished manuscript.

Keyes, E. F. (2000). Mental health status in refugees: An integrative review of current research. *Issues in Mental Health Nursing, 21,* 397–410.

Kira, I. A. (1999, August). *Type III trauma and the Iraqi refugees traumatic experiences.* Paper presented at the 107th annual convention of the American Psychological Association, Boston.

Kira, I. A. (2002). Torture assessment and treatment: The wraparound approach. *Traumatology, 8,* 23–51.

Kulwicki, A., & Miller, J. (1999). Domestic violence in the Arab American population: Transforming environmental conditions through community education. *Issues in Mental Health Nursing, 20,* 199–215.

Kulwicki, A., & Rice, V. H. (2003). Arab American adolescent perceptions and experiences with smoking. *Public Health Nursing, 20,* 177–183.

Laffrey, S. C., Meleis, A. I., Lipson, J. G., Solomon, M., & Omidian, P. A. (1989). Assessing Arab-American health care needs. *Social Science Medicine, 29,* 877–883.

Loza, N. (2001, May). *Insanity on the Nile: The history of psychiatry in pharaonic Egypt.* Paper presented at The Second Biennial National Conference on Arab American Health Issues, Dearborn, MI.

Meleis, A. I. (1991). Between two cultures: Identity, roles, and health. *Health Care for Women International, 12,* 365–377.

Nassar-McMillan, S. C. (2003a). Arab Americans. In N. A. Vacc, S. B. DeVaney, & J. Brendel (Eds.), *Counseling multicultural and diverse populations* (4th ed., pp. 117–139). New York: Brunner-Routledge.

Nassar-McMillan, S. C. (2003b). *Counseling Arab-Americans: Counselors' call for advocacy and social justice.* Denver, CO: Love.

Nassar-McMillan, S. C., & Hakim-Larson, J. (2003). Counseling considerations among Arab Americans. *Journal of Counseling and Development, 81,* 150–159.

Nobles, A., & Sciarra, D. (2000). Cultural determinants in the treatment of Arab Americans: A primer for mainstream counselors. *American Journal of Orthopsychiatry, 70,* 182–191.

Rasmussen, A. (2000). *The sound of culture, the structure of tradition.* In N. Abraham & A. Shryock (Eds.), *Arab Detroit: From margin to mainstream* (pp. 551–572). Detroit, MI: Wayne State University Press.

Read, J. G., & Bartkowski, J. P. (2000). To veil or not to veil? A case study of identity negotiation among Muslim women in Austin, Texas. *Gender & Society, 14,* 395–417.

Rice, V. H., & Kulwicki, A. (1992). Cigarette use among Arab Americans in the Detroit Metropolitan area. *Public Health Reports, 107,* 589–594.

Rice, V. H., Templin, T., & Kulwicki, A. (2003). Arab-American adolescent tobacco use: Four pilot studies. *Preventive Medicine, 37,* 492–498.

Rudy, D., & Grusec, J. E. (2001). Correlates of authoritarian parenting in individualistic and collectivistic cultures and implications for understanding the transmission of values. *Journal of Cross-Cultural Psychology, 32,* 202–212.

Sagy, S., Orr, E., Bar-On, D., & Awwad, E. (2001). Individualism and collectivism in two conflicted societies: Comparing Israeli-Jewish and Palestinian-Arab high school students. *Youth & Society, 33,* 3–30.

Salari, S. (2002). Invisible in aging research: Arab-Americans, Middle Eastern immigrants, and Muslims in the United States. *The Gerontologist, 42,* 580–588.

Samhan, H. (1999a). Not quite white: Race classification and the Arab American experience. In M. Suleiman (Ed.), *Arabs in America: Building a new future* (pp. 209–226). Philadelphia, PA: Temple University Press.

Samhan, H. (1999b). *Who are Arab Americans?* Article originally published in *Grolier's Multimedia Encyclopedia.* Retrieved October 26, 2004, from http://www.aaiusa.org/definition.htm

Sayed, M., Collins, D. T., & Takahashi, T. (1998). West meets east: Cross-cultural issues in inpatient treatment. *Bulletin of the Menninger Clinic, 62,* 439–454.

Schopmeyer, K. (2000). A demographic portrait of Arab Detroit. In N. Abraham & A. Shryock (Eds.), *Arab Detroit: From margin to mainstream* (pp. 61–92). Detroit, MI: Wayne State University Press.

Shaheen, J. (1991). The comic book Arab. *The Link, 24,* 1–11.

Shaheen, J. G. (2001). *Reel bad Arabs: How Hollywood vilifies a people.* Brooklyn, NY: Interlink.

Shakir, E. (1997). *Bint Arab: Arab and Arab American women in the United States.* Westport, CT: Praeger.

Shryock, A. (2000). Family resemblances: Kinship and community in Arab Detroit. In N. Abraham & A. Shryock (Eds.), *Arab Detroit: From margin to mainstream* (pp. 573–610). Detroit, MI: Wayne State University Press.

Shryock, A., & Abraham, N. (2000). On margins and mainstreams. In N. Abraham & A. Shryock (Eds.), *Arab Detroit: From margin to mainstream* (pp. 15–35). Detroit, MI: Wayne State University Press.

Simman, A. (2004, May). *Symptom severity as a factor in shaping the nature of stigmatization in the course of depression.* Paper presented at the Third Annual Symposium on Refugees & Victims of Torture, Dearborn, MI.

Simon, J. P. (1996). Lebanese families. In M. McGoldrick, J. Giordano, & J. K. Pearce (Eds.), *Ethnicity and family therapy* (pp. 364–375). New York: Guilford Press.

Triandis, H. C. (1994). Major cultural syndromes and emotion. In S. Kitayama & H. R. Markus (Eds.), *Emotion and culture: Empirical studies of mutual influence* (pp. 285–306). Washington, DC: American Psychological Association.

United Nations. (2004, August). *Unofficial map of Middle East.* Retrieved November 22, 2004, from http://www.un.org/Depts/Cartographic/map/profile/mideastr.pdf

U.S. Committee for Refugees. (2000). *Refugee reports, 21.* Retrieved October 14, 2004, from http://www.refugees.org/world/articles/nationality_rr00_12.cfm

Via, T., Callahan, S., Barry, K., Jackson, C., & Gerber, D. E. (1997). Middle East meets Midwest: The new health care challenge. *The Journal of Multicultural Nursing and Health, 3,* 35–39.

Walbridge, L. S., & Aziz, T. M. (2000). After Karbala: Iraqi refugees in Detroit. In N. Abraham & A. Shryock (Eds.), *Arab Detroit: From margin to mainstream* (pp. 321–342). Detroit, MI: Wayne State University Press.

Wingfield, M., & Karaman, B. (1995, March/April). Diverse learners in the social studies classroom: Arab stereotypes and American educators. *Social Studies and the Young Learner, 7,* 7–10.

Latino/Latina Americans

10

Edward A. Delgado-Romero,
Nallely Galván, Melissa R. Hunter,
and Vasti Torres

Although people often think that Melody is a Latina counselor because of her dark hair and brown skin, actually she is biracial: Asian (Filipino) and white. Melody took Spanish in school, but she never thought that she would have any practical use for it. Times have definitely changed; her Midwestern hometown has seen a tremendous growth in the immigrant Latino/Latina and Spanish-speaking population. Melody works as an outpatient drug and alcohol treatment counselor, and Latino/Latina clients have begun to enter the system. Melody knew it was only a matter of time before she would be assigned a Spanish-speaking client, and she dreaded putting her Spanish to the test.

That client was Miguel. Miguel entered her office and Melody noticed an expression of relief come across his face as he asked her, "¿Hablas español?" Melody hated to let him down and answered "un poco"—a little bit. Miguel smiled. Melody was sure he could tell from her accent that she was already struggling.

Miguel told Melody that he was an undocumented immigrant from Mexico. He entered the United States "by climbing and running" over a border fence. Miguel married a woman in a Texas border town and moved his family to the Midwest with the hope of finding a better job. He presented to counseling because he was addicted to cocaine and alcohol and was physically abusing his wife and three children. Miguel was concerned that if he were caught abusing substances or if the police were called on a domestic abuse call to his home, he would be deported.

As Melody listened to his story, she knew that she would need to be aware of the stereotypes that she had already formed about Latinos. One positive stereotype was her belief that Latino men were dedicated to their family and were hard working and community oriented. At the same time, she also believed that Latinos were domineering and macho. As Miguel's counselor, Melody knew that these stereotypes would have the potential to affect the entire counseling relationship.

Other factors that Melody considered when working with Miguel included her comfort level with her own culture and ethnic identity, as well as her own acculturation status. Because her monolingual and monocultural supervisor wasn't much help, Melody sought supervision from a former professor. In the process, she read all that she could about counseling Latino/Latina clients. Through supervision and research, Melody realized that she had to broach the relationship between acculturation struggles and substance abuse with Miguel, as well as help Miguel find a way to recognize and foster his cultural strengths.

Furthermore, due to her lack of expertise as a bilingual counselor and the facility's lack of bilingual resources for clients from different ethnic backgrounds, Melody did not feel that she had the necessary personal or professional supports to ethically work alone with Miguel, who wanted to speak Spanish exclusively in the sessions. Coming to this conclusion enabled Melody to have a trained bilingual interpreter brought in to assist them with the counseling process. Rather than seeing the interpreter as a sign of Melody's ineptitude, Miguel reported that he appreciated her attempts to be culturally sensitive and understand him.

❖

Angela, a 30-year-old Puerto Rican female, comes to a local counseling center on the advice of her physician. She meets with Terry, a European American of Scandinavian descent. Angela states that she is seeking counseling to help her develop assertiveness skills because she feels self-doubt and guilt when making decisions. She lives alone, is the youngest of five siblings, and has depressive symptoms. As the initial interview continues, Terry learns that Angela has been living in the United States for nine years. She has difficulty speaking English but has secured a job as a manager at a local fast food restaurant.

Angela has a history of broken relationships, including a divorce. Currently she is dating a man and reports being afraid of this relationship not working out. She is also fearful of losing the support of her family due to her relationships. She reports receiving critical comments from her family regarding her marital status and the number of partners she has had. Angela explains that, according to her family, her relationships do not work because she does what she wants (e.g., does not seek or follow her partner's approval), is not a good housekeeper (e.g., allows her partner to cook or do the dishes), and she is too independent. Angela explains that she is tired of putting aside her needs in order to help other people who do not appreciate her help or sacrifices.

In counseling, Terry helps Angela work on the assertiveness skills that she lacks. However, as part of the work, the counselor feels that it is important to explore Angela's family dynamics. Those dynamics include the role of women and men in the family and *in the Puerto Rican community and Angela's role as the youngest sibling and as a single divorced woman. Also, Angela and Terry discuss the process of acculturation and its impact on her personal and family life. The most challenging issue for the counselor is to remember the central role that family plays in Angela's decisions. Therefore, Terry tries to maintain an awareness of how her own enculturation into a more individualistic and Western mainstream culture could potentially influence her work with Angela. The counselor's seeing Angela's case from a collectivist point of view helps Angela feel understood. It also ensures that Angela includes family considerations when she makes decisions concerning her life, even if she goes against family norms.*

When the counselor who was described in the opening vignette met with Miguel, the term *Latino* served as a filter for her understanding the individual in context: By accounting for Miguel's ethnicity, Melody reflected on her own beliefs regarding what it means to be Latino/Latina in the United States, on her own identity as a biracial woman, and on the role this identity plays in Miguel's expectations of her. Similarly, in the second vignette, Terry remained culturally alert by keeping in mind the potential similarities and differences between herself and Angela regarding acculturation and enculturation, especially their views on gender roles, which might create conflict in their working relationship.

The two cases were presented from the viewpoints of the counselors in order to emphasize that the counselor's work is not simply to work on the client, but to be with the client. This alliance requires counselor self-reflection and personal cultural awareness. The cases of Melody, Miguel, Terry, and Angela will be referred to throughout this chapter. Before you proceed, answer the questions in Activity 10.1.

Due the dramatic increase in the U.S. Latino/Latina population over the past 20 years, it has become vitally important that counselors be prepared to work with Latino/Latina clients. Both of the above vignettes present some of the counseling issues (e.g., language, family values, culture, acculturation, gender roles) that counselors will encounter when they work with Latinos/Latinas. This chapter will explore these issues and their influence on the counseling relationship with a Latino/Latina client. It will begin by discussing the terms used to identify members of this large panethnic group and then present demographic information that could be useful in understanding Latinos'/Latinas' needs and

---

ACTIVITY 10.1

What do you think of when you think of Latinos/Latinas or Hispanics?

What are your preconceptions of what counseling will be like with a Latino/Latina or Hispanic client?

living conditions. From there, other salient variables needed for understanding Latino/Latina clients and implications for counseling will be discussed.

Hispanic or Latino/Latina: What's in a Name?

A name is often the introduction to identity for an individual or group of people. For Hispanic/Latino/Latina people, there are many names that have been used to describe them (e.g., Hispanic, Latino, Chicano, Raza, Spanish American, and specific country names like Mexican, Cuban, and Puerto Rican). Counselors need to be aware that the terms *Hispanic* and *Latino/Latina* have different political implications and origins. Some people argue that these terms reflect a legacy of colonialism in the Americas (i.e., the terms define a group of people by the names of the empires—Spanish [Hispanic] and Roman [Latino]—that historically colonized and oppressed them). In this section, we will discuss these controversial terms.

Hispanic is the official U.S. government term (U.S. Office of Management & Budget, 1997) for people of Mexican, Puerto Rican, Cuban, Central American, and South American origin. *Hispanic* is also an English word, one that is thought to emphasize the white European (Spanish and Portuguese) colonial heritage while excluding the indigenous, slave, mixed (*mestizo*), and non-European and non-Spanish-speaking heritages. For example, a Peruvian of Incan descent may feel the term *Hispanic* does not reflect who she or he is. Many scholars find the term *Hispanic* to be an undesirable panethnic term that can gloss over vital differences among many people (e.g., Jones-Correa & Leal, 1996). Santiago-Rivera, Arredondo, and Gallardo-Cooper (2002) point out that "to assume sameness about the different ethnic groups—such as Colombians, Cubans, Dominicans, and Puerto Ricans—would be tantamount to using stereotypes to know an individual and a group's worldview" (p. 12).

The term *Latino,* or the feminine form, *Latina,* has been thought of as a more inclusive and politically progressive term (Santiago-Rivera et al., 2002) and has, in many areas, become preferable to *Hispanic.* The term Latino/Latina is considered more inclusive because (a) the terms are gender specific; (b) the terms refer to all people from Latin America, including, for example, Brazilians (i.e., in contrast to the rest of South America, Brazil was colonized by the Portuguese and is, therefore, not Hispanic); and (c) the designation Latino/Latina to represent peoples from the Americas also prevents the inaccurate labeling of European Spaniards as an ethnic minority in the United States (Comas-Díaz, 2001).

However, what is often missing from the discussion on terminology is what this diverse group of peoples would call *themselves.* The power to name oneself represents liberation over colonization (Comas-Díaz, 2001). In this chapter, the general term Latino/Latina is used (unless U.S. government products such as the Census, which requires use of the term Hispanic, are mentioned). The authors recognize that for some people, national (e.g., Mexican or Mexican American), regional (e.g., *Nuyorican* or *Caribeño/ Caribeña*), political (e.g., *Chicano/Chicana*), panethnic (e.g., *Raza*), or racial (e.g., *LatiNegro/LatiNegra*) terms may be preferred. It is important for the counselor to assess how Latino/Latina clients identify themselves, both collectively and individually (e.g., the pronunciation and language of their name). The way in which clients choose to define their names and identities may reflect the importance of ethnic, racial, and cultural identity and political consciousness (or lack thereof). The terms a person uses to define herself or himself may change throughout the course of counseling as issues related to culture are addressed. A client's ethnic/racial identity can change in the process of counseling (see Chapters 3 and 4).

Latino/Latina Demographics

It is important for counselors to know how representative of the United States' overall population Latinos/Latinas are and the circumstances in which many Latinos/Latinas live. Culturally competent counselors need to especially understand the interplay between a group's demographic characteristics and existing mental health disparities in U.S. society. As addressed in Chapter 2, clients' living situations may influence their ability to access medical and mental health services, as well as give an indication of their mobility in career, academic, and social environments. For example, although it is generally true that counselors need to know about clients' financial situations regardless of their ethnicity or race, financial status becomes more salient in cases where the individual might be undocumented and/or uninsured. Having an awareness of Latino/Latina clients' financial positions and living circumstances will aid the counselor to better serve the needs of Latinos/Latinas. The following sections provide descriptions of Latino/Latina clients' demographic characteristics, historical background, and other contextual factors regarding race and ethnicity.

GENERAL DEMOGRAPHIC, HISTORICAL, AND CONTEXTUAL DESCRIPTORS

Although there have been Latinos/Latinas in the United States since the inception of the nation, awareness of the growing numbers of Latinos/Latinas has recently increased. The Latino/Latina population has expanded from 15 million in 1980 to nearly 39.9 million in 2003 (U.S. Census Bureau, 2004). This substantial growth means that Hispanics, to use the U.S. Census Bureau term, are the fastest growing minority mega-ethnic group in the United States. Among U.S. Hispanics, 58.6 percent are of Mexican origin, 9.6 percent are of Puerto Rican origin, 3.5 percent are of Cuban origin, and 28.3 percent are "other Hispanics." Approximately 10 million Hispanics fall into this "other" category, which includes (1) six million Hispanics whom the census has problems classifying (see Guzmán & McConnell, 2002; McConnell & Delgado-Romero, 2004) and (2) approximately four million Hispanics from Central America (1.7 million), South America (1.4

million), and the Dominican Republic (under 1 million) combined. Contrary to popular misconceptions, the growth of the Latino/Latina population can be attributed to high fertility rates rather than solely to immigration.

The Latino/Latina population tends to be young. Its median age is 26.7 years, compared to 39.6 years for non-Hispanic whites (Bernstein, 2004). Among Latinos/ Latinas, those of Mexican origin have the highest numbers of people under the age of 18 (37.1 percent) and Cubans have the lowest numbers (19.6 percent) (Ramirez & de la Cruz, 2003). The household size of Latinos/Latinas tends to be larger than that of non-Hispanic whites. Latinos/Latinas are also more likely to live in poverty and to be unemployed (Ramirez & de la Cruz, 2003) than non-Hispanic whites. Differences exist among Latinos/Latinas, with Puerto Ricans (31 percent) having higher rates of poverty than Mexicans (27 percent) and Cubans (14 percent) (U.S. Department of Health and Human Services [DHHS], 2001). More than two in five Hispanics over the age of 25 lack a high school diploma, with the two largest groups, Mexicans and Puerto Ricans, being the least likely to have a high school diploma (Bernstein & Bergan, 2003).

ACCESS TO COUNSELING

Latinos/Latinas are less likely than many other groups to have access to counseling. Age and education particularly affect Latinos'/Latinas' ability to receive counseling services. For example, younger adults are less likely than older adults to be insured. In turn, health insurance is a key to accessing health care. Only 40 percent of Latinos/Latinas have health insurance compared with 80 percent of whites and 65 percent of African Americans (Boushey & Wright, 2004). Of Latinos/Latinas with mental health disorders, only 1 in 11 contact a mental health provider (and this number is lower for immigrants) compared with 1 of 3 whites (Alegria, Perez, & Williams, 2003). For immigrants, only 1 of 20 Hispanic Americans uses mental health services and only 1 in 10 uses general health care services (DHHS, 2001). Such trends translate into large numbers of Latinos/Latinas having unaddressed issues like substance abuse, marital difficulties, anxiety, and depression.

HISTORICAL AND CONTEXTUAL FACTORS AFFECTING LATINO/LATINA CLIENTS

Historical and contextual factors are important in understanding characteristics of Latino/Latina clients, especially the circumstances of immigration and related attitudes toward the country of origin and the United States. For example, a Cuban who immigrated to the United States to escape Communism in the first wave of Cuban immigration (and was received in the United States with official resettlement programs) might have a reason to feel differently about the United States and her or his homeland than would a Puerto Rican individual who is able to travel freely between the United States and Puerto

Rico. Circumstances of immigration were important in both of the opening case vignettes. Miguel feared deportation. Angela, despite being a United States citizen by virtue of being born in Puerto Rico, still faced serious acculturation issues in the mainland United States.

Adjustment can be viewed through the lens of racial or cultural identity for Latino/Latina clients (e.g., cultural pride vs. shame), depending on the circumstances that brought them to the United States and where they choose to live. The circumstances of their immigration may also affect their attitudes toward counseling, other minority groups, and the importance of retaining the Spanish language and/or Latino/Latina culture. The rest of this section looks in greater detail at the important and often-overlooked issue of Latino/Latina ethnicity and race.

LATINO/LATINA ETHNICITY AND RACE

According the U.S. government, Hispanics are the only "official" ethnicity in the country. Therefore, U.S. Census takers expect Hispanics to choose both an ethnicity (Hispanic/non-Hispanic) and a race (white, black, Asian Pacific Islander, Native American). However, it is not clear that all U.S. Latinos/Latinas endorse this particular parsing of identity. Many Latinos/Latinas prefer national or panethnic terms instead of race or country of origin (McConnell & Delgado-Romero, 2004). This response represents the growing desire for a unique identity for Latinos/Latinas.

However, as is the case with any other group in the United States, race has historically played a complicated role within the Latino/Latina population and continues to do so. For example, three main racial groups of Hispanics have been found through analysis of census data: (1) white Hispanics, (2) black Hispanics, and (3) what the researcher termed "Hispanic Hispanics" (i.e., those who chose Hispanic as their racial designation; Logan, 2003). Logan found that success and educational attainment followed racial lines, with white Hispanics being more successful than Hispanic Hispanics and black Hispanics. Because the number of Hispanic Hispanics (now more than 16 million) is growing more rapidly than other Hispanic groups, it is even more important to be aware of the distinctiveness of Hispanics who identify neither as black nor as white. Many of those are of indigenous American ancestry (e.g., Mayan), and others see themselves as multiracial.

Racial and ethnic issues are not limited to self-identification. It is important to remember that clients also face daily interactions with others who want to classify them into categories. For example, those Latinos/Latinas with strong Spanish accents or those who outwardly represent what Latinos/Latinas are expected to look like (i.e., via skin and eye color, hair color and texture) may find that they are strongly identified as Latino/Latina by others. Conversely, light-skinned Latinos/Latinas without accents may struggle to be seen as legitimately Latino/Latina (Delgado-Romero, 2004). Dark-skinned Latinos/Latinas may face additional racial challenges when identified as black or African American by others (Comas-Díaz, 1994). Counselors should therefore be aware that racial and ethnic identity issues may be important to address with a client, in terms of both self-identification and potential discrimination or invalidation related to race and ethnicity that a client may encounter in society.

Although the growing panethnic identity of many U.S. Latinos/Latinas can be considered a positive development in terms of political unity, an imposed panethnic identity may also be distressing to a client who has a strong national or regional identity. It should be noted that upon entry into the United States, many Latinos/Latinas experience a transformation of identity as they enter the binary (black/white) racial and ethnic categorization system of the United States. They previously may have defined themselves nationally or regionally along a continuum of racial descriptors found in Latin American countries (Mörner, 1967). However, once in the United States, they may be given a new ethnicity (Hispanic or Latino/Latina) and race.

This transformation can be confusing and disorienting. For example, in the second vignette, Angela is a Puerto Rican who identifies herself as an *isleña*, someone from the island of Puerto Rico as opposed to a Puerto Rican who was born in the United States (Soto-Carlo, Delgado-Romero, & Galván, 2005), and as a *Tiana* (a reference to the indigenous people of Puerto Rico). However, she is now identified in the United States as simply Hispanic and/or black. This new identification can cause an identity crisis and marginalization. In response to accepting an imposed categorical system, several Latinos/Latinas have chosen racialized terms to describe themselves, such as *La Raza,* which means "the people" or "the race," to claim a place within the racial hierarchy of the United States (Vidal de Haymes, Kilty, & Haymes, 2002). Counselors might find it helpful to explore how their Latino/Latina clients' racial and ethnic identities affect their self-perceptions and the issues they bring to counseling.

Stereotypes, Racism, and Prejudice

Categorizations of race and ethnicity are also accompanied by stereotypes, racism, and prejudice. In the United States, Latinos/Latinas have to face several stereotypes that have been perpetuated in the media. Activity 10.2 invites the reader to generate such stereotypes.

STEREOTYPING BY NON-LATINOS/LATINAS

As the reader may recall from the first vignette, Miguel's counselor, Melody, was aware of the importance of knowing her stereotypes because they can influence the therapeutic relationship. Some of the stereotypes held by Melody are also typical of U.S. society. They include the idea that all Latinos are dedicated to their family yet are domineering, abusive *machos* or *machistas*. Latinas, by contrast, are seen as self-sacrificing and unassertive (a phenomenon called *marianismo,* which is discussed later). Other common stereotypes include

---

ACTIVITY 10.2

Can you think of some of the stereotypes of Latinos/Latinas?

What do you think are the stereotypical roles for men versus women in Latino/Latina cultures?

What are some stereotypes that you consider *positive* about Latinos/Latinas?

---

portraying Latino/Latina people as lazy, overly emotional, unreliable, illegally in the United States, speaking broken English, and criminal. There are also specific stereotypes according to country; for example, Cubans are sometimes portrayed as the "model" Latino/Latina population and Colombians are often portrayed as drug traders. Counselors should be aware of the power and pervasiveness of stereotypes because these stereotypes not only affect clients' self-perceptions, they also are related to counselors' decreased sense of client competence and a subsequent increase in clients' self-defeating behavior.

STEREOTYPES AND OPPRESSION FROM WITHIN THE LATINO/LATINA COMMUNITY

Latinos/Latinas not only face oppression and stereotypes from outside the Latino/Latina community, but *racismo*—discrimination—also exists within and between the Latino/Latina groups (Shorris, 1992). Latino/Latina people may internalize stereotypes about other Latino/Latina ethnicities (e.g., Mexican Americans might be seen as "lazy"), learn to devalue certain racial groups (e.g., disparage Latinos/Latinas who are also black or indigenous), or have long-standing rivalries or conflicts with other national groups (e.g., between Colombians and Venezuelans). For these reasons, a Latino/Latina client may resent being "lumped" into a generic racial or ethnic category with other groups or may have strong negative opinions of other Latino/Latina groups.

In sum, it is important for counselors to realize that Latinos/Latinas may face multiple oppressions from at least three sources: the majority culture, other minority cultures, and within the Latino/Latina community.

EMPHASIZING LATINO/LATINA FAMILY AS A STRENGTH

Because of pervasively negative stereotypes, it is important for counselors to focus on strengths in Latino/Latina culture. Family is one such asset. For example, there is evidence that family pride and cohesion play a particularly powerful role in the psychosocial development of Cuban American children, acting as buffers for acculturative stress (Vega, Gil, Warheit, Zimmerman, & Aposori, 1993). The power of the family context was seen in the case of Angela, along with her developing individual assertiveness skills. The counselor helped her make her changes within the family context, helping all of them see that they could continue to count on each other for support (thus lessening her feelings of guilt). Thus, counselors need to see Latino/Latina families as a potential source of strength for clients, rather than solely endorsing individualistic notions of independence and individuation. Family relationships are described more fully later in this chapter.

Latino/Latina Culture

As mentioned above, the use of one term, Latino/Latina, as a panethnic grouping of peoples creates the impression that all Latinos/Latinas are a monolithic racial or ethnic group and that they share a common culture. As noted earlier, the Latino/Latina population is widely diverse. The term is used to represent millions of people from the different countries in Central and South America and the Caribbean. Those peoples who are grouped together as Latino/Latina simultaneously represent indigenous, African, European, and Asian influences and speak an array of languages (including Spanish, Portuguese, English, and Amerindian languages). Each country and region of origin reflects a unique political, economic, social, religious, and cultural constellation. In addition, each has a unique history relative to the United States (e.g., Puerto Rico has been a commonwealth of the United States since the Spanish-American War; Mexico, which lost a border war to the United States, has free trade agreements and shares a common border). Each also has unique immigration issues that especially influence how Mexicans are perceived in the United States (Torres, 2004).

After a discussion of commonalities and differences among Latino/Latina people, Latino/Latina cultural attributes will be presented in terms of the following categories: region, language, family, gender, and acculturation.

COMMONALITIES AMONG LATINO/LATINA PEOPLES

Although there is considerable diversity within the U.S. Latino/Latina population, some general similarities define Latino/Latina people. Those similarities include the experience of colonization, ethnic mixing, and values.

Latinos/Latinas share histories of conquest and oppression; the struggle for liberation; and the destruction of indigenous cultures, religions, and people (Garcia-Preto, 1996). As a result, there is an ongoing struggle for social justice among Latino/Latina people.

Another common element among Latino/Latina people is the history of ethnic mixing. This phenomenon is a product of Central and South American participation in slavery. That history has resulted in *mestizo* (racially mixed) people such that, as Garcia-Preto acknowledges, "Latinos are descendants of [both] oppressors and the oppressed" (p. 143).

Additional similarities among Latino/Latina people include the widespread use of the Spanish language (with regional variations), the influence of Roman Catholicism, and an ambivalent perspective on U.S. foreign policies and political intervention in Caribbean and Central and South American countries (Delgado-Romero & Rojas, 2004).

At least five value orientations have been attributed to the Latino/Latina people (Altarriba & Bauer, 1998). They are *personalismo* (a preference for close personal relationships), *respeto* (esteem for elders and authority, which is maintained by all family members), *familismo* (an emphasis on the family, including the extended family and friends), *simpatia* (need for behaviors that promote pleasant and non-conflicting social relationships), and *allocentrism* (high levels of conformity, mutual empathy, willingness to sacrifice for the welfare of the group, and high levels of personal interdependence) (Marín & Marín, 1991). Clients will vary in the degree to which they endorse these value orientations.

REGIONAL DIFFERENCES IN THE UNITED STATES

In addition to cultural differences originating in the country of origin, the region of the United States in which the Latino/Latina individual lives can also contribute to the similarity (or dissimilarity) of Latino/Latina clients. Latinos/Latinas are increasingly found throughout the country, but they are still concentrated in several areas and states. According to the 2000 Census, half of all U.S. Latinos/Latinas live in two states: California and Texas. Approximately 77 percent of Latinos/Latinas live in the following seven states: California, Texas, New York, Florida, Illinois, Arizona, and New Jersey. Different groups of Latinos/Latinas live in different areas. Mexican Americans are most often found in California, Texas, Illinois, and Arizona; Puerto Ricans in New York, Florida, New Jersey, and Pennsylvania; and two-thirds of all Cubans live in Florida (U.S. Census Bureau, 2001).

The general point here is that in each region there is a dominant Latino/Latina culture that may differ significantly from the Latino/Latina culture in other regions. Consequently, a regional Latino/Latina identity may be more important than national origin, to some clients. For example, a Latino/Latina who is born and raised in Miami, Florida, may encounter "culture shock" when moving to Mexican American communities in Houston or Puerto Rican communities in New York City. Thus, it is important to consider the Latino/Latina client's relationship to both the dominant (white) culture and the dominant regional Latino/Latina culture.

In the case vignettes that were provided at the beginning of the chapter, the region of the country in which the clients Miguel and Angela live might be key to understanding the clients as well as providing resources. For example, if Miguel is in an area where there are many immigrant workers, the counselor may be able to find resources in the immigrant community. Similarly, if Angela, who is Puerto Rican, lives in an area where a different Latino/Latina group (e.g., Cubans) is dominant, her family may also be concerned that she is becoming less Puerto Rican and more like her Cuban peers. The family may be distressed to hear Angela speaking Spanish with a different accent.

Before common and varying Latino/Latina cultural norms are discussed further, the important issue of acculturation is presented. It is a significant concern for Latinos/Latinas in the United States and, therefore, one that should be recognized by counselors.

ACCULTURATION

The psychological stress of having to choose between cultures is referred to as *acculturative stress* (Smart & Smart, 1995). It can be expressed in familial discord, intergenerational conflict, and racial/ethnic identity conflicts and thus may be a topic for counseling sessions.

Acculturation is a controversial issue in the mental health treatment of Latinos/Latinas. As discussed in Chapter 4, acculturation in the United States was formerly framed in terms of cultural assimilation, guided by the experiences of European immigrants. It was expected that immigrants' racial, national, and ethnic differences would be replaced in successive generations by the characteristics of the dominant culture.

Because of the lingering ethos of assimilation, groups that choose to retain aspects of their indigenous culture (e.g., the use of the Spanish language) face intense pressure to conform to mainstream norms. They may be marginalized and face discrimination.

LANGUAGE: SPANISH, ENGLISH, AND SPANGLISH

Like Latino/Latina cultures, the Spanish language is not unitary. As with English, Spanish has national and regional variations and slang forms. Some U.S. Latinos/Latinas have combined English and Spanish into an idiosyncratic form of communication often referred to as *Spanglish*. According to Stavans (2000),

> It is commonly assumed that Spanglish is a bastard jargon: part Spanish and part English, with neither *gravitas* nor a clear identity. It is spoken (or broken) by many of the approximately 35 million people of Hispanic descent in the United States, who, no longer fluent in the language of Cervantes, have not yet mastered that of Shakespeare. (p. B7)

Consequently, due to the variations in the Spanish language, even counselors trained in technical Spanish may not be able to effectively communicate with

Spanish-speaking clients (see Rivas, Delgado-Romero, & Ozambela, 2004, for examples). In cases in which communication is compromised, the use of trained interpreters may be necessary (American Psychological Association, 2003). However, the use of untrained interpreters, who may not understand counseling or the profession of interpretation, is ethically inappropriate and potentially harmful.

It should be noted that most (75 percent) U.S. Latinos/Latinas who speak Spanish also report that they speak English. Thus, agreeing upon the language spoken in counseling might be a decision that is based on necessity (e.g., if the client does not speak English) or choice (e.g., if the client prefers to speak Spanish). For example, in the first vignette, Miguel preferred to speak Spanish even though he could speak English.

It is important to note that Latino/Latina clients do not need to be counseled by bilingual Latino/Latina counselors. It should also not be assumed that all Latino/Latina counselors are automatically "experts" on all Hispanic clients. Indeed, counselors from any racial or ethnic background can become competent to work with Latino/Latina clients, with the proper training. All counselors should strive to be culturally competent (American Psychological Association, 2003; Arredondo et al., 1996; Sue, Arredondo, & McDavis, 1992).

Language-Related Problems

There are three language-related problem domains central to working with Latino/Latina clients: language choice, resources, and attitude (Rivas et al., 2004). The reader is asked to refer back to Miguel's case, in which his counselor encounters all three of these problem domains.

Language Choice. The first domain, language choice, includes the following issues:

- the meaning behind a client's choice of language (e.g., which one he or she chooses at which points in the session and for how long);
- the implications of a counselor's choosing to address (or not) language use, that is, the power dynamics involved with language;
- the effect that these factors have on the therapeutic relationship;
- the extent to which language and related dynamics interfere with or deepen the counseling process.

In the case of Miguel, the counselor was unsure of her Spanish language ability; therefore, she opted to use an interpreter. Miguel reported feeling comfortable with that option, which possibly deepened their working relationship. However, this level of cultural awareness does not always exist, and language can become a barrier to helping.

Language-Related Resources. The second language-related domain concerns the availability of resources for alternate (to English) languages. Some of the current problems in this area are the inadequate training available for bilingual counselors, the lack of certification criteria for bilingual specialists, the lack of resources available to bilingual counselors (e.g., appropriately validated assessment tools and therapeutic instruments), agency policies regarding record keeping and other pragmatics of bilingual counseling, and the exploitation of bilingual counselors.

Language-Related Attitudes. The third domain, attitude, includes issues such as the counselor's level of comfort with both the client's and her or his own language proficiency (including reading, writing, speaking, and comprehending/communicating) and the counselor's own ethnic identity and acculturation status. Melody, the counselor in the opening vignette, took some risks in addressing these three domains, and the client seemed to benefit from the results.

LA FAMILIA: FAMILY RELATIONSHIPS IN LATINO/LATINA CULTURE

The strong familial relationships that presented conflict and strength in both the cases of Miguel and Angela are central to Latino/Latina culture. Latinos/Latinas should be conceptualized in the context of *La Familia,* that is, the whole family (Santiago-Rivera et al., 2002). However, the Latino/Latina notion of family is not the stereotypical nuclear family. Latino/Latina families often extend their notion of family to include relatives and close friends.

Most importantly, the family is a source of identity (and potential conflict) for Latinos/Latinas. Many Latinos/Latinas define themselves in the collectivist context of their families (Delgado-Romero, 2001). For example, Vasquez (2001) described her own family circle:

> I grew up in a small central Texas town during the 1950s. I was the first of seven children born to firstborn parents . . . . In other words, I had the privilege of a considerable amount of attention, adoration, and regard from my parents, large extended family (including 16 aunts and uncles and all 4 grandparents plus great uncles and aunts, second cousins, and so on!). (p. 65)

While traditional Latin notions of family are important, it is critical to understand that the concept of the Latino/Latina family is not static. It is something that is in transition and is variable because of the acculturation process (described later in this chapter), migration experience, language, race, nationality, and socioeconomic background of each family (Santiago-Rivera et al., 2002).

Types of Latino/Latina Family Structures

Four types of family structures are relevant to working with Latinos/Latinas (Santiago-Rivera et al., 2002). The first is the intact *familia,* which consists of parents who live together. This configuration may include grandparents or other members of the extended family. This family structure is likely to be patri-archal and the parents may take on designated gender roles. This is what is thought of as the "traditional" Latino/Latina family.

The second is the single-parent *familia,* which is most commonly headed by Latina single mothers. High rates of poverty and teen pregnancy in Latino/Latina communities contribute to the existence of this structure. It should be noted that single Latina mothers are at a high risk for depression.

The third type of family structure is the bicultural *familia.* There are two types of bicultural *familias:* acculturated bicultural families (in which a Latino/Latina family has some level of acculturation to the dominant culture) and cross-cultural bicultural families (i.e., those produced by intercultural marriage).

Finally, the fourth is the immigrant *familia.* Migration is a significant event in the life of a family. It can bring several forms of transformation to the family structure, such as new gender roles or increased responsibility for children. Some families migrate in stages, and separation and reunions are important events.

There are counseling implications for each one of these family types (Santiago-Rivera et al., 2002). One implication is that a distinction should be made between an intact family and other types of families. The issues that an intact *familia* will deal with in counseling can be very different from the issues faced by a single mother. Similarly, the intact *familia* will differ from a family whose members are either separated by geography (different times of immigration) or by cultural conflicts. Counselors should take care to assess the familial context of the client to understand the unique dynamics that each individual faces.

In the next section, traditional (and changing) gender roles that often have their origin in the traditional Latino/Latina family structure are addressed.

LATINO/LATINA GENDER ROLES

A common struggle for all ethnic minority family groups in the United States is the conflict between their own culturally traditional gender roles and those of the majority culture. Although Latinos/Latinas are a very diverse group, they share a history of European, particularly Spanish, influence on their religion and culture, which, in turn, has dictated what it means to be a man or a woman (Arredondo, 2002).

It would be to the counselor's advantage to be alert to how gender role ideolo-gies may affect relationships, the decisions clients make, and the reasons decisions are made. As stated earlier, many Latinos/Latinas define themselves in the context of their families (Delgado-Romero, 2001). Thus, understanding the role of gender in traditional Latino/Latina cultures is crucial. In the second vignette, Angela experienced a conflict with her family related to her independence and relation-ship history. This conflict was no doubt rooted in differing gender role expecta-tions for women versus men.

The following paragraphs provide an overview of Latinos'/Latinas' gender role ideologies, especially the traditional gender role characteristics of males (*machismo*) and females (*marianismo*). The influence of acculturation and economic status on *machismo* and *marianismo* are also discussed, as are other possible ways in which gender role conflict may play out in Latinos'/Latinas' personal and career decisions.

Machismo and *Marianismo*

In Latino/Latina culture, gender roles provide clear and rigid expectations for men and women. *Machismo* is a code for males. It can sometimes be characterized by male dominance, aggression, promiscuous behavior, excessive use of alcohol, and restricted emotions. It can also include positive characteristics, such as pride, honor, responsibility to be a good provider, and assertive behavior (Torres, Solberg, & Carlstrom, 2002). In the case of Latinas, *marianismo* has been associated with a number of stereotypical passive attributes for women, such as being self-sacrificing, submissive, and unassertive. These attributes have been shaped by the image of the Madonna or Virgin Mary, which indicates that women should put their needs last, be married, not be independent, or not want change (see Arredondo, 2002). However, there are also strengths inherent in female gender roles, such as dedication to family and being a keeper of tradition. Given these dual aspects of gender roles, counselors should not rush to view all traditional Latino/Latina gender roles as entirely negative.

Issues Related to Changing Gender Roles

As Latino men and Latina women acculturate into multiple cultures (e.g., their culture of origin and the dominant culture), they are likely to challenge more rigid and traditional prescribed gender roles. Clients' challenging and negotiating such gender roles can become very stressful, due to family and community attitudes. This was the case for Angela. She reported being criticized by her family for being too independent and for not acting on her duties as a woman (e.g., cooking for her husband). She had begun to acculturate to U.S. female gender roles and was negotiating her role as a woman in the community and her family. However, her family members did not appear to share her enthusiasm for changing her gender role and were demanding that she act in a traditional manner. This conflict is typical because not all members of a family will acculturate or integrate into the new culture at the same rate or on the same issues. Latinos/Latinas who are acculturating to another culture may feel a lack of support or understanding from their families or communities. Those communities might be pressuring them to adhere to the more traditional gender roles. The struggle to challenge traditional Latino/Latina gender roles can manifest itself as psychological stress, depression, and/or anxiety (Castillo & Hill, 2004; Fragoso & Kashubeck, 2000).

Counselor Responses to Gender Issues

Counselors can help Latinos/Latinas reduce their role-related stress by incorporating the following elements into their interventions. First, they can demonstrate understanding of Latino/Latina gender role expectations. Second, they can acknowledge the positive dimensions of *machismo* and *marianismo*. Finally, counselors can recognize the cultural values of *respeto* and *familismo*. As Falicov (1998) has explained, although Latinas are becoming more independent, for many, their family and their commitment to their culture remain very important. If a counselor mistakenly emphasizes independence from family, Latino/Latina clients might feel alienated and decline to participate fully in counseling because they may feel that their values are not shared or understood by the counselor.

In the case of Angela, the counselor first acknowledged *respeto*, or esteem for elders in the family, the importance of family (*familismo*), and the nature of Latino/Latina gender roles before working on her assertiveness skills. Angela's counselor also acknowledged the potential influence that her own Western mainstream culture might have on her work with Angela. The counselor kept in mind that Angela wanted to become assertive and make decisions that took her needs into account, but not at the expense of losing her connection with her family.

Particular Subgroups of Latinos/Latinas

Thus far, Latinos/Latinas have been presented in general. However, like the term Latino/Latina itself, much of the work on Latinos/Latinas is overly general and glosses over subgroups with unique mental health needs and risk factors. This section highlights some of the relevant subgroups that will need attention from counselors in the future. They include less well-known Latino/Latina ethnic groups, sexual minorities, Latino/Latina professionals and students, and the elderly.

NATIONAL GROUPS OUTSIDE THE "BIG THREE"

Because the majority of Latinos/Latinas in the United States are from Mexico, Puerto Rico, or Cuba, these groups rightfully receive the most attention in the counseling literature. However, much needs to be learned about the approximately 10 million Latinos/Latinas who are not from the "big three" countries. For example, Central Americans and Dominicans from the Caribbean constitute 5 percent of the U.S. Latino/Latina population. Another significant group, South Americans, makes up 4 percent of the U.S. Latino/Latina population. Although together they make up almost 10 percent of the Latino/Latina population, the experiences of these two groups are virtually untouched in the counseling literature (Delgado-Romero & Rojas, 2004).

Members of these groups may have unique needs. For example, Guatemalans, who often arrive from small villages and speak only indigenous (i.e., American Indian) languages, have to learn Spanish in addition to English as a way to adapt to their communities in the United States. Colombians are another example of an important but neglected group; they are the largest South American group in the

United States. They may be traumatized by a civil war that has raged in Colombia for over 40 years (Delgado-Romero & Rojas, 2004).

Clinical case studies are a helpful resource for counselors who are seeking greater familiarity with the unique needs of Latinos/Latinas who are not from the big three. Recent studies of counseling with a Dominican (Spanakis, 2004) or a Colombian (Wilczac, 2003) client are noteworthy. However, much work needs to be done to understand the needs of Latinos/Latinas outside of the big three.

LGBT LATINOS/LATINAS

Traditional Latino/Latina culture, steeped in a history of traditional Roman Catholicism, does not openly support lesbian, gay, bisexual, or transgendered (LGBT) people. In general, Latino/Latina families reject open admission of homosexuality or "coming out." Such an admission may lead to isolation, excommunication from the family, or even violence.

However, it should be noted that there is a gender difference in these attitudes. Sexual behavior for males is not extremely restricted, compared to sexual behavior of women. Traditional conceptualizations of sexual behavior in Latin American countries treat the male sex drive as overwhelming; therefore, there is less concern about a man's sexual attractions and activities.[1] In general, a man can have sex with other men and yet not be thought of as gay, as long as he continues to function in a gender role consistent with other phases of life. Conversely, the sexuality of Latinas is supposed to be confined to marriage and procreation. For women, sexual behavior outside of these confines is seen as sinful. As a result of these attitudes, the Latina lesbian faces the dual stigma that comes from both being sexually active outside of marriage and doing so with another woman.

When a Latino's/Latina's LGBT sexual behavior and orientation intersect with other oppressive conditions, the combination can prove to be a powerfully negative force in her or his life. For example, the combination of poverty, racism, and homophobia produce a higher risk of HIV for Latinos/Latinas (Diaz, Ayala, & Bein, 2004). Other problems can arise when Latino/Latina LGBT people who live in the majority white LGBT community experience racism, oppression, and dehumanization (e.g., being sought out by others for their "exotic" qualities). Counselors need to be aware of the multiple oppressions that Latino/Latina persons who are LGBT may face in their lives.

LATINO/LATINA PROFESSIONALS AND STUDENTS

Latinos/Latinas who have successfully acquired or are acquiring an education often, in Comas-Diaz's (1997) words, "represent a source of pride and joy for their families and communities," and "frequently they are identified as role models" (p. 143).

Such success comes with obligations for Latinos/Latinas: High-achieving Latinos/Latinas are expected to return to and give back to their families and communities. Latino/Latina professionals, therefore, face tremendous pressure in balancing the often-conflicting demands and values of the mainstream workplace (e.g., in predominantly white institutions of higher education) while maintaining ties to their culture.

Often, Latino/Latina professionals may feel that they are victims of their own success. Acculturation to the dominant culture, which is seen as a prerequisite for success, may lead to a sense of disconnection from the family and generational conflict. Therefore, Latino/Latina professionals may not feel sufficiently attached to or understood by their families as they struggle to achieve. Counselors should encourage Latino/Latina professionals and college students to reconnect with their families and help such clients find other support (Comas-Díaz, 1997; Gloria & Rodriguez, 2000; Ruiz, 1990).

The small number of Latinos/Latinas who are professionals makes the disconnection even greater. Illustrations of this alienation are found in personal narratives by Delgado-Romero, Flores, Gloria, Arredondo, and Castellanos (2003) and by Niemann (1999). They describe the challenges that Latino/Latina faculty members face as they try to advance in higher education. Being the single role model in a large organization can be a very lonely existence (Delgado-Romero, 2001).

Regarding Latinos/Latinas and academic success, counselors will need to challenge their own stereotypes. For example, counselors might associate Latinos/Latinas only with poverty or a lack of education. These stereotypes will be confronted when the counselor works with a Latino/Latina professional. In sum, counselors should be alert to the possible career discrimination and family conflicts that professionals may face as well as to their own biases.

THE ELDERLY

It is often emphasized that as a whole, Latinos/Latinas are the youngest population in the United States. Thus, much attention is paid to Latino/Latina adolescents. What is lost in that trend is attention to older people. As mentioned earlier, Cubans have the oldest mean age of Latino/Latina subgroups; consequently, counselors who work with Cuban Americans are more likely to deal with an older population. There is little guidance for counselors in this area.

The issues that Cuban elderly face can be instructive for counselors as the overall Latino/Latina population begins to age. For the Cuban elderly, acculturation brings with it social and economic mobility, but it consequently erodes available support and potential caregivers because children may not care for their parents or grandparents in the traditional way (Gonzalez, 1995). In the early and mid-1990s, Gonzalez (1991, 1995) studied the challenges facing the Cuban elderly. Cuban American elders tend to view the "Americanization" of their children and grandchildren in the United States with ambivalence. They are likely to have pride in the success of their family but also resent younger generations' losing cultural connection and/or intermarrying with non-Cubans.

In general, generational conflict, acculturative stress, medical decision making, and decisions on when to institutionalize Latino/Latina elderly (even when medically indicated) are challenges that face Latino/Latina families in dealing with elderly family members (Santiago-Rivera et al., 2002). These issues will intensify in the future as the Latino/Latina population ages. Counselors should be aware that generational conflicts may come into sharp focus as the issues of retirement and living arrangements for the elderly become issues for a Latino/Latina family.

OTHER VULNERABLE SUBGROUPS

As the U.S. Latino/Latina population grows, additional subgroups in the population will come to the attention of counselors. The following are a few vulnerable groups that are likely to have counseling needs.

Latino/Latina Military Veterans. Considering the overrepresentation of Latinos/Latinas in the military and the recent wars conducted by the United States, counselors must keep in mind the possible need for mental health services for current and future Latino/Latina war veterans and their families.

Latinos/Latinas Who Are Incarcerated. Members of this group have been found to have higher rates of mental health disorders when compared to community residents (DHHS, 2001). In addition, many incarcerated Latinos/Latinas may struggle with violence, substance abuse, and other health problems (e.g., HIV), which can complicate their mental health status.

Latino/Latina Children in the U.S. School System. More research needs to be done on the issues of Latino/Latina schoolchildren who are dropping out of the U.S. educational system at all levels and experiencing emotional, behavioral, and mental health problems from childhood to adolescence.

Latina College Students. Latinas have very few models of educational achievement. As a result, they are unlikely to attend college, and, if they do, they drop out at high rates. Counselors need to target Latina college students, in particular, with prevention and outreach programs.

Understanding Clients' Ethnic Identity

Generic ethnic and racial identity models were presented in Chapters 3 and 4. Those models, and the Chicano/Latino Model of Ethnic Identity that is described in this section, can be used to assess differences in ethnic identity among Latino/Latina clients. Early assessment of ethnic identity by counselors will help them to avoid overgeneralizations about what ethnicity means to a particular client.

It should be noted that ethnic identity is fluid and contextual. For example, Rivas (2004) remarked on the identity shift he experienced when he left Puerto Rico to attend college in the Midwestern United States:

> When I became a "minority" I certainly did not have a say over what that meant for me and how others were or were not to perceive me. Yet it affected, and still affects, my everyday life. No matter how many professional degrees I attain or how much good I may do in the world, people will still judge my character and me by the preconceived notions they have of others who are like me. (p. 87)

This quote illustrates the point made in Chapter 3 that ethnicity becomes salient when one is different from many others and/or is in a nondominant group.

In counseling, the individual racial and ethnic identities of both the client and counselor are important. In this regard, the reader is referred to the racial identity models in Chapter 4. Such models map how individuals evolve in their relationship to their and others' race and ethnicity. The majority of the work in racial identity development has been devoted to comparing black and white groups (e.g., Cross, 1971; Hardiman, 1982; Helms, 1990). More often than not, Latinos have either been ignored or placed in generic minority models, such as the Racial Identity Development for People of Color model described in Chapter 4 or the Minority Identity Development Model (Atkinson, Morten, & Sue, 1989), the Racial/Cultural Identity Model (Sue & Sue, 1990, 1999), and the Adolescent Ethnic Identity Development Model (Phinney, 1993). These generic models, however, may gloss over factors specific to being Latino/Latina as well as differences between national groups. Therefore, a model of identity that addresses Latino/Latina people in particular is reviewed next: the Bicultural Orientation Model (Torres, 1999).

THE BICULTURAL ORIENTATION MODEL

The Bicultural Orientation Model (Torres, 1999) is helpful for understanding the choices Latinos/Latinas make between their culture of origin and the majority white (Anglo) culture in the United States. The model assesses both acculturation to the majority Anglo culture and ethnic identity with the culture of origin. The measures used to assess bicultural orientation place an individual according to her or his cultural orientation (high to low on each of the scales). Latinos/Latinas were found to have four possible orientations:

- *Bicultural Orientation.* These individuals felt comfortable in both the dominant American and in the Latino culture. They had high scores on both acculturation and ethnic identity.

- *Latino Orientation.* These individuals preferred the Latino culture and preferred to interact more with Latinos than other Americans. They had low scores on acculturation and high scores on ethnic identity.

- *Anglo Orientation*. Overall, these individuals preferred the dominant American culture to the Latino culture. They had high scores on acculturation and low scores on ethnic identity.

- *Marginal Orientation*. The individuals identified as marginal were more likely to have spent less time in the United States and more likely to have parents who did not speak English. They had low scores on both acculturation and ethnic identity. (Torres & Delgado-Romero, in press, p. 9)

It is important to note that higher levels of adaptability to the majority culture do not necessarily correspond with a loss of ethnic identity. The Bicultural orientation includes both acculturation to the dominant culture and strong ethnic identity. In fact, it has been found that while individuals in areas where there were few Latinos/Latinas had higher levels of acculturation, they still had high ethnic identity (Torres, Winston, & Cooper, 2003). Counselors can help clients become more bicultural, if clients so wish. They can help those with an Anglo orientation to increase pride in their culture of origin by using Liberation Counseling, for example (see Chapter 16).

How Latinos/Latinas arrive at any of the four bicultural orientations is based on at least four conditions. Those conditions are delineated in Box 10.1 and can be used to assess a client's current orientation.

Counseling Latinos/Latinas

This chapter has provided the reader with some sensibilities and information that might prepare counselors for working with Latino/Latina clients. Given the limits of generalizations, individual clients will present unique problems. However, there will likely be some consistent themes (e.g., language, acculturation, family, and cultural values) across most Latino/Latina clients, as has been demonstrated in the cases of Miguel and Angela.

In order to provide the reader with more explicit direction for counseling Latinos/Latinas, four overall guidelines for working with Latinos/Latinas will be presented at this point. They will be followed by three special topics that must be kept in mind when working with Latino/Latina clients. Those are acknowledging racism, adapting language, and being accessible. These points are specific adaptations of the general practice guidelines that are in Chapter 16.

FOUR GUIDELINES

The following four recommendations for working with Latino/Latina clients are especially true for traditional Latino/Latina clients and families (Bernal & Shapiro, 1996). More acculturated Latino/Latina families may not differ much from European American clients and families. In working with most Latinos/Latinas, counselors should

> **BOX 10.1   Four Conditions That Affect Latinos'/Latinas' Bicultural Orientation and Related Questions for Assessment**
>
> 1. The environment in which a Latino/Latina individual grew up
>
>   Were there a large number of Latinos/Latinas in the area in which the client grew up?
>
>   If the client grew up in a predominantly white environment, how were Latinos/Latinas view by the majority?
>
> 2. Familial influences and generational status in the United States
>
>   What label does the client use to describe her or his ethnicity? Where did she or he first hear this label?
>
>   What generation in the United States is the family (first, second)? Does the client feel that his or her Latino parents have different expectations than non-Latino parents?
>
> 3. Self-perception of status in the United States
>
>   How does the client interpret what his or her peers think or see in the client? (Explore potentially negative messages that the client internalized.)
>
>   What is the client's association with negative messages about Latinos/Latinas in the popular media? (Pay attention to the client's dissociation from or internalization of negative stereotypes.)
>
> 4. Level of dissonance between the environment in which the person grew up and her or his current environment
>
>   Does the current environment (e.g., a college) differ? How is the client dealing with those differences or similarities?
>
>   Does the client define herself or himself as a minority or majority in the old or new environment?

- be present-oriented,
- focus on problem solving,
- involve the family in counseling,
- consider and incorporate the family hierarchy.

Traditional Latino/Latina culture tends to focus on the present rather than on the past or the future. Therefore, traditional Latino/Latina clients would expect a counselor to focus on current events and perceptions rather than explore the past. Regarding the second guideline, traditional Latinos/Latinas expect the counselor to focus on problem solving. Thus, many Latino/Latina clients may not respond well to less directive, insight-oriented counseling. Third, the family should be involved in counseling, whether in person or in the discussion with individual clients. Finally, when dealing with the family, traditional Latino/Latina family hierarchy should be respected, with the father's role being acknowledged as head of the household in traditional families.

The third and fourth guidelines are worth expanding on, as they address the all-important matter of family. In the area of family relations, counselors should particularly have skills in addressing intergenerational conflict in Latino/Latina immigrant families, especially conflict related to acculturation and assimilation (Gonzalez, 1991). Such conflict is likely because many Latino/Latina families immigrate in stages. Given the tendency for acculturation to happen at different paces in a family, the youngest members often acculturate and learn English first.

ACKNOWLEDGING RACISM AND PREJUDICE

A special topic that must be accounted for when working with members of any nondominant group is oppression. Not every Latino/Latina client will struggle with racism or prejudice; however, counselors should be open to introducing, hearing, and processing these issues (see Delgado-Romero, 2001). Simply said, counselors should not utilize denial, avoidance, or intellectualization in the face of racism.

ADAPTING LANGUAGE

Language issues were address in a previous section of this chapter. It is worth reiterating that language is often the major barrier to obtaining counseling for Latino/Latina clients who do not speak English (Preciado & Henry, 1997). However, not enough is known about this issue because language has traditionally been neglected as a counseling variable in the professional literature (Rivas et al., 2004). The reader is reminded of the case of Miguel, in which language choice was an issue. In general, counselors should not underestimate the power of language differences in counseling.

BEING ACCESSIBLE

Language is not the only barrier to Latinos/Latinas using counseling services. Many of the barriers to Latino/Latina use of counseling are related to access, including lack of (1) physical access to services, (2) affordability, (3) awareness of treatment options, and (4) Latino/Latina culturally competent and/or bilingual counselors and support staff. Chapter 16 offers suggestions for becoming more accessible to clients.

In addition to these barriers, there is the stigma attached to mental illness and counseling. Traditional Latino/Latina people, like people from other traditional cultures, are socialized to avoid openly sharing problems with non-family members. This reticence to disclose such matters can be compounded when the client is an undocumented immigrant and fears deportation by government officials. Although counselors may not think of themselves as government officials, they often have governmental ties (i.e., they work for governmental agencies and/or receive federal funding) that may scare a potential client. Therefore, access and trust-building should exist in the ways that will be described in Chapter 16.

Summary

In order to ensure social justice in their work with Latino/Latina clients, counselors are called to do many things: participate in and learn about Latino/Latina communities; recognize and reinforce the strengths of Latino/Latina clients; gain knowledge and specialized training in counseling Latino/Latina clients; and, most importantly, recognize and work through their own biases and assumptions. By doing so, counselors will be armed with an open attitude for work with the dynamically evolving Latino/Latina culture in the United States.

Trust is a central issue in working with people from oppressed cultures. Counselors must realize that when any client participates in counseling, she or he is taking a personal risk. That risk is even greater when that client is part of a group that historically has been oppressed and marginalized. Consequently, counselors must respond by taking risks of their own (e.g., stepping outside the office, participating in the community, learning some Spanish or at least learning to pronounce Spanish names, and/or becoming an advocate for Latino/Latina issues) as ways to demonstrate to clients that they are culturally committed and alert.

The call to be culturally alert is complicated by the fact that Latino/Latina culture in the United States is dynamic and constantly changing. It is not uncommon to see culture interpreted differently among Latinos/Latinas from the same country or even within the same family. Given these complications, the counselor has the daunting task of being aware of general cultural themes (e.g., importance of family, acculturation conflicts, the meaning of independence, gender roles) and, at the same time, needing to understand how these cultural themes are interpreted and lived by a Latino/Latina individual and her or his family. Given estimates that by the year 2050, one in four people in the United States will be Latino/Latina, counselors must do their best to be culturally alert in their work with Latinos/Latinas. Activity 10.3 invites the reader to consider her or his learning needs for working with this population.

ACTIVITY 10.3

What are some specific experiences and training that you can seek out to become culturally alert to Latino/Latina clients?

Do you have a Latino/Latina community in your area?

Is it established or emerging?

Who are some of the community leaders with whom you might consult?

Given that new immigrants may speak only Spanish, do you feel any need to learn Spanish?

If so, where might you get that training?

Note

1. In research regarding the sexual behavior of Latinos, this is known as MSM—men who have sex with men (e.g., Williams, Wyatt, Resell, Peterson, & Asuan-O'Brien, 2004).

References

Alegria, M., Perez, D. J., & Williams, S. (2003). The role of public policies in reducing mental health status disparities for people of color. *Health Affairs, 22,* 51–64.

Altarriba, J., & Bauer, L. M. (1998). Counseling the Hispanic client: Cuban Americans, Mexican Americans and Puerto Ricans. *Journal of Counseling and Development, 76,* 389–396.

American Psychological Association. (2003). Guidelines on multicultural education, training, research, practice and organizational change for psychologists. *American Psychologist, 58,* 377–402.

Arredondo, P. (2002). Mujeres Latinas—santas y marquesas. *Cultural Diversity and Ethnic Minority Psychology, 8*(4), 308–319.

Arredondo, P., Toporek, R., Brown, S., Jones, J., Locke, D., Sánchez, J., et al. (1996). Operationalization of multicultural counseling competencies. *Journal of Multicultural Counseling and Development, 24,* 42–78.

Atkinson, D. R., Morten, G., & Sue, D. W. (1989). A minority identity development model. In D. R. Atkinson, G. Morten, & D. W. Sue (Eds.), *Counseling American minorities* (pp. 35–52). Dubuque, IA: William C. Brown.

Bernal, G., & Shapiro, E. (1996). Cuban families. In M. McGoldrick, J. Giordano, & J. K. Pearce (Eds.), *Ethnicity and family therapy* (2nd ed., pp. 155–168). New York: Guilford Press.

Bernstein, R. (2004). Hispanic and Asian Americans increasing faster than overall population. *U.S Census Bureau News.* Retrieved September 7, 2005, from http://www.census.gov/Press-Release/www/release/archives/race/001839.html

Bernstein, R., & Bergan, M. (2003). Hispanic population reaches all-time high of 38.8 million, new Census Bureau estimates show. *United States Department of Commerce News.* Retrieved September 8, 2005, from http://www.census.gov/Press-Release/www?2003/cb03–100.html

Boushey, H., & Wright, J. (2004). *Health insurance coverage in the United States: Health insurance data brief #2.* Washington, DC: Center for Economic and Policy Research.

Castillo, L. G., & Hill, R. D. (2004). Predictors of distress in Chicana college students. *Journal of Multicultural Counseling and Development, 32,* 235–249.

Comas-Díaz, L. (1994). LatiNegra: Mental health issues of African Latinas. *Journal of Feminist Family Counseling, 5,* 35–74.

Comas-Díaz, L. (1997). Mental health needs of Latinos with professional status. In J. G. García & M. C. Zea (Eds.), *Psychological interventions and research with Latino populations* (pp. 142–165). Boston: Allyn & Bacon.

Comas-Díaz, L. (2001). Hispanics, Latinos, or Americanos: The evolution of identity. *Cultural Diversity and Ethnic Minority Psychology, 7,* 115–120.

Cross, W. E., Jr. (1971, July). The Negro-to-Black conversion experience. *Black World,* 13–27.

Delgado-Romero, E. A. (2001). Counseling a Hispanic/Latino client—Mr. X. *Journal of Mental Health Counseling, 23,* 207–221.

Delgado-Romero, E. A. (2004). No parece: The privilege and prejudice inherent in being a light skinned Latino with no accent. In S. K. Anderson & V. A. Middleton (Eds.), *Explorations in oppression, diversity and privilege* (pp. 119–126). Belmont, CA: Brooks/Cole.

Delgado-Romero, E. A., Flores, L., Gloria, A., Arredondo, P., & Castellanos, J. (2003). The majority in the minority: Developmental career challenges for Latino and Latina psychology faculty. In L. Jones & J. Castellanos (Eds.), *The majority in the minority: Retaining Latina/o faculty, administrators, and students in the 21st century* (pp. 257–283). Sterling, VA: Stylus Books.

Delgado-Romero, E. A., & Rojas, A. (2004). Other Latinos: Counseling Cuban, Central and South American clients. In C. Negy (Ed.), *Cross cultural counseling: Toward a critical understanding of diverse client populations* (pp. 139–162). Reno, NV: Bent Tree Press.

Díaz, R. M., Ayala, G., & Bein, E. (2004). Sexual risk as an outcome of social oppression: Data from a probability sample of Latino gay men in three U.S. cities. *Cultural Diversity & Mental Health, 10,* 255–267.

Falicov, C. J. (1998). *Latino families in counseling: A guide to multicultural practice.* New York: Guilford Press.

Fragoso, J. M., & Kashubeck, S. (2000). Machismo, gender role conflict, and mental health in Mexican American men. *Psychology of Men & Masculinity, 1,* 87–97.

Garcia-Preto, N. (1996). Latino families: An overview. In M. McGoldrick, J. Giordano, & J. K. Pearce (Eds.), *Ethnicity and family therapy* (pp. 141–154). New York: Guilford Press.

Gloria, A. M., & Rodriguez, E. R. (2000). Counseling Latino university students: Psychosociocultural issues for consideration. *Journal of Counseling and Development, 78,* 145–154.

Gonzalez, G. M. (1991). Cuban Americans: Counseling and human development issues, problems, and approaches. In C. C. Lee & B. L. Richardson (Eds.), *Multicultural issues in counseling: New approaches to diversity* (pp. 157–169). Alexandria, VA: American Association for Counseling and Development.

Gonzalez, G. M. (1995). Cuban-Americans. In N. A. Vacc, S. B. DeVaney, & J. Wittmer (Eds.), *Experiencing and counseling multicultural and diverse populations* (pp. 293–316). Bristol, PA: Accelerated Development.

Guzmán, B., & McConnell, E. D. (2002). The Hispanic population: 1990–2000 growth and change. *Population Research and Policy Review, 21,* 109–128.

Hardiman, R. (1982). *White identity development: A process oriented model for describing the racial consciousness of white Americans.* Unpublished doctoral dissertation, University of Massachusetts, Amherst.

Helms, J. E. (1990). *Black and white racial identity: Theory, research and practice.* New York: Greenwood.

Jones-Correa, M., & Leal, D. L. (1996). Becoming "Hispanic": Secondary panethnic identification among Latin American-origin populations in the United States. *Hispanic Journal of Behavioral Sciences, 18,* 214–215.

Logan, J. R. (2003). *How race counts for Hispanic Americans.* Albany, NY: University at Albany, Lewis Mumford Center for Comparative Urban and Regional Research.

Marín, G., & Marín, B. V. (1991). *Research with Hispanic populations.* Newbury Park, CA: Sage.

McConnell, E. D., & Delgado-Romero, E. A. (2004). Panethnic options and Latinos: Reality or methodological construction? *Sociological Focus, 4,* 297–312.

Mörner, M. (1967). *Race mixture in the history of Latin America.* Boston: Little, Brown.

Niemann, Y. F. (1999). The making of a token: A case study of stereotype threat, stigma, racism, and tokenism in academe. *Frontiers: A Journal of Women Studies, 20,* 11–34.

Phinney, J. S. (1993). A three-stage model of ethnic identity development in adolescence. In M. E. Bernal & G. P. Knight (Eds.), *Ethnic identity: Formation and transmission among Hispanics and other minorities* (pp. 61–79). Albany: State University of New York Press.

Preciado, J., & Henry, M. (1997). Linguistic barriers in health education and services. In J. G. García & M. C. Zea (Eds.), *Psychological interventions and research with Latino populations* (pp. 235–254). Boston: Allyn & Bacon.

Ramirez, G., & de la Cruz, P. G. (2003). The Hispanic population in the United States: March 2002. *Current population reports.* Washington, DC: U.S. Census Bureau.

Rivas, L. (2004). Visible and invisible minority: Double-whammy or double blessing? In G. S. Howard & E. A. Delgado-Romero (Eds.), *When things begin to go bad: Narrative explorations of difficult issues* (pp. 85–92). Dallas, TX: Hamilton Books.

Rivas, L., Delgado-Romero, E. A., & Ozambela, K. R. (2004). Our stories: Convergence of the language, professional, and personal identities of three Latino counselors. In L. Weliing & M. Rastogi (Eds.), *Voices of color: First-person accounts of ethnic minority counselors* (pp. 23–41). Thousand Oaks, CA: Sage.

Ruiz, A. S. (1990). Ethnic identity: Crisis and resolution. *Journal of Multicultural Counseling and Development, 18,* 29–40.

Santiago-Rivera, A. L., Arredondo, P. A., & Gallardo-Cooper, M. (2002). *Counseling Latinos and la familia: A practical guide.* Thousand Oaks, CA: Sage.

Shorris, E. (1992). *Latinos: A biography of the people.* New York: W. W. Norton.

Smart, J. F., & Smart, D. W. (1995). Acculturative stress of Hispanics: Loss and challenge. *Journal of Counseling and Development, 73,* 390–396.

Soto-Carlo, A., Delgado-Romero, E. A., & Galván, N. (2005). Challenges of Puerto Rican Islander students in the U.S. *Latino Studies Journal, 3,* 288–294.

Spanakis, N. C. (2004). Difficult dialogues: Interviewer, white inner voice, and Latina interviewee. *Journal of Multicultural Counseling and Development, 32,* 249–254.

Stavans, I. (2000, October 13). The gravitas of Spanglish. *The Chronicle Review,* p. B7.

Sue, D. W., Arredondo, P., & McDavis, R. J. (1992). Multicultural counseling competencies and standards: A call to the profession. *Journal of Counseling and Development, 70,* 477–483.

Sue, D. W., & Sue, D. (1990). *Counseling the culturally different: Theory and practice* (2nd ed.). New York: Wiley.

Sue, D. W., & Sue, D. (1999). *Counseling the culturally different: Theory and practice* (3rd ed.). New York: Wiley.

Torres, J. B., Solberg, S. H., & Carlstrom, A. H. (2002). The myth of sameness among Latino men and their machismo. *American Journal of Orthopsychiatry, 72*(2), 163–181.

Torres, V. (1999). Validation of a bicultural orientation model for Hispanic college students. *Journal of College Student Development, 40*(3), 285–299.

Torres, V. (2004). The diversity among us: Puerto Ricans, Cubans, Caribbean, Central and South Americans. In A. M. Ortiz (Ed.), *Addressing the unique needs of Latino/a American students* (pp. 5–16). San Francisco: Jossey-Bass.

Torres, V., & Delgado-Romero, E. A. (in press). Defining Latino/a identity through late adolescent development. In K. L. Kraus (Ed.), *Lifespan development theories in action: A case study approach for counseling professionals.* Boston: Houghton Mifflin/ Lahaska Press.

Torres, V., Winston, R. B., Jr., & Cooper, D. L. (2003). The effect of geographic location, type, and stress on Hispanic students' cultural orientation. *NASPA Journal, 40,* Article 10.

U.S. Census Bureau. (2001). *Census 2000 summary file 1.* Washington, DC: Author.

U.S. Census Bureau. (2004). *Facts for features and special editions.* Retrieved September 8, 2005, from http://www.census.gov/PressRelease/www/releases/archives/facts_ for_features_special_editions/002270.html

U.S. Department of Health and Human Services. (2001). Mental health care for Hispanic Americans. In *Mental health: Culture, race, and ethnicity. A supplement to Mental health: A report of the Surgeon General* (pp. 129–155). Rockville, MD: Author.

U.S. Office of Management and Budget. (1997). *Revisions to the standards for the classification of federal data on race and ethnicity.* Federal Register 62, No. 210 (October 30, 1997): 58782–58790.

Vasquez, M. J. T. (2001). Reflections on unearned advantages, unearned disadvantages and empowering experiences. In J. Ponterotto, J. M. Casas, L. A. Suzuki, & C. M. Alexander (Eds.), *Handbook of multicultural counseling* (pp. 64–77). Thousand Oaks, CA: Sage.

Vega, W. A., Gil, A. G., Warheit, G. J., Zimmerman, R. S., & Aposori, E. (1993). Acculturation and delinquent behavior among Cuban American adolescents: Toward an empirical model. *American Journal of Community Psychology, 21,* 113–125.

Vidal de Haymes, M., Kilty, K. M., & Haymes, S. N. (2002). Another kind of rainbow politics. *Journal of Human Behavior in the Social Environment 5,* 175–188.

Wilczak, C. (2003). A counselor trainee's conversations with a Colombian immigrant woman. In G. Roysircar, P. Arredondo, J. N. Fuertes, J. G. Ponterotto, & R. L. Toporek (Eds.), *Multicultural competencies 2003: Association for Multicultural Counseling and Development* (pp. 89–101). Alexandria, VA: Association for Multicultural Counseling and Development.

Williams, J. K., Wyatt, G. E., Resell, J., Peterson, J., & Asuan-O'Brien, A. (2004). Psychosocial issues among gay- and non-gay-identifying HIV-seropositive African American and Latino MSM. *Cultural Diversity and Ethnic Minority Psychology, 10,* 268–286.

South Asian Americans

Daya Singh Sandhu
and Jayamala Madathil

Anita is a 23-year-old international student from India. She comes from a middle-class family in South India. Anita has just completed her first semester in a social sciences program at a mid-sized university in the southern United States. Anita lives alone and finds herself in tears a lot. She is the first member of her family to come to the United States for higher studies. Her parents and her cousins helped to pay for her application fees and other expenses, such as an airplane ticket to the United States. The only reason she was able to attend the university was that she was offered a full scholarship with tuition waiver.

Since her arrival at the university, Anita has found that she feels very lonely. She is not sure to whom she can talk. She happened to mention her "crying" to one of her fellow American students in passing. The student suggested that Anita use the university counseling center. The concept of counseling is somewhat foreign to Anita. Because she has no one to talk to, she has decided to make a visit to the counseling center. She is very apprehensive about talking to a stranger about her problem. In addition, she is also afraid that the "American" counselor may not understand her concerns. Anita is even afraid that communication, due to language and different accents, might be a problem. During her first meeting with her counselor, who is a European American male, Anita is asked to share personal information about her relationships and whether she is sexually active. Anita finds these questions to be very inappropriate and is somewhat offended and embarrassed by them.

❖

Sameer is a 45-year-old businessman living in the Northeast. He immigrated to the United States five years ago from Bangladesh. Sameer was mandated to attend counseling sessions by the judge in a case of suspected domestic violence. He has been informed that attending counseling is not optional for him and that he would be in violation of the judge's orders if he did not attend the counseling sessions and he could be imprisoned. The judge gave Sameer the option of choosing his therapist for the individual counseling sessions. However, he was also required to attend the eight-week domestic violence offender group offered by Mandy, a therapist who is well-established and has an excellent reputation and respect in the community. Sameer started attending the groups. However, he did his best to distance himself from the other four members of the group, John, David, Jason, and Richard. He kept on insisting that he was not an "offender" and that he did not need to be in the counseling group. He also proceeded to inform the therapist that the only reason he was in the group was because of the judge's orders. Sameer was not willing to share anything in the group, nor was he responsive to receiving feedback from the therapist or the other group members.

Sameer informed the therapist that his wife, Nasreen, was getting to be "too smart and too Americanized" and that he needed to show her who was the boss in the house. For that reason, he hit her when she "talked back" to him. He had done this in their garage when the garage door was open. A neighbor across the street had seen Sameer hitting his wife and pulling her inside by her hair. The neighbor called the police. When the police arrived, there were marks on Nasreen's body. At first, Sameer's wife was hesitant and informed the police that nothing was wrong. However, after the officers talked with Nasreen for several minutes, she admitted that he had been beating her on a regular basis. On that particular day, she had not finished cleaning up the garage as ordered by Sameer, and he had "punished" her by beating her with a rolling pin. While Sameer was inattentive in the group, he made every effort to communicate to the therapist that he was a good man and that he provided well for his wife, Nasreen. He also insisted that as a husband he had the right to "discipline" his wife. Working with Sameer was a challenge for the therapist. Mandy was quite concerned with Sameer's attitude toward beating his wife. She was further concerned about Sameer's justification of his action and the lack of remorse.

❖

Mrs. Nooran Khan was brought to see a counselor in the San Francisco area by her daughter Sophia, a young physician in the area. The Khans immigrated from Pakistan 25 years ago and moved to the United States when Mr. Khan's eldest brother, Mr. Akbar Khan, sponsored them. They have lived in the San Francisco Bay Area ever since. The couple runs a small convenience store. Their only child, a daughter named Sophia, recently completed her residency in family medicine and is in the process of establishing a practice in the area. Mr. Khan passed away unexpectedly about six months ago.

The daughter suspects that Mrs. Khan is depressed. Mrs. Nooran Khan has never been to a therapist in her life and is very confused about why her daughter brought her to see the counselor. She is also afraid that her daughter and the other members of her community will think that she is "crazy." Meanwhile, her daughter has already talked with the therapist. The young Dr. Sophia Khan has communicated her guilt about not being able to help her mother as much as she should have during this emotionally difficult time. Sophia is struggling to establish her medical practice, and she admits that the past few months have been extremely difficult for her mother because of her "benign neglect" of her mother.

This chapter focuses on the experiences of individuals such as Anita, Sameer, and Mrs. Khan. It provides an introduction to South Asian cultures, especially ways in which counselors can help individuals from these cultures. It is also meant to provide mental health professionals with the means to become culturally sensitive and effective service providers to South Asian Americans. Before reading further, the reader is encouraged to assess her or his knowledge of important issues for working with this population by completing Activity 11.1.

Demographic Characteristics of South Asians

First, South Asian cultures must be distinguished from other Asian cultures. It is extremely important for mental health professionals to be careful not to lump all Asians into the "Asians/Pacific Islanders" category. South Asians are a distinct cultural grouping, one that is different in significant ways from the East and Southeast Asian grouping that includes people from countries such as Cambodia, China, the Philippines, Indonesia, and Japan. Those peoples were described in Chapter 6.

It is particularly important that counselors, while being culturally sensitive and aware of different cultural norms and expectations, do not use these similarities to stereotype their clients. This is something that the counselor has to be intentional about and must remind herself or himself about.

Who are South Asians as a group? What are some of the similarities among individuals from the South Asian cultures? What are some cultural factors that a mental health professional would need to remember while trying to help an individual from these cultures? These questions will be addressed in the next section.

South Asians, as defined here, are people who come from the seven nations of Bangladesh, Bhutan, India, Maldives, Nepal, Pakistan, and Sri Lanka. There is a great diversity within this population with regard to religious affiliations, language abilities, immigration history, socioeconomic status, education, and acculturation levels (Inman & Tewari, 2003). Despite all these differences, South Asians are presented here as a single group because of their common geographic origin. While it is not a homogenous group, South Asian culture, in general, has some common characteristics that set it apart from other major cultural and ethnic groups. These common characteristics include customs, values, individual and

ACTIVITY 11.1

Self-Assessment on South Asian American Culture and Issues

The following is a short self-assessment exercise about your knowledge of South Asian Americans. The purpose of this exercise is to help you become aware of your assumptions about this group and to increase your cultural awareness regarding South Asian Americans.

I can identify the South Asian countries on a world map: Yes/No

I know what the term "collectivist cultures" means: Yes/No

I agree with the media portrayal of South Asians: Yes/No

I am familiar with the mate selection process followed by the majority of South Asians: Yes/No

I can name three of the major religions widely practiced by South Asians: Yes/No

I have an accurate understanding of the variations in arranged marriages: Yes/No

I can name three different cultural/religious holidays observed by individuals from South Asian cultures: Yes/No

I have a clear understanding of how South Asian cultures regard the elderly individuals in their community: Yes/No

I can identify some of the struggles faced by South Asians in the United States: Yes/No

I can list cultural competencies that a mental health professional might need in order to work effectively with individuals from South Asian cultures: Yes/No

Give one point for each "Yes" response and add up your total. Calculate your knowledge by using the scale below.
Total Score out of 10: ___

Scoring Rubric:

	1 2 3 4	5 6 7	8 9 10
Your Knowledge About South Asians	Poor	Average	Superior

This activity is meant to help the reader to think further about her or his understanding of South Asian cultures. As described in Chapters 1 and 3, having an understanding of specific ethnic cultures helps a mental health professional to see key issues that she or he might otherwise miss or misinterpret (e.g., the South Asian client's experience of arranged marriage, views on care of the elderly). In addition, an increased awareness of these cultural factors helps counselors to become better advocates for these minority groups at the social and political levels.

family expectations, and beliefs about mental health problems (Maker, Mittal, & Rastogi, 2005).

Historically, these countries constituted one great nation called *Bharat.* Pakistan and Bangladesh were carved out of India as separate countries not long ago, when the British left India in 1947. South Asia is notably diverse in religious traditions. Hinduism, Buddhism, Jainism, Sikhism, Zoroastrianism, Islam, Judaism, tribal religions, and almost all denominations of Christianity are represented. South Asia is also known for a number of diverse languages. There are 22 official languages in India alone. The total number of languages listed for India is 428, of which 13 languages are considered extinct.

Immigration Patterns and Experiences of South Asians

The South Asian ethnic grouping is one of the fastest growing populations in the United States. South Asians' migration to the United States took place in three major waves. The first wave of immigrants from the Indian subcontinent arrived between 1897 and 1924. As is true with other immigrants, South Asians saw the United States as a land of opportunity and liberty. Most of the immigrants who arrived from South Asian countries during the 1800s were farmers and ship workers (Sheth, 1995). However, these immigrants were not allowed to own land, nor were they allowed to bring their spouses and other family members to the United States. Although these South Asians were invited as laborers, they were not seen by the host culture to be worthy of citizenship because of their racial and cultural differences (Takaki, 1989).

The Immigration and Naturalization Act of 1965 marked the beginning of the second wave of immigration. It also ended the racial discrimination against South Asians and other so-called tawny races of Asia. Entry into the United States was no longer determined by race but by the knowledge and skills of the potential immigrants, in terms of what they could offer to the United States (Prathikanti, 1997). Consequently, a large percentage of South Asians in the second wave were highly educated professionals. For instance, in a sample of 46,000 Asian Indian immigrants, Doshi (1975) found that at least 50 percent of them were working as medical doctors, scientists, and engineers. These newly arrived South Asian immigrants achieved great financial success and obtained United States citizenship. They were also allowed to bring their spouses and children with them.

A significant demographic shift took place during the 1980s, as many second-wave and well-established South Asian Americans started sponsoring their family members through the Family Reunification Act. Many of these immigrants were less educated and less fluent in English than their predecessors. Most of these new arrivals are now working as taxi drivers, convenience store clerks, and small motel operators. Also, some of them own small businesses (McMahon, 1995). Because this group is demographically and culturally quite different from the second wave of South Asian immigrants, they are classified as the third wave of South Asian immigrants (Prathikanti, 1997; Sandhu & Malik, 2001).

According to the 2000 U.S. Census data, there are over two million South Asian Americans living in the United States (U.S. Census Bureau, 2001). This group constitutes approximately 20 percent of the total Asian population in the United States. Among the South Asians, Asian Indians are the largest group (16 percent of the total Asian population). In fact, Asian Indians rank third behind Chinese (23 percent) and Filipino (19.9 percent) populations among the general grouping of all Asians/Pacific Islanders. Individuals vary in their levels of education, age, income, religious beliefs, and length of stay in the United States. It is important to remember that there could be a considerable difference between the first-generation immigrants who have arrived in the United States recently and second- or third-generation Asian American individuals who were born and raised in this country.

Cultural Values and Characteristics of South Asian Americans

One definition of culture is "a set of guidelines, both explicit and implicit, which individuals inherit as members of a particular society, and which tells them how to view the world, how to experience it emotionally, and how to behave in it in relation to other people" (Helman, 1990, pp. 2–3). Such guidelines vary as groups adapt to their environments in varying ways. Of special importance to South Asian Americans are four major values: *patriarchy, reticence, collectivism,* and *religion and spirituality.* These values are briefly explained below.

PATRIARCHY

South Asian families are traditionally patriarchal. The father or the eldest male in the extended family is generally the head of the household and is responsible for taking care of the financial and emotional needs of all family members. Patriarchy is related to the value of collectivism, which has been presented in previous chapters in this book and will be discussed later in this section. In collectivist cultures, the individual wishes of a person are sacrificed for the collective welfare of the family; what is best for the family is best for the individual (Chandras, 1997; Das & Kemp, 1997). For this reason, family members defer to the authority figures, who, it is assumed, can ensure the collective welfare.

The preferred method of solving individual problems is to defer to the authority figure in the family. Family members are discouraged from discussing personal concerns with strangers, including mental health professionals. South Asians consider the head of the household to have the prerogative to make final decisions (Abrahams & Salazar, 2005). Family members are expected to accept this person's decisions willingly.

Many other South Asian values can be described as extensions or corollaries of patriarchal values. Such values include nonconfrontation with older siblings and respect and reverence for the elderly. Wisdom gained through real-life experience is valued more than book knowledge. South Asian cultural values include filial piety, which is considered to be one of the greatest virtues in Asian cultures. It means taking care of one's parents; not being rebellious; showing love, respect, and support. It also includes accepting the advice of one's parents, concealing their mistakes, displaying sorrow for their sickness and death, and carrying out sacrifices in their names after their death. The shortcomings of parents are overlooked. Ancestors and parents are worshipped, and they are appreciated as role models for generations to come.

RETICENCE

Silence is considered another virtue in South Asian culture. South Asian parents admonish their children to talk less and think more. "Only an empty vessel makes a lot of noise" is an age-old adage popular among South Asians. Children should be seen but not heard around the parents. In addition, South Asians are taught at an early age to restrain themselves from strong emotional expressions. Thus, verbal and behavioral expressiveness are discouraged in South Asian populations (Atkinson, Morten, & Sue, 1998).

South Asian parents emphasize and value *self-control* more than *self-expression.* Some of these characteristics are similar to those of East and Southeast Asians.

In addition, open expression of sexual feelings is considered "cheap" and a sign of emotional immaturity. Modesty about sexual matters is encouraged. Public demonstration of sexual affection is considered offensive and characteristic of low or loose moral character. In South Asian cultures, even married couples refrain from holding hands, embracing, and kissing in public.

COLLECTIVISM

As opposed to the glorification of the individual, *collectivism* is the premiere cultural value of South Asians. Collectivism requires individual members to sacrifice their interests for the good of the family. Their personal interests and aspirations are less important. Generally speaking, in collectivist societies, authority and communication flow from top to bottom. Relationships are rigidly structured, and obedience from the young members toward their elders is expected and enforced.

Individuals' accomplishments are celebrated by the entire family, and a person's failure is considered to be the failure of the entire family. Therefore, all family members are expected to solve their problems within their familial context. One's duties to the family are of utmost importance, while one's individual rights are not emphasized (Sodowsky, Kwan & Pannu, 1995; Das & Kemp, 1997).

RELIGION AND SPIRITUALITY

In South Asian communities, importance is attached to preserving and practicing the original religion of one's ancestors. In addition to Hindu temples, Muslim mosques, and Sikh Gurudwaras, a special and sacred place is kept in many South Asian homes for daily worship and prayers. During family or personal crises or on the occasions of celebrations, South Asians hold special prayers to seek help and blessings from their beloved deities. While they are frequently fatalistic and believe in predestination, South Asians also believe that a sincere prayer from the heart can avert tragedies and change the course of their lives for the better.

SUMMARY AND IMPLICATIONS OF SOUTH ASIAN VALUES

The four major categories of values—patriarchy, reticence, collectivism, and religion or spirituality—significantly affect the psychological makeup of South Asians. Specific values include formality in interpersonal relationships, inhibition of strong feelings, obedience to the authority of elders, primary allegiance to the family, and deep respect for religion (Atkinson et al., 1998). It is also important for counselors to note that some of these values could be in direct conflict with the values and expectations of the majority European American culture, which emphasizes independence, individualism, and autonomy. Counselors particularly need to be aware of differences in values so that they do not inappropriately label South Asian clients' behaviors as dysfunctional.

These traditional values of South Asian Americans have significant implications for counseling. The values affect the manifestation of psychological problems, the expression of emotions, and help-seeking behaviors (Sue & Sue, 2003). Also, as mentioned in previous chapters, the generation since immigration to the United States is important. First-generation South Asian Americans might adhere to these values more than do second- or third-generation South Asian Americans (Kim, Atkinson, & Umemoto, 2001). Box 11.1 illustrates some of the important values issues in terms of the vignettes that began this chapter.

Acculturation Challenges and Strategies for South Asian Americans

For immigrants, adaptation to the cultural norms, behaviors, and values of the dominant group generally causes unavoidable psychological distress (Sandhu, Portes, & McPhee, 1996). This section of the chapter addresses acculturation stress and acculturation strategies as they relate to South Asian Americans. It concludes with a reminder for counselors to assess acculturation in their clients.

> ## BOX 11.1   The Three Vignettes and Cultural Values of South Asians
>
> Patriarchy, reticence, collectivism, and religion or spirituality have been identified as some of the notable cultural values of South Asian people. It is important for mental health professionals to examine the role and impact of their clients' values on their psychological problems before some viable and effective solutions are explored.
>
> The following discussion is focused on the three vignettes presented at the beginning of this chapter, to demonstrate the role of the cultural values of South Asian Americans. For brevity's sake, only the South Asian value of patriarchy is discussed here, with some specific information from each vignette.
>
> As stated in the first vignette, Anita migrated to the United States from India, apparently from a patriarchal family. Anita felt terribly lonely and lost. She did not know who she should talk to and what she should do. She was also very apprehensive about talking with strangers. Most likely, her father, as the head of the household, had been handling her problems as part of his patriarchal responsibilities, and Anita never had to learn how to take care of her problems on her own.
>
> In the second vignette, Sameer's domestic violence incident is directly related to his perceived patriarchal responsibilities to maintain discipline in the house as the head of the family. He kept on insisting that he was not an offender. On the contrary, he felt that as a husband, he had the right to discipline his wife. South Asian patriarchal responsibilities are not limited to the children; they also extend to all members of the household who are living together, including the wife and even brothers and sisters if they are members of the extended family.
>
> The third vignette is quite interesting. After the death of her father and due to her advanced level of education, Sophia has assumed patriarchal obligations in the Khan family. Since Mrs. Nooran Khan is unable to take care of her problems, her daughter, Dr. Sophia Khan, became a surrogate guardian of her mother and took her to a counselor for her depression-related problems.

ACCULTURATION STRATEGIES

Acculturation strategies are the plans or methods that individuals use in responding to stress-inducing cultural contexts (Bhatia & Ram, 2004). As presented in previous chapters, those strategies can be classified into four categories (Berry & Sam, 1997). The first is an *assimilation* strategy, which occurs when the individual decides not to maintain his or her own cultural identity and seeks extensive contact with the dominant group in his or her daily interactions. The second strategy, *separation,* refers to individuals holding on to their original culture and seeking no contact with the dominant group. A third strategy, *integration,* occurs when individuals express an interest in maintaining strong ties with their own ethnic group and with the dominant group. The fourth strategy, *marginalization,* happens when the individual loses contact with both her or his traditional culture and the larger society.

The acculturation level linked with the most positive outcome is *integration,* and the one associated with the most negative outcome is *marginalization.*

Separation and assimilation strategies fall somewhere in between as far as effectiveness is concerned (Berry & Sam, 1997). It can be concluded that South Asian immigrants would use these strategies to deal with acculturation stress as well. Therefore, helpers working with this population must be trained to recognize the different levels of acculturation and adaptation strategies. Box 11.2 illustrates some of the stages of acculturation for the four individuals in the vignettes that opened this chapter.

ACCULTURATIVE STRESS

The process of acculturation takes place when individuals from different cultures come into contact with a mainstream dominant group through sojourning, foreign study programs, and voluntary or involuntary migrations. Whatever the circumstances, individuals from different cultures experience inevitable psychological changes when they interact with one another (Furnham & Bochner, 1986; Sandhu et al., 1996). As with other minority groups, South Asians experience a wide variety of psychological stressors relating to the acculturation process when they attempt to adapt to the cultural values, norms, and behaviors and the political, social, and economic systems of the United States. Those acculturation-related stressors include culture shock, experiences of prejudice, changes in ethnic identity, shifting gender roles, family conflict, sense of inferiority, communication problems, sense of uncertainty, loss of support systems, nostalgia or homesickness, and feelings of guilt. Each of these stressors is described in the next sections.

Culture Shock

"Culture shock" is a term coined by anthropologists to describe the anxiety and other negative feelings experienced when a person is introduced to a radically new environment. Such culture shock is produced when immigrants encounter new expectations and social norms over a period of time while they strive to establish relationships with a host culture (Ozbay, 1994). The cumulative differences in climate, food, mannerisms, life styles, marriage customs, and religious practices contribute to culture shock. It is safe to assume that like many individuals from other migrating groups, South Asian persons experience culture shock when they enter the United States. Counselors need to be alert to culture shock as an explanation for anxiety and depression in South Asian immigrant clients.

Experiences of Prejudice or Perceived Prejudice

Acculturation stressors also include perceptions and actual experiences of prejudice and discrimination (Lay & Nguyen, 1998). Perceived discrimination and expectations of future discrimination are related to increased levels of depression and lower levels of self-esteem (Rumbaut, 1994). Therefore, mental health professionals who provide services to acculturating individuals must pay attention to clients' concerns about prejudice (Rahman & Rollock, 2004).

BOX 11.2   Acculturative Processes and Levels in the Three Vignettes

In reviewing the three vignettes presented at the beginning of the chapter, it is interesting to note that some of these acculturative stages and processes are represented. For instance, it is safe to assume that Anita is still at the second strategy of acculturation: separation. She has completed one semester and has not been residing in the United States very long. Apparently, she is still holding on to her original culture and has not made any appreciable efforts to contact people from the dominant European culture. She is even apprehensive about speaking with her white male counselor about her problems. However, it is important to note that her separation is not a deliberate effort to avoid the dominant culture: It seems to be caused by her lack of awareness and knowledge about the new culture.

In the second vignette, Sameer, on the contrary, had deliberately resisted assimilation into the dominant culture. Like Anita, Sameer could be classified as in the separation category of acculturation. For example, he told the counselor that he would not like to participate in the group sessions as required by the judge. He was not interested in sharing or in receiving any feedback from the other group members. He also tried his best to distance himself from the other four group members, who presumably belonged to other ethnic groups. Sameer's rejection of the dominant culture became even more evident when he justified striking his wife Nasreen for becoming "too smart and too Americanized." Sameer also insisted that he was a good husband who provided well for his wife, and as a husband he had the right to discipline her. It is interesting to note that even after living in the United States for 5 years, Sameer behaved as if he were still in Bangladesh. However, a significant difference remains in the acculturating process of Sameer and Anita. Anita's acculturating difficulties might be attributed to her innocence or ignorance about the new culture, while Sameer's resistance to acculturation is caused by his outright rejection of some American values.

The third vignette affords an opportunity to compare and contrast the acculturating process of a mother, Mrs. Nooran Khan, with that of her daughter, Sophia. It seems that Mrs. Nooran Khan is beginning the integration stage of acculturation, maintaining strong ties with her native culture of Pakistan while also taking on some those of the dominant culture through the counseling process. Despite the fact that Mrs. Khan had been living in the United States for 25 years, she had no prior knowledge of counseling and mental health services and she had never been to a therapist. Most likely, according to South Asian values, her late husband would have taken care of her psychological needs and provided her with necessary emotional support. On the other hand, Dr. Sophia Khan seems to be fully immersed in American culture. She has been raised and educated in the United States. Apparently, she is well informed about counseling services. She contacted a therapist and discussed her mother's depression-related problems. Sophia clearly has extensive contacts, daily interactions, and experiences with persons from the dominant culture. Consequently, Sophia is in the assimilation stage of acculturation.

It should be noted that acculturation seems to be facilitated more by the attitudes and proactive efforts of the immigrants rather than by mere length of time residing in a culture. Education, work, and other social opportunities where immigrants get a chance to mingle with others are ways to help newly arrived immigrants to participate in and become an integral part of the multicultural society of the United States.

There are several differences in perceived prejudice among South Asian subgroups, based on their religious affiliations. In an empirical study, Sodowsky and Plake (1992) reported that Muslims perceived prejudice more significantly than South Asians of other religious backgrounds. These differences might be a reflection of the contemporary sociopolitical climate in the United States as well as long-standing prejudices and stereotypes. These researchers also pointed out that South Asians who belonged to non-Western religions perceived more prejudice, were less acculturated, and used English less than did South Asians who were affiliated with traditional Western religious groups.

There have been numerous incidents of racism, prejudice, and hate crimes against South Asian Americans. Dotbusters (referring to the *bindi* on the forehead of Indian women), a group of hatemongers from New Jersey who are against Asian Indian women, is one example of prejudice. Since the tragedy of September 11, 2001, hate crimes against South Asian immigrants, especially against the Sikhs, have increased significantly. For example, in Mesa, Arizona, Balbir Singh Sodhi was shot to death by a man who mistook him for a follower of Osama Bin Laden. The South Asian American Leaders of Tomorrow (SAALT), a national nonprofit organization, documented 645 incidents of backlash in the first week after the September 11 terrorist attacks.

Experiences of prejudice might not be limited to the adults in the South Asian community. It is also likely that the children of South Asian immigrants will experience prejudice in their educational and social environments, such as in schools and on the playgrounds. Children of South Asian immigrants are socialized into two cultures: the culture of their own family and the culture of the larger American society. In the family, most parents try to inculcate ethnic pride and awareness of their cultural heritage into their children. They are also encouraged to practice their own religions, such as Hinduism, Islam, and Sikhism.

For young school-age children, acculturation into the larger society sometimes poses a difficult problem. These children stand out as distinctly different from the dominant community because of their physical appearance. For that reason, they are often teased or rejected by other children. Most young children lack the ability that adults have to deal with such hostility by basing positive self-esteem on their own ethnic heritage (Das & Kemp, 1997).

This issue of prejudice is an important one that mental health practitioners might have to directly address with their clients. Since it is possible that a client might not discuss this topic with the helper for fear of being further judged, a counselor might want to bring up this topic herself or himself.

Transformation of Ethnic Identity

Another source of acculturation stress is the transformation of ethnic identity. Immigrants and first-generation South Asians typically have a strong ethnic identity wherever they are in the world and are aware of the differences between them and the host culture. They do not feel that they have to deny such differences because their ethnic pride is extremely strong. While acculturating to American society, most South Asians also start acquiring a partially American identity; they become South Asian Americans. In short, now their self-identity is transformed from a single intact identity to a hyphenated or a hybrid identity.

Most of these immigrants are able to function with a dual identity or develop a fused identity as "Asian Indian Americans" or "Pakistani Americans," to name just two examples (Das & Kemp, 1997). For example, most South Asian men seem to adopt the Western mode of dress, etiquette, and manners used in the workplace or in formal social contacts with other Americans. However, they generally hold on to their cultural food preferences, family ideology and values, and religious beliefs and practices at home or in their private lives (Sodowsky & Carey, 1988). As with other groups, although the desire to maintain a distinct ethnic and cultural identity remains strong in the first generation, with every successive generation born and raised in the United States, the offspring become more and more acculturated and an integral part of the mainstream culture.

The acculturation of subsequent generations is affected by their experiences in the United States more than by their country of origin. Those experiences include racial encounters and discrimination, the culture of an inner-city area, the presence of other immigrant ethnic communities, and the South Asian community's emphasis on preservation of its home culture (Bhatia & Ram, 2004).

A mental health professional should attempt to assess the ethnic identity of the South Asian client early in the counseling process. A client's worldview, based on her or his cultural heritage, self-concept, and ethnic identity, shapes her or his values, beliefs, and behaviors (Grieger & Ponterotto, 1995). To understand and resolve clients' problems, it is important that counselors understand their clients' worldviews and their ethnic identity development. Table 11.1 provides some questions that counselors might ask regarding ethnic identity.

Gender Roles

A third acculturation issue is that of gender role and hierarchy. Gender attitudes of South Asian Americans vary with generation in the United States,

Table 11.1 Assessing Ethnic Identity

Here are some questions that counselors may find helpful to determine their client's ethnic identity:
How do you identify your cultural heritage?
What language or languages do you speak at home?
What languages do you teach your children (if the client has children)?
With whom do you associate during your leisure time?
What are some customs and practices that you value highly?
What (if any) aspects of the majority culture do you value?
What (if any) aspects of your own culture do you value?

educational level, social class, and economic stability. For example, the immigrant generation is more likely to adhere to traditional gender roles. The gender hierarchy among South Asians can range from extremely patriarchal to egalitarian. On the patriarchal extreme, the family of South Asian immigrants would expect men to act dominant in public in order to show the other cultural groups that the men are in control of the family. However, it should be noted that, in actuality, the power and control in the family reside with the oldest person, regardless of gender, even when the oldest person in the family lives 10,000 miles away in India, Pakistan, or Sri Lanka (Ibrahim, Ohnishi, & Sandhu, 1997).

The role of women in South Asian American families must be addressed carefully. South Asian women are generally considered to be the primary family caregivers. However, that role can become complicated as immigrant women struggle to find their new place in American society.

Men are traditionally identified with the higher-status roles of breadwinner and caretaker of the family (Inman & Tewari, 2003). For this reason, in traditional South Asian families, boys are preferred to girls. As a result, in many of the South Asian subcultures, mothers of male children are respected more than are mothers of only female children.

It should also be noted that even though men are generally considered to be the heads of the household in South Asian families, the exact gender roles within a family vary depending on social class, educational level, and economic status. There may be many South Asian families in which the family relationships are more egalitarian. However, it is rare that a woman would become the head of the household when the husband is still living.

South Asian American women experience intersectionality (see Chapter 1) in that as "brown" minority women, they face racial discrimination and prejudice from the larger American society, and at the same time, they also have to deal with gendered oppression within their own communities (Bhatia & Ram, 2004). In fact, female children are sometimes seen as a liability because of ancient dowry customs in South Asian cultures that require parents to pay large sums of money, jewelry, or property to the daughter's in-laws.

The acculturation process and identity formation of many South Asian American first- and second-generation immigrant women has been a painful, difficult, and complex process. Many South Asian parents become particularly concerned and experience high levels of anxiety as their daughters mature and are ready for marriage. Out-of-group and especially interracial marriages are discouraged. Dating is not an accepted phenomenon in South Asian cultures. Many South Asian American youth instead engage in secret dating (Inman & Sandhu, 2002; Inman & Tewari, 2003). Premarital sex is strictly prohibited. Under some extremely unfortunate circumstances, pregnant South Asian girls have been the victims of "honor" killings at the hands of their fathers or brothers, who believed they were saving the face, name, and honor of their family.

Both arranged marriages and love marriages, with the consent of the parents, are norms in many South Asian families at this time. Most South Asian American parents try their best to maintain their religious and cultural traditions by encouraging their children to marry individuals from families and subgroups that are similar or compatible with their own cultural or ethnic groups. Children who don't heed this advice commonly cause a significant amount of acculturative distress to their South Asian parents.

Family Conflicts

As mentioned earlier in regard to South Asian values, South Asian families place a high priority on the needs of the family as a unit, rather than on the individual or on specific needs of each family member (Inman & Tewari, 2003; Sodowsky et al., 1995). The family-first concept plays a pivotal role in maintaining and promoting stability and cohesiveness among all the family members (Sandhu, 1997). However, the obligation to attach more importance to family needs above one's own personal desires can become a source of psychological affliction for acculturating South Asian families. Dramatic and painful value conflicts occur when South Asian children, born and raised in individualistic American society, reject and defy their parents' ways of living (Sandhu, 1997).

Sense of Inferiority

In the process of acculturation, many South Asian immigrants are subject to downward mobility. South Asians might have been very successful in many ways in their native lands, such as in education, business, and high-status jobs. However, they often suffer from status loss upon arrival in the United States when they have to start all over with low-paying and low-status jobs. This downward mobility often occurs when the degrees, diplomas, and professional credentials earned from their native countries are not recognized. It is not uncommon for newly arrived Indian, Pakistani, or Bangladeshi doctors, engineers, scientists, and educators to drive cabs or work as store clerks for their economic survival. Suddenly becoming vulnerable in this way can result in a deep sense of inferiority (Das & Kemp, 1997; Sandhu, 1997; Sandhu & Malik, 2001).

Sense of Uncertainty

South Asian immigrants worry about their future in the newly adopted country and also lament the uncertainty of when they will see their loved ones who were left behind in their native country. This uncertainty produces a deep sense of guilt and the psychological pain of homesickness for many South Asian immigrants (Sandhu, 1997; Sandhu & Asrabadi, 1994, 1998).

Communication Problems

Not all South Asian immigrants are proficient or fluent in writing and speaking English. This lack of facility with the English language becomes a major obstacle for these immigrants when participating in social, cultural, and political processes in the United States. Consequently, many South Asian Americans are deprived of professional and economic opportunities. To exacerbate these problems, language barriers could also keep them from seeking professional help (Maker et al., 2005; Sandhu, 1995).

Loss of Support Systems

Separation from familiar economic, political, social, and cultural support systems, including abrupt separation from the extended family members, are major psychological stressors that are directly associated with the migration experience of South Asian Americans. This loss of support systems has been called the uprooting disorder, one that causes disorientation, alienation, feelings of isolation, and powerlessness for immigrants (Zwingman, 1978).

Nostalgia or Homesickness

Being separated from close friends and extended family members in a distant, strange land for an uncertain period of time causes a profound sense of loss. After migration, South Asian immigrants' contacts with their long-term acquaintances and familiar surroundings in their home countries end abruptly. This psychological void is never completely filled and generally becomes a painful source of nostalgia or homesickness for newly arrived immigrants and their first-generation offspring (Sandhu, 1997; Sandhu, Kaur, & Tewari, 1999).

Feelings of Guilt

A final expression of acculturative stress is guilt. Most South Asian people migrate for economic reasons, at the cost of their close relationships with parents and other family members. South Asians migrate from the most populous countries. For instance, India has a population of more than one billion people; Pakistan, more than 162 million; and Bangladesh, 145 million people. They rank number two, six, and seven, respectively, when compared with populations of other nations of the world. The natural and other economic resources have been depleted in these countries due to overpopulation, invasion, and colonization. Living comfortably in the United States while leaving loved ones behind in misery and wrenching poverty causes feelings of guilt for many South Asian immigrants (Sandhu, 1997; Sandhu & Asrabadi, 1998).

ASSESSING ACCULTURATION

Given the presence of these sources of acculturation stress in the life of many clients, one of the most important requirements for counselors who work with South Asian Americans is to recognize the acculturation levels of their clients. These acculturation levels guide the initiation and termination of counseling relationships, the making of necessary referrals, and recommendations for group therapy sessions. Box 11.3 illustrates acculturative stress in three of the individuals from the vignettes that began this chapter.

BOX 11.3   Acculturation Stress in the Cases of Anita, Sameer, and Mrs. Khan

Acculturative stress is one of the most difficult problems that afflicts South Asian immigrants. As discussed above, several contributing factors are responsible for causing this distress. Of course, not all these factors are applicable to each individual case. Some specific acculturative stress factors for each vignette are identified here:

Anita, the International Student

Anita is obviously experiencing a debilitating level of acculturative stress. It is impairing her ability to function effectively in her studies. This acculturative stress can be attributed to several factors, including nostalgia or homesickness, loneliness, loss of social support systems, and culture shock. Loneliness and nostalgia are clearly the salient factors that cause her to "find herself alone and in tears a lot." After leaving India, Anita has been abruptly cut off from her social support system of family and friends. For this reason, "She is not sure to whom she can talk."

Anita's acculturative stress is also caused by her lack of fluency in English. She is quite aware of it and "even afraid that communication, due to language and different accents, might be a problem." Anita experienced immediate culture shock when her counselor asked her "to share personal information about her relationships and whether she is sexually active." She was offended and embarrassed to answer such questions, which she considered culturally quite inappropriate, especially when asked by a male counselor.

Sameer, the Businessman

Sameer has been living in the United States for the past five years. He might have experienced acculturative stress due to all factors, such as nostalgia, loneliness, and language problems, that were mentioned in Anita's case. However, with time in the United States, during which he has achieved a higher acculturation level, he seems to have been able to cope with those acculturative stress factors.

Sameer's current acculturative stress seems to be caused by mandatory participation in group therapy because of domestic violence. This acculturative stress is also caused by culture shock because Sameer did not expect that in America he would be punished for hitting his own wife. He still insisted that he was not "an offender" because he did not do anything wrong by disciplining his wife, who was getting "too smart and too Americanized." Sameer failed to understand the new expectations and social norms of the American society. He still wanted to prove to his wife Nasreen that he was the boss and he could hit her when she "talked back to him."

As mentioned earlier, gender roles are changed, and even reversed, when South Asian immigrants arrive in the United States. But, even after migration, some South Asian immigrant men act dominant in public to prove that they have power and control over their wives and children. This attitude causes problems with the law. Sameer seemed to fit into that category. By hitting his wife Nasreen, Sameer unfortunately caused a lot of acculturative stress for her and himself.

Mrs. Khan, the Depressed Client

The third vignette brings up the acculturative stress issues of Mrs. Nooran Khan, the mother. After the unexpected death of her husband six months ago, naturally Mrs. Khan would feel depression to some degree.

(Continued)

(Continued)

It is interesting to note that even after residing in the United States for 25 years, Mrs. Khan did not know why her daughter brought her to see a counselor. As noted elsewhere, many South Asians lack awareness of available counseling services and question their appropriateness. In addition, South Asian Americans have cultural prohibitions against revealing personal problems to strangers, including mental health professionals. Also, South Asian Americans consider disclosing mental health problems to bring stigma and shame to the whole family. No wonder that Mrs. Nooran Khan is "afraid that her daughter and the other members of her community will think that she is 'crazy.'"

The main factors that contribute to Mrs. Khan's acculturative stress are her sense of uncertainty about working on her depression through a counseling process; communication problems; loss of support system, with the exception of some help from her daughter (who also acknowledges "not helping her mother through an emotionally difficult time"); and a profound sense of loss after the death of her husband.

Mental Health and South Asian Americans

South Asians, like all other human beings, experience emotional distress and personal disruption. A primary purpose of this section is to make counselors aware of the special needs, concerns, and issues of South Asian Americans. In the process, the model minority myth as it is applied to South Asian Americans will be debunked. However, the reader must continue to keep in mind the message of Chapter 1: The individual and universal dimensions of human life must also be factored into the work.

This section on mental health and South Asians is divided into four parts. First, reasons for the lack of information on mental health and South Asian Americans is presented. Then, misconceptions about South Asians and issues that are known to be especially relevant to South Asian mental health are discussed. Third, presenting problems of this client group are discussed. Finally, specific mental health concerns of South Asians are presented.

THE ABSENCE OF INFORMATION ON
MENTAL HEALTH AND SOUTH ASIAN AMERICANS

Objective, research-based information on significant aspects of the experience of South Asian Americans in the United States is lacking (Herrick & Brown, 1999). Unlike other Asian American groups, South Asian immigrants have not been studied by social scientists to any appreciable degree (Das & Kemp, 1997; Maker et al., 2005; Myers, Madathil, & Tingle, 2005; Rastogi, 2002; Sandhu, 1999). For example, not much is known about the quality of their lives, the stresses and strains of their day-to-day life, their mental health needs, and the degree to which they utilize mental health services. Two reasons for the neglect or oversight of South Asian Americans' adjustment and mental health problems are (1) their image as a model minority and (2) their infrequent use of mental health services.

Asian Americans as a Model Minority

The term "model minority" was mentioned in Chapter 6 as the view that Asian Americans in general function well in society and experience few adjustment difficulties. The author of the term, William Peterson (1966), compared the success of Asian Americans and Jewish Americans and described them as highly successful model minorities in contrast with other, so-called problem minorities.

The term model minority was also applied to the second wave of South Asians who immigrated to the United States under the Immigration and Naturalization Act of 1965, also known as the McCarran Immigration Act. This elite group of South Asian immigrants was highly educated and showed great promise for upward economic mobility. For instance, in a sample of 46,000 Asian Indian immigrants, Doshi (1975) found that at least 50 percent were working as medical doctors, scientists, and engineers.

This second wave of professional immigrants exhibited very little criminal activity and earned a higher income than many European Americans. Their children were also higher scholastic achievers and they did not demonstrate juvenile delinquency.

Due to the model minority myth, a common perception among mental health service providers is that members of South Asian communities do not suffer from mental health problems and that any problems they might have are easily resolved within their families and communities (Johnson & Nadirshaw, 2002). Their strong family ties, stability, and structure are cited as the contributing factors to South Asians' success on all fronts of life (Bell, 1996), including the mental health arena.

Model Minority Myth Debunked

The common perception of South Asian Americans as a model minority must be challenged. This label is problematic in that it has been overgeneralized. It fails to acknowledge the psychological, social, and academic problems that exist for many members of this group.

In fact, the model minority myth is especially less appropriate in recent years. Many of the more recent South Asian immigrants are less educated and lack English language skills. As mentioned earlier, they generally work as taxi or truck drivers, convenience store clerks, and small motel operators or small business owners (Inman & Tewari, 2003; Sandhu & Malik, 2001). Due to their low economic status and low educational background but greater acculturation difficulties, South Asian Americans now are at more serious risk of psychological problems than ever before.

It is therefore important that mental health professionals not buy into the popular model minority myth in order to adequately address the serious concerns of this generally overlooked population (Sandhu et al., 1999). In an interview with Morrissey (1997), Sandhu highlighted the mental health issues that are hidden by the model minority myth:

> The myth of Asians as a model minority, based on the success image of a few elite individuals, has a very negative and debilitating effect on the general population of Asian Americans. Several mental health concerns and psychological afflictions, such as threats to cultural identity, powerlessness, feelings of marginality, loneliness, hostility, and perceived alienation, and discrimination remain unaddressed and hidden under the veneer of the model minority myth. (pp. 1, 21–22)

Failure to Seek Professional Help

Another reason South Asians do not show up in the mental health literature is that they infrequently use mental health services (Beliappa, 1991; Leong, 1986; Sue & Sue, 2003). This phenomenon may be attributed to lack of awareness of available services, lack of confidence in the effectiveness and appropriateness of counseling, concerns about cultural and language barriers, and fear that confidentiality will not be preserved. Other reasons for infrequent use of counseling services include a cultural emphasis on restraining strong feelings, strict parental control of offspring, and cultural prohibitions against revealing family or personal problems to anyone outside the family. In South Asian families, disclosing mental problems or mental illness is viewed as bringing great shame and stigma to the whole family (Atkinson et al., 1998).

In particular, matters relating to sex are considered too personal to be discussed with others. Sex is a taboo subject in South Asian cultures because it is considered a strictly private matter. Discussing personal sexual matters with someone other than one's life partner is considered to be immature or a sign of looseness in character that invites embarrassment, shame, and insult to the self and the family. Thus, South Asian clients are extremely reticent to address their sex-related concerns such as sexual orientation or any episodes of sexual abuse.

MISCONCEPTIONS ABOUT MENTAL HEALTH AND SOUTH ASIAN AMERICANS

Through an extensive review of the available literature about South Asians residing in Britain, Johnson and Nadirshaw (2002) identified several misconceptions that might also have relevance for South Asians in the United States. Some are positive; some are negative. All are inaccurate and dangerous because counselors might be susceptible to them and not respond appropriately to South Asians. The misconceptions are followed by challenges to them.

1. South Asians are psychologically more robust than the indigenous populations of the countries to which they immigrate, and they do not need to use available therapeutic services.

Actually, the low rate of reported mental health problems among Asian Americans is attributed to their fear of stigmatization, lack of awareness of available mental health services, and cultural and language barriers, but definitely not due to an absence of mental health problems. As a matter of fact, Beliappa (1991) reported an alarmingly high rate of emotional distress among South Asians, with no outlet to express it.

2. South Asian culture is dominated exclusively by men; women play a dependent, submissive role. Therefore there is no role confusion.

This perception might be true in the native cultures and countries of origin; however, due to the Western emphasis on individualism, including economic independence, women are forced to re-examine their traditional passive gender roles in their newly adopted mainstream American culture (Sandhu, 1997). With more educational and economic opportunities available to women in Western countries, especially in the United States, women's traditional docile and passive roles are transformed to egalitarian and even to dominant roles when the women join the cadres of highly educated professionals.

3. South Asians are obsessed with religion.

As discussed above, this perception is misleading. It is fair to say that after immigration, South Asians are more concerned about earning money and meeting their financial obligations than with their religion. They are not just meditating or practicing yoga.

4. South Asians have arranged marriages and arranged marriages are not happy.

The practice of arranged marriages often becomes unacceptable to first- and second-generation South Asian offspring in the United States. The number of South Asian American children who have arranged marriages is relatively insignificant. South Asian parents strongly believe in arranged marriages and consider them to be more satisfying. One view of love in arranged marriage is that it "grows" rather than is "found," as in Western relationships.

On the contrary, one of the major concerns for South Asian parents, and a root cause of family discord, is their children's interethnic and interracial marital relationships, as well as dating in general. In extreme cases, South Asian parents cut off financial and emotional relations with their children if they marry someone who is from a non-South Asian cultural background and ancestry (Inman & Tewari, 2003). In general, intimate relationships and dating can be a source of intergenerational family conflicts for many South Asian American parents.

5. South Asian culture is stifling and denies freedom to the individual.

For first- and second-generation South Asian Americans, South Asian culture is not stifling. While South Asians may sacrifice their personal freedom for the sake of their extended family in their native countries, this changes when they arrive in the Western world. In their newly adopted land, more emphasis is placed upon the rights and glorification of the individual than on the demands of the family. A family member's personal needs become more salient than the needs of his or her family of origin.

6. Asians look after their own within extended family networks.

This misconception implies that South Asian Americans do not require any professional counseling services. As mentioned previously, members of this ethnic group are seen as either psychologically so robust and sound that they simply don't have any problems or as having strong family networks that are capable of solving all their problems. In reality, both assumptions are wrong. South Asian Americans do have their fair share of psychological problems (Beliappa, 1991), and their extended networks are usually disrupted after their migration to the United Sates.

Most of the perceptions about immigrant South Asians are accurate when viewed in the context of their original cultures and native countries. However, these stereotypes are either overgeneralizations or just mistaken beliefs about second- or third-generation South Asian Americans as acculturation occurs.

While counseling South Asian clients, mental health professionals must remember that, as with all other immigrants, acculturation is central. When South Asian immigrants enter the United States, their cultural transformation is immediately instantiated in new local settings. This transformation shakes up their identities, resulting in significant changes in their values, priorities, and behaviors (Sandhu et al., 1999; Weisner, 1993; Whiting & Edwards, 1988). They are now neither South Asians nor Americans, but South Asian Americans. Some of the stereotypes identified above by Johnson and Nadirshaw (2002) might be very important for newly arrived South Asians but might have very little relevance to first-, second-, and third-generation South Asian Americans.

PRESENTING PSYCHOLOGICAL PROBLEMS OF SOUTH ASIANS

Now that myths and misconceptions have been discussed, the chapter turns to trends in how South Asian Americans' mental health issues are expressed. The first topic is the presentation of psychological concerns.

South Asian Americans are likely to present their problems in a different way from mainstream American clients (Ananth & Ananth, 1996; Dasgupta, 1986; Jayakar, 1994; Prathikanti, 1997; Sandhu, 1999). They are likely to emphasize physical complaints, make external attributions, avoid exploring childhood experience, spiritualize emotional difficulties, and emphasize academic or career difficulties. Each will be discussed in turn.

Physical Complaints

South Asians' clinical presentations often consist of multiple somatic complaints, such as headaches, stomachaches, and bodily fatigue. As Asians generally view the body and mind as unitary rather than separate, clients tend to focus more on physical problems rather than on emotional afflictions, thus leading to a high number of expressions of somatic complaints for Asians (Lin & Cheung, 1999). These complaints may take them to medical doctors rather than to counselors (Prathikanti, 1997). Counselors should be keenly aware of the somatization of South Asian Americans' emotional problems and look beyond their physical ailments. In a sense, frequent headaches might signal frequent heartaches.

External Attributions

South Asians may also externalize emotional concerns in such ways as attributing their problems to supernatural forces, including black magic; the casting of evil eyes from people who are jealous of their successes; angry spirits of dead ancestors; and bad karmic deeds from their previous lives (Jayakar, 1994; Prathikanti, 1997). Many South Asian clients with such psychic distress often seek help from indigenous healers including palmists, herbalists, sorcerers, and a variety of shamans, whose therapeutic efforts include classical astrology, alchemy, and magic (Kumar, Bhugra, & Singh, 2005).

Avoiding Early Childhood Exploration

Out of deep respect for their parents and due to the aforementioned filial piety, South Asian clients rarely discuss problematic childhood experiences that might be contributing to their presenting problems. Children must show love and respect to parents and their ancestors and take care of them in their old age (Ikels, 2004). Children are also expected to conceal their parents' mistakes because they should not dishonor them. In addition, deceased parents and ancestors are worshipped in many South Asian families and are considered living members of the family. Related to filial piety is the concept of shame. Children must not bring shame to the family through inappropriate behaviors that might tarnish the family's reputation and prestige in the community (Schoen, 2005). Thus, a counselor's probing for childhood experiences will be resisted by most South Asians. However, since family is a central theme in South Asians' lives, it should be addressed in a respectful way through culturally educated inquiry, as discussed in Chapter 16.

Spiritualizing Emotional Difficulties

Many South Asian clients tend to present their problems as a manifestation of disturbance in body, mind, and soul, or lack of the fulfillment of social and religious duties, called *dharma* (Obeyesekere, 1977; Prathikanti, 1997; Sandhu, Leung, & Tang, 2003). Religion and spirituality play major roles in the daily lives of many Asian Indian and Nepalese Americans, especially those who profess their faith in Hinduism and Sikhism. For many South Asian Americans, the spiritual dimension is generally presented as integrated or intertwined with their emotional concerns.

Career Concerns

Generally speaking, concerns about career or academic matters are the major presenting problems for which South Asian Americans might seek professional counseling. Both academic and career success are paramount for South Asians and their families and are a source of pride or shame. There is much pressure to do well in those areas. Career uncertainty, career failure, or family disapproval of career choice are all potential presenting problems of South Asian Americans. These are also "safer" topics, ones that might cover other concerns. As mentioned, South Asian Americans rarely discuss personal and emotional problems that may bring shame to the family.

SPECIFIC MENTAL HEALTH CONCERNS OF SOUTH ASIANS

Although little is known about South Asians' mental health issues at this time, a few topics have been studied. Two particular, and related, sets of problems will be highlighted here. One set is youth-related issues around substance abuse and domestic violence. A second is conflict between parents and offspring.

Problems of South Asian American Youth

South Asian American youth now have serious problems related to substance abuse and domestic violence. In addition, according to Scalia (1997), criminal activity is much more serious among the Asian American juvenile population than would be expected. However, due to model minority myths and the other erroneous assumptions that were mentioned above, adolescent and young adult South Asian clients' mental health needs remain either unaddressed, overlooked, or handled inadequately.

South Asian American Parents' Concerns About Their Children

Another set of problems concerns parent-child conflict. Young South Asian adults are challenging parental authority in general and marrying outside the ethnic group. Most South Asian American parents worry about their children becoming too Americanized, especially when the children express their strong feelings through acting out or talking back to their parents. As discussed previously, South Asian families are patriarchal and the father is authoritarian.

Communication flows vertically from father downward to children. Any talking back to the father is considered insulting and unacceptable.

The previously mentioned disapproval of dating and interethnic relationships are a cause for conflict between offspring and parents. In fact, most of the dissatisfaction in South Asian American families is due to two main reasons: not marrying within one's own culture or not having a prestigious job that parents may approve.

Additional Concerns

In addition to the issues mentioned previously, recent research found three particular concerns that affect non-immigrant South Asian Americans (Das & Kemp, 1997):

- Minority status might predispose people to feelings of social isolation and heightened stress.

- Young school-age children of immigrants may become the target of negative stereotyping and social rejection.

- Second-generation South Asian Americans may find it offensive to be seen as foreigners.

As mentioned previously, second-generation South Asian Americans in particular may experience tension between mainstream American values and their ethnic cultural values. For example, a young, second-generation girl who finds her social life unduly restricted by traditional parents may find it irksome and begin to rebel.

With these manifestations and conflicts in mind, counselors are better prepared to work with this population. The chapter now turns to guidelines for practice with South Asian Americans.

Counseling and Psychotherapy With South Asian Americans

The counseling needs of South Asian Americans must be met within their cultural context (Sandhu et al., 2003; Tewari, Inman, & Sandhu, 2003). Thus, the applicability and effectiveness of Western models of treatment with South Asians who have different worldviews, values, and cultural systems must be examined (Maker et al., 2005). For this reason, the following sections provide (1) themes and guidelines for working with South Asian Americans, (2) applications for three stages of counseling, (3) four culturally specific helping methods, and (4) possibilities for group counseling.

SPECIAL GUIDELINES

The following 10 themes should be considered when working with South Asian clients, especially those who are less acculturated to the dominant American culture. This list will serve partly as a reiteration and summary of some of the themes that were discussed previously in this chapter.

Counselor Self-Examination

Counselors must examine their own unintentional biases toward South Asian clients and avoid stereotypes, including the model minority myth. This is a guideline for all culturally alert counseling.

Consultation With Healers in the South Asian Community

Consultation with *hakims* (wise men), *matas* (female priests), *yogis* (those who are expert in the practice of yoga), and *gurus* (teachers in Sikhism, Hinduism, and Buddhism) can prove quite helpful to South Asian clients (Johnson & Nadirshaw, 2002). These figures are acquainted with long-standing treatment modalities, such as yogic, tantric (i.e., concerned with powerful ritual acts of body, speech, and mind), and Ayurvedic (a set of ancient and contemporary medicine practices) methods. Counselors themselves are not likely to be acquainted with these indigenous helpers, but they can always encourage their clients to seek such help. Counselors working with South Asians would also benefit from acquainting themselves with some Asian psychotherapies (Walsh, 2000), possibly using them in conjunction with Western models.

The Role of Religion and Spirituality in Counseling

Religion and spirituality are extremely important for understanding and treating the mental health problems of South Asians (Hussain & Cochrane, 2002). South Asian clients may view their mental health problems not only as psychological or emotional as but also as spiritual and religious in nature. They might find it difficult to untangle them.

South Asians believe that if properly understood, all human problems, in the final analysis, are really spiritual problems (Sandhu, 2006). Counselors working with South Asian Americans must be prepared to answer their clients' religious or spiritual questions as they relate to their psychological problems.

The Family-First Concept

Counselors should recognize the power of familism in South Asian life (Paniagua, 2005). Familism is the notion that family is central for all life events and decisions. Since South Asians come from collectivist societies, an individual's problem is considered to be a family's problem (Triandis, 1994). For example, many South Asian clients first discuss their personal or economic problems with their parents or extended family members before seeking professional help. Some family members or friends may even accompany the client to see the counselor. Counselors should consider their client not only as an individual but also in relationship to the whole family.

As is true in most other collectivist societies, a South Asian father, as the head of the household, is responsible for taking care of all family members' problems. Thus, it is not uncommon that a father might receive counseling for his son, daughter, or even for his wife. This type of indirectness is generally more prevalent in collectivist societies than it is in individualistic societies like the United States (Vontress, 1991).

South Asians as Targets of Prejudice and Discrimination

Counselors must be aware that because they are physically different, politically powerless, and socially isolated from the dominant culture, South Asians may feel alienated and disconnected. Incidents of racism, discrimination, and hate crimes, including physical violence, are not unfamiliar to these ethnic groups (Sandhu, 1997). In that vein, counselors and other mental health professionals must acknowledge how power relationships between them and their clients might affect the therapeutic process (Johnson & Nadirshaw, 2002).

South Asians and Internalized Racism

Like many other nondominant ethnic groups, South Asian clients generally suffer from internalized racism, that is, the acceptance of negative and demeaning verbal and nonverbal messages from the dominant culture (Sharma, 2005). Self-devaluation, rejection of ancestral culture, hopelessness, and helplessness are some of the common characteristics of internalized racism that affect many South Asian Americans (Jones, 2000).

Level of Acculturation

It is important that counselors understand a South Asian client's level of acculturation before initiating any counseling or therapeutic interventions. Such knowledge for the counselor is critical to the success of the counseling process (Ibrahim et al., 1997). One tool that can be used to assess South Asian American clients' acculturation levels is The Cultural Adaptation Pain Scale (Sandhu et al., 1996). Generally speaking, higher levels of acculturation indicate that clients will be more receptive and able to benefit from counseling services (Vontress, Johnson, & Epp, 1999).

Generation Gap Issues of South Asian Immigrants and Their Children

Immigrants often face chronic difficulties specific to the acculturation experience, including conflicts with family members, members of their own ethnic group, and members of other ethnic groups (Lay & Nguyen, 1998). Children of immigrants may experience different acculturative stressors from their parents, such as conflicts between the children and parents regarding culturally acceptable behaviors. The offspring of immigrants report more in-group conflicts and marginally lower self-esteem than do immigrants (Abouguendia & Noels, 2001). The offspring of immigrants also experience conflict between parents' traditional cultural values and the contrasting values of the dominant culture (Lay & Nguyen, 1998). These results emphasize the need for considering the acculturation issues of the first-generation South Asian Americans as being different from those of the second- and third-generation immigrants.

Using a Relational Style of Counseling

A highly relational style, characterized by warmth and disclosure, should be used while counseling South Asian clients (Ibrahim, 1993). Both counselor and client should be willing to share their experiences and values. This exchange will likely increase trust and rapport with the client. A silent counselor who expects a South Asian client to reveal his or her deepest fears and anxieties is likely to fail.

Dealing With Sex-Related Concerns

As mentioned previously, discussion about sexual matters, especially with the opposite sex and with younger clients, is still taboo in the South Asian population. Counselors should refrain from abruptly asking questions or initiating conversation about sex, unless the clients themselves initiate the discussion of their sexual concerns.

INCORPORATING STRATEGIES INTO THREE MAIN STAGES OF COUNSELING

One model for counseling South Asian American clients can be conceptualized as incorporating particular elements into three main stages of counseling (Sandhu et al., 2003). These three stages are Exploration, Insight, and Action. The relational dimension of counseling is emphasized in each of these stages.

First Stage: Exploration

As mentioned earlier, South Asian clients are generally reluctant to discuss their concerns with strangers. For this reason, it is important that a counselor develop a special relationship with the South Asian client. Instead of being perceived only as an expert professional, an effective counselor would become personal and familiar, like a friend or another family member. Rogers's (1957) three facilitating conditions, empathy, respect, and genuineness, can prove quite helpful for building good rapport with South Asian clients. A professionally distant, neutral stance with these clients might be detrimental to therapeutic efforts because they most likely would withdraw prematurely from counseling sessions.

Second Stage: Insight

In the second stage, the client increases awareness of her or his motivations and behaviors. Such insight is usually thought of in individual terms. However, with South Asian American clients, such awareness should account for family, not only individual, needs. At this stage, counselors should keep in mind the aforementioned concept of "family first," or familism. South Asian Americans are generally willing to sacrifice their own interests for the sake of family members. They may prefer to suffer silently than to disrupt family harmony and peace. Thus, South Asian American clients might disagree with counselors' reflections and interpretations if they believe that those observations conflict with their desire to maintain family harmony and interpersonal relationships. Counselors can complement this concern by helping their South Asian American clients gain insight into how the counseling process ultimately can help their entire family.

Third Stage: Action

During the third and final stage, Action, the aim of counseling is for a client to think, behave, and feel differently. Methods for such change can be wide-ranging. It has been suggested that Asian American clients prefer a directive style of counseling and respond more favorably to problem-solving and cognitively oriented interventions (Sue & Sue, 2003). Such assertions have also been questioned (Sandhu et al., 2003). Culturally alert counselors must possess a full repertoire of intervention strategies and use them as needed to resolve the problems of their clients in the context of their cultural and family backgrounds. This repertoire should include ecological, spiritual, behavioral, and cognitive dimensions and approaches such as network therapy, narrative therapy, and feminist models (Ibrahim et al., 1997). Each of these are described elsewhere in this book. Chapter 16 expands on adapting counseling methods to culture.

FOUR STRATEGIES FOR WORKING WITH SOUTH ASIAN CLIENTS

Four specific types of interventions can be particularly useful for counseling South Asian Americans: (1) cultural genograms, (2) narratives and stories, (3) bibliotherapy and psychoeducation, and (4) group counseling (Inman & Tewari, 2003).

Using Cultural Genograms

Since family is an important source of support for South Asians, mental health providers need to address client issues in the familial context. A cultural genogram can help clients identify and understand the immigration history, family structure, and alliances in the extended family. The use of such a genogram can also help counselors assess the levels of acculturation of South Asian clients and their religious affiliations and ethnic identification. The making of a cultural genogram will be described in Chapter 16.

In Mrs. Khan's situation (from the third vignette at the beginning of the chapter), a cultural genogram could be used to identify the role of women in the family, especially after the death of a spouse. It can also help her daughter see the familial expectations and responsibilities that are placed on children after the death of a parent.

After Mrs. Kahn draws such a genogram, the counselor can explore the following with her: What aspects of your culture or values make you proud? Which ones might make you afraid or guilty? Which part of your cultural or familial expectations have you exceeded, and which ones have you compromised? What are the messages that are passed on from generation to generation regarding widowhood? How did this experience affect the lives of the women in your family? How did the other women in the family face it? What roles did their children play in these situations? What were their sources of support? What were the religious and cultural beliefs?

Information gathered from these questions could be helpful for Mrs. Khan and her daughter to understand their emotions and reactions in their cultural context. In addition, the information could also help them to recognize the strengths of the women in their family and how the women in their culture dealt with difficult times.

Narratives and Stories

Because of the possibility that South Asians might be more comfortable sharing their experiences through stories, as opposed to directly disclosing emotions, counselors can encourage South Asian families to share their experiences and struggles related to immigration and acculturation by using stories and narratives (Inman & Tewari, 2003). Stories and narratives can also serve as a powerful tool for exploring parents' expectations and relationship with their children.

To illustrate, narratives could be used to help Anita, the international student who was presented in the first vignette at the beginning of the chapter. She could be encouraged to narrate the story of her life, in which she is the "heroine" of the story. The counselor could help her to tell her story in such a way that Anita could perhaps see the themes in her life. She might identify the rewards and the obligations she has chosen and received and develop ways to address those topics in counseling. This may provide her with the means to explore the expectations placed on her and make helpful choices.

Bibliotherapy and Psychoeducation

Bibliotherapy and psychoeducation can be safer ways to help South Asians because they provide some distance from the personal issues. Reading about related phenomena and other people's experiences can normalize situations and feelings that otherwise are considered stigmatizing and shameful to clients and their families. For example, in the case of spousal abuse, the counselor could suggest a reading on anger or a workshop on spousal abuse at a local Hindu temple. Sameer, from the second vignette, might be encouraged to read literature from his own culture that focuses on taking care of one's spouse and treating the person with respect. That may make the message less foreign, less threatening, and less personal for Sameer.

Group Counseling With South Asians

Due to its cost effectiveness and practical efficacy, group counseling is a popular modality. Group counseling could be especially useful for South Asian clients, if the focus of the group is specifically on South Asian issues (Tewari et al., 2003). However, group counseling with South Asians can be a great challenge because their cultural values are diametrically opposed to the processes and dynamics of group counseling (Baruth & Manning, 2003; Mann & Duan, 2002; Merta, 1995). Group counseling requires directness, open expression of feelings, self-disclosure, and active participation. By contrast, South Asians are generally reluctant to express strong feelings in the presence of other group members, they lack verbal expressiveness, and they generally don't like to share personal or family problems with strangers. It can be helpful to have other South Asian clients in the group in order to encourage trust in the process. Thus, Sameer, the 45-year-old businessman from the second vignette, might find the group experience more beneficial if he were placed in a group with other individuals from similar cultural backgrounds. Perhaps, then, he might be more open and willing to share and be challenged by the other group members.

Another barrier to traditional group counseling for South Asian Americans is their expectation that a group leader will be an authority figure (DeLucia-Waack, 1996). Even when a challenge could be beneficial to all group members, South Asian clients are not likely to question or challenge the group leader (Gladding, 2003). Because a group leader is considered an expert, South Asian group members commonly would expect some concrete advice or solutions from the leader for solving their problems, not just the exploration of their feelings in the presence of others.

With those provisos in mind, counselors should first explain the goals, structure, and dynamics of group counseling before asking South Asians to join such groups. Careful screening, selection, explanation, and preparation can help South Asian clients benefit from group counseling like all other clients. It is also important that mental health professionals provide some individual counseling sessions first with South Asian American clients, before starting group counseling sessions with them.

Summary

This chapter introduced the readers to South Asian Americans as a rapidly increasing distinct ethnic minority group with unique characteristics, cultural values, special counseling needs, and mental health concerns. Several myths, misconceptions, and mistaken beliefs about this generally overlooked group were discussed. Acculturative experiences, threats to ethnic identity, barriers to seeking counseling, clinical presentations of mental health problems, and special recommendations for counseling were presented as special topics as they apply to South Asian American clients. In addition, various counseling considerations and strategies were presented to enhance counseling effectiveness with this group. Three case examples illustrated South Asian issues and counseling strategies that might be effective with South Asian American clients.

Now that you have completed this chapter, respond to the questions in Activity 11.2 to assess your understanding of South Asian Americans and counseling.

ACTIVITY 11.2

Discussion Questions

Who are South Asian Americans? Describe their demographic characteristics.

Discuss some of the cultural values of South Asian Americans. How do these cultural values contribute to the acculturative stress of South Asian Americans?

Generally, South Asian Americans have been recognized as a "model minority." Do you agree or disagree with this characterization? Please provide a rationale to support your answer.

Identify some common mental health problems of South Asian Americans. What are some beliefs and assumptions regarding these mental health problems?

Discuss intervention strategies that are culturally relevant and effective for helping South Asian Americans.

How would you incorporate counseling strategies into three stages—Exploration, Insight, and Action—while counseling South Asian Americans?

What are some of the major acculturative issues of South Asian Americans?

How would you help your clients to cope with acculturative stress?

Discuss the role of women in South Asian American families.

References

Abouguendia, M., & Noels, K. A. (2001). General and acculturation-related daily hassles and psychological adjustment in first- and second-generation South Asian immigrants to Canada. *International Journal of Psychology, 36,* 163–173.

Abrahams, S., & Salazar, C. F. (2005). Potential conflicts between cultural values and the role of confidentiality when counseling South Asian clients: Implications for ethical practice. In G. R. Walz & R. Yep (Eds.), *Vistas: Compelling perspectives on counseling 2005* (pp. 145–148). Alexandria, VA: American Counseling Association.

Ananth, J., & Ananth, K. (1996). *East Indian immigrants to the United States: Life cycle issues and adjustment.* East Meadow, NY: Indo-American Psychiatric Association.

Atkinson, D. R., Morten, G., & Sue, D. W. (1998). *Counseling American minorities* (5th ed.). Dubuque, IA: McGraw-Hill.

Baruth, L. G., & Manning, M. L. (2003). *Multicultural counseling and psychotherapy: A life span perspective.* Upper Saddle River, NJ: Merrill-Prentice Hall.

Beliappa, J. (1991) *Illness or distress? Alternative models of mental health.* London: Confederation of Indian Organizations.

Bell, D. A. (1996). America's greatest success story: The triumph of Asian-Americans. In R. C. Monk (Ed.), *Taking sides: Clashing views on controversial issues in race and ethnicity* (2nd ed., pp. 30–40). Guilford, CT: Dushkin.

Berry, J. W., & Sam, D. L. (1997). Acculturation and adaptation. In J. W. Berry, M. H. Segall, & C. Kagitcibasi (Eds.), *Handbook of cross-cultural psychology, Volume 3: Social behavior and applications* (2nd ed., pp. 291–326). Boston: Allyn & Bacon.

Bhatia, S., & Ram, A. (2004). Culture, hybridity, and the dialogical self: Cases from the South Asian diaspora. *Mind, Culture and Activity, 11,* 224–240.

Chandras, V. K. (1997). Training multiculturally competent counselors to work with Asian Indian Americans. *Counselor Education and Supervision, 37,* 50–59.

Das, A. K., & Kemp, S. F. (1997). Between two worlds: Counseling South Asian Americans. *Journal of Multicultural Counseling & Development, 25*(1), 23–34.

Dasgupta, S. D. (1986). Marching to a different drummer? Sex roles of Asian Indian women in the United States. *Women and Therapy, 5,* 297–311.

DeLucia-Waack, J. L. (1996). Multiculturalism is inherent in all group work. *Journal for Specialists in Group Work, 21,* 218–223.

Doshi, M. (1975). *Who is who among Indian immigrants in North America.* New York: B. K. Verma.

Furnham, A., & Bochner, S. (1986). *Culture shock: Psychological reactions to unfamiliar environments.* London: Methuen.

Gladding, S. (2003). *Group work: a counseling specialty* (4th ed.). Upper Saddle River, NJ: Merrill-Prentice Hall.

Grieger, I., & Ponterotto, J. G. (1995). A framework for assessment in multicultural counseling. In J. G. Ponterotto, J. M. Casas, L. A. Suzuki, & C. M. Alexander (Eds.), *Handbook of multicultural counseling.* Thousand Oaks, CA: Sage.

Helman, C. G. (1990). *Culture, health, and illness: An introduction for health professionals* (3rd ed.). Boston: Wright.

Herrick, C., & Brown, H. N. (1999). Mental disorders and syndromes found among Asians residing in the United States. *Issues in Mental Health Nursing, 20,* 275–296.

Hussain, F. A., & Cochrane, R. (2002). Depression in South Asian women: Asian women's beliefs on causes and cures. *Mental Health, Religion, and Culture, 5,* 285–311.

Ibrahim, F. A. (1993). Existential worldview theory: Transcultural counseling. In J. McFadden (Ed.), *Transcultural counseling* (pp. 23–57). Alexandria, VA: American Counseling Association.

Ibrahim, F. A., Ohnishi, I., & Sandhu, D. S. (1997). Asian American identity development: A culture-specific model for South Asian Americans. *Journal of Multicultural Counseling & Development, 25,* 34–51.

Ikels, C. (Ed.). (2004). *Filial piety: Practice and discourse in contemporary East Asia.* Stanford, CA: Stanford University Press.

Inman, A. G., & Sandhu, D. S. (2002). Cross-cultural perspectives on love and sex. In L. D. Burlew & D. Capuzzi (Eds.), *Sexuality counseling* (pp. 41–62). Huntington, NY: Nova Science.

Inman, A. G., & Tewari, N. (2003). The power of context: Counseling South Asians within a family context. In G. Roysircar, D. S. Sandhu, & V. E. Bibbins, Sr. (Eds.), *Multicultural competencies: A guidebook of practices* (pp. 97–107). Alexandria, VA: Association for Multicultural Counseling and Development.

Jayakar, K. (1994). Women of the Indian subcontinent. In L. Comas-Díaz & B. Greene (Eds.), *Women of color: Integrating ethnic and gender identities in psychotherapy* (pp. 161–181). New York: Guilford Press.

Johnson, A. W., & Nadirshaw, Z. (2002). Good practice in transcultural counseling: An Asian perspective. In S. Palmer (Ed.), *Multicultural counseling: A reader* (pp. 119–128). Thousand Oaks, CA: Sage.

Jones, C. P. (2000). Levels of racism: A theoretical framework and a gardener's tale. *American Journal of Public Health, 90,* 1212–1215.

Kim, B. S. K., Atkinson, D. R., & Umemoto, D. (2001). Asian cultural values and counseling process: Current knowledge and directions for future research. *The Counseling Psychologist, 29,* 570–603.

Kumar, M., Bhugra, D., & Singh, J. (2005). South Asian (Indian) traditional healing. In R. Moodley & W. West (Eds.), *Integrating traditional healing practices into counseling and psychotherapy* (pp. 112–121). Thousand Oaks, CA: Sage.

Lay, C., & Nguyen, T. (1998). The role of acculturation-related and acculturation nonspecific daily hassles: Vietnamese-Canadian students and psychological distress. *Canadian Journal of Behavioral Science, 30,* 172–181.

Leong, F. T. L. (1986). Counseling and psychotherapy with Asian Americans: Review of the literature. *Journal of Counseling Psychology, 33,* 196–206.

Lin, K., & Cheung, F. (1999). Mental health issues for Asian Americans. *Psychiatric Services, 50,* 774–780.

Maker, A. H., Mittal, M., & Rastogi, M. (2005). South Asians in the United States: Developing a systematic and empirically based mental health assessment model. In M. Rastogi & E. Wieling (Eds.), *Voices of color: The first person accounts of ethnic minority therapists* (pp. 233–254). Thousand Oaks, CA: Sage.

Mann, M., & Duan, C. (2002). Multicultural group counseling. In J. Trusty, E. J. Looby, & D. S. Sandhu (Eds.), *Multicultural counseling: Context, theory and practice, and competence* (pp. 247–259). Huntington, NY: Nova Science.

McMahon, S. (1995). *Overview of the South Asian diaspora.* Retrieved August 9, 2006, from http://www.lib.berkeley.edu/SSEAL/SouthAsia/overview.html

Merta, R. J. (1995). Group work: Multicultural perspectives. In J. G. Ponterotto, J. M. Casas, L. A. Suzuki, & C. M. Alexander (Eds.), *Handbook of multicultural counseling* (pp. 567–585). Thousand Oaks, CA: Sage.

Morrissey, M. (1997, October). The invisible minority: Counseling Asian Americans. *Counseling Today, 40,* 1, 21–22.

Myers, J. E., Madathil, J., & Tingle, L. R. (2005). Marriage satisfaction and wellness in India and the U.S.: A preliminary comparison of arranged marriages and marriages of choice. *Journal of Counseling and Development, 83,* 183–190.

Obeyesekere, G. (1977). The theory and practice of psychological medicine in the Ayurvedic tradition. *Culture, Medicine and Psychiatry, 1,* 155.

Ozbay, Y. (1994). An investigation of the relationship between adaptational coping process and self-perceived negative feelings of international students. *Dissertation Abstracts International, 54,* 2958A.

Paniagua, F. A. (2005). *Assessing and treating culturally diverse clients: A practical guide.* Thousand Oaks, CA: Sage.

Peterson, W. (1966, January 9). Success story: Japanese American style. *New York Times,* pp. VI-20.

Prathikanti, S. (1997). East Indian American families. In E. Lee (Ed.), *Working with Asian Americans: A guide for clinicians* (pp. 79–100). New York: Guilford Press.

Rahman, O., & Rollock, D. (2004). Acculturation, competence, and mental health among South Asian students in the United States. *Journal of Multicultural Counseling and Development, 32,* 130–142.

Rastogi, M. (2002). Mother-adult daughter questionnaire (MAD): Developing a culturally sensitive instrument. *Family Journal, 10,* 145–155.

Rogers, C. R. (1957). The necessary and sufficient conditions of therapeutic personality change. *Journal of Consulting Psychology, 21,* 95–103.

Rumbaut, R. G. (1994).Origins and destinies: Immigration to the United States since World War II. *Sociological Forum, 9,* 583–621.

Sandhu, D. S. (1995). An examination of the psychological needs of the international students: Implications for counseling and psychotherapy. *International Journal for the Advancement of Counseling, 17,* 229–239.

Sandhu, D. S. (1997). Psychocultural profiles of Asian and Pacific Islander Americans: Implications for counseling and psychotherapy. *Journal of Multicultural Counseling and Development, 25,* 7–22.

Sandhu, D. S. (Ed.). (1999). *Asian and Pacific Islander Americans: Issues and concerns for counseling and psychotherapy.* Commack, NY: Nova Science.

Sandhu, D. S. (2006). Seven stages of spiritual development: A framework to solve psycho-spiritual problems. In O. J. Morgan (Ed.), *Counseling and spirituality: Views from the profession* (pp. 64–92). Boston: Lahaska & Houghton Mifflin.

Sandhu, D. S., & Asrabadi, B. R. (1994). Development of an acculturative stress scale for international students: Preliminary findings. *Psychological Reports, 75,* 435–448.

Sandhu, D. S., & Asrabadi, B. R. (1998). An acculturative stress scale for international students: A practical approach to stress measurement. In C. P. Zalaquett & R. J. Wood (Eds.), *Evaluating stress: A book of resources* (Vol. 2, pp. 1–33). Lanham, MD: Scarecrow.

Sandhu, D. S., Kaur, K. P., & Tewari, N. (1999). Acculturative experiences of Asian and Pacific Islander Americans: Considerations for counseling and psychotherapy. In D. S. Sandhu (Ed.), *Asian and Pacific Islander Americans: Issues and concerns for counseling and psychotherapy.* Commack, NY: Nova Science.

Sandhu, D. S., Leung, S. L., & Tang, M. (2003). Counseling approaches with Asian Americans and Pacific Islander Americans. In F. D. Harper & J. McFadden (Eds.), *Culture and counseling: New approaches* (pp. 99–114). Boston: Allyn & Bacon.

Sandhu, D. S., & Malik, R. (2001). Ethnocultural background and substance abuse treatment of Asian Indian Americans. In S. L. A. Straussner (Ed.), *Ethnocultural factors in substance abuse treatment* (pp. 368–392). New York: Guilford Press.

Sandhu, D. S., Portes, P. R., & McPhee, S. (1996). Assessing cultural adaptation: Psychometric properties of the Cultural Adaptation Pain Scale. *Journal of Multicultural Counseling and Development, 24,* 15–25.

Scalia, J. (1997). *Juvenile delinquents in the federal criminal justice system. Special report.* Washington, DC: U.S. Department of Justice, Bureau of Justice Statistics.

Schoen, A. A. (2005). Culturally sensitive counseling for Asian Americans/Pacific Islanders. *Journal of Instructional Psychology, 32,* 253–258.

Sharma, M. (2005). Emerging identity: An Asian Indian female psychologist's perspective. In M. Rastogi & E. Wieling (Eds.), *Voices of color: First-person accounts of ethnic minority therapists* (pp. 13–22). Thousand Oaks, CA: Sage.

Sheth, M. (1995). Asian Indian Americans. In P. G. Min (Ed.), *Asian Americans: Contemporary trends and issues* (pp. 169–198). Thousand Oaks, CA: Sage.

Sodowsky, G. R., & Carey, J. C. (1988). Relationship between acculturation-related demographics and cultural attitudes of an Asian-Indian immigrant group. *Journal of Multicultural Counseling and Development, 16,* 117–136.

Sodowsky, G. R., Kwan, K. K., & Pannu, R. (1995). Ethnic identity of Asians in the United States. In J. G. Ponterotto, J. M. Casas, L. A. Suzuki, & C. M. Alexander, (Eds.), *Handbook of multicultural counseling* (pp. 123–154). Thousand Oaks, CA: Sage.

Sodowsky, G. R., & Plake, B. S. (1992). A study of acculturation differences among international people and suggestions for sensitivity to within-group differences. *Journal of Counseling and Development, 71,* 53–60.

Sue, D. W., & Sue, D. (2003). *Counseling the culturally diverse: Theory and practice.* New York: Wiley.

Takaki, R. (1989). *Strangers from a different shore.* Boston: Little, Brown.

Tewari, N., Inman, A. G., & Sandhu, D. S. (2003). South Asian Americans: Culture, concerns, and therapeutic strategies. In J. S. Mio & G. Y. Iwamasa (Eds.), *Culturally diverse mental health: The challenges of research and resistance* (pp. 191–209). New York: Brunner-Routledge.

Triandis, H. C. (1994). *Culture and social behavior.* New York: McGraw-Hill.

U.S. Census Bureau. (2001, May). *Profiles of general demographic characteristics 2000.* Retrieved March 5, 2006, from http://www.census.gov/prod/cen2000/dp1/2kh00.pdf

Vontress, C. E. (1991). Traditional healing in Africa: Implications for cross-cultural counseling. *Journal of Counseling and Development, 70*(1), 242–249.

Vontress, C. E., Johnson, J. A., & Epp, L. R. (1999). *Cross-cultural counseling: A casebook.* Alexandria, VA: American Counseling Association.

Walsh, R. (2000). Asian psychotherapies. In R. J. Corsini & D. Wedding (Eds.), *Current psychotherapies* (6th ed., pp. 407–444). Itasca, IL: F. E. Peacock.

Weisner, T. S. (1993). Overview: Sibling similarity and differences in different cultures. In C. W. Nuckolls (Ed.), *Siblings in South Asia: Brothers and sisters in cultural context* (pp. 1–17). New York: Guilford Press.

Whiting, B., & Edwards, C. (1988). *Children of different worlds: The formation of social behavior.* Cambridge, MA: Harvard University Press.

Zwingman, C. A. A. (1978). *Uprooting and related phenomena: A descriptive bibliotherapy* (Doc. MNH/78.23). Geneva, Switzerland: World Health Organization.

Part III

Social Groups

12

Social Class

Patricia Goodspeed Grant and Karen L. Mackie

> *We are what we know. We are, however, also what we do not know. If what we know about ourselves—our history, our culture, our national identity—is deformed by absences, denials, and incompleteness, then our identity—both as individuals and as Americans—is fragmented. Such a self lacks access, both to itself and to the world.*
>
> —William Pinar (1993)

Pinar's quote is particularly apt for the topic of social class in the United States. Americans know little about social class—both their own and that of others. It is one of the purposes of this chapter to fill in some of the absences and acknowledge some of the denial about social class so that counselors have "access," in Pinar's words, to themselves and to the world of their clients. Three vignettes that highlight the impact of social class follow.

The Bartons live in an upper middle-class neighborhood. Marvin is an executive for a large corporation, while Marge is a successful attorney. They typically enjoy yearly family vacations and are active in their children's schools and in community organizations. Their daughter, Eileen, and son, Ed, have always been top students. Eileen has just obtained her master's degree, and Ed is attending law school. The youngest, Alan, is considered by his family to be "different." He is socially awkward and doesn't seem as smart as his older siblings. However, with extra help from a tutor, he passed most of his classes in high school. Alan is pursuing a degree in automotive mechanics at the local community college. While they brag about Eileen and Ed to their friends, Alan is a source of some embarrassment, and they are reluctant to talk about his educational achievements.

---------------------------- ❖ ----------------------------

Annie, a married working class 34-year-old European American mother of two, has a bachelor's degree in business from the local state college. Her husband, a high school dropout, worked his way up to a $40,000-a-year factory job. After staying home to raise her family and then engaging in a fruitless four-year search for a job in her field, Annie is now turning to her college's career office for help. She is tearful, angry, and discouraged because so far she cannot find the secure job that she believes she "deserves," one in which she can use her education. The staff at the career office do not believe that she currently has the attitudes, skills, or appearance that would make her employable in the corporate world.

---------------------------- ❖ ----------------------------

Louise is a 52-year-old white female from a prominent, wealthy Anglo-Protestant family. Her husband recently left her for another woman. She had maintained their expensive home and entertained his colleagues for 22 years. She had been an active volunteer, working around her husband's schedule and commitments. Behind her facade of perfection, however, lay her misery that resulted from her husband's periodic physical assaults (sometimes resulting in serious bruises) and verbal assaults ("You're fat, ugly, you have no skills and no brains"). She has told no one of her problems, not even her best friend. Because the violence has been well concealed, and because her husband's power and standing in the community is so strong, she thinks that no one will believe her about the abuse, including a judge. She is frightened to be on her own because she must support herself for the first time in her life. Other than being a good hostess in the home, Louise believes she has no occupational skills.

The Barton family, above, exemplifies the "American Dream" of the middle class. They are successful. The two older children attended "good" universities. The offspring are on their way to successful careers, and their parents are very proud of them. However, when Alan began to exhibit difficulties in school, and to aspire to a working-class vocation rather than to a professional career, his family whispered about him because he was "different" and in need of remediation.

If middle-class aspirations and lifestyles are considered normal and desirable, non-middle-class values give rise to subtle feelings of embarrassment, inadequacy, and shame. Annie's disappointment that her college degree didn't result in achieving the American Dream of a middle-class life is one such class story. The attitudes, appearance, and behaviors that were valued in her parents' working-class world turned out to be barriers to finding the career she hoped for. Others labeled her as deficient ("The staff do not believe she has the attitudes, skills, or appearance that would make her employable in the corporate world"), when she was merely behaving in a manner consistent with her family's values. Unlike the Barton children, she had to pay her own way through college with needs-based grants, student loans, and part-time work to meet her expenses. She struggled academically, barely making it through her degree. She had particular difficulty with writing assignments because her instructors seemed to require a different use of language than she was familiar with. She believed that by working hard and sticking it out, though, she would raise her status to become "more respectable."

Finally, while many people believe that being a member of the upper class equates with being worry-free, individuals in this class are more isolated than those in other classes. Note that in the third vignette, Louise had hidden her husband's abuse for years (" . . . the violence has been well-concealed, and because her husband's power and standing in the community is so strong, she thinks that no one will believe her about the abuse, including a judge"). People in her class often feel pressure to maintain respectability at virtually all costs. She bore her burden alone because she was too ashamed to admit to anyone that she had problems.

The experiences and dilemmas of each of these individuals are rooted in social class. Class-related attitudes, values, and behaviors will be treated in this chapter as stories or narratives that people tell about what they expect, hope for, and know. The readers of this chapter are asked to reflect on their own class story, and its relationship to the experience of social life, as they explore the issues in class-alert counseling.

Social class intersects with other cultural factors, such as race and gender, to form lives. However, for the purposes of this chapter, the examples and stories presented are somewhat homogeneous. This, of course, is not the case in a culturally diverse society.

The chapter begins with definitions of class, then presents the notion of classism, continues with a discussion of counselor bias, and concludes with recommendations for class-alert practice.

Definitions and Implications of Class

The next sections of this chapter will discuss some of the many ways in which social class is defined in the literature and experienced by individuals. It begins with criteria for determining one's class; presents some of the ways in which subjective class is associated with values, gender roles, and family life; and ends with a discussion of the relational nature of class.

DEFINITIONS

Everyone experiences class, yet it is often invisible. It influences how individuals think, what they assume, what they expect, and how others treat them. A basic distinction will be made here between "socioeconomic status" (SES) and "class" (or social class). Although the terms are often used interchangeably, they describe different aspects of class.

SES is an objective notion (Marger, 1999; Zweig, 2000). It is usually measured by household income, education, and/or occupation (Marger, 1999; Zweig, 2000). By contrast, the term "social class" has a subjective quality. It is people's percep- tions about the social group to which they and others belong (Liu, Ali, Soleck, Hopps, Dunston, & Pickett, 2004). Social class indicates assumptions, rules, and hidden meanings that are shared among those of a similar class. For example, if an individual grew up in a middle-class family, she or he may have found the Barton family's expectations (in the first vignette) about achieving postgraduate education and professional status to be "normal." The fact that Alan wanted to become an automobile mechanic would have a very different meaning for them than it would for a working-class or poor family, who might be proud that their child aspired to a skilled occupation such as mechanic.

In this chapter, the terms may sometimes be used interchangeably. However, most often, unless SES is specifically indicated, the term "class" will be used because counselors work with clients' subjective experiences of their and others' status. The following discussion explores social class from three perspectives: the objective, subjective, and relational.

Objective Dimensions of Class

The classic sociological definition of class is based on combinations of three factors: income, occupation, and education (Hollingshead & Redlich, 1958; Zweig, 2000). Based on these criteria, groups can be roughly divided into rank- ings that may include upper class, upper middle class, lower middle class, work- ing class, the working poor, and the underclass. There are no distinctive markers that distinguish cutoffs from one class to another. Table 12.1 outlines Marger's (1999) categories of class.

Objective Descriptions of Class

The following are brief descriptions of these objective class distinctions. Note that while the highest and lowest classes are quite distinct from one another, the broad categories of "middle class" are much less so.

The Upper Classes. Individuals in the upper classes at the current time are predominantly Anglo American Protestants who were born into their posi- tions (Kliman & Madsen, 1999; Marger, 1999). In the upper class, according to Marger, income is largely derived from inherited wealth, investments, and real estate, rather than from wages. Upper-class individuals are likely to hold major shares in large corporations. Their occupational positions are highly esteemed in society. Individuals in this class have significant authority and make important societal decisions, such as creating corporate or public policy and making large-scale financial deals. A high percentage of U.S. presidents,

Table 12.1   Categories of SES

	% of Population	Annual Household Income	Education	Examples of Occupations
Upper	<1	>$1 Million	Prestigious prep schools, colleges	Corporate executives with enormous ownership of shares in companies
Upper Middle	18–20	$75,000– 1 Million	College, post-graduate training	Physicians, attorneys, engineers, scientists, professors
Lower Middle*	20–30	$35,000– $75,000	High school, some have college degrees	Middle managers, nurses, skilled technicians, craftspersons, retail sales workers, police, firefighters, public school teachers, small business owners
Working*	25–30	$25,000– $40,000	High school, some college	Skilled, semi-skilled factory workers; bank tellers; truck drivers; routine computer programmers; postal workers
Working Poor	12–15	$12,000– $15,000	Jobs require least education	Housekeepers, waiters and waitresses
Underclass	9–10	<12,000		Unemployed, work "under the table"

SOURCE: Marger (1999).

NOTE: *These two are combined in some of the discussion below, due to shared values and lifestyles.

for example, were born into upper-class families (e.g., the Roosevelts, Kennedy, the Bushes).

The Upper Middle Classes. The upper middle class is generally distinguished from the classes below it by the criterion of a college education. Middle-class occupations include the professions and upper management positions. These occupations command a high degree of respect, for example, physicians, attorneys, college professors, and corporate CEOs. This segment of the middle class has greater income, occupational prestige, and social power than do those in the classes below it.

The Lower Middle and Working Classes. The lower middle and working classes are the least clearly definable and most diverse. While many in these two groups have attended some college, the percentage of college graduates in these categories is far below that of the upper middle class. Annie, in the second vignette, is an example of a working-class college graduate. The working class may include a broad range of occupations of both blue- and white-collar workers. Jobs tend to be relatively routine and procedure-driven, with little opportunity for creativity or innovation and with little authority. Working-class occupations include licensed practical nurse, receptionist, trash collector, medical technician, plumber, police officer, customer service representative, and technical help desk personnel. Incomes are generally below society's median. Most lower middle- and working-class individuals are paid an hourly wage rather than an annual or monthly salary.

The Poor: Working Poor and Underclass. The poor, or lower class, are defined as individuals or families whose income or assets either fall below the official U.S. government poverty line or are slightly above it. There are two categories of poor people: the working poor and the underclass. A further distinction can be made between situational and generational poverty, that is, those who are temporarily poor and families who have been chronically poor over at least two generations. These will be discussed in turn.

The Working Poor

The working poor are those who are poor but who work at jobs. They drift in and out of poverty, experience periodic unemployment, and earn wages that are too low to enable them to rise above the poverty line. Their jobs require the least education and are the least desirable and the least skilled, for example, restaurant servers and day laborers.

The Underclass

Members of the underclass derive their income primarily from social welfare funds. They may also operate on the margins of the mainstream economy, for example, working "under the table" or engaging in petty crime. In the latter case, income may actually be quite high, but economic security is tenuous and temporary because it may be partly derived from illegal work activities (Kliman, 1998). Although all ethnicities are represented in this group, the underclass in the United States disproportionately comprises African Americans living in urban areas (Marger, 1999).

Situational and Generational Poverty

People can be poor in two general circumstances: situational and generational (Payne, 2001). Situational poverty is a transient condition resulting from a lack of resources due to a particular event such as death, divorce, unemployment, or chronic illness. Those who experience situational poverty may have acquired the education, cultural capital, attitudes, and aspirations that are typical of the middle or working classes, but they are experiencing a temporary reduction in income. They may identify with middle- or working-class values and strive to restore their former status. A graduate student is one example of a person who might be experiencing situational poverty. In pursuit of a career, many students temporarily subsist on student loans and part-time jobs. They know that they will be "poor students" for a relatively brief time. In the meantime, they continue to maintain their previous interests and social networks and identify with their previous lifestyles.

Generational poverty, by contrast, is more pervasive. It spans at least two generations (Payne, 2001) and may include those in Marger's (1999) working poor and underclass categories. Individuals in generational poverty may be caught in the "victim" system (Pinderhughes, 1982), which is a vicious cycle in which individuals must adapt to both oppression and poverty. These adaptations then become permanent patterns in communities in which barriers to opportunity and education limit the chance for achievement, employment, and skill attainment (Payne, 2001).

Subjective Dimensions of Class

Class is also experienced at a personal level. The subjective experience of class can be generalized to some degree, although individuals vary greatly on the subjective level. Individuals within a social class are socialized toward particular values, attitudes, and lifestyles. Class influences preferences for entertainment, foods, leisure activities, tastes in the arts, and patterns of speech. For example, those in the upper classes may tend to play golf or tennis, drink fine wines, and drive classic luxury vehicles, while those in the working classes may enjoy bowling, drink domestic beer, and drive pickup trucks. Some of those choices are related to access to money, while others are associated with peer influence (Kliman & Madsen, 1999; Pinderhughes, Dodge, Bates, Pettit, & Zelli, 2000).

Attitudes toward family life, education, and work roles are also class-related and learned in the family. The following discussion reviews the literature on class-related differences in cultural patterns and lifestyles. It is important to remember that there is a great deal of within-group variation in a class. These generalizations are not meant to stereotype. They should be read as approximations that might help counselors to be alert to hidden client assumptions and aspirations.

Characteristics of Class Culture

Much of the following discussion will focus on those in the middle, working, and poor classes, that is, the groups from which most clients come. It should be noted that the private lives of the upper class are not studied as much as other classes because they tend to maintain greater privacy in their affairs (Kliman & Madsen, 1999).

OVERVIEW OF CLASS VALUES

In general, middle-class values are represented by individualism, the work ethic, a desire for material gain, expectations of upward mobility, an action orientation, and an internal locus of control (Bellah Madsen, Sullivan, Swidler, & Tipton, 1996). The Barton family, in the first vignette, exhibited these very typical middle-class characteristics and values.

These values are not necessarily shared by those in lower social classes, partly because of a lack of opportunities (Bellah et al., 1996). Those in the working class generally find identity from groups, such as friends, family, religion, or recreational groups. That identification with the group contrasts with the more individualistic identity of the middle classes around career and other individual statuses (Sennett & Cobb, 1977).

Working-class individuals are often pragmatic and value functional, rather than reflective, thinking (Shelvin, Zandy, & Smith, 1999). In the working and poor classes, communication tends to be direct, even blunt. Emotions are often expressed vividly, and arguing is usually seen as acceptable.

One value held in common by the middle and working classes is the work ethic. There are some class differences, however, in its expression. For working-class individuals, work means providing for the family, having a good job, and working hard, particularly for men. That focus contrasts to the middle class, where professionals derive personal identity from their careers. Time is money for those in the working class because they are usually paid an hourly wage. By contrast, a middle-class professional is commonly paid a monthly or yearly salary. Working class culture tends toward the functional and practical. It is focused on getting things done (Shelvin et al., 1999).

For poor persons who are experiencing generational poverty, much of life operates on a survival basis (Payne, 2001). Low-income neighborhoods are more dangerous, with poorer municipal services, more deterioration, and higher crime than middle- or working-class neighborhoods (Evans, 2004). As a result, life is dominated by a survival, present-time orientation. Individuals generally live in the moment, do not consider future ramifications, and tend to be fatalistic. Relationships are important for survival, and there is fear and resistance to leaving the community. The ability to entertain, tell stories, and have a sense of humor is highly valued because they provide a diversion from the difficulties of daily living (Payne, 2001).

The next sections describe subjective experiences of class in some specific areas, including (1) marriage, (2) childhood and parenting, and (3) education. Table 12.2 summarizes some of these trends. Each trend is just that, a general possibility that a high percentage of people in that grouping will exhibit those values and behaviors. As Chapter 3 made clear, individuals can be more or less enculturated, acculturated, and/or multicultural in the subjective aspects of social class.

Table 12.2   Summary of Some Subjective Dimensions of Class

	Upper	Upper Middle	Lower Middle and Working	Poverty
General	Often born into class Family traditions and history	Upward mobility Materialism Individualism Future orientation Make things happen Be productive	Many resist class mobility Identity derived from the group	Fear about leaving community Relationships important for survival Survival orientation Live in present Fatalistic
Marriage, Gender, Family Roles	Patriarchal Men have more power Division of labor rigid Men attend to familyfortune Women arrange social and home life, entertain, manage household and children	Egalitarian Women pursue careers, financially independent Marriage and children occur later Family role conflict for women, work-family balance Physical displays orverbal expressions of love	Patriarchal Marriage and children occur earlier Both parents usually work Men show less emotion Affection tied to rules and chores	Traditional Rely on marriage or domestic partnerships for economic survival Poor black women expect to support themselves Gender roles restricted Men work hard physically Women take care of men Men show less emotion Affection tied to rules and chores
Childhood and Parenting	Supported by trust funds Children leave home for boarding school or travel Pressure to carry out parents' choices of	Teens relatively free of family or work obligations Children remain home until they leave for college Children have choices	Teens may work to pay expenses or contribute to the family Older children may do housework, care for younger siblings	Teens may work to pay expenses or contribute to the family Children considered adults upon marriage and/or full-time employment

	Upper	Upper Middle	Lower Middle and Working	Poverty
	schools or marriage partners	Competence, achievement, curiosity, self-direction, self-control, and responsibility encouraged	Transition directly from secondary school to work Respect for parents Obedience to authority Physical punishment	Respect for parents Obedience to authority Physical punishment
Education	Best private universities Entry through name and connections	Parents actively involved in children's schooling College, graduate, and professional degrees Entry through academic achievement	Excluded from and resentful of schools Trade, technical, and two-year schools Entry sometimes nonselective College may be source of tension for families who resist class mobility	Parents feel disconnected from schools School subjects unimportant and irrelevant
Career	Managing finances, investing, volunteering, leadership roles, pursuing hobbies	Career choices based upon self-fulfillment, good pay, and career progression	Occupational security and predictability Expects to be a worker	Jobs are about making enough money to survive

MARRIAGE AND FAMILY ROLES

Gender roles vary greatly, and somewhat paradoxically, among all of the classes. Upper-class marriages are typically quite patriarchal, with the husband having greater business, government, social, and marital power. He may control his wife's access to money and require her to account for her expenditures. This imbalanced power relationship may seem surprising because the upper-class wife usually has a college degree. However, the division of labor in upper-class marriages tends to be rather rigid. Men are responsible for the family's finances, and women maintain a high public profile, often through charity work. Women are also expected to manage the household and the children, arrange their social and home life, accompany their husbands on business or social trips, and entertain lavishly (Wolfe & Fodor, 1996). Louise, in the third vignette, illustrates some of these phenomena.

Middle-class marriages tend to be more egalitarian than those in working- and upper-class families (Stillson, O'Neil, & Owen, 1991; Wolfe & Fodor, 1996). In the middle class, there are less strictly defined gender roles. Young women are expected to pursue careers and to be financially independent (Dickerson, 2004). However, the prevailing belief that young women can "have it all" creates conflict and thus a struggle to balance work and family roles. Middle-class couples tend to marry and have children later, often waiting until their mid-thirties or later so that the wife can establish her career (Leeder, 1996).

Working-class and poor women, by contrast to the middle class, often rely on marriage or domestic partnerships for economic survival (Wells & Zinn, 2004). Marriages tend to be traditional, in the sense that women are expected to take care of men's domestic needs (Payne, 2001). Out of economic necessity, however, both partners in working-class and poor families are usually employed. They often rely on relatives for child care. This is especially true for poor African American women, who generally expect to have to work to support themselves due to the effects of institutional racism on poor black men (Wells & Zinn, 2004). Working-class parents often sacrifice their own wants and needs to provide for their children because disposable income is typically lower than for middle and upper classes (Shelvin et al., 1999).

A number of other characteristics of working-class and poor individuals are worth noting. For the poor and the working class, family ties are highly valued, and family members typically stay close to home rather than relocate for career advancement (Shelvin et al., 1999). Finally, men in working-class and poor families tend to show less positive emotion than those in the middle class, with affection tied to rules and chores rather than physical displays or verbal expressions of love.

CHILDHOOD AND PARENTING

A second subjective dimension of class culture is related to rearing children. A key characteristic of upper-class childhood is that upper-class youth are often supported by trust funds rather than parental wages. Thus, children have little concern about earning a wage income or learning daily money management or domestic skills. However, financial support may be coupled to family expectations and obligations, and children can be threatened with disinheritance for not carrying out parents' choices of schools or marriage partners (Wolfe & Fodor, 1996).

The middle class and the working and poor classes have contrasting parenting styles. Middle-class parents generally value their children being curious and self-directed and want them to demonstrate self-control and responsibility (Luster, Rhoades, & Haas, 1989). These characteristics prepare them to succeed in managerial and professional occupations. Middle-class parents encourage competence and achievement (Minton, Shell, & Solomon, 2004). By contrast, working-class parents are likely to value obedience to external authority, use physical punishment, and restrict the actions of their children (Luster et al., 1989; Minton et al., 2004). These behaviors ostensibly prepare working-class children to succeed in subordinate adult work roles.

It follows that class affects young persons' work responsibilities. Upper-middle-class adolescents are relatively free of serious family or work obligations, although they may work for luxuries. By contrast, lower-middle- and working-class teens often work to pay expenses through high school (Kliman & Madsen, 1999). They may even contribute financially to the family. In the working and poor classes, older children often carry responsibilities for housework and for younger siblings because parental wages are so low that child care is unaffordable.

How long and when children stay in the family home is related to class. Whereas children in upper-class families may leave home for boarding school or for travel, middle-class children typically leave home to attend college. Members of the lower social classes are likely to make a transition directly from secondary school to work or to enter the military (Blustein et al., 2002). If they work locally, they generally stay in the family home. Poor and working-class children are considered adults when they marry and/or get full-time employment, which could occur as early as age 16 (Kliman & Madsen, 1999). Parents with limited resources may look forward to relieving their financial load. Thus, the sooner a working-class young person can start to earn a living, the fewer financial stresses there will be on the family.

EDUCATION AND CAREER

The attitude toward education can be radically different among the social classes. Middle-class parents, regardless of ethnicity, value reading and literacy (Bialostok, 2002; Haynes, 2000) and are actively involved in their children's schooling (Diamond & Gomez, 2004; McNeely, Nonnemaker, & Blum, 2002). They expect their children to attend college, and they actively help them meet competitive standards for college admissions. It is becoming increasingly common for middle-class individuals to also attend graduate or professional schools before beginning a career. The Barton family, in the first vignette, was typical in this regard. Upper-class children are expected to attend the best private schools and universities. Admission to such institutions is often guaranteed through name and connections rather than only through academic achievement (Wolfe & Fodor, 1996).

Those in the working class are likely to value basic education as a means to achieving a good job rather than for the inherent value of learning and ideas. On the other hand, too much education is looked down upon in the working class (Shelvin et al., 1999). Because many lower-middle- and working-class families resist class mobility (Gorman, 1998), attending college can become a source of family tension. This trend may be changing. As the labor market requires more training, more working-class youth are pursuing higher education, often in public, community, or technical colleges, and financing themselves through loans (Kliman & Madsen, 1999). This was the case with Annie, in the second vignette, who sought upward class mobility. Her family did not know how to help her, nor did they have the financial resources to do so. Therefore, she paid her own way at the local state four-year college.

In the poor class, school is often seen as foreign. School subjects are considered unimportant and irrelevant because they do not relate to getting along in life. The experiences and worldviews of poor families are often at odds with the middle-class culture of schools. Therefore, the poor tend to view education less favorably than do those in higher classes. Parents feel excluded from and resentful of schools and academic learning (Diamond & Gomez, 2004; McNeely et al., 2002). Some barriers to being involved in children's schooling are very basic. Low-income parents often lack transportation and have inflexible work schedules. For example, mothers who enter the work force after being on government aid usually end up with jobs that leave them little choice about working conditions and hours, making it difficult to meet with teachers (Heymann, 2000) or attend school functions. They may lose wages or be threatened with termination if they miss work to attend a school meeting.

Career choices for the middle class tend to be based upon self-fulfillment, good pay, and career progression. Work provides a sense of identity and is an expression of interests and values that is not necessarily the case for those in lower classes. Whereas a middle-class individual may value a professional occupation, those in the working class have high respect for tools and maintenance (Shelvin et al., 1999). Occupational security and predictability predominate over self-fulfillment (Chaves et al., 2004). They may, therefore, take whatever jobs are open and available rather than plan a career. For poor persons, jobs are about making enough money to survive, rather than being about fulfillment and advancement. This value fits with their learned fatalism and with the nature of jobs that poor persons see around them.

CHANGE IN CLASS STATUS

It is possible for an individual to have the subjective values of one class, yet, by virtue of income, education, or occupation, to fall into another class. This juxtaposition is particularly true for those who change class positions in adulthood because many class-related values persist, regardless of changes in income. As individual values and worldviews are learned within one's class of origin, it can be difficult for those who cross class lines successfully to ever fully unlearn the set of values and perspectives with which they were raised (Liu et al., 2004; Tingle, 2004). This disjuncture between existing values and new class position can produce tensions and conflicts, both intrapsychically and within families. For example, a janitor with a high school education who grew up in a working-class family and who wins the lottery would probably not feel comfortable at the upper-middle-class country club, despite being able to now afford its yearly membership fees. Conversely, a professional engineer who has been laid off and currently works as a clerk at the local hardware store is not likely to change her or his leisure interests and social network merely because of a new economic class position.

Those who do cross class lines sometimes exist in a state between two worlds, where they often feel different from the group they have adopted, harbor "secret doubts" about belonging, feel ashamed, and hide their class background in order to manage a new, tenuous identity (Granfield, 1991). This dissonance may be a particular problem for those who are the first in their families to attend college. They may find themselves at a disadvantage because they have not grown up with middle-class values, yet they find they must learn them in order to succeed and "fit in."

Before continuing, complete Activity 12.1.

ACTIVITY 12.1

Identifying Your Social Class of Origin

Review both Tables 12.1 and 12.2. Which class grouping best describes your family of origin?

Does your family fit into more than one category?

Did your grandparents or other family members grow up in a different class from your parents?

If so, which best describes their class position(s)?

RELATIONAL DIMENSIONS OF CLASS

The relational dimension of class refers to a person's economic and social status being intertwined with that of others (Kliman, 1998, p. 51). Each class is dependent upon the others to maintain class status. For example, those in the upper or middle class may utilize domestic services, such as a housekeeper or a gardener. These lower-class jobs have relatively low status and low pay. Yet, if no one were willing to perform these services, those in the upper classes could not maintain a lifestyle free of menial work. The classes are intertwined. Conversely, those in the lower classes depend upon those in higher classes for their livelihoods. This can be problematic in the sense that it sets up an unequal power relationship that has the potential for oppression. The relational nature of class is important because it affects how resources are distributed.

The relational dimension also affects how satisfied or dissatisfied a person is likely to be with her or his class situation (Kliman, 1998; Lucal, 1994; Vanneman & Cannon, 1987; Zweig 2000). Classes can "see" each other, either in person or through the media. When individuals are exposed to the manners, values, and material things of those in a higher class, they may become dissatisfied with their own class-related lifestyle. For a poor person, the experience of scarcity amid affluence invites devaluation by others and, consequently, devaluation of oneself. Beyond the basic necessities, satisfaction is not usually based on the number of material possessions but on how much a person has in relation to someone else. People living in relative poverty today may actually have more material goods and income security due to governmental entitlement programs than did most persons during the Great Depression, but they may be more dissatisfied. It has been said that a person who was selling apples on the street during the Great Depression could be relatively satisfied with her or his economic class, in the context of near-universal economic distress. That same person might bemoan her or his fate when surrounded by affluence. One of the implications of the relational nature of class, with its embedded systems of hierarchy, is classism, which will be discussed next.

Classism

The misuse of hierarchy and power were discussed in Chapter 2, under the topic of oppression. Classism is a specific expression of oppression. Classism can take three forms: First, it can be external, in the form of one person's attitudes and behaviors toward another who is of a different class. Second, it can be internalized. Finally, it can be institutionalized. The following section begins with a discussion of external classism and then moves on to descriptions and examples of internalized and institutional classism. Before reading farther, the reader is encouraged to complete Activity 12.2.

ACTIVITY 12.2

What Is Your Response to This Story?

Read the following scenario. Notice your reactions, perhaps relating it to a similar situation that you might have encountered.

Laura is a 34-year-old single mother of three school-aged children. She is participating in a support group for women who are adult survivors of sexual abuse. She is the only woman in the group who is receiving government assistance. The other participants either work outside the home or have partners who provide financially for the family. Laura mentioned that she was going home to make baked ham for dinner, with artichoke salad, fresh asparagus, and ice cream for dessert. Two of the other women clearly resented the fact that Laura, who is receiving food stamps, was able to purchase what they saw as expensive food. They considered themselves to be self-sufficient, in contrast to their view of people on government assistance. As they saw it, they had worked hard, put themselves through graduate school, and were paying off student loans. You, as a counseling intern, have been working as the facilitator of this group for four months and have, in fact, not been able to afford to treat yourself to a movie and dinner out for quite some time, and you and are also paying off your student loans. You are exhausted from putting in internship hours while also working at a job at which you get paid very little. Your resentment starts to interfere with your ability to provide Laura with the support, respect, and positive regard she needs. One woman said exactly what you were thinking: "I could never afford such expensive meals."

What was your initial reaction to Laura's statement that she planned to seemingly splurge on an expensive meal with food stamps? Did you feel somewhat critical of her decision to use food stamps in this way?

Have there been times when you've been unable to offer support for and respect to others because of the decisions they have made?

What alternative explanations would change the significance of this story for you?

The purpose of this Activity is to help you to be more deliberate and less judgmental in response to clients' stories.

EXTERNAL CLASSISM

External classism refers to negative prejudice and discrimination by an individual from one class toward someone of another class. Classism in the United States is largely based on the desire for and expectation of upward social mobility, a value especially prevalent in the American middle classes (Bellah et al., 1996). The middle-class values of focusing on the future, delaying gratification, abstract reasoning, doing well in school, and getting a college degree can be the basis for classism because these values come from privileges that those in lower classes don't have. The middle or upper classes have sufficient material and cultural, and therefore emotional, resources to gain the rewards of these values.

The classist dimension of this formula for class participation is that Americans often attribute these values purely to the individual, as if they didn't generate from opportunities and the environment. If someone doesn't succeed, it is assumed that she or he is lazy or deficient in some way and not that there are social structural factors at play (i.e., institutions such as jobs, education, and informal groups that are set up to favor members of one group over the other in different ways, as discussed in Chapters 2 and 4). This failure to acknowledge social structural factors in turn affects social policy, for example, the existence of compensatory financial aid and academic assistance programs in schools and colleges.

"Downward classism" occurs when one holds negative stereotypes and discriminates against those of lower social classes. It may include making jokes at the expense of the poor or assuming that workers in low-status jobs are stupid, uneducated, unworthy of respect, irresponsible, hostile, or illogical (Lott & Saxon, 2002).

There can also be "upward classism," in which lower-class persons stereotype more affluent people, putting down their tastes and manners. That type of classism carries less power in actual societal terms than does downward classism. Counselors may be guilty of upward classism when they underestimate the problems of affluent clients.

INTERNALIZED CLASSISM

Internalized classism refers to the process by which individuals come to believe negative attributes about their class and themselves as members of that class. It occurs when dominant class groups are portrayed as the models for "normal" human relationships. In the process, other class-related lifestyles and attitudes are presumed to be of lesser value. Members of subordinate class groups subsequently find it difficult to believe in their own abilities (Liu et al., 2004).

Internalized classism influences self-concept and relationships with others. For example, children come to believe in their own abilities through interactions in the classroom. When educational values between parents and teachers differ, teachers even see the children as less competent, treat them accordingly (Hauser-Cram, Sirin, & Stipek, 2003), and hold lower expectations for academic success (Alexander, Entwisle, & Thompson, 1987). These lower expectations become internalized. Children then expect less from themselves and perform to those expectations, resulting in a self-fulfilling prophecy. Counselors should be alert to internalized classism.

INSTITUTIONAL CLASSISM

Institutional classism is the class dominance that becomes embedded in the social structure and perpetuates class inequality. It occurs largely because upper- and middle-class groups make most of the policy decisions relative to the distribution of resources. They define what is health and what is illness. These policies and norms can function to systematically provide advantages to the upper and middle classes over working-class and poorer persons.

Institutional classism can be found in schools and colleges. Due to disparities in school funding, school districts attended by poor and minority children receive far less money than the districts that serve white and more affluent children (Education Trust, 2005). Poor schools are staffed by less-qualified teachers. For example, 27 percent of high school math teachers in low-income school districts majored in mathematics in college, compared with 43 percent of those in more affluent school districts (Ingersoll, 1999). There is a similar trend for colleges, where financial aid is increasingly awarded to more affluent students (Nichol, 2003). From 1995 to 2003, college grants to students with family incomes of more than $100,000 increased at a faster rate than to students with family incomes of less than $20,000. When colleges succumb to pressure to inflate their average SAT scores and *U.S. News & World Report* rankings, they make admission decisions that favor the very best students, most of whom are from highly educated, affluent households, at the expense of low-income peers (Hancock, 2006).

Institutional Classism in Public Policy

Lower-class individuals are often not consulted when policies are made. Public policies and funding decisions, which are partly based on voters' and politicians' attitudes, disproportionately and negatively affect the poor and working class. An example of institutional classism in government is the government providing poorer municipal services to low-income neighborhoods, resulting in greater physical deterioration (Evans, 2004). Or it can be as simple as building private beachfront property with no public access, so that poorer persons are excluded from those facilities. Classism is also present when government watchdogs target Medicaid recipients for fraud, but do not do so equally for the service providers who file false claims. Another instance of classism occurs when middle-class families can legally transfer assets while remaining eligible for Medicaid funding in nursing homes, yet basic health services for the poor are reduced (Wegner & Yuan, 2004).

Counselors can counter institutional classism by providing models, incentives, information, strategies, and encouragement for poorer clients to pursue education and financial aid. On the public policy level, classism is countered, for example, when investment in low-income neighborhoods is encouraged by government incentives and assistance. Programs that create low-income housing and neighborhood rehabilitation, with public input, can improve people's lives through public investment.

Mental Health and Class Differences

Class position wends its way into all aspects of a person's life, including experiences of emotional distress. Thus, class has profound implications for counselors. The following sections review class differences in the prevalence, prognosis, and symptoms of mental disorders, and some possible explanations for these observations.

Virtually all indicators of physical and mental health favor persons of higher socioeconomic status. For example, blue collar workers experience more psychological distress than do white collar workers (Belek, 2000). Poorer persons get sicker more often, for longer periods, and with more serious consequences than people with sufficient means. Further, such effects are cumulative; those who have experienced hardship over a sustained period of time are at the greatest risk (Evans, 2004).

PREVALENCE OF DISORDERS

Counselors should be aware of the relationship between social class and health so that they understand the class-related hardships faced by some of their clients. Counselors of children, for example, should know that children in lower socioeconomic classes are more likely to have problems in at least three areas: (1) severe disorders requiring hospitalization, (2) higher injury rates, and (3) higher rates of school absences due to ear or respiratory infections (Chen, Matthews, & Boyce, 2002).

Counselors in all settings should be aware that both adults and children in lower social classes experience higher rates of depression, anxiety, substance abuse, and antisocial behavior. Rather than blame individuals for the behaviors that accompany these conditions, counselors should consider the context in which these conditions develop—namely, stress, a lack of resources, and environments characterized by discrimination based in classism.

Table 12.3 presents a summary of some correlations between various disorders and social class. For example, body weight, body image, and eating disorders are related to class, age, race/ethnicity, and gender. Lower-class individuals are generally heavier than those in upper classes. Severe obesity is thought to cause or aggravate depression (Dixon, Dixon, & O'Brien, 2003) and can lead to other health problems such as diabetes. It should also be noted that regardless of actual weight, white women tend to be more dissatisfied with their body size than men and black women.

Persons in the upper classes experience many of the same mental health problems as others, which contradicts stereotypes that the wealthy "have it made." Individuals with higher class standing can even be disadvantaged in some ways. For example, middle- and upper-class individuals diagnosed with schizophrenia experience more depression and hopelessness when coping with career losses than do lower-class persons. Since they have higher occupational aspirations (Lewine, 2005), they regret the loss of their career potential to a greater extent. Another example of wealth being a disadvantage is the case of affluent women with histories of child abuse and domestic violence who feel ashamed to seek help for those problems, as illustrated in the case of Louise

Table 12.3   Social Class and Mental Disorders

Variables	Major Findings	Authors
Depression, anxiety, chronic diseases, and SES	Low income and low SES are associated with high rates of mental disorder, chronic diseases, depression, anxiety, and diabetes.	Belle, 1990; Everson, Maty, Lynch, & Kaplan, 2002; Judda, 1995; Lewis et al., 2003; Lynch, Kaplan, & Salonen, 1997; Norman, 2004
Substance use in lower classes Substance use in low-income minorities	Alcohol regulates feelings of anxiety and depression; substance abuse is influenced by culture and class. Persons in high-poverty neighborhoods are exposed to violence and disorder, experience more health problems, and abuse alcohol than persons in more affluent neighborhoods.	Nichter, 2003 Fauth, Leventhal, & Brooks-Gunn, 2004
Substance use in upper classes	Fifty percent of upper-middle-class and upper-class adults are frequent drinkers, compared to 30 percent of the general population. Affluent children engage in frequent substance use.	Luthar & Latendresse, 2002; Priory Group, 2004
Depression, antisocial disorder, ADD	Anxiety, depression, antisocial disorder, and attention deficit disorder each has a unique relationship with SES.	Miech, Caspi, Moffitt, & Wright, 1999
Obesity	Obesity is inversely related to social class; lower-class women are more obese than upper-class women; black women are more obese than white women and all men; white men are more obese than white women.	Rand & Kuldau, 1989; Wardle, Waller, & Jarvis, 2002
Dieting behavior and race, class	Upper-class girls tend to diet, count calories, binge, and engage in vigorous physical exercise, whereas boys and women of color do not.	Drewnowski, Kurth, & Krahn, 1993; Ogden & Thomas, 1999
Anorexia nervosa and class	Serious and chronic anorexia is higher in middle classes.	McClelland & Crisp, 2001
Antisocial behavior	Higher rate of antisocial behavior in lower class	Dishion, French, & Patterson, 1995
Suicide	Higher rates in males of lower social class	Kposowa, 2001

from the third vignette. They may, instead, present with chronic pain syndromes and other psychosomatic complaints (Kendall-Tackett, Marshall, & Ness, 2003).

REASONS FOR CLASS DIFFERENCES IN MENTAL HEALTH

Several explanations for social class differences in health have been offered. Three common influences of social class will be discussed: the effects of the environment, class-related values, and counselor bias.

Effects of the Environment

Adverse environments have both direct and indirect effects on health. Those who live in poverty are exposed to more crime, violence, and aggressive peers (Evans, 2004). Thus, they are at greater risk for physical and psychological problems due to the quality of these environments (Pilisuk, 1998). The more threatening the neighborhood, the more common are symptoms of depression, anxiety, oppositional defiant disorder, and conduct disorder.

The environment affects physical health directly when poor children live in substandard housing. They are more likely to ingest paint chips contaminated with lead; lead is a known toxin that has adverse affects on intellectual, neurological, and behavioral development. Poor and working-class families are also more likely to live near industrial sites, where industrial pollution and hazardous waste have a direct negative impact on physical and mental health (Downey & van Willigen, 2005).

Environments also have indirect effects on health through increased vulnerability to the effects of stress (Hudson, 2005), and such stress is class-related. Lower-class individuals struggle with inadequate resources and difficulties of daily living. This stress can cause tension and frustration, which in turn affect health (Adler, Epel, Castellazzo, & Ickovics, 2000).

Class-Related Values

Class-related values can contribute to emotional distress in any class. For example, in the upper middle class, excessive pressures to achieve and adolescents' isolation from parents may contribute to depression and substance abuse (Luthar & Latendresse, 2005). Similarly, upper-middle-class family values and wider social pressures to achieve play a part in the development of disorders such as anorexia nervosa (McClelland & Crisp, 2001).

Class Bias in Counseling

Social class is a psychological and social phenomenon that powerfully shapes clients' and counselors' experience (Constantine, 2002; Kliman, 1998). Until now, the counseling profession has failed to substantively focus on the disparity between counselors' own middle-class/professional culture and the varied class cultures of their clients. This, in turn, has led to at least four middle-class assumptions, or potential biases, that must be accounted for in research and practice with non-middle-class clients. These assumptions are that (1) the research that informs counseling theory and practice is objective and unbiased, (2) all mental health issues are intrapsychic, (3) humans are largely self-determining, (4) communication should be extensively verbal, and (5) vulnerability and self-disclosure must be promoted. Each of these will be discussed next.

The assumption of the social sciences is that the research upon which mental health is based is objective and value-free, yet this is clearly not the case. Early research tended to label lower-class persons as deficient, poorly adjusted, and in need of change. Poor clients have been blamed for not following through in counseling, for lacking insight, and for preferring advice and immediate solutions (Baum & Felzer, 1964; Brill & Storrow, 1960). The poor have also been characterized as having intellectual limitations, low creativity, restricted capacity for emotional depth, and lack of impulse control (Lott & Saxon, 2002; Shen & Murray, 1981). These broad generalizations about poor persons ignore the realities of living in stressful environments, especially the matter of chronic and persistent lack of resources. For example, those who drop out of counseling are more likely to be poor and to lack insurance coverage for mental health treatment (Edlund et al., 2002). The above pronouncements reveal a lack of understanding about daily living in poverty and blame victims for their own problems.

The second assumption of counseling is that individual problems are intrapsychic and are rooted in childhood and family experiences. That assumption can be classist in the sense that responsibility, or sometimes blame, is assigned completely to individuals for problems that may arise from the social context. Consider a father who is a factory worker who works 10-hour days and whose boss is extremely demanding and critical. Upon arrival home after a difficult day at work, he is unresponsive, drinks a beer, and relaxes in front of the TV rather than playing with his children. A counselor might view him as an uninvolved father who should spend more "quality" time with his children. The scenario, however, should also be understood from the working-class perspective. He may be so stressed and exhausted from hard physical labor and ill treatment at work that he has few physical or emotional resources left to give to his family. A counselor who sees this family or the children would need empathy for the father's plight. With that empathy, the counselor can generate solutions for all members of the family rather than merely demonize the father.

The third assumption of traditional middle-class counseling is that people have relatively free choices to determine their lives. This view assumes that clients can and should fully control their lives and their environments, that they should have a goal orientation, and that they need to take action to solve their problems (Katz, 1985). This extreme emphasis on free choice is rooted in the American Anglo-Protestant middle-class notion of "rugged individualism," which declares that individuals can achieve anything they wish if they try, regardless of social context. Working-class and poor clients are more likely than others to believe that forces outside themselves control their lives—a phenomenon sometimes called fatalism. This acceptance of fate is countercultural to the American middle-class ethos. However, acceptance, rather than striving, can be adaptive. It is one coping mechanism for working-class and poor persons. Fatalism is often based on generations of very real experiences where people have had very few choices in their lives in areas of work, housing, or public policies that may affect them. Counselors must acknowledge that worldview while discussing the notion of relative choice in client's lives.

The fourth middle-class counseling assumption is that communication must emphasize verbal processing, accompanied by counselor reflective listening. Such a style is more relevant for the dominant, white middle class. As noted, those in the lower and working classes are more likely to take a direct, pragmatic approach to communication. Working-class and poor clients usually seek counseling because of extreme emotional distress resulting from a crisis in their lives that needs immediate attention (Chalifoux, 1996; Leeder, 1996). When immediacy issues predominate, clients look for a problem-solving and efficacy approach that will help them manage their lives, rather than personal growth or insight into emotional patterns (Chalifoux, 1996; Leeder, 1996).

A fifth assumption of middle-class counseling is that self-disclosure is valuable, even necessary, for problems to be solved. However, the poor are not as likely as middle-class clients to reveal their vulnerabilities. In fact, it may even be unsafe for some clients to do so. Consider the case of an unmarried mother who is trying to survive with only social service assistance. She would face very real consequences—losing her social service benefits—should she reveal that the father of her children is living with her, providing emotional and financial support. While she may feel guilty about lying to the authorities, this is one of the moral compromises that she must make in order to get her material and emotional needs met at the same time.

The above five assumptions play out in counseling practice. When one is counseling working-class and poor clients, class is a factor in the following areas: diagnosis, counselor focus, values, stigma, and work with upper-class clients. Each of these topics will be addressed in the next segments. The section will conclude with a discussion of potential bias in two particular settings, schools and agencies.

BIAS IN DIAGNOSIS

The prevalence, definitions, and symptoms of disorders are infused with cultural meaning and interpreted through the lens of social class. Sometimes, class differences in mental health can be accounted for by looking at the counselor. In order to counteract classism in diagnosis, counselors must uncover their class-based assumptions and values, beginning with "excavating" their own class identifications—whether they were raised in a middle-, upper-, working-, or poor class culture.

When conceptualizing the nature and extent of a client's problem, a counselor can be biased in either a positive or negative way due to social class. For example, the classist assumption that more material wealth is better may lead the counselor to wrongly assume that those from higher classes are in good mental health (Csikszentmihalyi, 1999; Leeder, 1996; Robinson, 1999). In fact, there may be a tendency to under-diagnose upper-class clients and to over-diagnose those in lower classes. Negative stereotypes held by counselors toward lower-class clients may lead to pathologizing attitudes and behaviors that may be perfectly functional in a lower-class environment.

BIAS IN COUNSELOR FOCUS

The counseling profession selectively studies issues based upon assumptions about economic class. One example of mismatch can be found in career counseling. Career theories were founded on middle-class assumptions, a point made by Richardson (1993): "The concept of career that implies some sort of developmental progression over a period of time is inherently biased in favor of middle-class populations that have access to occupational opportunities that enable progressive movement over time" (p. 427). This assumption is borne out in practice. For example, career guidance is one function of a school counselor. Theoretically, the counselor is available to all students, so access should not be an issue. Yet, in practice, guidance is often limited to helping students with the college selection process—selectively attending to middle-class concerns. For those students not bound for college, counseling is usually limited to graduation requirements, ignoring career planning issues. Class-alert counselors should familiarize themselves with career theories that acknowledge the constricted expectations that are related to lower social class status (Gottfredson, 1981). By doing so, counselors may recognize that career choice is not so free, and they can consider the vocational aspirations of all students, not just those who are college-bound.

BIAS IN VALUES

Middle-class values include being self-fulfilled, self-sufficient, respectable, and thrifty. Those values are often not possible for poor persons. Counselors must recognize the compromises that poor clients must make in order to survive. For example, a working-class or poor woman may choose to stay in an unhappy marriage to ensure that her children get what they need financially. While a middle-class counselor may earn sufficient income to provide for a family on her or his own, a poor client may not earn enough, even with two incomes, to provide even a basic standard of living. Clients may want confirmation of the value of their choices, which are grounded in survival (Leeder, 1996).

STIGMA ATTACHED TO COUNSELING

Even though counselors themselves are likely to treat counseling as a positive experience, counselors should be aware of the common class-related stigma that is attached to being in counseling. Low-income clients are often embarrassed about seeing a mental health provider (Edlund et al., 2002). The very idea of the therapeutic relationship, with its disclosure, vulnerability, verbal sharing, and expression of emotion, is unacceptable in some groups, particularly among the poor and the working class (Chalifoux, 1996; Schore, 1990). For members of those classes, attending counseling often implies that they are deficient in some way, that they are not doing something "right."

BIAS AGAINST UPPER-CLASS CLIENTS

Since most of the discussion concerns poor and working class clients, a special mention of bias against upper-class clients is warranted. Upper-class clients are not immune to the effects of class bias. Similar to the problem of stigma for lower-class clients, problems are often hidden in upper-class families. Because of the upper-class (combined often with the Anglo-Protestant) cultural imperative of not making problems public, upper-class persons are not likely to initiate conversations about difficult emotional topics with either friends or counselors. This might lead counselors to underestimate upper-class clients' difficulties (Wolfe & Fodor, 1996).

As mentioned previously, counselors who come from middle- or working-class families may also have negative preconceived notions about those in the upper classes, which may affect their ability to provide support. Louise, in the third vignette at the beginning of the chapter, presented herself in counseling as aloof, which might have been interpreted by a class-unaware counselor as a superior attitude. A class-alert assessment revealed severe depression, anxiety, and feelings of worthlessness. This awareness led to Louise getting the help she needed.

CLASS BIAS IN SCHOOLS AND SCHOOL COUNSELING

Schools sometimes perpetuate classism through bias in favor of middle-class norms. One such school-related instance of classism is evident in the area of measured intelligence. Higher IQ scores are reported in upper- and middle-class children (Suzuki & Valencia, 1997) than in working- and poor-class persons. These facts are often attributed to biological differences rather than environmental factors. However, lower-class parents are more stressed, have fewer resources, and have more demands on their time than do higher-class parents. Even the definition of intelligence itself reflects a class bias. Individuals from lower socioeconomic classes often hold a practical view of intelligence, viewing with suspicion those who are "book smart" but who cannot get by in the everyday world using practical resourcefulness (Leeder, 1996).

Other examples of class bias in schools relate to the clothing, appearance, and resources expected. For example, poor families cannot afford music lessons for their children. The result is that talented poor children are less likely to experience being in costly activities such as orchestra or band. Box 12.1 demonstrates a case in which class differences between school staff and a poor family almost resulted in an inappropriate referral, which could have led to a negative outcome had a class-alert counselor not intervened.

CLASS BIAS IN COMMUNITY AGENCIES

Mental health services are not easily available for poorer persons (Leeder, 1996; Schore, 1990). The lack of access for this group of people lies in stark contrast to the need: Poorer persons have more mental health problems, especially depression, than do those from other classes (Belle, 1990).

Cost is one class bias factor. Community service boards and other agencies are charged largely with serving the poorest clients. Because poverty is associated

---

BOX 12.1   A Class-Conscious School Counseling Intervention

A classic example of class-related problems with basic needs is the case of Alice, a 13-year-old girl. Alice's teachers brought her to the attention of the counselor because she was friendless. She was ostracized because she wore the same dirty outfits day after day, never seemed to wash or comb her hair, and exhibited body odor.

Alice's teachers had also referred her to the health office, hoping that if she knew how to practice personal hygiene, including combing her hair, she would be less offensive to her peers and she could then develop a support network. From a middle-class perspective, a regular shower is normative and thus is the standard from which judgments about those living in poverty are made.

School personnel concluded that the parents had neglected their children. School staff pressured them to change their attitudes and behavior, threatening to report the parents to Child Protective Services when no changes were forthcoming.

Fortunately, the school counselor was sensitive to class circumstances and able to understand the child's experiences. It turned out that the family lived in a rented trailer and had no washing machine and no hot water. Alice had been showering at a friend's house, but she didn't feel comfortable imposing on them any more often than once a week.

During a home visit, the counselor learned that the parents were loving toward their children. However, they didn't always have enough money to pay their rent in a timely manner and the landlord had neglected, in turn, to repair the hot water heater. Thus, the family had lived without hot water for several months. Alice didn't want to risk alienating one of the few friends she had by asking her to use her shower too often.

Reporting the family for neglect would have been an abuse of the reporting system and insensitive to the needs of the family. The counselor arranged for Alice to use the school's gym shower as an additional resource. Without being condescending, she also volunteered to help Alice learn to style her hair. Counseling sessions were utilized to practice hair styling, thus providing a creative activity that was focused on something other than problems.

with greater prevalence and severity of problems, the need for services is greater than are available resources. Because social service agencies operate with limited funding that is frequently subject to budget cuts, they can provide mental health services for only the most extreme problems, leaving many issues, like anxiety, career distress, and most versions of depression, unattended.

Another cost issue for working-class clients and poor clients is their strong resentment about the cost of counseling in private practice or other settings (Leeder, 1996)—that is, being charged what they see as high fees for "only" talking with someone. Even for those who have insurance, a $50 co-pay may well represent one-fourth of a week's take-home pay for a poor, working single parent. Thus, more direct interventions, a solution focus, self-help resources, and sliding scales are more class sensitive when clients are concerned with finances.

Class-Alert Counseling: Assessment and Intervention

Now that class-related mental health issues and counselor class bias have been discussed, positive strategies for class-alert counseling will be presented. This section is organized around the three themes of counselor self-awareness, class-alert client assessment, and the practices that follow from that assessment. The case of Jean will be used to illustrate these guidelines.

COUNSELOR SELF-AWARENESS

Awareness is a primary competency in culturally alert counseling. It guides what information a counselor considers and what interventions are used. Table 12.4 presents six self-awareness questions that counselors can ask themselves about class.

The questions in Table 12.4 represent a switching of perspectives, from one that assumes a common middle-class worldview and circumstance to one that sees unique values and environments that affect members of different classes. With lower-class clients, counselors can, therefore, properly attribute at least a portion of client difficulties to socially oppressive practices. The following sections will discuss class-alert assessments and interventions that honor class-related experiences.

ASSESSING FOR CLASS CONTEXT

The general recommendation for assessing clients' situations is that counselors should elicit class-related values during the assessment process. The notion of culturally educated questioning, as described in Chapter 16, suggests that the counselor use her or his prior knowledge of class issues to inquire about the client's experience.

Table 12.4   Class Awareness Checklist for Counselors

When working with a client who has a different class background from their own, the following questions, adapted from Parry and Doan (1994), can assist counselors to be class alert:

Do I have a negative label or story about this client based on different class values?

What class-related factors and influences might have led to her or his view that I need to understand?

Do clients seem to show "resistance" because they believe that their class stories cannot be spoken to the counselor?

What gender roles, family experiences, expectations, and stresses are related to class?

Am I even being seen as the enemy due to class differences?

Do I have a conception of class-related strengths, that is, how clients can thrive within the context of their social class?

One model that can help the counselors do a comprehensive, class-alert assessment is Wilbur's Integrative Model (Wilber, 1995, 1996). It will be adapted to class issues here. The model is conceptualized in four quadrants (see Table 12.5), representing (1) Objective Observations ("Outside") and (2) Subjective Experiences ("Inside") across (3) Group and (4) Individual levels. Wilbur's model can alert the counselor to look for each of those four dimensions of a client's life. Each of the quadrants is explained further below, with some specific examples related to class.

Assessing the "Outside"

The "Outside" (right side) represents characteristics that can be measured objectively without understanding the client's internal state of mind. At the Individual level (upper right), these Outside observations may include results of psychological testing and a mental status exam. The Group level (lower right) represents trends and group outcomes that have been observed by social scientists, of which the individual may not be aware. Such components might include class-related health trends and educational attainment. The counselor can consider these in assessing clients' experiences, strengths, and sources of difficulty.

Assessing the "Inside"

The "Inside" (left side) represents the subjective characteristics of a client's experience. At the Individual level (upper left), Inside consists of client thoughts and feelings that can be elicited through dialogue between the counselor and the client.

Table 12.5   Wilber's Integrative Model Applied to Social Class

	Inside	*Outside*
Individual	Client's subjective thoughts and feelings made known through dialogue in the counseling interview	Results of psychological and IQ testing Nonverbal behaviors Mental status exam Symptom patterns
Group	Parenting practices Gender roles and expectations Attitudes toward education and careers	Class-based health outcomes Working conditions Occupational positions Educational attainment SES criteria

SOURCE: Wilber (1995, 1996).

At the Group level (lower left), the Inside alerts the counselor to the class-related images and symbols that give meaning to client experiences. "Group-Inside" includes the "social-in-the-individual," such as gender expectations, parenting practices, and career expectations. These are the classed meanings that the client brings to the world. By being alert to these meanings, the counselor can subsequently help the client recognize them and change, if that is desirable, or honor and validate their experiences.

The following actual case will illustrate how Wilber's Integrative Model can be used to incorporate social class factors into client assessment. The actual disposition of the case will be presented toward the end of this discussion. The case will also guide the rest of this discussion of class-alert counseling.

The Case of Jean

Jean is a 55-year-old home health aide who was referred to the mental health agency because she had been feeling anxious, depressed, and was having difficulty sleeping. She had been eking out a living but was having increasing difficulty paying her bills. Several assignments had, in her words, "not worked out" because of "personality conflicts" and tardiness. She didn't drive, and her records indicated that she had a DWI. She was being evicted from her apartment in two weeks and had no place to go. During the initial interview, Jean was very agitated: "I don't need someone to talk about my feelings. I know how I feel. I need help NOW!" (See Activity 12.3.)

ACTIVITY 12.3

Initial Assessment of Jean

Based on the information so far, what is your initial assessment of Jean?

What else would you like to know about Jean to help you with your assessment?

During the session, the counselor learned that Jean's mother had died three months ago and that Jean missed her terribly. Jean also said she lost her driver's license because she had been "tricked" into pleading guilty to DWI. However, Jean avoided any discussion related to drinking alcohol. Jean also expressed anger because she had gotten the "runaround" when she tried to contact the social services office to apply for assistance. The counselor suspected that chemical dependency might be the source of many of Jean's personal, financial, and work-related problems.

The counseling agency required the counselor to make a diagnosis at the first meeting. However, due to Jean's agitation, it was difficult to gather sufficient information to do so. Based on the evidence, however, the counselor considered an initial diagnosis of a nonspecific anxiety disorder and substance dependence. (See Activity 12.4.)

ACTIVITY 12.4

Considering the Individual-Outside Factors in the Case of Jean

Given this new information, and considering the types of data that are utilized in the "Individual-Outside" quadrant of Wilbur's Integrative Model (upper right quadrant in Table 12.5), does your impression of Jean change in any way?

What other information would help you to understand Jean and her situation?

What is your "Individual-Outside" assessment of Jean (e.g., possible diagnosis, aspects of her mental status)?

CLASS-ALERT ASSESSMENT OF JEAN

Given the pressure to come up with a diagnosis, there are many chances for the counselor to make class-biased judgments and to engage in misperceptions. A class-alert assessment would take into account the assumptions that a middle-class counselor might make based on her or his own experience and contrast them with working-class assumptions. A way to do such a class-alert assessment is to consider data from Wilber's four perspectives. Table 12.6 shows such an assessment. It was based partly on using basic counseling skills (reflection of feelings, questioning and probing, advanced empathy) in the initial interviews.

It might be seen from the analysis that the differing class-based assumptions of a middle-class counselor and a working-class client could lead to some misunderstandings. For example, given Jean's presentation as demanding, uncooperative, and rude, along with the loss of her license due to a DWI, it would be easy to attribute Jean's troubles only to her inability to perform satisfactorily at her job due to an alcohol problem.

CLASS-ALERT INTERVENTION WITH JEAN

Intervention with Jean focused on four matters: (1) the need for immediate attention to Jean's survival needs, (2) the client's following the hidden rules for survival, (3) Jean's communication style, and (4) client substance abuse as a consequence of the loss of employment as well as the cause of work-related problems. Each will be discussed in turn.

Paying Immediate Attention to Survival Needs

One pressing problem for Jean was the urgency of her survival needs. With financial, legal, housing, and food problems bearing down on her, Jean felt desperate, fearing that she would have no place to live or anything to eat. Given that working-class and poor clients often seek counseling only when they are in crisis (Chalifoux, 1996; Leeder, 1996), Jean's immediate, pressing concerns were temporary financial assistance and affordable housing. She had previously depended on her mother to help her manage her life. However, since her mother's death, she simply did not know where to turn for help. The counselor should acknowledge her fears at this point and focus on her immediate needs.

Recognizing the Hidden Working-Class Rules

As can be seen in Table 12.6, Jean's job as a computer programmer had previously provided enough money for her to get by. After she was laid off, however, finances became increasingly problematic. Had the counselor not considered the Group-Inside quadrant, she or he might not have understood that Jean knew the hidden rules of survival in the working class. These rules include obeying policies and taking orders in return for keeping a relatively well-paying, secure job.

Table 12.6   Assessing Jean's Situation Using Wilber's Model

	Inside	*Outside*
Individual	Frustrated and scared, no money, will have no place to live in two weeks, social services doesn't return calls Was a computer programmer for large manufacturer, but unable to find comparable work since being laid off seven years ago Home health aide assignments become more scarce, for reasons noted above Mother was her only support system, paid her bills, filed her taxes for her	Appears anxious, agitated Speech demanding, blunt Uncooperative Record of DWI, license suspension
Group	*Hidden working-class rules:* Subordination and passivity in the face of authority *Strong work ethic:* Obey the rules, take orders in return for job security Union negotiates contracts, ensures everyone treated fairly Communication style blunt, direct Conformity to external authority, therefore preference for advice in counseling	People in lower social classes have higher incidence of depression, anxiety, and substance disorders. Migration from industrial to service economy results in low-paying, part-time, working-class jobs with no benefits, erosion of economic security

Those rules served her well as long as steady work was available. Her skills in this regard were exemplified by her having held her job for over 20 years.

The Group-Outside quadrant revealed that Jean was a low-level computer programmer. Based on Table 12.1 presented earlier in this chapter, this is considered a working-class occupation characterized by little autonomy and requiring little formal education beyond high school. For all of her working life, job security, adequate income, and good benefits prevailed for this type of work. She had had no reason to believe that this would change. However, with the new "service economy," low-level computer programming jobs have been disappearing, and the rules that Jean knew were no longer relevant. She was desperate and consequently took the home health aide job to survive because, as she said, "It was available, and near my home." She thought that it would be only temporary. Jean was unaware that these unskilled service jobs would not allow her to earn enough money to meet her basic survival needs. Jean had never had contact with a social service system in the past, so she had no idea how to navigate the complex networks that have been established in order to discourage welfare-savvy clientele from "cashing in" on the social service system.

Being Alert to Class-Related Communication Style

The direct and blunt manner in which she expressed her needs were normative in her working-class culture. A counselor who was accustomed to polite clients who talk about their feelings could easily view Jean as having a difficult personality accompanied by an anxiety disorder, rather than as an individual under stress caused by a crisis in her life. Yet, given her very realistic fears for survival and the direct, blunt communication style often seen in working-class persons, Jean was merely expressing her needs to the counselor. She rightly believed that a counselor's sympathetic listening was not going to solve her immediate problem of finding a place to live. Her communication style and her demands were consistent with the scope and intensity of her presenting problems.

Identifying Mental Symptoms as a Consequence of Substance Abuse

A further misleading piece of evidence was Jean's DWI. Because she had lost her license, the counselor might have assumed that Jean contributed to her own problems by her drinking. The counselor might simply assume that if Jean received treatment, she would be better able to manage her life. Yet, it is also known that substance abuse can sometimes be a consequence of an issue like long-term unemployment. Drinking is a legal way to self-medicate, to dull the pain of the difficulties of daily living.

The counselor could also interpret Jean's symptoms of agitation and worry as symptoms of an anxiety disorder. Yet, given her life circumstances, these symptoms might not fit the criteria for a disorder because her anxiety is based on a very real concern for her survival needs. Her anxiety could be considered normal and expected, given her life circumstances. (See Activity 12.5.)

ACTIVITY 12.5

Further Considerations in the Case of Jean

Based on all of the information so far and based on Wilber's model, what else would you like to know to help you reinterpret Jean's story?

What strengths can you see in Jean that might be viewed as a deficit by someone who was not class alert?

THE CLASS ALERT COUNSELOR'S ACTIONS

Fortunately, Jean's counselor was class alert. First, the counselor paid attention to trust and rapport-building, using reflection and self-disclosure. For example, the counselor appropriately mentioned the loss of his own mother a few years ago. He also used empathic responses to Jean's desire to be soothed, for which she used alcohol. These steps were important because lower-class clients often mistrust the "professional" middle-class atmosphere of counseling.

In the process of listening to Jean, the counselor noted the meaning that Jean made of her situation. He acknowledged both her anxiety and her strengths. Thus, the focus was not only on negative emotions and difficulties. The counselor was able to attribute much of Jean's behavior to extreme distress due to the social context, rather than to her having a difficult personality or only a substance use problem. The counselor pointed out to Jean that she felt powerless because she was no longer able to provide for herself, due to structural unemployment. He validated three positive assets: (1) Jean's strengths in being able to survive the loss of her mother when she had no other source of support, (2) her ability to keep her job for 20 years, and (3) the fact that she had been able to complete some home health assignments despite having no license.

By eliciting Jean's employment history and by being aware of current labor market trends, the counselor was able to prioritize Jean's needs in a class-consistent way and provide the direct assistance that Jean needed. He helped Jean contact the housing authority and gave Jean a direct contact for social services so that she could avoid the automated voice messaging system that had frustrated her.

Once her food and shelter needs were addressed, Jean's counselor helped her to understand the broader social problems associated with a service economy, thereby locating the problem within the context rather than blaming Jean for her situation. Because Jean's employment situation was not of her own doing, the counselor referred Jean to a government-funded displaced-worker retraining program, where those who have been laid off are eligible to receive retraining funds. These actions were far more useful at this point to Jean than only exploring her emotions and meanings.

Summary

This chapter has explored the major groupings of social class and their implications for counseling. Class was defined first through objective categories that influence life chances and power. Class is also experienced subjectively, and class groupings are associated with differences in values, lifestyles, family roles and expectations, parenting practices, and attitudes toward school and work. The relational dimension of class contributes to attitudes and experiences of external, internalized, and institutionalized classism, which are based in differential distribution of resources and power.

There are class differences in the prevalence and severity of mental disorders, with those in the lower classes typically at a disadvantage due to stress and inadequate resources. However, the relationship between class and health is complex. Complex relationships among social class, gender, and ethnicity must be accounted for. And not all health disorders are greater for the lower classes. Problems can occur in individuals in all classes, and those in the upper class are also disadvantaged in some ways due to the need to maintain social status and keep problems hidden.

Helping professionals are not immune to class bias, and counseling research and practice has been slow to recognize classism. There has been a tendency to blame clients for their own problems and to blame them for not engaging in the counseling process when, in fact, it is the helpers that have not understood the class experiences of their clients. Some specific suggestions for class-sensitive counseling assessment and interventions were offered.

Counselors must not only learn about class. They must develop greater consciousness of their own class identities. In gaining a perspective on their own class narrative, middle-class counselors can learn that not all clients share the same class-related values, aspirations, or life goals as themselves. When a client's perspective and needs conflict with the middle-class value system of counseling, it is the counselor's responsibility to bridge the class gap (Lott, 2002) and to avoid imposing middle-class solutions when other, more workable solutions can be found (Payne, 2001). Counselors can help clients reinterpret their life stories to see strength and resilience in the face of classism rather than deficits and pathology.

References

Adler, N. E., Epel, E. S., Castellazzo, G., & Ickovics, J. R. (2000). Relationship of subjective and objective social status with psychological and physiological functioning: Preliminary data in healthy white women. *Health Psychology, 19,* 586–592.

Alexander, K. L., Entwisle, D. R., & Thompson, M. (1987). School performance, status relations, and the structure of sentiment: Bringing the teacher back in. *American Sociological Review, 52,* 665–682.

Baum, O. E., & Felzer, S. B. (1964). Activity in initial interviews with lower-class patients. *Archives of General Psychiatry, 10,* 345–353.

Belek, I. (2000). Social class, income, education, area of residence and psychological distress: Does social class have an independent effect on psychological distress in Antalya, Turkey? *Social Psychiatry and Psychiatric Epidemiology, 35,* 94–101.

Bellah, R. N., Madsen, R., Sullivan, W. M., Swidler, A., & Tipton, S. (1996). *Habits of the heart: Individualism and commitment in American life.* Berkeley: University of California Press.

Belle, D. (1990). Poverty and women's mental health. *American Psychologist, 45,* 385–389.

Bialostok, S. (2002). Metaphors for literacy: A cultural model of white, middle-class parents. *Linguistics & Education, 13,* 347–371.

Blustein, D. L., Chaves, A. P., Diemer, M. A., Gallagher, L. A., Marshall, K. G., Sirin, S., et al. (2002). Voices of the forgotten half: The role of social class in the school-to-work transition. *Journal of Counseling Psychology, 49,* 311–323.

Brill, N. Q., & Storrow, H. A. (1960). Social class and psychiatric treatment. *Archives of General Psychiatry, 3,* 340–344.

Chalifoux, B. (1996). Speaking up: White, working class women in therapy. *Women and Therapy, 18,* 25–34.

Chaves, A. P., Diemer, M. A., Blustein, D. L., Gallagher, L. A., DeVoy, J. E., Casares, M. T., et al. (2004). Conceptions of work: The view from urban youth. *Journal of Counseling Psychology, 51,* 275–285.

Chen, E., Matthews, K. A., & Boyce, W. T. (2002). Socioeconomic differences in children's health: How and why do these relationships change with age? *Psychological Bulletin, 128,* 295–329.

Constantine, M. G. (2002). The intersection of race, ethnicity, gender, and social class in counseling: Examining selves in cultural contexts. *Journal of Multicultural Counseling and Development, 30,* 210–215.

Csikszentmihalyi, M. (1999). If we are so rich, why aren't we happy? *American Psychologist, 54,* 820–827.

Diamond, J. B., & Gomez, K. (2004). African American parents' educational orientations. *Education & Urban Society, 36,* 383–427.

Dickerson, V. C. (2004). Young women struggling for an identity. *Family Processes, 43,* 337–348.

Dishion, T. J., French, D. C., & Patterson, G. R. (1995). The development and ecology of antisocial behavior. In D. Cicchetti & D. J. Cohen (Eds.), *Developmental psychopathology: Risk, disorder, and adaptation* (Vol. 2, pp. 421–471). New York: Wiley.

Dixon, J. B., Dixon, M. E., & O'Brien, P. E. (2003). Depression in association with severe obesity: Changes with weight loss. *Archives of Internal Medicine, 163,* 2058–2065.

Downey, L., & van Willigen, M. (2005). Environmental stressors: The mental health impacts of living near industrial activity. *Journal of Health & Social Behavior, 46,* 289–305.

Drewnowski, A., Kurth, C. L., & Krahn, D. D. (1993). Body weight and dieting in adolescence: Impact of socioeconomic status. *International Journal of Eating Disorders, 16,* 61–65.

Edlund, M., Wang, P. S., Berglund, P. A., Katz, S. J., Lin, E., & Kessler, R. C. (2002). Dropping out of mental health treatment: Patterns and predictors among epidemiological survey respondents in the United States and Ontario. *American Journal of Psychiatry, 159,* 845–851.

Education Trust. (2005). *The funding gap 2005: Low-income and minority students shortchanged by most states.* Retrieved October 1, 2006, from http://www2.edtrust.org/NR/rdonlyres/31D276EF-72E1-458A-8C71-E3D262A4C91E/0/FundingGap2005.pdf

Evans, G. (2004). The environment of childhood poverty. *American Psychologist, 59,* 77–92.

Everson, S. A., Maty, S. C., Lynch, J. W., & Kaplan, G. A. (2002). Epidemiologic evidence for the relation between socioeconomic status and depression, obesity and diabetes. *Journal of Psychosomatic Research, 53,* 891–895.

Fauth, R. C., Leventhal, T., & Brooks-Gunn, J. (2004). Short-term effects of moving from public housing in poor middle-class neighborhoods on low-income, minority adults' outcomes. *Social Science & Medicine, 59,* 2271–2284.

Gorman, T. (1998). Social class and parental attitudes toward education: Resistance and conformity to schooling in the family. *Journal of Contemporary Ethnography, 27,* 10–44.

Gottfredson, L. S. (1981). Circumscription and compromise: A developmental theory of occupational aspirations. *Journal of Counseling Psychology, 28,* 545–579.

Granfield, R. (1991). Making it by faking it: Working-class students in an elite academic environment. *Journal of Contemporary Ethnography, 20,* 331–351.

Hancock, K. (2006). *Promise abandoned: How policy changes and institutional practices restrict college opportunities.* Retrieved October 1, 2006, from http://www2.edtrust .org/NR/rdonlyres/B6772F1A-116D-4827-A326-F8CFAD33975A/0/Promise AbandonedHigherEd.pdf

Hauser-Cram, P., Sirin, S. R., & Stipek, D. (2003). When teachers' and parents' values differ: Teachers' ratings of academic competence in children from low-income families. *Journal of Educational Psychology, 95,* 813–820.

Haynes, F. E. (2000). Gender and family ideals: An exploratory study of black middle-class Americans. *Journal of Family Issues, 21,* 811–837.

Heymann, J. (2000). What happens during and after school: Conditions faced by working parents living in poverty and their school-aged children. *Journal of Children & Poverty, 6*(1), 5–20.

Hollingshead, A. B., & Redlich, F. C. (1958). *Social class and mental illness.* New York: Wiley.

Hudson, C. G. (2005). Socioeconomic status and mental illness: Tests of the social causation and selection hypothesis. *American Journal of Orthopsychiatry, 75,* 3–18.

Ingersoll, R. (1999). The problem of underqualified teachers in American secondary schools. *Educational Researcher, 28,* 26–37.

Judda, L. L. (1995). Prevalence, lifecourse and disability in social phobia. *European Neuropsychopharmacology, 5,* 224–225.

Katz, J. H. (1985). The sociopolitical nature of counseling. *The Counseling Psychologist, 13,* 615–624.

Kendall-Tackett, K., Marshall, R., & Ness, K. (2003). Chronic pain syndromes and violence against women. *Women & Therapy, 26,* 45–66.

Kliman, J. (1998). Social class as relationship: Implications for family therapy. In M. McGoldrick (Ed.), *Re-visioning family therapy: Race, culture, and gender in clinical practice* (pp. 50–61). New York: Guilford Press.

Kliman, J., & Madsen, W. (1999). Social class and the family life cycle. In B. Carter & M. McGoldrick (Eds.), *The expanded family life cycle: Individual, family and social perspectives* (pp. 88–105). Boston: Allyn & Bacon.

Kposowa, A. J. (2001). Unemployment and suicide: A cohort analysis of social factors predicting suicide in the U.S. National Longitudinal Mortality Study. *Psychological Medicine, 31,* 127–138.

Leeder, E. (1996). Speaking rich people's words: Implications of a feminist class analysis and psychotherapy. *Women & Therapy, 18,* 45–57.

Lewine, R. J. (2005). Social class of origin, lost potential, and hopelessness in schizophrenia. *Schizophrenia Research, 76,* 329–335.

Lewis, G., Pebbington, P., Brugha, T., Farrell, M., Gill, B., Jenkins, R., et al. (2003). Socioeconomic status, standard of living, and neurotic disorder. *International Review of Psychiatry, 15,* 91–96.

Liu, W. M., Ali, S. R., Soleck, G., Hopps, J., Dunston, K., & Pickett, T., Jr. (2004). Using social class in counseling psychology research. *Journal of Counseling Psychology, 51,* 3–18.

Lott, B. (2002). Cognitive and behavioral distancing from the poor. *American Psychologist, 57,* 100–110.

Lott, B., & Saxon, S. (2002). The influence of ethnicity, class, and social context on judgments about U.S. women. *Journal of Social Psychology, 142,* 481–499.

Lucal, B. (1994). Class stratification in introductory textbooks: Relational or distributional models? *Teaching Sociology, 22,* 139–150.

Luster, T., Rhoades, K., & Haas, B. (1989). The relations between parental values and parenting behaviors: A test of the Kohn hypothesis. *Journal of Marriage and the Family, 51,* 139–147.

Luthar, S. S., & Latendresse, S. J. (2002). Adolescent risk: The costs of affluence. *New Directions for Youth Development 2002, 95,* 101–122.

Luthar, S. S., & Latendresse, S. J. (2005). Children of the affluent. *Current Directions in Psychological Science, 14,* 49–53.

Lynch, J. W., Kaplan, G. A., & Salonen, J. T. (1997). Why do poor people behave poorly? Variation in adult health behaviors and psychosocial characteristics by stages of the socioeconomic lifecourse. *Social Science and Medicine, 44,* 809–819.

Marger, M. (1999). *Social inequality: Patterns and processes.* Mountain View, CA: Mayfield.

McClelland, L., & Crisp, A. (2001). Anorexia nervosa and social class. *International Journal of Eating Disorders, 29,* 150–156.

McNeely, C. A., Nonnemaker, J., & Blum, R. W. (2002). Promoting school connectedness: Evidence from the National Longitudinal Study of Adolescent Health. *Journal of School Health, 72,* 138–146.

Miech, R. A., Caspi, A., Moffitt, T. E., & Wright, B. R. E. (1999). Low socioeconomic status and mental disorders: A longitudinal study of selection and causation during young adulthood. *American Journal of Sociology, 104,* 1096–1139.

Minton, J., Shell, J., & Solomon, L. Z. (2004). A comparative study of values and attitudes of inner-city and middle class postpartum women. *Psychological Reports, 95,* 235–249.

Nichol, G. (2003, October 13). Educating for privilege. *The Nation,* pp. 22–24.

Nichter, M. (2003). Smoking: What does culture have to do with it? *Addiction, 98,* 139–145.

Norman, J. (2004). Gender bias in the diagnosis and treatment of depression. *International Journal of Mental Health, 33,* 32–43.

Ogden, J., & Thomas, D. (1999). The role of familial values in understanding the impact of social class on weight concern. *International Journal of Eating Disorders, 25,* 273–279.

Parry, A., & Doan, R. E. (1994). *Story re-visions: Narrative therapy in a postmodern world.* New York: Guilford Press.

Payne, R. K. (2001). *A framework for understanding poverty.* Highlands, TX: aha! Process.

Pilisuk, M. (1998). The hidden structure of contemporary violence. *Journal of Peace Psychology, 43,* 197–216.

Pinar, W. (1993). Notes on understanding curriculum as a racial text. In C. McCarthy & W. Crichlow (Eds.), *Race identity and representation in education* (p. 61). New York: Routledge.

Pinderhughes, E. E. (1982). Afro-American families and the victim system. In M. McGoldrick, J. K. Pearce, & J. Giordano (Eds.), *Ethnicity and family therapy* (pp. 108–122). New York: Guilford Press.

Pinderhughes, E. E., Dodge, K. A., Bates, J. A., Pettit, G. S., & Zelli, A. (2000). Discipline responses: Influence of parents' socioeconomic status, ethnicity, beliefs about parenting, stress and cognitive-emotional processes. *Journal of Family Psychology, 14,* 380–400.

Priory Group. (2004). Alcohol for the soul. *Counselling & Psychotherapy Journal, 15,* 10.

Rand, C. S. W., & Kuldau, J. (1989). The epidemiology of obesity and self-defined weight problem in the general population: Gender, race, age, and social class. *International Journal of Eating Disorders, 9,* 329–343.

Richardson, M. S. (1993). Work in people's lives: A location for counseling psychologists. *Journal of Counseling Psychology, 40,* 425–433.

Robinson, T. (1999). The intersections of dominant discourses across race, gender, and other identities. *Journal of Counseling & Development, 77, 73–79.*

Schore, L. (1990). Issues of work, workers, and therapy. *New Directions for Mental Health Services, 46,* 93–100.

Sennett, R., & Cobb, J. (1977). *The hidden injuries of class.* New York: W. W. Norton.

Shelvin, D., Zandy, J., & Smith, L. R. (Eds.). (1999). *Writing work: Working class writers on writing.* Huron, OH: Bottom Dog Press.

Shen, J., & Murray, J. (1981). Psychotherapy with the disadvantaged. *American Journal of Psychotherapy, 35,* 268–275.

Stillson, R. W., O'Neil, J. M., & Owen, S. V. (1991). Predictors of adult men's gender-role conflict: Race, class, unemployment, age, instrumentality-expressiveness, and personal strain. *Journal of Counseling Psychology, 38,* 458–464.

Suzuki, L. A., & Valencia, R. R. (1997). Race-ethnicity and measured intelligence: Educational implications. *American Psychologist, 52,* 1103–1114.

Tingle, N. (2004). The vexation of class. *College English, 67,* 222–230.

Vanneman, R., & Cannon, L. W. (1987). *The American perception of class.* Philadelphia: Temple University Press.

Wardle, J., Waller, J., & Jarvis, M. J. (2002). Sex differences in the association of socioeconomic status with obesity. *American Journal of Public Health, 92,* 1299–1305.

Wegner, E. L., & Yuan, S. C. (2004). Legal welfare fraud among middle-class families. *American Behavioral Scientist, 47,* 1406–1418.

Wells, B., & Zinn, M. (2004). The benefits of marriage reconsidered. *Journal of Sociology and Social Welfare, 3,* 59–80.

Wilber, K. (1995). *Sex, ecology, spirituality: The spirit of evolution.* Boston: Shambhala.

Wilber, K. (1996). *A brief history of everything.* Boston: Shambhala.

Wolfe, J. L., & Fodor, I. G. (1996). The poverty of privilege: Therapy with women of the "upper" classes. *Women & Therapy, 18,* 73–90.

Zweig, M. (2000). *The working class majority: America's best well kept secret.* Ithaca, NY: Cornell University Press.

Gender

13

Kelly L. Wester and
Heather C. Trepal

The scene is a birthing room, with the mother in the late stages of delivery, the excited father recording it all with his video camera, and the doctor ready to receive the newborn infant. "You have a beautiful baby..." The doctor's voice trails off. "A beautiful baby what?" demands the father. "I don't know," the doctor responds, "I can't tell."... Subsequent tests reveal that the baby is chromosomally male; however, it would be easier medically to perform surgery to give him female genitalia (more extensive surgery would be needed for male genitalia, which could not be "fully functional" in adulthood) (Glick & Fiske, 1999, p. 365).

A new client comes in seeking counseling to deal with feelings of depression and helplessness related to a career transition. The transition includes resigning from a lucrative position in the corporate world at a Fortune 500 company to stay at home with three young children. The client mentions wanting to stay home with the children, yet reports frustration over leaving a rewarding career at a company that has offered a pay raise in order to entice the client to stay and wasting so many years in college attempting to achieve this career. The client reports having many hobbies and interests, including cooking, sports, spending time with friends, spending time with family (including a spouse and three kids), and gardening, yet reports recently not having a desire to partake in any of them. The client has no history of depression, nor does the client's family of origin. When asked about family of origin, the client mentions that they are all healthy, alive, and living close to home. The client's mother was a full-time homemaker and the father worked as a corporate lawyer to support the family.

The first vignette describes a scene from a dramatic television series (Glick & Fiske, 1999). This illustration of ambiguous biological sex demonstrates how important biological sex is. Sex is the primary category by which people automatically classify others. Classifying people by sex is an automatic response that has been found to develop within the first few years of life (Beal, 1994), earlier than other characteristics, such as skin color. When an individual encounters another person, she or he is typically categorized as male or female within seconds, and it is usually done unconsciously. Indeed, some readers may have found the second vignette, chosen to illustrate and stimulate thinking on topics covered in this chapter, frustrating to read because the vignette does not specify the biological sex of the client. Before reading the rest of this chapter, answer the questions in Activity 13.1.

Sex classification is important because it helps people determine how to interact with each other and identify expectations of the other person. Have you ever been unsure of someone's sex? If so, what was your response to this person? Did you know how to interact? Did you find yourself attempting to figure out whether the person was female or male throughout the entire interaction? Were you uncomfortable? Activity 13.2 illustrates the power of sex classification in our experience of the world.

In this chapter, the nature of gender and socialization will be presented, followed by specific issues in counseling women and men.

Gender: History, Socialization, Theory

Gender and sex are often confused. A review of the history of these distinctions will help the reader to appreciate the socialization that creates gender roles. That appreciation can then be brought to the counseling session, where gender role conflict can be explored and client options can be discussed.

SEX VERSUS GENDER

Margaret Fuller, whose work profoundly influenced the nineteenth-century women's rights movement, once wrote, "Male and female represent the two sides of the great radical dualism. But in fact they are perpetually passing into one another. . . . There is no wholly masculine man, no purely feminine woman" (Fuller, 1845/1999, p. 103). But societal gender roles often mask that subtlety because biological sex and gender are often seen as interchangeable.

In Western and other societies, people usually attribute characteristics, features, and traits to a person's biological sex. However, this assignment of traits and characteristics is more accurately referred to as *gender*. In Simone de Beauvoir's words, "one is not born, but rather becomes a woman [or man]" (as cited Gilbert & Scher, 1999, p. 3).

ACTIVITY 13.1

Beginning to Examine Gender

Take a moment and write down your thoughts on the following questions related to the second vignette. Other activities in this chapter will further explore your thinking about this client's situation.

Although more information is needed, what might a provisional diagnosis for this client be?

What do you think the prognosis is for this client? Explain your thoughts.

What are the strengths of the client?

What are some weaknesses that might hinder the client's prognosis?

What are a few goals that you would select to work on with this client?

What did you approximate the client's age to be?

The client's race?

The client's biological sex?

Explain your reasoning about how you came to the answers regarding the demographics of the client.

What aspects of the vignette caused you to come to these conclusions?

Many people tend to use the terms *sex* and *gender* synonymously, even though these terms do not mean the same thing. Sex refers to "whether one is born biologically female or male" (Gilbert & Scher, 1999, p. 3). Gender, by contrast, is what is *assumed* of an individual who is born into a particular *sex*, that is, "the psychological, social, and cultural features and characteristics that have become strongly associated with the biological categories of male or female" (Gilbert & Scher, 1999, p. 3). A female's and a male's biological sex roles differ in any society or culture (unless the person is intersexed), due to the distinct male and female sex and

---

ACTIVITY 13.2

Communication Without Identifiers

At home or in class: Have a three-minute conversation with a person in which you describe something you did this weekend with a friend, family member, or partner. However, do *not* mention that person's name and do *not* reveal that person's sex through any identifiers.

After the conversation, comment on the following:

What did you observe about yourself?

Was the conversation easy or difficult?

How much thought did you have to put into not mentioning the individual's biological sex?

Did you succeed in this conversation?

What did you observe about the listener?

Now switch roles in this activity, and for three minutes listen to someone else tell you about an activity that she or he did this weekend with someone, but, again, without revealing the biological sex.

What was it like for you to listen to a conversation without knowing someone's biological sex?

Did you have difficulty listening to the conversation?

Did you attempt to try and figure out the biological sex of the person he or she was talking about?

Were you able to listen to the content of the conversation, or were you too involved in attempting to figure out the sex of the person?

---

reproduction organs. By contrast, a person's gender role consists of the actions and behaviors that are seen as acceptable and appropriate for a female or male to engage in within a culture. For example, in Western society, it is more acceptable for a female to wear a skirt or makeup than it is for a male to do so, while it is more appropriate for males to show aggressive or angry behaviors. Now, take a moment to consider the second vignette above, the one in which the client has left a corporate position. What biological sex did you assign to the client? Does the biological sex you assigned appear to align itself with the characteristic gender roles from your culture or society for males or females?

Despite these strictures, however, men and women cross society's gender lines. For example, female athletes rate themselves as more traditionally masculine (i.e., assertive, independent, and goal-oriented) than non-athletes (Miller & Levy, 1996). Similarly, a man who stays home to raise children may score low on masculine characteristics and high on feminine characteristics, according to Western society.

As a general rule, however, male and female gender roles are distinct from each other, based on the culture in which one is socialized. Societies vary in the specific norms, however. For example, in the Wodaabe tribe in North Nigeria, men, rather than women, are considered to be beautiful and physically attractive.

> At annual gere wol festivals, hundreds of people gather, and the young men spend hours painting their faces and ornamenting their bodies. The men also dance vigorously for seven full nights, showing off their health and endurance. Towards the end of the week-long ceremony, the men line up and display their beauty and charm to the young women. Each woman invites the man she finds most attractive for a sexual encounter. Wodaabe women usually prefer the tallest men with the whitest teeth, the largest eyes, the straightest nose, the most elaborate body-painting, and the most creative ornamentation. (Miller, 2001, pp. 276–277)

Thus, gender is not innately related to an individual's biological sex, but is constructed socially, within the family and society. Activity 13.3 might illustrate the social construction of gender.

Gender Role Development and Socialization

As discussed, sex and gender are not synonymous, although they are inappropriately used interchangeably. In Pearson's (1996) words, "by using 'gender' as a synonym for 'sex,' we confuse the language and perpetuate the myth that biology is destiny" (p. 329). It has been a difficult endeavor to separate gender from sex. This effort and current socialization practices will be briefly discussed.

In the 1970s, feminist theorists made a distinction between sex and gender (Connell, 1999). This distinction was considered to be a breakthrough because it no longer suggested that differences between men and women could be totally ascribed to biology. Instead, the distinction suggested that people could *choose* the gender they wished to adhere to. Mintz and O'Neil (1990) went further in suggesting that it is possible, and common, for men and women to vary in the degree to which they adopt, endorse, and are affected by gender roles.

Although Feminist Theory has suggested that men and women can *choose* their gender, gender roles still have strong association with biological sex in the United States and elsewhere. Men and women are typically socialized to have differing characteristics (e.g., Gilbert & Scher, 1999; Mintz & O'Neil, 1990;

ACTIVITY 13.3

Free Association Activity

Take a moment to look at each of the words listed below.

When you read a word, take note of your immediate mental picture before you move on to the next word.

Then think about the roles you assign to each of these words. What characteristics and status are involved with each?

Female	Male	Fortune 500 CEO
Nurse	Interior Decorator	Firefighter
Surgeon	Homemaker	

More than likely, the mental picture you had of each of the words listed above included a biological sex. For example, most individuals will mentally picture a female when they think of the profession "nurse" or "interior decorator," but will picture a male when they hear professions such as "Fortune 500 CEO," "firefighter," or "surgeon." Although it is more than likely that you attached a biological sex of female or male to each word, none of the words has anything to do with biological sex, except for the first two: male and female. Thus, these are some of the gendered stereotypes you have that have been constructed by Western society. Further, you probably made some assumptions regarding characteristics and status involved with each word.

Which words conjured up nurturing images?

Which ones seemed more autonomous?

Which seem to have higher status in society?

Did any of these characteristics pertain to the biological sex you attached to the occupation?

Prentice & Carranza, 2002) and to be viewed as "opposites" based on their biological sex. Gilbert and Scher (1999) depicted these differences as the Traditional Model of "Opposite" Sex (Gender) Identity. This Traditional Model, which pits men and women against each other as opposites in every respect, portrays the dominant U.S. gender formulation. In that model, males and females are conceptualized differently in various aspects of life (e.g., biological sex, life roles, personality, and sexual partner), and one's gender identity is prescribed directly according to one's biological sex.

Gender identity is the gender with which a person identifies. For example, one person can be a biological male (i.e., sex) but identify more with the typical gendered characteristics of females, such as a desire to be closer and more intimate in relationships, focus on fashion and styles, and getting one's nails done at a salon. Based on this definition of gender identity, therefore, there is no one *true, direct* connection between sex and gender because one's gender identity can diverge from one's biological sex. Gender may be affected by a variety of social structures, including a person's ethnicity, employment status, religion or absence of religion, and family.

The Traditional Model, which treats men and women's sex *and* gender as opposites, results in the gender stereotypes of Western society. Based on these gender stereotypes, biological males should avoid all things seen as feminine, such as expressing emotions other than anger. They should also be more competitive, act tough and aggressive, and have women as sexual partners. On the other hand, women should try hard to make relationships work, should be emotional and expressive, should be the caretaker of a family, should make children a priority, and should have a male as a sexual partner (Gilbert, 1987; Gilbert & Scher, 1999; Kaplan, 1979).

As mentioned previously, and contrary to the Traditional Model, *gender* is not directly related to biological *sex*. Gender is a social construction that occurs within a cultural environment. That process creates what is appropriate and acceptable for women and men within a particular society (e.g., Deaux & LaFrance, 1998). It is a process that starts with birth, when the doctor says, "It's a boy (or girl)"—or even before birth when ultrasound tests are done—and the socialization continues until death.

These prescribed gender roles are revealed early to children. Most children indicate at a young age that they have clearly learned gender roles (Beal, 1994; Etaugh & Liss, 1992) and have a sense of their own gender identity by 24 to 36 months of age (e.g., Powlishta, Sen, Serbin, Poulin-Dubois, & Eichstedt, 2001). Beal (1994) suggested that in the United States, boys are expected to dress in pants, play outdoors, be active, get dirty, and hold their tears back when they are frightened, while girls are expected to stay clean, play close to home, be pretty, and be nice to other children.

It should be noted that gender roles may not be as rigid as they have been in the past. Nevertheless, subtle differences still exist and traditional role restrictions remain in effect. For example, in many current popular songs, the artists sing of a culture where women are valued as sexual objects and men as monetary providers. Another traditional gender role assumption is made when one drives up to the take-out window at a fast-food outlet and orders a child's special meal with a toy in it. The customer will be asked, "boy or girl?" to determine which toy to give to the child. In this case, boys are usually given superheroes or cars—more action-oriented toys—while girls are given little dolls or ponies.

HISTORICAL SHIFTS IN GENDER ASSUMPTIONS

Throughout the years, ideas and stereotypes of gender roles have changed in Western society in many ways (Beal, 1994). For example, before 1920, women were denied the right to vote in the United States because men were supposed to make all the decisions for women. Males were considered to be more rational and, therefore, to know what was in the community's best interest.

Most women did not work outside the home, although it should be noted that working-class women always supplemented the family income by having such jobs as taking in wash, putting up boarders, and taking care of other people's children. The exception occurred during the two World Wars, when women had to take on physical, low-wage factory jobs.

Obviously, times have changed. Women can now vote and run for government office. They commonly work outside the home. Moreover, due to high divorce rates, women are often the major breadwinners of a family. However, women continue to earn a lower average wage than men (Longley, 2004), and they continue to be the primary caregivers in the family. These phenomena may be related to traditionally prescribed gender roles in some cases, but in other cases may be related to the occupational choices women make. Activity 13.4 evokes such a gender expectation.

Women tend to choose occupations that are considered to be more nurturing and service-oriented, such as nursing, teaching, or counseling. These positions also tend to pay less and are considered lower in prestige than occupations that are considered to be more masculine and are typically chosen by males, such as CEO, entrepreneur, and engineer (Betz, 1994; National Center for Education Statistics, 2002; Spraggins, 2000). It is unclear whether or how much these occupational selections are due to innate biological qualities (e.g., many women being more nurturing or caring) or socialization into gender roles.

Although it appears that the idea of males and females being "opposites" has disappeared through the centuries and that gender role socialization has become more flexible, the Traditional Model still holds sway. Over three decades ago, Broverman and her colleagues found that both college students and counselors described different desirable traits for men and women (Broverman, Broverman, Clarkson, Rosenkrantz, & Vogel, 1970). Men's desirable traits reflected "competency," including attributes such as being independent, objective, active, competitive, and logical. These traits were identified by mental health workers as the characteristics of a *healthy adult*. However, these same participants reported that desirable traits for men, and healthy adults, were not the same as the desirable traits for women. Traits desirable for women included warmth and

ACTIVITY 13.4

Stereotypical Assumptions?

Think back to the second vignette from the beginning of the chapter. What biological sex did you assign—male or female? Did the "lucrative position at a Fortune 500 company" sway you in this decision?

expressiveness as well as being less independent, less rational, and less ambitious. These were not seen as key characteristics of a healthy adult. Similar findings have been reported more recently (e.g., Prentice & Carranza, 2002; Wester & Trepal, 2004). Traditional gender prescriptions persevere, with women being seen as more relational relative to societal standards, yet also more dependent and weak in nature. Men are seen as more aggressive and independent, which, in turn, has been viewed as being more competent overall.

THE POWER OF SOCIALIZATION

As described in Chapter 2, humans learn how to think and act through the process of socialization. The socialization that creates gender occurs through families' expectations and modeling, as well as through the media and other environments (such as schools). Parents describe their newborn children differently by gender within 24 hours after birth, portraying their daughters as more delicate and their sons as hardier and more coordinated than their daughters (Rubin, Provenzano, & Luria, 1974). Parents continue to describe their children in much the same way as their children get older, believing that boys are more competent, better able to take care of themselves, and accomplish tasks earlier than girls and describing their girls as needing more protection because they are more fragile and physically vulnerable (Beal, 1994). That latter belief is contradicted by the fact that boys are, in fact, more vulnerable to infectious diseases than are girls when they are first born (Robinson & Howard-Hamilton, 2000).

Many families begin training their children in gender-appropriate behavior through both subtle and overt communications about how to behave, speak, and dress according to the social norm (Philpot, Brooks, Lusterman, & Nutt, 1997) and by modeling behavior, rewards, and consequences. Teachers and children in schools promote conformity to gender-appropriate behavior through direct instruction, encouragement, exclusion in play, and teasing (Martin, 1998; Thorne, 1993).

Some parents report attempts to raise their children at home as "gender neutral." However, when the children go to school they begin to alter their behavior to become more gender "appropriate" (Gilbert & Scher, 1999). Thus, although it has been suggested that adherence to gender identity is a choice, that choice seems to be constricted by the pressure to conform to the gender role deemed appropriate by society for a particular sex. Activity 13.5 provides the reader with an opportunity to examine the role of socialization in gender.

Theories of Gender Development

Over the years, there have been a number of theories of gender development. A common thread running through some of the theories is the "nature versus nurture" debate. This debate surrounds the relative influence of biology (nature) or

ACTIVITY 13.5

Checking In on Socialization

Look again at your responses in Activity 13.1 about the second vignette at the beginning of this chapter.

1. How were the client's parental roles related to the biological sex that you assigned to the client?

   (Did you assign "male" to the client because the client had worked in the corporate world, as had the client's father? Or did you deem the client "female" because the client had a desire to stay home, regardless of a rewarding career?)

2. What were the characteristics that drove you to select the biological sex of the client in the vignette? For example, what did you select as the strengths of the client?

3. Were the strengths more caring and family-oriented or were they more ambitious and career-oriented?

4. Are these strengths, along with the biological sex you assigned to the client, associated with how *you* were socialized (regardless of whether your socialization is through Western society, family values, or cultural messages)?

5. What was it like to grow up in your family?

6. What chores were you responsible for as a child/adolescent?

7. What were your brothers and sisters responsible for, if you had any?

8. Were the chores assigned on the basis of biological sex differences, or were they assigned based on skills?

Fill in the blanks:

9. As a boy/girl I was encouraged to _____
   _____ and from this I learned
   that girls/boys should _____
   _____

10. As a girl/boy I was discouraged from _____
    _____ and from this I learned that girls/boys should not
    _____

11. During traditional holiday meals, women and men performed certain roles, which were
    _____

12. The women and men I was closest to as a child modeled that women and men
    _____

13. Now describe what your family's expectations were for men and women, thinking of both immediate and extended family.

14. Were there any gender-related patterns in the above questions between the men and women in your family? (Were men given specific chores related to outdoor activities or strength-based tasks? Were women given more homemaker chores? Was individuality stressed more than gender-stereotyped activities, behaviors, or expectations?)

15. What messages might this these patterns have given you?

16. How do the gender messages you received in your family play a role in your beliefs about men and women today?

Optional class activity: After you have responded to these questions and sentence starters, discuss this information in a small group or class setting in order to compare the differences and similarities of gender socialization that occurred in various families.

socialization (nurture) on gender. Although a discussion of all theories is beyond the scope of this chapter, the two emphases are briefly described here (see Table 13.1 for a summary).

Although discussion of the impact of gender socialization is emphasized in this chapter, counselors need to understand the biological dimension of gender, which is commonly called sex. Biology has been found to play a role in some differences between men and women. In fact, one extreme view posits that biology is primarily responsible for creating and structuring gender identity. This view places importance on the impact of genes and hormones on the mind and the body.

EMPHASIS ON NATURE IN GENDER DEVELOPMENT

Evidence for the nature dimension includes the significant physical differences between the sexes that can affect behavior. For example, women and men respond differently to medication; they require different dosages for the same body weight. Nature-oriented theorists also cite as evidence of a biological difference the fact that women are much more likely to experience depression and

Table 13.1   Summary of the Biological and Nature-Based Gender Development Themes

Theory	Explanation of Male Behavior	Explanation of Female Behavior	Explanation of Differences	Conclusion
Biological (Nature)	XY chromosomes	XX chromosomes	Attributed to having different genes and hormones; having a different biology explains the differences	Males and females look, act, and respond differently based on their different biological make-up.
Social (Nurture)	Imitate males they encounter in society	Imitate females they encounter in society	Attributed to social learning (rewards and punishments) from others based on societal standards of masculine and feminine behavior	Culture transforms the male or female.

anxiety than are men (Padgett, 1997). For example, hormone secretion differences have been implicated in increased rates of depression among female adolescents (Moreau, 1996).

Other biology-oriented writers have pointed to brain composition and chemistry as playing a role in gender differences and behavior (Quartz & Sejnowski, 2002). Brain tissue has been found to be different between men and women, with females seeming to have the capability to use both sides (left and right hemispheres) of the brain for language and speech, while males' language seems to be associated more with the left side of the brain (Sax, 2005). This may account for why females tend to be more talkative or engage in communication more than males do, which ultimately may enhance relationships.

Additional biological differences have been found between women and men. For example, males hear less well than females do. Thus, a male student who does not seem to be paying attention or is gazing out into space in a classroom setting may not have attention deficit disorder (ADD) but instead may be unable to hear the teacher at the front of the room (Sax, 2005). In addition, from birth, boys are more interested in action-oriented items than in relational items. For example, in a study of 102 infants, males were more interested in a mobile than in a woman's face, while the female babies were more likely to look at the person's face than at the mobile (Sax, 2005). Thus, researchers are suggesting that sex differences in social interest may be "biological in origin." Girls have also been found to be better at tasks that involve object discrimination, thus answering the question of "what is it" versus "where is it," while boys are better at object location (Sax, 2005).

Interestingly, it has been found that at birth and in the first few months after, males tend to be more emotionally expressive than female infants (Mejia, 2005). That fact is ironic in the sense that women tend to be socialized in Western society to exhibit a wide array of emotions. Male infant expressiveness may be related to men's tendency to be more physically aggressive. By age five, very few boys are likely to express feelings other than anger (Pollack, 1998), which can at least be partly explained by the nurture dimension.

EMPHASIS ON NURTURE IN GENDER DEVELOPMENT

Theories that emphasize nurture propose that gender differences largely stem from socialization. In these views, gender is an invisible societal structure that organizes the world into masculine and feminine. These gender categories are conceptualized as polar opposites, and men and women are seen as being rewarded for assimilating their behavior to the socially "correct" pole. For example, women in Western cultures are socialized to dress and look attractive and sexy, which is typically defined as being thin (e.g., Sneddon, 1999). When women do not "achieve" this physical appearance, people tend to have a lower opinion of them; they actually view such women as less intelligent. Such women tend to be more depressed and less satisfied with their body image. They may punish themselves in other ways in order to "fit" this gender stereotype that has been created by society (Davis & Scott-Robertson, 2000). According to the nurture perspective, these behaviors, desires, and actions are not biologically driven, but tend to be socialized and accepted through social learning.

Gender Stereotypes

Gender stereotyping is one of the ways in which people structure, organize, and categorize the world around them (Scher & Good, 1990; Stevens-Smith, 1995). Such stereotyping can be useful in organizing social discourse, and it can seriously limit human potential.

THE FUNCTION OF GENDER STEREOTYPES

Indeed, as noted in Chapter 1, categorizing is an act of assimilation that can be functional. Categorizing is a "cognitive label-saving device" that allows humans to determine quickly how to treat people without having to take in the holistic, unique aspects and the surrounding context for every individual (Glick & Fiske, 1999). Gender stereotypes guide a person's behavior so that she or he fits into expected roles. Such assimilation can act as an organizer that structures society in terms of behaviors, expectations, and personalities. For children, gender acts, in Beal's (1994) words, as "a powerful tool" that helps them to "make sense of their social world" (p. 92). Beal continues, "In other words, gender becomes an 'organizing principle' for children, helping them understand and interpret the behavior of those around them" (p. 92). Gender stereotypes thus help shape a child's development, leading children to master the skills they will require as adults as well as assisting in socializing them so that they "fit" into their culture in terms of what society believes is a well-functioning adult (Beal, 1994).

DRAWBACKS OF GENDER STEREOTYPES

Although gender stereotypes can be functional, they can also have serious drawbacks and implications, both for society in general and for counseling. Gender development theories, whether fundamentally based on biological, social, or psychological assumptions, are still rooted in the "men versus women" paradigm. Thus, although at times they can be helpful, stereotypes can exaggerate the notion of men and women as "opposites," suggesting that behavior, activities, dress, and other traits are directly a result of biological sex (Beal, 1994). When individuals adhere rigidly to the restrictions of gender stereotypes, they constrain their own experiences and abilities and may possibly inhibit or judge others.

Expecting oneself to adhere firmly to a gender stereotype might take away opportunities, perhaps leading to feelings of depression, loneliness, or anger. For example, a woman who adheres strictly to the Traditional Model might give up her career to be a stay-at-home mother and raise her children while her husband goes to work to advance his career and be the breadwinner in the family. That might occur even if her goal in life was to advance in her career and be the CEO of a Fortune 500 company. In another example, a gay male who adheres to gender stereotype might marry a woman and possibly have children with her. In both of these examples, the individuals adhered to the Traditional Model of gender, or what they identified as appropriate expectations for someone of their biological sex. However, placing themselves into the rigid box of a gender stereotype may ultimately lead them into a counselor's office due to depression and disappointment.

Expecting others to adhere to a strict gender stereotype may inhibit and direct interactions with others. Although one can choose the level at which one adheres to stereotypic gender roles (Connell, 1999; Mintz & O'Neil, 1990), violations of gender stereotypes are met with forms of punishment, devaluation, and exclusion (Fiske, Bersoff, Borgida, Deaux, & Heilman, 1991; Rudman & Glick, 1999). Those who deviate from the traditional, expected gender stereotype tend to pay a price (e.g., being teased, being excluded from groups, being less likely to make friends, having a difficult time establishing intimate relationships, or becoming a victim of violence). For example, O'Neil (1982) noted the terms "sissy" for boys and "tomboy" for girls who deviate from gender role expectations. Men who are emotionally sensitive tend to be labeled as weak (Philpot et al., 1997), and boys who play with dolls are more likely to be ostracized by their peers (Bailey, 2003). Women who identify excessively with masculine gender stereotypes tend to be characterized as overly aggressive. It should be noted that men who deviate from masculine gender stereotypes often pay a greater societal price than women who deviate from feminine stereotypes.

In sum, gender stereotypes can be beneficial; however, when adhered to inflexibly, stereotypes can be damaging. It is important, instead, to keep in mind that in actuality, women and men have many characteristics that overlap, leading to the concept of "fluid gender." Gender is fluid in that, for example, both sexes experience sexual desire and similar feelings and emotional reactions (e.g., sadness, happiness, frustration, anger, and pain). In addition, both sexes can perform many of the same occupations and roles within a family (homemaker, breadwinner, parenting). Gender thus can be a constriction on human potential.

Gender and Counseling

Gender, like all culture, is a two-way street in counseling because it is present in both the client and the counselor. That presence may, at times, be central. The presenting concerns that clients bring into counseling can be explicitly related to their gender and may particularly be related to violations of society's gender stereotypes. In turn, counselors themselves come into their work as gendered beings, bringing their own biases, stereotypes, and expectations (Kaplan, 1979; Mintz & O'Neil, 1990). Thus, with the counseling process mirroring the societal context, gender roles influence session content (Mintz & O'Neil, 1990).

There are several important topics to consider regarding gender in counseling. First, a discussion on the typical concerns and experiences of men and women in counseling will be presented. Then, the impact of gender stereotypes in counseling will be presented. In addition, the influence of the four combinations of sex dyads in counseling, namely (a) male to male, (b) female to male, (c) female to female, and (d) male to female, will be discussed.

MEN AND WOMEN IN COUNSELING

According to the Traditional Model of "Opposite" Sex (Gender) Identity discussed earlier, men in Western society are generally socialized to be more emotionally controlled, independent, assertive, powerful, and heterosexual (i.e., be attracted to women), and to be providers (Gilbert & Scher, 1999). It follows, then, that men do not often seek counseling because requesting help goes against the bias to be autonomous, strong, and unemotional. When men do come into counseling, they may have been forced there by a spouse, significant other, friend, or the court system (Allen & Laird, 1991). A small percentage of men may come into counseling on their own volition.

Lest gender stereotypes be promoted in the following sections, it should noted that not all clients fit into the Traditional Model "mold." Also, it should be reiterated that some genuine sex differences exist between men and women.

Counseling Men

In counseling, some men may tend to show avoidant behaviors, such as fidgeting or averting eye contact as a result of fear (Mintz & O'Neil, 1990). As mentioned previously, seeking help is discontinuous with many men's self-concepts and socialization (Allen & Laird, 1991; Wilcox & Forrest, 1992). To receive counseling, men must step out of their "typical" role of being autonomous, aggressive, and in control. As clients, males move into a position of vulnerability, one in which they are challenged to acknowledge weakness (Robinson & Howard-Hamilton, 2000).

When men are in counseling, they tend to present certain main issues, particularly (1) the lack of ability to express emotions (Gilbert & Scher, 1999; Goodman, Koss, & Russo, 1993), (2) violent behavior (Goodman et al., 1993), (3) lack of intimacy and a desire to connect interpersonally (Gilbert & Scher 1999), and (4) career- and work-related stress issues (Gilbert & Scher 1999; Mintz & O'Neil, 1990). In couples counseling, it has been found that men will typically depend on women to express the emotions in the counseling session (Pleck, 1981). For example, instead of crying or stating that he is sad, a male may expect or wait for his partner or wife to mention and/or exhibit these emotions so that he does not have to. This lack of emotional expression may especially occur in the male-client-to-male-counselor dyad (Gilbert & Scher, 1999; Scher, 2001) because men sometimes have an increased difficulty expressing emotions in front of other men.

More information is provided later in this section about the makeup of sex dyads in counseling.

Counseling Women

Women tend to enter counseling more often than men because women tend to be more relationship oriented, expressive, and verbal. When women come into counseling, they are more likely to present with relationship problems, such as fear of upsetting a partner, frustrations with non-expressive male partners, or problems in general with relationships, than are men (Gilbert & Scher, 1999; Mintz & O'Neil, 1990). Women also tend to present issues of low self-confidence, even though that may not be consistent with their actual academic or work performance; feeling marginalized at work; having overwhelmed feelings due to responsibilities and multiple roles and role conflict; dissatisfaction with physical appearance and body image; and sexual harassment or abuse (Gilbert & Scher, 1999). In general, women will be more expressive and show more emotions and affect in counseling than will men.

THE POWER OF GENDER STEREOTYPES AND BIASES IN COUNSELING

Counselors need to be acutely aware of how their own gender socialization and beliefs affect what they consider to be "appropriate" behavior for others, including clients who may or may not fit within the Traditional Model. Thus, it is imperative that counselors examine the stereotypes and biases that they bring into the counseling session.

Most clients and many counselors are unaware of the role that gender plays in their lives. In particular, highly educated counselors often consider themselves to be immune to the influence of gender stereotypes (Philpot et al., 1997). These biases play a role in clinical judgment, diagnoses, and other aspects of counseling.

Counselors' own gender role socialization is a powerful determinant of how they work with clients (Daniluk, Stein, & Bockus, 1995). Counselors form impressions of their clients very quickly (Sandifer, Horden, & Green, 1970; Vogel, Epting, & Wester, 2003), often resulting in inaccurate assumptions and decisions based on easily identifiable information. For example, biological sex is easily identifiable. People are unconsciously classified by biological sex within seconds (Beal, 1994; Glick & Fiske, 1999). Thus, counselors' initial "understanding" of a client tends to be based on biological sex (e.g., Deaux, 1976; Knudson-Martin, 1997; Knudson-Martin & Mahoney, 1996; Stabb, Cox, & Harber, 1997)—or, in actuality, on the assumptions of expected gendered traits of a client's biological sex.

In the next sections, the influence of the various gender dyads will be presented. Then the effects of counselor biases on career counseling, couples and/or family counseling, and diagnosing will be presented. In addition, bias in relation to sexual orientation will be briefly discussed, although that topic is addressed more fully in the next chapter of this book. Activity 13.6 asks the reader to examine assumptions that might influence counseling.

ACTIVITY 13.6

Re-Examining Your Thoughts

Thinking of the second vignette at the beginning of this chapter, respond to the following questions:

Does the sex you assigned and the strengths, weaknesses, or characteristics you selected for the client match the presenting concerns that researchers have shown men and women typically bring into counseling? (For example, since the client is freely expressing depression and battling with multiple roles in life, did you assume the client was female? Or since there is depression over leaving a rewarding career at a Fortune 500 company for childrearing, did you assume the client was male? Or were the characteristics you selected not similar to the typical presenting concerns for men and women?)

Use your responses at the beginning of the chapter in Activity 13.1 to assess your assumptions about men and women when they come into counseling. Specifically, note what your ideas of presenting concerns for each sex might be and some characteristics associated with each sex.

The Effects of Sex Combinations in Counseling

There are four typical biological sex combinations that can occur in counseling: female counselor to female client, female counselor to male client, male counselor to female client, and male counselor to male client (see Table 13.2). Each of these combinations comes with typical counseling dynamics.

MALE COUNSELOR-MALE CLIENT

A male-male counseling dyad, or pairing, may be characterized by competitiveness, lack of emotion and/or empathy, and possibly homophobia. Due to the traditional male gender role being characterized by independence, competitiveness, and aggressiveness, male counselor-client dyads can sometimes become competitive, particularly when the male client questions the male counselor's judgment (Gilbert & Scher, 1999; Scher, 2001). In addition, male counselors who have identified with the Traditional Model may find it difficult to show warmth,

Table 13.2   Possible Counselor Bias and Counseling Issues Based on Sex Dyads

Traditional Male Gender Attributes	Traditional Female Gender Attributes
Independence	Caretaking
Competitiveness	Relationally oriented
Aggressiveness	More verbal
Male Client ~ Male Counselor	**Female Client ~ Male Counselor**
Possible counseling dynamics:	Possible counseling dynamics:
Competition	Power issues
Difficulties with empathy	Sexuality issues
Difficulties sharing emotions	Tentative to reveal presenting concerns
Male Client ~ Female Counselor	**Female Client ~ Female Counselor**
Possible counseling dynamics:	Possible counseling dynamics:
Client discomfort	Questioning counselor's capabilities
Power issues	Emotionally intense
Client may be more open	

concern, or caring to male clients because this would go against their male gender role. Conversely, male clients may have difficulty with a male counselor who *is* empathic (Heppner & Gonzalez, 1987). Such male clients may have difficulty expressing emotions and may feel shame and embarrassment about seeking or needing help from another male because such behaviors are stereotypically viewed as weak.

One study that examined male counselor-male client dyads found that when confronted with a male client who did not quite fit the male counselor's gender stereotype, the counselor felt less empathic, less comfortable with the client, and had less willingness to see the client (Wisch & Mahalik, 1999). For example, if a client fit the Traditional Model for males (i.e., aggressive, independent) *or* if the client was a gay man who was more emotional and passive, then the male counselor was more empathic toward the client and willing to work with him. However, if a male client stepped outside of the expected stereotype that the male counselor held (e.g., a gay male client who exhibited anger and aggression), then the male counselor reported a higher level of gender role conflict and reported less empathy, comfort, or willingness to work with the client (Wisch & Mahalik, 1999).

FEMALE COUNSELOR-MALE CLIENT

Female counselor-male client dyads may exhibit power struggles and sexuality issues. Male clients with a female counselor may be uncomfortable due to the degree of power that the counselor may be perceived to have (Mintz & O'Neil,

1990). On the other hand, male clients may reveal more emotions with a female counselor than with a male counselor because females are stereotypically seen as empathic, nurturing, and good listeners.

MALE COUNSELOR-FEMALE CLIENT

In the male counselor-female client dyad, sexual tension must be dealt with. The counselor may believe that female clients are flirting with them, or, if they are heterosexual, male counselors may view female clients as sex objects (Gilbert & Scher, 1999). That dynamic encourages a traditional sex role of females as sexual objects. The result in counseling can be that the client's goal is not adequately worked on, due to counselor discomfort in the relationship or inability to focus, incorrectly judging the female client's behavior and nonverbals, and/or abandoning the client by terminating counseling or referring her. In one research study, female clients who dressed up to look physically attractive received more supportive comments from male counselors than female clients who were not seen as physically attractive (Schwartz & Abramowitz, 1978). Male counselors may also adopt a power position (i.e., be more directive and authoritarian) in a session with female clients (Heatherington & Allen, 1984; Robinson & Howard-Hamilton, 2000). In turn, female clients may automatically assume a subordinate role in this male/female dyad (Kaplan, 1979). Along these same lines, fearful that they might be judged, women working with male counselors may be overly careful about what they reveal in counseling (Mintz & O'Neil, 1990). They may not reveal certain emotions that feel intolerable due to embarrassment or concern with what the counselor will think (Robinson & Howard-Hamilton, 2000). Indeed, it has been reported that male counselors are more annoyed with female clients than with males when females question the counselor's judgment (Gilbert & Scher, 1999) and see themselves as less open and more self-critical than do female counselors working with female clients (Robinson & Howard-Hamilton, 2000). Male counselors should, therefore, be alert to all of these tendencies.

FEMALE COUNSELOR-FEMALE CLIENT

When the counseling dyad was female-female, female clients were found to challenge the role of the female counselor and question her training, experience, and competence (Kaplan, 1979). However, it has also been found that the female counselor-client dyad tends to be the most emotionally intense therapeutic dyad. This dyad has been shown to result in full exploration of presenting concerns, childhood experiences, and interpersonal relationship problems, as well as have more expression of affect in the session (Jones, Krupnick, & Kerig, 1987; Jones & Zoppel, 1982). It should be noted, however, that while this dyad is emotionally intense and the female counselor elicits a wide array of emotions from her female client, aggression and anger are still less accepted by counselors from female clients—regardless of the sex of the counselor (Kaplan, 1987; Robinson & Howard-Hamilton, 2000).

OVERALL GENDER BIAS TOWARD MEN

Regardless of the dyad combination, some typical counselor gender bias must be attended to. Overall counselor gender bias in relation to men ranges from applying constraints to men that are consistent with conventional roles (e.g., a man must be the breadwinner; a man cannot be emotional) to assuming that men who engage in traditional feminine activities or roles are weak or sissies. Counselors must be wary of encouraging men to be stoic, emotionally distant, or solely reliant on women for meeting their emotional needs and not seek out experiences where they can discuss and share their feelings (Gilbert & Scher, 1999; Pasick, Gordon, & Meth, 1990). Counselor bias against men also includes discouraging a man from leaving his occupation to stay home and take care of his children. Such a stance ultimately limits his choices to one rigid career-related gender role. This bias also works in reverse when a counselor commends or accepts a man's inclination to disregard family and make career a priority. Similarly, a counselor may discount the responsibility that a male has in making a relationship work, discounting or discouraging the client's expressing his feelings to a partner or family, and putting this accountability on the female in the relationship.

OVERALL GENDER BIAS TOWARD WOMEN

Three specific biases against women in counseling have been found: (a) discouraging or disapproving of behavior that does not adhere to the Traditional Model (e.g., aggression, career orientation); (b) dissuading the expression of anger; and (c) not confronting or exploring passive, submissive, or compliant behavior with the client (Bernardez, 1987). Overall counselor gender bias against women includes fostering only traditional feminine roles for women (Gilbert & Scher, 1999). Also, counselors might see women only as being emotional, dependent, and oriented toward relationships. In that vein, both counselors and clients tend to view women as being better able than men to make relationships work. However, counselors also fault women more than men if there are problems in a relationship (Fitzgerald & Nutt, 1986; Hare-Mustin, 1983). Counselor bias may also support and communicate the stereotypical view that it is more important for a woman to make sacrifices and/or quit her career in order to take care of the children because she is more nurturing.

The next sections discuss gender bias against both men and women in the areas of client assessment, career issues, family and couples counseling, and heterosexism.

Counselor Bias in Assessment and Diagnosis

Bias exists in clinicians' judgments of psychological disturbances as a function of gender and gender role (e.g., Becker & Lamb, 1994; Biaggo, Roades,

Staffelbach, Cardinali, & Duffy, 2000; Broverman et al., 1970; Danzinger & Welfel, 2000; Vogel et al., 2003). As noted earlier, mental health professionals have equated the characteristics of a healthy adult with those of a healthy man (Broverman et al., 1970). By contrast, healthy women were characterized as less aggressive, more submissive, more excitable, and less competitive—characteristics associated more with less healthy or pathological adults. Similar results have been found more recently (Danzinger & Welfel, 2000). For example, in a survey of 99 mental health professionals, including licensed social workers, psychologists, and counselors, female clients were seen as less competent than male clients, regardless of age.

Fitting into gender-stereotypical roles seems to be a sign of health to counselors because they tend to describe male and female clients in gender stereotypical terms (O'Malley & Richardson, 1985; Vogel et al., 2003). When clients do not conform to the traditional gender roles represented in the Traditional Model of "Opposite" Sex (Gender) Identity (Gilbert & Scher, 1999), counselors tend to view them as pathological (e.g., Garfinkle & Morin, 1978; Portland, 1994; Robertson & Fitzgerald, 1990). Counselors make stereotypical gender attributions in at least two ways. First, they assign gender responsibility for presenting concerns (e.g., women are responsible for making the relationship work; men are responsible for the lack of emotions in a relationship). In addition, counselors express gender bias by formulating diagnoses (including the severity of the problem) and treatment recommendations based on biological sex and gender stereotypes (e.g., Cook, Warnke, & Dupuy, 1993; Lopez, 1989; Nelson, 1993; Vogel et al., 2003). This second source of gender bias will be discussed next.

GENDER BIAS IN DIAGNOSIS

One way in which gender stereotypes are problematic in the counseling process is in the diagnosis of clients: Males and females with identical symptomology may earn different diagnoses (Hamilton, Rothbart, & Dawes, 1986). For example, in one study, clinicians rated females as significantly more histrionic than males who exhibited the identical symptoms (Hamilton et al., 1986).

The *Diagnostic and Statistical Manual of Mental Disorders* (*DSM*) itself has also been found to be gender biased. According to Cook et al. (1993), disorders in the *DSM* have a great deal of overlap with stereotypes of men and women in Western society. Most of the diagnoses that men are given include behaviors that are considered to be "acting out," such as antisocial behavior, oppositional defiant disorder, conduct disorder, and attention deficit disorder, while diagnoses bestowed on women tend to include more "acting in" behaviors, such as major depressive disorder, dysthymia, and post-traumatic stress disorder.

In order to avoid errors in diagnosis based on gender stereotypes, a counselor should assess a client's beliefs about gender roles and stereotypes, her or his experiences as a man or woman, and current stressors. The counselor's own views of gender must also be accounted for.

The counselor, therefore, should begin to formulate her or his assessment of client issues based on the client's beliefs about her or his role as a member of a particular sex, especially the gendered characteristics to which she or he adheres. The counselor would then examine the possible interaction among demographic factors (such as race, ethnicity, age, and social class), the client's biological sex, and gender identity (Brown, 1986). After taking demographic interactions into account, the counselor would look at the presenting concern (e.g., in the vignette at the beginning of the chapter, depression) and consider the possible life events and subsequent stressors related to gender (e.g., the client's beliefs about her or his current business professional role and her or his competing aspirations to take a larger childrearing role).

Collection and examination of this information throughout the intake process will assist the counselor to determine useful diagnoses and intervention plans (Cook et al., 1993). The reader is encouraged to complete Activity 13.7 in order to examine gender issues in diagnosis.

Counselor Bias in Career-Related Counseling

Career is an area where gender bias may play a role in both society and counseling. Both women and men experience gender-based career and job pressures. Men and women are socialized to value different types of work (e.g., paid work for men vs. unpaid work, such as cooking, buying, and child care, for women). These differences exacerbate power imbalances because men traditionally do less of the unpaid labor and still receive the comforts of women's unpaid labor (Glenn, 1999).

WOMEN AND CAREER

For women, such issues affect career aspirations and choices and the actual state of the workplace as well (Cook, 1993). A rigid view of traditional gender career development, where women are valued for working in the home and men for working outside, may cost women the ability to advance in organizations and men to share in the joys of family (Tavris, 1992).

Assessing career goals for women and men may involve more than just focusing on stated aspirations. In women's cases, career goals tend to be related to whether a female believes she can succeed based on her biological sex or whether she will be discriminated against due to being a woman (Betz, 2002). In addition, women's career goals are related to the understanding or knowledge that one might have multiple roles in life (i.e., career, partner, parent). For most women, determining a career path may also be a result of balancing the multiple roles she has, or sees in the future. For example, if a woman wants children, she typically considers this ambition earlier in her career choice, choosing a career that might provide her with the ability to have time to raise her children; a male is less likely

---

ACTIVITY 13.7

Diagnostic Assessment

Respond to the following questions:

When thinking about the depressed homemaker in the vignette at the beginning of the chapter, what was your provisional diagnosis?

Did your diagnoses tend to relate to the "acting-in" or "acting-out" diagnoses as suggested by Cook et al. (1993), or did the severity increase and the prognosis decrease if the diagnosis crossed typical gender lines? For example, if the client was male, was he not diagnosed with depression and instead considered to have more of an adjustment disorder? Or if he was diagnosed with a depressive disorder, was it considered to be more severe in terms of the level of depression or have a poorer prognosis?

Comment on how the client's sex interacts with other demographic variables. Think of other chapters on ethnicities, race, social class, and religion in this book to determine what stereotypes might exist for men and women from different groupings.

Finally, how might current life events affect the client's depression?

Keep in mind that society's expectations of gender cannot be removed from this vignette. Thus, if the client is a woman, how might expectations to be a mother and homemaker versus being a career woman affect her decision and feelings? Or, conversely, how might these expectations play a role in the desire of a man to stay home with his children, and how might the expectations of his company, friends, and society impact his emotions and decisions?

---

to think about the potential role of fatherhood when he is entering college and selecting a career.

Gender also factors into the workplace itself. For women, the effects of gender on the economy can translate into lower-wage employment, silent discrimination against working mothers (i.e., being passed over for a promotion or chance to advance based on the assumption that having children means less interest in work), and possible harassment (Moghadam, 1999).

Although wage discrimination is sometimes treated as a thing of the past, in 2004, female employees won the right to launch a class action lawsuit against Wal-Mart—the largest sex discrimination lawsuit of its kind in history. On behalf of 1.6 million current and former female employees, the lawsuit alleged gender discrimination in pay and promotions (Equal Rights Advocates, 2004).

In addition to wage disparities, when women do work in traditionally male-dominated professions, they may too often be subject to harassment (Marshall, 1995). Such harassment takes two forms: men may sexually harass them or men may undermine their credibility. Sexual harassment can particularly serve to dissuade women from persevering in traditional male work environments (Farmer, 1997).

MEN AND CAREER

For men, traditional career identity-related expectations about being the primary breadwinner may contribute to work dominating their lives (Pasick et al., 1990). Men may feel societal pressure to work more to bring in more income than women. They justify this socialized assumption by rationalizing that they are providing better for their families. But this bias about being the main monetary provider may backfire because overwork can lead to marital and familial dissatisfaction on the part of the man, his partner, or his family (Pasick et al., 1990).

HELPING WOMEN AND MEN IN CAREER

In the area of career and gender, counselors should pay attention to the gendered context of career choice and the work environment, particularly when people are preparing for career transitions (Cook, 1993). In the workplace, some work environments might tend to employ recent graduates. This may be problematic for a woman who is returning to the workforce after raising children. Also, the absence of accessible childcare may be a factor for women and sometimes for men (Farmer, 1997). The culture of the work environment itself can be problematic. Long hours, weekend work, and frequent travel may be the norm for an organization. A male client who is interested in spending more time with his family might have to evaluate the fit of such a career opportunity.

In light of these gender-related career factors, clients should be encouraged to do gender role analysis (Enns, 2000), that is, to explore and challenge the gendered context of their career aspirations, choices, and workplace experiences. They should be encouraged to examine their values and expectations regarding their career choices so that they can feel positively about them. It is important to consider that there may not be much support for clients' nontraditional gender career choices in society. Activity 13.8 asks the reader to give her or his perceptions of gender-related factors in career.

Counselor Bias in Couples and Family Counseling

Relationships and family are another area in which gender bias may exist in counseling. Although there are many different types of relationships (e.g., dating, partnered, married, heterosexual, homosexual), the focus in this section

ACTIVITY 13.8

Career and Gender

Reflect on the second vignette at the beginning of the chapter.

In what ways was your conceptualization of the client's sex and strengths influenced by the occupational choices?

Do you know both men and women who have nontraditional careers?

How might you begin to pay attention to these issues in counseling?

is on heterosexual relationships because Chapter 14 focuses on lesbian, gay, bisexual, and transgender issues and counseling.

With respect to heterosexual couples, gender issues may create challenges in problem solving, connection, and intimacy (Knudson-Martin & Mahoney, 1999). Many couples re-create gender-learned patterns from their own development in their relationships. Although partners (i.e., male-female, female-female, male-male) may rely on each other in a relationship to meet each other's physical and emotional needs, they may define and express intimacy in different ways (Hook, Gerstein, Detterich, & Gridley, 2003).

PATTERNS FOR MEN

Men typically do not outwardly express emotions that can make them seem vulnerable, thus creating potential difficulties in intimacy with a partner. As mentioned earlier, although male infants express more emotion than female infants at birth, by early childhood, males typically do not exhibit as wide a range of emotions as do females. In particular, Western culture limits men's opportunities to receive physical contact (Allen & Robinson, 1993). Men do not usually physically touch friends, whereas female friends might commonly hug. However, it is acceptable for men to exhibit aggression, anger, or physical urges. Thus, men have often not learned how to emote or relate intimately.

In reality, love relationships and intimacy mean a great deal to men. However, they often do not know how to foster or nurture intimacy (Allen & Robinson, 1993). While women tend to show intimacy through emotional and physical closeness, men tend to show intimacy through actions, such as making time to do activities with their partner, giving up friends, and doing romantic things such as making dinner or lighting a candle (Allen & Robinson, 1993). However, most of the actions men do in a relationship tend to be concentrated in the earlier, more romantic stages of dating. Thus, by doing so much in the beginning of the relationship, men can either lose part of who they are (e.g., giving up friends) or be unable to decide what they want emotionally because they often allow their partners to take the lead in intimacy. They then are surprised when a woman wants more than money, sex, or time (Allen & Robinson, 1993).

PATTERNS FOR WOMEN

Women are expected to be the emotional caretakers. When traditional gender roles are dominant in heterosexual relationships, it is often the woman who ends up with the larger share of the emotional/relational work in the relationship (Knudson-Martin, 2003). For women, romantic heterosexual relationships can be, at times, a source of turmoil (e.g., exacerbating depression) and a strength or source of support (e.g., having a close confidante) (Romans, 1998). The assumption that women should be responsible for intimacy and connectedness in a relationship, or that a man is not responsible for nor capable of emotional expression and intimacy in heterosexual relationships, is a bias that may present in counseling—by the client *or* the counselor. For example, if a man and woman come in for couples counseling, lacking intimacy in their relationship, the counselor may suggest that the female partner enhance the relationship by increasing her sexual engagement with her male partner in order for the couple to become closer. The same counselor may not encourage the male partner to share more about his feelings, making the assumption that, as a male, the client needs only to exhibit his emotions in a physical way, implying that increasing the sexual contact should help to increase the intimacy in the relationship.

Heterosexual Bias

Counselors can sometimes show bias about sexual orientation by making an incorrect assumption that a client is heterosexual (Phillips & Fischer, 1998). Mental health professionals have acknowledged negative attitudes toward lesbian and gay clients (Portland, 1994) and have reported not feeling adequately equipped or prepared to deal with gay, lesbian, or bisexual clients, and they report retaining anti-gay biases (Green, 2000). In general, heterosexual clients are perceived to be more psychologically healthy than are homosexual clients (Garfinkle & Morin, 1978). For example, although therapists reported that they did not view "male" homosexuality as being pathological, it was conceptualized as being less good, less masculine, and less rational than heterosexuality (Davison & Wilson, 1973). In addition to holding negative attitudes, or feeling ill-equipped to work with lesbian and gay clients, a counselor who attempts to use heterosexual standards to make sense of homosexual relationships, or attempts to apply male and female roles to gay and lesbian partners in order to understand their relationship, is displaying heterosexual bias (Gilbert & Scher, 1999). For example, in the second vignette at the beginning of this chapter, the student might have assumed that the client's partner was the opposite sex. Thus, counselors need to assess their knowledge, biases, and assumptions in working with clients from different sexual orientations. For more discussion of being culturally alert to a client's sexual orientation in counseling, see Chapter 14.

Summary: Consequences of Gender Bias for Counseling

Assumptions made by counselors, consciously or unconsciously, based on biological sex and gender stereotypes can harm a client (Tsui & Shultz, 1988). Because of gender bias, the client may receive inappropriate or inadequate treatment in counseling, incorrect diagnoses may be given, or restrictive notions may be applied to the roles that men and women should assume, thereby limiting behaviors available to the client because the client is not encouraged to "step outside of the gendered box."

It needs to be noted, however, that if a client is comfortable within the Traditional Model, and this model is not causing distress, then it is not a counselor's role to convince the client otherwise. Gender differences can be respected if each member of the couple shows flexibility and choice in gender roles and throughout the relationship. For example, division of labor is not, in itself, a problem in couples, but when problems arise, the refusal to adapt because of inflexibility in gender roles can become a problem.

Implications for Practice

Every client who comes in for counseling is a gendered being. As discussed above under counselor bias, it is imperative that counselors be aware of the impact of their gendered selves, as well as the impact that clients, as gendered beings, have on the counseling process. Therefore, a brief overview and discussion of the implications and expectations for counseling men and women is provided, as well as a discussion of how to develop a process of gender-fair counseling.

Women tend to seek out counseling services more readily than men (Fisher & Turner, 1970). Thus, when men seek out counseling services they are more likely to be in a crisis (Neukrug, 2003) or be externally forced (Mejia, 2005) by a spouse, partner, or system (e.g., work or court). They are also less likely to talk, share feelings, or collaborate with the counselor. This reticence may be due to the socialized masculine gender role in Western society, which encourages men to be strong, independent, and competitive—not collaborative, self-revealing, and weak. As mentioned earlier, men tend to reveal feelings and emotions, especially intimacy, with action-oriented behaviors—not necessarily through "talk." Thus, methods other than talk may need to be considered by the counselor to help men learn to share feelings and be intimate. Counselors should note that because men tend to take on more competitive roles and talk about intimate concerns less, they are also at an increased risk of experiencing a crisis, have overwhelming feelings, attempt or commit suicide, and have a shorter life expectancy than women (Neukrug, 2003).

As stated earlier, women are more likely than men to seek counseling services. This readiness may be related to their relational and communicative orientation. Most women will open up and discuss presenting concerns and feelings to a counselor fairly easily. However, given conventional Western gender socialization, women are also taught to place a value on relationships. They may thus also feel responsible, and may be criticized, if a relationship is failing—regardless of the reasons. In addition, given the effects of gender socialization, women may have difficulty establishing and maintaining self-boundaries (Collier, 1982). Counselors should note women's self-imposed roles in relationships, both with themselves (e.g., self-esteem) and with others (importance of others related to self). Women may think of others' needs to the exclusion of their own.

In light of these trends, counselors need to make an effort to implement gender-fair counseling (Van Buren et al., 1989), which explicitly addresses the influence of gender in counseling. Gender-fair counseling aims at facilitating the development of full client potential based upon an individual's unique characteristics, regardless of her or his gender.

Van Buren (1992) proposed four steps for gender-fair counseling: (1) examination of values and beliefs of both the counselor and the client, (2) confrontation of biases that may exist in the counselor or client that may limit client options, (3) initiation of action toward gender-fair goals, and (4) evaluation of the outcomes. These steps are discussed next in some depth.

EXAMINING THE VALUES AND BELIEFS OF COUNSELOR AND CLIENT

As has been emphasized throughout this chapter, it is imperative that counselors examine their own and their clients' gender identities and socialization. Research has revealed that gender has a significant impact on counseling, from the presenting issues that are brought into counseling; to the relationship between counselor and client; to assessment, diagnoses, and interventions. According to the ethical standards of the American Counseling Association (2005), counselors must be "aware of their own values, attitudes, beliefs, and behaviors and avoid imposing values that are inconsistent with counseling goals" (§ A.4.b.). Given these ethical guidelines, the possibility of gender bias is an area for counselors to consider, and they must recognize their own beliefs about gender. These beliefs may not be in their conscious awareness because sex classification, along with beliefs about gender, tends to occur instantaneously.

Along with exploring their own gender identity and beliefs, counselors must proactively help clients examine their gender identities and beliefs. A counselor should inquire about the history of the client's gender roles and behaviors, with such questions as, "How have others, for example your friends and family, reacted to your choice to quit your job and stay home with your kids? What about your co-workers or your boss? How has this choice affected you, your spouse, your family, or your lifestyle?" These types of questions are discussed further in Chapter 16 as culturally educated questions, in the sense that the counselor uses knowledge of the cultural trends to frame probing culture-related questions.

These questions can be asked of both women and men. Counselors should also not ask these types of questions only when a client steps out of the Traditional Model—that would not be gender-fair counseling. Question 9 in Activity 13.5 is a good example of how a counselor might do a gender analysis by exploring a client's history, background, and socialization of gender (e.g., "As a girl/boy I was discouraged from _____ and from this I learned that girls/boys should not _____"). For the client in the second vignette that began this chapter, a counselor might ask how the client's parental roles of homemaker and corporate lawyer had an impact on her or his career choice and on the struggle with leaving her or his career and staying at home. In addition, the client might be asked what were the messages about life, career, and family the client received from his or her parents and how did these messages align or conflict with society's messages.

The role of a counselor in this part of gender analysis is to make patterns and assumptions about gender in the client's life visible and help clients see that there are options for making changes in their lives (Knudson-Martin, 2003). For example, the counselor might say, "I notice that you always seem to take on the responsibility in your relationships without handing any of that accountability over to your partners," or ask, "Based on what you are telling me, have you ever expressed your desire to stay home with your kids instead of working? What might be your partner's reactions to this desire?" By pointing out these patterns and assumptions, the counselor is able to assist the client to examine them and their role in her or his life.

Also, as part of examining gendered values and beliefs, it is helpful to encourage clients to process how developmental aspects of their manhood or womanhood have changed over time (Pasick et al., 1990). For example, a female's assumptions of gender, ideas about gender roles, and her own gender identity might change when she becomes a mother, or a man's might change when he becomes a father. A counselor might ask, "What are your expectations of your partner? Have these expectations changed now that your son is born?" Or ask, "What changed when you moved out of your childhood home? Did your gender identity and roles change?" A client's responses should not be judged as right or wrong, but instead simply listened to and validated while continuing to search for the patterns and themes in the client's life.

Links between the client's gender identity, expectations, and her or his presenting concerns may begin to arise during this examination. However, the counselor's role is not to push a client to pick up a gendered role or expectation that she or he does not want, or is not ready for, based on the counselor's own expectations or agenda. Instead, simple statements identifying the pattern of the client can be made in order to bring these gendered blueprints into awareness. The Gender Lens Activity can be used with clients to evoke gender socialization and assumptions (see Activity 13.9).

CONFRONTING BIASES

The second step in gender-fair counseling is for counselors to help clients discover the ways in which gender biases take effect in their lives and to help clients explore and challenge old gendered patterns (Knudson-Martin, 2003). In this vein, counselors can reframe gender differences, which may or may not be influenced by nature, as choices. This type of discourse leaves open the possibility of change.

Counselors should assume that clients can have flexible gender behaviors and that they can be developed by both sexes (Knudson-Martin, 2003). For example, as indicated previously, with heterosexual couples it is important to assume that both men and women are capable of developing skills that are stereotypically associated with the other sex (e.g., men can be emotional and women can be aggressive). Instead of viewing one gender role or the other as correct or right, counselors can focus on the strengths of all potential roles and behaviors (Heesacker & Prichard, 1992).

ACTIVITY 13.9

Gender Lens Activity

Each of us has her or his own personal experiences, including educational, ethnic, familial, and religious experiences. These experiences make up our Gender Lens.

For example, think about your past educational, ethnic, familial, and religious experiences and try to think of an example of a gendered message or perception you heard or experienced. Then, think of an image, word, phrase, or color that might represent these experiences or messages. Then, take a few minutes and make a drawing that reflects your own set of gendered experiences.

Awareness of your Gender Lens is the first step in understanding your socialization, culture, and judgments or biases toward gender and/or sex.

This activity can be done with clients.

SOURCE: © Wester & Trepal (2003).

Counselors can also confront clients' overt gender biases. Consider the following example. A female client says that she cannot become more assertive because for her whole life, people have been telling her that she is kind, so she doesn't see any other way of acting as appropriate. The client has a gender bias—thinking that she can act only a *certain* way, based on her history. In this situation, the counselor may choose to confront the client's bias by helping her to uncover some exceptions (e.g., surely there was a time, however minute, when she was mildly assertive) or assisting her to find opportunities to experiment with a new behavior. The goal is to help the client expand her choices, both in behaviors and in attitudes (Collier, 1982).

ACTION TOWARD GENDER-FAIR GOALS

The third step in gender-fair counseling is to present gender-fair strategies that should be used within and outside the counseling setting to make gender fairness a reality in U.S. society (Knudson-Martin & Mahoney, 1999; Van Buren, 1992). These strategies can include actively encouraging clients to be gender fair to themselves and others, as well as "going public" by presenting and writing about gender-fair counseling and treatment.

It should be noted, in setting goals, that it is difficult for counselors to be "neutral" while also being ethical regarding gender. On the one hand, counselors are trained to take a neutral stance and not to impose their own values and beliefs on clients. In addition, they are trained to conceptualize clients and enact related subsequent treatments based on the symptoms clients present and their diagnosis (Allen & Robinson, 1993). However, gender cannot be treated as a neutral factor; it is fraught with power and equity issues. Therefore, counselors need to be perceptive with regard to social and political issues in order to accurately conceptualize the gendered context of counseling (Van Buren, 1992). Counselors must ask, in helping to set gender-fair goals, "What degree of a client's concern is due to mostly internal struggle or is a problem stemming from societal pressure (e.g., to conform when one is not conforming and/or when one does not want to conform)?" The answer to each will determine the goals.

Counselors must keep in mind that some clients may not be ready to actively engage in gender-fair behaviors or discussions within a counseling session, let alone outside a counseling session. Thus, the first step should always be validating the client's feelings and presenting concern, regardless of what they are; validating the client's gender identity; and exploring patterns and/or desires to alter some gender roles—or, conversely, understanding that the client does not yearn to change gender roles or alter her or his expectations. If a client does want and need to alter his or her behaviors or perceptions, counselors need to realize that this may be a slow process, depending on how aware the client is about her or his gendered expectations and socialization.

EVALUATION OF OUTCOMES

The final step in gender-fair counseling is continuing evaluation. Once clients make a change, the counselor and the client need to examine the change that has been made. How is the client doing with the change? Does she or he like it? Does the change seem to "fit" with him or her? Do other people in the client's life (e.g., family, friends) agree with and support the change? Is there any conflict? Do any additional changes need to occur? For example, suppose that a female client has made a change and is trying to become more assertive. She may have a history of not being assertive and, consequently, there may be some uncomfortable moments, both for the client and for others in her life, when she attempts to change long-standing patterns that can have gendered messages (i.e., women are not rewarded for being assertive). The counselor should evaluate by asking the client about the change that she has made and follow up by exploring the effects of the new behavior in her life.

Summary

As demonstrated in this chapter, there are several ways in which gender emerges in counseling, including stereotypes and biases that both the counselor and the client might have and the important role of values, beliefs, and socialization. Gender stereotypes can be beneficial. However, when adhered to inflexibly, stereotypes can serve to limit clients' options. It is important to keep in mind that, in actuality, men and women have many characteristics that overlap, leading to the concept of fluid gender. It is imperative that counselors take a critical look at their own gendered lives, as well as those of their clients, in order to establish culturally alert practice.

References

Allen, J., & Laird, J. (1991). *Feminist approaches for men in family therapy.* New York: Harrington Park Press.

Allen, M., & Robinson, J. (1993). *In the company of men: A new approach to healing for husbands, fathers, and friends.* New York: Random House.

American Counseling Association. (2005). *Code of ethics.* Alexandria, VA: Author.

Bailey, J. M. (2003). *The man who would be queen: The science of gender-bending and transexualism.* Washington, DC: Joseph Henry Press.

Beal, C. R. (1994). *Boys and girls: The development of gender roles.* New York: McGraw-Hill.

Becker, D., & Lamb, S. (1994). Sex bias in the diagnosis of borderline personality and posttraumatic stress disorder. *Professional Psychology: Research and Practice, 25,* 55–61.

Bernardez, T. (1987). Gender-based countertransference of female therapists in the psychotherapy of women. In M. Braude (Ed.), *Women and therapy* (pp. 25–39). New York: Haworth Press.

Betz, N. E. (1994). Basic issues and concepts in career counseling for women. In W. B. Walsh & S. H. Osipow (Eds.), *Career counseling for women* (pp. 1–42). Hillsdale, NJ: Erlbaum.

Betz, N. E. (2002). The 2001 Leona Tyler Award address: Women's career development: Weaving personal themes and theoretical constructs. *The Counseling Psychologist, 30,* 467–481.

Biaggo, M., Roades, L., Staffelbach, D., Cardinali, J., & Duffy, R. (2000). Clinical evaluations: Impact of sexual orientation, gender, and gender role. *Journal of Applied Social Psychology, 30,* 1657–1669.

Broverman, I. K., Broverman, D. M., Clarkson, F. E., Rosenkrantz, P. S., & Vogel, S. R. (1970). Sex-role stereotypes and clinical judgments of mental health. *Journal of Counseling and Clinical Psychology, 34,* 1–7.

Brown, L. S. (1986). Gender role analysis: A neglected component of psychological assessment. *Psychotherapy, 23,* 243–248.

Collier, H. V. (1982). *Counseling women: A guide for therapists.* New York: Free Press.

Connell, R. W. (1999). Making gendered people: Bodies, identities, sexuality. In M. M. Ferree, J. Lorber, & B. B. Hess (Eds.), *Revisioning gender* (pp. 449–471). Thousand Oaks, CA: Sage.

Cook, E. P. (1993). The gendered context of life: Implications for women's and men's career-life plans. *The Career Development Quarterly, 41,* 227–237.

Cook, E. P., Warnke, M., & Dupuy, P. (1993). Gender bias and the *DSM-III-R. Counselor Education and Supervision, 32,* 311–322.

Daniluk, J. D., Stein, M., & Bockus, D. (1995). The ethics of inclusion: Gender as a critical component of counselor training. *Counselor Education and Supervision, 34,* 294–307.

Danzinger, P. R., & Welfel, E. R. (2000). Age, gender and health bias in counselors: An empirical analysis. *Journal of Mental Health Counseling, 22,* 135–149.

Davis, C., & Scott-Robertson, L. (2000). A psychological comparison of females with anorexia nervosa and competitive male bodybuilders: Body shape ideals in the extreme. *Eating Behaviors, 1,* 33–46.

Davison, G. C., & Wilson, G. T. (1973). Attitudes of behavior therapists toward homosexuality. *Behavior Therapy, 4,* 686–696.

Deaux, K. (1976). Sex: A perspective on the attitudinal process. In J. H. Harvey, W. J. Ickes, & R. F. Kidd (Eds.), *New directions in attribution research* (Vol. 1, pp. 335–352). Hillsdale, NJ: Erlbaum.

Deaux, K., & LaFrance, M. (1998). Gender. In D. Gilbert, S. Fiske, & G. Lindzey (Eds.), *Handbook of social psychology* (pp. 788–827). New York: McGraw-Hill.

Enns, C. Z. (2000). Gender issues in counseling. In S. D. Brown & R. W. Lent (Eds.), *Handbook of counseling psychology* (3rd ed., pp. 601–638). New York: Wiley.

Equal Rights Advocates. (2004). *Federal judge orders Wal-mart Stores, Inc., the nation's largest private employers, to stand trial for company-wide sex discrimination.* Retrieved November 30, 2004, from http://www.equalrights.org/media/walmart 062204.asp

Etaugh, C., & Liss, M. B. (1992). Home, school, and playroom: Training grounds for adult gender roles. *Sex Roles, 26,* 129–147.

Farmer, H. S. (1997). Future directions for research in women's career development. In H. S. Farmer (Ed.), *Diversity and women's career development: From adolescence to adulthood* (pp. 293–306). Thousand Oaks, CA: Sage.

Fisher, E. H., & Turner, I. (1970). Orientation to seeking professional psychological help: Development and research utility of an attitude scale. *Journal of Consulting and Clinical Psychology, 35,* 79–90.

Fiske, S. T., Bersoff, D. N., Borgida, E., Deaux, K., & Heilman, M. E. (1991). Social science research on trial: Use of sex stereotyping research in Price Waterhouse v. Hopkins. *American Psychologist, 46,* 1049–1060.

Fitzgerald, L. F., & Nutt, R. L. (1986). The Division 17 principles concerning the counseling/psychotherapy of women: Rationale and implementation. *The Counseling Psychologist, 14,* 180–216.

Fuller, M. (1999). *Woman in the nineteenth century.* New York: Dover. (Original work published 1845)

Garfinkle, E. M., & Morin, S. F. (1978). Psychologists' attitudes toward homosexual psychotherapy clients. *Journal of Homosexuality, 34,* 101–113.

Gilbert, L. A. (1987). Female and male emotional dependency and its implication for the therapist-client relationship. *Professional Psychology: Theory, Research, and Practice, 18,* 555–561.

Gilbert, L. A., & Scher, M. (1999). *Gender and sex in counseling and psychotherapy.* Needham Heights, MA: Allyn & Bacon.

Glenn, E. N. (1999). The social construction and institutionalization of gender and race. In M. M. Ferree, J. Lorber, & B. B. Hess (Eds.), *Revisioning gender* (pp. 129–160). Thousand Oaks, CA: Sage.

Glick, P., & Fiske, S. T. (1999). Gender, power dynamics, and social interaction. In M. M. Ferree, J. Lorber, & B. B. Hess (Eds.), *Revisioning gender* (pp. 365–398). Thousand Oaks, CA: Sage.

Goodman, L. A., Koss, M. P., & Russo, N. F. (1993). Violence against women: Physical and mental health effects. Part I: Research findings. *Applied and Preventative Psychology, 2,* 79–89.

Green, R. J. (2000). Lesbians, gays, and family psychology: Resources for teaching and practice. In B. Green & G. C. Croom (Eds.), *Education, research, and practice in lesbian, gay bisexual, and transgendered psychology: A resource manual* (pp. 207–225). Thousand Oaks, CA: Sage.

Hamilton, S., Rothbart, M., & Dawes, R. M. (1986). Sex bias, diagnosis, and *DSM-III. Sex Roles, 15,* 269–274.

Hare-Mustin, R. T. (1983). An appraisal of the relationship between women and psychotherapy: 80 years after the case of Dora. *American Psychologist, 32,* 889–890.

Heatherington, L., & Allen, G. J. (1984). Sex and relational communication patterns in counseling. *Journal of Counseling Psychology, 3,* 287–294.

Heesacker, M., & Prichard, S. (1992). In a different voice revisited: Men, women and emotion. *Journal of Mental Health Counseling, 14,* 274–290.

Heppner, P. P., & Gonzalez, D. S. (1987). Men counseling men. In M. Scher, M. Stevens, G. Good, & G. A. Eichenfield (Eds.), *Handbook of counseling and psychotherapy with men* (pp. 30–38). Newbury Park, CA: Sage.

Hook, M. K., Gerstein, L. H., Detterich, L., & Gridley, B. (2003). How close are we? Measuring intimacy and examining gender differences. *Journal of Counseling and Development, 81,* 462–472.

Jones, E. E., Krupnick, J. L., & Kerig, P. K. (1987). Some gender effects in brief psychotherapy. *Psychotherapy, 24,* 336–352.

Jones, E. E., & Zoppel, C. L. (1982). Impact of client and therapist gender on psychotherapy process and outcome. *Journal of Consulting and Clinical Psychology, 50,* 259–272.

Kaplan, A. G. (1979). Toward an analysis of sex-role related issues in the therapeutic process. *Psychiatry, 43,* 112–120.

Kaplan, A. G. (1987). Reflections on gender and psychotherapy. In M. Braude (Ed.), *Women and therapy* (pp. 11–24). New York: Haworth Press.

Knudson-Martin, C. (1997) The politics of gender in family therapy. *Journal of Marital and Family Therapy, 23,* 421–437.

Knudson-Martin, C. (2003). Gender and biology: A recursive framework for clinical practice. *Journal of Feminist Family Therapy, 15,* 1–21.

Knudson-Martin, C., & Mahoney, A. R. (1996). Gender dilemmas and myth in the construction of marital bargains: Issues for marital therapy. *Family Process, 35,* 137–153.

Knudson-Martin, C., & Mahoney, A. R. (1999). Beyond different worlds: A "postgender" approach to relational development. *Family Process, 38,* 325–335.

Longley, R. (2004). *Gender wage gap widening, census data shows.* Retrieved October 10, 2006, from http://usgovinfo.about.com/od/censusandstatistics/a/paygapgrows.htm

Lopez, S. R. (1989). Patient variables biases in clinical judgment: Conceptual overview and methodological considerations. *Psychological Bulletin, 106,* 184–203.

Marshall, J. (1995). *Women managers moving on: Exploring life and career choices.* London: Routledge.

Martin, K. A. (1998) Becoming a gendered body: Practices of preschools. *American Sociological Review, 63,* 494–511.

Mejia, X. E. (2005). Gender matters: Working with adult male survivors of trauma. *Journal of Counseling and Development, 83,* 29–39.

Miller, G. (2001). *The mating mind: How sexual choice shaped the evolution of human nature.* New York: Anchor.

Miller, J. L., & Levy, G. D. (1996). Gender role conflict, gender-typed characteristics, self-concepts, and sport socialization in female athletes and non-athletes. *Sex Roles, 35,* 111–122.

Mintz, L. B., & O'Neil, J. M. (1990). Gender roles, sex, and the process of psychotherapy: Many questions and few answers. *Journal of Counseling and Development, 68,* 381–387.

Moghadam, V. M. (1999). Gender and the global economy. In M. M. Ferree, J. Lorber, & B. B. Hess, (Eds.), *Revisioning gender* (pp. 129–160). Thousand Oaks, CA: Sage.

Moreau, D. (1996). Depression in the young. In J. A. Sechzer, S. M. Pfafflin, F. L. Denmark, A. Griffin, & S. J. Blumenthal (Eds.), *Women and mental health* (pp. 31–44). New York: New York Academy of Sciences.

National Center for Education Statistics. (2002). *Integrated Postsecondary Education Data Systems (IPEDS) Completions Survey.* Washington, DC: U.S. Department of Education. Retrieved June 23, 2004, from http://www.nces.ed.gov/programs/digest/d02/tables/dt265.asp

Nelson, M. L. (1993). A current perspective on gender differences: Implications for research in counseling. *Journal of Counseling Psychology, 40,* 200–209.

Neukrug, E. S. (2003). *The world of the counselor: An introduction to the counseling profession* (2nd ed.). Pacific Grove, CA: Brooks/Cole.

O'Malley, L. M., & Richardson, S. S. (1985). Sex bias in counseling: Have things changed? *Journal of Counseling and Development, 63,* 294–299.

O'Neil, J. M. (1982). Gender role conflict and strain in men's lives: Implications for psychiatrists, psychologists, and other human-services providers. In K. Solomon & N. Levy (Eds.), *Men in transition: Theory and therapy* (pp. 5–44). New York: Plenum.

Padgett, D. (1997). Women's mental health: Some directions for research. *American Journal of Orthopsychiatry, 67,* 522–534.

Pasick, R. S., Gordon, S., & Meth, R. L. (1990). Helping men understand themselves. In R. L. Meth & R. S. Pasick (Eds.), *Men in therapy: The challenge of change* (pp. 152–180). New York: Guilford Press.

Pearson, G. A. (1996, October 21). Of sex and gender. *Science, 274,* 328–329.

Phillips, J. C., & Fischer, A. R. (1998). Graduate students' training experiences with lesbian, gay, and bisexual issues. *The Counseling Psychologist, 26,* 712–734.

Philpot, C. L., Brooks, G. R., Lusterman, D., & Nutt, R. L. (1997). *Bridging separate gender worlds: Why men and women clash and how therapists can bring them together.* Washington, DC: American Psychological Association.

Pleck, J. H. (1981). *The myth of masculinity.* Cambridge: MIT Press.

Pollack, W. (1998). *Real boys: Rescuing our sons from the myths of boyhood.* New York: Random House.

Portland, C. (1994). *Mental health professionals' attitudes toward lesbian and gay clients.* Unpublished doctoral dissertation, Pacific University.

Powlishta, K. K., Sen, M. G., Serbin, L. A., Poulin-Dubois, D., & Eichstedt, J. A. (2001). From infancy through middle childhood: The role of cognitive and social factors in becoming gendered. In R. K. Unger (Ed.), *Handbook of the psychology of women and gender* (pp. 116–132). New York: Wiley.

Prentice, D. A., & Carranza, E. (2002). What women should be, shouldn't be, are allowed to be, and don't have to be: The contacts of prescriptive gender stereotypes. *Psychology of Women Quarterly, 26,* 269–281.

Quartz, S., & Sejnowski, T. (2002). *Liars, lovers, and heroes: What the new brain science reveals about how we become who we are.* New York: HarperCollins.

Robertson, J. M., & Fitzgerald, L. F. (1990). The (mis)treatment of men: Effects of client gender role and life-style on diagnosis and attribution of pathology. *Journal of Counseling Psychology, 37,* 3–9.

Robinson, T. L., & Howard-Hamilton, M. F. (2000). *The convergence of race, ethnicity and gender.* Upper Saddle River, NJ: Merrill.

Romans, S. (1998). Women and social relatedness. In S. Romans (Ed.), *Folding back the shadows: A perspective on women's mental health* (pp. 97–114). Dunedin, New Zealand: University of Otego Press.

Rubin, J. Z., Provenzano, F. J., & Luria, Z. (1974). The eye of the beholder: Parents' views on sex of newborns. *American Journal of Orthopsychiatry, 44,* 512–519.

Rudman, L. A., & Glick, P. (1999). Prescriptive gender stereotypes and backlash toward agentic women. *Journal of Social Issues, 57,* 743–762.

Sandifer, M., Horden, A., & Green, L. (1970). The psychiatric interview: The impact of the first three minutes. *American Journal of Psychiatry, 126,* 968–973.

Sax, L. (2005). *Why gender matters: What parents and teachers need to know about the emerging science of sex differences.* New York: Random House.

Scher, M. (2001). Male therapist, male client: Reflections on critical dynamics. In G. R. Brooks & G. E. Good (Eds.), *The new handbook of psychotherapy and counseling with men* (Vol. 2, pp. 719–734). San Francisco: Jossey-Bass.

Scher, M., & Good, G. E. (1990). Gender and counseling in the twenty-first century: What does the future hold? *Journal of Counseling and Development, 126,* 388–391.

Schwartz, J. M., & Abramowitz, S. I. (1978). Effects of female client physical attractiveness on clinical judgment. *Psychotherapy: Theory, Research and Practice, 15,* 251–257.

Sneddon, P. S. (1999). *Body image: A reality check.* Springfield, NJ: Enslow.

Spraggins, R. E. (2000). *Census brief: Women in the United States: A profile.* Washington, DC: U.S. Census Bureau.

Stabb, S. D., Cox, D. L., & Harber, J. L. (1997). Gender-related therapist attributions in couples therapy: A preliminary multiple case study. *Journal of Marital and Family Therapy, 23,* 335–346.

Stevens-Smith, P. (1995). Gender issues in counselor education: Current status and challenges. *Counselor Education and Supervision, 34,* 283–293.

Tavris, C. (1992). *The mismeasure of women.* New York: Simon & Schuster.

Thorne, B. (1993). *Gender play: Girls and boys in school.* New Brunswick, NJ: Rutgers University Press.

Tsui, P., & Shultz, G. L. (1988). Ethnic factors in group process: Cultural dynamics in multi-ethnic therapy groups. *American Journal of Orthopsychiatry, 58,* 136–142.

Van Buren, J. (1992). Gender-fair counseling. *Counseling and Human Development, 24,* 1–12.

Van Buren, J. B., Miller, K. L., Deason, M. G., Gipson, R. A., Goldstein, A. E., Patton, D. M., et al. (1989). *A model for gender-fair counseling: Viewer's guide.* Indianapolis: Indiana Common Vocational and Technical Education.

Vogel, D. L., Epting, F., & Wester, S. R. (2003). Counselors' perceptions of female and male clients. *Journal of Counseling and Development, 81,* 131–141.

Wester, K. L., & Trepal, H. C. (2003). *Gender lens activity.* Unpublished manuscript.

Wester, K. L., & Trepal, H. C. (2004). *Identifying and working through our gendered stereotypes.* Athens, GA: Southern Association for Counselor Education and Supervision.

Wilcox, D. W., & Forrest, L. (1992). The problems of men and counseling: Gender bias or gender truth? *Journal of Mental Health Counseling, 14,* 291–304.

Wisch, A. F., & Mahalik, J. R. (1999). Male therapists' clinical bias: Influence of client gender roles and therapist gender role conflict. *Journal of Counseling Psychology, 46,* 51–60.

14

Lesbian, Gay, Bisexual, and Transgendered Clients

Dawn M. Szymanski

Roger is a junior in high school. He is doing well academically and is a star quarterback on the school's football team. College scouting agents are beginning to watch him play and offer sports scholarships. He is also dating one of the most popular and prettiest girls in the school. From an outsider's perspective, Roger seems to have everything going for him, yet he presents to his high school counselor with feelings of loneliness and feeling different from the other guys on the football team, confusion concerning his lack of romantic interest in his girlfriend, and an unspoken speculation that he might be gay. He wonders what all of this might mean for him and his football career, particularly given all the "fag" jokes and anti-gay remarks that he hears in the locker room. He has barely begun to consider what it would mean in his family.

❖

June was at a lesbian bar hanging out with a group of friends. Because she had to work early in the morning, she drank only two beers and left at 11:30 P.M. It was a crowded night at the club and her truck was parked about three blocks away. As she left the bar, a group of guys drove by her in a blue car, laughing and screaming out, "Dyke! You lezzie! I'll show you what you need." June ignored their bantering and quickened her pace. When she arrived at her truck, two of the men from the blue car were there to meet her. June turned around to run but one of the men grabbed her by the arm and attempted to sexually assault her. Thankfully, some other bar patrons were passing by and were able to scare off the two men. June enters counseling two weeks after this incident complaining of difficulty sleeping, disturbing memories of the attempted assault, anxiety, feeling emotionally numb, and being hyper-alert.

In her song "Silent Legacy," Melissa Etheridge (1993) sings about her own struggle with sexual orientation. She describes the pain of individuals concealing who they are despite their powerful attractions, ones that are automatic and natural. She describes the shame that comes from societal rejection and its transformation into anger. Her lyrics touch on people's lack of accurate information about sexual orientation issues; the negative attitudes and myths about lesbian, gay, bisexual, and transgendered (LGBT) persons that exist in U.S. society; and the pain and isolation that many LGBT persons experience in their coming out process. If the reader has access to the song, she or he might listen to it and try to identify some of the feelings and experiences that may be associated with the coming out process, so that she or he has a feel for what it might be like to be LGBT. These lyrics also evoke the power of heterosexism, that is, the privileging of heterosexual forms of relating while concurrently devaluing non-heterosexual forms of relating, which can negatively affect the psychological well-being of LGBT persons. Her song lyrics also relate to the two vignettes above; that is, Roger's grappling with his sexual identity and June's traumatic experience of heterosexism.

Chapter 1 presented an overview of the competencies associated with culturally alert counseling (Sue, Arredondo, & McDavis, 1992). Those competencies are presented in full in Chapter 16. In those competencies, there are three overarching steps to becoming a multiculturally competent counselor: (1) becoming more *aware* of one's attitudes and biases toward sexual minority persons, (2) increasing one's *knowledge* about sexual orientation and gender identity issues, and (3) learning *skills* to provide culturally sensitive practice with sexual minority persons. Thus, this chapter is organized along these lines—self-awareness, knowledge, and skills—as it describes the ways in which counselors can become more culturally competent clinicians when working with LGBT clients.

Before beginning, it is worth mentioning that it was difficult to write this chapter because lesbian, gay male, bisexual, and transgendered issues are here lumped together, yet these groups have unique differences. Most of the research and theoretical writings have focused predominantly on gay male, followed by lesbian, then bisexual, then transgendered issues. Furthermore, lesbian, gay, and bisexual (LGB) issues fall under the category of sexual orientation (i.e., attraction to someone of the same or different sex), while transgendered issues fall under the category of gender identity (one's internal or self-identification as a gender or one's psychological sense of being male or female; American Psychological Association [APA], 2004).

Thus, one's sexual attraction to an individual, or sexual orientation, should not be confused with one's gender identity. For example, many transgendered persons have heterosexual identities, but because they face some of the same discrimination that LGB persons face, they often work together with LGB persons to advocate for those who challenge the dominant societal conceptions of sex, gender, attraction, and behavior and who are considered outside the heterosexual norm (Sausa, 2002).

The main focus of this chapter is sexual orientation. What follows focuses primarily on LGB issues, with attention given to similarities and differences among lesbians, gay men, and bisexual women and men. Then, a special section is devoted to addressing the unique issues of transgendered persons.

Self-Awareness

Self-awareness is a process of becoming aware of and challenging one's values, biases, and personal limitations with regard to working with LGB clients. This section will focus on general information concerning attitudes toward LGB persons and demonstrate how these attitudes can impact counselor's therapeutic work with LGB clients.

One of the first steps in this process is for the reader to assess her or his own attitudes and beliefs about homosexuality, bisexuality, and transgenderism. The reader is invited to take the Self-Assessment in Activity 14.1, to measure some of her or his own attitudes, knowledge, and experiences with LGBT persons.

Attitudes toward LGB persons range on a continuum from condemnation to acceptance to affirmation. At the most negative end of the continuum is viewing same-sex attraction and behavior as crimes against nature. Persons with these attitudes believe that LGB persons are immoral, sick, and inferior. They believe that anything, including hospitalization, prison, and electric shock therapy, is justified to change them. Those with more accepting attitudes tend to view sexual minority individuals as no different from heterosexual persons, believe in equal rights for sexual minority persons, and accept a person's sexuality as long as sexual minority persons don't "flaunt it." At the most positive end of the continuum is viewing same-sex attraction as a natural expression of human sexuality. Such individuals appreciate, validate, and affirm LGB individuals and communities and believe that LGB persons are indispensable to a society. They are willing to reject and confront negative stereotypes and discriminatory practices. They actively work to eradicate oppression and improve the lives of LGB persons (Herek, 1994, 1995; Riddle, n.d.).

Many heterosexuals hold hostile attitudes toward lesbians and gay men (Herek, 1994). For example, in a community sample of self-identified heterosexuals, over 60 percent believed that sex between two members of the same sex was wrong, and 60 percent believed that lesbians and gay men are disgusting (Herek, 1994). Furthermore, 49 percent of heterosexuals indicated they would object to having a gay doctor, and 55 percent would object to having a gay elementary school teacher (Schmalz, 1993). Consistent with community and national samples, research on heterosexual college students' attitudes toward lesbian and gay students also

ACTIVITY 14.1

Self-Assessment

Instructions: Please indicate your agreement or disagreement with each of the following statements by writing in the appropriate number from the scale below.

Strongly Disagree	Disagree	Neither Agree nor Disagree	Agree	Strongly Agree
1	2	3	4	5

_____ 1. I believe homosexuality is a sin.

_____ 2. I would feel disappointed if I learned that my child was lesbian, gay, bisexual, or transgendered (LGBT).

_____ 3. Same-sex couples should be allowed to marry.

_____ 4. Children should be taught that being gay is a normal and healthy way for people to be.

_____ 5. If a member of my sex asked me out for a date, I would feel flattered.

_____ 6. Most lesbians hate men.

_____ 7. Lesbianism is the result of traumatic relationships with men.

_____ 8. Gay men are more likely than heterosexual men to be pedophiles.

_____ 9. Most men who display effeminate traits are gay.

_____ 10. Bisexual men and women are really "closeted" gay men and lesbians.

_____ 11. I have LGBT friends.

_____ 12. Someone has "come out" to me in the past two years.

_____ 13. I am familiar with religious groups that welcome and affirm LGBT persons.

_____ 14. I know someone who has been beaten up or murdered because of her or his sexual orientation.

_____ 15. I have attended LGBT establishments and events, such as a gay bar or a gay pride festival.

_____ 16. I understand the costs of "coming out" that LGBT persons face.

_____ 17. I am knowledgeable about a variety of reactions a parent might have after learning that her or his child is LGB.

_____ 18. I am familiar with the community resources in my area for LGBT persons (e.g., bookstores, hotlines, support groups, bars).

_____ 19. I understand the significance of the Stonewall riots to the LGBT community.

_____ 20. I am knowledgeable about the conditions of "triple jeopardy" that affect lesbians and bisexual women of color.

(Continued)

(Continued)

Scoring: Reverse score (that is, 1 = 5, 2 = 4, 3 = 3, 4 = 2, 5 = 1) the following items: 1, 2, 6, 7, 8, 9, and 10. Then add up all the items for a total score. Scores can range from 20 to 100. Items 1 to 5 reflect attitudes toward LGBT persons, items 6 to 10 reflect commonly held myths about LGBT persons, and items 11 to 20 reflect knowledge about and experiences with LGBT persons and communities. Higher scores reflect positive attitudes and more knowledge and experiences with LGBT persons and communities. Lower scores reflect negative attitudes and limited knowledge and experiences with LGBT persons and communities.

---

indicate an intolerant climate. For example, over half of college students surveyed believed that lesbians and gay men should try to be heterosexual, 22 percent reported that they had verbally harassed gay men, and 54 percent described themselves as disapproving or very disapproving of homosexuality (Comstock, 1991).

Perhaps as you completed the Self-Assessment in Activity 14.1, you noticed that you, too, hold some of these negative attitudes and myths about LGBT persons and lack information about sexual minority persons. Keep your current attitudes in mind as you work through this chapter. Be open to the data presented here, even if it counters your current views.

CORRELATES OF HETEROSEXUALS' ATTITUDES TOWARD LGB PERSONS

Negative attitudes toward LGB persons are often not based on actual experiences but on stereotypes and prejudice (APA, 2004). Attitudes toward LGB persons tend to be related to a variety of factors. For example, negative attitudes toward lesbians and gay men are associated with being male, having a low educational level, belonging to a conservative religious denomination, being politically conservative, accepting traditional gender roles for women and men, and lacking interpersonal contact with lesbians and gay men. In contrast, positive attitudes toward lesbians and gay men are associated with being female, reporting a high educational level, not being religious or belonging to a liberal religious denomination, being politically liberal or moderate, accepting nontraditional gender roles for women and men, and having positive interpersonal experiences with lesbians and gay men (Herek, 1994). Consistent with these findings, positive attitudes regarding bisexuality among heterosexuals are related to more positive attitudes toward lesbians and gay men, lack of or infrequent religious attendance, more liberal political ideology, and prior contact with LGB persons (Mohr & Rochlen, 1999). Information concerning correlates of anti-LGB attitudes gives counselors a sense of the task of eradicating heterosexism and anti-LGB prejudice and discrimination. It also helps counselors know the context of the lives of LGB persons who are making decisions about coming out to others and dealing with hetero-sexism in their lives.

COUNSELORS' ATTITUDES TOWARD LGB PERSONS

Counselors tend to be more open-minded about sexual minority identities than people in general. The majority of counselors have lower levels of hetero-sexism than does the general public, counselors generally do not view same-sex attraction as psychopathology, and they would be supportive of LGB clients who are coming to terms with their sexual identity (Bieschke, McClanahan, Tozer, Grzegorek, & Park, 2000).

Despite these overarching positive trends, negative attitudes toward LGB clients still persist in the counseling profession. For example, Jordan and Deluty (1995) found that 12.9 percent of counselors reported that they considered a lesbian and gay orientation to be a psychosexual disorder, 5 percent considered it a personality disorder, and 11 percent reported using counseling methods to try to change clients' sexual orientation. In addition, counselors generally rate LGB clients as being weaker and more powerless than heterosexual clients (Glenn & Russell, 1986). Furthermore, experiences of heterosexist bias in the training of counseling and psychology students and within the profession itself have been well documented (cf. Croteau, Lark, Lidderdale, & Chung, 2005; Pilkington & Cantor, 1996).

HETEROSEXIST BIASES IN COUNSELING WORK

Heterosexist counselor attitudes, behaviors, and language negatively affect LGB clients (Dorland & Fischer, 2001). Even among counselors who reported low levels of heterosexism in themselves, negative views of homosexuality were found and were correlated with inaccurate information processing, cognitive errors, and verbal avoidance behaviors that discouraged or inhibited lesbian and gay clients from expressing or exploring sexual orientation themes during coun-seling sessions (Gelso, Fassinger, Gomez, & Latts, 1995; Hayes & Gelso, 1993). In addition, Liddle (1996) found that client-reported heterosexist behaviors and attitudes were positively related with the risk of terminating after one session and were negatively related with perceptions of counselor helpfulness. It makes sense, therefore, that most lesbian and gay clients pre-screened their counselors for LGB affirmativeness (Liddle, 1997). This screening was linked to greater client satisfaction with counseling.

Examining the power of language in counseling, Dorland and Fischer's (2001) analogue study found that LGB participants exposed to a counseling vignette that was free from heterosexist language bias were more likely to express a desire to return to see the counselor, to perceive the counselor as more credible, to indi-cate greater willingness to disclose personal information in counseling, and to express greater comfort in disclosing her or his sexual orientation to the coun-selor than participants exposed to a similar counseling vignette that contained heterosexist language.

TYPES OF PROBLEMATIC COUNSELOR HETEROSEXIST RESPONSES

Sexual minority clients might encounter four types of heterosexist counselor responses (Falco, 1991). The reader might consider which one, if any, would typify her or his current tendency.

The first one is "You're not really an LGB person." This type of response can vary from the extreme of counselors telling clients that they are outright liars to counselors suggesting that clients are going through a phase or that they don't really know what they want. The effects of this type of response are to silence clients and convey to them that they are not able to trust their own perceptions.

The second type of heterosexist counselor reaction is "the inadequate response," where the counselor either automatically assumes a client is heterosexual or treats sexual identity issues with avoidance. Thus, when a client tells the therapist that she or he is LGB, the counselor ignores the relevance and importance of this social identity to the client, refuses to discuss this topic in any depth, and often changes the subject when the client brings it up.

The third response is "the liberal response," where the counselor seems open to sexual minority identities but tries to treat LGB clients as if they were heterosexual. This type of response denies all of the unique dynamics and stressors, such as experiences of external and internalized heterosexism, that sexual minority clients experience and bypasses very important counseling material.

The fourth heterosexist counselor behavior is "the lecture," where the counselor provides an unfounded description of sexual minority persons as immature, developmentally arrested, acting out, unhealthy, or pathological. An extreme form of this type of heterosexist bias can be seen in proponents of "conversion" or "reparative" therapies that aim to change clients' sexual orientation. These types of therapies assert that same-sex feelings are unacceptable and pathological and need to be "cured." Conversion therapies are based on misleading, oppressive, and unsupported hypotheses. They have been shown to cause considerable damage, such as increased self-hate, psychological distress, and suicidality, to those who undergo them (Beckstead & Morrow, 2004; Morrow & Beckstead, 2004; Shidlo & Schroeder, 2002). In addition, they violate many principles of the American Psychological Association's ethical code, including respect for people's rights and dignity, competence, integrity, and social responsibility (Tozer & McClanahan, 1999).

IDENTIFYING AND CHALLENGING HETEROSEXISM

The culture of North America is predominantly heterosexist and homophobic and conveys negative messages about LGB identities, persons, and communities. Thus, future counselors have internalized these messages to some degree or another. For some counselors, these attitudes and beliefs are overt and conscious (e.g., believing that homosexuality is a sin) and for others they are covert and unconscious (e.g., assuming that a client is heterosexual). So the question is not, "Am I heterosexist?" but "How am I heterosexist and how might that affect my work with LGB as well as heterosexual clients?" (Morrow, 2000).

For counselors, self-awareness about LGB issues is a continual process of self-examination, of identifying and challenging their values, beliefs, attitudes, biases, and personal limitations in working with LGB clients. Counselors must examine their own sexual orientation and how it has affected their development and identity. From there, they have to study their own heterosexist socialization and identify specific attitudes and beliefs from their upbringing that indicate both respect and a lack of respect for LGB persons. In other words, counselors must look at how their personal feelings influence their interactions with their LGB clients (see Activities 14.2 and 14.3).

Knowledge About Sexual Orientation

As mentioned earlier, part of the process of becoming a culturally alert counselor involves increasing one's knowledge of historical, social, and psychological issues pertaining to LGBT persons and communities. This section addresses the "why" and "how much" questions about sexual orientation by presenting sexual orientation as a continuum, the pervasiveness of same-sex attraction, and the causes of sexual orientation. Then, the social and psychological dimensions of minority sexual orientation are discussed: the history of the LGB rights movement and impact of heterosexism, internalized heterosexism, and the effect of the coming out process on an LGB person's psychosocial well-being. Finally, the unique issues of bisexuals, transgendered persons, sexual minority women, and LGB persons of color are explored.

SEXUAL ORIENTATION AS A CONTINUUM

Sexual orientation refers to the direction of emotional, romantic, and sexual feelings or behavior. The orientation can be toward (1) people of the opposite sex (heterosexuality), (2) people of the same sex (homosexuality), and (3) people of both sexes (bisexuality). Kinsey, Pomeroy, and Martin (1948) found that rather than these being discrete categories, romantic and sexual attraction and behavior could be categorized on a seven-point continuum: (1) exclusively heterosexual, (2) predominantly heterosexual with incidental homosexuality, (3) predominantly heterosexual with more than incidental homosexuality, (4) equal amounts of heterosexual and homosexual activity, (5) predominantly homosexual with more than incidental heterosexuality, (6) predominantly homosexual with incidental heterosexuality, and (7) exclusively homosexual.

SAME-SEX ATTRACTION

Same-sex attraction and sexual behavior are forms of sexuality that occur consistently in humans, as well as in other species of the animal world. Same-sex

ACTIVITY 14.2

Examining Messages Learned About Sexual Orientation

As a part of becoming more self-aware concerning sexual orientation issues, it is important for you to examine both the overt and subtle messages that you learned about heterosexuals, lesbians, gay men, and bisexual women and men. In doing so, you might consider the following questions:

What are your earliest memories related to hearing others speak about sexual orientation?

How did you learn about heterosexuality, homosexuality, and bisexuality as a child, adolescent, and adult?

What messages did you hear from the government, media, school, religious institutions, colleagues, acquaintances, friends, and family of origin about heterosexuality, homosexuality, and bisexuality?

What stereotypes exist in the general culture (e.g., dominant U.S.) about lesbians, gay men, and bisexual persons? What impact do you think these stereotypes might have on both heterosexuals and sexual minority clients?

When was the first time, or a significant time, if ever, when you were forced to rethink or were challenged about your attitudes concerning sexual orientation?

How have your attitudes about sexual orientation issues developed over time?

How do you feel about interacting with and counseling others whose sexual orientation is the same as yours?

How do you feel about interacting with and counseling others whose sexual orientation is different from yours?

ACTIVITY 14.3

Becoming Aware of Heterosexual Privilege

Heterosexual privilege refers to unearned benefits and social advantages that are enjoyed by heterosexual people but not by sexual minority people. Many heterosexuals are likely to consider these privileges to be "natural." They frequently go unarticulated and unexamined by those who benefit from them. Examples of heterosexual privilege include showing affection to your romantic partner in public without fear of retaliation, having the tax benefits associated with marriage, and talking openly to a co-worker about the vacation you had with your romantic partner.

Make a list of at least three examples of heterosexual privilege that occur in daily living. This activity can be particularly insightful when done with others in small groups consisting of persons of various sexual orientations.

1.

2.

3.

---

sexual behavior has been documented in almost every animal species including cats, cows, dogs, fish, frogs, lions, and rabbits (Roughgarden, 2004; Weinrich, 1982). For example, observations of bird species, such as Western gulls, provide examples of two animals of the same sex engaging in committed, long-term attachments (Hunt & Hunt, 1977).

In humans, same-sex romantic attraction and relationships have occurred in both Western and non-Western societies, from ancient Greece to modern times (Bohan, 1996). Reactions to sexual minority persons have differed across time and culture and range from affirmation and celebration to persecution (Bohan, 1996; Weinrich & Williams, 1991). For example, same-sex marriage was permitted among many Native American tribes, but it is not allowed in 49 of the 50 states in the United States as of this writing, with Massachusetts being the exception (Bohan, 1996).

Estimates of the number of LGB persons vary dramatically, depending on definitions (e.g., engaging in same-sex sexual behaviors vs. self-identifying as LGB) and sampling methods used (e.g., random vs. convenience samples). A generally accepted statistic is that up to one in 10 persons is lesbian or gay (Kinsey, Pomeroy, & Martin, 1948; Kinsey, Pomeroy, Martin, & Geebhard, 1948; Singer & Deschamps, 1994). LGB persons come from all cultural backgrounds, socioeconomic levels, educational levels, religions, personality styles, career paths, and life philosophies (Bell & Weinberg, 1978). LGB persons are demographically as diverse as their heterosexual counterparts and, therefore, cannot be described as a unitary group. However, as will be discussed later in this chapter, certain stressors associated with being a sexual minority person are unique to LGB persons and can have an effect on psychological well-being and interactions with counselors (Meyer, 2003).

CAUSES OF SEXUAL ORIENTATION

Sexual orientation is shaped through a complex interaction of biological, cognitive, and environmental factors. Sexual attraction typically emerges in early adolescence without any prior sexual experience (APA, 2004). Although how a particular sexual orientation develops is not well understood by scientists, there is considerable evidence suggesting the important role of hereditary or genetic factors in determining sexual orientation.

Hereditary and genetic investigations of sexual orientation consist of family pedigree studies, twin studies, adoption studies, and DNA linkage analysis. A pedigree analysis is founded on the principle that if a trait—in this case, homosexuality—is genetically influenced, it will tend to aggregate in families. Thus, by studying the degree and patterns of familial aggregation, inferences can be made concerning the possible number of genes involved in the expression of a trait and how these genes may act (Pillard, Poumadere, & Carretta, 1981). Family studies indicate that homosexual participants have more homosexual siblings and relatives than do heterosexual participants and more than would be expected given population frequencies (Pattatucci & Hamer, 1995; Pillard & Bailey, 1998; Pillard et al., 1981).

Twin and adoptee studies investigate the comparison of concordance between monozygotic/identical twins (those developed from the splitting of a single fertilized egg), dizygotic/fraternal twins (those developed from the fertilization of two separate eggs by two separate sperm), and adopted siblings (biologically unrelated individuals) reared together. If the influence of genes is paramount, monozygotic twins will frequently be concordant, whereas dizygotic twins will have the same concordance as non-twin biological siblings. It is significant that adopted siblings, sharing the family's environment but not its genes, will share the trait no more often than an average sample of the population (Pillard & Bailey, 1998). Reviews of the twin studies indicate that the rate of adult homosexuality is higher among monozygotic than dizygotic twins and that twin, sibling, and adoptee concordance rates are compatible with the hypothesis that genes may account for half of the variance in sexual orientation (Pillard & Bailey, 1998; Pillard et al., 1981).

DNA linkage studies of families in which the homosexuality trait appears to be genetically segregating are done by chromosomal mapping of the loci of the relevant DNA sequences. Those studies have revealed statistically significant correlations between sexual orientation and the inheritance of genetic markers on chromosomal region Xq28 of the sex chromosome in males, but not females (Hu et al., 1996). Evidence for the relative contribution of biology and environment to sexual orientation is still accumulating.

A BRIEF HISTORY OF THE LGB RIGHTS MOVEMENT

Social attitudes toward LGB persons have evolved over time. In her historical review, Esther Rothblum (2000) described three key events or factors contributing to the evolution of the LGB rights movement and the current increased understanding of LGB mental health The first factor in social change for gays and lesbians was the Stonewall riots that occurred in New York City's Greenwich Village during late June and early July of 1969 and their aftermath. The uprising occurred in a working-class gay and lesbian bar called the Stonewall Inn after the police attempted a routine raid; at that time, harassment against gay bars was common. Unexpectedly, the patrons resisted and the incident escalated into a riot that continued for several days. Most people view this event as the beginning of the modern LGB rights movement, and most U.S. cities hold a Gay Pride Celebration Festival each June to commemorate the Stonewall riots.

The second factor was the influence of psychological and sex-related research. Most notable were research studies conducted by Alfred Kinsey and Evelyn Hooker (Hooker, 1957; Kinsey, Pomeroy, & Martin, 1948; Kinsey, Pomeroy, Martin, & Geebhard, 1948). Kinsey's research indicated that (a) sexual orientation could be measured on a continuum; (b) same-sex sexual attraction, fantasies, and behavior occurred among individuals who were married or otherwise conventional; and (c) homosexuality and bisexuality were normative, that is, common and pervasive across all populations and historical eras. Hooker's research indicated that gay men were as well adjusted as heterosexual men. In contrast to previous pathology-based studies of gay men who were either prisoners or psychiatric clients, Hooker's study was the first to examine "normal" gay men. Her landmark study set the stage for future psychological research that would indicate that LGB individuals are as well adjusted as heterosexuals.

The third factor consisted of changes that were made to the *Diagnostic and Statistical Manual of Mental Disorders* (*DSM*). Most notable was the removal of homosexuality from the list of mental disorders on December 15, 1973. This change led to more affirmative stances on minority sexual orientation by the counseling and psychology professions (Rothblum, 2000).

HETEROSEXISM AND ITS RELATIONSHIP TO LGB MENTAL HEALTH

Heterosexism refers to attitudes and behaviors that deny, devalue, or stigmatize any non-heterosexual form of community, relationship, identity, or behavior and can manifest on individual, familial, institutional, political, and cultural levels (Herek, 1995). Examples of heterosexism include anti-gay jokes; LGB harassment and violence; rejection by family due to sexual orientation; religious condemnation of homosexuality; sexual orientation-based discrimination in housing and employment; loss of child custody due to being a sexual minority parent; failure of the federal government to grant the more than 1,000 federal rights, benefits, and protections associated with marriage (e.g., inheritance rights and tax benefits) to lesbian and gay couples; and infrequent or negative portrayals of LGB persons in the media.

Heterosexism is sometimes subtle and passive, but it is also too often overt and aggressive. Two examples of its most violent expressions are the following. They would likely not happen without a pervasive anti-gay sentiment in society. On October 6, 1998, a student from the University of Wyoming named Matthew Shepard was brutally tortured, tied to a fence, fell into a coma, and ultimately died. The abduction, beating, and burning were due solely to the fact that he was an openly gay man. On February 2, 2006, a teenager armed with a hatchet and handgun opened fire inside a gay bar in New Bedford, Massachusetts, wounding at least three people, after asking whether it was a gay bar. The police deemed it a hate crime.

These incidents, unfortunately, are not rare; anti-gay violence occurs in all regions of the United States. In 1999, a large study found that approximately 20 percent of sexual minority women and 25 percent of sexual minority men had been victims of a sexual orientation-based hate crime or attempted hate crime, such as physical assault, sexual assault, robbery, and vandalism (Herek, Gillis, & Cogan, 1999). In a related study, the same researchers asked participants about their hate crime victimization experiences. Here is one example in which a man describes having his house fire-bombed and his car windows smashed:

> I was asleep on the front porch and a Molotov cocktail was lobbed up onto the second-story front porch where I was at. . . . And it immediately ignited the porch. I was asleep in that porch. As the building was burning I could hear the windows being broken out of the cars. And the people doing it laughing and screaming "Faggot" at the top of their lungs. . . . There was a note attached to the windshield of my car: "The faggot that lives here will be dead within a week." (Herek, Cogan, & Gillis, 2002, p. 326)

In addition to hate crime victimization, many LGB persons have experienced other types of anti-gay harassment and discrimination. For example, a summary of 24 anti-gay violence studies indicated that a full 80 percent of LGB respondents had been verbally harassed, 44 percent had been threatened with violence, 33 percent had been chased or followed, and 25 percent had been pelted with objects because someone knew or presumed them to be LGB (Berrill, 1992). A 2001 study by Vickie Mays and Susan Cochran revealed pervasive anti-gay discrimination. Over 50 percent of LGB participants reported lifetime experiences of sexual orientation-based discrimination, including not being hired for a job, being fired from a job, being prevented from renting or buying a home, being hassled by the police, and being denied or given inferior services.

Similar results have been found in U.S. high schools. For example, the Gay, Lesbian, and Straight Education Network's (GLSEN) 2003 National School

Climate Survey revealed that 84 percent of sexual minority students reported being verbally harassed because of their sexual orientation, 39 percent of LGBT students reported being physically harassed because of their sexual orientation, 45 percent of sexual minority youth of color reported being verbally harassed because of both their sexual orientation and their race/ethnicity, 92 percent of LGBT students reported hearing derogatory heterosexist remarks such as "dyke" and "faggot" frequently or often, 83 percent reported teachers intervening rarely or never when heterosexist comments were made, and 64 percent reported feeling unsafe at school.

Like the case of June presented at the beginning of this chapter, studies also indicate that the victims of anti-gay violence experience poor mental health. For example, the 1999 study by Herek, Gillis, and Cogan revealed that LGB survivors of sexual orientation-based hate crimes manifested greater anger, anxiety, depression, and posttraumatic stress than did LGB survivors of non-sexual orientation based crime victimization and LGB non-victims. Additional studies have confirmed further that experiences of heterosexist stressors such as anti-LGB violence, harassment, and discrimination are related to poorer mental and physical health, negative job-related outcomes, and poorer academic performance (GLSEN, 2003; Lewis, Derlega, Berndt, Morris, & Rose, 2001; Mays & Cochran, 2001; Szymanski, 2005b; Waldo, 1999). The price paid by LGB individuals in the United States is high and is experienced daily. Activity 14.4 provides the student with an opportunity to see the consequences of heterosexism.

ACTIVITY 14.4

Experiencing Heterosexism

One way for counselors to begin to understand what it is like to live with heterosexism on a daily basis is to engage in experiential exercises that provide a feeling for heterosexism. A good way to do this is to rent or buy the 2000 HBO film *If These Walls Could Talk 2*.

Watch the first segment where Vanessa Redgrave plays an elderly woman whose lesbian partner of 50 years dies and she finds herself unprotected and alone as she deals with her in-laws. After viewing the film segment, note your own feelings and your reactions to what transpired.

Identify the ways in which heterosexism operated and affected the lesbian characters' lives and psychological well-being.

INTERNALIZED HETEROSEXISM AND
ITS RELATIONSHIP TO LGB MENTAL HEALTH

In addition to experiencing external oppression, LGB persons frequently inter-nalize the negative attitudes toward and images about homosexuality and bisexu-ality that permeate a culture. Internalized heterosexism is the presence of negative attitudes in LGB persons about their same-sex attractions. It also includes anti-gay religious and moral attitudes in LGB persons, resulting in their isolation from the LGB community, attempting to "pass" and live a lie, subsequent fear of discovery concerning their LGB identity, and negative attitudes toward other LGB persons (Szymanski & Chung, 2001).

Internalized heterosexism can be both overt, for example, "There have been times when I've felt so awful about being LGB that I wanted to be dead; if I could take a pill to become heterosexual, I would," and subtle, for example, "I get nervous when people around me talk about homosexuality; I act as if my same-sex lovers are merely friends" (Mayfield, 2001; Shidlo, 1994; Szymanski & Chung, 2001).

Internalized heterosexism is typically greatest and most overt during the early phases of sexual identity development, which will be discussed in the next sec-tion. However, it often continues in more covert and subtle ways even in LGB persons who hold positive sexual identity attitudes. Reviews of the empirical literature (Shidlo, 1994; Szymanski, 2005a; Szymanski & Chung, 2002) indicate that internalized heterosexism is related to a variety of psychosocial difficulties in LGB persons at any age. These difficulties include low self-esteem, loneliness, depression, psychological distress, and lower levels of social support. In addi-tion, internalized heterosexism is related to lower levels of openness, responsi-bility, and motivation for the counseling process and appears to impede clients' discussion of sexual identity issues.

THE COMING OUT PROCESS

Positive sexual identity development is often a critical dimension of gay-affirmative counseling. It can be a guide for the counselor and client and an indi-cator of related issues (McCarn & Fassinger, 1996). The coming out process will be described in the context of LGB identity development.

Sexual Identity Development Models

Several models of sexual identity development have been proposed in the literature. The first and most widely cited model was developed by Vivian Cass in 1979. Several more models followed her lead (e.g., Coleman, 1982; Lewis, 1984; Sophie, 1982). Those models are combined here in the form of four phases that seem to be similar across each of the models, although differences exist among the proposed models. The first phase, which was illustrated in the case of Roger at the beginning of this chapter, is called *Being Different* by Lewis and *Identity Confusion* by Cass. It typically involves a general feeling of being different, feelings of confusion, and an initial wondering if one is lesbian or gay. The second phase, called *Coming Out to Self* by Sophie and *Identity Comparison* by Cass, involves acknowledging that one is lesbian or gay, working toward self-acceptance of one's sexual identity, and reducing internalized heterosexism.

The third phase, called *Coming Out to Others* by Sophie (1982), involves making decisions about disclosing one's sexual identity to others. Many LGB persons first come out to others who are LGB-supportive. Individuals typically come out to other LGB people first, which helps them to decrease feelings of isolation and shame and increase their social support network. During this phase, LGB individuals are likely to become immersed in gay culture, for example, attending LGB clubs and organizations and gay pride events. Coming out to heterosexuals is often the next step in this phase. It is more difficult for many LGB persons because it increases the chances of their encountering heterosexism, rejection, discrimination, and violence. The decision to come out to others needs to be weighed against the possible negative consequences that may follow (Falco, 1991). However, research supports the notion that hiding one's sexual identity is costly in terms of psychological health (Jordan & Deluty, 1998; Morris, Waldo, & Rothblum, 2001). See Activity 14.5 for a vivid illustration of the coming out process. Cass (1979) adds three additional phases at this point, called *Identity Tolerance, Identity Pride,* and *Identity Acceptance.* However, for simplification, those are omitted from this description.

The fourth phase, called *Identity Synthesis* by Cass (1979), involves a feeling of pride concerning one's lesbian/gay identity, an integration of one's sexual identity into other aspects of the self, and confrontation of heterosexism.

Sexual minority identity models provide a useful framework to guide counselors who work with LGB clients. However, such models have limitations. First, there is much variation in how a person establishes a sexual minority identity. Many LGB persons do not follow the steps outlined in the aforementioned models (Garnets & Peplau, 2001). For example, a lesbian who views sexual orientation as a private matter may be less likely to disclose her sexual orientation to others, yet she may still feel pride about herself as a lesbian. Similarly, a Latino gay man may feel good about himself as a gay man but choose not to disclose his sexual orientation in his ethnic community in order to maintain respect within his community and to avoid ridicule and outcast status (Greene, 1997). Second, gender differences exist in the coming out process for sexual minority women and men. These differences parallel gender-related trends in the general heterosexual population. For example, lesbians are more likely than gay men to come out in the context of an emotionally connected same-sex romantic relationship and to emphasize affectional rather than sexual experiences (McCarn & Fassinger, 1996). A third limitation of sexual minority identity development models is that many such models confound *individual* sexual identity development (i.e., the process of recognizing and accepting one's own same-sex attraction and lifestyle preferences) with *group* membership identity development (i.e., the process of accepting one's status as a member of an oppressed group and the confrontation of societal oppression as a member of that group) (Fassinger & Miller, 1996; McCarn & Fassinger, 1996). A final limitation of the

ACTIVITY 14.5

An Illustration of Coming Out and Family Members' Reactions

An illustration of coming out and family members' reactions to an LGB person's self-disclosure of sexual identity can be found in the 2001 Starlight Signature Series/Hearst Entertainment film *The Truth About Jane* starring Stockard Channing and Ellen Muth.

Watch the film, and then answer the following questions:

How does heterosexism manifest in Jane's and her family's life? Discuss specific examples.

What did you see in the film that is illustrative of each of the four different phases of sexual identity development described in this chapter?

How do Jane's teacher and mother's friend help Jane accept her sexuality?

If their response to her had not been so positive, how might this have affected Jane?

Discuss the reactions of family members (mother, father, brother) to Jane's disclosure of her sexual orientation.

How do these reactions fit or not fit with the three typical reactions of family members to an LGB person's disclosure discussed earlier in this chapter?

Stop the film right after Jane's teacher confronts Jane's mother and father about their behavior and her daughter's suicidal ideation (about 70 minutes into the movie). If Jane and her family were to come see you for counseling at this time to help them in their "coming out process" struggles, what goals and strategies would you implement?

developmental models is that many phase models fail to acknowledge the existence of bisexuality and the impact of multiple identities (e.g., race, ethnicity, class) on sexual identity development (Garnets & Peplau, 2001).

The Reactions of Family Members to Coming Out

LGB clients are confronted with the unique dilemma of having to decide whether or not to come out to family members. Because openness, honesty, and congruence are important in establishing intimate relationships, many LGB persons decide to come out to family members (Brown, 1989). Family members' responses can range from negative to neutral to positive.

In their review of the literature, Matthews and Lease (2000) identified several typical family reactions to a family member's self-disclosure of her or his same-sex attraction. They generally follow Kübler-Ross's (1969) formulation of the grieving and acceptance process. A typical early reaction to a family member's disclosure of her or his sexual identity is *denial*. Frequently, family members will suggest that the LGB person is simply "going through a phase" and does not really know what she or he wants. At other times, family members may be overtly rejecting, even trying to change or "cure" their family member's sexual orientation or disown her or him.

Anger toward the LGB person is another reaction that often stems from family members' beliefs that the LGB person's sexual orientation is a rejection of them and their values. Another possible response is depression, which often manifests itself in family members' worries about what a sexual identity status means for their LGB family member and for themselves. Guilt feelings may also surface, and family members may question whether they have done something wrong to cause this to happen. Another common reaction is grief. This may take the form of grieving for the child or sibling they thought they had and a loss of dreams associated with a traditional heterosexual lifestyle.

Whatever the initial reaction, family members must face the negative cultural stereotypes and myths that they have learned about LGB persons as they confront those negative images in light of their daughter, son, sibling, grandchild, niece, or nephew. Family members must begin to re-evaluate and challenge these heterosexist messages (Matthews & Lease, 2000).

Family members of LGB persons often find it helpful to engage in bibliotherapy, that is, reading relevant and informative gay-affirmative materials (e.g., Fairchild & Hayward, 1998), and to connect with formal support systems, such as PFLAG (Parents and Friends of Lesbians and Gays). These activities can help family members to accept and affirm their daughter, son, or sibling's sexual orientation, as well as help in their own "coming out" as the parent or sibling of a LGB family member (Brown, 1989).

UNIQUE ISSUES OF BISEXUAL PERSONS

Bisexual persons deal with many of the same issues, such as heterosexism and internalized heterosexism, that lesbians and gay men contend with; however, they also face unique issues. This section will provide information about these unique issues, which include the myths about bisexuality, forms of bisexuality, coming out issues, and biphobia.

Myths

Several myths in U.S. culture about bisexuality can negatively influence both a bisexual person's self-acceptance of her or his sexual identity and a counselor's attitudes, behaviors, and therapeutic work with bisexual clients. These myths include the following: (a) bisexuals are "closeted" lesbians and gay men who are in denial of their homosexual identity, (b) bisexuals are stuck in the transition phase from heterosexuality to homosexuality, (c) bisexuals are indecisive and ambivalent "fence sitters," (d) bisexuals are incapable of monogamy and unable to make relationship commitments, and (e) bisexuals need concurrent relationships with both genders for personal satisfaction (Dworkin, 2001; Firestein, 1996; Guidry, 1999). These myths arise in part out of socially constructed assumptions that sexual orientation is dichotomous and fixed rather than continuous and fluid (Morrow, 2000).

Forms of Bisexuality

Bisexuality can take at least four forms. "Historical bisexuality" is the case for individuals who currently define themselves as heterosexual or gay who had past experiences of attraction or sexual behavior with members of the same sex or opposite sex, respectively. Another form is "transitional bisexuality," which represents the process of individuals moving through the phase of coming out as either gay or bisexual. A third form of bisexuality is "sequential bisexuality," which consists of individuals having relationships with members of both sexes but with only one individual during a particular time. Finally, there is "concurrent bisexuality," in the case of persons who have both female and male partners during the same period (Guidry, 1999).

Coming Out Issues

Bisexual women and men face various issues and concerns in the coming out process that frequently make it a difficult transition. These include fear of isolation, alienation, rejection, being considered an outsider from a previously identified heterosexual or gay group, lack of community social support, feeling marginalized, experiencing identity confusion, and dealing with a lack of social confirmation for one's bisexual identity (Dworkin, 2001; Fox, 2000; Guidry, 1999).

Although there are similarities in the coming out process among bisexuals, lesbians, and gay men, there are distinct differences for bisexual clients. Lesbians and gay men need to acknowledge and affirm only their same-sex attractions and relationships in order to achieve positive and integrated sexual identities. By contrast, bisexuals need to acknowledge and affirm both the homosexual and heterosexual components of their identities (Fox, 2000). Such a dual acknowledgment and affirmation process for bisexuals can be confusing and challenging and, therefore, may be a core focus in counseling.

Biphobia

Bisexual women and men must also deal with biphobia and internalized biphobia in addition to dealing with heterosexism and internalized heterosexism (Dworkin, 2001; Fox, 2000; Guidry, 1999; Ochs, 1996). *Biphobia* is defined as a fear or dislike of those who do not identify as either heterosexual or lesbian/gay (Dworkin, 2001). Biphobia manifests itself in the denial of the very existence of bisexual people and in the "double discrimination" that many bisexual woman and men experience. They often experience rejection and alienation both by some members of the lesbian and gay community, who criticize them for possessing a degree of heterosexual privilege, and by some members of the heterosexual community, who view them as amoral, hedonistic spreaders of disease and disrupters of families (Ochs, 1996).

As a result of biphobia, bisexual women and men often struggle to have their sexual orientation recognized as legitimate. For example, if a bisexual person is in a relationship with a person of the same sex, she or he often struggles to be recognized as bisexual rather than being immediately perceived as lesbian or gay. Similarly, if a bisexual person is in a relationship with a person of the opposite gender, she or he often struggles to be seen as legitimately bisexual. Thus, the sexual identities of bisexual women and men are often rendered invisible because of existing notions that portray simplified pictures of sexual orientation as defined by the sex of one's romantic partner (Bieschke, Croteau, Lark, & Vandiver, 2005).

Internalized biphobia refers to the internalization of negative messages about bisexuality and experiences of rejection and alienation that result in self-hatred, self-doubt, and low self-esteem (Guidry, 1999). Internalized biphobia can be overpowering, and the experience of isolation, illegitimacy, shame, and confusion felt by many bisexuals can be debilitating (Guidry, 1999; Ochs, 1996). Internalized biphobia includes feelings of conflict and shame concerning one's bisexuality. These feelings often result from not fully fitting into either lesbian/gay or heterosexual worlds. They also stem from a sense of betraying one's identity group. Guilt may be present, for example, when a bisexual person ends a relationship with a member of the same sex and later gets involved with a member of the opposite sex (Ochs, 1996). In that case, the bisexual person might feel guilty about reinforcing negative stereotypes about bisexuals in general.

UNIQUE ISSUES OF TRANSGENDERED PERSONS

Transgender refers to "a range of behaviors, expressions, and identifications that challenge the pervasive bipolar gender system in a given culture" (Carroll, Gilroy, & Ryan, 2002, p. 139). A vast range of often unrelated identity categories, such as transgenderists, transsexuals, intersex, transvestites, drag queens, and drag kings, fall under the classification of transgendered behaviors (Carroll et al., 2002; Gainor, 2000). Each will be defined here.

The term *transgenderist* refers to an individual, such as a cross-dresser or non-surgical transsexual, who has chosen to live life as the other gender on a continuous basis but does not wish to have sex reassignment surgery (Gainor, 2000). The term *transsexual* refers to individuals whose gender identity is different from their anatomical sex, who frequently seek sex hormones and/or sex reassignment surgery, and who desire to permanently live their lives as members of the other gender. The terms *intersex* or *hermaphrodite* refer to individuals who are born with some mixture of ambiguous genitalia (Carroll et al., 2002). The term *transvestite* refers to individuals who wear clothing of the opposite gender for emotional satisfaction and/or sexual stimulation (Gainor, 2000), but who are not necessarily sexually attracted to members of the same sex. The terms *drag queen* and *drag king* refer to individuals who identify themselves as gay or lesbian and who cross-dress for entertainment purposes in lesbian and gay clubs (Carroll et al., 2002).

Due to the diversity of identity categories within this population, self-definition is a complicated process for many transgendered persons. This process is often made more difficult due to the marginalization of, discrimination against, and alienation of transgendered persons in U.S. society (Carroll et al., 2002; Gainor, 2000). These cultural and societal pressures also create or exacerbate clinical issues that transgendered persons might present in counseling, such as anxiety, depression, low self-esteem, substance abuse, hate crime victimization, and physical and emotional abuse (Carroll et al., 2002; Gainor, 2000).

Transgendered clients are often skeptical of the counseling and medical communities due to their experiences of discrimination by service providers. Counselors and medical doctors often play the role of gatekeeper—the person who makes decisions about who can or cannot go through the gender transition process (Carroll et al., 2002; Gainor, 2000). When working with transgendered clients, counselors should avoid medical and psychiatric perspectives that pathologize transgenderism, use correct terminology to identify or label such clients, be aware that feminine and masculine behaviors are generally the creation of cultural standards and not of biological specification, and use approaches that give transgendered clients a voice to tell their story and help them overcome negative feelings of powerlessness, such as client-centered, feminist, and constructivist therapies (Butler, 1990; Carroll et al., 2002).

INTERSECTIONS OF OPPRESSIONS FOR SEXUAL MINORITY WOMEN AND PERSONS OF COLOR

This chapter so far has focused on heterosexism as a main form of oppression faced by LGB persons. As mentioned in Chapter 1 under intersectionality, other, nondominant statuses may intersect in one person's life. Many LGB persons have multiple identities and may experience oppression based on other minority statuses (e.g., gender, race/ethnicity, socioeconomic status, ability level, religious affiliation). The intersection of minority sexual orientation and (1) gender and (2) race/ethnicity will be discussed next.

Heterosexism and Sexism

Lesbian and bisexual females must deal with sexism as well as heterosexism (Szymanski, 2005b). Research has demonstrated that many lesbian and bisexual women have experienced sexist stressors such as child sexual abuse, sexual assault, gender discrimination, and hearing degrading sexual jokes about women. These experiences themselves are related to poorer mental health (Bradford, Ryan, & Rothblum, 1994; Descamps, Rothblum, Bradford, & Ryan, 2000; Szymanski, 2005b). In addition, research has demonstrated that women who experience both heterosexist and sexist stressors report more psychological distress than women who report experiencing only one form of oppression (either heterosexism or sexism; Descamps et al., 2000; Szymanski, 2005b). These research findings indicate that the experience of multiple forms of oppression can have a profound impact on psychological health.

Bias Against LGBT Persons of Color

Racism intersects with sexual minority status for lesbian and gay people of color. Lesbian and bisexual women of color have to deal with what Beverly Greene (1994) called "triple jeopardy": the interactive influences of racism, heterosexism, and sexism. Research has demonstrated that many persons of color have experienced racial discrimination, such as being treated unfairly by employers, being accused of stealing or breaking the law, and being called a racist name, and that these experiences are related to adverse psychological and health outcomes. For example, Landrine and Klonoff (1996) found that 98 percent of African Americans reported experiencing some type of racial discrimination in the past year. They also found that more experiences of racial discrimination were related to greater psychological distress and, interestingly, to cigarette smoking.

In addition to the negative effects of racism on LGB persons of color, it is important for counselors to recognize that LGB persons of color also experience a minority racial identity formation process that has many parallels to the minority sexual identity development process. It can be a challenge to effectively maintain the two minority identities, for example, as a Latino or as an African American and as a gay or lesbian person.

An added burden for a person of color might be having one's own ethnic group reject non-heterosexual identities. In that sense, LGB persons of color can have conflicting dual identities. A person may want to strongly identify with her or his ethnicity, but experience that group's rejection of non-heterosexual identities. For example, Chung and Katayama (1998) pointed out that the intensity of heterosexism is much stronger in Asian cultures than in the dominant U.S. culture because Asian cultures tend to maintain traditional gender roles for men and women and tolerate less openness about sexuality. Thus, an Asian gay man's disclosure of his sexual minority status may be seen as a rejection of his appropriate roles within the culture and as a threat to the continuation of the family line. In ethnic communities where heterosexism is rampant, LGB members may be more vulnerable, may experience more anxiety during the coming out process, and may choose not to disclose their sexual minority identity to members of their own family and ethnic community.

Given rejection by their own communities, a double oppression can confront many LGB people of color because they may find it difficult to connect with mainstream LGB communities. Their race may prove to be a barrier to support and they may be subject to shunning, stereotyping, outright rejection, or blatant racism for their racial/ethnic minority identity. Thus, counselors need to understand that the combined effects of heterosexism, racism, and sexism can create especially intense stressors for racial and ethnic minority LGB persons (Greene, 1997).

This section on knowledge of LGBT cultures and issues concludes with the invitation in Activity 14.6 to learn more.

ACTIVITY 14.6

Learning About LGBT Identities and Cultures

To increase your knowledge of LGBT identities and cultures, you might consider reading an LGBT novel or magazine; watching television shows and movies with LGBT themes and characters (e.g., *Will and Grace, Queer as Folk, The L Word, Boys Don't Cry, Desert Hearts, Philadelphia, The Birdcage, Latter Days, Doing Time on Maple Drive, Two Mothers for Zachary, Serving in Silence, Maupin's Tales of the City*); attending LGBT community events, such as a gay pride festival or a gay comedy or music performance.

NOTE: Many of the films mentioned in this chapter can be found at your local video store, through www.wolfevideo.com or www.amazon.com, or at a gay bookstore, if there is one in your community.

Skills

The final step in becoming a culturally alert counselor involves practicing relevant and sensitive counseling interventions in working with LGB clients. These interventions will be described next under the following nine rubrics: (a) avoiding heterosexist assumptions, bias, and language; (b) responding appropriately to clients' disclosures of their sexual identities; (c) conceptualizing the role of sexual orientation in the counseling process; (d) facilitating sexual identity development and the coming out process; (e) attending to external oppression; (f) identifying and challenging internalized heterosexism and biphobia; (g) exploring multiple identities of LGB clients; (h) addressing the issue of whether, and how, the counselor's sexual orientation should be disclosed; and (i) supporting the elimination of homophobia and heterosexist bias in institutions and among colleagues and peers.

USING NON-HETEROSEXIST, GENDER-NEUTRAL INCLUSIVE LANGUAGE

Counselors need to remain current with the LGB literature and monitor their own use of language, stereotypes, and bias. Terms that describe individuals who are in nondominant or minority groups require particular sensitivity because they have the power to hurt and can be backed up by oppressive action. That is the case with sexual minorities.

As described in Chapter 1, terms for nondominant cultural groups are fluid; they are products of times and attitudes. The counselor needs to be flexible in determining what terms to use with sexual minorities. Asking clients for the terms they prefer for themselves is, of course, recommended.

The term "homosexuality" is currently acceptable as a description of the overall phenomenon of same-sex attraction. However, in reference to an individual, the terms "lesbian" or "gay man" are preferred to the term "homosexual," for at least three reasons. "Homosexual" has been used in the past with negative, stereotypical connotations. It has also been the term used to label lesbian and gay identity as a psychological disorder. Finally, "homosexual" emphasizes the sexual aspect of LGB experience rather than the multifaceted nature of LGB identity and community (APA, 2004; Bohan, 1996).

The currently preferred terms for referring to people who have same-sex attraction are "lesbians," "gay men," "sexual minorities," or "LGB persons" (APA, 2004). The terms "gay" or "gay persons" generally refer to all LGB persons. However, those terms have their origins in reference only to gay men, leaving lesbians in a subordinate position and thus replicating societal sexism.

Finally, counselors should make language inclusive. They should avoid language that assumes universal heterosexuality. Instead, they might use non-heterosexist language with all clients. For example, a counselor working with a client might ask, "Do you have a partner?" or "Are you involved in a romantic relationship?" rather than "Are you married?" or "Do you have a boyfriend/husband/girlfriend/wife?" Furthermore, it is important for counselors not to assume that current romantic partners are the same sex as past partners. In a similar vein, the heterosexist use of marital status (single, married, divorced, widowed) on a counseling intake form ignores LGB relationships, thereby rendering them invisible. The word "partnered" might be added to counselors' vocabulary and to intake forms.

RESPONDING TO CLIENTS' DISCLOSURES OF THEIR SEXUAL IDENTITIES

At some point in the counseling relationship, many sexual minority clients will make the decision to disclose their sexual identity to their counselor. For clients who have been "out" for a long period of time and are accepting of their sexual identity, disclosing their sexual identity may feel very comfortable and be "no big deal." It is important for counselors to respond to such disclosures with acceptance and acknowledgment of the realistic obstacles of being a sexual minority client in a heterosexist society. Thus, a counselor might respond to client disclosure by saying, "I'm glad that you felt comfortable enough to come out to me. I know that coming out can be a difficult process. What has your experience been like?" In addition, counselors might ask clients to tell their coming out story; in particular, ask to whom the client has disclosed her or his sexuality, how others have reacted to their disclosures, and how much support the client has from LGB persons and heterosexual allies.

For clients who are in the early phases of the sexual minority development process, coming out to a counselor may feel very threatening. Such a self-disclosure is apt to be of great significance to the client, even though it may be obscured by how the client chooses to disclose her or his sexual identity. For example, a client may indicate that she or he has something to talk about, but be unable to state what it is. In that case, the counselor should honor the client's hesitance and not push disclosure. In other cases, a client may disclose her or his sexual minority status indirectly. For example, the client may refer to a "partner" or provide hints of her or his LGB status without directly disclosing sexual identity. Or the client may do so defiantly, as in, "I'm gay. I hope you are not a homophobe." Finally, the client may disclose covertly, for example, in a written note to the counselor. In each case, the client may then wait for the counselor's reaction before deciding whether it is safe to continue on this topic (Sophie, 1987).

However the client chooses to disclose, it is important that the counselor realize how difficult such a disclosure may be. The counselor's nonjudgmental acceptance is crucial. Examples of counselors' responses to such disclosures might include, "Thanks for coming out to me. That took a lot of courage. How long have you known you were gay?" and "I feel honored that you came out to me. How are you feeling about sharing this part of yourself with me?"

CONCEPTUALIZING THE ROLE OF SEXUAL ORIENTATION IN THE COUNSELING PROCESS

One of the tasks for counselors who work with sexual minority clients is to determine what role, if any, sexual orientation plays in a client's clinical issues and in the counseling process. The importance of sexual minority orientation can range from being central to a person's life to being relatively inconsequential, depending on the environment in which she or he exists and her or his identity development phase.

For some clients, sexual orientation issues will be central in the counseling process. For example, it is likely to be a core counseling issue for a client who is in the early phases of coming out. She or he is likely to be struggling to overcome internalized heterosexism and is possibly dealing with sexual orientation-based family rejection. In these cases, exploring the meaning of being lesbian, gay, or bisexual is important, as is checking on the implications for family and religion. Finally, sharing gay resources, such as literature and support groups, can help the early-phase client move toward a positive gay identity. Two learning resources that demonstrate sessions with LGBT clients are the training videos *Lesbian, Bisexual, Gay & Transgendered Counseling* (Chen-Hayes & Banez, 2001) and *Counseling Gay and Lesbian Youth: A Multiethnic Demonstration Video* (McAuliffe, 2005).

For other clients, sexual orientation issues may be relevant but not central to the client's issues and counseling process. For example, while sexual orientation issues might not be central to a client who is dealing with grief issues over a parent's death, they still might be relevant (e.g., additional loss associated with losing an LGB-affirmative parent). Finally, in the case of a gay person who has achieved an integrated sexual identity (e.g., Cass's Identity Synthesis), a counseling issue may barely touch on sexual minority matters. However, "gay stressors"— that is, the strains of living in an oppressed status in a heterosexist society—are always potentially factors in an LGB client's mental health.

FACILITATING SEXUAL IDENTITY DEVELOPMENT AND THE COMING OUT PROCESS

Counselor responses to clients' minority sexual orientation should vary with client readiness. The phases described previously can serve as a general guide to counselor behavior.

Responding to the Early Identity Phases

When clients such as Roger (from the vignette at the beginning of this chapter) are in the early phases of the sexual identity development process, they often are not ready to declare themselves to be LGB. They only wonder if they might be LGB. Counselors working with clients in these early phases need to help them explore their feelings and thoughts free from evaluation or labeling by using unconditional positive regard and responding empathically.

As clients' recognition of same-sex attraction begins to emerge, counselors should affirmatively provide support and complete acceptance of their clients' same-sex feelings as well as their worries and doubts about these feelings. For example, a counselor could validate Roger's feelings of confusion about whether he is really gay or not and his feelings of worry about what being gay might mean for him in his future, while also supporting his attraction to other men at the same time. At this early phase, counselors should discourage clients from adopting an LGB label as long as that identity has primarily negative meaning for them (Sophie, 1987). As mentioned above, it is also important for counselors to identify, explore, and challenge the client's negative stereotypes and maladaptive beliefs about LGB persons.

Responding to Coming Out Issues

Once clients who are in the early phases of sexual minority identity development have worked through some of their internalized heterosexism and have developed positive feelings about being LGB, it is useful to help them with the decision to come out to others, such as family, friends, and co-workers (Brown, 1989; Padesky, 1988; Sophie, 1987).

One of the first steps in the process of counseling a client who is considering coming out is to help the client explore some of the reasons for deciding to come out, or not to come out, to a particular person. Expressions of why a client might want to come out to a parent include, "I'm sick of silence in my family" and "I won't have to come up with excuses for not visiting anymore."

Expressions of why a client might not want to come out to a parent include, "My support system isn't strong enough right now" and "I'm afraid my father might get violent."

In addition to helping clients explore the risks and benefits associated with coming out to each individual of concern, counselors might facilitate clients' awareness of the costs of hiding and denying one's sexuality (Brown, 1989; Gartrell, 1984; Neisen, 1993). Once clients have decided to self-disclose their sexual identity, counselors can work collaboratively with them to develop a sequence of high- to low-priority persons to whom they will come out (Gartrell, 1984). Counselors might help clients explore their fears, hopes, and expectations about coming out to others. Subsequently, they might help them to select an appropriate time and setting in which to do so (Gartrell, 1984; Sophie, 1987).

In order to prepare clients for the coming out disclosure, counselors might model various ways that clients can present their sexual minority identity in an affirmative, proud, and direct manner (Gartrell, 1984). "Empty chair" role plays, in which the client plays both parts of a conversation, are particularly useful for rehearsing a self-disclosure. This technique can serve at least three purposes. First, it helps clients to anticipate what reactions they expect and fear from the target person. Second, it can provide information about a client's relationship with the target person and that person's assumptions about sexual minorities. Third, such experiential activities can help clients appreciate the difficulties of the target person's role. The role plays can be amplified by discussing best- and worst-case scenarios (Sophie, 1987).

Beyond role-playing coming out, counselors might also educate clients about common initial reactions of family and friends to a disclosure (e.g., shock, hurt, anger, guilt, possible rejection). They can remind clients that the family member, friend, or co-worker may go through her or his own developmental process of coming to accept the client's sexual minority identity. The counselor can, therefore, encourage clients to provide interested family members and friends with articles and books that contain accurate information about LGB issues and inform clients about support groups and LGB-affirmative counselors who can help the target person come to terms with the client's disclosure, if needed (Brown, 1989; Gartrell, 1984; Padesky, 1988).

After each disclosure has been achieved, counselors might facilitate the client's expression of his or her feelings about both positive and negative responses received from others (Falco, 1991). If the client experiences a rejection from an important person as a result of the disclosure, the counselor's task is to help the client deal with these negative reactions without permanent damage to her or his positive self-identity (Padesky, 1988). Clients who have experienced rejections that are particularly meaningful often internalize these rejections and deny their feelings of anger and hurt. In that case, counselors can help them to experientially express their feelings. This visceral experience can frequently move clients to a more comfortable resolution of the loss, or perhaps lead them to try a different approach with the person who rejected them (Falco, 1991). Additionally, by role play and discussion of others' possible reactions, counselors might find out what meaning these negative reactions have for clients. For example, some clients might believe that they can't trust anyone and therefore might be inclined stay in the closet. Counselors then might facilitate the mourning process that accompanies the loss of trust or relationship. Or, on the other hand, they might help clients see where their conclusions might be distorted (Padesky, 1988).

Beyond Coming Out

Beyond the major challenges of initial disclosure to family and friends, LGB persons must continue to make choices about being out as LGB every day of their lives. The development of a positive LGB identity does not protect an individual from the additional pressures that LGB persons face. For example, an LGB person will face whether, where, when, and how to express affection toward a same-sex partner in public (Gartrell, 1984). Having to hide a relationship can be a constant source of tension. Other special pressures include gay or lesbian couples frequently having to deal with financial and legal constraints on their partnership and family pressures to appear at holidays without their partners (Padesky, 1988). In addition, there are important career considerations, especially for people with high public profiles such as politicians, sports stars, physicians, and movie stars, that may make the decision to come out more difficult and place added pressures on LGB individuals and their families.

Counselors can assist clients to deal with these situations by helping them to clarify their values and what is important to them; evaluating the disadvantages and advantages of varying responses to the situations; assisting with ongoing development of social support networks; and facilitating the perspective that being a sexual minority is only one, albeit a central one, of the many aspects of their life (Gartrell, 1984; Padesky, 1988; Sophie, 1987).

The next two sections offer strategies for working with external and internal oppression.

EXTERNAL OPPRESSION: ATTENDING TO THE HETEROSEXIST CONTEXT OF CLIENTS' LIVES

The continuing heterosexist context of LGB clients' lives must be accounted for in the work. This can be done in two phases: (1) assessment of the impact of heterosexism and (2) incorporating the heterosexist dimension of LGB client's lives in the ongoing counseling.

Counselors should first assess the negative impact of heterosexist experiences on sexual minority clients. The counselor can proactively ask LGB clients about their experiences of prejudice, discrimination, harassment, violence, rejection, and invisibility. Questions at this phase might include, "What has it been like for you living as a gay man/lesbian/bisexual woman/bisexual man in a heterosexist society?" and "Have you had incidents where you thought you were treated unfairly because you are a sexual minority person?" The second phase of this process involves conceptualizing clinical issues in a heterosexist context. The counselor here tries to note the ways that heterosexism may be influencing a client's presenting problems and psychological well-being. For example, a counselor working with an LGB client who is struggling with anxiety might include minority stress and heterosexist experiences in his or her client conceptualizations, along with other LGB-related factors that may be contributing to anxiety issues (e.g., parental criticism and overly high expectations, suppression of feelings, anxious self-talk, and a high-stress lifestyle). In a similar vein, a counselor can incorporate the heterosexist context with a gay client who is struggling with whether or not to come out to a work colleague. The counselor might assist her or him to see how heterosexism in the workplace, the absence of sexual orientation-based nondiscrimination workplace policies, and the client's previous experiences of rejection after such self-disclosures might be contributing to her or his indecision.

INTERNALIZED OPPRESSION: IDENTIFYING AND CHALLENGING INTERNALIZED HETEROSEXISM

In addition to acknowledging external pressures on LGB clients, counselors should be able to assess their LGB clients' levels of internalized heterosexism or biphobia. In that vein, they should determine the extent to which these internalized negative messages are influencing clients' presenting concerns. In many cases, counselors will need to help the client explore the impact of internalized heterosexism or biphobia on their lives and, in addition, continually challenge various aspects of the client's internalized heterosexism or biphobia (Brown, 1989; Gartrell, 1984; Szymanski, 2005a).

To facilitate clients' awareness and expression of these internalized negative beliefs, counselors might ask them about attitudes and stereotypes about LGB people that they have heard while growing up and explore what impact these stereotypes might have on the clients and their levels of acceptance of their sexual minority identity. In a related vein, counselors might ask clients about times when they felt ashamed or embarrassed about their sexual orientation and, conversely, about times they felt proud of their sexual orientation.

Once internalized negative messages have been identified, counselors can use several methods to challenge those internalizations. Simple instruction and bibliotherapy can be useful; the counselor might provide factual information or affirmative readings about homosexuality or bisexuality. In addition, the counselor might use cognitive methods to help clients evaluate the validity of these beliefs. Finally, the counselor can encourage contact with other LGB persons (Gartrell, 1984; Sophie, 1987; Szymanski, Chung, & Balsam, 2001), which, in turn, can provide affirmation, role models, and self-acceptance.

A counselor might assist clients to see how their internalized heterosexism or biphobia may be related to any of their current struggles (Szymanski, 2005a). For example, a counselor working with a gay male couple might help them explore ways that their internalized negative beliefs that "gay men are not capable of monogamy" and that "gay male relationships don't last" might be contributing to their relationship problems.

EXPLORING MULTIPLE IDENTITIES OF LGB CLIENTS

As mentioned earlier, many LGB persons have more than one minority status. It is important for counselors to attend to the intersections of oppression for such clients. Counselors can use the feminist model of an "Integrated Analysis of Oppression" in such a situation. That analysis can serve three purposes: (1) to increase LGB clients' awareness of their other relevant nondominant social identities (e.g., gender, race, physical abilities, class), (2) to facilitate identity development within these identities, and (3) to promote an awareness of how clients' multiple identities influence both external and internalized heterosexism and psychosocial difficulties (Szymanski, 2005a). For example, a counselor might encounter an African American lesbian client who has heard racist messages in the LGB community and, conversely, heterosexist messages from her family and racial/ethnic community. In the latter case, she is accused of betraying her people as a black lesbian because lesbianism is seen by her community as a "white problem." A counselor can intervene by helping this client explore how racism within the LGB community is contributing to her feelings of alienation and distress and how heterosexism within her racial community is compounding her experiences of external and internalized heterosexism (Szymanski, 2005b). In addition, the counselor might (1) help her to discuss the impact of racism on herself and other African Americans, (2) identify beliefs about gay persons within the African American community, (3) explore the client's realistic fears of rejection by other African Americans if she comes out as a lesbian, and (4) provide her with readings about the issues confronting African American lesbians (cf. Greene, 1994).

COUNSELORS' SELF-DISCLOSURE OF THEIR SEXUAL ORIENTATION

One of the challenges that counselors face when working with sexual minority clients is the issue of whether, and how, the counselor's sexual orientation should be disclosed. Both nondisclosure and disclosure of one's sexual identity can convey important messages to the client. For example, by not disclosing her or his sexual identity, a counselor might be colluding with the larger culture in perpetuating the norm of secrecy. This might, in turn, make it more difficult for a client to disclose her or his sexual identity to others (Morrow, 2000). Likewise, by the counselor disclosing her or his sexual identity, she or he might convey an affirmation of LGB identities and serve as a positive role model for clients. Alternatively, there may be good reasons not to disclose one's sexual orientation to a client. For example, a gay client might ask you directly not to disclose personal information about yourself so that she or he can find her or his own strength and healing.

Whatever their sexual orientation, counselors should explore with clients what the counselor's own sexual identity might mean for the client. For example, a counselor might ask LGB clients what it would mean to them if she or he were lesbian, gay, bisexual, or heterosexual and how this might affect their relationship with her or him. A client might, or might not, indicate that she or he might feel more comfortable talking with a sexual minority counselor about certain issues.

A client might ask the counselor directly about her or his sexual orientation. Sophie (1987) asserts that counselors finding themselves in such a situation should be aware that refusal to self-disclose in response to a direct request for this information is likely to lead to distrust, which can negatively affect the counseling relationship. Important questions for the counselor to consider are whether the client wants this information and what this information would mean to her or him. If the client's motivation is to find out whether an LGB counselor has or has not gone through the coming out process, it is a legitimate concern and should be acknowledged with an honest response. The counselor may then wish to explore the meaning of this response to the client. If, on the other hand, the client's motivation is based on stereotyped and homophobic assumptions, or on distorted thought processes due to severe disturbance, it is probably advisable to risk some distrust by refraining from responding to her or his question until further work has occurred. It might be clear at this point that the issue of counselors' self-disclosure is complex and should be evaluated on a case-by-case basis (Sophie, 1987).

For counselors who themselves are sexual minorities, it is important to have worked through some of their own internalized heterosexism and biphobia. They should be comfortable with their own sexual orientation before they decide to come out to a client.

For counselors who are heterosexual, it is important for them to have worked through some of their own heterosexism, biphobia, and heterosexual privilege. It is also important for heterosexual counselors to be aware that offhanded self-disclosures of their heterosexual identity, such as casual references to a spouse or children, may be interpreted by the client as an expression of discomfort with the client's sexuality or pressure toward a heterosexual orientation (Sophie, 1987).

ENGAGING IN ACTIVISM TOWARD THE ERADICATION OF HETEROSEXISM

As part of their professional responsibility, counselors need to actively work to eradicate heterosexism and other forms of oppression. As Coretta Scott King said at the 1996 Atlanta Gay Pride Celebration, "Gay bashers and church burners drink from the same poisonous well. The civil rights movement I support believes in unity and inclusion, not division and exclusion. I will continue to support elimination in this country of all forms of bigotry—of racism, of sexism, of homophobia." Counselors can work in various ways as advocates and activists to make the world a better and safer place for LGB persons. For example, they can discourage heterosexist behavior by, for example, refusing to laugh at jokes about LGB persons and by confronting others' stereotypes about homosexuality and bisexuality. Counselors can model non-heterosexist behaviors, such as being equally affectionate with women and men; not teasing someone for nontraditional gender behaviors; avoiding "heterosexual credentializing" (i.e., making a point of one's heterosexuality); and using gender-neutral language, such as using "partner" rather than "wife" or "husband."

Counselors can make their own offices or agencies welcoming places for LGB clients by placing something LGB-related, such as a rainbow flag sticker, LGB books, and an affirmative brochure on sexual orientation, in an easily viewed place. Counselors might also recruit LGB employees to their workplaces and advocate for sexual orientation to be included in their agencies' non-discrimination policies. They also can analyze their agency's counseling materials for heterosexist bias and make the needed changes (Szymanski, 2005a). For example, instead of offering "marriage" and family counseling, counselors might change the term to "couples" and family counseling.

Outside their offices, counselors should be familiar with community resources for LGB persons in their areas, such as bookstores, hotlines, support groups, clubs, and religious groups. They can provide LGB-affirmative outreach programs as part of their work in schools, agencies, or colleges. Finally, they can become actively involved in an LGB organization in the community or in the counseling profession. Even if a counselor is not LGB, she or he can proudly be an "ally" of LGB persons by engaging in the activities enumerated above (see Activity 14.7).

CASE EXAMPLE ILLUSTRATING SKILLS

Jason is a 21-year-old white gay male. He is a senior majoring in biology. He has a 3.6 GPA and is president of the Biology Club, research assistant for the

---

ACTIVITY 14.7

Activist Reflections

Part of becoming a social change agent is being able to make a commitment to specific ways that you can work toward the eradication of heterosexism. To help you first reflect on your experiences of injustice, address the following questions. First write responses alone, then discuss in pairs or small groups:

1. Describe a time when you felt angry about heterosexism or biphobia in society.

2. Describe a time when you felt helpless as an individual to create change regarding heterosexism or biphobia in society.

3. Describe a time when you decided to actively resist heterosexism or biphobia.

4. Make a list of three ways that you will actively resist heterosexism and biphobia in both your personal and professional lives over the next few weeks.

Biology Department Chair, and mentor for new students majoring in biology; however, he still fears failure and feels he should be getting all A's and doing more biology-related activities. In the past, his father told him he would never amount to anything because he was gay, and this increases his fear of failure. He describes himself as a perfectionist and is very hard on himself. Jason is also dealing with stress about multiple responsibilities at school and at home. Jason decides to enter counseling because he is feeling overwhelmed and stressed out and is experiencing symptoms of anxiety, such as difficulty sleeping, shallow breathing, and racing thoughts.

As he enters the university counseling center, Jason is feeling very anxious and unsure of what his experience will be like, particularly since he had a bad experience with a homophobic therapist in the past. While waiting for his counselor, he sees a pamphlet on coming out issues and a couple of LGBT magazines on the table in the lobby. His therapist, a white female, comes out to greet him and leads him to her office. As they enter her office, Jason sees a Safe Zone sticker on her door and several LGBT books in her bookcase, and this begins to put him at ease.

During the initial intake interview, the counselor asks Jason about his previous counseling experience. He states that he saw a therapist in high school for about three sessions when he was dealing with coming out as a gay man but stopped going to that therapist when he suggested that Jason's homosexuality was caused by having an "overbearing and smothering" mother. Jason's counselor responds to his past therapy experience with shock and states that she is sorry that Jason had to deal with such an uninformed and biased counselor. She makes it clear to Jason that she does not believe that his being gay was caused by his mother, and she normalizes homosexuality as a natural form of emotional/sexual attraction. At this point, Jason asks his counselor what her sexual orientation is. She states that she is a heterosexual woman and asks what her sexual orientation means to him and how he feels about working with her, given that she is both heterosexual and a woman. Jason responds that he feels comfortable working with her and was just curious because she seemed so gay-friendly.

The counselor proceeds to ask Jason about his coming out experience and his experiences of being a gay man in a heterosexist society. Jason states that he had difficulty in high school accepting being gay but that he feels good about himself now as a gay man. He states that he is out to his family and some heterosexual and LGB friends. He reports that reactions to his self-disclosures of his sexual orientation have been good, except for his father's response, which was very negative. Jason states that his father, a successful businessman, and he have a conflictual, distant relationship and that when they do talk, his father is very critical of him, believes he needs to be doing more to be successful in his career, and frequently makes derogatory comments about his being gay. After further exploration, Jason admits that he has internalized some of his father's heterosexist comments about gay men not being successful in work and that he doesn't feel good enough at times because he is gay. Jason also states that he is not out as a gay man at school because he believes it could ruin his career, and he doesn't believe it is safe because he has heard his department chair make heterosexist comments.

The counselor continues with the clinical interview, finding out more information about Jason's family history; medical history; alcohol and drug use; and educational, interpersonal, and vocational histories. She also checks for any suicidal and homicidal ideation/attempts and checks for a history of abuse, rape, and assault. At the end of the session, she checks in with Jason to see how he is feeling about their first session. Jason states that he feels good and would like to continue their work together.

After Jason leaves, the counselor reviews the session and feels she has a good beginning case conceptualization and some ideas for treatment. She believes that Jason's presenting issues of stress and anxiety are fueled and maintained by several sources. First, she identities two sub-personalities, The Critic and The Perfectionist, which tend to be prominent in people who are prone to anxiety (see Bourne, 2005, for a full discussion of these sub-personalities). She believes that it might be helpful to assist Jason to identify when he is engaging in these negative self-talks (e.g., "I should be more involved in biology-related activities"), demonstrate how they are contributing to his anxiety issues, illustrate how they may be connected with his family of origin issues (e.g., growing up in a family that set excessively high standards and was overly critical), help him replace his negative self-talk with more positive talk (e.g., "It's important to have a balance in my life, and it's okay to take care of my personal needs"), and teach him self-nurturing skills. In addition, she would like to explore Jason's fears related to failing and not feeling good enough, even though he is at the top of his class. Using cognitive therapy, she would like to challenge some of his catastrophizing thoughts that are not reality-based.

The counselor also believes that Jason's high-stress lifestyle, juggling of multiple responsibilities, and lack of personal time are also contributing to his anxiety. She would like to discuss ways that Jason might achieve more of a balance between his school demands and personal time. Also, she might discuss other stress management techniques, such as exercising, deep breathing, progressive muscle relaxation, and listening to music, to help him decrease his stress level.

The counselor would also like to further discuss Jason's feeling that he needs to be the best at everything and an overachiever and to make connections to how this relates to both external (e.g., heterosexist behaviors from father and department chair) and internalized heterosexism (e.g., "gay men are not successful at work" and "to be gay is to be not good enough"). She would like to explore and challenge Jason's s internalized heterosexism using cognitive and feminist methods, bibliotherapy, and encouraging his making connections with gay men who are successful in their careers. She also wonders whether Jason has unfinished business with his father, and she would like to further discuss their relationship, his father's rejection of his being gay, and his feelings of anger and hurt toward his father. She thinks it also might be helpful to further explore his school situation and decision not to come out at school, noting both the pros and cons of staying closeted in the area. At some point in therapy, she would also like to discuss more fully Jason's experiences of heterosexism, ways he dealt with these behaviors, and possibly discuss and role-play ways Jason might confront and deal with other people's heterosexist beliefs and behaviors.

Activity 14.8 encourages the reader to gain deeper knowledge of LGB issues through personal contact. Further, the reader is encouraged to try offering counseling responses to various situations by completing Activity 14.9.

ACTIVITY 14.8

Interviewing an LGB Person

Locate an LGB person who is willing to be interviewed, for example, through a local college LGB organization, a gay-friendly religious organization, or through a local PFLAG chapter. Conduct a personal interview with that person and ask her or him about her or his coming out experiences, how she or he handled the disclosure or non-disclosure of her or his sexual identity, reactions of others to the self-disclosures, experiences with heterosexism and internalized heterosexism, and challenges and coping strategies for living in a heterosexist environment. Green (1996) provides additional structured and detailed questions you might ask concerning families of origin, lesbian and gay couple relationships, parenting issues, and families of choice. When conducting this interview, be sure to implement some of the LGB affirmative counseling skills you learned in this chapter.

ACTIVITY 14.9

Based on the reading, respond to each of the following client statements with a potentially helpful response. Give a short reason for each.

"I just don't want to go the prom with a boy. My mom is pressuring me to get a date though. I just want to hang out with girls. Is there something wrong with me?" _____

_____

_____

"I know that gay people are wrong and sinful. When I am attracted to other men, I loathe myself." _____

_____

"It all happened so quickly. I just remember hearing someone screaming 'faggot' at me. Then all of a sudden, two big guys jumped me and started punching and kicking me. When they were done, I could hardly move, and there was blood everywhere." _____

_____

_____

Summary

Heterosexist bias, prejudice, and discrimination often go unchallenged in U.S. culture and are often tolerated and accepted. As demonstrated in this chapter, these oppressive conditions can make managing a sexual minority identity complex, challenging, and difficult. Even within the multicultural counseling profession, LGBT issues are often marginalized. Thus, it is imperative for counselors to engage in growth-producing dialogues about LGBT issues and move sexual orientation issues from the margin to the center of counseling discourses.

References

American Psychological Association. (2004). *Answers to your questions about sexual orientation and homosexuality.* Retrieved October 24, 2004, from http://www.apa .org/pubinfo/answers.html

Beckstead, A. L., & Morrow, S. L. (2004). Mormon clients' experiences of conversion therapy: The need for a new treatment approach. *The Counseling Psychologist, 32,* 651–690.

Bell, A. P., & Weinberg, M. S. (1978). *Homosexualities: A study of diversity among men and women.* New York: Touchstone.

Berrill, K. T. (1992). Antigay violence and victimization in the United States: An overview. In G. M. Herek & K. T. Berrill (Eds.), *Hate crimes: Confronting violence against lesbians and gay men* (pp. 19–45). Newbury Park, CA: Sage.

Bieschke, K. J., Croteau, J. M., Lark, J. S., & Vandiver, B. J. (2005). Toward a discourse of sexual orientation equity in the counseling professions. In J. M. Croteau, J. S. Lark, M. A. Lidderdale, & Y. B. Chung (Eds.), *Deconstructing heterosexism in the counseling professions: A narrative approach* (pp. 189–210). Thousand Oaks, CA: Sage.

Bieschke, K. J., McClanahan, M., Tozer, E., Grzegorek, J. L., & Park, J. (2000). Programmatic research on the treatment of lesbian, gay and bisexual clients: The past, the present, and the course for the future. In R. M. Perez, K. A. DeBord, & K. J. Bieschke (Eds.), *Handbook of counseling and psychotherapy with lesbian, gay, and bisexual clients* (pp. 309–335). Washington, DC: American Psychological Association.

Bohan, J. (1996). *Psychology and sexual orientation.* New York: Routledge.

Bourne, E. J. (2005). *The anxiety & phobia workbook.* Oakland, CA: New Harbinger.

Bradford, J., Ryan, C., & Rothblum, E. D. (1994). National Lesbian Health Care Survey: Implications for mental health care. *Journal of Consulting and Clinical Psychology, 62,* 228–242.

Brown, L. (1989). Lesbians, gay men and their families: Common clinical issues. *Journal of Gay and Lesbian Psychotherapy, 1,* 65–77.

Butler, J. (1990). *Gender trouble: Feminism and the subversion of identity.* New York: Routledge.

Carroll, L., Gilroy, P. J., & Ryan, J. (2002). Counseling transgendered, transsexual, and gender-variant clients. *Journal of Counseling & Development, 80,* 131–139.

Cass, V. C. (1979). Homosexual identity formation: A theoretical model. *Journal of Homosexuality, 4,* 219–235.

Chen-Hayes, S., & Banez, L. (2001) *Lesbian, bisexual, gay & transgendered counseling.* Framingham, MA: Microtraining Associates.

Chung, Y. B., & Katayama, M. (1998). Ethnic and sexual identity development of Asian-American lesbian and gay adolescents. *Professional School Counseling, 1,* 21–25.

Coleman, E. (1982). Developmental phases of the coming out process. *Journal of Homosexuality, 7,* 31–43.

Comstock, G. D. (1991). *Violence against lesbians and gay men.* New York: Columbia University Press.

Croteau, J. M., Lark, J. S., Lidderdale, M. A., & Chung, Y. B. (2005). *Deconstructing heterosexism in the counseling professions: A narrative approach.* Thousand Oaks, CA: Sage.

Descamps, M. J., Rothblum, E., Bradford, J., & Ryan, C. (2000). Mental health impact of child sexual abuse, rape, intimate partner violence, and hate crimes in the National Lesbian Health Care Survey. *Journal of Gay and Lesbian Social Services, 11,* 27–55.

Dorland, J. M., & Fischer, A. R. (2001). Gay, lesbian, and bisexual individuals' perceptions: An analogue study. *The Counseling Psychologist, 29,* 532–547.

Dworkin, S. H. (2001). Treating the bisexual client. *JCLP in Session: Psychotherapy in Practice, 57,* 671–680.

Etheridge, M. (1993). Silent legacy. On *Yes, I am* [CD]. New York: Island Records.

Fairchild, B., & Hayward, N. (1998). *Now that you know: What every parent should know about homosexuality.* San Diego: Harcourt Brace Jovanovich.

Falco, K. L. (1991). *Psychotherapy with lesbian clients: Theory into practice.* New York: Brunner/Mazel.

Fassinger, R. E., & Miller, B. A. (1996). Validation of an inclusive model of sexual minority identity formation on a sample of gay men. *Journal of Homosexuality, 32,* 53–78.

Firestein, B. A. (1996). Bisexuality as paradigm shift: Transforming our disciplines. In B. A. Firestein (Ed.), *Bisexuality: The psychology and politics of an invisible minority* (pp. 263–291). Thousand Oaks, CA: Sage.

Fox, R. C. (2000). Bisexuality in perspective: A review of theory & research. In B. Greene & G. L. Croom (Eds.), *Psychological perspectives on lesbian and gay issues: Education, research, and practice in lesbian, gay, bisexual, and transgendered psychology* (Vol. 5, pp. 161–206). Thousand Oaks, CA: Sage.

Gainor, K. A. (2000). Including transgender issues in lesbian, gay and bisexual psychology: Implications for clinical practice and training. In B. Greene & G. L. Croom (Eds.), *Psychological perspectives on lesbian and gay issues: Education, research, and practice in lesbian, gay, bisexual, and transgendered psychology* (Vol. 5, pp. 131–160). Thousand Oaks, CA: Sage.

Garnets, L. D., & Peplau, L. A. (2001). A new paradigm for women's sexual orientation: Implications for therapy. *Women & Therapy, 24,* 111–121.

Gartrell, N. (1984). Combating homophobia in the psychotherapy of lesbians. *Women & Therapy, 3,* 13–29.

Gay, Lesbian, and Straight Education Network. (2003). *National School Climate Survey.* Retrieved June 1, 2005, from http://www.glsen.org

Gelso, C. J., Fassinger, R., Gomez, M. J., & Latts, M. G. (1995). Countertransference reactions to lesbian clients: The role of homophobia, counselor gender, and countertransference management. *Journal of Counseling Psychology, 42,* 356–364.

Glenn, A. A., & Russell, R. K. (1986). Heterosexual bias among counselor trainees. *Counselor Education and Supervision, 26,* 222–229.

Green, R. (1996). Lesbians, gays, and family psychology: Resources for teaching and practice. In B. Greene & G. L. Croom (Eds.), *Psychological perspectives on lesbian and gay issues: Vol. 5. Education, research, and practice in lesbian, gay, bisexual, and trans-gendered psychology.* Thousand Oaks, CA: Sage.

Greene, B. (1994). Lesbian women of color: Triple jeopardy. In L. Comas-Díaz & B. Greene (Eds.), *Women of color: Integrating ethnic and gender identities in psychotherapy* (pp. 389–427). New York: Guilford Press.

Greene, B. (1997). Ethnic minority lesbians and gay men: Mental health and treatment issues. In B. Greene (Ed.), *Psychological perspectives on lesbian and gay issues: Ethnic and cultural diversity among lesbians and gay men* (Vol. 3, pp. 216–239). Thousand Oaks, CA: Sage.

Guidry, L. L. (1999). Clinical intervention with bisexuals: A contextualized understanding. *Professional Psychology: Research and Practice, 30,* 22–26.

Hayes, J. A., & Gelso, C. J. (1993). Male counselors' discomfort with gay and HIV-infected clients. *Journal of Counseling Psychology, 40,* 86–93.

Herek, G. M. (1994). Assessing heterosexuals' attitudes toward lesbians and gay men: A review of empirical research with the ATLG scale. In B. Greene & G. M. Herek (Eds.), *Lesbian and gay psychology: Theory, research and clinical application* (pp. 206–228). Thousand Oaks, CA: Sage.

Herek, G. M. (1995). Psychological heterosexism in the United States. In A. D'Augelli & C. Patterson (Eds.), *Lesbian, gay, and bisexual identities over the lifespan: Psychological perspectives* (pp. 321–346). New York: Oxford University Press.

Herek, G. M., Cogan, J. C., & Gillis, J. R. (2002). Victim experiences in hate crimes based on sexual orientation. *Journal of Social Issues, 58,* 319–339.

Herek, G. M., Gillis, J. R., & Cogan, J. C. (1999). Psychological sequelae of hate crime victimization among lesbian, gay, and bisexual adults. *Journal of Consulting and Clinical Psychology, 67,* 945–951.

Hooker, E. (1957). The adjustment of the male overt homosexual. *Journal of Projective Techniques, 21,* 18–31.

Hu, S., Pattatucci, A. M. L., Patterson, C., Lin, L., Fulker, D. W., Cherny, S. S., et al. (1996). Linkage between sexual orientation and chromosome Xq28 in male but not females. *Nature Genetics, 11,* 248–256.

Hunt, G. L., & Hunt, M. W. (1977). Female-female pairing in Western gulls in southern California. *Science, 196,* 1466–1467.

Jordan, K. M., & Deluty, R. H. (1995). Clinical interventions by psychologists with lesbians and gay men. *Journal of Clinical Psychology, 51,* 448–456.

Jordan, K. M., & Deluty, R. H. (1998). Coming out for lesbian women: Its relationship to anxiety, positive affectivity, self-esteem, and social support. *Journal of Homosexuality, 35,* 41–63.

Kinsey, A. C., Pomeroy, W. B., & Martin, C. E. (1948). *Sexual behavior in the human male.* Philadelphia, PA: W. B. Saunders.

Kinsey, A. C., Pomeroy, W. B., Martin, C. E., & Geebhard, P. H. (1948). *Sexual behavior in the human female.* Philadelphia, PA: W. B. Saunders.

Kubler-Ross, E. (1969). *On death and dying.* New York: Macmillan.

Landrine, H., & Klonoff, E. A. (1996). The Schedule of Racist Events: A measure of racial discrimination and a study of its negative physical and mental health consequences. *Journal of Black Psychology, 22,* 144–168.

Lewis, L. A. (1984, September/October). The coming out process for lesbians: Integrating a stable identity. *Social Work,* 464–469.

Lewis, R. J., Derlega, V. J., Berndt, A., Morris, L. M., & Rose, S. (2001). An empirical analysis of stressors for gay men and lesbians. *Journal of Homosexuality, 42,* 63–88.

Liddle, B. J. (1996). Therapist sexual orientation, gender, and counseling practices as they relate to ratings of helpfulness by gay and lesbian clients. *Journal of Counseling Psychology, 43*, 394–401.

Liddle, B. J. (1997). Gay and lesbian clients' selection of therapists and utilization of therapy. *Psychotherapy, 34*, 11–18.

Matthews, C., & Lease, S. H. (2000). Focus on lesbian, gay, and bisexual families. In R. M. Perez, K. A. DeBord, & K. J. Bieschke (Eds.), *Handbook of counseling and psychotherapy with lesbian, gay, and bisexual clients* (pp. 249–273). Washington, DC: American Psychological Association.

Mayfield, W. (2001). The development of an internalized homonegativity inventory for gay men. *Journal of Homosexuality, 41*, 53–76.

Mays, V. M., & Cochran, S. D. (2001). Mental health correlates of perceived discrimination among lesbian, gay, and bisexual adults in the United States. *American Journal of Public Health, 91*, 1869–1876.

McAuliffe, G. J. (2005). *Counseling gay and lesbian youth: A multiethnic demonstration video* [Video]. Framingham, MA: Microtraining Associates.

McCarn, S. R., & Fassinger, R. E. (1996). Revisioning sexual minority identity formation: A new model of lesbian identity and its implications for counseling and research. *The Counseling Psychologist, 24*, 508–534.

Meyer, I. H. (2003). Prejudice, social stress, and mental health in lesbian, gay, and bisexual populations: Conceptual issues and research evidence. *Psychological Bulletin, 129*, 674–697.

Mohr, J. J., & Rochlen, A. B. (1999). Measuring attitudes regarding bisexuality in lesbian, gay male and heterosexual populations. *Journal of Counseling Psychology, 46*, 353–369.

Morris, J. F., Waldo, C. R., & Rothblum, E. D. (2001). A model of predictors and outcomes of outness among lesbian and bisexual women. *American Journal of Orthopsychiatry, 71*, 61–71.

Morrow, S. L. (2000). First do no harm: Therapist issues in psychotherapy with lesbian, gay and bisexual clients. In R. M. Perez, K. A. DeBord, & K. J. Bieschke (Eds.), *Handbook of counseling and psychotherapy with lesbian, gay, and bisexual clients* (pp. 137–156). Washington, DC: American Psychological Association.

Morrow, S. L., & Beckstead, A. L. (2004). Conversion therapies for same-sex attracted clients in religious conflict: Context, predisposing factors, experiences, and implications for therapy. *The Counseling Psychologist, 32*, 641–650.

Neisen, J. H. (1993). Healing from cultural victimization: Recovery from shame due to heterosexism. *Journal of Gay & Lesbian Psychotherapy, 2*, 49–63.

Ochs, R. (1996). Biphobia: It goes more than two ways. In B. A. Firestein (Ed.), *Bisexuality: The psychology & politics of an invisible minority* (pp. 3–50). Thousand Oaks, CA: Sage.

Padesky, C. A. (1988). Attaining and maintaining positive lesbian self-identity: A cognitive therapy approach. *Women & Therapy, 8*(1/2), 145–156.

Pattatucci, A. M. L., & Hamer, D. H. (1995). Development and familiarity of sexual orientation in females. *Behavior Genetics, 25*, 407–420.

Pilkington, N. W., & Cantor, J. M. (1996). Perceptions of heterosexual bias in professional psychology programs: A survey of graduate students. *Professional Psychology: Research and Practice, 27*, 604–612.

Pillard, R. C., & Bailey, J. M. (1998). Human sexual orientation has a heritable component. *Human Biology, 70*, 347–365.

Pillard, R. C., Poumadere, J., & Carretta, R. A. (1981). Is homosexuality familial? A review, some data, and a suggestion. *Archives of Sexual Behavior, 10*, 465–475.

Riddle, D. (n.d.). *Attitudes toward differences: The Riddle Scale.* Retrieved September 15, 2006, from http://www.glsenco.org/Resources/the_riddle_ scale.htm

Rothblum, E. D. (2000). "Somewhere in Des Moines or San Antonio": Historical perspectives on lesbian, gay, and bisexual mental health. In R. M. Perez, K. A. DeBord, & K. J. Bieschke (Eds.), *Handbook of counseling and psychotherapy with lesbian, gay, and bisexual clients* (pp. 137–156). Washington, DC: American Psychological Association.

Roughgarden, J. (2004). *Evolution's rainbow: Diversity, gender, and sexuality in nature and people.* Berkeley: University of California.

Sausa, L. A. (2002). Updating college and university campus policies: Meeting the needs of trans students, staff, and faculty. *Journal of Lesbian Studies, 6,* 43–55.

Schmalz, J. (1993, March 5). Poll finds an even split on homosexuality's cause. *New York Times,* p. A14.

Shidlo, A. (1994). Internalized homophobia: Conceptual and empirical issues in measurement. In B. Greene & G. M. Herek (Eds.), *Lesbian and gay psychology: Theory, research and clinical application* (pp. 176–205). Thousand Oaks, CA: Sage.

Shidlo, A., & Schroeder, M. (2002). Changing sexual orientation: A consumers' report. *Professional Psychology: Research and Practice, 33,* 249–259.

Singer, B. L., & Deschamps, D. (1994). *Gay and lesbian stats: A pocket guide to facts and figures.* New York: The New York Press.

Sophie, J. (1982). Counseling lesbians. *Personnel and Guidance Journal, 60,* 341–345.

Sophie, J. (1987). Internalized homophobia and lesbian identity. *Journal of Homosexuality, 14,* 53–65.

Sue, D. W., Arredondo, P., & McDavis, R. J. (1992). Multicultural counseling competencies and standards: A call to the profession. *Journal of Counseling and Development, 70,* 481–483.

Szymanski, D. M. (2005a). A feminist approach to working with internalized heterosexism in lesbians. *Journal of College Counseling, 8,* 74–85.

Szymanski, D. M. (2005b). Heterosexism and sexism as correlates of psychological distress in lesbians. *Journal of Counseling & Development, 83,* 355–360.

Szymanski, D. M., & Chung, Y. B. (2001). The Lesbian Internalized Homophobia Scale: A rational/theoretical approach. *Journal of Homosexuality, 41,* 37–52.

Szymanski, D. M., & Chung, Y. B. (2002). Internalized homophobia in lesbians. *Journal of Lesbian Studies, 7,* 115–125.

Szymanski, D. M., Chung, Y. B., & Balsam, K. (2001). Psychosocial correlates of internalized homophobia in lesbians. *Measurement and Evaluation in Counseling and Development, 34,* 27–38.

Tozer, E. E., & McClanahan, M. K. (1999). Treating the purple menace: Ethical considerations of conversion therapy and affirmative alternatives. *The Counseling Psychologist, 27,* 722–742.

Waldo, C. R. (1999). Working in a majority context: A structural model of heterosexism as minority stress in the workplace. *Journal of Counseling Psychology, 46,* 218–232.

Weinrich, J. D. (1982). Is homosexuality biologically natural? In W. Paul, J. D. Weinrich, J. C. Gonsiorek, & M. E. Hotvedt (Eds.), *Homosexuality: Social, psychological, and biological issues* (pp. 197–208). Beverly Hills, CA: Sage.

Weinrich, J. D., & Williams, W. L. (1991). Strange customs, familiar lives: Homosexuality in other cultures. In J. C. Gonsiorek & J. D. Weinrich (Eds.), *Homosexuality: Research implications for public policy* (pp. 44–59). Newbury Park, CA: Sage.

15

Religion and Spirituality

Karen Eriksen, Shelley A. Jackson, and Chet Weld

Brittany is a single 34-year-old Evangelical Christian. She attends a small Evangelical Baptist church in her rural town. Recently she has been struggling with not being married because being married and raising a family are the desires of her heart. She has been wondering why God has waited so long to bring a partner into her life, why He has not answered her prayers. Although she lives in a small town and attends a small church, there are a number of available men her age both in her town and in nearby towns; most of these men are Christian. However, it seems that those in whom she is interested are not interested in her, and those interested in her, she is not interested in. She has been questioning whether she is faithful enough for God to answer her prayers. She is also questioning whether there is something wrong with her that keeps her from forming successful relationships with men. She presents to you for counseling because she has been feeling depressed about her life situation.

Geoff is a 19-year-old Orthodox Jewish American undergraduate student majoring in pre-med at a large metropolitan university. He grew up in a relatively small city in another part of the state. He recently began attending a relationship support group at the campus counseling center because he is feeling depressed and isolated from friends and family. During the third session, Geoff shares with the group that he has found himself developing a phone relationship with the campus late night male disc jockey. The phone calls have led to Geoff's masturbating to sexual fantasies about the disc jockey. Geoff's understanding of the Torah is that both homosexuality

and masturbation are sins, so he feels that he can't go to the rabbi with his struggle. But he wonders if masturbation is really wrong. He feels torn between his and his family and temple's orthodox commitments and his attraction to this man. The struggle creates a sense of isolation as he wonders with whom he can talk—his faith community doesn't seem to offer support or answers, while the secular perspectives challenge the faith and community that have supported him since birth.

❖

Joseph is a 65-year-old man who has faithfully practiced Christian Science for 30 years. He now finds himself ill. His doctors say that he is dying of cancer. Because Christian Science is a healing faith that involves praying for people when they are ill and eschewing most medical services, and because he has not been healed despite many years of his own and healers' prayers, he and his family find themselves in a quandary. As his parents are not believers in Christian Science, his wife is somewhat less committed to Christian Science, and his children left the faith years ago, and he is experiencing extreme pressure to do "what most people would do," that is, to see a doctor and undergo medical treatment. He is now doubting his faith because it seems to be deserting him at a key point in his life. He thinks that, after all, if God is not healing him now, perhaps there is no heaven, and God will not greet him when he dies. He comes into family counseling with his wife and three adult children.

Religion has been at the heart of some of the best and some of the worst impulses and events in U.S. history—for example, it played a part in the events of 9/11 and the subsequent wars, the Salem witch trials of 1692, the pro-life and pro-choice debates, the evolution and intelligent design controversies, and the debate over legalizing gay marriage (Kosmin, Mayer, & Keysar, 2001). It is evident that, throughout history, people have considered spiritual or religious beliefs to be fundamental to who they are.

Some authors have proposed that spirituality and religion are universal impulses in human beings. For instance, Unger (1966) stated,

There is that in a [human being's] nature which prompts him [sic] to some sort of faith and worship . . . he [sic] requires the satisfaction and consolation and guidance, which comes from faith in the unseen and the eternal. (p. 916)

More recently, Wong (1998) agreed, stating,

Religion has been and remains one of the most potent forces in human existence because it is rooted in human nature. Deep within all people, there is a yearning for connection with the sacred and the transcendent. Like an orphan, there is a void, a restlessness compelling individuals to search for their parent, their destiny, and their home. Even without being aware of it, people desperately and secretly want to believe in God, so that they can have the faith and courage to face the unknown. (p. 361)

Some, such as agnostics and atheists, would disagree with the universality of those statements. But religiosity is a major facet of many, if not most, Americans' lives. According to the Gallup Organization (2004), approximately 60 percent of Americans say that religion is very important and more than 8 in 10 Americans identify themselves as Christian, at least by birth.

The Case for Including Religion and Spirituality in Counseling

Because the quest for the sacred is so common, many mental health professionals believe that spiritual concerns should be part of counseling. Wade and Worthington (2003) stated that "religion and spirituality are important to many people seeking counseling" (p. 3). That fact has spurred counselor interest in the topic. Genia (2000) proposed that "because many potential clients have religious as well as secular concerns, secular counselors . . . are striving to become more empathic and competent in treating religious individuals." Genia further stated, "If they are informed about important issues regarding the treatment of religious clients, psychocounselors will be better prepared to address the needs of this population" (p. 214). Similarly, Miranti and Burke (1995) indicated,

> Counselors must be prepared to deal with all issues, including that quality that lies at the very core and essence of the clients' being. . . . Clients themselves often suggest that spirituality is the sustaining core or essence that keeps them going when all else seems to fail. (p. 2)

These trends have resulted in ethical and professional mandates related to counseling and spirituality. For instance, the American Counseling Association (ACA) *Code of Ethics* (ACA, 2005) indicates that ACA "members recognize diversity and embrace a cross-cultural approach in support of the worth, dignity, potential, and uniqueness of people within their social and cultural contexts" (Preamble). In addition, "counselors actively attempt to understand the diverse cultural backgrounds of the clients they serve" and "explore their own cultural identities and how these affect their values and beliefs about the counseling process" (§ A, Introduction). These cultural identities include religion and spirituality. The standards of the Council for Accreditation of Counseling and Related Educational Programs (CACREP) specifically includes counselor sensitivity to "spiritual values" (CACREP, 2001, § 2, Standard K. 2).

Ignoring faith issues can, at a minimum, be considered "passively prejudicial" (Esau, 1998, p. 32). At worst, counselors can do harm if they fail to grasp the significance of a client's organizing belief system, a system that, for religious people, may be based on their traditions and interpretation of scriptural teachings (Johnson & Johnson, 1997). Thus, if counselors are to remain within the bounds of ethical standards when counseling spiritual or religious clients, they must understand the beliefs and values of these clients (Bishop, 1992; Genia, 2000; Ridley, 1985).

Beyond ethical considerations are practical matters: Most people's counseling choices have been restricted by managed care, and clients may not have the luxury of receiving counseling from someone who shares their faith. These clients, particularly when they are religiously conservative, may reject necessary counseling services when a counselor fails to understand and respect their belief system. That is a problem today because many counselors feel unprepared to work competently with religious material (Shafranske, 1996; Shafranske & Malony, 1990).

Consider the vignettes at the beginning of this chapter. Each clearly includes religious challenges and requires a degree of competence on the part of the counselor concerning religious issues. Brittany, who is a single Evangelical Christian, is questioning whether there is something wrong with her that keeps her from forming successful relationships with men. Geoff, an Orthodox Jewish American, wonders if masturbation and homosexuality are sins. He is depressed and torn between his family's orthodox beliefs and a secular society. Joseph, a Christian Scientist, is sick and being pressured by his family to receive traditional medical treatment for his cancer.

Counseling each of these clients requires the counselor to have spiritual competencies such as those developed by the Association for Spiritual, Ethical, and Religious Values in Counseling (ASERVIC; see Table 15.1).

This chapter addresses each of the ASERVIC competencies while exploring (1) the definitions, history, and importance of religion and spirituality in the United States; (2) the social and psychological dimensions of religion and spirituality; (3) the characteristics and issues facing various religious and spiritual groups in the United States; and (4) counseling interventions that incorporate spirituality and religion.

Definitions of Religion and Spirituality

Religion and spirituality need to be distinguished from each other. Religion usually has a group element and a set of beliefs or principles, and spirituality is an individual experience that is creedless.

DEFINING RELIGION

Most definitions of religion refer to a belief in a personal deity or some supernatural entity. Unfortunately, those definitions exclude faith communities that do not necessarily require belief in a deity, such as Buddhism and Unitarian Universalism (Stifoss-Hanssen, 1999).

Table 15.1　　Competencies for Working With Spiritually and Religiously Diverse Clients

Knowing the similarities, differences, and relationship between spirituality and religion
Being able to describe faith practices and beliefs within a cultural (e.g., ethnic) context
Engaging in self-exploration to become aware of one's own beliefs
Being able to explain faith from a developmental perspective
Demonstrating sensitivity to and acceptance of a variety of client religious and/or spiritual expressions
Knowing the limits of one's own competencies, and being able to make appropriate referrals when necessary
Knowing how to assess the relationship between the client's faith and the presenting problem
Being sensitive and receptive to religious and/or spiritual themes expressed during counseling
Being able to use the client's faith, as relevant and desired by the client, to pursue therapeutic goals

SOURCE: G. Miller (1999).

The English word *religion* may derive from the Latin word *religio*, which means "good faith" or "ritual." Or, it may have come from the Latin *religāre*, which means "to bind back or to tie fast," as in "ligament" (Stifoss-Hanssen, 1999). From these origins comes the idea of religion as an element that ties people together in a faith commitment. This chapter will use the broad definition of religion that was given in Chapter 1: *the organized set of beliefs that encode a person or group's attitudes toward, and understanding of, the essence or nature of reality.*

Religion is generally communal. It brings people together in a group to share their spirituality and to ponder the meanings of living. This chapter discusses some of the main belief systems found in the United States: Christianity, Islam, Judaism, Hinduism, Buddhism, Paganism, Unitarian Universalism, agnosticism, humanism, and atheism.

DEFINING SPIRITUALITY

Spirituality derives from the Latin root word *spirare*, which means "to breathe." In that sense, spirituality is a means for people to stay consciously connected with a life force, like the air they breathe and the universe around them. Spirituality variously connects individuals to their inner self, relationships with other people, and universal elements such as a divine force (Richards & Bergin, 1999). Myers (1990) defined spirituality broadly as "a continuing search for meaning and purpose in life; an appreciation for the depth of life, the expanse of the universe, and natural forces which operate" (p. 11). In the traditional religious literature, spirituality is defined as (a) values and beliefs connected to a formal religion; (b) metaphysical, mystical, or transcendent experiences; or (c) a sense of connectedness with another person or persons, nature, and/or God (Jankowski, 2002). Hartz (2005) delineates his "Primary Colors of Spirituality" (p. 5) as the search for meaning and purpose and for highest values; transcendence beyond the day-to-day and beyond the individual; and morality, or bringing happiness to self and others that is inspired by love. For the purpose of this chapter, spirituality is defined, as it was in Chapter 1, as as *a mindfulness about the existential qualities of life, especially the relationship between self, other, and the world.*

COMPARING RELIGION AND SPIRITUALITY

Religion and spirituality are often conflated. Yet, according to Richards and Bergin (1999), three major differences exist between them. First, spirituality has no doctrines, while religion relies on principles or rules. Second, religion is primarily external, while spirituality is fundamentally internal. Finally, religion is exclusive, while spirituality is usually inclusive. Each of these distinctions will be discussed in turn.

Doctrine

Spirituality is doctrineless and places its primary emphasis on individual experiences of the Divine. There is no "creed" in spirituality. Instead, each person brings something different to her or his relationship with and perceptions of Spirit. By contrast, religion has the aforementioned group dimension. Religion ties people together with common principles, doctrines, and rules. The doctrines vary from religion to religion and from denomination to denomination within each religion. This distinction between religion and spirituality can be confusing when both meet in one individual (Goud, 1990). For example, Roman Catholic teaching indicates that a human being's highest authority is her or his individual conscience. However, the Church endorses the notion of a just war. A Catholic might decide, after sincerely searching her or his conscience, that she or he takes a pacifist position on war. That spiritual stance can stand alongside the Church's general doctrine of there being the possibility of a just war.

As seen in the previous example, spirituality makes each person responsible for his or her own relationship with the "Holy." While spiritual guides may recommend practices that have helped others in their spiritual journeys, each person has to do her or his own "work." Spirituality embraces intangibles, gray areas, and paradoxes. Its ambiguity may make spirituality unattractive to those who are more comfortable with certainties. It might be said that religions, with some exceptions, are systems of answers, whereas spirituality is about questions.

External Versus Internal

The second distinction between religion and spirituality is that religion has an external dimension, as opposed to being primarily internal. External expressions of religion include rituals, requirements, or practices, such as accepting Jesus as Savior and studying the Bible (Protestant Christianity), going to confession and Mass (Roman Catholic Christianity), adhering to the rules of the Talmud and Torah (Judaism), praying five times daily and making a pilgrimage to Mecca (Islam), or meeting as a community to raise questions through readings and discussion (Unitarian Universalism).

By contrast, spirituality, as an internal proposition, encourages humans to pursue communion with a force more pervasive and powerful than themselves. Spirituality stresses integration with the divine and all of creation by bringing a personal relationship with the divine into all other relationships. In spirituality, such integration is largely achieved through meditation, prayer, and contemplation rather than through external, group ritualistic expression (Goud, 1990).

Exclusivity Versus Inclusivity

The final distinction between religion and spirituality is the exclusivity of religion versus the inclusivity of spirituality (Goud, 1990). Only those who agree with the beliefs and follow the principles and rules may become part of a religious group. Those who belong often must be brought somehow into the group, whether they are baptized, sign a membership book, or go through whatever other initiation rituals the religion practices. Failing to comply means that one can't be part of the group. This exclusiveness offers an identity and a sense of community solidarity for the members of the religion. Also, positive feelings are attached to being part of the "right" group or to being "saved." Members may often feel supported by religion in their spiritual journeys. People who are part of a religion generally feel free from the stresses of challenges by outsiders because outsiders are not allowed in or, if they are already in, they are removed, excommunicated, or disciplined. Members may gain a sense of comfort from knowing that everyone in their group generally thinks the way they do. In this sense, the exclusivity of religion may provide a kind of safety in comparison with the often uncertain and individual journey of spirituality.

The Limits of the Distinctions Between Religion and Spirituality

In some ways, distinctions between religion and spirituality may be a bit arbitrary and somewhat artificial. Therefore, the terms will sometimes be used interchangeably in this chapter. Although some people are spiritual without participating in a religion and some religious people lack spirituality, many people find their religion empowered and enlivened by spirit. Conversely, individuals' spirituality is supported by the rituals and communal experiences of religion.

In reflecting on the cases that begin this chapter, it seems apparent that the clients' religious beliefs are challenged by their recent life experiences. In the long run, they may find guidance from within their religions; however, they might also engage in spiritual and cognitive growth to increase the complexity of their thinking about those religions. Either choice might assist them in resolving the conflicts that they are currently experiencing. Activity 15.1 is designed to help counselors articulate an understanding of their own spirituality and its development throughout their lives.

Cultural Dimensions of Religion

Religion, through its beliefs, rituals, and moral codes as well as its emotional and communal aspects, can be considered a culture (Saroglou, 2002). Traditional religion identifies itself as integral to most aspects of people's life style and community. Even in the United States, where separation of religion and state is institutionalized, reference to religion is found on the currency, in the Pledge of Allegiance, and in the Declaration of Independence. Religion can be synonymous with ethnicity at times, as in Polish Catholic, Greek Orthodox, or Arab Muslim faiths. While not universal, these groups often claim an identity that includes spiritual beliefs, codes for living, and identification with a people who share a common ancestry or place (Smith, Faris, Denton, & Regnerus, 2003).

THE CULTURE OF RELIGION IN THE UNITED STATES

Religion is a particularly powerful force in U.S. life, especially in comparison to other industrialized nations. Religion or spirituality is regarded by many U.S. citizens as the deepest source of meaning and belonging in life. The impact of religion goes beyond worship and family life; it also shapes and reinforces the political and social views of vast numbers of citizens.

Varieties of Religion in the United States

The United States has moved beyond the largely Protestant pluralism of its early history and the Protestant, Catholic, and Jewish triumvirate of the last century to a diversity that includes almost every religious expression in the world. This pluralism also includes the 15 percent of Americans who define themselves as secularists, humanists, agnostics, and nonbelievers (Kosmin et al., 2001).

Not only does diversity in beliefs exist, but there is diversity in the intensity of belief. Sometimes the most profound religious and cultural differences are not between traditional denominations or religious groups, but between liberals and conservatives within denominations. Those with more liberal perspectives generally assume that societal change is both desirable and achievable. They also believe that their religious writings are symbolic and metaphorical, a set of principles

ACTIVITY 15.1

Assessing One's Own Spirituality and Religion

Frame (2003) indicated, "Counselors and other mental health clinicians must address their own personal issues regarding religion and spirituality before they can help their clients" venture into this arena (p. xi). In that vein, this activity is designed to help counselors articulate an understanding of their own spirituality and its development throughout their lives.

A. Read the following statements made by thinkers and theologians about the nature of spirituality. Use these definitions to help you develop a better understanding of the spiritual dimension in your life and work. Decide which statements resonate with your views.

Spirituality is	Your views on each:
the search for harmony and wholeness in the universe (Cervantes & Ramirez, 1992).	
that which is related to one's ultimate concern and is the meaning-giving dimension of culture (Tillich, 1959).	
an appreciation for the sacredness of life; a balanced appreciation of material values, altruism toward others, a desire for the betterment of the world, and an awareness of life's tragic side (Elkins, Hedstrom, & Hughes, 1988).	
"any experience of transcendence of one's former frame of reference that results in greater knowledge and love" (Chandler, Holden, & Kolander, 1992, p. 170).	
awareness, felt in the body, of the transcendent dimension of life that brings new meanings and leads to growth (Hinterkopf, 1994).	
"less a method than an attitude, a posture of one's very being that allows seeing not different things but everything differently" (Holifield,1983, p. 88).	
"an inner-generated, thoughtful and sometimes skeptical search—a process rather than a product— for universal connections, with no quid pro quo from a higher power sought or intended. People who consider themselves to be spiritual may or may not participate in organized religion. Some may find solace in readings, discussion groups, and the like" (Winarsky, 1991, p. 186).	

B. Briefly write your own personal definition of spirituality.

Spirituality is	Your views on each:

C. Now ask another person who has significantly different religious beliefs from your own to read the quotes above and give you her or his definition of spirituality. Report that person's responses here:
 	
  1.
 	
  2.	

D. Ask yourself and that person the following questions and record the responses:
 	
  1. Where do your beliefs come from? (e.g., From your parents? From being involved in a church, synagogue, mosque, temple?)
 	
  2. Briefly describe your religious beliefs. (This description can be very different from describing spiritual beliefs. As a counselor, it is important that you ask clients about both their spiritual beliefs and their religious beliefs.)
 	
  3. What sources of authority, if any, do you use for your religious beliefs? (e.g., the Torah, the Bible, the Qur'an, a particular philosophy system, other sources and books)
 	
  4. Does your belief system encourage reasoning and questioning or urge/require you to have faith in and acceptance of the established beliefs? (e.g., can the leader of your belief system be wrong?)
 	
  5. Why have you chosen your belief system over all others? If you consider it the best choice, on what basis did you reach this conclusion?	

rather than literal rules. Those with more conservative tendencies prefer to pre-serve traditions and may, therefore, resist change. They may also subscribe to a more "literal" religion. In American Protestantism, for example, conservatives are sometimes criticized by liberals for being overly strict on moral issues, closed-minded, intolerant of other religious views, fanatical about their beliefs, too harsh, overly focused on guilt or sin, too concerned about their own salvation, and unrea-sonably rigid and simplistic. Liberals are sometimes faulted by conservatives for substituting social concerns for the true gospel, compromising with the world, being morally loose, having a shallow knowledge of the scripture, and being too heavily influenced by secular humanism (Hoge, 1996).

Results of research on the intensity of belief are inconsistent. The Center for the Study of Religion at Princeton University (Wuthnow, 2004) found that one in four people in the United States is devoutly religious, one in four is secular, and the remaining two are moderately interested in religion. Bergin and Jensen (1990) found that religious beliefs are very important to an estimated two-thirds of the U.S. population. Other national polls report that 9 out of 10 Americans believe in God and consider religion to be an important part of their lives (Elkins, 1999).

The inconsistency of the research results may be explained by the effects of "history," that is, by the fact that religious practices were observed or measured at different points in time and when it was highly likely that particular events had affected religious practice or feeling at a particular time (Silk, 2005). For instance, there was a surge in religious observation after the terrorist attacks on New York City and Washington in 2001. Some religious leaders predicted that the phenomenon would be short lived. Others saw it as the start of a major revival in the United States. It appears that the increase lasted only about two months. By November 2001, attendance at religious services had returned to usual levels (Gallup International Association, 2002). Measuring intensity of faith before, during, or after this event (or others) might, therefore, explain the inconsistent research results

Inconsistencies may also be due to the difficulty of collecting religious data. The naming and identification of religious groups is itself difficult (Silk, 2005). This problem is compounded by the lack of government data on religion. The U.S. Census Bureau feels proscribed by the First Amendment from including religious affiliation questions on either the Census or the Current Population Survey (CPS; Petersen, 2003).

A national census of religious bodies was last conducted in 1936, and the CPS has not asked about religion since 1957 (Mueller & Lane, 1972). Therefore, authoritative, fine-grained statistics on religion are in short supply (Silk, 2005). However, a large comprehensive survey on religious identification, The National Survey of Religious Identification (NSRI), was conducted by Kosmin, Mayer, and Keysar in 2001. The results are shown in Table 15.2, which lists the top 20 religious affiliations in the United States in 2001, and Table 15.3, which lists the largest denominations/denominational families in the United States.

Table 15.2   Top 20 Religious Affiliations in the United States, 2001

Religion	Estimated Adult Population, 2001	Percentage of U.S. Population, 2001
Christianity	159,030,000	76.5
Nonreligious/Secular	27,539,000	13.2
Judaism	2,831,000	1.3
Islam	1,104,000	0.5
Buddhism	1,082,000	0.5
Agnostic	991,000	0.5
Atheist	902,000	0.4
Hinduism	766,000	0.4
Unitarian Universalism	629,000	0.3
Wiccan/Pagan/Druid	307,000	0.1
Spiritualism	116,000	
Native American Religion	103,000	
Baha'i	84,000	
New Age	68,000	
Sikhism	57,000	
Scientology	55,000	
Humanism	49,000	
Deity (Deist)	49,000	
Taoist	40,000	
Eckankar	26,000	

SOURCE: Kosmin et al. (2001).

Religions are not uniform across the United States. Particular faiths tend to be concentrated within regions. For example, Catholicism is the largest single group in the New England, Middle Atlantic, East North Central, Mountain, and Pacific regions; Southern Baptist is the single largest group in the West North Central, South Atlantic, East South Central, and West South Central regions (Guiso, Sapienza, & Zingales, 2003). Lutherans are the largest group in the upper Midwest (Chalfant, Beckley, & Palmer, 1994). Southern U.S. culture, in general, embraces religion more substantially than other regions in the United States (Smith et al., 2003). In particular, Baptist adults and youth in the South have the highest levels of church participation of any group (Smith et al., 2003).

Table 15.3   Largest Denominations/Denominational groupings in the United States, 2001

Denomination	Estimated Adult Population, 2001	Percentage of U.S. Population, 2001
Catholic	50,873,000	24.5
Baptist	33,830,000	16.3
Methodist/Wesleyan	14,150,000	6.8
Lutheran	9,580,000	4.6
Presbyterian	5,596,000	2.7
Pentecostal/Charismatic	4,407,000	2.1
Episcopalian/Anglican	3,451,000	1.7
Judaism	2,831,000	1.3
Latter-day Saints/Mormon	2,697,000	1.3
Churches of Christ	2,593,000	1.2
Congregational/ United Church of Christ	1,378,000	0.7
Jehovah's Witness	1,331,000	0.6
Assemblies of God	1,106,000	0.5

SOURCE: Kosmin et al. (2001).

Guiding Ethic of Religious Tolerance

One striking aspect of the culture of religion in the United States is the ethic of religious tolerance. This country has managed to avoid any kind of major religious strife, which contrasts with worldwide experiences. Worldwide, more people died because of their religious convictions during the twentieth century than in any previous century. More than two-thirds of the wars in the 1990s were caused by religious or ethnic differences. For example, serious outbreaks of religious and ethnic bigotry and division have occurred in Eastern Europe despite their tremendous advances in democracy. Tensions between Muslims and Christians have resulted in violence in Bosnia, Azerbaijan, Armenia, and elsewhere. Hindus and Muslims clash in India. One of the most frightening developments has been the dramatic rise of anti-Semitism throughout Eastern Europe (Hoge, 1996). The Sunni and Shiite factions of Islam are often contentious, and Northern Ireland continues to be a religiously divided province.

By contrast, the United States, one of the most intensely religious nations and *the* most religiously diverse nation in the world, has managed to avoid the "holy wars" so prevalent throughout history. This remarkable achievement may be traced directly to the religious liberty clauses of the First Amendment (Gaustad & Dishno, 2000). The founding fathers, especially Thomas Jefferson, were adamant that no

religion would be favored by government. In spite of occasional setbacks and outbreaks of religious bigotry, religious tolerance has generally held. It should be noted
that the choice not to participate in a religion is also part of the U.S. ethos.

THE INTERSECTION OF RELIGION WITH RACE/ETHNICITY

The relationship between ethnicity and religion varies. As mentioned previously, for some groups, religion and ethnicity are integrally connected. Sixty-four
percent of Latino congregations and half of African American congregations
consider their churches to be a primary means of preserving cultural heritage
(Kosmin et al., 2001). About one-third of white congregations tend to link ethnic
traditions with the religious community, as in Italian Catholic or Scandinavian
Lutheran churches. In particular, religion has played a central role in the political
and social history of African Americans from the Colonial period to the present.
Indeed, black Christian churches shaped the lives of all Americans by providing
much of the moral and political leadership of the civil rights movement. Among
African Americans, the Baptist denomination dominates, with more than half (55
percent) professing an affiliation with that tradition (Levin, Chatters, & Taylor,
2005). It should be noted that this Baptist tradition is affiliated with the National
Baptist Convention, which is separate from the predominantly white Southern
Baptist and American Baptist traditions. Among Hispanic Americans, Catholicism
dominates, with 64 percent practicing that faith (Kosmin et al., 2001). Table 15.4
shows the makeup of each of 22 major religious groups by race. Faith seems to
unite people who believe similarly. However, it has generally not bridged the
racial/ethnic gap. Sunday morning religious hours are still considered to be the
most racially segregated hours in the United States (Kosmin et al., 2001).

Psychological Dimensions of Religion and Spirituality

Now that the cultural dimensions of religion have been discussed, the important
psychological dimension of religion and spirituality in individual lives will
be presented. Four such psychological aspects of religion and spirituality are
important: (1) their contribution to a sense of meaning in life, (2) their place in
the experience of support and community (Saroglou, 2002), (3) how people
choose a religion, and (4) how religious identity develops. These dimensions are
important indicators of how clients think about religion in their lives.

PROVIDING MEANING

Religion can satisfy a fundamental human need to find meaning in life and to
feel in control (Baumeister, 1992). Humans, aided by an enormously imaginative
brain, have for thousands of years sought to connect to a "higher power" that will

Table 15.4   Race and/or Ethnic Makeup of Selected Religious Groups, 2001

Group	Percentage White	Percentage Black	Percentage Asian	Percentage Hispanic	Percentage Other
Catholic	64	3	3	29	2
Baptist	64	29	1	3	2
No Religion	73	8	5	11	4
Christian	67	12	3	14	3
Methodist	86	11	1	1	1
Lutheran	96	1	0	1	1
Presbyterian	91	3	2	3	1
Protestant	87	4	0	6	3
Pentecostal	58	22	0	17	3
Episcopalian/ Anglican	89	9	1	0	1
Jewish*	92	1	1	5	1
Mormon	91	0	0	8	1
Church of Christ	89	6	1	2	2
Non-denominational	73	11	1	13	2
Congregational/ UCC	93	0	0	5	2
Jehovah's Witnesses	46	37	0	14	3
Assemblies of God	80	5	5	8	2
Muslim/Islamic	15	27	34	10	14
Buddhist	32	4	61	2	1
Evangelical/ Born Again	77	3	0	20	0
Church of God	84	12	0	4	0
Seventh Day Adventist	67	26	0	7	0
Total	70	10	3	12	5

SOURCE: Kosmin et al. (2001).

NOTE: *This category refers only to religious Jews.

protect and provide for them, make sense of natural events, and give purpose or meaning to life (Baumeister, 1992). Historically speaking, human needs and fears have motivated the development of religions that embodied and reinforced a group's values. Many of the promises of religion have helped adherents handle life's misfortunes and deal with their fear of death. Religion evokes hope in troubling situations (Yahne & Miller, 1999) and creates serenity despite difficulties (Connors, Toscova, & Tonigan, 1999). Religious experience may also help members find acceptance and forgiveness and a subsequent sense of relief (Sanderson & Linehan, 1999). Pargament (2002) found that faith that is internalized and that provides meaning in life fosters well-being. The payoffs of religion, therefore, are so attractive and comforting that participants in a religion may find questions about their faith or religion to be extremely threatening (Baumeister, 1992).

SUPPORT AND COMMUNITY

A second psychological dimension of religion is the sense of belonging and social support that it provides. Many studies find that religious affiliation, when accompanied by frequent attendance and prayer, is associated with positive mental health and a decreased likelihood of mental illness (Ellison, 1991; Koenig, George, & Peterson, 1998; Levin & Chatters, 1998; Levin & Taylor, 1998). Greater benefit in religion is found particularly by socially marginalized groups, more religiously committed people, and those experiencing very stressful situations (e.g., death). Studies using overt indicators of public religious behaviors and activities (e.g., attendance) explain their positive relationship with mental health as an outcome of the increased social integration and support that institutionalized religion provides (Ellison, 1991; Idler, 1995). Several studies found that people who attended religious services exhibited higher levels of social support than did people who didn't participate in a religious community (Bradley, 1995; Ellison & George, 1994). Thus, social support has tended to be a significant explanation for the mental health benefits of religious behavior.

In cases of chronic illness or disability, spirituality and religion are recognized as important sources of motivation, strength, and social support for individuals who are adjusting to those situations (Chibon, 1992; Eckes, 2004; Landis, 1996; Larson, Wood, & Larson, 1993; Nathanson, 1995; Nino, 1997). Such religious coping efforts often involve a search for spiritual meaning, while religion plays a part through congregations providing an array of instrumental, informational, and emotional support resources (e.g., economic assistance and spiritual assistance).

Even the most controversial religions seem to have psychological benefits (Pargament, 2002). For instance, fundamentalism correlates both with greater prejudice toward those who are different from oneself *and* with increases in well-being. It should be noted, however, that there can also be negative consequences of religious involvement (Krause, 1998). Religious duties may be demanding, and some people may feel that their congregation is overly critical of them. Far from reducing stress, these forms of interaction may exacerbate it. Since these negative effects of religious involvement exist alongside the positive effects, both must be considered by counselors to form a realistic picture of the effects of religious activity on clients' lives.

The case of Geoff at the chapter's beginning is a perfect example of both the strengths and difficulties of belonging to a religious tradition. Geoff had found support in his Orthodox Jewish faith since birth. It had provided him a sense of safety, support, belonging, and answers to life's big questions. When he experiences challenges to the orthodoxy, he experiences a true loss and great confusion. He no longer feels he can approach his rabbi with his struggle about masturbation, and yet his longstanding Orthodox commitments prevent him from really believing that other answers can be justified. The struggle creates a sense of isolation as he wonders with whom he can talk—his faith community doesn't seem to offer support or answers, but secular answers challenge a faith and community that has supported him since birth.

RELIGION OF CHOICE AND RELIGION OF ORIGIN

People in the United States and in most of the world are usually enculturated into a religion, which would then be considered their religion of origin. The enculturation process is powerful. For instance, a strong religious upbringing is a leading indicator of adult religious participation and religious identity. A study of 6,000 white adult respondents revealed that members of all religions showed a strong tendency to maintain their background affiliations (Kluegel, 1980). For some, the religion chosen by their parents and community continues as a life practice. However, not all religion is inherited passively; for others, an inherited religion may develop into a more conscious choice, or a person may deliberately choose a religion distinct from that of the parents or community. This phenomenon can be referred to as religion of choice.

Whether or not people practice an inherited religion is strongly related to their faith development and maturity. That is, those who progress from more received ways of knowing to more self-authorized ways of knowing, as described in Chapter 1, tend also to move from the practice of their religion of origin to a religion of choice. Such developmental change, as explained by the neo-Piagetian model of cognitive development (e.g., Fowler, 1991, 2004; Kegan, 1982, 1994; Kohlberg, 1981; Loevinger, 1976; Perry, 1970), requires that an individual experience internal conflict about an old way of knowing accompanied by support and challenge to a new way of knowing.

Religion of Origin

Those who have inherited their religion from their families of origin can be characterized by various terms, all of which refer to a relatively unquestioned receiving of inherited norms and values. Following Chapter 1, this tendency will be called received knowledge here. From such a perspective, the conventions of the community are treated as the ultimate source of knowledge. Such a way of knowing may be characterized by being a good and productive citizens, being trustworthy and employable, taking others into account, and developing a meaningful life based on clear ideals. Individuals characterized by received knowledge are fully socialized, or enculturated; that is, they have internalized the values of society or their religion (Kegan, 1982, 1994). They will adhere loyally to their religion of origin, or be followers of a religion based on peer or authority influence. In a fundamental sense, they do not ultimately "think for themselves" about religious issues.

There are limitations to this "received" way of knowing. The automaticity of received knowledge makes it difficult for individuals to emerge beyond a mentality characterized by, "That's the way I was brought up" or "That's the way it has always been done." Great stress may be experienced when such individuals are required to think outside of their religion, when something about their religion isn't working for them, or when they must deal intimately with those whose values and beliefs differ from their own. In the first vignette at the beginning of this chapter, Brittany may be experiencing the stress caused by challenges to her received view as she struggles with being a single Evangelical Christian. She seems to be questioning whether her faith has the answers she needs: "Will God answer my prayers?" or "Is there something wrong with me that I can't form relationships with men?" In the second vignette, Geoff certainly finds his received knowledge challenged by his attractions and his encounters with alternative perspectives. Finally, in the third vignette, Joseph's received faith is challenged by his impending death, which raises seemingly unanswerable questions for both him and his family. Individuals who are characterized by received knowledge may not yet have the capacity to carefully weigh the challenges and develop their own value systems

Religion of Choice

Those who can make relatively independent decisions about their faith, by weighing what they have inherited from their culture against their experiences, are characterized by a self-authorized way of knowing (Kegan, 1982, 1994), as described in Chapter 1. Individuals who are self-authorizing can stand back from their relationships, roles, rules, spiritual leaders, and religious denomination and evaluate objectively or individually what they will claim for themselves. They can use their own "theory" to carefully weigh what they believe and what this means about how they will behave. Their positions do not rely ultimately on whether others agree. This self-direction helps them to negotiate conflicts that may emerge among relationships, roles, and rules. In their families and religious groups, individuals who are self-authorizing are able to be leaders; to institute a vision and invite family and co-religionists into it; to manage boundaries effectively; and to set limits on children, friends, and on themselves. They are able to define a sense of self or separate identity, so that others do not organize or define them. They are self-initiating, self-correcting, and self-evaluating. They take responsibility for what happens to them.

Self-authorized knowing is characterized by increased autonomy or a sense of self as distinct from others. Such knowers are thus not bound by the faith that they may have inherited, although they can choose parts of it at some points by using a self-determined method of weighing alternatives and generating evidence. Research indicates that only about 20 percent of adults achieve self-authorized knowing in a consistent way (Allison, 1988; Alvarez, 1985; Bar-Yam, 1991; Beukema, 1990; Binner, 1991; Dixon, 1986; Goodman, 1983; Greenwald, 1991; Jacobs, 1984; Lahey, 1986; Roy, 1993; Sonnenschein, 1990).

The Benefits of Self-Authorized Knowing

As ways of knowing evolve, thinking becomes less rigid, exclusive, simplistic, and dogmatic and more flexible, open, complex, and tolerant of differences. In the domain of religion or spirituality, those demonstrating a more mature religious adjustment exhibit (a) an awareness of complexity and ambiguity in sacred texts, (b) religious affiliation based on a thoughtful decision-making process, (c) congruence between values and behaviors, (d) recognition of their shortcomings, and (e) respect for boundaries (Lovinger, 1996).

Self-authorized knowing is desirable for counselors also. More complex ways of knowing are associated with higher empathy levels, which is a fundamental element of good counseling (Benack, 1988; Bowman & Reeves, 1987; Lovell, 1999; McAuliffe & Lovell, 2006). It is also associated with internal locus of control and open-mindedness in counselors (Neukrug & McAuliffe, 1993), as well as with the abilities to tolerate ambiguity, be reflective, use evidence for choices, and demonstrate insight into clients' issues (McAuliffe & Lovell, 2006). Self-authorized knowing may be important if counselors are to avoid imposing their values on clients and are to help clients to move toward a religion of choice (Brendel, Kolbert, & Foster, 2002).

Encouraging Development

When clients or prospective clients experience a dilemma in which the old rules of their religion of origin don't fit their experience, they find that their received knowledge limits them. Such is the case for people like Brittany or Geoff, who discover their sexuality in new ways or find their old ways less satisfactory. It may also be the case for a person trapped by rigid gender roles.

In order to assist such clients, counselors must optimally match (support) and mismatch (challenge) clients' current way of knowing. "Matching" implies relating to clients from within their currently dominant way of knowing and mismatching clients means relating to them from the next potential way of knowing (McAuliffe & Eriksen, 1999).

To *match* or *support* people operating from received knowledge, counselors would give clear direction and a lot of structure, particularly using the authority of the client's religious precepts because clients operating out of this stage need an authority-based experience (Kegan, 1982, 1994). In order to *mismatch* or *challenge* people toward a religion of choice, counselors would urge clients to think about why they are doing what they are doing, to examine their inner urges, and to establish a separateness from others' definitions. Counselors might ask clients to investigate inconsistencies in religious texts, to pray about how to resolve them, and to come to a religiously grounded and justifiable decision about beliefs that might be more helpful. Counselors, teachers, and other leaders might also create ambiguous value discussions (e.g., ethical dilemma discussions) to challenge the more rigid received knowledge toward self-authorization (Kegan, 1982, 1994). Activities 15.2 and 15.3 can challenge counselors to move toward self-authorized knowing in terms of a religion of choice.

Many people seeking counseling may be doing so as a result of conflicts that have the potential to be resolved by movement to a more complex way of knowing. However, such movement is not without risks. For instance, transitions between stages are fraught with feelings of formlessness, "not knowing," and "being out at sea but not in sight of any shore." This experience can be quite stressful. Further, movement from religion of origin to religion of choice may put clients at odds with their families and their religious communities. If the religious community encompasses a client's whole cultural group, as sometimes occurs in more traditional societies, clients may find themselves quite literally ostracized and without a people. Geoff, for example, believed that he would be ostracized by his religious community and family. Counselors, therefore, must carefully consider the risks as well as the benefits of development and use informed consent procedures to help clients carefully weigh the benefits and risks of moving beyond traditionalism. During a move to self-authorized religious choice, individuals will

---

ACTIVITY 15.2

Religious De-Centering

Describe your past and current ways of religious knowing by using the descriptions in this text of "religion of origin" and "religion of choice" to make a list of those characteristics that fit you, and give examples.

a. Characteristics of my received knowledge of a religion of origin (in the past or present): (e.g., treating the conventions of your community as the ultimate source of knowing; adhering loyally to your religion of origin, or being a follower of a religion based on peer or authority influence)

b. Characteristics of my self-authorized knowledge of a religion of choice (if you have at least partially engaged in such thinking up to this point): (e.g., not being automatically bound by the faith that you may have inherited; being able choose a spiritual or religious direction by using a relatively autonomous method of weighing alternatives and self-generated evidence)

ACTIVITY 15.3

Experiencing Alternate Religious Perspectives

In an effort to promote your own spiritual development, take a "plunge" into another religious experience, meet the people, and experience the rituals.

Afterwards, ask yourself the following questions:

How did it feel to be with people who believe differently?

Do you see your group as "dominant" (e.g., generally in a position of greater power and/or favor at the current time and place) or as "nondominant" in comparison with the group you visited? How might this affect your perceptions of them?

What rituals or procedures were different from your own? Similar?

What was it like to experience their rituals? How did the experience differ from your own faith?

What does your faith say about other faith experiences? What do you think about that?

How might this experience assist you with clients whose faith is different from your own?

need "bridge people," that is, others like themselves who share their journey. Counselors can help them to find a supportive group of peers who are exploring religious or spiritual meaning.

Religion and Counseling

Historically speaking, the mental health professions have had a contentious relationship with religion, frequently considering it to be part of clients' pathology and preferring to leave spirituality to spiritual leaders (Wiggins-Frame, 2005). Some of the struggle evolved from the different philosophical underpinnings of science and religion (Wiggins-Frame, 2005). Mental health professionals have endeavored to understand the psychological and behavioral aspects of human life (Patterson, Hayworth, Turner, & Raskin, 2000), while religion has usually focused on people's spiritual dimension and the influence of a supreme being on human behavior (Richards & Bergin, 2002). This section of the chapter presents, in this order, the different philosophical foundations of counseling and religion, trends in integrating the two, the dangers of harmful faith, guidelines for assessing clients' relationship to faith, and the risks of religious countertransference.

DIFFERENTIAL FOUNDATIONS
OF COUNSELING AND RELIGION

The historical separation of counseling and religion comes from the different foundations of psychology and religion. Bergin (1980) identifies two primary philosophical underpinnings of counseling: *clinical pragmatism,* which embodies predominant cultural values on what works to improve clients' lives; and *humanistic idealism,* which embraces positive values such as human dignity and self-actualization but manifests "a relative indifference to God" (p. 98). Bergin proposes that a third view, *theistic realism,* should be considered an underpinning for the work of mental health professionals. Theistic realism posits that God exists, that human beings are creations of God, and that there are unseen spiritual processes by which the link between God and humanity is maintained.

THE RAPPROCHEMENT BETWEEN
COUNSELING AND RELIGION

In the past 10 years, the separations between counseling and religion have started to break down (Richards & Bergin, 2002). The ongoing rapprochement between counseling and religion is evidenced by a growing eclecticism of models of counseling, including transpersonal counseling, recognition of the importance of values in counseling, and the articulation of spiritual views by mental health professionals (Elkins, 1995; Richards & Bergin, 2002). Specialty fields have evolved that make it possible for clients to seek out counselors who have skill in addressing spiritual issues in counseling (Genia, 2000).

More evidence of the growing inclusion of religious or spiritual issues in the framework of recent psychological thought is the addition of "Religious or Spiritual Problem" to recent editions of the *Diagnostic and Statistical Manual of Mental Disorders* (American Psychiatric Association, 1994, 2000). Similarly, the increasing number of studies being conducted to evaluate the links among people's spirituality, their mental health, and effective counseling (e.g., Gordon et al., 2002; Wade & Worthington, 2003) indicates that counseling professionals are taking a more amiable posture toward religion, and vice-versa, than has been previously been seen.

The multicultural counseling movement has spurred more inclusion of religion and spirituality in practice. This inclusion is mandated by ethical standards (ACA, 1995; American Psychological Association, 2002). Recognition of spiritual issues encourages counselors to attend to the benefits of faith, which, in turn, helps counselors to more easily maintain the therapeutic alliance with religious or spiritual clients (Genia, 2000).

Mental health professionals themselves also demonstrate a high degree of personal spiritual commitment. The majority of mental health practitioners claim some type of religious affiliation, believe that spirituality is personally relevant, and value personal prayer (Bergin & Jensen, 1990; Shafranske & Malony, 1990). In particular, marriage and family counselors incorporate religion into their personal and professional lives more than other mental health professionals. Ninety-five percent of marriage and family counselors believe that there is a relationship between spiritual and mental health, 94 percent believe that spirituality is an important aspect of their personal lives, 82 percent report regularly spending time getting in touch with their spirituality, and 71 percent report praying regularly (Carlson, Kirkpatrick, Hecker, & Killmer, 2002).

Despite the high regard given to spiritual issues by mental health providers, not all believe that spirituality should be integrated into counseling. Only 62 percent of marriage and family counselors believe that a spiritual dimension should be included in clinical practice and only 47 percent believe that it is necessary to address a client's spirituality in order to help her or him (Carlson et al., 2002). In one study, only 29 percent of clinical psychologists, psychiatrists, clinical social workers, and marriage and family counselors "expressed a belief . . . that religious matters are important for treatment efforts with all or many of their clients" (Bergen & Jensen, 1990, p. 6). Carlson et al. (2002) attribute the disparity between beliefs in the importance of spirituality and the integration of spirituality in counseling to (a) a lack of education on how to integrate spirituality and counseling and (b) "the newness of spirituality as a viable topic for counseling" (p. 167). Wiggins-Frame (2005) attributes the disparity to counselors' unresolved religious/spiritual issues.

HARMFUL FAITH

In the past, many counselors maintained that religion itself was psychologically limiting, even harmful, and was often part of clients' psychopathology. Although more recent evidence, cited above, counters this perspective, it is certainly true that in some cases, clients with mental health problems may act out their problems in religious terms.

One instance of harmful uses of faith is religious addiction. The religiously addicted "adhere to a hurtful religion to dodge the emotional turmoil that comes with facing the reality of their circumstances" (Arterburn & Felton, 1992, p. 114). Consequently, certain religious interventions are contraindicated if they encourage religious behavior that interferes with attention to the central problems. For example, religious addiction is often accompanied by compulsive prayer. Therefore, an uninformed counselor may reinforce such compulsivity by praying with this type of client (Taylor, 2002). Another example of harmful uses of faith might occur in couples work. A religiously addicted and authoritarian spouse may force "sessions of prayer and scripture quoting" (p. 304) and engage in physical abuse when the other partner violates a dogmatic rule. Including spirituality in treatment with this couple may reinforce the controlling behavior of the religiously addicted spouse (Taylor, 2002). Table 15.5 lists indications of religious pathology.

Table 15.5   Indications of Religious Pathology

The following are 10 indications of probable religious pathology:

- Self-oriented or narcissistic displays

- Religion used to gain rewards from a divine power

- Scrupulosity in avoiding sin or error

- Relinquishing responsibility for problematic behavior to "the devil" or other evil forces (Lovinger, 1996, p. 348)

- Ecstatic frenzy or intense emotionality

- Persistent church/temple/mosque shopping

- Inappropriate sharing of one's religious experiences

- Religiously inspired "love" that causes pain or confusion

- Using the scriptures to answer "ordinary questions about daily living" (Lovinger, 1996, p. 349)

- Reports of possession by evil spirits or the devil

SOURCE: Lovinger (1996).

SUMMARY: HELPFUL AND HARMFUL FAITH

The counselor should, therefore, be alert to both the harm and benefits that may accrue from religious faith. Counselors should do an ongoing assessment, especially early in counseling, of the client's uses of faith. Counselors can assess four matters in this area: (1) the role of faith in a client's life, (2) the ways in which the client expresses his or her faith, (3) the client's expectations about the role of spirituality in the counseling sessions, and (4) the most helpful ways to intervene with religious clients (Magaletta & Brawer, 1998). Such assessment allows counselors to investigate religious behavior or beliefs that may be related to the client's presenting problem (Spero, 1982; Yarhouse, 1999) and to exercise caution in using spiritual interventions if religion seems to contribute to the client's problem (Richards & Potts, 1995; Spero, 1982).

AVOIDING COUNTERTRANSFERENCE

Appropriately interacting with the client's faith system requires a great deal of counselor self-awareness. Ongoing self-examination, in Spero's (1982) words, is a "technical and ethical obligation . . . [for] anti- and nonreligious counselors encountering religious patients, and religious counselors encountering anti- or nonreligious patients" (p. 566). Activity 15.4 offers an opportunity for the reader to examine her or his relationship to religion.

Self-awareness in relation to religion may be hampered by counselors' unresolved issues that come from damaging experiences with or without religion. Thus, countertransference may emerge in both religious and secular counselors. Table 15.6 summarizes types of religious countertransference.

ACTIVITY 15.4

Integrating Counseling With Religion and Spirituality

Readers are encouraged to complete the following activity in order to become more aware of how they are integrating (or not) their beliefs about counseling with religion and/or spirituality.

What is your overall worldview and how does it relate to your religious and spiritual beliefs? Carefully elaborate your worldview and its implications for counseling practice.

What are the religious and spiritual dimensions of your definition of ethical practice?

Consider the core conditions for effective counseling (empathy, unconditional positive regard, genuineness). What are the spiritual and religious dimensions of these concepts?

With which counseling skills and concepts do you feel particularly comfortable? How would clients from different religious backgrounds respond to these concepts?

What theories of counseling and therapy appeal to you? From what approach do you personally plan to practice? What influence do your own spiritual and religious beliefs have on your choice?

1. Examine how your personal religious and spiritual developmental history, as influenced by your family and culture, affects your answers to the above questions.

2. How will you continue to reflect on the influence of your personal history and your present religious and spiritual beliefs on your performance as a counselor?

   a. Are you participating in your own therapeutic processes?

   b. What is your developmental goal?

   c. How are your concepts of well-being, disease, pathology, healing, and "cure" evolving?

Table 15.6   Types of Religious Countertransference

Below are six types of countertransference, as they relate to religious issues, that counselors might exhibit (Case, 1997):

1. The *Sibling Complex* engenders excessive agreement or loose interpersonal boundaries with the client because of commonalities such as similar values and similar expectations from one's religious community.

2. The *Missionary* counselor uses the therapeutic relationship to proselytize clients.

3. The *Spiritualizer* views all client issues as requiring a spiritual intervention when many other legitimate interventions may be appropriate, a view that may be encouraged by the client's misinformed expectations about a counselor's role.

4. The *Reactionary* counselor experiences "aggressive feelings against the (religious) group, or unresolved rebelliousness" that can result in inappropriately avoiding religious interventions or acting in defiance of the client's religious traditions, behaviors, or spiritual statements.

5. The *Window Shopper* exhibits excessive curiosity about the client to gratify her or his own needs (e.g., asking clients to divulge all of their sexual secrets due to the counselor's perhaps restrictive religious beliefs regarding sexuality).

6. *My Way Is Yahweh* counselors pose as the experts in spiritual matters, instead of recognizing that many different and valid opinions and interpretations exist about specific spiritual issues, some of which may be held by the client.

Counselors should pursue their own counseling or supervision in order to become aware of and appropriately manage countertransference (Agass, 2002; Astor, 2000; Wolitzky, 1995). During such a process of self-examination, they can scrutinize their own religious attitudes or lack of them to determine whether their perspectives are useful or dysfunctional, mature or immature. Counselors should aim to counter their own anxiety, anger, and frustration when encountering clients who are religiously different from themselves. Counselors must be tolerant of the client's need for emotional, but not necessarily rational, commitment and belief and learn to contain their own need to impart insight into every aspect of the client's life (Spero, 1982).

At times, referral is in order. While counselors are in the process of resolving countertransferential reactions to clients, clients need protection from the potentially harmful effects of the counselor's inability to work with spiritual issues. Therefore, Genia (2000) and the ACA *Code of Ethics* (ACA, 2005) advocate making appropriate referrals, either to other counselors who share a worldview with the client or to spiritual advisors who are trained to address spiritual issues.

Beliefs of the Major Religious Groups in the United States and Implications for Counseling

This section briefly explores some beliefs of the following major religions in the United States: Christianity, Islam, Judaism, Hinduism, and Buddhism. In addition, paganism, agnosticism, and humanism, although not usually considered mainstream religions, are discussed at the end of this section. Each segment offers a brief history, a chart indicating any religious practices and customs that might manifest in the counseling room, and recommendations for practice

CHRISTIANITY

The religion based on the life and teachings of Jesus, or Yehoshua in Hebrew, is called Christianity (Keller, 1999). Jesus was also named the "Christ" ("the Anointed One" in Greek), thus leading to the common name Jesus Christ. About one-third of the world's population is considered Christian and can be divided into three main branches: (1) Roman Catholicism (the largest coherent group, representing over one billion baptized members); (2) Orthodox Christianity (including Eastern Orthodoxy and Oriental Orthodoxy); and (3) Protestantism (comprised of many denominations and schools of thought, including Anglicanism, Reformed, Presbyterianism, Lutheranism, Methodism, Evangelicalism, and Pentecostalism). Christians believe that because of humanity's fall from God's grace through sin, people were separated from God. Christ's death on the cross was necessary to pay for or atone for that sin in order for people to regain a relationship with God. Christians maintain their relationship with God in various ways; therefore, the denomination to which a person belongs tends to determine how that relationship is expressed. Prayer, reading the Bible, and meeting in congregations for worship, confession, and celebration of communion are examples of common Christian practices.

Roman Catholicism

The Catholic Church is the Westernmost of two churches that were created by the East/West split of Christianity in 1054. The term "catholic," at its root, comes from the Latin *catholicus,* which means "universal." Catholicism's headquarters are in Rome at the Vatican. Its leader is the Pope, who occupies the top point of a hierarchy that begins at the lower end with the laity and the priests and climbs up through bishops, archbishops, and cardinals. Catholics emphasize the importance of the Church's teaching authority and the sacraments. The central acts of worship are the Mass, which is the complex of prayers and ceremonies that make up the service of the Eucharist. The Eucharist is a ceremony of giving thanks that parallels what Jesus did with His disciples at the last supper before his death. Holy Communion is part of the Mass also: Congregants partake of the consecrated bread and wine as a means of receiving "grace" (Hoge, 1996).

Table 15.7 outlines some of the traditional Catholic beliefs that may intersect with counseling concerns. Great variance exists among Catholics in terms of the influence of religion and spirituality on their lives; however, the table outlines some general reminders for counseling with Catholics.

Protestant Christianity

The Christian Protestant churches originated during the Reformation in the sixteenth century when many European Christians broke away from the Catholic Church—that is, they "protested." The German Martin Luther is considered the founder of Protestantism; his followers become "Lutherans." The Frenchman John Calvin (born Chauvin) was influential as well, and his followers became Calvinists who later, in the United States under the influence of the Scotsman John Knox, became Presbyterians. The Englishman John Wesley's followers became Methodists. From Switzerland came the followers of Ulrich Zwingli, who were called Anabaptists; they later became the Baptists and Mennonites. In the beginning, there were few Protestant denominations. Later, however, Protestantism experienced many further divisions. As a result, there are now numerous Protestant denominations in the United States.

Mainstream Protestant Christianity. Mainstream Protestants are generally characterized by a progressive theology and an openness both to other churches and, at times, even other religions. Historically speaking, mainstream Protestants have practiced a "social gospel," which strongly emphasizes activism to address social problems as a primary outward expression of a faithful life. For instance, mainstream Protestants have often been in the forefront of movements such as the abolition of slavery, prison reform, orphanage establishment, hospital building, and the founding of educational institutions. Today, this activism is also expressed in literacy training, adoption agencies, food banks, and daycare centers for children (Esau, 1998). Some of the groups that are considered mainstream Protestants are the United Church of Christ (historically known as the Congregationalists), the American Baptist Church (Northern Baptists), the Episcopal Church, the Presbyterian Church, the United Methodist Church, the Evangelical Lutheran Church, and Disciples of Christ. Table 15.8 lists some of the traditional mainstream Protestant beliefs that may intersect with counseling concerns and offers treatment recommendations.

Evangelical and Fundamentalist Protestant Christianity. Evangelical and/or fundamentalist Christian denominations generally emerged in the United States as a reaction against the perception that mainstream denominations, in emphasizing the social gospel, were "falling away" from God and scripture. Evangelicals expressed the desire to practice faith as they saw it described in the New Testament.

Commentators and historians have described four distinctive characteristics of evangelicals (Bebbington, 1989). The first is an emphasis on the conversion experience. The conversion is also called being "saved" or being "born again"

Table 15.7   Catholic Beliefs and Counseling

Marriage and Divorce	Family is viewed as holy, permanent, and monogamous. The marriage ceremony is a sacrament. The family's holy role is to cooperate with God by procreating children, who are destined to be the adopted children of God, and instructing them for His kingdom. The absence of offspring as a result of artificial devices (birth control) is thus considered immoral. The Roman Catholic Church regards marriage as permanent and indissoluble, except upon the death of a spouse. However, the church can—in some circumstances—issue an annulment. That document, in effect, states that a valid marriage never existed. This allows individuals to remarry in the church.
Sexuality	Premarital, homosexual, and extramarital sexual behaviors are considered sinful.
Abortion and Birth Control	Abortion and artificial birth control are considered sinful.
View of Counseling	Catholics may prefer a counselor whose faith is consistent with their own, but there is a wide degree of variance in opinions among Catholics about the importance of the faith of the counselor. Catholics are open to the use of medication.
Spiritual Practices and Healing Traditions	There are many sacraments that are part of ritual worship, including anointing the sick, use of holy water, prayer, and devotion.
Potential Religious/ Clinical Issues	Conflicts about the relationship to authority, sexuality, interfaith marriage, divorce, abortion, suicide, artificial insemination, genetic engineering, and euthanasia
Treatment Recommendations	Be aware of Church teachings about suffering, death, resurrection, confession, and reconciliation. Explicitly integrate religious resources. Consult with clergy.

SOURCE: Adapted from Richards & Bergin (1999).

Table 15.8 Mainstream Protestant Beliefs and Counseling

Marriage and Divorce	Marriage is considered a union blessed by God. Divorce is tolerated though not encouraged, as are single-parent families and remarriage.
Sexuality	Many Protestant religions advocate responsible sexual behavior, understood as sexual expression that matches the seriousness and permanence of the relationship. Teenage and extramarital sex are seen as morally unacceptable in most cases. No clear positions are stated on masturbation. Homosexuality, in some mainstream Protestant religions, is morally acceptable, but many denominations will not conduct same-sex unions or ordain homosexual ministers.
Abortion and Birth Control	Mainstream Protestants acknowledge legitimate diversity of opinion related to abortion. Abortion may be acceptable under circumstances of rape or incest, physical or mental deformity of the fetus, or threats to the physical or mental well-being of the mother. Most oppose its use as a method of birth control and acknowledge that the state has at least a limited interest in regulating abortion, but they believe in safe and affordable access to abortions in acceptable situations. Contraceptive use is acceptable in most Protestant religions.
View of Counseling	Protestants tend to have a positive view of counseling. Sometimes clients might fear counseling will not integrate their religious beliefs.
Spiritual Practices and Healing Traditions	Worship services, prayer, meditation, Bible reading, teachings about grace and forgiveness
Potential Religious/ Clinical Issues	Sexuality, divorce, substance abuse, abortion, euthanasia
Treatment Recommendations	Usually comfortable with secular approaches to counseling. Use forgiveness as a therapeutic tool, collaborate with pastoral care in using spiritual interventions.

SOURCE: Adapted from Richards & Bergin (1999).

(King James Bible, John 3:3). Evangelicals are sometimes referred to as "born-again Christians" because of this emphasis. The second is the use of the Bible as the primary source of God's revelation to people and, therefore, the ultimate religious authority. That is why the term "fundamentalist" is sometimes used to describe this type of belief—because of an allegiance to the fundamental inerrancy of the Bible. The third is evangelism, which is the act of sharing one's beliefs with others, either in organized missionary work or through personal evangelism, in order that others, too, may be "saved." The fourth characteristic is a central focus on Christ's redeeming work on the cross, especially as the means for salvation and the forgiveness of sins (Esau, 1998).

Evangelicals try to follow the biblical injunction to be in the world yet not "of" the world (King James Bible, John 17:14–18), which means to make a difference in the world while not adopting the world's "ungodly" ways. Evangelicals primarily engage with those who believe similarly to themselves, or with those whom they are evangelizing. As a result, evangelicals may not be open to secular counseling, instead only feeling safe with a counselor of their own faith. During such counseling, spiritual interventions, such as forgiveness, prayer, examining distorted religious beliefs, and consultation with clergy may be expected and therefore necessary (Esau, 1998).

Evangelicals are also very active in promoting conservative social causes, including anti-abortion, same-sex marriage prohibition, the elimination of pornography, the promotion of abstinence education in schools, and school prayer. Within Protestantism there is often a political dichotomy, with the mainstream denominations and the evangelicals both actively lobbying in Washington, but on opposite sides of the same issues (Hannon, Howie, & Keener, 1994). Table 15.9 lists some of the traditional Evangelical and Fundamentalist Protestant beliefs that may intersect with counseling concerns. It also offers treatment recommendations.

In the cases presented at the beginning of the chapter, Brittany would be considered an Evangelical Christian. She struggles with how to date and find a mate while remaining godly. A counselor would need to remember that "secular" dating behaviors would probably appear to be "of the world" and therefore ungodly in her eyes. Eriksen et al. (2002) provide one guide to counseling conservative Christians.

ISLAM

Islam was founded by Mohammed (ca. 570–632). Orphaned at the age of six, he worked as a shepherd and camel driver. Muslims believe that when Mohammed was 40 years old and married, he was visited in Mecca by the Angel Gabriel. Subsequently, he believed himself to be a prophet and began converting people to his new religion. At first he faced stiff opposition. However, through military activity and political negotiation, he eventually became a powerful leader, firmly establishing Islam in the Middle East as the dominant faith and as the second largest religion in the world (Council on American-Islamic Relations, 2000).

Table 15.9   Evangelical and Fundamentalist Protestant Beliefs and Counseling

Marriage and Divorce	Evangelicals oppose divorce and remarriage except in cases of spouse's infidelity.
Sexuality	They oppose premarital, homosexual, and extramarital sex.
Abortion and Birth Control	Evangelicals oppose abortion as a means of birth control or a means of eliminating unwanted pregnancies. Contraception is acceptable.
View of Counseling	Evangelicals often have a positive view of counseling as long as the counselor shares their faith.
Spiritual Practices and Healing Traditions	Social support is gained through the church and congregation, through prayer, Bible study, and participation in services and activities.
Potential Religious/ Clinical Issues	Fear of authority figures and of emotional conflict, repression of negative feelings, group dependency, perfectionism, excessive guilt and shame, low self-esteem, dogmatism, sexual addiction
Treatment Recommendations	Use forgiveness, prayer, relevant scriptures; challenge distorted religious beliefs; consult with religious leaders.

The Arabic word "Islam" means "submission" or "peace," referring to the peace experienced by the person who completely submits himself or herself to God or Allah. A person who follows Islam is called a Muslim. The Qur'an is the holy book of Islam, believed to be the literal and final word of God in Arabic as it was revealed to Mohammed. Also important to Muslims is the Sharia, or the Islamic law, also known as the Law of Allah. Classic Islam draws no distinction between religious and secular life; hence, Sharia covers not only religious rituals but many aspects of day-to-day life, politics, economics, banking, business or contract law, and social issues (Council on American-Islamic Relations, 2000). Table 15.10 lists some of the traditional Muslim beliefs that may intersect with counseling concerns.

JUDAISM

According to the Exodus story, the Jews settled on a thin strip of land at the eastern end of the Mediterranean Sea, probably sometime in the thirteenth century B.C.E. Their history is one of dispersion throughout the world (called "the Diaspora") and expulsion from non-Jewish communities. Jews established communities throughout much of the world after the original Diaspora. They

Table 15.10   Muslim Beliefs and Counseling

Marriage and Divorce	Marriage and children are encouraged. Polygamy is permitted but rarely practiced in the United States. Romantic love is not a prerequisite to marriage. Divorce is discouraged but is permitted and is easier for men to obtain than for women.
Sexuality	All sexual relationships outside of marriage are forbidden. Homosexual behavior is forbidden.
Abortion and Birth Control	Abortion is discouraged but permitted under certain circumstances. Contraception is permitted.
View of Counseling	Muslims commonly view counseling with suspicion.
Spiritual Practices and Healing Traditions	Ritual prayers, fasting, pilgrimage, visiting a mosque, reading or listening to the Qur'an, participating in holidays.
Potential Religious/ Clinical Issues	Conflicts with mainstream secular culture and values, depression, somatization of problems, suicidal ideation.
Treatment Recommendations	Gain knowledge about Muslim religion and cultural values, involve the family, and consult with members of the Muslim community.

SOURCE: Adapted from Richards & Bergin (1999).

continued to experience forced expulsions and persecution. The centers of Jewish life moved during the last two millennia from Judea to Babylonia to Spain to Poland to the United States and finally back to Israel. During the Middle Ages, Jews divided into distinct regional groups. These groupings are the Ashkenazi (Northern and Eastern European Jews) and Sephardic Jews (Spanish, Mediterranean, and Middle Eastern Jews).

Two major organizing events of contemporary Judaism are the Holocaust and the defense of Israel's statehood. In the Holocaust, the Nazis killed over six million Jews and rendered hundreds of thousands homeless. The Holocaust spurred the creation of the nation of Israel in 1948. The country was immediately besieged by armies from several Arab countries. After weeks of fighting, Israel remained, holding more territory than it had originally claimed. At this point, Jews sent out a call for all Jews to return to Israel. And Jews came, often being airlifted out of Arab countries just ahead of persecution. They also came from the European countries where they had often been outcasts. The support of Israel and the defense of its borders has captured a great deal of Jewish energy since Israel first became a country (Heilman & Cohen, 1989).

There are three general strands in Judaism: Reform, Conservative, and Orthodox. The most liberal strand comprises Reform Jews. Beliefs vary among adherents, including that of nonbelief or questioning belief. They generally see scripture as a cultural product to be interpreted as an ethical guide and in historical terms. Reform Jews generally do not believe in original sin or hell. Conservative Judaism affirms belief in God and in the divine inspiration of the Torah; however, it also affirms the legitimacy of multiple interpretations of these issues. The term "conservative" signifies that Jews should attempt to conserve Jewish tradition, rather than reform or abandon it; it does not mean that the movement's adherents are politically conservative. Orthodox Judaism adheres to a relatively strict interpretation and application of the written and oral laws and ethics. All branches of Judaism encourage asking questions about how to live ethically.

Not all Jews are religious. The American Jewish Identity Survey of 2000 (Kosmin et al., 2001) concluded that there are 5.5 million ethnic Jews in the United States. Of these, about 3 million, or 51 percent of ethnic Jews, are religious. Jews also vary in their degree of orthodoxy. Table 15.11 lists some of the traditional Jewish beliefs that may intersect with counseling concerns and offers treatment recommendations.

Geoff, one of the clients presented at the beginning of the chapter, is a religious Jew from an Orthodox sect. It would seem that his small-town upbringing and his orthodoxy, rather than his Jewishness, are the factors leading to his emotional distress at this time. These factors would make it difficult for him to integrate or relate to the vast array of beliefs present in a large city or on a metropolitan college campus.

HINDUISM

Hinduism is the dominant religion of the Indian subcontinent and the third largest religion in the world, after Christianity and Islam. Established over 3,000 years ago, Hinduism is based on ancient scriptures known collectively as the Vedas. Although the Vedas serve as a foundation for Hinduism, many modifications have been made over the years, resulting in a religion characterized by a multitude of often-conflicting ideologies and practices. Hindus believe in a supreme spiritual force called Brahman, with which an individual will become one after cleansing his or her karma through a cycle of birth, death, and rebirth (reincarnation). Karma represents the total of all that an individual has done, is currently doing, and will do. In life, Hindus follow the laws of dharma, or the doctrine of the rights and duties of each individual. Hinduism's salient characteristics include an ancient mythology, an absence of a specific recorded origin or founder, a cyclical notion of time, a pantheism that infuses divinity into the world around, a relationship between people and divinity, a priestly class, and a tolerance of diverse paths to the Ultimate. Its sacral language is Sanskrit, which came to India about 5,000 years ago with a tribe called the Aryans, from Central Asia (Kumar, Bhugra, & Singh, 2005). Table 15.12 presents some of the traditional Hindu beliefs that may intersect with counseling concerns and offers treatment recommendations.

Table 15.11 Jewish Beliefs and Counseling

Marriage and Divorce	Marriage and children are highly valued. Divorce is permitted and remarriage is encouraged.
Sexuality	Conservative and Reform Jews allow premarital sex as a matter of personal choice but view adultery and incest as sinful. Male homosexual behavior is viewed as more unfavorable than female homosexual behavior. Some Orthodox Jews view premarital, homosexual, and extramarital sex as sinful.
Abortion and Birth Control	Orthodox Jews view abortion as a sin, except if the mother's life is in danger or when a rabbi sanctions it. For the Orthodox Jew, contraception is discouraged and usually permitted only for medical reasons. Conservative and Reform Jews allow abortion when the life or health of the mother is threatened. For them, contraception is acceptable.
View of Counseling	There are various views of counseling. Some may be reluctant to seek counseling for fear it will undermine or conflict with their values. Psychoanalysis, however, has been especially attractive.
Spiritual Practices and Healing Traditions	Study of the Torah, Mishna, and Talmud; prayer and worship, holidays, and ceremonies
Potential Religious/ Clinical Issues	Depression, identity conflicts, intellectualization, guilt, interfaith marriage, family enmeshment, marital discord, sexual problems, homosexuality, masturbation, feelings of spiritual inadequacy
Treatment Recommendations	Psychodynamic and cognitive approaches may be more acceptable. Debate, discussion, and argument may be appropriate. Consult with rabbis.

SOURCE: Adapted from Richards & Bergin (1999).

BUDDHISM

For centuries, Buddhism has been the dominant religion of the Eastern world. Today, it remains the predominant religion in China, Japan, and much of Southeast Asia and is one of the largest religions in the world. With the rise of the Asian population in the United States, Buddhism has expanded tremendously in the United States (Das & Kemp, 1997).

Table 15.12   Hindu Beliefs and Counseling

Marriage and Divorce	Marriage and childrearing are highly valued. Arranged marriages. are common. Divorce is discouraged but allowed in certain circumstances.
Sexuality	Premarital and extramarital sex are discouraged. Homosexuality is tolerated. Chastity is valued.
Abortion and Birth Control	Abortion and contraception are acceptable.
View of Counseling	Counseling may be viewed with skepticism. Importance is placed on families taking care of their own.
Spiritual Practices and Healing Traditions	Meditation, yoga, religious devotions and prayers, rituals, festivals and pilgrimages
Potential Religious/ Clinical Issues	Acculturation and value conflicts, family and marital problems, dating and marriage concerns, domestic violence, incest
Treatment Recommendations	Use the concept of karma; explore contradictions; learn more about the Hindu religion

SOURCE: Adapted from Richards & Bergin (1999).

Buddhism began in India as an offshoot of Hinduism. Siddhartha Gautama, the founder of Buddhism, was born in approximately 560 B.C.E. in northern India. Deeply distressed by human suffering, he began a quest to find the answer to the problem of suffering. Gautama eventually turned to a life of meditation. While deep in meditation, Gautama experienced the highest degree of God-consciousness, called nirvana. Subsequently, he became known as the Buddha, or the "enlightened one." As he began his teaching ministry, he gained an audience with the people of India because many had become disillusioned with Hinduism. By the time of Gautama's death at age 80, Buddhism had become a major force in India. Three centuries later, Buddhism had spread to all of Asia (Muramoto, 2002).

The basic teachings of Buddhism are found in the Four Noble Truths and the Eightfold Path. The First Noble Truth is that there is pain and suffering in the world. The Second Noble Truth relates to the cause of suffering. The Third Noble Truth says that suffering will cease when people can rid themselves of all desires. The Fourth Noble Truth is that all desire can be extinguished by following the Eightfold Path. The Eightfold Path is a system of living designed to develop habits that will release people from the restrictions caused by ignorance and craving (Muramoto, 2002).

Three important concepts in Buddhism are karma, samsara, and nirvana. Karma, as in Hinduism, refers to the law of cause and effect in a person's life— reaping what one has sown. Samsara holds that everything is in a birth and rebirth cycle and that every person must go through a process of birth and rebirth until he or she reaches the state of nirvana. Nirvana is not a place like heaven, but rather a state of being in which there is no suffering and there are no desires. Buddha taught that the existence of an individual self or ego is an illusion; therefore, nirvana is also the state in which individual consciousness ends. Buddhists believe that through self-effort one can attain the state of peace and eternal bliss called nirvana (Richards & Bergin, 1997).

In general, Buddhists are pantheistic in their view of God. Many view God as an impersonal force composed of all living things that holds the universe together. Buddhism is a moral philosophy, an ethical way of life (Muramoto, 2002). Table 15.13 lists some of the traditional Buddhist beliefs that may intersect with counseling concerns and offers treatment recommendations.

EARTH-BASED RELIGIONS/PAGANISM

Paganism, which since the 1960s has been referred to as Neo-Paganism, is a set of spiritual paths and traditions in which reverence for the Earth and all of its creatures are celebrated. Pagans generally believe that all life is interconnected and try to experience this interconnectivity as part of their religious practices. Some may do this by taking care of the space they inhabit, while others try to deal with the problems that are harming the Earth on a wider scale. These Earth-based religions focus on connection to divinity through nature. Pagan religions are characterized by personal autonomy, polytheism, and immanent divinity. That is, the belief that there is a single divinity, a life force of the universe who is immanent in the world. Pagans value diversity, good works, living lightly on the Earth, individual freedom, personal responsibility, community service, gender equity, and spiritual development (Seymour, 2005). Table 15.14 lists some of the pagan beliefs that may intersect with counseling concerns and offers treatment recommendations.

AGNOSTICISM/HUMANISM

Agnosticism is the philosophical and theological view that the existence of God, gods, or deities is either unknown or inherently unknowable, but that to deny the existence of God is also untenable. It is used to describe those who are unconvinced or noncommittal about the existence of deities as well as other matters of religion. The word "agnostic" comes from the Greek *a* (no) and *gnosis* (knowledge) (Agnosticism, 2006).

Humanism, though not a religion in a full sense, is an extremely influential and important belief system. Humanism is oriented toward the satisfaction of human needs, both material and spiritual, and the fulfillment of human potential, here and now. Humanists, therefore, lack interest in the supernatural and theological or in an afterlife. Religious and secular humanists hold in

Table 15.13 Buddhist Beliefs and Counseling

Marriage and Divorce	No specific Buddhist teachings exist about marriage and divorce or childrearing.
Sexuality	Buddhists believe that sex before marriage is not immoral if there is love and consent between the two parties involved. As long as the act of sex does not cause harm, it is permissible. Homosexuality is accepted.
Abortion and Birth Control	Respect for all life is important. Abortion is unethical; contraception is acceptable.
View of Counseling	A range of attitudes exists among Buddhists.
Spiritual Practices and Healing Traditions	Meditation, being one's own spiritual teacher, daily worship, prayers, holy days, festivals, studying Buddhist teachings
Potential Religious/ Clinical Issues	Self-contempt, addictions, pathological selfishness
Treatment Recommendations	Be supportive of and encourage meditative practices; consult with Buddhist teachers; use insight-oriented approaches.

SOURCE: Adapted from Richards & Bergin (1999).

common the belief that nothing should be accepted on faith. Rather, there must always be good evidence for beliefs, religious or otherwise. This is the most fundamental tenet of rationalism. Nothing specific to humanism precludes belief in God. In the humanist view, the controversy over the existence of God is far less relevant to ethical living than is ordinarily supposed by believers in God (Firth, 1996).

Humanism has two core beliefs:

1. People should think for themselves, rather than blindly accept what they are told by authorities. Authority figures too often have agendas of their own, frequently for the enhancement of their own wealth or power, or may be uninformed or confused.

2. Values are based in the human person. In order to know whether a given course of conduct is meaningful or right, an individual can ask herself or himself whether it promotes the maintenance or development of the normal capabilities of human beings, such as thinking, feeling, and physical health (Firth, 1996).

Table 15.14 Pagan Beliefs and Counseling

Marriage and Divorce	"Handfasting" is practiced. It represents making a one-year trial marriage commitment, after which time the couple can stay together or "handpart," that is, choose to separate. Both the male and the female are considered essential to the creation of new life, and therefore, neither should be subordinate to the other.
Gender Roles Sexuality	Pagans have no set rules against homosexuality, nudity, or premarital sex. Sex is viewed positively as the generative force in nature and is seen by most pagans as something utterly sacred. The physical act of love is to be approached with great respect and responsibility.
Abortion and Birth Control	The majority of modern pagans favor safe and legal access to abortions.
View of Counseling	Pagans may view counselors with distrust and apprehension, fearing that their faith will be misunderstood.
Spiritual Practices and Healing Traditions	Diverse kinds of divination; altered states of consciousness or trances; magic spells and incantations; special rites for seasonal holy days
Potential Religious/ Clinical Issues	Prior prejudices about the word "pagan." The frequent, inaccurate association between paganism and evils such as satanic abuse.
Treatment Recommendations	Recognize that paganism is a nature religion in which self-realization is a central tenet. Acknowledge spirituality and respect indigenous traditions.

SOURCE: Adapted from Seymour (2005).

Table 15.15 provides some of the traditional agnostic/humanistic issues that may intersect with counseling concerns.

General Interventions That Are Alert to Religion and Spirituality

Counselors must respect clients' religious perspectives. Multicultural sensitivity around religion is required by both religious counselors and secular counselors. Religious counselors run the risk of believing that all encounters are spiritual

Table 15.15   Traditional Agnostic/Humanist Beliefs

Abortion	The American Humanist Association endorses elective abortion, and Unitarian Universalists, many of whom are humanists, "believe in the right of every woman to safe and affordable abortion services, including federally funded abortion counseling and abortion provision, and [have] called for governmental protection for abortion providers and women who receive abortions" (http://www.uua.org/actions/women/93abortion.html).
Other Contemporary Issues	Agnostics, humanists, and atheists generally support equality for lesbian, gay, bisexual, and transgendered people; gender equality; a secular approach to divorce and remarriage; working to end poverty; promoting peace and nonviolence; and protecting the environment.
View of Counseling	Views of counseling are positive.
Spiritual Practices and Healing Traditions	No specific practices but open to many
Potential Religious/ Clinical Issues	May overemphasize personal responsibility, intellectualize as a defensive strategy, and fear appearing dependent or weak.
Treatment Recommendations	Be open to exploring beliefs, but do not make assumptions. Be inclusive in language.

SOURCE: Adapted from Richards & Bergin (1999).

and may be inclined to impose spiritual interventions on clients. Secular counselors, by contrast, may resist incorporation of any spirituality in the counseling process.

How might counselors effectively incorporate spirituality and/or religion into their work, given their agreement with the need to do so? Two ways are possible: *explicit* integration and *implicit* integration (Tan, 1996b). Explicit integration directly incorporates spiritual approaches, such as prayer or discussion and interpretation of sacred writings, with traditional therapeutic methods (Richards & Bergin, 2002). Counselors who wish to explicitly incorporate religion into practice clearly need religious training beyond what is provided in most counselor education programs (Richards & Bergin, 2002; Shafranske & Malony, 1996). *Implicit* integration consists of respectfully and sensitively responding to religious themes as they emerge in the counseling process. In the more implicit approach, the counselor does not initiate the discussion of religious or spiritual issues, but respectfully responds to those brought up by the client. In implicit integration, the counselor does not openly, directly, or systematically use spiritual resources like prayer and sacred texts in counseling (Tan, 1996b).

Further discussion of religiously alert counseling intervention is guided by the three multicultural competency themes of awareness, knowledge, and skills (Sue, Arredondo, & McDavis, 1992). Following the discussion of counseling based on the multicultural competencies, religiously alert counseling is illustrated using the cases from the vignettes at the beginning of the chapter.

INCORPORATING THE MULTICULTURAL COMPETENCY THEMES

Counselors need to have spiritual self-awareness, knowledge about particular faiths, and skill in practicing counseling interventions appropriate to religious clients (W. R. Miller, 1999). This chapter has, thus far, offered some exercises designed to increase readers' self-awareness and has offered some specific knowledge about particular faiths. Competent counseling with spiritual or religious clients, however, will require continuing study in each of these areas.

SELF-AWARENESS AND COUNTERTRANSFERENCE

Spiritual self-awareness includes two facets: (a) awareness of one's own faith and faith development, including how one's faith has been or might be beneficial; and (b) awareness of countertransference issues that may hinder one's work with clients.

Regarding one's own faith, in Hagedorn's (2005) words, counselors need to "acknowledge and be comfortable with [their] own spiritual and religious beliefs, values, and spiritual journey" in order to help others in that area (p. 69). Counselors may use the same assessments that they would use with clients to evaluate themselves, or may ask themselves the questions posed in Activities 15.1 and 15.2 in this chapter. Those activities can help students to gain clarity on their spiritual history and development and the benefits that they have experienced as a result of their faith or from their nonbelieving. Counselors should be able to respond to the following questions: "Where did I come from?" "Where am I going?" "What does life mean [for me]?" "What is worth living for?" (Helminiak, 2001, p. 163).

More specifically, counselors need to consider their understanding of the role of the following in their and others' lives: "forgiveness, transcendence, . . . the purpose of tragedy, sin, faith, the afterlife, morality, sacredness, leading a religious/spiritual life, altruism and high ideals, . . . relationship with God or a higher power, [and] value of material possessions" (Hagedorn, 2005, p. 69). They need to reflect on spiritual themes that permeate their lives or set the tone of life, on spiritual influences, and on life lessons that may be useful to pass along to others (Faiver & Ingersoll, 2005). Counselors need to ask and answer questions about how they will integrate their value/faith system with the counseling process. Finally, they need to assess how comfortable they are with exploring such issues with clients.

Benefits of Spiritual Self-Assessment

Participation in such self-exploration may promote counselors' development away from their own religious or antireligious dogmatism and countertransference, which could harm the therapeutic relationship. Such self-assessment can help religion-skeptical counselors to consider the benefits of faith for clients, particularly if client worldviews differ from those of the counselor (Hagedorn, 2005).

Overcoming Bias

As with any hindrances to carrying out their responsibilities to clients, counselors need to get help in overcoming biases. Supervision, of course, may assist in this process (ACA, 2005). Other means to overcoming bias include counselors building meaningful relationships with people who differ in faith perspectives from themselves (Bishop, 1992), gaining knowledge about other faiths, and educating themselves through reading. These strategies may build understanding, appreciation, and knowledge of how to work with clients from different faith positions. Knowledge about others may increase one's sense of competence enough to reduce counselor uncertainty about meeting clients of different faiths. That is the topic of the next major section.

KNOWLEDGE ABOUT FAITHS

Along with developing self-awareness, counselors need to be competent in the second area of multicultural competence, namely knowledge of different religious groups, especially as seen through the eyes of clients. This chapter has offered a very brief overview of different faiths, but adequate understanding requires more substantive reading, as well as "plunges" into the activities and rituals of different faiths (Bishop, 1992), especially the faiths practiced by the clients in one's practice.

Counselors must be knowledgeable in four domains. Each of the following domains has been introduced in this chapter. Counselors should (1) be able to define and understand the differences between spirituality and religion, which was discussed in the beginning of this chapter; (2) have a general understanding of the tenets of the major world religions and familiarity with helping resources within spiritual and religious traditions; (3) understand the interactions between professional ethical standards and spiritual and religious issues (especially where they clash); and (4) be able to differentiate positive and negative spiritual and religious beliefs, that is, those attitudes and practices that support awareness, growth, and flexibility from those that do not (W. R. Miller, 1999).

Knowing the Benefits of Spiritual Practices

Non-religious counselors might familiarize themselves with research on the benefits of various spiritual practices in order to appreciate the healthy potentialities of religious involvement (Genia, 2000). They might further strive to understand how faith practices and beliefs can be integrated with psychological theory and counseling practice (Bishop, 1995). At a minimum, a counselors should be sensitive to the world's mainstream religions, including Hinduism, Buddhism, Islam, Judaism, and Christianity (Kelly, 1995).

Knowing Harmful Practices

In addition to knowing the benefits of various faiths, counselors also need to understand the ways in which people's misinterpretation of faith principles could lead to harm and the idiosyncrasies of particular faiths that may serve as pitfalls for well-intentioned counselors (Eriksen et al., 2002). For instance, the Bible asks Christians to be in the world but not of the world (King James Bible, John 17:14–18) and indicates that it would be better if one plucked out one's eye rather than have this body part cause one to sin (King James Bible, Matthew 5:29). Healthy Christians do not interpret these scriptures to mean that they should live in complete isolation or do themselves bodily harm, although believers with psychological problems might. Harmful faith has been more clearly articulated earlier in this chapter.

The Risks of Being Misinformed

Counselors who are unfamiliar with idiosyncrasies of particular faiths can hinder the work of counseling. For instance, one cannot talk glibly about a marriage of equals to conservative Christian clients because they believe strongly in the Bible's mandate that husbands are to be the head of the family (King James Bible, Ephesians 5:22–24). Similarly, counselors should probably not ask abused conservative Christian wives why they are staying with their husbands because the wives may then believe the counselor is advocating for divorce, which, from their perspective, would be a sin (King James Bible, Matthew 5:31–32). The client would likely not return for counseling if the counselor were to simplistically push such issues. Counselors should not only be aware of the idiosyncrasies, but of how people within that faith tradition address complexities that arise because of the idiosyncrasies. Should these complexities be too difficult for the counselor to ferret out, she or he should refer to or consult with clergy who can help with alternative interpretations of teachings.

Particular Applications of Counseling Skills to Religious and Spiritual Clients

There are four counseling skill areas to which counselors need to attend when incorporating religious dimensions: informed consent, assessment, intervention, and networking. Considerations in those four areas are discussed next.

INFORMED CONSENT

Keeping in mind many religious clients' sensitivities about faith issues and about including spiritual interventions in counseling, counselors need to inform clients about the nature of counseling and the presence or absence of an explicit religious dimension in the counselor's practice. Clients have the right to participate in the decisions about how spiritual interventions may be incorporated in the counseling process (ACA, 2005, A.2). Particularly important would be developing a straightforward language with which to communicate with clients about religious values (Bishop, 1995), initiating a discussion about values with clients, and discussing counselor perspectives on religion or spirituality with clients.

ASSESSMENT

Counselors need to assess clients' spirituality in order to fully understand what interventions might be appropriate (or inappropriate) or needed. Each client will have her or his own understanding of religion and how it might be incorporated in the counseling process. Richards and Potts (1995) advised counselors to respect individual differences and learn about clients' unique religious understanding: "Even when the client belongs to the same religion as the counselor, major differences in belief can exist, and so counselors should not make assumptions about the religious beliefs and values of the client" (p. 169). In assessing clients' religious and spiritual perspectives, counselors might use the following informal or formal assessment procedures.

Informal Religious Assessment Strategies

Four approaches to inquiring about client religion are possible. Most simply, in the process of informal assessment, the counselor might ask the following questions: "Do you have a religious preference?" "Do you currently attend religious services?" "What are your reasons for attending services?" and "How important are your religious beliefs to you?" (Griffith & Griggs, 2001, p. 22).

A more complex exploration may include the following five questions:

"How does your faith give your life meaning?"

"What are the advantages and disadvantages of your faith?"

"Does your faith help you with some situations more than with others?"

"Who can support you so that you can grow in your faith in helpful ways?"

"Might there be a solution to your problems that includes other personal strengths besides your faith?" (Pargament, 2002)

A third informal assessment of religious meaning explicitly integrates client issues with religious themes while assessing the client's general religious orientation and meaning-making (Hartz, 2005). In that vein, the counselor can ask clients

- how their spirituality could contribute to their understanding of the problem or solutions;
- how they chose their religious community and how helpful this community is in supporting them with the current problems;
- what spiritual practices they engage in and how these are helpful;
- what their relationship with God is like and how this has changed over the years.

In that vein, counselors can ask how clients find their faith to be helpful in coping with difficult situations (McCullough & Larson, 1999).

A fourth, and deeper, assessment of client religiosity consists of counselors taking a thorough spiritual history in order to fully understand the client's religious upbringing, feelings, beliefs, and practices.

Regardless of the method of assessment, counselors need to include clients in the decision-making process about the place of religion in counseling by asking, "In what ways do you want to include spirituality in our counseling sessions?" By introducing any of these questions during the initial interviews, the counselor both gains important information and conveys to the client the notion that religious material is a legitimate topic in counseling.

Formal Religious Assessment Strategies

More formal assessment might include use of available religious assessment instruments or strategies. First, the Religious Background and Behaviors Questionnaire (Hartz, 2005) offers a more formal way of asking the questions listed above.

Second, the Spiritual Surrender Assessment Scales (Cole & Pargament, 1999) measure the degree to which clients defer, plead, self-direct, collaborate, or surrender to a higher power in very difficult situations. On the spiritual surrender instrument, it is considered better for one's mental health to surrender in situations over which one has no control.

Other quantitative instruments are presented and evaluated by Harper and Gill (2005). They may include assessments of values, beliefs, lifestyle, and spiritual experiences. More qualitative approaches may include a values assessment, a sentence completion task, a spiritual autobiography, and a spiritual genogram (Harper & Gill, 2005).

INTERVENTION

The third area of multicultural competency is, of course, skill, or intervention. Religion-inclusive interventions may be either *implicit* or *explicit*. Both are discussed next.

Implicit Interventions

Implicit interventions consist of the attitudes that the counselor expresses toward a client's spirituality. Three of the implicit ways to incorporate religion into counseling are discussed next: validating helpful facets of religion, reinterpreting religious meanings into psychological terms, and challenging maladaptive religious beliefs.

Validating Positive Aspects of Religion. Most simply, the counselor can appreciate and validate a client's religious understanding and its helpfulness in her or his life, using reflection and affirmation. Such encouragement is consistent with understandings from the psychology of religion, namely that religious belief and practice can facilitate psychological healing and personal integration (Bergin, 1980, 1991; Bergin, Payne, & Richards, 1996; Ellis, 1980; Hood, Spilka, Hunsberger, & Gorsuch, 1996; Jones, 1994; Moberg & Brused, 1978; Wulff, 1997). Therefore, a counselor can encourage the use of the helpful facets of a client's religion (Clinebell, 1995; Patterson, 1992), such as the client's belief in a loving and caring God; the need to make some sense of life's happenings; a commitment to honesty, compassion, and goodwill; the faith's approaches to repentance and forgiveness; the client's membership in a supportive community; participation in reassuring rituals; practice of private devotions and meditative exercises; and opportunities for transcendence beyond day-to-day existence.

Reinterpreting Religious Meanings. In the implicit domain, it may be helpful at times to reinterpret or reframe some aspects of a client's religion in psychological terms. Certain facets of a client's spirituality may hinder authentic growth and must be adjusted. For example, people may pray, expecting a miracle. For them, God may still fit the childhood fantasy of the "Great Magician in the Sky" (Woodward, 1997). It can be maladaptive to build one's life around the expectation of external miracles, especially if the personal effort that could contribute to a needed counseling outcome is neglected. Therefore, without taking a theological stand on the validity of such a practice, the counselor can understand the psychological significance of the belief for the person and express empathic understanding about how such a practice can sustain hope and trust (Bergin et al., 1996). The counselor is thus able to deal with matters of the human spirit without being explicitly religious or theological herself or himself.

There are other psychological reinterpretation strategies that might help clients to bridge their religious and psychological experiences (Prest & Keller, 1993):

1. The counselor can determine a client's spiritual solutions that are no longer working and then help the client to explore alternative spiritually grounded solutions. For example, if a client is increasing her or his suffering from depression in hopes that it will ensure entrance into an afterlife, the counselor might help the client get into a religious discussion group that is both supportive and encourages participants to cope positively with mental distress.

2. The counselor can elicit fundamental beliefs and attribute alternative meanings to metaphors. For example, the "rod" metaphor in the Bible (Proverbs 13:24) that is used to justify corporal punishment can be reframed to include time-outs or other non-corporal punishments.

3. The counselor can initiate a discussion about "incongruent spiritual maps" (Prest & Keller, 1993, p. 143). For example, with a husband whose "spiritual map" tells him to be the spiritual authority of the home, the counselor can suggest that spiritual authority can be manifested in sacrificial love and that this would also contribute to the effectiveness of the "head" of the household. Ways to demonstrate sacrificial love may then become a topic of discussion.

In the overall reinterpretation strategy, counselors might first validate the client's valuing of doctrine, but challenge the interpretation if it is proving to be harmful (Lovinger, 1996; Spinney, 1991). This alternative interpretation requires reading the verses in context, exploring other translations and the historical context of the writing, and examining alternative interpretations. These are clearly efforts that involve a good deal of religious education on the counselor's part or consultation with spiritual experts.

Challenging Clients' Beliefs. Counselors may, in some cases, actually confront the legitimacy of some of the client's spiritual and religious beliefs (Helminiak, 2001). Client-counselor trust is required when this is done, accompanied by the client's sense that the counselor does not reject the client's religion outright. Although counselors need to understand the client's need for and valuing of a belief, some beliefs are antithetical to psychological healing, personal integration, and wholesome growth (Helminiak, 2001). The client's protest that, for example, "Evil forces made me do it," poses some questions for the culturally alert counselor. While individuals with collectivistic values may actually get better when problems are attributed to outside forces, other clients may be abdicating their responsibilities. Therefore, the counselor would not reject this belief without exploring its meaning with the client. Other harmful religious practices have been discussed above.

Explicit Interventions

More *explicit* spiritual interventions may also be used by both spiritual and non-religious counselors. For instance, counselors can attempt to enter client worldviews with vocabulary and imagery that are congruent with clients' faith experiences (Ingersoll, 1995). Table 15.16 suggests some explicit religion-based interventions.

Each of the specific strategies in Table 15.16 reflects the old adage, "You need to get into someone's house before you can help them rearrange the furniture." Counselors need to demonstrate respect for the client by speaking in language that reflects an understanding and acceptance of the client's faith as a condition of encouraging a client to change. Both W. R. Miller's (1999) and Sperry and Shafranske's (2005) books effectively discuss a range of ideas about how one

Table 15.16 Religious and Spiritual Interventions

Counselors might

1. use religious images during guided imagery (Worthington, 1978; Yarhouse, 1999), including images that decrease anxiety or increase a sense of comfort (Tan & Johnson, 2005);

2. offer scriptural passages or other religious textual materials that correspond to therapeutic prescriptions (Eriksen et al., 2002);

3. use prayer as a means to shift cognitions (McCullough & Larson, 1999);

4. introduce religious texts to dispute cognitions that are not working (Tan & Johnson, 2005);

5. ask clients to journal about beliefs and values, how they developed, and how they might help in the current situation (Basham & O'Connor, 2005);

6. suggest books related to spiritual issues (O'Connor, 2002);

7. use liberation, transformation, or celebration rituals from different religious traditions (Basham & O'Connor, 2005);

8. incorporate "inner healing" to help to heal unresolved developmental issues or childhood traumas (Tan, 1987; see Tan, 1996a, for a seven-step model for inner healing prayer);

9. use religious perspectives that help the client move toward the ideal—from a Christian perspective, for example, it would be becoming more Christ-like; in the Buddhist tradition, it would be getting closer to one's Buddha nature;

10. stress the healing power of God's Spirit (Tan, 1987);

11. join the resistance when clients express doubt by indicating that there is no faith without doubt (Lovinger, 1979);

12. consider God a member of the family or place God in an empty chair and thereby bring God directly into the counseling process (Hannon et al., 1994);

13. consider the clients' experiences of God to be "similar to their experiences of other significant psychological *objects* [italics added]" (Shafranske, 2005, p. 110);

14. self-disclose one's own spiritual journeys to encourage change; for example, speak of both the times that the counselor thought that God answered prayer and other times that she or he wondered whether God existed.

might integrate spirituality into clinical practice, from a variety of theoretical perspectives.

NETWORK, REFERRAL, CONSULTATION, AND PARTNERSHIP WITH INDIGENOUS HEALERS

Counselors who do not share their client's faith need to develop a cadre of experts with whom to consult. Counselors can engage and network with religious leaders; become familiar with community resources, such as churches, synagogues, prayer groups, 12-step programs, and lay religious counselors; and develop a referral network that is composed of religious professionals from a variety of faiths (Yarhouse, 1999).

Consultation and partnership can be important when religion is explicitly brought into counseling. As will be discussed in Chapter 16, counselors might further consult with the client's other "healers," such as clergy, when questions arise about how intervene (Ingersoll, 1995; Tan, 1987). In that vein, they might coordinate care with the client's pastor (with the client's permission) (Johnson & Johnson, 1997). Counselors can also partner with local religious groups in order to gain their support when developing programs and services (Johnson & Johnson, 1997). And. of course, if the various suggested strategies are not working, counselors need to know when and how to refer clients to other professionals who might be more facile with those clients' religions.

Applying Religiously Alert Interventions to the Vignettes

Application of the multicultural counseling competencies of religious self-awareness, knowledge, and intervention will now be demonstrated using the three vignettes that were presented at the beginning of the chapter. The first vignette was about Brittany, a single 34-year-old Evangelical Christian. The second case told the story of Geoff, a 19-year-old Orthodox Jewish American undergraduate student majoring in pre-med at a large metropolitan university. The third situation was about Joseph, a 65-year-old man who has faithfully practiced Christian Science for 30 years. Some of the multicultural competencies may be applied in similar fashion for all of the clients presented, while other interventions might more appropriately matched to specific clients in the vignettes.

UNIVERSAL COMPETENCIES

For each of the cases of Brittany, Geoff, and Joseph, counselors would need to begin with their own self-awareness, that is, awareness of their own attitudes and beliefs about spirituality and religion and a sense of their preconceived notions about their clients' religious perspectives. Strategies for increasing such awareness have been delineated in a previous section. Counselors would also need to know, or inform themselves, about the faiths practiced by each of these clients, namely Evangelical Christianity, Orthodox Judaism, and Christian Science.

In each case, counselors working with each of the clients would, in addition, need to fully assess the nature of each client's spiritual or religious experiences, beliefs, and development. That assessment would include the salience of the religion for the client and the level of enculturation into it. Counselors would have to acknowledge both the centrality of faith to the clients' lives and the strong connections between religious issues and the presenting problems.

As part of the informed consent process, counselors would need to openly negotiate with the clients the desired role of spirituality/religion in the counseling process. Further, because of the importance of religion to Brittany, Geoff, and Joseph, counselors would need to respond to religious themes as they arose in counseling. These responses would fall under the *implicit* integration of religion into counseling. In that vein, the counselors could (1) acknowledge the positive impact of faith on these client's lives, (2) use the resources provided by the clients' faith communities, (3) network with consultants who could offer information about the particular faiths, and (4) be alert to client beliefs becoming psychologically harmful.

COUNTERTRANSFERENCE

Another implicit dimension of intervening in these cases is being aware of religious countertransference, as has been discussed previously. In one or more of the vignette cases, counselors might find their countertransference to be aroused by the strength—perhaps dogmatism—of each of the client's faith experiences and beliefs. Even those counselors who are ready to integrate spirituality into all counseling with all clients may find that the orthodoxy, evangelicalism, conservatism, and powerful faith commitments of these particular clients trigger personal challenges.

One such challenge might be the fact that clients with such powerful faith commitments nearly always demand that mental health professionals explicitly integrate religion into the helping process, which would tax most providers' competence. In addition, unless the counselors share the same commitments, counselors may find themselves somewhat put off by the intensity of their clients' commitments.

Such potential for countertransference can be illustrated in the case of Joseph, the Christian Scientist. A counselor might have difficulty not "siding" with Joseph's family in insisting that Joseph receive standard Western medical care. How does one not label Joseph "crazy" for refusing medical care when he is in such dire straits? Might one feel ethically challenged by someone who is seeming to harm himself in this way?

Counselors might also experience surprise, and perhaps bias, should they ask Brittany during assessment about her prior and current sexual relationships. Her conservative beliefs probably preclude sexual activity prior to marriage and may also forbid activities that are sexually arousing (even without actual intercourse). She may, therefore, be shocked or embarrassed to even be asked the question. Thus, the very asking of the question may damage the therapeutic alliance.

In both Joseph's and Brittany's cases, counselors need to know enough about each of these clients' faiths to appreciate and work with the positive aspects and, when confronted with problems related to the faith, to find alternative answers from *within* the faith. They need to consult with experts in each faith to discover ways in which those from that particular faith live differently than the general population, in order to avoid surprises, or at least to prevent expressions of dismay when clients first introduce these beliefs. Counselors need to be sufficiently aware of their own beliefs, faith development, and biases to distinguish between, on the one hand, negative reactions that cue them to an area that the client might need to change and, on the other hand, negative reactions that are countertransferential and require the counselor herself or himself to examine problematic attitudes, perhaps through supervision.

One way to reframe countertransference is for counselors to view dogmatism from a developmental perspective. They might then intervene by matching and mismatching clients' developmental levels in order to help clients become more flexible and open. As Fowler (1981, 2004) indicates, such development is not movement away from faith, but toward a more mature faith.

EXPLICIT INTERVENTIONS

Boxes 15.1, 15.2, and 15.3 present explicit interventions for each of the cases presented in the beginning of this chapter. Such explicit interventions may require a level of religious knowledge not common to all counselors. These interventions need to be grounded in the client's faith position and the counselor's theory. Accurate and relevant decisions about such interventions would require greater information about the clients than has thus far been presented in the vignettes. However, a number of possibilities are presented below as examples. Initially, a number of expected cultural phenomena within these cases are discussed, followed by a number of ways in which the clients may demonstrate psychological difficulties no different than other clients. Finally, theoretically grounded and spiritually sensitive interventions are offered.

BOX 15.1   Intervening in the Case of Brittany

Brittany has clearly remained single beyond what is typical in rural and conservative Christian communities. In rural communities, early marriage and childbearing may result from less education; fewer opportunities for women; and traditional values that place women in the home, bearing and caring for children. In conservative Christian communities, early marriage seems to be especially related to the requirement for sexual abstinence before marriage. Early childbearing seems grounded in strong beliefs about the value of family. Brittany would be unlikely to value any life vocation or occupation more than marriage and raising a family. Within such Christian communities, because others have usually married in their early 20s, unmarried persons beyond their 20s often feel left behind, as though all of the "good" partners have been taken and as though God is not being faithful to them in providing a life partner. In some cases, clients like Brittany may wonder what "sin" God wants them to discover and repent of in order to be ready for the sacrament of marriage.

Brittany's own individual struggles may be further exacerbated by her church community's belief that Brittany should be married and raising children and that she is failing in God's purpose for her life by not "getting on with it." They may "encourage" her with prayer and by bringing men to her doorstep, expecting her to respond with gratitude for their assistance. She may instead feel pressured to accept others' answers when her own heart is not in agreement.

Brittany may also struggle with her faith's demands for premarital sexual abstinence and for being "equally yoked," that is, partnered only with a Christian. Men who are her age may be less patient with her belief in abstinence, which may generate conflict as relationships become more emotionally intimate. Thus, relationships may end before they can flower. And Brittany may, as a result of her dissatisfaction with available Christian men, find her gaze wandering outside of her faith. However, her guilt and those men's struggle with the conservativeness of her faith may also end relationships with non-Christians before they can begin.

Counselors would clearly need to be knowledgeable about these possibilities, which differ from mainstream culture, during assessment. Counselors can use culturally educated questioning (see Chapter 16) to inquire about these possibilities, along with the more typical questions for assessing the reasons for Brittany's continuing singleness. Spiritually sensitive assessment would thus include asking Brittany about her feelings/beliefs about being single; her beliefs, hopes, or images about her life at this age; the messages she is currently receiving from her family and community about this issue; her experiences with relationships to this point; how she currently experiences God's will in her life since she is without the desired husband and children; and how her relationships with friends her age and with her church community may have been affected by her remaining single. Assessment goals would include determining possible reasons for Brittany's singleness and the degree to which faith and/or interpersonal issues might contribute to her difficulties in finding a marital partner. Treatment goals would include either making peace with singleness or resolving spiritual, interpersonal, cultural, or geographic hindrances to marriage.

Spiritually alert counseling might operate from a range of different theoretical perspectives. If a male counselor operated from a family counseling or systems perspective, he might observe the here-and-now process between Brittany and himself as illustrative of the ways in which Brittany relates to men and perhaps to God. If the counselor then observed any problematic ways of being, he could make Brittany aware of his observations and could assist her in relating to men in more helpful ways. However, any counselor would need to exercise caution in order to ensure that these "more helpful ways" were congruent with conservative biblical understandings. In pursuit of understanding biblical perspectives, counselors might ask Brittany what the Bible would say or advise given their observations. They might ask her to consult and pray with her spiritual mentors about the observations and to solicit their perspectives. Counselors might also consult with a minister from a conservative Christian church before proposing possible solutions.

If a counselor preferred a Gestalt perspective, she or he might ask Brittany to place God in a chair and have a conversation with God about her disappointment. Or the counselor might teach Brittany deep relaxation and walk her through guided imagery related to singleness and marriage. Both interventions would serve to bring to Brittany's awareness all of her feelings about and historical needs related to this situation. The counselor might ask Brittany to journal about her feelings related to this issue or to write a letter to God. Full catharsis of these feelings, and congruence in expression, might be the therapeutic goals and the means toward insight. However, once all of the feelings were "out" verbally or on paper, the counselor might go beyond "human" insight to suggest that Brittany pray about everything she has thus far discovered in order to obtain God's guidance. The counselor would also need to know whether Brittany would find experiencing and expressing such emotions to be contradictory to biblical injunctions about "the greatest of these" being "charity" or "love" (King James Bible, I Corinthians 13:13) or contradictory to the biblical injunction to focus on others rather than herself. Again, Brittany's homework might include consulting and praying with prayer partners, spiritual elders, or her pastor. The counselor might also consult with Brittany's pastor (with permission) in order to safeguard against potential "landmines," that is, controversial topics that could be shocking to clients, and to determine the best of the possible interventions.

BOX 15.2   Intervening in the Case of Geoff

Geoff finds himself on the cusp of a great number of developmental opportunities. He has moved from a small city to a large metropolitan area, which entails exposure to a wide variety of possibilities and life choices that he never previously imagined. He finds himself, as do many college students, comparing the values, choices, faith, and lifestyles that he inherited with a vast array of new possibilities presented by his peers. But he most likely lacks the capacities to carefully weigh which of the old ways he wishes to reject and which of the new ones he wants to adopt. He finds himself attracted to a man, which may undermine all that he has ever been taught about marriage and family life. He may, as a result of each of these challenges, feel as though he straddles a great chasm between his previous life and some new life that he has yet to create or discover. This chasm threatens to engulf him and does not allow him to easily move backward or forward. He may feel as though it is an either/or choice and that to choose to move forward is to reject all that he has previously valued, that is, to reject his family and his religion. Thus, it is no surprise that Geoff finds himself depressed, torn, isolated, and having difficulty deciding among the myriad choices that confront him.

Geoff may find it very difficult to consult a rabbi or family member, due to shame, but he may also find it equally difficult to have complete faith in those who differ from his family or religion. The orthodoxy of his faith (or his family's faith) increases the challenge, as orthodoxy's message is likely to promote thinking such as "all or nothing," "in or out," "with God or without God." Or he may be overinterpreting the Torah's messages due to his small-town and possibly more traditional upbringing. That is, the Torah offers a faith that comes with many traditions but rarely requires Jewish people to literally follow all of them. Deciding which traditions to preserve is often left up to individual conscience and discussion. Assessment would need to more fully explore these areas and hypotheses.

Treatment goals would include helping Geoff to recognize the potential of a developmental process for him and to gain the supports he needs in the journey. As a means to normalizing his experience, he may be helped to gain information about internalized homophobia and about the stages of the "coming out" process. He may be helped by being aware that his experience is fairly common for those who are moving out of a received, traditional, or conventional, way of knowing toward a more self-authorized or autonomous way of knowing (Kegan, 1982, 1994). He may benefit from knowing that developmental progression doesn't have to mean rejecting all that has come before. In fact, in the best of cases, it means incorporating or reconstructing the old into some new way of knowing and being. Further, he may be ideally situated—because of an available college counseling center—for receiving developmental counseling because college counselors and student affairs practitioners are more likely to be cognizant of Adult Developmental Theory.

These counselors may be able to structure his counseling and other college experiences so as to support Geoff firmly "at each point along the bridge" (Eriksen, 2006) between the two developmental stages. Support would mean having him talk about his traditions and how they have worked for him and for his family and friends and then reflecting, appreciating, and honoring these traditions. It might also mean finding "authorities" from his faith community to respond to his questions. Challenge might mean focusing on the value that the Jewish faith places on asking questions; posing different and opposing views; and asking people to struggle with, discuss, and reflect upon possibilities and then asking him to use that value, and the skills he has thus developed within his tradition, to consider and make decisions about the conflicting perspectives that he is facing.

Geoff may find himself "over his head" (Kegan, 1994) if a counselor from outside his faith attempts to promote development; he may fear that the counselor could lead him away from God as he has understood Him. Therefore, Geoff may be supported in his developmental progression by "bridge people." That is, he may benefit from meeting with a support group of Jewish gay men who are struggling to integrate their faith with their sexual orientation. This opportunity would both honor his faith and make him more comfortable with knowing that he doesn't have to abandon his faith in order to make sense of his sexual feelings. Bibliotherapy might serve as a bridge by introducing Geoff to scholars of the Torah who have written about homosexuality and masturbation from both sides of the debate (e.g., Heilman & Cohen, 1989; Schneer, 2002). Clearly, the counselor would need connections within the Jewish community in order to assist in finding such books and support groups. Geoff might also find a bridge in connecting with an Orthodox Jewish man (or men) who is from a metropolitan area or who is a transplant like himself, but who has already moved through his developmental struggle. Again, careful networking would be necessary so as not to introduce Geoff to someone who would stand in judgment of him at a time when he would need the space to explore more freely.

BOX 15.3   Intervening in the Case of Joseph

Joseph is most likely feeling scared and alone with his illness at this point. Christian Science believes strongly in the healing power of prayer, and unless bones are broken, people of this faith do not typically pursue traditional medicine or visit medical practitioners. The religion instead offers healers who pray with the person for healing. Clearly, if Joseph has visited doctors, it must be because the healing rituals have not worked. And those same doctors must be recommending treatment for the cancer, which he is probably not taking advantage of.

Herein lies his individual struggle: God is not healing him through prayer alone for some reason. The doctors indicate that he is dying. Joseph may be questioning why God is not healing him. Will he betray his faith and his God if he pursues more traditional medical treatment? Can he really believe God's promises about salvation and an afterlife if God is not "following through" with the promised healing? Added to these spiritual concerns is the fact that, in waiting this long, he may have reduced the chances that traditional medicine will prove curative. Further, "traditional" cancer treatment is far from universally successful even in the best of circumstances. Joseph may find himself questioning himself and his God about whether he should now pursue traditional medical treatment or whether he should have pursued it long ago. He is also probably wondering if this is "his time," that is, wondering whether it is time to make peace with death and move on.

Joseph's family members may find themselves in a different sort of quandary. His parents, wife, and children do not want to lose him prematurely to cancer. The typical end-of-life questions about the right time to "make peace and let go" may be complicated by their worries about his mental health, given his persistent belief in faith healing despite evidence of its ineffectiveness in this situation. They may find themselves angry at God for not healing Joseph, or angry at Joseph for adhering so strongly to something they have at least partially rejected. They may find that his end-of-life issues trigger their own fears about death, particularly given that they have rejected or are not fully participating in their faith.

During assessment, the counselor will need to attend fully to this range of possibilities of beliefs, feelings, thoughts, and challenges to relationships.

The assessment goals would be

- discovering what is realistic regarding Joseph's treatment and chances for recovery so as to aid in his and his family's end-of-life decisions;
- discovering what the condition of family relationships have been historically and are currently and what relationship issues might need to be resolved, regardless of Joseph's treatment choices;
- discovering how the family members' spiritual lives may hinder or help the current dilemma in which they find themselves.

(Continued)

(Continued)

Treatment goals could include

- making clear decisions about whether to stop pursuing healing options or whether to keep hoping, and for how long;
- improving family relationships so that the family can be fully functional as they make very important life decisions, perhaps using this situation to resolve past pains;
- assisting each family member to grow spiritually, perhaps developing spiritual relationships with one another, and helping them to make peace with God as they understand Him or Her.

Clearly God will be "in the room" when counseling this family, whether or not the counselor chooses to acknowledge it, and so it is probably better to recognize God's presence explicitly. This might be done in a variety of ways. An empty chair could be placed in the family circle (or outside of it if the non-believing family members would prefer it) and could be named "God's chair." As in Brittany's case, the family members might be encouraged to voice their struggles directly to God or could merely use the chair to remain aware of God's involvement with the family's struggle. Family members might be instructed to journal or write a letter to God about this situation and then might share their letter with other family members. And the counselor could include God as a key part of any interpretation or observation of family process.

The usual family counseling or end-of-life interventions would include

- assisting all family members to talk openly with one another about their thoughts, feelings, needs, and beliefs about the illness, impending death, faith, and medical treatment;
- helping them to address conflicts in these and to negotiate ways to be at peace with each other and with each others' decisions, despite differences;
- discovering in the process "inadequacies" in the ways that the family functions and creating change strategies to shift to healthier functioning;
- acknowledging family strengths, including their spirituality, and building on these to address the presenting dilemma.

In all of these efforts, their faith may be helpful in finding and offering forgiveness and in moving from a past position of "sinfulness" or failures to a place of understanding and acceptance.

Summary

The United States was birthed out of religious persecution and the desires of its foreparents to practice their religions freely. Americans seem to have persisted in their passion for spiritual and religious involvement throughout the years, being more intent on practicing faith than those in many other countries and continuing to be a refuge for those fleeing religious persecution. Further, constitutional mandates for free practice of one's religion seem to have allowed those of differing faiths to live relatively harmoniously next door to one another, in comparison with people in other countries. During the past 20 years, the mental health professions seem to have "caught up" with these initial and continuing popular culture impulses, and they now acknowledge that competence with spiritual or religious clients is necessary for ethically mandated multicultural competence. In this spirit, therefore, this chapter has provided a place for mental health providers to begin their journey toward such competence. It began with the definitions, history, and importance of religion and spirituality in the United States. It described the social and psychological dimensions of religion and spirituality and the characteristics and issues facing various religious and spiritual groups in the United States. The chapter outlined specific counseling interventions and professional growth options for providers pursuing competence in counseling religious or spiritual clients. Finally, this chapter began to illustrate application possibilities with the clinical vignettes presented at the beginning of the chapter. It is hoped that such beginnings will draw readers' attention to the spiritual issues affecting their work and their clients and will whet readers' appetites for pursuing more in-depth and comprehensive competence at the intersections of counseling and spirituality.

References

Agass, D. (2002). Countertransference, supervision, and the reflection process. *Journal of Social Work Practice, 16,* 125–133.

Agnosticism. (2006). Retrieved May 27, 2006, from http://en.wikipedia.org/w/index.php?title=Agnosticism&oldid=55354656

Allison, S. (1988). *Meaning-making in marriage: An exploratory study.* Unpublished doctoral dissertation, Massachusetts School of Professional Psychology.

Alvarez, M. (1985). *The construing of friendship in adulthood: A structural-developmental approach.* Unpublished doctoral dissertation, Massachusetts School of Professional Psychology.

American Counseling Association. (2005). *Code of ethics and standards of practice.* Alexandria, VA: Author.

American Psychiatric Association. (1994). *Diagnostic and statistical manual of mental disorders* (4th ed.). Washington, DC: Author.

American Psychiatric Association. (2000). *Diagnostic and statistical manual of mental disorders* (4th ed., Text rev.). Washington, DC: Author.

American Psychological Association. (2002). *Ethical principles of psychologists and code of conduct.* Retrieved January 20, 2005, from http://www.apa.org/ethics

Arterburn, S., & Felton, J. (1992). *Faith that hurts, faith that heals.* Nashville, TN: Thomas Nelson.

Astor, J. (2000). Some reflections on empathy and reciprocity in the use of countertransference between supervisor and supervisee. *Journal of Analytical Psychology, 45,* 367–383.

Bar-Yam, M. (1991). Do women and men speak in different voices? A comparative study of self-evolvement. *International Journal of Aging and Human Development, 32,* 247–259.

Basham, A., & O'Connor, M. (2005). Use of spiritual and religious beliefs in pursuit of clients' goals. In C. S. Cashwell & J. S. Young (Eds.), *Integrating spirituality and religion into counseling* (pp. 143–167). Alexandria, VA: American Counseling Association.

Baumeister, R. F. (1992). *Meanings of life.* New York: Guilford Press.

Bebbington, D. (1989). *Evangelicalism in modern Britain: A history from the 1730s to the 1980s.* London: Unwin Hyman.

Benack, S. (1988). Relativistic thought: A cognitive basis for empathy in counseling. *Counselor Education and Supervision, 27,* 216–232.

Bergin, A. E. (1980). Counseling and religious values. *Journal of Counseling and Clinical Psychology, 48,* 95–105.

Bergin, A. E. (1991). Values and religious issues in counseling and mental health. *American Psychologist, 46,* 394–403.

Bergin, A. E., & Jensen, J. (1990). Religiosity of psychotherapists: A national survey. *Counseling, 27,* 3–7.

Bergin, A. E., Payne, I. N., & Richards, P. S. (1996). Values in counseling. In E. P. Shafranske (Ed.), *Religion and the clinical practice of psychology* (pp. 297–325). Washington, DC: American Psychological Association.

Beukema, S. (1990). *Women's best friendships: Their meaning and meaningfulness.* Unpublished doctoral dissertation, Harvard Graduate School of Education.

Binner, V. F. (1991). *A study of Minnesota entrepreneurship: Balancing personal, business, and community demands.* Unpublished doctoral dissertation, Graduate School of the Union Institute.

Bishop, D. R. (1992). Religious values as cross-cultural issues in counseling. *Counseling and Values, 36,* 179–191.

Bishop, D. R. (1995). Religious values as cross-cultural issues in counseling. In M. T. Burke & J. G. Miranti (Eds.), *Counseling: The spiritual dimension* (pp. 59–71). Alexandria, VA: American Counseling Association.

Bowman, J. T., & Reeves, T. G. (1987). Moral development and empathy in counseling. *Counselor Education and Supervision, 26,* 293–298.

Bradley, D. E. (1995). Religious involvement and social resources: Evidence from the Americans' Changing Lives data. *Journal for the Scientific Study of Religion, 34,* 259–267.

Brendel, J. M., Kolbert, J. B., & Foster, V. A. (2002). Promoting student cognitive development. *Journal of Adult Development, 3,* 217–227.

Carlson, T. D., Kirkpatrick, D., Hecker, L., & Killmer, M. (2002). Religion, spirituality, and marriage and family counseling: A study of family counselors' beliefs about the appropriateness of addressing religious and spiritual issues in counseling [Electronic version]. *The American Journal of Family Counseling, 30,* 157–171.

Case, P. W. (1997). Potential sources of countertransference among religious counselors. *Counseling and Values, 41,* 97–107. Retrieved January 10, 2005, from Academic Search Premier database.

Cervantes, J. M., & Ramirez, O. (1992). Spirituality and family dynamics in counseling with Latino children. In L. A. Vargas & J. D. Koss-Chioino (Eds.), *Working with culture: Psychotherapeutic interventions with ethnic minority children and adolescents* (pp. 103–128). San Francisco: Jossey-Bass.

Chalfant, P., Beckley, R. E., & Palmer, E. (1994). *Religion in contemporary society* (3rd ed.). Itasca, IL: F. E. Peacock.

Chandler, H. C., Holden, J. M., & Kolander, C (1992). Counseling for spiritual wellness: Theory and practice. *Journal of Counseling and Development, 71,* 168–175.

Chibon, J. (1992). Healing and spirituality. *Pastoral Psychology, 40,* 235–245.

Clinebell, H. (1995). *Counseling for spiritually empowered wholeness: A hope-centered approach.* New York: Hawthorn Press.

Cole, B. S., & Pargament, K. I. (1999). Spiritual surrender: A paradoxical path to control. In W. R. Miller (Ed.), *Integrating spirituality into treatment: Resources for practitioners* (pp. 179–198). Washington, DC: American Psychological Association.

Connors, G. J., Toscova, R. T., & Tonigan, J. S. (1999). Serenity. In W. R. Miller (Ed.), *Integrating spirituality into treatment: Resources for practitioners* (pp. 234–250). Washington, DC: American Psychological Association.

Council for Accreditation of Counseling and Related Educational Programs. (2001). *CACREP accreditation standards and procedures manual.* Alexandria, VA: Author.

Council on American-Islamic Relations. (2000). *About Islam and American Muslims.* Retrieved October 5, 2006, from http://www.cair-net.org/default.asp?Page= aboutIslam

Das, A. K., & Kemp, S. F. (1997). Between two worlds: Counseling South Asian Americans. *Journal of Multicultural Counseling & Development, 25,* 23–33.

Dixon, J. W. (1986). *The relation of social perspective stages to Kegan's stages of ego development.* Unpublished doctoral dissertation, University of Toledo, Ohio.

Eckes, G. (2004, September). Spirituality vs. religion. *The Edge Newspaper.* Retrieved March 27, 2005, from http://www.edgenews.com/issues/2004/ 09/eckes.html

Elkins, D. N. (1995). Psychotherapy and spirituality: Toward a theory of the soul. *Journal of Humanistic Psychology, 35,* 78–99.

Elkins, D. N. (1999). Spirituality. *Psychology Today, 32,* 45.

Elkins, D. N., Hedstrom, L., & Hughes, L. (1988). Toward a humanistic-phenomenological spirituality: Definition, description, and measurement. *Journal of Humanistic Psychology, 28,* 5–18.

Ellis, A. (1980). Counseling and atheistic values: A response to A. E. Bergin's "Counseling and religious values." *Journal of Counseling and Clinical Psychology, 48,* 635–639.

Ellison, C. (1991). Religious involvement and subjective well-being. *Journal of Health and Social Behavior, 32,* 80–99.

Ellison, C., & George, L. (1994). Religious involvement, social ties, and social support in a southeastern community. *Journal for the Scientific Study of Religion, 33,* 46–61.

Eriksen, K. (2006). Robert Kegan, Ph.D.: Subject-object theory and family counseling. *The Family Journal, 14*(3), 1–9.

Eriksen, K., Marston, G., & Korte, T. (2002). Working with God: Managing conservative Christian beliefs that may interfere with counseling. *Counseling and Values, 47,* 48–72.

Esau, T. G. (1998). The evangelical Christian in counseling. *American Journal of Counseling, 52,* 28–36.

Faiver, C., & Ingersoll, R. E. (2005). Knowing one's limits. In C. S. Cashwell & J. S. Young (Eds.), *Integrating spirituality and religion into counseling* (pp. 169–183). Alexandria, VA: American Counseling Association.

Firth, R. (1996). *Religion: A humanist interpretation.* London: Routledge.

Fowler, J. W. (1981). *Stages of faith: The psychology of human development and the quest for meaning.* San Francisco: Harper & Row.

Fowler, J. W. (1991). Stages in faith consciousness. *New Directions for Child Development, 52,* 27–45.

Fowler, J. W. (2004). Stages of faith and identity: Birth to teens. *Child and Adolescent Clinics of North America, 13,* 17–33.

Frame, M. W. (2003). *Integrating religion and spirituality into counseling.* Pacific Grove, CA: Brooks/Cole.

Gallup International Association. (2002). *Gallup International Millennium Survey.* Retrieved August 13, 2006, from http://www.gallup-international.com

The Gallup Organization. (2004). *American public opinion about religion.* Retrieved May 14, 2004, from http://www.gallup.com/poll/focus/sr040302 .asp

Gaustad, P. L., & Dishno, R. W. (2000). *New historical atlas of religion in America.* New York: Oxford University Press.

Genia, V. (2000). Religious issues in secularly based counseling [Electronic version]. *Counseling and Values, 44,* 213–222.

Goodman, R. (1983). *A developmental and systems analysis of marital and family communication in clinic and non-clinic families.* Unpublished doctoral dissertation, Harvard University.

Gordon, P. A., Feldman, D., Crose, R., Schoen, E., Griffing, G., & Shankar, J. (2002). The role of religious beliefs in coping with chronic illness. *Counseling and Values, 46,* 162–174.

Goud, N. (1990). Spiritual and ethical beliefs of humanists in the counseling profession. *Counseling and Values, 68,* 571–574.

Greenwald, J. M. (1991). *Environmental attitudes: A structural developmental model.* Unpublished doctoral dissertation, University of Massachusetts.

Griffith, B. A., & Griggs, J. C. (2001). Religious identity status as a model to understand, assess, and interact with client spirituality. *Counseling and Values, 46,* 14–25.

Guiso, L., Sapienza, P., & Zingales, L. (2003). People's opium? Religion and economic attitudes. *Journal of Monetary Economics, 50,* 225–282.

Hagedorn, W. B. (2005). Counselor self-awareness and self-exploration of religious and spiritual beliefs: Know thyself. In C. S. Cashwell & J. S. Young (Eds.), *Integrating spirituality and religion into counseling* (pp. 63–84). Alexandria, VA: American Counseling Association.

Hannon, J. W., Howie, C. C., & Keener, R. J. (1994). Counseling conservative and fundamentalist Christians: Issues and implications for the counselor. *Journal of Humanistic Education and Development, 32,* 121–132.

Harper, M. C., & Gill, C. S. (2005). Assessing the client's spiritual domain. In C. S. Cashwell & J. S. Young (Eds.), *Integrating spirituality and religion into counseling* (pp. 31–62). Alexandria, VA: American Counseling Association.

Hartz, G. W. (2005). *Spirituality and mental health.* New York: Haworth Pastoral Press.

Heilman, S. C., & Cohen, S. M. (1989). *Cosmopolitans and parochials: Modern Orthodox Jews in America.* Chicago: University of Chicago Press.

Helminiak, D. A. (2001). Treating spiritual issues in secular counseling. *Counseling and Values, 45,* 163–189.

Hinterkopf, E. (1994). Integrating spiritual experiences in counseling. *Counseling and Values, 38,* 165–175.

Hoge, D. (1996). Religion in America: The demographics of belief and affiliation. In E. Shafranske (Ed.), *Religion and the clinical practice of psychology* (pp. 21–41). Washington, DC: American Psychological Association.

Holifield, E. G. (1983). *A history of pastoral care in America: From salvation to self realization.* Nashville, TN: Abingdon.

Hood, R. W., Spilka, B., Hunsberger, B., & Gorsuch, R. (1996). *The psychology of religion: An empirical approach* (2nd ed.). New York: Guilford Press.

Idler, E. L. (1995). Religion, health, and nonphysical senses of self. *Social Forces, 74,* 683–704.

Ingersoll, R. E. (1995). Spirituality, religion, and counseling: Dimensions and relationships. In M. T. Burke & J. G. Miranti (Eds.), *Counseling: The spiritual dimension* (pp. 5–18), Alexandria, VA: American Counseling Association.

Jacobs, J. (1984). *Holding environment and developmental stages: A study of marriage.* Unpublished doctoral dissertation, Harvard University.

Jankowski, P. J. (2002). Postmodern spirituality: Implications for promoting change. *Counseling and Values, 46,* 69–79.

Johnson, W. B., & Johnson, W. L. (1997). Counseling conservatively religious fathers: Salient treatment issues. *Journal of Psychology and Christianity, 16,* 36–50.

Jones, S. (1994). A constructive relationship for religion with the science and profession of psychology: Perhaps the boldest model yet. *American Psychologist, 49,* 184–199.

Kegan, R. (1982). *The evolving self.* Cambridge, MA: Harvard University Press.

Kegan, R. (1994). *In over our heads.* Cambridge, MA: Harvard University Press.

Keller, R. R. (1999). Religious diversity in North America. In P. S. Richards & A. E. Bergin (Eds.), *Handbook of counseling and religious diversity* (pp. 27–55). Washington, DC: American Psychological Association.

Kelly, E. W., Jr. (1995). *Spirituality and religion in counseling and psychotherapy: Diversity in theory and practice.* Alexandria, VA: American Counseling Association.

King James Bible. (1983). Grand Rapids, MI: Zondervan Bible Publishers.

Kluegel, J. R. (1980). Denominational mobility: Current patterns and recent trends. *Journal for the Scientific Study of Religion, 19,* 26–40.

Koenig, H. G., George, L. K., & Peterson, B. L. (1998). Religiosity and remission from depression in medically ill older patients. *American Journal of Psychiatry, 155,* 536–542.

Kohlberg, L. (1981). *The philosophy of moral development.* San Francisco: Harper & Row.

Kosmin, B. A., Mayer, E., & Keysar, A. (2001). *American Religious Identification Survey, 2001.* New York: The Graduate Center of the City University of New York.

Krause, N. (1998). Stressors in highly valued roles, religious coping and mortality. *Psychology of Aging, 13,* 242–255.

Kumar, M., Bhugra, D., & Singh. J. (2005). South Asian (Indian) traditional healing: Ayurvedic, Shamanic, and Sahaja counseling. In R. Moodley & W. West (Eds.), *Integrating traditional healing practices into counseling and psychotherapy* (pp. 112–121). Thousand Oaks, CA: Sage.

Lahey, L. (1986). *Males' and females' construction of conflict in work and love.* Unpublished doctoral dissertation, Harvard University.

Landis, B. (1996). Uncertainty, spiritual well-being, and psychosocial adjustment to chronic illness. *Issues in Mental Health Nursing, 17,* 217–231.

Larson, D., Wood, G., & Larson, S. (1993). A paradigm shift in medicine toward spirituality. *ADVANCE: The Journal of Mind-Body Health, 9,* 39–49.

Levin, J. S., & Chatters, L. M. (1998). Religion, health, and psychological well being in older adults. *Journal of Aging and Health, 10,* 504–531.

Levin, J, S., Chatters, L. M., & Taylor, R. J. (2005). Religion, health and medicine in African Americans: Implications for physicians. *Journal of the National Medical Association, 97,* 237—249.

Levin, J. S., & Taylor, R. J. (1998). Panel analyses of religious involvement and well-being in African Americans: Contemporaneous vs. longitudinal effects. *Journal for the Scientific Study of Religion, 37,* 695–709.

Loevinger, J. (1976). *Ego development.* San Francisco: Jossey-Bass.

Lovell, C. W. (1999). Empathic-cognitive development in students of counseling. *Journal of Adult Development, 6,* 195–203.

Lovinger, R. J. (1979). Therapeutic strategies with "religious" resistances. *Counseling: Theory, Research, and Practice, 16,* 419–427.

Lovinger, R. J. (1996). Considering the religious dimension in assessment and treatment. In E. P. Shafranske (Ed.), *Religion and the clinical practice of psychology* (pp. 327–364). Washington, DC: American Psychological Association.

Magaletta, P. R., & Brawer, P. A. (1998). Prayer in counseling: A model for its use, ethical considerations, and guidelines for practice. *Journal of Psychology and Theology, 26,* 322–330.

McAuliffe, G. J., & Eriksen, K. P. (1999). Toward a constructivist and developmental identity for the counseling profession: The context-phase-stage-style model. *Journal of Counseling and Development, 77,* 267–280.

McAuliffe, G. J., & Lovell, C. W. (2006). The influence of counselor epistemology on the helping interview: A qualitative study. *Journal of Counseling and Development, 84,* 308–317.

McCullough, M. E., & Larson, D. B. (1999). Prayer. In W. R. Miller (Ed.), *Integrating spirituality into treatment: Resources for practitioners* (pp. 85–110). Washington, DC: American Psychological Association.

Miller, G. (1999). The development of the spiritual focus in counseling and counselor education. *Journal of Counseling and Development, 77,* 498–501.

Miller, W. R. (Ed.). (1999). *Integrating spirituality into treatment: Resources for practitioners.* Washington, DC: American Psychological Association.

Miranti, J., & Burke, M. T. (1995). Spirituality: An integral component of the counseling process. In M. T. Burke & J. G. Miranti (Eds.), *Counseling: The spiritual dimension* (pp. 5–18). Alexandria, VA: American Counseling Association.

Moberg, D. O., & Brused, P. M. (1978). Spiritual well-being: A neglected subject in quality of life research. *Social Indicators Research, 5,* 303–323.

Mueller, S. A., & Lane, A. V. (1972). Tabulations from the 1957 Current Population Survey of Religion: A contribution to the demography of American religion. *Journal for the Scientific Study of Religion, 11,* 76–98.

Muramoto, S. (2002). Buddhism, religion and counseling in the world today. In P. Young-Eisendrath (Ed.), *Awakening and insight: Zen Buddhism and counseling* (pp. 15–29). New York: Brunner-Routledge.

Myers, J. E. (1990). Wellness through the lifespan. *Guidepost, 32,* 11.

Nathanson, I. (1995). Divorce and women's spirituality. *Journal of Divorce and Remarriage, 22,* 179–188.

Neukrug, E. S., & McAuliffe, G. (1993). Cognitive development and human services education. *Human Services Education, 13,* 13–26.

Nino, A. (1997). Assessment of spiritual quests in clinical practice. *International Journal of Counseling, 2,* 193–212.

O'Connor, M. (2002). Spiritual dark night and psychological depression: Some comparisons and contrasts. *Counseling and Values, 46,* 137–149.

Pargament, K. I. (2002). The bitter and the sweet: An evaluation of the costs and benefits of religiousness [Electronic version]. *Psychological Inquiry, 13,* 168–181.

Patterson, J., Hayworth, M., Turner, C., & Raskin, M. (2000). Spiritual issues in family counseling: A graduate-level course. *Journal of Marital and Family Counseling, 26*(2), 199–210.

Patterson, R. B. (1992). *Encounters with angels: Psyche and spirit in the* counseling *situation.* Chicago: Loyola University Press.

Perry, W. G. (1970). *Forms of intellectual and ethical development in the college years: A scheme.* New York: Holt, Rinehart & Winston.

Petersen, W. (2003). Social consequences of religion. *Society, 40,* 53–57.

Prest, L. A., & Keller, J. F. (1993). Spirituality and family counseling: Spiritual beliefs, myths, and metaphors. *Journal of Marital and Family Counseling, 19,* 132–148.

Richards, P. S., & Bergin, A. E. (1997). Western and Eastern spiritual worldviews. In P. S. Richards & A. E. Bergin (Eds.), *A spiritual strategy for counseling and psychotherapy* (pp. 49–74). Washington, DC: American Psychological Association.

Richards, P. S., & Bergin, A. E. (1999). Toward religious and spiritual competency for mental health professionals. In P. S. Richards & A. E. Bergin (Eds.), *Handbook of counseling and religious diversity* (pp. 3–26). Washington, DC: American Psychological Association.

Richards, P. S., & Bergin, A. E. (2002). *A spiritual strategy for counseling and psychotherapy*. Washington, DC: American Psychological Association.

Richards, P. S., & Potts, R. W. (1995). Using spiritual interventions in counseling: Practices, successes, failures, and ethical concerns of Mormon psychocounselors. *Professional Psychology: Research and Practice, 26*(2), 163–170.

Ridley, C. R. (1985). Imperatives for ethnic and cultural relevance in psychology training programs. *Professional Psychology: Research and Practice, 16,* 611–622.

Roy, N. S. (1993). *Toward an understanding of family functioning: An analysis of the relationship between family and individual organizing principles*. Unpublished doctoral dissertation, Harvard Graduate School of Education.

Sanderson, C., & Linehan, M. M. (1999). Acceptance and forgiveness. In W. R. Miller (Ed.), *Integrating spirituality into treatment: Resources for practitioners* (pp. 199–216). Washington, DC: American Psychological Association.

Saroglou, V. (2002). Religion and the five factors of personality: A meta-analytic review. *Personality and Individual Differences, 32,* 15–25.

Schneer, D. (2002). *Queer Jews*. New York: Routledge.

Seymour, E. (2005). Pagan approaches to healing. In R. Moodley (Ed.), *Integrating traditional healing practices into counseling and psychotherapy* (pp. 233–245). Thousand Oaks, CA: Sage.

Shafranske, E. (1996). Religious beliefs, affiliations, and practices of clinical psychologists. In E. Shafranske (Ed.), *Religion and the clinical practice of psychology* (pp. 149–162). Washington, DC: American Psychological Association.

Shafranske, E. (2005). A psychoanalytic approach to spiritually oriented counseling. In L. Sperry & E. Shafranske (Eds.), *Spiritually oriented counseling* (pp. 105–130). Washington, DC: American Psychological Association.

Shafranske, E., & Malony, H. (1990). Clinical psychologists' religious and spiritual orientations and their practice of counseling. *Counseling, 27,* 72–78.

Shafranske, E., & Malony, H. (1996). Religion and the clinical practice of psychology: A case for inclusion. In E. Shafranske (Ed.), *Religion and the clinical practice of psychology* (pp. 561–586). Washington, DC: American Psychological Association.

Silk, M. (2005). Religion and region in American public life. *Journal for the Scientific Study of Religion, 44,* 265–270.

Smith, C., Faris, R., Denton, M. L., & Regnerus, M. (2003). Mapping American adolescent subjective religiosity and attitudes of alienation toward religion: A research report. *Sociology of Religion, 64,* 111–123.

Sonnenschein, P. C. (1990). *The development of mutually satisfying relationships between adult daughters and their mothers*. Unpublished doctoral dissertation, Harvard Graduate School of Education.

Spero, M. H. (1982). Countertransference in religious counselors of religious patients. *American Journal of Counseling, 35,* 565–575.

Sperry, L., & Shafranske, E. P. (Eds.). (2005). *Spiritually oriented counseling*. Washington, DC: American Psychological Association.

Spinney, D. H. (1991). How do fundamental Christians deal with depression? *Counseling and Values, 35*(2), 114–128. Retrieved December 13, 2004, from Academic Search database.

Stifoss-Hanssen, H. (1999). Religion and spirituality: What a European ear hears. *International Journal for the Psychology of Religion, 9,* 25–33.

Sue, D. W., Arredondo, P., & McDavis, R. J. (1992). Multicultural counseling competencies and standards: A call to the profession. *Journal of Counseling and Development, 70,* 481–483.

Tan, S. Y. (1987). Cognitive-behavior counseling: A biblical approach and critique. *Journal of Psychology and Theology, 15,* 103–112.

Tan, S. Y. (1996a). Practicing the presence of God: The work of Richard J. Foster and its applications to psychotherapeutic practice. *Journal of Psychology and Christianity, 15,* 17–28.

Tan, S. Y. (1996b). Religion in clinical practice: Implicit and explicit integration. In E. Shafranske (Ed.), *Religion and the clinical practice of psychology* (pp. 365–387). Washington, DC: American Psychological Association.

Tan, S. Y., & Johnson, W. B. (2005). Spiritually oriented cognitive-behavioral counseling. In L. Sperry & E. P. Shafranske (Eds.), *Spiritually oriented counseling* (pp. 77–103). Washington, DC: American Psychological Association.

Taylor, C. Z. (2002). Religious addiction: Obsession with spirituality [Electronic version]. *Pastoral Psychology, 50,* 291–315.

Tillich, P. (1959). *Theology of culture.* New York: Oxford University Press.

Unger, M. F. (1966). *Unger's Bible dictionary* (3rd ed.). Chicago: Moody Press.

Wade, N. G., & Worthington, E. L., Jr. (2003). *Religious and spiritual interventions in counseling: An effectiveness study of Christian counseling.* Unpublished manuscript, Iowa State University and Virginia Commonwealth University.

Wiggins-Frame, M. (2005). Spirituality and religion: Similarities and differences. In C. S. Cashwell & J. S. Young (Eds.), *Integrating spirituality and religion into counseling* (pp. 11–29). Alexandria, VA: American Counseling Association.

Winarsky, M. (1991). *AIDS-related counseling.* New York: Pergamon.

Wolitzky, D. L. (1995). The theory and practice of traditional psychoanalytic counseling. In A. S. Gurman & S. B. Messer (Eds.), *Essential psychotherapies: Theory and practice* (pp. 12–54). New York: Guilford Press.

Wong, P. T. (1998). Spirituality, meaning, and successful aging. In P. T. Wong & P. S. Fry, *The human quest for meaning: A handbook of psychological research and clinical applications* (pp. 359–394). Mahwah, NJ: Erlbaum.

Woodward, K. L. (1997, March 31). Is God listening? *Newsweek,* 56–64.

Worthington, E. (1978). The effects of imagery content, choice of imagery content, and self-verbalization on the self-control of pain. *Cognitive Counseling and Research, 2,* 225–240.

Wulff, D. (1997). *Psychology of religion: Classic and contemporary* (2nd ed.). New York: Wiley.

Wuthnow, R. (2004). *Saving America? Faith-based services and the future of civil society.* Princeton, NJ: Princeton University Press.

Yahne, C. E., & Miller, W. R. (1999). Evoking hope. In W. R. Miller (Ed.), *Integrating spirituality into treatment: Resources for practitioners* (pp. 217–233). Washington, DC: American Psychological Association.

Yarhouse, M. A. (1999). When psychologists work with religious clients: Applications of the general principles of ethical conduct. *Professional Psychology: Research and Practice, 30*(6), 557–562. Retrieved January 10, 2005, from Academic Search Premier database.

Part IV

Implications for
Practice

16

The Practice of Culturally Alert Counseling

Garrett McAuliffe,
Tim Grothaus, David Paré,
and Ali Wininger

Mario is a 17-year-old biracial young man of Puerto Rican and Italian heritage who has just moved to suburban Denver, Colorado. He is originally from a multiethnic community in Queens, New York. He speaks English and Spanish fluently. He was raised as a Roman Catholic and had, until recently, attended Catholic schools in Queens. He had experienced little or no negative bias from his peers or others in his school there. His family's move to Colorado was due to his father's being transferred by the airline for which he works as a mechanic. The family members miss their close extended family in the New York area, especially the father's mother, who lived next door and helped to raise Mario and his younger sister. There are only a handful of Latino/Latina students in his school. Mario is not accepted by the few Latino/Latina students, who are mostly Mexican children of farm workers. He is ignored by most of the European American students, being seen by them as "not like us," especially given his Latin-New York accent. Most of the students are Protestant, with a large segment being Evangelical Christians. Mario has been unsuccessful in meeting girls as well. He is isolated and shows very low mood. The school counselor is alerted to his situation by an attentive English teacher who had read a paper that he wrote, called "I Am No One." The counselor, a middle-class European American woman from Minnesota, of German and Norwegian descent, calls Mario into her office in order to check on his situation.

The story of Mario is infused with important cultural issues. Mario has experienced cultural displacement in a number of ways. He is disconnected from his culture of origin. His accent and communication style are different from those of his peers. He looks different from the dominant group. He feels inadequate to meet the dominant standard for appearance, language, and religion. He is also in an important developmental phase as an adolescent, one in which peers are central to his sense of identity. These and other issues play parts in Mario's distress. This chapter is particularly dedicated to helping counselors know what to do with clients like Mario. The counselor who is working with Mario must especially bring culture to the foreground, at least part of the time, to help Mario trust the process, to incorporate specific ethnic dimensions (e.g., language, the nature of family, and communication style), and to help him find strength from his heritage. Each client's world is constructed by cultural factors such as ethnicity, race, gender, social class, sexual orientation, age, abilities/disabilities, and religion/spirituality. This chapter will present culturally alert counseling strategies. Activity 16.1 allows the reader to identify some of the key elements in working with Mario and with other clients.

This chapter will provide readers with guidelines for culturally alert practice. First, issues in culturally alert counseling practice are presented. Then, after an illustration of the cultural dimensions in a counseling interview, guidelines for culturally alert practice are discussed in terms of three overall themes: accessibility, assessment, and intervention. Two specific counseling theories, namely liberation counseling and the narrative approach to counseling, are integrated into this discussion in some detail, as they are particularly oriented toward infusing culture into the work.

Culturally Alert Intervention: An Inexact Art

No single counseling theory, construct, or tradition adequately suits all of the cultural groups in the U.S. (Corey, 1996; Fuertes & Gretchen, 2001).

> Multicultural counseling is neither a theoretical orientation on its own nor is it an outgrowth of any one traditional orientation. [It consists of] using awareness of culture during counseling. . . . [It is] an added dimension to the therapy process, much like relationship building and other core conditions of counseling. (Kincade & Evans, 1996, p. 90)

It is, therefore, unrealistic to look for a complete prescription for culture-specific interventions. Instead, culturally alert counseling consists of counselor vigilance about the impact of culture on people accompanied by a set of culturally alert practices. In fact, many of the existing counseling approaches can be used, but in a culturally intentional way.

ACTIVITY 16.1

In the case of Mario, what combination of the following should a counselor do? Check off the items that you believe would be important in this case:

Establish rapport by sharing aspects of herself or himself as an adolescent who had also moved to a new school. _____

Show warmth and caring by attending to the client with a concerned facial expression and some casual physical touching on the shoulder. _____

Assess depression and suicide by asking where he is on a 10-point scale of sadness. _____

Help him to identify the strengths of his heritage by reading and talking to others of similar heritage in the community. _____

Form a group in the school for the 10 or so students who share Latino/Hispanic heritage. _____

Talk to the teachers and the principal about the situation so that it is addressed in a school assembly, for example, through a film presentation and discussion on diversity. _____

Bring in Mario's parents in order to explore the situation and their experiences. _____

Initiate or participate in efforts to reach out to the larger Hispanic community, which is composed mostly of Central American agricultural workers. _____

Go to his classes and open up the discussion of bias. _____

Refer Mario to a psychotherapist for his adjustment difficulties. _____

All of these interventions are actually worthy of consideration. They range from simple empathy and rapport, to parental involvement, to group psychoeducation, to community activities. The consequences of the counselor's action, or inaction, in such culturally infused situations can be enormous. In particular, clients from less dominant or marginalized groups are especially at risk, as can be seen in counseling attrition rates for clients of color, suicide rates for gay and lesbian youth, and rates of violence against women. For clients from dominant groups, culture is less a source of externally imposed distress. However, like all cultures, it can still be a source of internal conflict, as well as of strength.

CULTURE AND COUNSELING METHODS: CURRENT STATUS AND DEBATES

The whole domain of culturally alert counseling intervention is new and emergent. Until about 20 years ago, the great psychodynamic, humanistic, and behavioral counseling meta-theories competed with each other to explain human nature and to suggest related helping strategies. Their proponents shared the modernist ambition to find and spread comprehensive, universal truths about humans. Each vied for dominance and sought arguments to prove its case. Of course, many voices also spoke for an intelligently eclectic approach to counseling.

Counselors who enter the field at the present time are joining a humbler, more complex endeavor. The cultural construction of all counseling approaches, including "universal theory," is recognized. This so-called postmodern awareness posits that people tell stories based on their assumptions in order to explain the world. In that vein, counselors must recognize that counseling theories are stories themselves, each relatively useful or not in particular cultural contexts.

Today, therefore, counselors are challenged to know their own cultural story, the story of their counseling theories, and their clients' stories. The great Western counseling theories must be judiciously utilized by counselors who recognize that these theories are not universal solutions to universal human problems. They may be quite useful, but the theories, the counselors who utilize them, and their clients are always "in culture." This recognition has resulted in culturally alert counseling being called the emerging "fourth force" (after psychodynamic, humanistic, and behaviorist) in the field (Pedersen, 2001).

There is a catch: Knowledge about culturally oriented counseling skills is limited at this time. In that vein, Rodriguez and Walls (2000) observe, "Current multicultural training efforts are 'top-heavy': understandably preoccupied with the development of multicultural awareness and with the dissemination of culture-specific facts and trends but neglectful of the skill-driven mechanisms by which such knowledge is translated into effective interventions" (p. 90). It should be noted that, of course, the first two multicultural counseling competencies, cultural self-awareness and knowledge of other cultures, are important foundations for practice (Hunt, Matthews, Milsom, & Lammel, 2006; Pedersen, 2004; Sciarra, Chang, McLean, & Wong, 2005). As Ponterotto, Utsey, and Pedersen (2006) note, "the first step for counselors . . . is to work through their own ethnocentrism" (p. 151).

While the skills domain of multicultural competency is still relatively new and evolving, there have been some promising research results, particularly in the area of trust and the therapeutic alliance. Studies have linked culturally alert counseling practice with enhanced perception of the counselor's credibility, trustworthiness, and effectiveness (Ancis, 2004b; Zang & Dixon, 2001). Clients experiencing culturally alert practice report feeling "more understood and respected" (Smith, Richards, Granley, & Obiakor, 2004, p. 5). Given the acknowledged importance of the therapeutic relationship (Murphy, 1997), a culturally alert stance is a significant advantage.

While evidence of culturally based practice is only emerging, the counselor must practice. Therefore, this chapter outlines what is currently known, as best that can be done at this point, about effective culturally alert intervention.

The Particularist-Universalist Debate

The current central discussion about how to do multicultural counseling revolves around the particularist-universalist tension. The particularist view, in its extreme expression, would prescribe specific ("particular") culturally matched practices for certain cultural groups. Examples of particular practices include indigenous healing methods and the use of more structured, directive methods for heavily enculturated members of some ethnic groups. By contrast, as mentioned in Chapter 1, the universalist approach emphasizes the general application of Western counseling theories to individuals, regardless of culture. Counselors need not embrace either extreme position.

There is little empirical evidence to support the strict particularist matching of specific culturally based counseling methods with corresponding clients from those cultures (Atkinson & Israel, 2003). Any such practices must always be qualified by individual client differences, due to such factors as enculturation, acculturation, and the convergence of multiple cultural identities (e.g., gender, class, multiple ethnicities) in one person (Ancis, 2004b; Robinson, 2005). Particularism is also limited by the fact that culture is not a total explanation for human behavior. While culture is always present in clients' lives, it may not be central to their concerns at any given time. Instead, individual personality, situational, and universal human issues may be more prominent.

The universalist stance is also suspect and inadequate. A universalist view of applying a particular counseling theory to all clients without regard for culture is a form of cultural imperialism imposed by individualistic Western practitioners, as discussed in Chapter 1. Draguns (2002) refers to the folly of applying humanism, for example, as a cure-all for all clients:

> Opportunities for misunderstanding . . . are prodigious. For example, a therapist's encouraging the client to search for his or her own solutions [i.e., in the person-centered tradition] can be misconstrued as indifference or even incompetence. . . . [Further,] what a therapist may intend as . . . egalitarianism may be interpreted by the client as a lack of respect and violation of dignity and decorum. (p. 43)

The Culturally Alert Alternative

Given the limitations of relying solely on either universalism or particularism, counselors need an alternative path to culturally alert counseling. Draguns (2002) provides a balance: "[Counseling], wherever it is applied, constitutes a blend of universally effective and culturally specific components" (p. 29).

It follows, then, that counselors can use traditional Western methods while being aware of culture, but do so selectively. They can also apply some culturally specific strategies, such as varying structure and directiveness, emotionality, and the use of silence and pause time. However, counselors must remind themselves of the limits of generalizations: Individuals within groups vary greatly in their levels of acculturation, enculturation, and cultural identity, as well as in other characteristics (Matsumoto & Juang, 2004). Thus, all generalizations must be qualified.

ILLUSTRATION OF CULTURALLY ALERT COUNSELING

What follows is an illustration of how the universal, the individual, and the cultural are integrated in one case. In this example, one of the counselor's intentions is to establish trust in the context of a cultural difference, gender. Another is to explore the client's concerns and to educate the client, if that is warranted, about the gender dimensions of her situation.

In this interchange, empathic listening is mixed with six particular counseling skills, all of which will be discussed later in the chapter:

1. Broaching cultural differences

2. Culturally oriented questioning

3. Intentional self-disclosure

4. Instruction and information-giving

5. More directive leads

6. Advocacy (specifically the empowerment competencies enumerated in Appendix B)

In the process of responding to the client, the counselor must consider all three previously mentioned dimensions that affect lives:

1. the *particulars* of gender and other cultural factors;

2. the *individual's* situation, history, personality, and temperament;

3. the *universal* human emotions and dilemmas of living.

The client, Andrea, is discussing her male partner's emotional unavailability and lack of involvement in their children's upbringing. He is sometimes verbally abusive to her and to the children, especially when he is under the influence of alcohol. She is very unhappy with him and is thinking of separating. This segment picks up in the middle of the session.

Client: I don't know if you can understand my need to make sure that my children are okay and also my fear of being left without a partner who can provide for them and keep me from being alone.

Counselor: It seems that you're uncertain that I, as a male, can appreciate your dedication to your children's welfare and, perhaps, recognize your financial worries. Is that correct? How does it feel to work with me on these issues?

    [COUNSELOR INTENTIONALLY BROACHES THE GENDER DIFFERENCE TO SEE IF IT NEEDS TO BE EXPLORED.]

Client: Well, I don't know. You seem okay. I guess we'll have to see. A lot of men seem to forget that children need much, almost constant care. My husband stays away both physically and mentally from us and leaves their total caretaking to me. And I feel very alone. I don't have family in the area, so I need his emotional support and involvement.

Counselor: I hear some anger about his not doing his part, which is made worse by your aloneness.

    [EMPATHIC RESPONSE WITH EMPHASIS ON TWO FEELINGS]

Client: Yes. But I feel stuck. He says he has to be gone most of the time to make money for the family. But I think he does it for himself. He says he can't stand kids most of the time. However, I'd still rather have him around more and have less money. Plus, if it were about money, I could even add some income by working for pay myself. But I can't put in many hours of work outside of family duties, with the children to care for and all.

Counselor: That is an issue for many women—being torn between their commitments to family, work, and a partner. I sense that you are clear that the children are your current top priority and that you want help in raising them. Your dedication to your children is clear. I can sense the strong nurturing you give them. The other side of your dedication is what might be called "caretaking exhaustion," which many women experience—taking care of others and not leaving room for themselves.

    [COUNSELOR EMPOWERS BY (1) INFORMING THE CLIENT OF SOME GENDER PATTERNS (2) POINTING OUT CLIENT STRENGTHS. ADDITIONALLY, COUNSELOR (3) NOTES MIXED FEELINGS/DILEMMA BETWEEN DEDICATION AND EXHAUSTION.]

Client: Yes! But what am I supposed to do? The three kids are all under six years old!

Counselor: [Pause] Tell me what you learned in your religious tradition and from your family about women's and men's roles.

    [COUNSELOR PROBES RELIGIOUS, ETHNIC, AND SOCIAL CLASS CULTURAL MESSAGES ABOUT GENDER]

    [SEGMENT DELETED, INCLUDING PORTIONS ON CULTURAL MESSAGES AND ASSESSMENT OF ANY PHYSICAL ABUSE, OF WHICH THERE HAS BEEN NONE.]

    [TEN MINUTES LATER]

Counselor: How would you like things to be in the ideal?

Client: I'd like my husband to be around, to treat us right, and to bring in the income we need.

Counselor: Let's look at all of these wishes plus your needs for self-care. It is not uncommon for men to believe that they have to prove themselves in the world at the expense of family and relationships. Sometimes I even have to catch myself when I get buried in reading the newspaper after work while my kids need care and attention. Your husband hasn't caught himself it seems.

              [COUNSELOR POINTS OUT MALE PATTERN AND SELF-DISCLOSES.]

Client: That's for sure, to say the least! He justifies it. And he expects sex after all that! It feels like there is nothing left between us. I should end the marriage. But I never thought I would be without a man. I do try to please him so he'll stay. But I'm at the end of my rope.

Counselor: You mentioned previously your anxiety about "being alone" and your panic attacks when you were a child. Could you tell me more about that?

              [SEGMENT DELETED]

              [LATER IN THE SESSION]

Counselor: Your husband seems to you to be one more person to take care of. In fact, *you* want some emotional care taken of you too, by him. Your needs get lost in the process. And I hear that you don't want to do that any more but can't figure out how. I know that you said that you were raised to believe that the man is both the provider and authority at all times. Let's hold that aside for a moment and talk about your needs.

              [MATERIAL DELETED IN WHICH COUNSELOR AND CLIENT EXPLORE SUPPORT GROUPS, INCLUDING RELIGIOUS COMMUNITIES, FOR HER TO CONNECT WITH]

              [TOWARD THE END OF THE SESSION]

Counselor: Our time is nearly up. We have done a lot of work today, it seems to me. I'd like to ask you two things: What did you think of our session today? And what might you want to ask me, about anything? I see us as working together to help you get your own needs met while continuing to nurture those you love.

              [COUNSELOR GIVES CLIENT A CHANCE TO SHARE PERCEPTIONS, TO PARTICIPATE IN THE HELPING PROCESS.]

Activity 16.2 asks the reader to think critically about the cultural dimensions in Andrea's situation and the interaction between Andrea and her counselor.

ACTIVITY 16.2

A. Identify at least one each of the cultural, individual, and universal elements in the case of Andrea:

Cultural:

Individual:

Universal:

B. Tell what, in your view, the counselor might do differently or add to the counseling work as it proceeds in the future:

In this scenario, the male counselor attempted to gain the trust of the female client by responding empathically, self-disclosing, acknowledging the gender difference, showing awareness of distinct behavior patterns for men and for women, directing the client to resources, affirming strengths, and using the term "us" to show his alliance with her. He also checked in with the client on how the session was working for her.

Overall, the counselor acknowledged the cultural *particulars* of gender, religion, ethnicity, and social class as well as the *individual's* unique life circumstances and temperament, all the while knowing that such phenomena as fear, longing, loneliness, intimacy, and security are *universal* human emotions.

The counselor had many additional choices. One was to suggest outside supportive resources, such as a women's group, books that provide relevant information and support for her situation, and referral to financial counseling and/or social services guidance so that she might have a financial plan. Another issue that could have been addressed in this session was the client's and her husband's ethnic communities and their influence on each of their expectations for family life. All of the above can be held in the counselor's mind as possibilities.

Guidelines for Culturally Alert Practice

The remainder of this chapter is devoted to presenting strategies for culturally alert practice. In order to determine the current state of knowledge in that regard, a content analysis of the multicultural counseling literature was executed (McAuliffe, Grothaus, Wininger, & Corriveau, 2006). What emerged were three major themes for culturally alert counseling practice: accessibility, assessment, and intervention. This section will be organized around those three themes. It should be noted that some of the practices described here are important for any counseling relationship. However, they are especially significant when there is a cross-cultural encounter or when the client is a member of a nondominant group.

THEME ONE: ACCESSIBILITY

Counseling can be intimidating to anyone. It requires client vulnerability—admitting that something is not working in her or his life. Clients put their emotions, time, and resources on the line to work with a counselor.

Counseling is especially intimidating to members of many ethnic and religious groups. For example, it might be seen by many clients of color as a largely European American enterprise, from the nature of its origins to the ethnicity of most of its current practitioners. Cross-cultural counselor-client combinations often cause clients to wonder, "Can this counselor understand me? Does this male 'get' women's issues? Does that counselor resonate with the concerns of people like me?" In fact, people prefer to see counselors who are like them in some way. But that is not possible at all times, nor does it guarantee successful work.

In order to counter these culturally related doubts that clients bring, counselors must be accessible. To paraphrase the previously mentioned expression: "You have to get in the door before you can rearrange the furniture." In that vein, counselors cannot assume that clients can find them, afford them, understand them, or trust them. Three ways for counselors to be accessible are described below: being approachable, adapting language, and showing trustworthiness.

Being Approachable

Being approachable begins with counselors making services physically accessible to clients in the following ways: place and time, atmosphere, cost, and outreach. Approachability may make the difference in whether a client even ventures into counseling or returns for it. Being approachable can be expressed even before clients appear.

Place and Time. Many clients do not access counseling because of the location, the times services are offered, and/or difficulties with issues such as childcare or transportation. As noted in the chapter on social class, for example, low-income working parents often have little choice about jobs, working conditions, and hours and cannot take time off from work to attend counseling or school events without the risk of losing pay or even their jobs. Accessible programs make place and time convenient for clients. Regarding place, accessible programs have easily reached central or satellite locations that are accessible to people with disabilities. Accessibility by time is represented, for example, by scheduling accommodations, as illustrated by school counselors and mental health agencies being available on some evenings and late afternoons or on some weekends, as well as by making home visits (Kim, 2005). Additionally, they allow for extended sessions when needed. Culturally alert counselors also make a culturally sensitive choice in deciding how to "confront" a client about showing up late for sessions.

Atmosphere. A second dimension of approachability is atmosphere. The physical counseling setting should be inclusive and welcoming, with culturally diverse décor, evidence of commitments to social justice, and hospitable front-line staff (Neukrug, 2002). Paniagua (2005) suggests that there be multicultural training for all in the office, including support staff. Decorating one's office with posters and other artifacts (e.g., gay-supportive symbols, multiethnic artifacts, multiple religious symbols) shows some clients that the counselor is aware of nondominant groups' cultures and struggles. Given that, in Hanjorgiris and O'Neill's (2006) words, "people with disabilities (PWD) constitute the largest minority group in the United States" (p. 321), so accommodations should be made. Examples of such accommodations include having particular materials for people with visual impairments (Hunt et al., 2006), such as large print, Braille, and/or audio versions of consent forms, and counselors being familiar with various assistive technologies that might be needed by persons with disabilities (Olkin, 2004).

Cost. Approachability also includes cost. It is a simple fact that clients with fewer financial resources often cannot see private practitioners because most counselors do not accept Medicaid (see Chapter 12). Even with insurance, co-payments are daunting to people with low income. Yet persons of lower socioeconomic status have higher rates of certain mental disorders, such as depression. Individuals who have low incomes include many college students and young adults, who are in a life phase in which money is scarce. One form of demonstrating cost approachability is to offer pro bono counseling services and sliding fee scales based on client income.

Outreach. A final area in which counselors can be approachable to diverse clients is in reaching out to potential clients who might not come to counseling before crisis occurs. Counselors need to anticipate the concerns of particular populations and be creative in reaching them (Rayle, 2005). Such outreach can be planned if counselors are "familiar with and active in the communities in which their clients reside" (Vera, Buhin, & Shin, 2006, p. 280; see also Sue, Arredondo, & McDavis, 1992). One recommended means of planning and accomplishing outreach is to collaborate with leaders and/or indigenous healers in the community (Simcox, Nuijens, & Lee, 2006; Wallace, 2006). Thus, for example, the school counselor might link with local religious organizations to provide tutoring programs after school.

Counselors are charged with balancing remediation with proactive prevention work in the communities they serve (D'Andrea, 2006; Ponterotto et al., 2006; Vera et al., 2006). A school counselor who actively engages parents with lower incomes by helping to arrange for transportation to evening school assemblies and by making phone calls is making the school accessible. Another form of outreach for school counselors is paying significant attention to the career plans of non-college-bound students by running career planning groups and other efforts. Other prevention efforts include conducting study skills and test-taking workshops for lower-achieving college students; providing support groups for lesbian, gay, and bisexual clients; reaching out to unemployed men; offering groups for immigrant students and adults; facilitating community forums about issues of concern (Wallace, 2006); and providing culturally sensitive life skills training (D'Andrea, 2006). Counselors can assist in enhancing social support systems; participation in such support systems, such as extended family, religious communities, and ethnic organizations, is linked with a decreased chance of experiencing psychological distress (Ancis, 2004a).

Adapting Language

The second major category under the Accessibility theme is language. There are two dimensions of language usage in counseling. One is the literal tongue of the client and counselor. The other is related to slang, jargon, and terms for cultural groups.

Using a Translator. Language is obviously a basic issue in communication, whether it is auditory or sign language. The most basic concern is whether the counselor and client speak the same language; that is not assured in the United States. According to data from the 2000 U.S. Census, 11 million people in the United States indicated that they speak English "not well" or "not at all" (cited in Paniagua, 2005, p. 28). The Multicultural Counseling Competencies (Sue et al., 1992) provide guidance in this regard:

> Culturally skilled counselors take responsibility for interacting in the language requested by the client and, if not feasible, make appropriate referral. A serious problem arises when the linguistic skills of a counselor do not match the language of the client. This being the case, counselors should (a) seek a translator with cultural knowledge and appropriate professional background and (b) refer to a knowledgeable and competent bilingual counselor. This guideline is basic but too often ignored, resulting in miscommunication, frustration, and loss of trust. (p. 483)

Language is particularly important in diagnosis, as diagnosis tends to be less accurate when clients are not allowed to utilize their language of preference (Paniagua, 2005).

When a client does not speak English, or speak it well, a translator can be used. In the case of translators, the following guidelines should be considered:

- Translators should have training in mental health and culturally related mental disorders/syndromes.
- It is preferable for the translator to share the client's racial and ethnic background and dialect, and there should not be a major difference in their levels of acculturation.

- Early in the process, the counselor should allow the client and translator to have some time together (without the counselor) to discuss common interests.

- Plan ahead for extra time, as translated exchanges are likely to take longer.

- Avoid using a friend or relative (especially the client's children) as a translator. (Paniagua, 2005, pp. 16–17)

There is some controversy in the field about whether translators should be used at all. Paniagua (2005) points out two problems with the use of a translator:

> First, the translator introduces a third person into the psychotherapy process, and this can lead to distortion and misrepresentation of the client's verbalizations. Omissions, additions, and substitutions are examples of common distortions or errors associated with the process of translation in the practice of psychotherapy. . . . Second, the client may find communicating through a translator to be a disagreeable experience. (p. 15)

Obviously, there is a tradeoff in using a translator. However, having one shows interest in and respect for the language differences, and it provides a means of communication when there may be no other.

Jargon, Inclusive Language, and Terms. Language access also includes how language is used. Many clients are already intimidated by the jargon of the professional counseling and education fields. Clients can be daunted merely by entering a school or agency building to meet with a "professional." One way to be accessible is for counselors to speak in commonly understood language, to avoid jargon. Thus, acronyms for programs and diagnoses, such as IEP and ADHD, should be explained in clear terms.

A related notion is using inclusive language that shows respect for clients' cultures. As mentioned in Chapter 1, that can be a subtle undertaking, as terms evolve, taking on negative and positive connotations. Thus, the formerly neutral term "retarded," meaning delayed, took on a derogatory meaning. As a result, the new term, "developmentally delayed," which denotes the same condition, came into use. A similar evolution has occurred with terms such as "girl" (for an adult woman), "Negro," "Oriental," and "homosexual." Each of these terms was once acceptable for members of nondominant groups. But nondominant groups recognized that those names were given by the dominant group. Nondominants often wish to claim their own name for themselves. It takes an effort to learn and use language that is preferred by members of a group, for example, to say "woman," "African American," "Asian," and "lesbian" or "gay man."

In addition to the issue of who does the naming, there is the issue of how to be more inclusive. A counselor must be sensitive to the exclusiveness of the dominant terms, how they serve to marginalize nondominant persons, and the unearned power they promote. For example, counselors can be inclusive by saying "her or him" when speaking generically instead of only "him," "humankind" instead of "mankind," "staffing" instead of "manning," "partner" instead of "husband/wife" or "boyfriend/girlfriend," and "place of worship" instead of the Christian term "church." Counselors should scan their intake forms and other paperwork for inclusive language (Miville & Ferguson, 2006).

It should be noted, paradoxically, that formerly negative terms can reverse their meanings when nondominant groups reclaim them as positive labels, as some gay men and lesbians have done with "queer," some Appalachian people with "hillbilly," and some activist women's groups have done with "girl."

Finally, counselors should respond to clients' preferred language. Clients themselves may use such familiar terms as "girl," "Oriental," or "wife." Counselors must balance their sense of inclusiveness with clients' preferred language and not seek to instruct them at all times in currently preferred terms. The counselor can also ask clients what terms they prefer.

Showing Trustworthiness

The final, and essential, dimension of cultural accessibility is trustworthiness. It is a precondition and an ongoing requirement for clients to reveal themselves and listen to the counselor. Trust is especially crucial in cross-cultural counseling, even more important than the specific intervention choices a counselor makes (Slattery, 2004). Clients must believe that the counselor can understand them and not use their revelations against them. In fact, a trustworthy relationship, or alliance, between counselor and client is more important than counselor-client cultural differences in the success of the work (Ridley & Kleiner, 2003).

Trust is particularly important if the counselor is a member of the dominant group and the client is not.

> Many clients from cultural . . . groups that have historically been at the bottom of the class structure . . . have developed coping mechanisms that may make it difficult for them to trust counselors but [those coping mechanisms] are appropriate within the context of their lives. (Kincade & Evans, 1996, p. 104)

Pedersen (2003) proposes, therefore, that the counseling context must be an especially "safe space" because "dangerous questions" must be asked (p. 29). These include questions related to sensitive gender and racial differences and attitudes, or a particular social group's negative social stigma, as is still often the case for homosexuality, poverty, and disability. As Lewis (2003) says, "Creating safety and trust while having difficult dialogs is central to multiculturalism, as is creating an environment in which clients from oppressed groups feel secure enough to engage in the counseling process" (p. 262). In Lewis's view, trust development can be especially important, for example, between African American clients and white counselors, heterosexual counselors and lesbian and gay clients, female clients and male counselors, and clients from lower SES statuses and middle-class counselors. It should be noted that trust will be easier to establish with any client who is in significant distress (Kopta, Howard, Lowry, & Beutler, 1994). Thus, a culturally different client who has urgent emotional needs will likely disclose even if trust issues have not been dealt with extensively.

Trust is promoted by counselors and clients recognizing shared worldviews or other commonalities. As Ibrahim (2003) declares, "The key to establishing a trusting and respectful relationship [is] . . . being able to find common ground or creating a shared worldview in an emotionally warm environment" (p. 198). Some of the ways for increasing trust that are discussed next are making explicit efforts to establish rapport; providing informed consent; proactively "leaning in" to client mistrust and anger; demonstrating knowledge of clients' cultures; and broaching cultural differences, especially if they seem to be a concern.

Establishing Rapport. Establishing rapport is an early task of all counseling relationships. It is most easily established when the counselor and client share similar cultures. In cross-cultural encounters, counselors should consciously attend to rapport. Warmth, small talk, and self-disclosure are three ways to establish rapport. For example, at some point in the early part of the relationship, counselors can share something of themselves (Wehrly, 1995). In many cultures, disclosure is considered part of trust building. Such revelation can increase the common bond by helping clients see the counselor as an authentic person with a "real life" (Davies & Neal, 2003). In fact, counselor self-disclosure has often been found to be a prerequisite to client disclosure with people from communitarian cultures, such as many Native American Indians and Asian Americans (Sue & Sue, 2003). Simple disclosures about interests, relatives, and family can be valuable. Of course, such disclosure should be brief, relevant, true, and followed by a quick return to the client's concerns.

Providing Informed Consent. Another way to increase rapport that is related to self-disclosure is to provide "culturally informed consent" (Davidson, Yakushka, & Sanford-Martens, 2004). Such information is most important to members of non-dominant groups who have had less access to counseling culture than others. In that vein, the writers of the Multicultural Counseling Competencies urge counselors to "educat[e] their clients to the processes of psychological intervention, such as goals, expectations, legal rights, and the counselor's orientation" (Sue et al., 1992, p. 483; see also Appendix A, this volume). The statement describes an open, transparent counseling environment that includes sharing diagnoses, notes, the counselor's background, awareness of a client's culture, approach to counseling, and aspects of medications. This type of informed consent is especially important for members of nondominant ethnic groups and persons with low incomes, for whom counseling might seem like a mysterious, middle-class, foreign practice.

"Leaning In" and Being Empathic. Another element in establishing trust is an especially proactive form of empathy. It is called "leaning in" by McGoldrick (1998). Empathy involves stepping back from one's perspectives to "really

listen" (Belenky, Clinchy, Goldberger, & Tarule, 1986) to another. Leaning in is especially important when counselors are confronted with ideas and customs that are foreign, even distasteful, to them. There are legitimate grounds for counselors to have an initial negative reaction to some client disclosures, manners, and attitudes. For example, a client may make an ethnically prejudicial remark, or she or he may advocate a custom, such as corporal punishment of children, that is distasteful or even morally questionable to the counselor.

As mentioned in Chapter 1, it is easier to psychologically assimilate, that is, to take in what is familiar and therefore comfortable, than to accommodate. For that reason, when a counselor meets a "foreign" idea or custom, she or he is likely to have at least momentary difficulty with it. However, culturally alert counseling requires the ability to pause, reflect, and consider alternative responses. Leaning in allows that counselor to accommodate unsettling newness and contradiction.

Leaning in consists of actively hearing the legitimacy of customs and ideas that are initially irritating to the counselor. McGoldrick (1998) proposes that counselors do so to counter their prejudices and other cultural blinders when they are confronted with unfamiliar or difficult cultural differences. McGoldrick recommends the following to the counselor who is feeling resistant: "Just listen. Try to take in the pain of what [the other] is saying, instead of thinking of the exceptions" (p. 225). She offers the example of having to lean in to appreciate men's dilemmas when she was initially immersed in feminism. At first, she couldn't hear that men had gender-related dilemmas also. Leaning in helped her to let go of her bias and hear the new perspective.

McGoldrick (1998) proposes that leaning in is especially important when there are power differences and cultural controversies. Leaning in might be especially important for the agnostic who is working with the Evangelical Christian, and vice versa, or the feminist counselor who is working with the woman client who adheres to strict gender roles. Cultural empathy and leaning in are especially important for dominant group members when they are confronted with client claims of oppression. Dominant group members might be inclined to think, regarding oppression, "Everyone has equal opportunity. Let's drop the subject and move on." Such leaning in requires pausing and working hard to enter another's framework. It is an important attitude for any counselor who thinks, "I just don't get it" about a value or cultural dimension.

Cultural empathy might be considered a special version of empathy because it entails counselors putting aside their discomforts and prejudices about individuals as members of whole groups, whether those groups are, for example, the working class, the affluent, adolescents, or people of a particular religion. In cases where there are significant cultural differences between counselor and client, a strong effort to vicariously experience the client's world is especially important. For example, in Chapter 15, the authors challenge the counselor to develop an attitude of appreciation, empathy, and respect for a variety of spiritual and religious traditions, experiences, and practices. Such attitudes can be applied to all cultural differences.

Having and Using Cultural Knowledge. Trust is also engendered by the counselor's having and demonstrating specific knowledge of clients' cultures and their experiences of oppression (Pieterse & Collins, 2004). The counselor should not have to ask the client to completely educate her or him on the client's cultures (Davies & Neal, 2003). Empathy and questioning are not substitutes for cultural knowledge. For example, as described in Chapter 6, in East and Southeast Asian cultures, gifts are part of relationship acknowledgment. The counselor who knows about gift giving might share a problem-solving strategy, a tentative diagnosis, or a reframe early in the process (Paniagua, 2005; Wehrly, 1995).

Counselors should have a solid working knowledge about each of the cultural groups that are discussed in this book, for they are the dominant ones in American society. If the counselor does not know much about a client's cultures, she or he should do research between sessions. To educate themselves, counselors can participate in cultural events, read, watch, and consult with "cultural informants." Such informants are "people who provide insight about an indigenous group . . . usually, cultural informants are bicultural, meaning they can maneuver fluently both in mainstream American culture and in their own indigenous culture" (Day-Vines, Patton, & Baytops, 2003, p. 49).

There are at least two general areas of culture that counselors should know about: communication styles and cultural phenomena. In the first area, culturally alert counselors should also be able to engage appropriately in a variety of verbal and nonverbal helping responses. They should not be tied down to only one method or approach to helping but should recognize that helping styles and approaches may be culture-bound. When they sense that their helping style is limited and potentially inappropriate, they can adjust it or bring up the question, using cultural immediacy, which is discussed next. Head nodding is a simple example of showing cultural knowledge of communication. For many Japanese people, vigorous head nodding is not necessarily a sign of agreement, but instead shows attentive listening.

Knowledge of cultural communication styles would include, for example, being oriented to the importance of the relationship for more collectivist, status-oriented, and uncertainty-avoidant cultures (Matsumoto, 1991). In those cases, counselors might need to regularly acknowledge the relationship with the client and with family members, using compliments and statements of appreciation. They might also learn to be less confrontational and more indirect when challenging client thinking, due to the collectivist emphasis on preserving harmonious relationships.

Other cultural phenomena that a counselor should be familiar with are artistic expressions, verbal expressions, values about health and family, and core beliefs. Counselors could know about such phenomena as the meaning of Afrocentric hair styles; gay "chosen families"; hip-hop music; salsa; sickle-cell anemia; women's career-family conflicts; working-class values; the Rule of Opposites for Native American Indians; the central place of family involvement in the counseling process for Middle Eastern clients; and fundamental Islamic, Jewish, Christian, pagan, and other beliefs. There is no substitute for cultural knowledge.

A qualifier about how much cultural knowledge a counselor can expect to have is in order. Counselors cannot be expected to know everything about clients' cultures. In cases where counselors are unaware of aspects of a client's culture, they can ask (Wehrly, 1995). That topic is discussed later as "culturally oriented questioning."

Broaching Cultural Differences. At times, the counselor will sense a tension in the room that might be trust related. In fact, clients tend to initially seek out counselors of the same race, gender, sexual orientation, and ethnicity as themselves. Uncertainty, even mistrust, can be dealt with by the counselor's broaching the cultural differences that are on individuals' minds. Another term for such a here-and-now acknowledgment is "cultural immediacy." Cultural immediacy consists of acknowledging the presence of cultural differences. The counselor is the initiator of such immediacy (Rayle, 2005; Wehrly, 1995). In the words of Day-Vines et al. (in press), the need to broach the subject of race, ethnicity, and culture "places the onus of responsibility to initiate race-related dialogues on the counselor, [ones that] might otherwise remain unexamined due in large measure to the taboo nature of race within a racially charged society."

Here are some questions that a counselor might introduce, or broach, the topic of culture:

People have different perspectives based on their experiences and cultures. You and I from different cultures. How do you feel about working with me, a [fill in race/ethnicity/sexual orientation], on your concerns?

How do you feel about working with a culturally different counselor?

What is this experience like for you as a [fill in race/ethnicity/sexual orientation] man/woman?

Thus, the "elephant in the room" is acknowledged. Culture may or may not be seen as a salient issue at that point. Either way, the client now is more likely to feel comfortable in bringing up the topic if it becomes a concern. If it is an issue, it can be explored. The client feels invited to ask the counselor questions about herself or himself and to share any doubts about the counselor's ability to assist the client. The result of such conversations is likely to be increased trust between counselor and client.

THEME TWO: ASSESSMENT

The process of assessment is an ongoing task in all counseling. Assessment may even precede the initial client-counselor encounter. For example, even before the first session, counselors might have referral information or records to preview. When the client arrives, counselors also assess by observing the client's verbal and nonverbal behavior skills to evaluate her or his functioning.

Assessment is powerful because it is likely to influence the course of counseling. That is especially why assessment must account for culture. In Ancis's (2004b) words, "Understanding the client's cultural and sociopolitical context is essential for accurate assessment, interpretation, and treatment" (p. 8).

Unfortunately, instances of cultural ignorance and bias in assessment have occurred. For example, African American clients score lower on intelligence tests administered by European American evaluators than they do on the same tests when evaluated by an African American (Paniagua, 2005). The test takers' self-beliefs seem to be affected by the test giver, especially in tests that require interactions.

Diagnosis can be affected by skin color and dialect. For example, Paniagua (2005) notes that "when clinicians are not aware of a client's racial/ethnic identity, they tend to arrive at the correct diagnosis, whereas when they know the racial/ethnic identity of a non-Anglo client, their diagnoses tend to be more severe" (p. 134). In addition, Hays, Chang, and Dean (2007) found that some counselors resent wealthy clients and assessed them as having few serious problems when that is not the case.

Culturally alert assessment asks the counselor to have a "third ear" open for cultural dimensions that help to explain a client's situation. In order to know the client better, counselors must find out about the client's world; that includes the inevitable cultural dimension (Pedersen, 2004). Such assessment comes in four forms: culturally oriented questioning in the interview, the cultural genogram, culturally sensitive diagnosis, and the culturally sensitive use of tests. In each of these cases, the client should be a participant. She or he should know the nature and foundations of the questions or instrument used and be part of the meaning-making that results from the assessment activity.

Doing Culturally Oriented Questioning

Culturally oriented questioning refers to the practice of asking clients about the meaning and nature of the cultural dimensions of their lives. Counselors can inquire about at least three topics: (1) the importance, or salience, of culture for a client; (2) the experiences of oppression for members of nondominant groups; and/or (3) the cultural values that guide a person's life.

The importance of asking for clients' cultural stories is emphasized by Rodriguez and Walls (2000): "Client self-report is the most reliable source of information regarding the relevance of cultural factors. [It] always supersedes the counselor's textbook knowledge of that culture" (p. 93). Even when counselors know much about a client's culture, checking how it plays out for that particular client is essential. By inquiring, counselors can avoid making incorrect assumptions about the nature and impact of clients' cultures. Such questions will especially help counselors to assess clients' acculturation and enculturation.

Such questioning is common practice in everyday life: People who find themselves with a culturally different person commonly ask questions about the other culture in order to reduce the uncertainty of the situation and increase predictability. Box 16.1 contains examples of culturally oriented questions that a counselors might ask.

BOX 16.1   Suggestions for Culturally Oriented Questions

Following are some suggested questions, organized by their general intent, that bring the cultural dimension into the work

1. *Overall Importance of Culture*

   What place did a gender [and/or social class] script play in your career [or relationship] choices?

   Help me understand what you are going through as a [Fill in ethnicity/race/ sexual orientation] woman/man.

   In what way has your ethnicity influenced your life?

   Different people have different perspectives based on their experiences. In our [school, community, agency], we have a wide range of cultures. How do you feel that your culture affects your relationship with others?

   How do you think people perceive you as a result of your ethnicity [disability, sexual orientation, upbringing, etc.]? What is that like for you?

2. *Comfort Level With the Topic of Culture*

   On a scale of 1 to 5, what is your comfort level in addressing issues of [race, ethnicity, gender, sexual orientation, religion, etc.]?

3. *Counselor Interest in Learning About Client's Culture*

   What would you like me to know about your experience in your culture?

4. *The Client's Experience With Cultural Others, Including Experiences of Bias*

   What was your first experience with someone different from you?

   What has been your experience with other races (ethnic groups, etc.)?

5. *Local Impact of Culture, Including Oppression*

   What has your experience as a(n) [Fill in ethnicity/race/sexual orientation] woman/man been at this [school/college/workplace/other institution]?

Ironically, with such questioning, counselors can avoid overemphasizing culture. After all, they might assume that culture wields more power in some clients' lives than it actually does. In fact, the importance of culture will vary from person to person. Merely knowing a person's gender, sexual orientation, ethnicity, religion, or social class does not indicate the power of those factors in her or his worldview. If a client is in a nondominant group or is an immigrant, culture will likely be central. If clients are in stages of cultural identity development in which their culture has become prominent for them, it will also probably be very important.

Having Clients Do a Cultural Genogram

The cultural genogram is a cultural assessment activity that potentially can increase awareness (Hardy & Laszloffy, 1995). One of the strengths of a genogram is that the client generates the data. In the process, she or he reflects on the influence of this dimension of her or his life. The genogram can be adapted for any cultural dimension; it is most often used for ethnicity. Box 16.2 describes the making of a cultural genogram and some of the questions that can be used to evoke meaning from the activity.

BOX 16.2   Making a Cultural Genogram

The Cultural/Gender Genogram is intended to illuminate and highlight the influences, beliefs, and assumptions that influence our systemic interactions as individuals and as therapists.

I. Defining One's Culture of Origin

   Culture of origin refers to the major group(s) from which you have descended that were the first generation to come to America. For example, an individual may have been born and raised in America, but if his or her grandparents were Irish and Greek, then the culture of origin consists of these two groups.

   a. Selecting colors: A different color should be selected to represent each group that makes up your culture of origin. The colors are used to identify the different groups and to depict how each group contributes to the cultural identity of each individual. For instance, if a female is half Swedish (yellow), a quarter Ugandan (red), and a quarter Venezuelan (blue), then the circle that identifies her on the genogram would be color-coded half yellow, a quarter red, and a quarter blue.

   b. Identifying intercultural marriages: Use a ~ symbol to represent intercultural marriages in your genogram.

II. Mapping Organizing Principles and Pride/Shame Issues

   a. Organizing principles: Organizing principles are fundamental constructs that shape the perceptions, beliefs, and behaviors of members of a group. (For instance, in Jewish culture, fear of persecution is an organizing principle). Organizing principles regarding gender roles and gender relations should also be addressed.

   b. Pride/Shame issues: Pride/shame issues are the aspects of a culture that are sanctioned as distinctively negative or positive. They are similar to organizing principles in that they organize the perceptions, beliefs, and behaviors of group members. However, pride/shame issues punctuate behaviors as negative or positive, while organizing principles do not. (For example, in traditional Latino cultures, masculine assertiveness is a pride/shame issue because not being assertive is seen as negative.) Pride and shame issues pertaining to each gender and gender relations should be discussed.

   To identify organizing principles and pride/shame issues, you may have to use several sources: personal knowledge experience, interviews with members of that culture, reviewing reference materials.

c. Creating symbols: Symbols should be designed to denote all pride/shame issues and should be placed directly on the genogram to depict graphically the prevalence of pride/shame issues and to highlight their impact on family functioning.

d. Cultural framework charts: The cultural framework chart is like a legend to your cultural genogram. One cultural framework chart should be included for each group that makes up your culture of origin. It should list the major organizing principles and pride/ shame issues along with their corresponding symbols. The cultural framework chart will allow the interpretation of your pictorial genogram.

III. Putting It All Together

The following questions can be discussed with the client:

1. How was conformity to your family's/culture's gender norms rewarded? How was nonconformity punished?

2. What was your family's/culture's criteria for a successful woman? A successful man?

3. Have there been conflicts between the gender norms of your family/culture and those of your peer group? If so, how have you handled those conflicts?

4. At this time, how would you describe the ideal male/female?

5. What are your family's beliefs and feelings about the group(s) that make up your culture of origin? What parts of the group(s) do they embrace or reject? How has this influenced your feelings about your cultural/gender identity?

6. What aspects of your culture of origin do you have the most comfort "owning" and the most difficulty "owning"? What aspects of your culture of origin's view of gender do you have most comfort owning and most difficulty owning?

Questions for students of counseling:

1. What groups do you think you will have the most difficulty working with and the least difficulty?

2. What did you learn about yourself and your cultural/gender identity? How might this influence your work as a counselor?

SOURCE: Adapted from Dunn (2000).

Practicing Culturally Sensitive Diagnosis

Diagnosis is an attempt to succinctly capture key characteristics of a person's mental state. Diagnosis can be a reminder that there is "more than meets the eye" to clients. In fact, diagnosis may especially help counselors who, due to their developmental and humanistic tradition, might underestimate the seriousness of clients' disorders. Diagnosis has not been popular with counselors in the past because it seemed to interfere with an egalitarian, authentic relationship between counselor and client. It was also seen as objectifying clients instead of treating them as whole persons. However, when diagnosis is used judiciously and not treated as an absolute, it can help counselors form hypotheses about the client. Diagnosis, at its best, can also help counselors plan actions that correspond to the nature and severity of a client's distress and avoid imposing arbitrary, unethical interventions.

Diagnosis can help clients; a clear set of terms and explanations for emotional distress can transform self-blame into self-acceptance of a known phenomenon. Thus, clinical depression and generalized anxiety, to name two examples, can be framed as expressions of a combination of biological and psychological concomitants, none of which are the "fault" of the individual. In its best sense, therefore, diagnosis can be a humanizing and comforting phenomenon. Diagnosis can counteract the historical tendency to blame individuals for mental distress, which was common in pre-psychological Western societies. It can be concluded, therefore, that when used carefully, diagnosis can be a complement to good interviewing and ongoing assessment.

Diagnosis also has well-known risks. It is a problem when a diagnostic category is viewed as an essential characteristic of an individual. A diagnostic category is not an entity. It is a socially constructed generalization that fits, more or less, with a person's experience. As such, there can be as many expressions of, for example, generalized anxiety disorder as there are persons, in terms of the frequency, internal experience, and triggers for what is called anxiety. Therefore, diagnosis must always be done tentatively, with the recognition of individual and cultural variation in how disorders are experienced and expressed.

Like all psychological constructions, diagnosis is an expression of culture. The accepted guide in much of the world for such diagnosis is a U.S. product, the latest version of which is the *Diagnostic and Statistical Manual of Mental Disorders* 4th edition text revision, or *DSM-IV-TR* (American Psychiatric Association, 2000). While it is an attempt to objectify observations about people, those observations are always made within a language and a culture. That, in itself, does not discount the value of diagnosis. In fact, the same basic patterns of mental disorders have been found around the world (Westermeyer, 1987). However, these disorders are influenced by culture in their expression and by the way a community treats those who suffer from them. Therefore, it is important for the culturally alert counselor to consider diagnostic categories as social constructions, not entities. They have been assembled through a process of consensus by Western psychiatrists, social workers, and psychologists.

Following is a three-step guide to culturally alert diagnosis: (1) assessing client cultural identity and salience before diagnosing, (2) considering local descriptions of mental distress, and (3) working through the *DSM-IV-TR* in an Axis IV-III-I-II order. Additional information on cultural factors in diagnosis can be found in three places in the *DSM-IV-TR:* on p. xxxiv, in Appendix I, and in the descriptions of some disorders throughout the manual.

Assessing Cultural Identity and Salience. Before doing a *DSM-IV-TR* diagnosis, a counselor should, early in the relationship, assess the client's level of enculturation and cultural identity development and salience. The culturally oriented questioning that was discussed in a previous section of this chapter should precede a diagnosis. By doing so, a combination of factors that add to the client's distress can be acknowledged. It may be that a client is mainly experiencing an acculturation problem, which is described in the "Other Conditions" (i.e., not official mental disorders) section of the *DSM-IV-TR*. For example, a young immigrant may find that her young adult identity problem around career or relationships is exacerbated by her acculturation difficulties and is inseparable from them. Culture can also play a significant role in religious, academic, or occupational problems, none of which are themselves mental disorders. Thus, a cultural explanation for the client's distress can begin the assessment, especially for members of nondominant groups.

Recognition of Cultural Terms for Mental Distress. A second step in culturally alert diagnosis is to consider the "local" cultural description of a client's symptoms. For example, many European and African Americans describe a family member or co-worker who has become unable to function well as having had a "nervous breakdown." That culture-bound designation was the Western folk term from the 1930s through the 1970s for a host of possible conditions, especially major depression. Past Western terms for such a syndrome were "melancholia" and, later, "neurasthenia." Other common Western cultural descriptions of mental disorders include "having the blues" and "a case of nerves." Each comes with a corresponding explanation and sometimes treatment suggestions. The *DSM-IV-TR* now terms such notions "folk categories," although, curiously, it leaves out the preceding Western folk terms. *DSM-IV-TR* folk categories include such notions as *zar,* a term used in parts of North Africa and the Middle East to describe dissociative episodes ascribed to being possessed by a spirit; *ataque de nervios,* a Hispanic term for a sense of being out of control, often as a result of a stressful event; and *hwa byung,* which translates literally from the Korean as "anger syndrome" and includes a host of symptoms that are related to the suppression of anger, such as insomnia, fatigue, dysphoria, indigestion, and palpitations. The culturally alert counselor should know, or learn about, such categories when working with specific populations. Then the counselor can complement that understanding with the Western diagnostic descriptions of those symptoms and explain those to the client, if warranted.

Utilizing the DSM-IV-TR *With Cultural Alertness.* The counselor can do culturally alert diagnosis by considering the *DSM-IV-TR* in this order: Axis IV, III, I, and II. First, the counselor can consider the Psychosocial and Environmental Problems, or Axis IV. Many emotional difficulties can be related to cultural factors, such as inadequate social support, discrimination, disruption of family, illiteracy, unemployment, inadequate housing, insufficient finances, inadequate health care services, lack of transportation, or exposure to disasters and war. Each of those problems is delineated in Axis IV.

In line with looking at psychosocial or environmental problems, counselors should consider culturally related problems that can cause distress, such as religious or spiritual problems, acculturation problems, or identity problems. For example, the children of immigrants from collectivist cultures are often caught between a Western emphasis on (1) autonomy or separation from family and (2) an ethnic expectation to have ultimate loyalty to the group. These concerns are listed under "Other Conditions" in the *DSM-IV-TR*.

Next, the culturally alert counselor should weigh the medical conditions (Axis III) that might contribute to, trigger, or be the source of distress. In some cultures, medical conditions are commonly hidden from oneself and from others, and it may take some effort for the client to even know or acknowledge physical pain (McGoldrick, 2005).

Clinical disorders or other conditions that may be a focus of clinical attention (Axis I) can next be considered. Here, cultural considerations are also warranted. Some seeming disorders are actually acceptable cultural expressions, such as talking to spirits or hearing direction from a deity. Knowing those cultural phenomena should not, of course, rule out more serious mental disorders.

Finally, Axis II, which includes personality disorders, must be addressed with special care. Culture particularly affects personality. For example, what is seen as aggressive in Midwestern U.S. culture might be seen as merely direct and involved by New Yorkers (Tannen, 1990). Similarly, what is avoidant in one culture can be merely respectful in another. However, it should be reiterated that cultural elements do not preclude serious disorder in the area of personality. Counselors can use the filter of culture to distinguish the merely culturally acceptable, but perhaps contextually inappropriate, from the consistent pattern of dysfunction that is called a personality disorder.

Using Tests in a Culturally Alert Fashion

A final dimension of client assessment is formal testing. When tests are used well, they can help a client decide on a course of action, recognize issues that need to be confronted, optimize strengths, and manage weaknesses. However, when formal tests are used, they must be put in cultural context. Tests can masquerade as universal when they are in fact culture-bound. Two dimensions of testing call for cultural alertness: One is the validity of tests themselves and the other is their use.

Cross-Cultural Validity. Two important factors in the cross-culture fairness of tests are their content and their norming. The content of tests is constructed from material that is inevitably more or less culture-bound. For example, a mental status examination commonly asks, "Who is the President of the United States?" or "What are the four seasons?" Each of those questions relies on local knowledge. In tropical climates, there are different concepts of seasons. Thus, a first requirement for a psychological test is that its content acknowledges the culture of the client, if the counselor is to make generalizations about the client's mental status.

If items on a test seem to be particularly culture-bound, counselors should go over the specific items with clients instead of relying on simple summary scores. For example, a recent immigrant from the Middle East who is taking the

Self-Directed Search (Holland, 1990) might not know what a "Human Relations course" is or "income tax forms" are, or even what "the Red Cross" is.

A second concern about the validity of tests for all populations is their standardization on particular populations. A counselor should note the group on which a test was normed. If tests are used to make predictions about the future (e.g., how well a person will perform on a job), they must show that they predict accurately for all groups.

The Use of Tests. In addition to determining the validity of tests, it is also important for counselors to monitor the use of test results. Such results affect educational and career opportunities for clients. For example, aptitude and achievement tests have been used to strictly assign students into lower and higher academic tracks in school. This assignment early in life can have long-term consequences for students of color and for lower-class students. This "cumulative deficit problem" (Deutsch, 1967) evolves in this way:

> At the very outset of their educational careers, on the basis of low test results, these students are placed in classes for poor performers; when they fail to make progress, which is again measured in terms of tests not geared for them, they fall further and further behind their white [and middle-class] peers. (Samuda, 1998, p. 9)

When counselors see members of one ethnic group disproportionately placed in lower-level tracks, they must raise questions about such tracking.

Guidelines for Culturally Alert Testing

Counselors might apply the following "test for culturally valid tests" (Paniagua, 2005, p. 126) by asking these questions:

Content Equivalence. Are the items relevant for the cultures being tested? Items featuring dominant-culture customs, games, or history may be less meaningful or unknown to members of nondominant cultures.

Semantic Equivalence. Is the meaning of each item the same in all cultures that are being tested? Some terms have different connotations or meanings across cultural lines; for example, in Ireland and Britain, the word "bonnet" refers to the part of a car that covers the engine.

Technical Equivalence. Is the method of assessment comparable across cultures? Sole reliance on verbal questioning may disadvantage individuals from nondominant cultures who rely more heavily on nonverbal communication.

Criterion Equivalence. Would the interpretation of variables remain the same when compared with the norms for all cultures studied? Desired levels of measured variables, such as "autonomy" or "masculinity," may be specific to the dominant culture. Their values may not be shared by nondominant cultures.

Conceptual Equivalence. Does the test measure the same theoretical construct across cultures? A construct such as "self-esteem" in an individual from a culture that reinforces modesty and collective identity may result in inaccurate interpretation of the results. (p. 126)

Paniagua (2005) asserts that no existing psychological test meets all five criteria. Counselors should use the least-biased instrument available. They should also complement such tests with culture-specific assessments, including assessing socioeconomic factors in test performance and asking culturally appropriate questions—all in the client's preferred language (Paniagua, 2005; Pedersen, 2004).

THEME THREE: INTERVENTION

The third theme in culturally alert counseling is, of course, actual intervention. In addition to being accessible and doing culturally sensitive assessment, counselors must help clients make positive changes in a culturally intentional way. Intervention is, of course, the heart of the work of the counselor. Therefore, this chapter recommends specific culture-inclusive intervention practices.

This section is organized around five types of strategies for culturally alert intervention. First, methods are presented for addressing internalized oppression, namely, evoking cultural strengths and doing liberation counseling. The second overall strategy is adapting common clinical interventions to cultural diversity. The third is utilizing the narrative approach in order to incorporate culture into counseling. The fourth strategy is advocacy. The fifth is using or referring to indigenous healing practices.

Intervention Strategy One: Challenging Internalized Oppressions

A primary task of the culturally alert counselor is to help all clients free themselves from self-limiting attitudes based on cultural membership. Both dominants and nondominants can suffer from limiting internalized cultural assumptions. For example, males can be captives of cultural stereotypes, as can females.

It is especially important, however, for counselors to assist clients from nondominant cultures to challenge their self-limiting internalized oppressions. Examples of such inaccurate negative self-perceptions include believing that one's group can't achieve academically, can't take on leadership roles, is less competent, is immoral, is less attractive, has an inferior culture, or should be second class. Two means of challenging internalized oppression are presented here: The first is strengths-oriented counseling; the second is applying liberation counseling.

Emphasizing Cultural Strengths. Throughout the chapters in this book, reference has been made to the positive dimensions of all cultures. Not all clients believe in the strengths of their cultures. A strengths focus is particularly important for nondominant group members in light of the fact that (1) in general, counseling often focuses on deficits and (2) dominant cultures have often viewed themselves as superior.

In the latter regard, the hegemony of European American, Christian, male, and middle-class standards in the United States leads to the denigration of other cultural groups. The terms "internalized colonization" (Said, 1994) and "auto-colonialism" (Utsey, Bolden, & Brown, 2001) have been used to describe oppressed peoples' acceptance of the dominant culture's ideology. Thus, for example, women are autocolonized when they devalue their gender-related tendencies, such as cooperativeness and nurturing, seeing them as less valid than traditional male standards of autonomy and competition (Belenky et al., 1986; Gilligan, 1982). Similar self-denigration has occurred throughout the world when particular ethnic groups have been oppressed. It is expressed in oppressed peoples' embarrassment at languages, accents, physical appearances, clothing, and names, to mention a few examples.

Counselors can counter oppression by explicitly helping clients discover their cultural strengths (Ancis, 2004a; Constantine, 2006; Miville & Ferguson, 2006). Such strengths exist in every culture. In particular, an overarching strength of nondominant cultures is their resilience in the face of daily oppression and discrimination. They have made adaptations, such as religious gatherings and traditions; code languages; musical expressions; and strong, positive attitudes that allow them to thrive despite ongoing oppression.

There are also more generic strengths of cultures, of course. In previous chapters, cultural strengths of each group were mentioned. For example, in Chapter 5, the African American cultural strengths of resilience, flexibility, persistence, extended family, religiosity, and forgiveness were named. In Chapter 7, American Indian cultural strengths such as belonging, generosity, and tradition were evoked. In Chapter 9, Middle Eastern American strengths that were presented include extended family support and expression through dance.

Cultural strengths searches can also be done for members of dominant cultures because they may have discarded some elements of their culture, or only see the oppressive dimensions of their culture. The men's movement has attempted to reclaim aspects of men's culture. Members of Northern European American ethnic groups can similarly find strength in such values as individualism and the work ethic. White Southerners can identify with white Southern civil rights activists, rather than with the oppressors. Thus, counselors can help any client find and build on cultural strengths.

The counselor might bring out such strengths in at least three ways. First, a simple positive cultural asset search might suffice to bring out cultural strengths. This asset search can be done by simply asking the client, "What positive qualities do you see in your ethnic group, gender, social class, sexual orientation, or religion?" The counselor can also suggest some strengths based on her or his knowledge of the client's life and cultures. Activity 16.3 can serve as a guide.

A more explicit way of evoking cultural strengths is the Guided Imagery Using Positive Cultural Symbols Activity (Ivey, D'Andrea, Ivey, & Simek-Morgan, 2002). During a counseling session, clients imagine a positive cultural symbol, such as a stained glass window, a revered ethnic figure, or a sacred place,

---

ACTIVITY 16.3

Cultural Strengths Search

In order to help clients find strengths, it is helpful for the counselor to have discovered her or his own cultural assets. Consider your ethnic or regional culture(s). Think about the values, humor, habits, norms, and other cultural expressions. List as many positive assets of your culture(s) as you can. This exercise is best completed after you have had a chance to read and think about your culture, perhaps through an ethnicity self-awareness project.

Some of the strengths of my culture:

In work: _____

In humor: _____

In interpersonal support (e.g., family, networks): _____

In leisure/recreation: _____

In arts: _____

In the community/neighborhood: _____

In cultural artifacts, places, or symbols that can evoke pride and strength: _____

In activities: _____

Other areas of strength: _____

---

with their eyes closed. Later, outside the session, they can mentally access that symbol when they experience doubts and difficulties. See Box 16.3 for this Guided Imagery Activity that counselors can use to help clients to identify their cultural strengths.

A final cultural strengths activity is to have clients create a "community genogram" (Holcomb-McCoy, 2005; Paniagua, 2005; Rigazio-DiGilio, Ivey, Grady, & Kunkler-Peck, 2005). In the community genogram, clients make a chart of people and places from their community of origin or current community so that they might see the context that gives them strength.

Liberation Counseling. Psychotherapy as liberation (Ivey, 1995), here called liberation counseling, directly helps client to challenge both internal and external limitations. In Ivey's (1995) words, psychotherapy as liberation aims at helping clients "see how their difficulties are the logical result of social history" (p. 54). With that knowledge, clients might then be able to consider what relationship they wish to have with their cultures of origin and what aspect of their difficulty is due to external oppression. In a sense, liberation counseling is a way of helping clients to have more choices about their relationship to their cultures.

BOX 16.3   Guided Imagery With Positive Cultural Symbols

The following exercise is designed to help clients recognize and use strengths from their cultural background. When employed carefully, using concrete language, the exercise also can be effective with children.

Inform your client about your process and intent. Rather than surprise the client, tell her or him what is about to happen and why it is potentially helpful.

Generate an image. Ask your client to relax and then to generate a positive image that can be used as a resource. Suggest that the image be related to cultural background. A black person might imagine a picture of an African or African American hero, a Navajo a mountain or religious symbol, an Egyptian the pyramids, a Chinese person Confucius, and so on.

Focus on the image. Ask the client to see the image in her or his mind. What does she or he see, hear, feel? Ask the client to locate the positive feelings in the body. Then identify that image and feeling as a positive resource that is always available to the client.

Take the image to the problem. Using relaxation and free association techniques, guide the client to the problem that has previously been discussed or to any problem the client chooses. Suggest to the client that he or she use the positive resource image to help work with the problem. It is important to stress to the client that the image may or may not solve the problem. If the problem seems too large, the image should be used to work on a small part of the problem rather than to solve it.

SOURCE: Adapted from Ivey et al. (2002).

Liberation counseling strategies are tied to the client's cultural identity level, or stage. They aim to enhance their cultural identity development, when that seems appropriate, given clients' life situations. It is not the counselor's job to "force" changes in cultural identity on clients. The decision to engage in liberation work must be made in consultation with the client, based on client needs and cultural context. Liberation counseling can give clients more choices. However, in some contexts, so-called liberation might increase frustration and disconnection from the client's community. For example, Garrett McAuliffe once worked with a woman from a conservative Islamic culture who was an international student in the United States. Her increasing awareness of Western feminism led to frustration. She recognized that when she returned to her country, she might be ostracized for taking on a more equal role with men. In this case, the counselor helped her to weigh her behavioral options, rather than merely encouraging her to forge a public feminist identity in her country. For some clients, it is difficult to return "home" after certain liberating experiences (Montgomery, Marbley, Contreras, & Kurtines, 2000).

Ivey (1995) describes five cultural identity levels (or stages) to guide the counselor. The stages that Ivey uses parallel those of the Cultural Group Orientation Model (CGOM) from Chapter 1. In the following discussion, the first two stages (Naïveté and Acceptance) have been combined because they share many characteristics, yielding four stages. Each stage has accompanying counselor actions that might move the client along in her or his development. It should be noted that a person is never fully "in" a stage of cultural identity. Instead, a person uses thinking from a number of stages, likely centered on one way of thinking (Middleton, Erguner-Tekinalp, & Petrova, 2005).

In order to illustrate liberation counseling at each stage, the case of a woman who has been living in an abusive situation with her husband and two children is presented.

Naïveté/Acceptance

Clients who are "Naïve" or "Acceptant" are unaware of their culture and its effects on their opportunities and limitations. In the case of the woman who was in an abusive partnership, she at first merely accepted that she, as a woman, was powerless due to financial dependence and internalized notions that a woman "needs" to be married. She did not consider the gender factor in her experience nor think about how to empower herself.

In liberation counseling, the counselor would *encourage her to first describe her experience in concrete terms*, thereby transforming her story from inchoate physical expressions, such as stomach disorders, anxiety, and anger, into a story that is partially outside her sensory experience. The counselor can then *point out discrepancies as well as the cultural dimension:* "You say that he treats you well much of the time, but you are angry when he puts you down and raises his voice. Women sometimes get caught up in taking such abuse because of financial needs. Is that possibly what is going on for you?" Here, the gender issue is intentionally raised through culturally oriented questioning. The client is prepared to challenge any internalized oppressions, which might take the forms of self-blame, automatic receipt of a problematic status quo, and a sense of hopelessness.

Naming and Resistance

At this stage, a client has at least acknowledged that she has learned some behaviors as part of enculturation and is beginning to be aware that they might affect her life situation. At Ivey's "Naming and Resistance" stage (equivalent to "Encountering" in the CGOM in Chapter 1), a counselor might help the client to *explicitly name the contradictions between herself and society* through discussion in the session or via out-of-session reading or support groups.

The counselor then *encourages the client to gather resources,* so that she might have alternatives to her previous acceptant stance. She might read a book on gender roles, contact a lawyer who specializes in women's issues, meet with an advocate for women who have endured domestic violence, and see a financial counselor. By venturing down this road, the client will be taking the first steps toward separating herself from the automatic thinking of the Acceptance stage—that women must depend on men, that women cannot work on their own finances, that women must accept verbal and even physical abuse. The counselor can also help the client discover strong women role models and confirm the assets of women's culture.

Redefinition and Reflection

Through those beginning awareness activities, the client can move toward "Redefinition and Reflection" (the "Immersed" and "Reflective" orientations of the CGOM). Here, she becomes aware of her internal responsibility to rethink socially prescribed roles that are no longer acceptable. She is beginning to take a perspective on her culture rather than to be unthinkingly wedded to its social roles and internal prescriptions for thinking and acting in certain ways.

The counselor might then *affirm the growth* by saying, "I hear a strong voice in you that is saying, 'I'm not going to play out a powerless script as a woman. I can stand up for myself and for my children at the same time.'" The client at this stage might declare, "Yes. I called the women's advocate at the shelter and got great support and advice. I've hired a lawyer. I've learned a lot in a short time about finances. I've gotten support from friends. I'm not going to be a victim. The children and I can live well in this house without him, without his abusing us with his financial and physical power. I have met a group of women through the local college women's center who help each other be strong and assertive."

Multiperspective Integration

At the stage of Multiperspective Integration (called "Multicultural/Critically Conscious" in the CGOM), the client is now engaged in continually creating her cultural identity and is actively seeking multicultural experiences, including understanding men's issues. She can now move back and forth from reflection, to anger, to taking action, to taking some responsibility for her choices, to recognizing external barriers.

At this point, the counselor can *help the client take action for herself and others.* The counselor (or the client) can also *affirm progress* with a statement such as, "You have been advocating for other women by speaking with them about similar situations to the one you were in, and by speaking to men also. You recognize the trap that women can fall into—being caregivers to others while not taking care of themselves. You also realize that men are caught up in this gender context too, as they scramble to prove themselves by being breadwinners and being strong at the expense of being nurturing and relationship-oriented. But you know that is no excuse for abuse." The counselor can now help the woman make difficult but more intentional choices about career, family, and housing. She might now help others who are abused or who might be helped by rethinking gender roles.

This example has emphasized the internal transformation of one woman. The counselor can also work to change external oppressions, a topic that was discussed in Chapter 2 and is addressed later in this chapter. Activity 16.4 asks the reader to apply counseling strategies to a particular case.

Intervention Strategy Two: Adapting Common Counseling Approaches to Culture

Evoking cultural strengths is, therefore, a primary piece of work for the proactive, culturally alert counselor. The second set of methods is culture-specific adaptation of common counseling approaches.

In a review of the multicultural counseling literature, nine counseling practices emerged that have particular cultural implications: (1) authority and

---

ACTIVITY 16.4

Here is the case of Ronaldo. Read the case. Imagine him evolving through each of Ivey's (1995) cultural identity stages. Write suggestions for counselor or client activity at each stage.

Ronaldo is a working-class Mexican American man from rural western Texas who was heard to say, "I've never seriously considered going back to school in the field I'd love, school teaching. I've always just assumed, somehow, that was something out of my reach as a farm worker's son. I've never had high career aspirations. That's why I've always followed my friends, first into the Navy and now back here as a stockman in this department store. I just have to make a living. Plus, I don't know any Mexican Americans who have college degrees. And, I have an accent. I don't think I would be hired as a teacher."

Cultural Identity Stage Counselor and/or Client Activities That Might Promote Growth

Naïve/Acceptant:

Naming and Resistance:

Redefinition and Reflection:

Multiperspective Integration:

---

directiveness, (2) group work, (3) emotionality, (4) career, (5) the use of insight, (6) cognitive behavioral approaches, (7) use of humor, (8) positive reframing, and (9) bibliotherapy. Each will be discussed in turn.

Authority and Directiveness. Authority, directiveness, and solution focus in counseling are recommended with members of particular ethnic groups. While no universal and absolute generalizations can be made, there are some trends. It is suggested that counselors be more solution-focused and more directive in general with persons of lower socioeconomic status, Asians, Middle Easterners, and Latinos, as described in those particular chapters in this book. For example, in Chapter 6 on East and Southeast Asians, the authors propose that counselors are likely to be more successful if they selectively use authority with clients, in the form of directives and advice. With persons from low socioeconomic status, a practical and advisory role is often effective, rather than immediate exploration of inner psychological states.

Communicating one's expertise is also recommended when working with clients from hierarchical cultures. One way to help clients gain confidence in your capability early in the counseling relationship is to mention previous successes with similar clients or display degrees and certifications earned (see Chapter 6). This presentation of qualifications shouldn't be done in a bragging or overbearing way, however. Such strategies can appeal to those cultures' valuing of hierarchical relationships.

It is also recommended that counselors help such clients see some immediate, concrete benefits early in the counseling relationship (Sue & Zane, 1987). The solution-focused approach, which addresses immediate concerns in concrete fashion, would suit many members of those cultural groups.

The Use of Groups. Group work has cultural implications. Groups help clients connect with others; they are communities themselves. In fact, groups can be particularly important for European Americans, who often lack extended family and community support.

With people from more communitarian cultures, groups can reflect the existing community. For example, bringing the family—as defined by the client—into the work for Asian Americans and others, either for discussion or in sessions, is recommended (Ancis, 2004a; Kim, 2005; Vera et al., 2006; Wehrly, 2003).

Finally, nondominant group members might benefit from support groups in general because they can experience solidarity in such settings and reduction in feelings of isolation and powerlessness in the larger society (Day-Vines et al., 2003; Holcomb-McCoy, 2005). In addition, a group format can be used to promote understanding of diverse cultures and culturally sensitive interpersonal skills. For example, Simcox et al. (2006) suggest students from diverse cultural backgrounds can participate in a psychoeducational group at school, which can be called a "Friendship Group." A goal for group members is to learn about and practice using social skills that are appropriate for different cultures. The results could include the acquisition of positive social skills for all students, such as basic friendship-building tools, as well as enhanced openness to diversity and prevention of bullying and related social problems, such as ostracizing and teasing students from minority groups at the school.

Expression and Emotion. Physical and emotional expression vary according to ethnic group norms. In more emotionally restricted cultures, such as Northern European American cultures (McGoldrick & Giordano, 2005) and male culture in general, expressive approaches such as music, art, dance, or guided imagery can be liberating. They would balance those cultures' emphasis on rationalism and emotional control. Of course, expressive counseling methods would have to be folded in carefully, with clear trust established in the counseling relationship, for them to not scare those clients away.

Expressive counseling approaches are particularly inappropriate for cultures in which stoicism and reticence are seen as signs of psychological strength, such as in East Asian cultures, and should be avoided. See Chapter 6 for more on that topic.

Career Counseling. Career counseling strategies need to vary with culture. First, members of nondominant groups should not be discouraged from striving for nontraditional occupations. Such has been the case, as illustrated in

Chapter 4 by the case of a bright Latino youth who was directed toward a non-academic track.

Career is an especially complex area for women. Their career patterns can be quite varied during the lifespan as they balance multiple commitments. The lack of support for childcare in U.S. society makes many women's career lives stressful and disappointing. That pattern is reinforced by the stereotypes of males as breadwinners and high achievers. The existing gender ethos also discourages men from making nontraditional choices, such as childrearing and less lucrative occupations.

Another side of career is balancing work and other dimensions of life. For European Americans, it could be important to introduce the idea of balancing work, family, and leisure. Such a perspective can help to modify the extreme so-called Protestant work ethic that may drive European Americans to succeed at the expense of family and leisure.

Finally, some career counseling methods may need to be modified for ethnic groups. For example, naming achievements and skills is common practice in career counseling (e.g., Bolles, 2006). That practice can be countercultural for Asian clients, who value self-effacement.

The Use of Insight. A fifth issue in adapting counseling to particular cultural groups is the use of psychological insight. Some insight-oriented counseling approaches might not be helpful with particular groups. For example, psychodynamic approaches might be countercultural for Asians. Such methods often challenge the client to explore unresolved issues with family members or other significant figures in her or his early life. For traditional Asian Americans, who value avoiding family shame, such exploration might leave them feeling disloyal to their family.

Similarly, in the area of social class, a pure person-centered, insight-oriented approach might not be effective for many poor clients. Persons in the lower and working class often take a more direct and pragmatic approach to communication, whereas verbal communication and self-disclosure are highly valued in counseling work.

Applying Cognitive and Behavioral Approaches. Some voices in the professional literature also suggest that behavioral or cognitive behavioral therapies (CBT) show promise for work with people with non-Western cultural backgrounds (Ancis, 2004a; Harper & Stone, 2003; Paniagua, 2005; Pedersen, 2004; Ponterotto et al., 2006). Ponterotto et al. (2006) suggest that helping clients restructure their cognitions "is a powerful tool in the fight against prejudice and racism" (p. 157). Changing thinking patterns not only holds promise for ameliorating negative or undesired behavior, it also can be used to combat autocolonialism; that is, the internalization of oppression by the subjects of oppressive systems. In Paniagua's (2005) words,

> Many culturally diverse clinicians and researchers believe that behavioral approaches
> are probably the most effective strategies for the assessment and treatment of clients

from the four [non-European] cultural groups. . . . This is because these strategies are authoritative and concrete, and they emphasize learning focused on the immediate problem—all characteristics of treatment that members of these groups generally prefer. (p. 7)

Replacing negative, or dysfunctional, thoughts with positive, more functional ones can help clients access their inner strengths and their outer community and family resources. They can use these new ways of thinking to take action toward a culturally congruent positive change. However, there is a limit to the exclusive use of CBT with clients from nondominant groups; addressing only individual thinking leaves out the social dimension that affects clients' lives. In that vein, D'Andrea (2006) observes that CBT is "often less effective when used among persons of color who are adversely impacted by white racism" (p. 259). He proposes that any individually oriented counseling theory be complemented by advocacy, possibly involving interventions in the community, as described later in this chapter.

Use of Humor. Humor in the counseling process may increase trust and a sense of connectedness in the counseling relationship, lessen anxiety and discomfort, relieve stress, help clients cope with painful and/or oppressive situations, and assist clients to gain a new perspective on their concerns or situation (Garrett, Garrett, Torres-Rivera, Wilbur, & Roberts-Wilbur, 2005; Rayle, Chee, & Sand, 2006; Vereen, Butler, Williams, Darg, & Downing, 2006). Humor is esteemed by many cultures and can sometimes offer insight into a culture's perspective and values.

In general, humor is most appropriately utilized in the context of a trusting and respectful counseling relationship (Stone & Dahir, 2006). Four further caveats for the use of humor are needed, however. First, a counselor who is not a member of the client's cultural group should exercise caution in using humor about painful historical or current oppressive situations. What may be appropriate for members of the cultural group to joke about may be considered offensive coming from an "outsider." Second, the counselor should also be wary of sending a message that she or he is not taking the client's concerns seriously. Third, humor has the potential to mask issues that might be helpful for clients to explore. Fourth, humor can also be ill timed, seen as disrespectful, or irrelevant to the process at hand. It may be wise to wait for the client to initiate or invite the use of humor before a counselor engages in the use of therapeutic wit (Garrett et al., 2005). With the aforementioned cautions in mind, counselors are encouraged to educate themselves about cultural expressions of wit and consider using humor to enhance the effectiveness of the counseling process.

Positive Reframing. Reframing consists of looking at a seemingly negative client characteristic or relationship from a positive perspective (Ivey & Ivey, 2007). It is often a part of an overall strengths-based or empowerment strategy (Ancis, 2004a; Kim, 2005). Reframing an internalized concern by acknowledging the external pressures or oppressions involved in a situation might ameliorate the sense of shame some clients might feel about seeking assistance from a counselor. For example, a counselor could reframe the tension within an immigrant family as an understandable response to the difficulties of cultural transitions. Framing their concerns this way opens up the possibility of counseling as an empowering educational intervention, one that provides an opportunity for the client family to learn and educate themselves about more effective strategies.

Bibliotherapy. Bibliotherapy, that is, asking the client to read or watch culturally relevant material that might enhance her or his understanding, is recommended when counselors are familiar with a client's culture, acculturation status, and reading level. Clients' abilities to see themselves and their situation in a book or film is a key component of this counseling modality (McFadden & Banich, 2003; Wehrly, 2003). Given the vicarious nature of the experience, a client may experience this technique as a safer means of exploring important issues. Reading about or watching others deal with similar issues can also assist the client to normalize the feelings or concerns that she or he may be experiencing. The client may feel encouraged or empowered by learning about other people who successfully resolved comparable issues. Bibliotherapy is thought to be especially effective with visual (vs. auditory) processors (McFadden & Banich, 2003).

To implement bibliotherapy, once clients' issues are identified, a counselor can select culturally and developmentally appropriate material that is salient to the specific situation or client concern. The text or film can be read or watched together or given to the client as "homework." After the reading or viewing is done, the counselor and client should process the material by analyzing the content and applying it to the client's own situation. Such processing can prevent the possibility of the experience being miseducative. Discussion of the material chosen may be a catalyst for further discussion of culture and its impact on the presenting concerns.

One example of the use of bibliotherapy with a young individual or small group is reading the children's book *Amazing Grace* by Mary Hoffman. In the text, the lead character (an African American girl named Grace) lives with her mother and grandmother. In aspiring to play the lead in a school production of "Peter Pan," Grace experiences both racist and sexist remarks from peers. The story continues with Grace feeling initially discouraged, sad, and angry. With the help of her mother and "nana," Grace experiences success; she is empowered to believe that she can accomplish anything she sets her mind to. One can see several potent themes in this text that can be processed and applied to the lives of elementary school-aged youth.

Intervention Strategy Three: Applying the Narrative Approach to Culture

An approach to counseling that is particularly suited to cultural issues is narrative therapy. A fundamental notion in narrative therapy is that individuals experience the "realities" of their lives through the stories they tell about themselves, others, and life in general (White & Epston, 1990). In narrative-oriented counseling, culture is not seen as a variable that can be separated out for special attention; instead, it is the container in which meaning is forged. Thus, the stories that clients tell, and live, are infused with ethnicity, gender, class, religion, and other cultural meanings (Semmler & Williams, 2000). For this reason, the narrative therapy approach is especially well adapted for engaging persons who are struggling with cultural strictures that cause conflict.

Following is a brief description of narrative counseling. Narrative theorists begin by noting that the stories that clients bring to counseling are often "problem-saturated" (White & Epston, 1990). These stories are dominated by what is going wrong. A central theme of clients' narratives is often that the problems are expressions of their own inherent flaws.

A narrative counselor gently challenges this internalization of problems by helping clients to "externalize" the problems. The counselor treats such problems as socially constructed stories rather than their being "inside" the client. The counselor helps the client to see that these problem stories are constructed from cultural experience, as communicated by family, peers, her or his ethnic group, and others.

The Case of Eduardo. Following is an example of the narrative approach as it incorporates culture. A client named Eduardo reported that he suffered from panic attacks, agoraphobia, and general anxiety. From a narrative perspective, these "disorders" are seen as constructions of culture, in that the very language used to describe them and the meanings ascribed to those words are products of society. That description does not deny the physical experience of distress, but it offers Eduardo an alternate way of making sense of his experience, one that might be more helpful to him. Within Eduardo's family and ethnic group, let us suppose that fear and anxiety are seen as shameful. Eduardo has experienced powerful cultural stories in his second-generation Latino American family about not revealing vulnerable feelings, especially for males. As a result, he feels depressed, inadequate in the company of others, and emotionally isolated. Faced with negative conclusions about himself, Eduardo attempts to hide the anxiety from others and perhaps even from himself, and in so doing, also avoids seeking help. A narrative approach involves the counselor's joining Eduardo in constructing an alternative account of his experience.

Strategies for Narrative Counseling. For simplicity's sake, narrative counseling will be seen as having two overall processes:

The Current Story: Helping individuals name problems and their consequences and determining their foundations ("deconstructing").

The Alternative Story: Helping individuals story their lives around their preferred, more useful purposes, values, and commitments.

This depiction of two overall processes makes narrative counseling look more linear than it is in practice. To lay down a prescribed sequence beforehand would be to overlook the way that clients very actively shape the direction of the work. Narrative conversations can be seen as occasions for constructing new meanings, and clients are very active in the process. In that sense, narrative counseling is a "co-construction" of meaning by counselor and client together.

Nevertheless, these two overall processes can be helpful for characterizing the general flow of narrative counseling. It is probably fair to say that narrative conversations generally start with that first process, namely, counselors helping clients to dislodge problem stories from clients' sense of who they are. This separation of story from the person then "opens space" for the second process, that is, the counselor joining with clients in constructing accounts of their lives that are more in line with their preferences. What follows is a brief description of the narrative counseling process, with a highlight on cultural issues.

Phase One: The Current Story. In this phase, clients and counselors join in putting words to problems and in examining their effects. Problems are spoken of as separate from persons' identities, or "externalized." Externalizing problems makes it easier for the client to stand back and examine how the meanings of problems have arisen from the cultural context. This externalizing process has an interesting impact—the stories that once seemed like irrefutable "truths" begin to look more like influential cultural narratives.

The externalizing process mostly rests on careful questioning by the counselor. Here is a more explicit description of this first phase, with illustrations. It will be broken into three processes, which, again, are not necessarily sequential: (1) naming, (2) consequences, and (3) deconstructing the foundations. In the process, the story can be viewed as external to the client. It is a culturally induced story.

Naming

The client might first tell the problem story and give it a name. The story can then be treated as external to the client—a way that her or his community told a story that the client believed and acted on. In the case of Ayita, a working-class Cherokee woman from rural western North Carolina, the story was called, "The Reservations Story." It captured her mixed feelings—pride in her heritage but her feelings of holding herself back, especially career-wise, from engaging in the wider American culture. The aforementioned Eduardo called it "The Uncle Jorge's Macho Story," reflecting Eduardo's particularly stern and rigid uncle who mocked any signs of weakness in boys and men.

Consequences

A next step is to probe the existing consequences of the story. To evoke the negative power that the story has on the client's life, the counselor asks, "How is this problem affecting and/or interfering with your life/relationship(s)?" The counselor might further ask, "Does the problem have you do things that go against your better judgment?" In this process, the client becomes aware of how the problem story affects the perception the client has of herself or himself and of others, and how it limits her or his actions. Clients often realize at this point how the problem story limits them. Eduardo told of "suffering in silence," pretending he was "tough" (and getting into trouble with authorities), hiding his artistic inclinations, and putting other people down in order to feel superior. Ayita acknowledged at this point that she was unhappy with her career but was not exploring options due to her acceptance of the "reservations script." Ayita reported that she "squashed" any dreams of professional work in the problem story.

The counselor might now continue to probe the consequences of the problem story by encouraging the client to evaluate its effects. The counselor might ask, "Are you comfortable with the effects or not? Which effects are most distressing?" and "Why is this such a problem for you?" Eduardo was tired of the shame he felt for being who he was. Ayita found that "The Reservations Story" trapped her into feelings of powerlessness. She said, "As a result of this story, I am beholden only to what some others think I should do and be. How can I be loyal to my people and their traditions while pursuing my dreams?"

Deconstructing the Foundations

Another process is called "deconstruction." What has been constructed can be taken apart by looking at its foundations in a particular narrative. The foundations of the problem story can later be exposed as one particular construction among many possible ones.

Foundations of the Old Story

In order to the probe the foundations, the counselor can ask such questions as, "When and from what source did you first hear that (in Eduardo's case) men shouldn't reveal hurt or scared feelings?" or "When and from what source did you first hear (in Ayita's case) that women shouldn't aspire to professional work?" These probes bring forth the context of the problem story. In the social constructionist vein, these patterns are not seen as self-created. Instead, they are seen as familial or cultural in nature. In that vein, the counselor asks such questions as, "How did you get recruited into these ways of thinking/feeling/acting?" "Have you witnessed these ways of being in others?" and "If so, whose? And did these witnessings influence your ways of being?" Again, in this way, the cultural story is unearthed. Eduardo talked of his macho uncle, one who never married but lived with his elderly mother. That uncle had called him a "crybaby." Eduardo also recognized that the boys with whom he associated in his working-class neighborhood were from very disrupted home situations, unlike his, and that he was always uncomfortable being around these would-be "gangsters." He was recruited by those discourses. The counselor can further evoke the constructed foundations of the problem story with questions such as, "How come you had a vision that your experience had to be like this? That your identity had to be this one?" Ayita responded with, "All I knew were people who worked with their hands. Women cared for children. It was the only story I knew, except for what I saw on TV."

Foundations for a New Story

The counselor can then introduce "preferred possibilities" with the question, "What is your better judgment?" In response, Eduardo said, "I am not 'damaged goods.' I come from a loving, well-functioning family. I have fond memories of close family times in childhood. I have told myself this story of being 'damaged' because I am just sensitive to some things." He provided foundations for an alternative story with descriptions of his artistic talents, good friendships, and attractiveness to women. Ayita reported on her brilliance in math and science classes in high school and her continuing fascination with how nature worked. These clients' discoveries of their "better judgment" further challenged the problem story. The problem story is often based in a gender, ethnic, social, or other cultural class narrative.

In sum, naming the problem story, exploring its effects, and identifying the processes of recruitment to it undermine the essentialist fallacy that these stories are "reality." Non-narrative approaches might identify the client as "irrational," "inauthentic," or "neurotic." These initial processes provide a space for the client herself or himself to take a clear position on the problem and its effect on her or his life. In Kegan's (1982) terms, the client can have a relationship to her or his cultural stories, rather than being subject to them. By the client's identifying the preferred story, the counselor is freed from being put into the "convincing position" as expert.

What can instead be created, in the second phase of the work, is an identity that is apart from the now-externalized problem.

Phase Two: The Alternative Story. The second major process of narrative counseling proceeds from the naming and deconstructing of the problem story. In this "re-storying" phase, the counselor helps the client to explore alternatives to the dominant stories. The client brings out aspects of her or his life that have not been overwhelmed by or "dictated to" by the problem, experiences that don't fit the dominating patterns that surround the problem.

These aspects often consist of exceptions (e.g., when the person felt competent, or worthy, or acted assertively). Eduardo remembered the power of revealing his fears to a friend and the help that a high school counselor had offered. He also thought of how he felt good about his "sensitive" side—the part that liked music, poetry, and reading. Ayita remembered having career dreams, passionate interests, and ideas of her own on many occasions. She further remembered her intelligent responses in science discussions in high school.

Discovering New Foundations

Part of the process of re-storying is to reclaim the foundations of the old story in new ways. New foundations are sought in alternative family or ethnic models, or in seeking new stories about one's group. The counselor asks, "How can you know that things could be different from the original problem story you told?" Eduardo might tell of his father's gift for music and his sentimentality about movies. He might think of a valued high school teacher who passionately expressed feelings and words. He thought of Latino Americans who modeled non-stereotypical masculinity. In the case of an African American woman who is feeling powerless in her professional context, it might be "I saw powerful, competent African American women at my school and in my church. Plus I think about Maya Angelou and Oprah Winfrey, both of whom I saw on television recently."

This part of the work is extensive. It parallels the "Working" stage of counseling (Ivey & Ivey, 2007; Neukrug, 2002). In the case of Ayita, the counselor helped her discover the stories of women who thought for themselves and held professional careers. She remembered a woman from another part of the reservation who went to college and entered law school. She learned about her grandmother's friend, who had protested the sending of native people to Indian boarding schools in the early 1900s. More important, she remembered times when she herself had dreams of a career as a veterinarian. She also remembered how well she did academically in most subjects and how effective she had been in high school as a horse trainer. Eduardo thought about people who could seek help; he had seen men in movies go to therapists. He participated in a support group for people with anxiety problems and noted the willingness of the men in the group to reveal their feelings. He read about panic disorder and noted the possible biological dimension for it, helping him to consider a medical consult.

The narrative counselor lets the client decide whether the alternative story is positive or negative and asks the client, "Why is it positive or negative?" Again, the counselor doesn't evaluate or justify. The client finds aspects of her or his experience that are constructive and the counselor asks, "How have these achievements contributed to your life?" Eduardo found his delight in "deep conversations" with others and his "soaring" when moved by great art. They formed a new story that he called "La Historia Masculina Fuerte del Artista" ("The Strong Male Artist Story"). Ayita found her academic success and her voracious interest in biology to be sources of satisfaction and pleasure. She relished stories of American Indians' relationship to nature and saw herself as carrying on that tradition in new ways. She called the new story "Ayita: A Native Woman of Science."

At this point in narrative counseling, clients might fully recognize that cultural dimensions are the foundations for the stories that they have told. Parts of the cultural stories might be useful; others can be discarded. The client is asked to find other examples of alternative cultural stories and to include them as elements of the alternative plot. In the process, the client decides the foundation for a story that works; the counselor does not advise. Activity 16.5 offers the opportunity for the reader to work through narrative counseling with a partner.

Intervention Strategy Four: Advocacy

As was emphasized in Chapter 2, the historical roots of the counseling field are in empowerment and advocacy work (e.g., Frank Parsons's initiatives). Clients' difficulties are not "all in their heads." Counselors must acknowledge the real

ACTIVITY 16.5

Trying Out the Narrative Approach

After reading the following sections, work with a partner who tells of a discrepancy or conflict in her or his life that can possibly be related to ethnicity, social class, gender, sexual orientation, or religion. Go through each of the processes of narrative counseling to work on the discrepancy, seeking out the client's cultural stories that contribute to the problem story and that can contribute to alternative stories.

The Problem Story

A. **Give the problem story a name.**

B. **Probe the consequences of the problem story by encouraging the client to evaluate its effects. Ask the client the following:**

How is this problem affecting and/or interfering with your life/relationship(s)?

What has the problem talked you into/convinced you of about yourself and others?

Does the problem have you doing things that go against your better judgment?

What is your better judgment?

Are you comfortable with the effects or not? Which effects are most distressing?

Look for the foundations of the problem story.

When did you first hear that [fill in the theme of the problem story]?

How did you get recruited into these ways of thinking/feeling/acting (including ethnic, religious, gender, and social class bases for the story)?

How come you had a vision that experience had to be like this or that your identity had to be this one?

Have you witnessed these ways of being in others? If so, who?

Did these witnessings influence your ways of being?

Re-storying (Reclaiming the foundations of the old story in new ways)

How can you know that things could be different from the original problem story you told? (Probe for foundations for a new story; e.g., people in the client's life or awareness who demonstrate a different story.)

What is an alternative story? When did you witness such an alternative story for your [gender, ethnic group, social class, etc.]?

Help the client decide whether the alternative story is positive or negative and ask the client, "Why is it positive or negative?"

impact of prejudice and oppression on clients' lives. Counselor actions that can promote social justice are subsumed here under the umbrella concept of advocacy. Advocacy was introduced in Chapter 2 in the discussion of social justice.

What Is Advocacy? Advocacy is the act of empowering individuals or groups through actions that increase self-efficacy, remove barriers to needed services, and promote systemic change. Advocacy calls counselors to incorporate an activist function into their role as helper. McGoldrick (1998) declares that the counselor is part of the problem unless she or he is actively working against inequities.

Advocacy is a broad notion that takes many forms; however, in all types of advocacy, counselors are asked to support clients and groups who have less power in society—to alter, in D'Andrea's (2000) words, "those environmental conditions that adversely impact clients' psychological health" (p. 14). Advocate can mean spokesperson, supporter, pleader, defender, empowerer, intercessor, proponent, change agent, mediator, collaborator, monitor, petitioner, coordinator, ombudsperson, expediter, promoter, protector, instigator, investigator, and exposer.

The Expectation for Advocacy. Counselors cannot close their eyes and minds to the need for advocacy. Counseling "business as usual" is a handmaiden to the status quo. It is oblivious to sociopolitical and economic factors. That kind of counseling is not effective nor ethical. Herlihy and Watson (2003) make the case in this way:

> The traditional one-on-one, in-the-office approach may have limited value with clients whose problems originate in social discrimination and oppression. Counselors operating as advocates, social change agents, and consultants can help minority clients learn skills they can use to interact successfully with various forces within their community. The client and counselor, working together collegially, can address unhealthy forces within the system and design prevention programs to reduce the negative impact of discrimination and oppression. (p. 368)

The literature is replete with calls for counselors to effectively assume advocacy roles (Ancis, 2004b; Constantine, 2006; Day-Vines et al., 2003; Kim, 2005; Roysircar, 2006; Simcox et al., 2006; Smith et al., 2004; Vera et al., 2006).

The Need for Advocacy. Some oppression is subtle. For example, many clients from nondominant cultural groups see few people who look like them in positions of power and prestige, or encounter few people who look like them anywhere in the workplace, school, or street. Each of these can be considered an external factor that clients must deal with, rather than a psychological "weakness" or a lack of coping ability. Of course, there are also more obvious oppressions, such as job discrimination and social exclusion. These need to be acknowledged and addressed, not ignored or minimized, by counselors. Box 16.4 provides some examples of everyday situations that call for advocacy.

BOX 16.4   Examples of Situations Needing Advocacy

School/agency décor and events that do not represent people of color or are not accessible to persons with disabilities

African American males receiving disproportionately harsh sentences and being overrepresented in jails and prisons (as well as the phenomenon of this same group receiving a disproportionate number of discipline referrals and harsher consequences in schools)

One religion being over-represented in a public display or in an organization's symbols, décor, or invocations

Schools in lower socioeconomic status neighborhoods and/or with a higher percentage of people of color having fewer resources, inadequate facilities, and a higher percentage of underqualified teachers

De facto segregation in public school activities or in parent-teacher associations, for example, due to the cost of extracurricular materials and private lessons or leadership being an exclusive domain of folks from the dominant and privileged culture

Inadequate services for students with learning disabilities or those who are lower-achieving

An inordinate percentage of students from dominant groups in counselor training programs and/or special education

Counselors choosing to work in affluent agencies and schools and/or running exclusive practices for only dominant group and/or affluent clients

Student harassment, for example, anti-gay slurs, without prevention programming or school policies that are enforced or have effective consequences

Imbalance in academic tracking, such as racial imbalance in special education, advanced classes, and in gifted and talented programs

The absence of a ramp for the disabled at an entrance to a building or nearby curb

Exclusion of students, women, younger staff members, or support staff from decision making

African Americans being diagnosed for schizophrenia at twice the rate of whites (and Latino/Latinas at a 50 percent greater rate), regardless of income or education levels (Paniagua, 2005).

Each of the situations in Box 16.4 requires counselors to ask difficult questions and to take risks.

The culturally alert counselor must be oriented not only to overt acts of discrimination and oppression but also to instances of institutionalized racism and to the daily stresses involved in being a member of a nondominant group. In order to be effective and culturally competent, counselors must recognize the impact of racism, sexism, ableism, heterosexism, and other forms of oppression on clients. In action, they must validate those experiences (Ancis, 2004a; Constantine, 2006; Liu, Hernandez, Mahmood, & Stinson, 2006).

While the work of counseling usually focuses on the act of interpersonal helping, there are more proactive and systemic interventions that counselors are called to do, including organizational and community advocacy. The culturally alert counselor needs to engage in any or all of those roles when an individual or systemic injustice is present. Toward that end, counselors have the assistance of a guiding framework. The American Counseling Association (ACA) developed a set of 43 "Advocacy Competencies" in six domains (see Appendix B).

An examination of the competencies makes the scope of advocacy skills more clear. Interventions range from individual empowerment to collaborating with or supporting allies to effect systemic change. Counselors work both *for* and *with* clients, depending on the need. At times, counselors act on behalf of clients (with the goal to also teach self-advocacy skills so clients are empowered to advocate for themselves). At other times, counselors collaborate with clients and allies for individual and/or systemic concerns.

Advocacy can take place on the individual level, in which case it is called case advocacy, or the group level, in which case it is called class advocacy.

Advocate as Ally. One way to conceive of the role of advocate is as an ally (Washington & Evans, 2000). An ally is a member of a dominant group who acts to counter oppression, in the belief that such action benefits everyone in a society. Allies take a stand against social injustice by speaking and acting against oppressive patterns. If counselors are members of a dominant group, they recognize their privilege and take responsibility to learn more about the unearned benefits of this privilege and the contrasting oppressions for members of nondominant groups. They then use their privilege and skills to take risks to change inequity.

Almost everyone can be an ally at some point for those in nondominant groups. An African American male can be an ally for women, a heterosexual woman can be an ally for lesbians and gay men, and an able-bodied Latino/Latina person can be an ally for individuals with a disability.

The Personal Requirements for Advocacy. Advocacy can be a particularly difficult role for counselors. Counselors are often not inclined, by personality or training, to engage in political and institutional advocacy. Many counselors are primarily attracted to the interpersonal and emotional dimensions of experience. Advocacy, therefore, requires many counselors to "stretch" beyond their comfort zone.

Another reason advocacy can be difficult is that it may be received negatively by those in power. At times, people may feel fearful, confused, or threatened and will react defensively to counselors' advocacy efforts. In those cases, counseling training can be put to good use in addressing concerns. Even with such training one should expect resistance, however. As Frederick Douglass observed, power does not cede its privilege easily, and the work can be taxing. The counselor who would be an advocate should seek support, guidance, and supervision. Such support can help prevent ineffectiveness and feelings associated with burnout.

A number of personal qualities are needed for advocacy. They include a positive, integrated cultural identity of one's own; non-defensiveness; and persistence. Each will be discussed in turn.

Counselors who would be advocates must first feel good about their own social group memberships and feel some pride in their own identity before they can overcome the fear to take the risks needed for nondominant groups (Griffin, 2005). The white person who is resentful of opportunities for people of color cannot be an effective ally. The Christian who has a defensive attitude about the standing of her or his religion cannot be an ally for non-Christians.

Advocates must be non-defensive: They must "lean in" to ideas that challenge their current positions. Allies are consistent in that way; they are willing to be confronted about their own behavior and attitudes because they are committed to rectifying inequities.

Finally, when a strong cultural identity is achieved, the potential advocate must appreciate the unglamorous persistence that advocacy requires. Griffin (2005) notes that advocates must understand that social change is not a single event but a lifelong process that involves learning from mistakes and trying again.

Methods for Engaging in Advocacy. Particular methods for being an advocate will be highlighted here. First, the simple act of asking challenging and difficult questions about practices is discussed. Then suggested strategies for specific types of advocacy are presented.

Asking Challenging Questions

Advocacy asks the counselor to unveil the daily and hidden slights, make the familiar unfamiliar, or help the seemingly certain and fixed oppressive practices to be questioned and ameliorated. Culturally alert counselors can begin by asking some of the following critically conscious questions about who is served and how they are served by their organizations and by society:

- What are the beliefs, assumptions, and values behind a particular policy, structure, action, or orientation?

- If we act according to the identified beliefs, who prospers? Who loses? Who is disempowered or dehumanized?

- What do the disaggregated data show us in terms of patterns of inclusiveness and/or oppression?

- How can we make a given situation more equitable and democratic?

- How can we encourage a diversity of views and alternatives?

- Who is included in the decision-making process (e.g., hiring, selection, policy making)?

Advocacy on the Organizational Level

Oppression does not play out just on the societal or individual levels. In between lies the zone of organizations. Individuals belong to some combination of workplaces, educational institutions, recreation centers and community clubs, religious groups, and work units. Those institutions can be characterized in terms of their exclusiveness or inclusiveness, their monoculturalism or their multiculturalism.

Box 16.5 presents a model of multicultural organizational development. Like all developmental models, it offers a guide for change. At each stage, specific advocacy actions can be taken to help an organization become more multicultural. In their model, called Stages of Multicultural Organizational Development, Jackson and Holvino (1988) spell out six levels of exclusiveness or inclusiveness. The model is useful for counselors who would create a more inclusive school, agency, college, or department. Counselors can use it to assess the current multicultural status of organizations and to set goals for helping organizations to become more inclusive. To do so would be to act systemically, that is, on multiple dimensions of a group, rather than only on an individual or subgroup. Such systemic action can be larger and have more lasting impact than individual interventions. Activity 16.6 asks the reader to speculate about the multicultural stance of specific organizations.

BOX 16.5   Jackson and Holvino's (1988) Stages of Multicultural Organizational Development

Stage 1: *The Exclusionary Organization* is devoted to maintaining dominance of one group over other groups based on race, gender, ethnicity, or other social identity characteristics (e.g., the males-only country club, the white supremacist organization).

Stage 2. *The Club* stops short of explicitly advocating anything like one group's supremacy but does seek to maintain the privilege of those who have traditionally held social power (e.g., the exclusive business club).

Stage 3. *The Compliance Organization* is committed to removing some of the discrimination inherent in the "club" by providing access for members of nondominant groups. However, it accomplishes this objective without disturbing the structure, mission, and culture of the organization (e.g., some private schools). If a person from a nondominant group is hired, she or he must be a "team player" and not openly challenge the organization's practices, such as admissions or board memberships.

Stage 4. *The Affirmative Action Organization* is also committed to eliminating the discriminatory practices and inherent "riggedness" of the Stage 2 club by actively recruiting nondominant group members, that is, ones who are typically denied access to organizations. All organization members are encouraged to think in non-oppressive manners. However, members are still required to conform to the norms derived from the dominant group's worldview (e.g., many liberal religious denominations).

Stage 5. *The Redefining Organization* is a system in transition. It is not just satisfied with being "anti-sexist," for example, but it is committed to examining all of its activities for their impact on all members' ability to participate in the success of the organization (e.g., some universities).

Stage 6. *The Multicultural Organization* reflects the contributions and interests of diverse cultural groups in its mission, operations, and product or service. It acts on a commitment to eradicate social oppression in all of its forms within the organization. Members of diverse groups are full participants. The organization follows through on broader external social responsibilities to eradicate oppression and educate others in multicultural perspectives (e.g., the Southern Poverty Law Center, Multicultural Student Services Organizations on a campus, the National Council for Community and Justice).

ACTIVITY 16.6

Name organizations that you perceive to be at each stage of the model described in Box 16.5.

The Exclusionary Organization:

The Club:

The Compliance Organization:

The Affirmative Action Organization:

The Redefining Organization:

The Multicultural Organization:

When they engage in class advocacy on the organizational level, counselors cast a socially critical eye on the routines and rituals of their organizations. They uncover oppressive conditions that might otherwise be ignored. For example, counselors can examine client admissions and intake processes, programs offered and not offered, evaluation practices, professionalization models, allocation of resources, and decision-making processes in order to discover the patterns and sources of legitimacy. They would further support continuous subjecting of an organization's methods to critical inquiry.

Advocacy on the Community Level

Beyond the individual and organizational levels, counselors are further challenged to intervene in the larger community sphere. This is a type of class advocacy that is sometimes called "citizen advocacy." It includes such acts as volunteering outside one's professional role to mentor youth, lobbying for civil rights laws or more inclusive policies, participating in events for oppressed groups, or encouraging community groups to be more inclusive. In Box 16.6 there is a description of an actual community advocacy project.

Specific Advocacy Actions

Advocacy can be done in small ways as well as large ways. In addition to the interventions and strategies listed throughout this chapter, following are examples of actions that can be taken in five settings: home and family, school or college, workplace, house of worship, and community. They are derived from the Anti-Defamation League's work on "101 Ways to Combat Prejudice" (http://www.adl.org) and the Southern Poverty Law Center's "101 Tools for Tolerance"(http://www.tolerance.org). Both are available as brochures. Another excellent resource for educational issues is The Education Trust at http://www2.edtrust.org/edtrust. It features a wealth of examples of "success" stories as well as incisive analysis of

> ## BOX 16.6 The Give Kids Their Chance Project
>
> A powerful example of class advocacy is the *Give Kids Their Chance Project*. With a modest budget from a nonprofit group, Dr. Karen Eriksen established an after-school enrichment program for children and parents from a poor urban neighborhood. She built a collaborative program that involved a university, a school principal, a school counselor, teachers at the school, the PTA, parks and recreation, and local clergy and their churches in recruiting at-risk second graders in an urban, African American, Title I school and their parents for weekly mentoring, reading assistance, and music and art experiences. She recruited undergraduate and graduate counseling interns to administer the program and to be available to offer individual and family counseling and psychoeducational groups (job skills and placement and "build your child's self-esteem"). She recruited undergraduate human services students who were required to participate in service learning experiences to work one-to-one as mentors. Onsite at the local school, the children participated in music and art while the parents discussed difficulties and successes in parenting. The mentors tutored the children in reading and generated various age-appropriate activities for the children to participate in. Awards and celebrations were provided, turning late afternoons from unstructured time to loosely structured learning and esteem-building experiences.

educational inequities. The counselor is advised to try a few of the recommended actions. Here are some examples in each category of the brochure:

Begin at Home

- Speak out against jokes and slurs that target people or groups. Silence sends a message that you are in agreement. It is not enough to refuse to laugh.
- Appreciate and model enthusiasm for differences in people, including the abilities and disabilities each of us brings to the table of life.
- Give a multicultural doll, toy, or game as a gift.

In Your School or College

- Initiate classroom discussions of terms such as anti-Semitism, racism, homophobia, sexism, exclusion, and bias. Then compose a list of definitions and post it in a prominent place.
- Encourage representation of all students and/or families on every board, committee, group, publication, or team.
- Participate in activities that expand the role of the counselor—particularly in K–12 schools—so that counselors have opportunities to guide school efforts focused on social injustice.

In the Workplace

- Publish and distribute to all staff a list of ethnic and/or religious holidays and the meaning of the customs associated with celebrating them.
- Sponsor a mentoring program and reach out to colleagues from diverse cultures and to students in local schools.

- Fight against "just like me" bias—the tendency to favor those who are similar to ourselves.

- Advocate for domestic partner benefits.

In Your House of Worship

- Urge your leaders to use the pulpit to condemn all forms of bigotry.

- Encourage friends of other faiths to visit your religious services and share your religious knowledge with each other, without proselytizing.

In the Community

- Suggest to your local newspaper that it devote part of the editorial page each week or month to at least one opinion piece relating to anti-prejudice and pro-diversity themes. Advocate for diverse programming on local radio and television stations.

- Initiate conversations with school administrators to ensure that school policies and procedures are proactive on behalf of members of all social classes, ethnic groups, sexual orientations, ability levels, religions, and genders.

- Research your community's involvement in struggles for civil and human rights throughout history, and create an exhibit for the local library or city hall. Include a section on goals for creating a more inclusive community.

Advocacy, even as seen in the small acts named here, requires a consistent commitment to examining institutional arrangements that result in inequity. Small and large acts are all important. Thus, counselors can be comforted by knowing that their advocacy does not often result in major societal changes, although it can. The seemingly small acts described in such materials express the spirit of the Hebrew Talmud, which states, "It is not our job to finish the work, but we are not free to walk away from it."

Intervention Strategy Five: Indigenous Healing Practices

Ancient forms of physical, spiritual, and emotional healing are still practiced in many parts of the world, having survived cultural shifts and the introduction of Westernized mental health care. Even if counselors do not utilize such practices, they can know and appreciate the practices from clients' viewpoints.

The following section will introduce major culturally specific healing practices and traditions in order to increase counselor knowledge about these traditions. It is also hoped that the curiosity triggered by this section will lead to the reader learning more about such practices. Four categories of healing practices will be discussed next: African/Caribbean, Latin American, Asian, and American Indian. It should be noted that European traditional healing practices have largely given way to Western medical and scientific practices, although religious practices such as prayer and ritual are also healing traditions in the West; those are discussed in Chapter 15.

African/Caribbean. In the African tradition, much of which was carried over into the Caribbean, the most powerful healing is believed to come from the group itself and from spiritual connections, rather than by isolated effort alone and purely rational thinking. In the African/Caribbean tradition, it is hoped that those who are "afflicted" with both physical and emotional pain can find spiritual and community connections (Bojuwoye, 2005). Positive change is aided by relationships with the spirit world, specific healers, and rituals.

One of the core beliefs that is the baseline for many of the traditional African/Caribbean healing practices is the concept of animism—the idea that there is one spirit that animates the entire universe, living and non-living, material and supernatural alike. Those traditional practices have been translated into implicit and explicit approaches to healing today. In general, African American and Caribbean values tend to center on the parallel themes of community, religion, and petitionary prayer (Torres-Rivera, Garrett, & Crutchfield, 2004).

African/Caribbean cultures have many different types of traditional healers, each with her or his own specialty, focus, and methods:

- Herbalists use plants and herbs as healing agents.

- Fetish men provide amulets, potions, and lotions that are said to be natural beneficial healing sources.

- Mediums are those people who have the power to communicate with the spirit world.

- Sorcerers have the ability to control and manipulate another person's vital force and are often connected to black magic.

- Indigenous spiritual doctors, known as diviners, are seen as being connected to the universal therapeutic power. They use many of the same healing methods as the herbalists and fetish men, but also incorporate prayer and massage.

In the Caribbean, there are two particular types of healers, *shango* and *vodun.* Shango healers are thought to use communication with the spirits and dreams to find guidance for treating their patients. Shango healers also lead cleansings, a practice in which a wrongdoer spends seven or nine days in different churches. Vodun (also known as Vodoun, Voudou, and Voodoo) can be traced to the West African Yoruba people. Vodun is described by Marshall (2005) as "a socioreligious activity possessing magical features" (p. 76). It is especially practiced by Haitian Americans. Vodun priests focus on the relationship between the living and the dead because illness is seen as associated with evil spirits and curses. Therefore, healing comes from appeasing the dead. This practice involves dancing, offering gifts, and animal sacrifices (Marshall, 2005).

Since people from African-derived cultures, including African immigrants, are more likely to be connected to these types of healers, counselors should have a basic knowledge of all types and the location of such healers in the client's community (Vontress, 2005).

Latin American. In the Latin American tradition, illnesses are seen as having multiple, connected causes from each of the spheres of life: emotional, relational, material, supernatural, and organic. Illnesses are categorized as being either good or bad, hot or cold. They are often treated through both traditional indigenous methods and through prayer to Christian saints (Gonzalez-Chevez, 2005). Diagnosis of physical, emotional, and spiritual problems in the Latin American tradition is threefold: It is done through a combination of the patient's information, observations, and "magicoreligious processes" (Gonzalez-Chevez, 2005; Constantine, Myers, Kindaichi, & Moore, 2004). The latter processes may include the healer reading an egg, corn, or cards in order to discover into what category the illness falls and what the best healing method may be.

Traditional Latino diagnoses and treatments are often categorized as hot or cold. Cold conditions are treated with hot remedies, and vice versa. An example of hot conditions being treated with cold remedies would be hypertension (a "hot" condition) being treated with passionflower tea (a "cold" remedy). This method reflects the balance often seen in other traditional therapies, especially those derived from Asian and American Indian cultures (Jucket, 2005). Both mental and physical imbalance is often believed to be restored through *yerberia,* the ingestion of wild or domestic herbs (Constantine et al., 2004).

The traditional Latino healers are called *curanderos, espiritistas,* and *santeros. Curanderos* are individuals who are believed to have gained their power to heal directly from God. They involve family members in the curative process of using cleansing rituals and objects to heal by means of curanderos' own personal awareness of the suffering they can detect in those surrounding them. *Espiritistas* are believed to have the ability to communicate with spirits and the power to heal though this connection. They are considered mediums to the dead, rather than having a direct connection to a divine power. *Santeros* come from the religion of Santeria and are thought to be able to communicate with the saints and other spirits to resolve life situations (Constantine et al., 2004).

Asian. Within this subgroup there exist many different religions, types of spiritualities, and healing practices. In this section, the East Asian, South Asian, and Islamic traditions will be discussed. It is important to distinguish the traditions from each other and not make the mistake of overgeneralizing within the overall Asian population. The common theme among them all is the focus on the interconnectedness between the mind, body, and spirit (Yeh, Hunter, Madan-Bahel, Chiang, & Arora, 2004).

East and Southeast Asian healing methods are especially influenced by Chinese traditions. Those traditions focus on balance and the harmony of the earth, heavens, and people. The driving forces of the *qi* (pronounced "chi"), or vital energy, and the *li,* or order, are defined by the oppositional characteristics of the *yin* and *yang.* Yin and yang are also often described in terms of the balancing forces of hot and cold or male and female (Constantine et al., 2004; Jucket, 2005; Thobaben, 2004; Yeh et al., 2004). Each of these concepts and words describes the important concept of balance that is the primary goal for most indigenous healing in this cultural group. It is believed that mental illness comes from an imbalance of yin and yang in the qi (the body's vital energy) and in the blood of various organs in the body.

These imbalances can be managed and alleviated through acupuncture, yoga, herbal medicine, and Qigong, all of which help in the conscious directing of the qi (So, 2005; Tseng, 1999). Acupuncture involves inserting needles into specific pressure points in the body (Thobaben, 2004). Yoga consists of controlled movements of the body during meditation (Tseng, 1999). Herbal medicine is characterized by the prescribing of a combination of herbs and foods specific to each type of illness. Qigong is a series of controlled meditation-related physical movements. The triumvirate of Qigong, herbs, and acupuncture make up the three aspects of traditional Chinese medicine (Yeh et al., 2004).

In the South Asian (e.g., Asian Indian) tradition, there are two central concepts of mental health, *Ayurveda* and *Siddha.* The Ayurveda tradition sees mental health as directly related to dual harmonies: within oneself and with society. Mental illness is categorized by whether or not the illness is of mental or physical origin, as indicated by psychological or physical symptoms. It is treated through three methods: (1) purification through purging, enemas, or bleeding; (2) pacification through the use of ointments and ingestion of plant and/or metal combinations; or (3) changes in lifestyle and environment known as "the removal of the cause" (Kumar, Bhugra, & Singh, 2005). Treatment incorporates diet, meditation, herbal preparations, and other techniques aimed at reducing stress and tension and regaining harmony (Thobaben, 2004).

In the *Siddha* tradition, for mental health, there is a diagnosis of the person as a whole, using such methods such as pulse reading and urine examination. Treatment involves a restoration of equilibrium through cleansing or the application of oils and pressure on vital points (Kumar et al., 2005). In *Siddha,* there are two types of traditional healers, the shaman and the mystic. The shaman uses divine powers to heal through rituals, yoga, mantras, and exorcism. Mystics have unity with the deity and lead others to self-realization and transformation by example, showing the importance of sacrifice and life change through the model of their own lives (Kumar et al., 2005).

Islamic tradition holds that it is faith that protects against bad physical and mental health. As was discussed in Chapters 9 and 15, it is through faith that Muslims handle problems when they arise. It is believed that illness occurs by the will of Allah and that the pain will be felt in the heart because this is where the human psyche resides. Religious interventions are used to heal mental distress. These interventions include *sawm* (fasting), *taubah* (repentance), and the recitation of the Qur'an. Spiritual healers in this tradition focus on restoring the balance of energy within the body by working on the *lateefa,* or energy points (Inayat, 2005). It is believed that the *zar*, or evil spirit, is the cause of distress and disorders. The shamanic *zar* ceremony involves having both healer and client experience a dissociated state in hopes of purging the evil *zar* spirit. It is hoped that by purging this spirit through ceremony and sacrifice, balance in life can be restored (Tseng, 1999).

American Indian. Although a multitude of tribal nations compose the Native American population, there are beliefs and healing practices that are common to them all. Those practices include cultural narratives, ceremonies, and rites of passage. Native American practices are characterized by the themes of balance, harmony, and self-awareness.

In American Indian tradition, the healer is also seen as a leader or helper. The healer is someone who assists others to obtain balance and harmony. This person is seen as a guide, rather than an authority, and can be a mental, physical, natural, or spiritual leader (Garrett & Garrett, 2002). Ceremonies are used as a large part of the healing process in this culture. They are a way to maintain balance and harmony with oneself, the group, the environment, and the spirit world. Ceremonies include, but are not limited to, "sweat lodge, vision quest, clearing-way ceremony, blessing-way ceremony, pipe ceremony, sunrise ceremony, Sun dance, and the powwow" (Torres-Rivera et al., 2004, p. 299). The vision quest incorporates some of these ceremonies. In the vision quest, individuals concentrate their life energy though sweat lodges and herbal treatments, as well as learning from elder teachings, in order to more clearly define their life goals and experiences and their relationship with the universe (Constantine et al., 2004). It is through these group ceremonies, similar to the group ceremonies of the African tradition, that healing is found for the individual. In sum, for the majority of Native Americans, healing comes through introspection, balance with nature, and harmony with the group.

As counselors begin to see clients from cultures other than their own, it will become increasingly important to have a basic understanding of indigenous healing practices and what the concept of mental health means in these various cultures. In contrast to a prior rejection of the non-rational sphere by psychology, "issues of spirituality, divinity, the supernatural, god, and religion are once again appearing to surface in our consciousness. It seems reasonable, perhaps inevitable, that these issues will be apart of the healing process in the twenty-first century" (Moodley & West, 2005, p. xxi). It will be imperative for new counselors, as well as veterans, to become aware of and open to indigenous forms of healing.

Concluding Thoughts

This chapter has tried to bring together the current thinking on generally effective methods for culturally alert counseling. The search for "method" should not, however, overshadow the dynamic dimension of any counseling work. It is only in the spontaneity of the encounter that method can be applied. The timing and manner of applying culturally alert methods are choices that each counselor must make with each client. Competency as a culturally alert counselor requires not only method, but prior cultural self-awareness and knowledge of other cultures. In Smith et al.'s (2004) words,

> Practicing multiculturalism means internalizing the principles of multicultural competency and acting accordingly. . . . A book or class cannot provide for multicultural competence because multiculturalism is not just a set of facts, guidelines, or principles. It is a way of life. (p. 15)

It also demands a set of attitudes. One is openness to stories that are not one's own and a commitment to the work of reducing human suffering by challenging inequality and prejudice. Then, through alert action, counselors will be part of the solution.

References

American Psychiatric Association. (2000). *Diagnostic and statistical manual of mental disorders* (4th ed., Text rev.). Washington, DC: Author.

Ancis, J. R. (2004a). Culturally responsive interventions. In J. R. Ancis (Ed.), *Culturally responsive interventions: Innovative approaches to working with diverse populations* (pp. 213–222). New York: Brunner-Routledge.

Ancis, J. R. (2004b). Culturally responsive practice. In J. R. Ancis (Ed.), *Culturally responsive interventions: Innovative approaches to working with diverse populations* (pp. 3–21). New York: Brunner-Routledge.

Atkinson, D., & Israel, T. (2003). The future of multicultural counseling competence. In D. B. Pope-Davis, H. L. K. Coleman, W. M. Liu, & R. L. Topoek (Eds.), *Handbook of multicultural competencies in counseling and psychology* (pp. 591–606). Thousand Oaks, CA: Sage.

Belenky, M., Clinchy, B., Goldberger, N., & Tarule, J. (1986). *Women's ways of knowing: The development of self, voice, and mind*. New York: Basic Books.

Bojuwoye, O. (2005). Traditional healing practices in southern Africa. In R. Moodley & W. West (Eds.), *Integrating traditional healing practices into counseling and psychotherapy* (pp. 61–72). Thousand Oaks, CA: Sage.

Bolles, R. N. (2006). *What color is your parachute workbook*. Berkeley, CA: Ten Speed Press.

Constantine, M. G. (2006). Institutional racism against African Americans: Physical and mental health implications. In M. G. Constantine & D. W. Sue (Eds.), *Addressing racism: Facilitating cultural competence in mental health and educational settings* (pp. 33–41). Hoboken, NJ: Wiley.

Constantine, M. G., Myers, L. J., Kindaichi, M., & Moore, J. L., III. (2004). Exploring indigenous mental health practices: The roles of healers and helpers in promoting well-being in people of color. *Counseling and Values, 48*, 110–125.

Corey, G. (1996). Theoretical implications of MCT theory. In D. W. Sue, A. E. Ivey, & P. B. Pedersen (Eds.), *A theory of multicultural counseling and therapy* (pp. 99–111). Pacific Grove, CA: Brooks/Cole.

D'Andrea, M. (2000). Postmodernism, constructivism, and multiculturalism: Three forces reshaping and expanding our thoughts about counseling. *Journal of Mental Health Counseling, 22*, 1–16.

D'Andrea, M. (2006). In liberty and justice for all: A comprehensive approach to ameliorating the complex problems of white racism and white superiority in the United States. In M. G. Constantine & D. W. Sue (Eds.), *Addressing racism: Facilitating cultural competence in mental health and educational settings* (pp. 251–270). Hoboken, NJ: Wiley.

Davidson, M. M., Yakushka, O. F., & Sanford-Martens, T. C. (2004). Racial and ethnic minority clients' utilization of a university counseling center: An archival study. *Journal of Multicultural Counseling and Development, 32*, 259–271.

Davies, D., & Neal, C. (2003). *Pink therapy: A guide for counselors and therapists working with lesbian, gay, and bisexual clients.* Philadelphia: Open University Press.

Day-Vines, N., Patton, J. M., & Baytops, J. L. (2003). Counseling African American adolescents: The impact of race, culture, and middle class status. *Professional School Counseling, 7*, 40–51.

Day-Vines, N., Woods, S., Grothaus, T., Holman, A., Douglas, M., Dotson-Blake, K., et al. (in press). Broaching the issues of race and culture in the counseling process. *Journal of Counseling and Development.*

Deutsch, C. P. (1967). Minority groups and class status as related to social and personality factors in scholastic achievement. In M. Deutsch et al. (Eds.), *The disadvantaged child* (pp. 89–131). New York: Basic Books.

Draguns, J. G. (2002). Universal and cultural aspects of counseling and psychotherapy. In P. Pedersen, J. Draguns, W. Lonner, & J. E. Trimble (Eds.), *Counseling across cultures* (5th ed., pp. 29–50). Thousand Oaks, CA: Sage.

Dunn, A. B. (2000). *Cultural/gender genogram assignment.* Retrieved October 25, 2006, from http://pirate.shu.edu/~dunnadri/CPSY7615.html

Fuertes, J. N., & Gretchen, D. (2001). Emerging theories of multicultural counseling. In J. G. Ponterotto, J. M. Casas, L. A. Suzuki, & C. M. Alexander (Eds.), *Handbook of multicultural counseling* (2nd ed., pp. 509–541). Thousand Oaks, CA: Sage.

Garrett, J. T., & Garrett, M. T. (2002). *The Cherokee full circle: A practical guide to ceremonies and traditions.* Rochester, VT: Bear & Co.

Garrett, M. T., Garrett, J. T., Torres-Rivera, E., Wilbur, M., & Roberts-Wilbur, J. (2005). Laughing it up: Native American humor as a spiritual tradition. *Journal of Multicultural Counseling and Development, 33*, 194–204.

Gilligan, C. (1982). *In a different voice: Psychological theory and women's development.* Cambridge, MA: Harvard University Press.

Gonzalez-Chevez, L. (2005). Latin American healers and healing. In R. Moodley & W. West (Eds.), *Integrating traditional healing practices into counseling and psychotherapy* (pp. 85–99). Thousand Oaks, CA: Sage.

Griffin, P. (2005). *Becoming an ally.* Retrieved April 17, 2005, from http://www.eiu.edu/~safezone/becoming_an_ally.htm

Hanjorgiris, W. F., & O'Neill, J. H. (2006). Counseling people with disabilities: A sociocultural minority perspective. In C. C. Lee (Ed.), *Multicultural issues in counseling: New approaches to diversity* (3rd ed., pp. 321–342). Alexandria, VA: American Counseling Association.

Hardy, K. V., & Laszloffy, T. A. (1995). The cultural genogram: Key to training culturally competent family therapists. *Journal of Marital & Family Therapy, 21*, 227–237.

Harper, F. D., & Stone, W. O. (2003). Transcendent counseling: An existential, cognitive-behavioral theory. In F. D. Harper & J. McFadden (Eds.), *Culture and counseling: New approaches* (pp. 233–251). Boston: Allyn & Bacon.

Hays, D. G., Chang, C. Y., & Dean, J. K. (2007). Addressing privilege and oppression in counselor training and practice: A qualitative analysis. *Journal of Counseling and Development, 85,* 317–324.

Herlihy, B., & Watson, Z. E. (2003). Ethical issues and multicultural competence in counseling. In F. D. Harper & J. McFadden (Eds.), *Culture and counseling: New approaches* (pp. 363–378). Boston: Allyn & Bacon.

Holcomb-McCoy, C. (2005). Ethnic identity development in early adolescence: Implications and recommendations for middle school counselors. *Professional School Counseling, 9,* 120–127.

Holland, J. L. (1990). *The self-directed search assessment booklet.* Odessa, FL: Psychological Assessment Resources.

Hunt, B., Matthews, C., Milsom, A., & Lammel, J. A. (2006). Lesbians with physical disabilities: A qualitative study of their experiences with counseling. *Journal of Counseling and Development, 84,* 163–173.

Ibrahim, F. A. (2003). Existential worldview counseling theory: Inception to applications. In F. D. Harper & J. McFadden (Eds.), *Cultural and counseling: New approaches* (pp. 196–208). Boston: Allyn & Bacon.

Inayat, Q. (2005). Islam, divinity, and spiritual healing. In R. Moodley & W. West (Eds.), *Integrating traditional healing practices into counseling and psychotherapy* (pp. 159–169). Thousand Oaks, CA: Sage.

Ivey, A. E. (1995). Psychotherapy as liberation. In J. G. Ponterotto, J. M. Casas, L. A. Suzuki, & C. M. Alexander (Eds.), *Handbook of multicultural counseling* (pp. 53–72). Thousand Oaks, CA: Sage.

Ivey, A. E., D'Andrea, M., Ivey, M. B., & Simek-Morgan, L. (2002). *Theories of counseling and psychotherapy: A multicultural perspective.* Boston: Allyn & Bacon.

Ivey, A. E., & Ivey, M. B. (2007). *Intentional interviewing and counseling.* Belmont, CA: Thomson Brooks/Cole.

Jackson, B. W., & Holvino, E. (1988). Developing multicultural organizations. *Journal of Religion and the Applied Behavioral Sciences, 9,* 14–19.

Jucket, G. (2005). Cross-cultural medicine. *American Family Physician, 72*(11), 2267–2275.

Kegan, R. (1982). *The evolving self: Problem and process in human development.* Cambridge, MA: Harvard University Press.

Kim, Y. S. E. (2005). Guidelines and strategies for cross-cultural counseling with Korean American clients. *Journal of Multicultural Counseling and Development, 33,* 217–231.

Kincade, E. A., & Evans, K. M. (1996). Counseling theories, process, and interventions within a multicultural framework. In J. L. DeLucia-Waak (Ed.), *Multicultural counseling competencies: Implications for training and practice* (pp. 89–113). Alexandria, VA: Association for Counselor Education and Supervision.

Kopta, S. M., Howard, K. I., Lowry, J. L., & Beutler, L. E. (1994). Patterns of symptomatic recovery in psychotherapy. *Journal of Consulting and Clinical Psychology, 62,* 1009–1016.

Kumar, M., Bhugra, D., & Singh, J. (2005). Southern Asian (Indian) traditional healing. In R. Moodley & W. West (Eds.), *Integrating traditional healing practices into counseling and psychotherapy* (pp. 112–121). Thousand Oaks, CA: Sage.

Lewis, J. (2003). The competent practice of multicultural counseling: Making it happen. In G. Roysircar, D. S. Sandhu, & V. E. Bibbins (Eds.), *Multicultural competencies: A guidebook of practices* (pp. 261–267). Alexandria, VA: Association for Multicultural Counseling and Development.

Liu, W. M., Hernandez, J., Mahmood, A., & Stinson, R. (2006). Linking poverty, classism, and racism in mental health: Overcoming barriers to multicultural competency. In M. G. Constantine & D. W. Sue (Eds.), *Addressing racism: Facilitating cultural competence in mental health and educational settings* (pp. 65–86). Hoboken, NJ: Wiley.

Marshall, R. (2005). Caribbean healers and healing. In R. Moodley & W. West (Eds.), *Integrating traditional healing practices into counseling and psychotherapy* (pp. 73–84). Thousand Oaks, CA: Sage.

Matsumoto, D. (1991). Cultural influences on facial expressions of emotion. *Southern Communication Journal, 56,* 128–137.

Matsumoto, D., & Juang, L. (2004). *Culture and psychology* (3rd ed.). Belmont, CA: Wadsworth/Thompson Learning.

McAuliffe, G. J., Grothaus, T., Wininger, A., & Corriveau, S. (2006). *Content analysis of the multicultural counseling intervention literature.* Unpublished paper, Old Dominion University, Norfolk, VA.

McFadden, J., & Banich, M. A. (2003). Using bibliotherapy in transcultural counseling. In F. D. Harper & J. McFadden (Eds.), *Cultural and counseling: New approaches* (pp. 285–295). Boston: Allyn & Bacon.

McGoldrick, M. (1998). Belonging and liberation: Finding a place called home. In M. McGoldrick (Ed.), *Re-visioning family therapy: Race, culture, and gender in clinical practice* (pp. 215–228). New York: Guilford Press.

McGoldrick, M. (2005). Irish families. In M. McGoldrick & J. Giordano (Eds.), *Ethnicity and family therapy* (pp. 595–615). New York: Guilford Press.

McGoldrick, M., & Giordano, J. (2005). *Ethnicity and family therapy.* New York: Guilford Press.

Middleton, R. A., Erguner-Tekinalp, B., & Petrova, E. (2005, October). *Clinical applications of racial identity development.* Presentation to the meeting of the Association for Counselor Education and Supervision, Pittsburgh, PA.

Miville, M. L., & Ferguson, A. D. (2006). Intersections of sexism and heterosexism with racism: Therapeutic implications. In M. G. Constantine & D. W. Sue (Eds.), *Addressing racism: Facilitating cultural competence in mental health and educational settings* (pp. 87–103). Hoboken, NJ: Wiley.

Montgomery, M., Marbley, A., Contreras, R., & Kurtines, W. M. (2000). Transforming diversity training in counselor education. In G. J. McAuliffe & K. P. Eriksen (Eds.), *Preparing counselors and therapists: Creating constructivist and developmental programs* (pp. 148–169). Alexandria, VA: Association for Counselor Education and Supervision.

Moodley, R., & West, W. (Eds.). (2005). *Integrating traditional healing practices into counseling and psychotherapy.* Thousand Oaks, CA: Sage.

Murphy, J. J. (1997). *Solution-focused counseling in middle and high schools.* Alexandria, VA: American Counseling Association.

Neukrug, E. (2002). *Skills and techniques for human service professionals: Counseling environment, helping skills, treatment issues.* Pacific Grove, CA: Brooks/Cole.

Olkin, R. (2004). Making research accessible to participants with disabilities. *Journal of Multicultural Counseling and Development, 32,* 332–343.

Paniagua, F. A. (2005). *Assessing and treating culturally diverse clients: A practical guide* (3rd ed.). Thousand Oaks, CA: Sage.

Pedersen, P. B. (2001). Multiculturalism as a generic approach to counseling. *Journal of Counseling and Development, 70,* 6–12.

Pedersen, P. B. (2003). "Walking the talk:" Simulations in multicultural training. In G. Roysircar, D. S. Sandhu, & V. E. Bibbins (Eds.), *Multicultural competencies: A guidebook of practices* (pp. 29–38). Alexandria, VA: Association for Multicultural Counseling and Development.

Pedersen, P. B. (2004). The multicultural context of mental health. In T. B. Smith (Ed.), *Practicing multiculturalism: Affirming diversity in counseling and psychology* (pp. 17–32). Boston: Pearson.

Pieterse, A. L., & Collins, N. M. (2004, February). *Active multicultural awareness and counselor training: A critique and extension of current approaches to competence.* Paper presented at the 21st Annual Winter Roundtable on Cultural Psychology and Education, New York.

Ponterotto, J. G., Utsey, S. O., & Pedersen, P. B. (2006). *Preventing prejudice: A guide for counselors, educators, and parents* (2nd ed.). Thousand Oaks, CA: Sage.

Rayle, A. D. (2005). Cross-gender interactions in middle school counselor-student working alliances: Challenges and recommendations. *Professional School Counseling, 9,* 152–155.

Rayle, A. D., Chee, C., & Sand, J. K. (2006). Honoring their way: Counseling American Indian women. *Journal of Multicultural Counseling and Development, 34,* 66–79.

Ridley, C. R., & Kleiner, A. J. (2003). Multicultural counseling competence. In D. B. Pope-Davis & H. L. K. Coleman (Eds.), *Handbook of multicultural competencies in counseling and psychotherapy* (pp. 3–20). Thousand Oaks, CA: Sage.

Rigazio-DiGilio, S. A., Ivey, A. E., Grady, L. T., & Kunkler-Peck, K. P. (2005). *Community genograms: Using individual, family, and cultural narratives with clients.* New York: Teachers College Press.

Robinson, T. L. (2005). *The convergence of race, ethnicity, and gender: Multiple identities in counseling* (2nd ed.). Upper Saddle River, NJ: Pearson.

Rodriguez, R. R., & Walls, N. E. (2000). Culturally educated questioning: Toward a skills-based approach in multicultural counselor training. *Applied & Preventive Psychology, 9,* 89–99.

Roysircar, G. (2006). Research in multicultural counseling: Client needs and counselor competencies. In C. C. Lee (Ed.), *Multicultural issues in counseling: New approaches to diversity* (3rd ed., pp. 369–387). Alexandria, VA: American Counseling Association.

Said, E. W. (1994). *Culture and imperialism.* New York: Vintage.

Samuda, R. J. (1998). *Psychological testing of American minorities.* Thousand Oaks, CA: Sage.

Sciarra, D., Chang, T., McLean, R., & Wong, D. (2005). White racial identity and attitudes towards people with disabilities. *Journal of Multicultural Counseling and Development, 33,* 232–242.

Semmler, P. L., & Williams, C. B. (2000). Narrative therapy: A storied context of multicultural counseling. *Journal of Multicultural Counseling and Development, 28,* 51–62.

Simcox, A. G., Nuijens, K. L., & Lee, C. C. (2006). School counselors and school psychologists: Collaborative partners in promoting culturally competent schools. *Professional School Counselor, 9,* 272–277.

Slattery, J. M. (2004). *Counseling diverse clients: Bringing context into therapy.* Belmont, CA: Thomson Brooks/Cole.

Smith, T. B., Richards, P. S., Granley, H. M., & Obiakor, F. (2004). Practicing multicul-turalism: An introduction. In T. B. Smith (Ed.), *Practicing multiculturalism: Affirming diversity in counseling and psychology* (pp. 3–16). Boston: Pearson.

So, J. K. (2005). Traditional and cultural healing among the Chinese. In R. Moodley & W. West (Eds.), *Integrating traditional healing practices into counseling and psychotherapy* (pp. 100–111). Thousand Oaks, CA: Sage.

Stone, C., & Dahir, C. (2006). *The transformed school counselor*. Boston: Lahaska Press.

Sue, D. W., Arredondo, P., & McDavis, R. J. (1992). Multicultural counseling competen-cies and standards: A call to the profession. *Journal of Counseling and Development, 70*, 477–486.

Sue, D. W., & Sue, D. (2003). *Counseling the culturally diverse*. New York: Wiley.

Sue, S., & Zane, N. (1987). The role of culture and cultural techniques in psychotherapy: A critique and reformulation. *American Psychologist, 42*, 37–45.

Tannen, D. (1990). *You just don't understand: Women and men in conversation*. New York: William Morrow.

Thobaben, M. (2004). Alternative approaches to mental health care. *Home Health Care Management and Practice, 16*, 528–530.

Torres-Rivera, E., Garrett, M. T., & Crutchfield, L. B. (2004). Multicultural interventions in groups: The use of indigenous methods. In J. L. DeLucia-Waack, D. Gerrity, C. Kalodner, & M. Riva (Eds.), *Handbook of group counseling and psychotherapy* (pp. 295–306). Thousand Oaks, CA: Sage.

Tseng, W. S. (1999). Culture and psychotherapy: Review and practical guidelines. *Transcultural Psychiatry, 36*(2), 131–179.

Utsey, S. O., Bolden, M. A., & Brown, A. L. (2001). Visions of revolution from the spirit of Frantz Fanon: A psychology of liberation for counseling African Americans confronting societal racism and oppression. In J. G. Ponterotto, J. M. Casas, L. A. Suzuki, & C. M. Alexander (Eds.), *Handbook of multicultural counseling* (2nd ed., pp. 311–336). Thousand Oaks, CA: Sage.

Vera, E. M., Buhin, L., & Shin, R. Q. (2006). The pursuit of social justice and the elimi-nation of racism. In M. G. Constantine & D. W. Sue (Eds.), *Addressing racism: Facilitating cultural competence in mental health and educational settings* (pp. 271–287). Hoboken, NJ: Wiley.

Vereen, L. G., Butler, S. K., Williams, F. C., Darg, J. A., & Downing, T. K. E. (2006). The use of humor when counseling African American college students. *Journal of Counseling & Development, 84*, 10–15.

Vontress, C. E. (2005). Animism. In R. Moodley & W. West (Eds.), *Integrating traditional healing practices into counseling and psychotherapy* (pp. 124–137). Thousand Oaks, CA: Sage.

Wallace, B. C. (2006). Healing collective wounds from racism: The community forum model. In M. G. Constantine & D. W. Sue (Eds.), *Addressing racism: Facilitating cul-tural competence in mental health and educational settings* (pp. 105–123). Hoboken, NJ: Wiley.

Washington, J., & Evans, N. J. (2000). Becoming an ally. In M. Adams, W. Blumenfeld, R. Casteneda, H. Hackman, M. Peters, & X. Zuniga (Eds.), *Readings for diversity and social justice* (pp. 312–318). New York: Routledge.

Wehrly, B. (1995). *Pathways to multicultural counseling competence: A developmental jour-ney*. Pacific Grove, CA: Brooks/Cole.

Wehrly, B. (2003). Breaking barriers for multiracial individuals and families. In F. D. Harper & J. McFadden (Eds.), *Cultural and counseling: New approaches* (pp. 313–323). Boston: Allyn & Bacon.

Westermeyer, J. (1987). Cultural factors in clinical assessment. *Journal of Consulting and Clinical Psychology, 55,* 471–478.

White, M., & Epston, D. (1990). *Narrative means to therapeutic ends.* New York: W. W. Norton.

Yeh, C. J., Hunter, C. D., Madan-Behel, A., Chiang, L., & Arora, A. K. (2004). Indigenous and interdependent perspectives of healing: Implications for counseling and research. *Journal of Counseling and Development, 82,* 410–419.

Zang, N., & Dixon, D. N. (2001). Multiculturally responsive counseling: Effect on Asian students' rating of counselors. *Journal of Multicultural Counseling and Development, 29,* 253–262.

Appendix A

Multicultural Counseling Competencies

A Conceptual Framework

I. Counselor Awareness of
Own Assumptions, Values, and Biases

A. BELIEFS AND ATTITUDES

- Culturally skilled counselors have moved from being culturally unaware to being aware and sensitive to their own cultural heritage and to valuing and respecting differences.

- Culturally skilled counselors are aware of how their own cultural background and experiences, attitudes, and values and biases influence psychological processes.

- Culturally skilled counselors are able to recognize the limits of their competencies and expertise.

- Culturally skilled counselors are comfortable with differences that exist between themselves and clients in terms of race, ethnicity, culture, and beliefs.

B. KNOWLEDGE

- Culturally skilled counselors have specific knowledge about their own racial and cultural heritage and how it personally and professionally affects their definitions and biases of normality-abnormality and the process of counseling.

- Culturally skilled counselors possess knowledge and understanding about how oppression, racism, discrimination, and stereotyping affect them personally and in their work. This allows them to acknowledge their own racist attitudes, beliefs, and feelings. Although this standard applies to all groups, for white counselors it may mean that they understand how they may have directly or indirectly benefited from individual, institutional, and cultural racism (white identity development models).

- Culturally skilled counselors possess knowledge about their social impact upon others. They are knowledgeable about communication style differences, how their style may clash or facilitate the counseling process with minority clients, and how to anticipate the impact it may have on others.

C. SKILLS

- Culturally skilled counselors seek out educational, consultative, and training experiences to enrich their understanding and effectiveness in working with culturally different populations. Able to recognize the limits of their competencies, they (a) seek consultation, (b) seek further training or education, (c) refer out to more qualified individuals or resources, or (d) engage in a combination of these.

- Culturally skilled counselors are constantly seeking to understand themselves as racial and cultural beings and are actively seeking a nonracist identity.

II. Understanding the Worldview of the Culturally Different Client

A. BELIEFS AND ATTITUDES

- Culturally skilled counselors are aware of their negative emotional reactions toward other racial and ethnic groups that may prove detrimental to their clients in counseling. They are willing to contrast their own beliefs and attitudes with those of their culturally different clients in a nonjudgmental fashion.

- Culturally skilled counselors are aware of their stereotypes and preconceived notions that they may hold toward other racial and ethnic minority groups.

B. KNOWLEDGE

- Culturally skilled counselors possess specific knowledge and information about the particular group that they are working with. They are aware of the life experiences, cultural heritage, and historical background of their culturally different clients. This particular competency is strongly linked to the minority identity development models available in the literature.

- Culturally skilled counselors understand how race, culture, ethnicity, and so forth may affect personality formation, vocational choices, manifestation of psychological disorders, help-seeking behavior, and the appropriateness or inappropriateness of counseling approaches.

- Culturally skilled counselors understand and have knowledge about sociopolitical influences that impinge upon the life of racial and ethnic minorities. Immigration issues, poverty, racism, stereotyping, and powerlessness all leave major scars that may influence the counseling process.

C. SKILLS

- Culturally skilled counselors should familiarize themselves with relevant research and the latest findings regarding mental health and mental disorders of various ethnic and racial groups. They should actively seek out educational experiences that enrich their knowledge, understanding, and cross-cultural skills.

- Culturally skilled counselors become actively involved with minority individuals outside the counseling setting (community events, social and political functions, celebrations, friendships, neighborhood groups, and so forth) so that their perspective of minorities is more than an academic or helping exercise.

III. Developing Appropriate Intervention Strategies and Techniques

A. ATTITUDES AND BELIEFS

- Culturally skilled counselors respect clients' religious and/or spiritual beliefs and values about physical and mental functioning.

- Culturally skilled counselors respect indigenous helping practices and respect minority intrinsic help-giving networks in the community.

- Culturally skilled counselors value bilingualism and do not view other languages as impediments to counseling (monolingualism may be the culprit).

B. KNOWLEDGE

- Culturally skilled counselors have a clear and explicit knowledge and understanding of the generic characteristics of counseling and therapy (culture bound, class bound, and monolingual) and how they may clash with the cultural values of various minority groups.

- Culturally skilled counselors are aware of institutional barriers that prevent minorities from using mental health services.

- Culturally skilled counselors have knowledge of the potential bias in assessment instruments and keep in mind the cultural and linguistic characteristics of the clients when using procedures and interpreting findings.

- Culturally skilled counselors have knowledge of minority family structures, hierarchies, values, and beliefs. They are knowledgeable about the community characteristics and the resources in the community as well as the family.

- Culturally skilled counselors should be aware of relevant discriminatory practices at the social and community level that may be affecting the psychological welfare of the population being served.

C. SKILLS

- Culturally skilled counselors are able to engage in a variety of verbal and nonverbal helping responses. They are able to send and receive both verbal and nonverbal messages accurately and appropriately. They are not tied down to only one method or approach to helping but recognize that helping styles and approaches may be culture bound. When they sense that their helping style is limited and potentially inappropriate, they can anticipate and ameliorate its negative impact.

- Culturally skilled counselors are able to exercise institutional intervention skills on behalf of their clients. They can help clients determine whether a "problem" stems from racism or bias in others (the concept of healthy paranoia) so that clients do not inappropriately blame themselves.

- Culturally skilled counselors are not averse to consulting with traditional healers or religious and spiritual leaders and practitioners in the treatment of culturally different clients, when appropriate.

- Culturally skilled counselors take responsibility for interacting in the language requested by the client; this may mean appropriate referral to outside resources. A serious problem arises when the linguistic skills of the counselor do not match the language of the client. This being the case, counselors should (a) seek a translator with cultural knowledge and appropriate professional background or (b) refer to a knowledgeable and competent bilingual counselor.

- Culturally skilled counselors have training and expertise in the use of traditional assessment and testing instruments. They not only understand the technical aspects of the instruments but are aware of the cultural limitations. This allows them to use test instruments for the welfare of diverse clients.

- Culturally skilled counselors should attend to as well as work to eliminate biases, prejudices, and discriminatory practices. They should be cognizant of sociopolitical contexts in conducting evaluations and providing interventions and should develop sensitivity to issues of oppression, sexism, and racism.

- Culturally skilled counselors take responsibility for educating their clients about the processes of psychological intervention, such as goals, expectations, legal rights, and the counselor's orientation.

SOURCE: From Sue, Derald Wing; Arredondo, Patricia; & McDavis, Roderick J. (1992). Multicultural Counseling Competencies: A Call to the Profession. *Journal of Counseling and Development, 70,* 481–483. © 1992 The American Counseling Association. Reprinted with permission. No further reproduction authorized without written permission from the American Counseling Association.

Appendix B

Advocacy Competencies

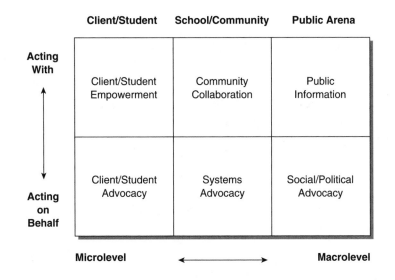

Figure 1 Advocacy Competency Domains

I. Client/Student Empowerment

An advocacy orientation involves not only systems change interventions but also the implementation of empowerment strategies in direct counseling. Advocacy-oriented counselors recognize the impact of social, political, economic, and cultural factors on human development. They also help their clients and students understand their own lives in context. This lays the groundwork for self-advocacy.

EMPOWERMENT COUNSELOR COMPETENCIES

In direct interventions, the counselor is able to

- Identify strengths and resources of clients and students;
- Identify the social, political, economic, and cultural factors that affect the client/student;
- Recognize the signs indicating that an individual's behaviors and concerns reflect responses to systemic or internalized oppression;
- At an appropriate development level, help the individual identify the external barriers that affect his or her development;
- Train students and clients in self-advocacy skills;
- Help students and clients develop self-advocacy action plans;
- Assist students and clients in carrying out action plans.

II. Client/Student Advocacy

When counselors become aware of external factors that act as barriers to an individual's development, they may choose to respond through advocacy. The client/student advocate role is especially significant when individuals or vulnerable groups lack access to needed services.

CLIENT/STUDENT ADVOCACY COUNSELOR COMPETENCIES

In environmental interventions on behalf of clients and students, the counselor is able to

- Negotiate relevant services and education systems on behalf of clients and students;
- Help clients and students gain access to needed resources;
- Identify barriers to the well-being of vulnerable individuals and groups;
- Develop an initial plan of action for confronting these barriers;
- Identify potential allies for confronting the barriers;
- Carry out the plan of action.

III. Community Collaboration

Their ongoing work with people gives counselors a unique awareness of recurring themes. Counselors are often among the first to become aware of specific difficulties in the environment. Advocacy-oriented counselors often choose to respond to such challenges by alerting existing organizations that are already working for change and that might have an interest in the issue at hand. In these situations, the counselor's primary role is as an ally. Counselors can also be helpful to organizations by making available to them our particular skills: interpersonal relations, communications, training, and research.

COMMUNITY COLLABORATION COUNSELOR COMPETENCIES

- Identify environmental factors that impinge upon students' and clients' development.
- Alert community or school groups with common concerns related to the issue.
- Develop alliances with groups working for change.
- Use effective listening skills to gain understanding of the group's goals.
- Identify the strengths and resources that the group members bring to the process of systemic change.
- Communicate recognition of and respect for these strengths and resources.
- Identify and offer the skills that the counselor can bring to the collaboration.
- Assess the effect of counselor's interaction with the community.

IV. Systems Advocacy

When counselors identify systemic factors that act as barriers to their students' or clients' development, they often wish that they could change the environment and prevent some of the problems that they see every day.

Regardless of the specific target of change, the processes for altering the status quo have common qualities. Change is a process that requires vision, persistence, leadership, collaboration, systems analysis, and strong data. In many situations, a counselor is the right person to take leadership.

SYSTEMS ADVOCACY COUNSELOR COMPETENCIES

In exerting systems-change leadership at the school or community level, the advocacy-oriented counselor is able to

- Identify environmental factors impinging on students' or clients' development;
- Provide and interpret data to show the urgency for change;
- In collaboration with other stakeholders, develop a vision to guide change;
- Analyze the sources of political power and social influence within the system;

- Develop a step-by-step plan for implementing the change process;
- Develop a plan for dealing with probable responses to change;
- Recognize and deal with resistance;
- Assess the effect of counselor's advocacy efforts on the system and constituents.

V. Public Information

Across settings, specialties, and theoretical perspectives, professional counselors share knowledge of human development and expertise in communication.

These qualities make it possible for advocacy-oriented counselors to awaken the general public to macro-systemic issues regarding human dignity

PUBLIC INFORMATION COUNSELOR COMPETENCIES

In informing the public about the role of environmental factors in human development, the advocacy-oriented counselor is able to

- Recognize the impact of oppression and other barriers to healthy development;
- Identify environmental factors that are protective of healthy development;
- Prepare written and multimedia materials that provide clear explanations of the role of specific environmental factors in human development;
- Communicate information in ways that are ethical and appropriate for the target population;
- Disseminate information through a variety of media;
- Identify and collaborate with other professionals who are involved in disseminating public information;
- Assess the influence of public information efforts undertaken by the counselor.

VI. Social/Political Advocacy

Counselors regularly act as change agents in the systems that affect their own students and clients most directly. This experience often leads toward the recognition that some of the concerns they have addressed affected people in a much larger arena.

When this happens, counselors use their skills to carry out social/political advocacy.

SOCIAL/POLITICAL ADVOCACY COUNSELOR COMPETENCIES

In influencing public policy in a large, public arena, the advocacy-oriented counselor is able to

- Distinguish those problems that can best be resolved through social/political action;
- Identify the appropriate mechanisms and avenues for addressing these problems;
- Seek out and join with potential allies;
- Support existing alliances for change;
- With allies, prepare convincing data and rationales for change;
- With allies, lobby legislators and other policy makers;
- Maintain open dialogue with communities and clients to ensure that the social/political advocacy is consistent with the initial goals.

SOURCE: Lewis, J., Arnold, M. S., House, R., & Toporek, R. (2002). *Advocacy competencies.* Retrieved May 18, 2007, from http://www.counseling.org/Counselors/. © 2002 The American Counseling Association. Reprinted with permission. No further reproduction authorized without written permission from the American Counseling Association.

Index

About the Editor

Garrett McAuliffe has worked as a counselor educator, counselor, and school teacher for over 35 years. In his professional life, he has worked toward ensuring equity in society through his counseling, teaching, and writing. He is committed to empowering learners and has taught in the public schools of New York City and counseled at the community college and university levels in Massachusetts, where he also served as the director of Learning Assistance Programs at Greenfield Community College. Since 1988, he has been a counselor educator at Old Dominion University in Norfolk, Virginia. His work has been dedicated to improving the lives of all learners. He grew up in a tightly connected extended family in a multiethnic neighborhood in New York City, and is the grandchild of Irish immigrants. He received his Bachelor of Arts magna cum laude in English literature, with Highest Honors, from Queens College of the City University of New York, in 1971. He was named to Phi Beta Kappa for his academic performance at Queens College in 1971. He took from his undergraduate education both a love of ideas and words and a desire to turn ideas into social and personal change actions. Toward that end, he pursued his graduate counseling studies at the University at Albany and at the University of Massachusetts at Amherst, receiving his doctorate in 1985. His dissertation was named the Outstanding Dissertation in the Nation for that year. In his time at Old Dominion University, he has produced five books, over 40 articles, over 25 book chapters, and two training videos. His great love continues to be teaching, in all of its forms.

About the Contributors

Mona Danner is a sociologist. She specializes in criminological, sociological, and feminist theory; cross-national research; social inequality (gender, race/ethnicity, class, and nation); and criminal justice policy. She received her Ph.D. from the American University in 1993 and is currently associate professor at Old Dominion University.

Edward A. Delgado-Romero received his doctorate in counseling psychology from the University of Notre Dame in 1997. He is currently an associate professor, training director, and program chair of the counseling psychology program at the University of Georgia. His primary research interests are multicultural psychology, race and racism in the psychotherapy process, and Latino/Latina psychology. He is a fellow of APA Division 45 and a founding member of the National Latina/Latino Psychological Association.

Lynn Doyle is currently an associate professor in the Department of Educational Leadership and Counseling at Old Dominion University in Norfolk, Virginia. She received her doctorate in administrative leadership and urban education from the University of Wisconsin, Milwaukee. She has served as a speech and language pathologist and special education administrator in a variety of educational settings. Her research interests include equity and social justice with diverse populations, pupil personnel services, special education administration, and leadership and its relationship to learning and teaching.

Karen Eriksen received her doctorate from George Mason University and her master's degree from California State University, Fullerton. She practiced as a licensed professional counselor and marriage and family counselor in Virginia. She has specialties in family therapy, addictions, survivors of sexual abuse, and the intersection of spirituality and counseling. She has authored or co-edited five books on the topics of counselor advocacy, counselor education, and diagnosis. Her research areas are counselor preparation, constructive development, multiculturalism, and spirituality. She has been active in leadership of several state and national professional associations.

Kathy M. Evans received her doctorate in counseling psychology from Pennsylvania State University and is an associate professor of counselor education at the University of South Carolina. Her research, publications, and national presentations address issues important to African Americans, multicultural and feminist issues, and multicultural career development. She has been active in many professional counseling organizations including serving as Secretary to the Chi Sigma Iota Counseling, Academic and Professional Honor Society International for the 2004–2006 term. She has also been President-Elect of the Southern Association for Counselor Education and Supervision.

Nallely Galván is currently a doctoral student in the Educational Counseling Psychology program at the University of Illinois at Urbana-Champaign. She also works for the Mental Health Center of Champaign County as a bilingual counselor (Spanish-English) and conducts therapy primarily in Spanish. She holds an educational specialist degree and a master's degree in counseling psychology from Indiana University-Bloomington. Her research interests include multicultural issues, women's health, the mental health needs of immigrant Latinas/Latinos, and violence against women.

Michael Tlanusta Garrett, Eastern Band of the Cherokee Nation, is associate professor in the Department of Counselor Education at the University of Florida. He holds a doctorate in counseling and counselor education and an M.Ed. in counseling and development from the University of North Carolina at Greensboro. He is author and coauthor of more than 50 articles and chapters dealing with multiculturalism, group work, wellness and spirituality, school counseling, working with youth, and counseling Native Americans. His specialized focus has been in advancing professional understanding of working with Native people.

Rebecca George is a doctoral candidate in the Counselor Education Program at the University of South Carolina. She holds an M.A. in rehabilitation counseling from South Carolina State University. Her research interests include multiculturalism, diversity, women's issues, and mentoring.

Patricia Goodspeed Grant is an assistant professor in the Department of Counselor Education at the State University of New York College at Brockport. She holds a doctorate in counseling and human development from the University of Rochester and an M.S. in organizational psychology from Springfield College in Massachusetts. She specializes in qualitative research methodologies. Her research and writing interests center on the meaning of work and unemployment, the loss of relationships through death or divorce, issues related to social class and counseling, and the emotional aspects of obesity and weight loss.

Edwin Gómez is an associate professor in the Department of Exercise Science, Sport, Physical Education and Recreation at Old Dominion University. He earned his doctorate from Michigan State University in parks, recreation, tourism and urban studies. His M.S. was from Rochester Institute of Technology in hospitality and travel management. His research interests include urban recreation issues, sense of community in neighborhoods, and recreation issues related to ethnic group inclusion. His most recent research looks at the relationship between acculturation processes as they relate to bilingualism, cultural identity, and use of public spaces, such as urban parks.

Tim Grothaus is an assistant professor and coordinator of the school counseling specialty area in the Department of Educational Leadership and Counseling at Old Dominion University. He received a doctorate in counselor education from the College of William & Mary after serving over 20 years as a school counselor, teacher, therapist, coordinator of a youth leadership development program, and youth minister. His primary research interests include professional development of school counselors, multicultural competence, and supervision.

Mary H. Guindon is associate professor and chair of the Department of Counseling and Human Services at Johns Hopkins University. She holds a Ph.D. in counselor education from the University of Virginia. Her areas of expertise are mental health and career management, adult transitions, relationship building, self-esteem, and occupational stress.

Julie Hakim-Larson is currently an associate professor of child clinical psychology at the University of Windsor in Ontario. She received her Ph.D. in life-span developmental psychology from Wayne State University in Detroit, Michigan, and received postdoctoral training in child clinical psychology. She is a licensed psychologist in Michigan and Ontario. Her research interests include emotion and families and mental health and culture. In addition to studies involving the general population, since 1997 she has been involved in collaborative projects involving Arab Americans in Southeastern Michigan, which has the largest concentration of immigrants from the Middle East in North America.

Melissa R. Hunter is a mental health counselor in private practice at Southeast Indiana Mental Health Professionals in North Vernon, Indiana. She holds an educational specialist degree and a master's degree in counseling psychology from Indiana University–Bloomington. Her research interests include multicultural/ acculturation issues surrounding the mental health needs of immigrants. She provides individual and family counseling as well as group counseling for specific individuals including domestic violence, alcohol/substance abuse, and court-ordered probationers.

Shelley A. Jackson is an associate professor at Texas Woman's University in the Department of Family Sciences. Her teaching and research interests include spirituality and counseling, school counseling, and the use of expressive arts in counseling, particularly with young children. She is a registered play therapist supervisor and has maintained a private play therapy practice in addition to teaching. Her most memorable spiritual and counseling experience occurred while swimming with dolphins in Key Largo.

Bryan S. K. Kim is an associate professor in the Department of Psychology at the University of Hawai'i at Hilo. He holds a doctorate in counseling/clinical/school psychology (counseling psychology emphasis) from the University of California at Santa Barbara. His research focuses on multicultural counseling process and outcome, the measurement of cultural constructs, and counselor education and supervision. He serves on several editorial boards of counseling-related journals and was a recipient of the 2006 Fritz and Linn Kuder Early Career Scientist/Practitioner Award from the Society of Counseling Psychology (Division 17 of APA).

Karen L. Mackie is an assistant professor (clinical) in the Department of Counseling and Human Development at the University of Rochester. She holds a doctorate in counseling and human development from the University of Rochester and is a licensed mental health counselor and permanently certified school counselor in New York. Her scholarly and research interests include feminist and cultural perspectives on the work of counselors and counseling; postmodern understandings and approaches to work with families over the life-course; creativity and improvisation in the counselor education process; and the impact of globalization, multinational identity, and cultural plurality on counseling theories and practices.

Jayamala (Mala) Madathil is an assistant professor in the Department of Counseling at Sonoma State University in California, where she teaches in the community counseling/MFT track. She received her doctorate in counseling and counselor education from the University of North Carolina at Greensboro. She has experience working in community mental health agencies, particularly with children, adolescents, and families, on a wide variety of mental health concerns. Her research areas include multicultural counseling and working with families.

Sylvia Nassar-McMillan is currently an associate professor of counselor education at North Carolina State University. She earned her doctorate in counseling and counselor education from the University of North Carolina at Greensboro. She has served in a variety of community mental health settings. Her scholarship includes gender and multicultural issues, with a special focus on Arab Americans. She is a past board member of the National Board for Certified Counselors and currently serves as a member of the Census Information Center advisory board to the Arab American Institute and member of the North Carolina Board of Licensed Professional Counselors.

Lee J. Richmond is professor of education at Loyola College in Maryland, where she teaches counseling courses in the school counseling program and career counseling in both the school and the pastoral counseling programs. She received her Ph.D. from the University of Maryland and her M.Ed. from Johns Hopkins Univers ity. She is past president of the American Counseling Association, the National Career Development Association, and the Maryland Counseling Association. She received the 2002 Eminent Career Award of the National Career Development Association, its highest accolade. She is co-author of three books and author of numerous book chapters and articles in the areas of multicultural counseling, career counseling, and school counseling.

Daya Singh Sandhu is professor and former chairperson in the Department of Educational and Counseling Psychology at the University of Louisville. He received his doctorate in counselor education from Mississippi State University and has taught graduate courses in counseling and counseling psychology for the past 20 years. He has an interest in school counseling, multicultural counseling, neurolinguistic programming, and the role of spirituality in counseling and psychotherapy. In addition to more than 50 refereed journal articles, he has authored or edited 12 books and was recognized as one of the 12 pioneers in the field of multicultural counseling in the *Handbook of Multicultural Counseling* (2001).

David Paré is an associate professor of counseling in the Faculty of Education at the University of Ottawa and the director of the Glebe Institute, a center for constructive and collaborative practice. A psychologist and family therapist, his research focuses on collaborative therapeutic practice and the postmodern turn in family therapy and psychotherapy.

Yong S. Park is currently a doctoral student in the Counseling/Clinical/School Psychology Program at the University of California, Santa Barbara. He also serves as the co-chair of the Division of Students for the Asian American Psychological Association. His research interests revolve around the cultural and psychological aspects of providing professional services to Asian Americans. More specifically, he is interested in examining how relational expectations, family dynamics, and racism experiences affect the counseling process and outcome with Asian American clients.

Dawn M. Szymanski is an assistant professor in the Department of Psychology at the University of Tennessee–Knoxville. She holds a Ph.D. in counseling psychology from Georgia State University. Her research interests include feminist therapy and supervision; lesbian, gay, and bisexual issues; multicultural counseling; psychology of men and masculinity; scale construction; and research training.

Vasti Torres is associate professor of higher education and student affairs administration at Indiana University. Prior to joining the faculty, she served as associate vice provost and dean for enrollment and student services at Portland State University. She was the principal investigator for a multiyear grant investigating the choice to stay in college for Latino students. She has been honored as a Diamond Honoree and Emerging Scholar by the American College Personnel Association and Program Associate for the National Center for Policy in Higher Education. She holds a Ph.D. in student affairs administration from the University of Georgia.

Heather C. Trepal is an assistant professor in the Department of Counseling, Educational Psychology, Adult and Higher Education at the University of Texas at San Antonio. She holds a Ph.D. in counseling and human development from Kent State University. Her primary research interests include self-injurious behaviors, at-risk youth, women's issues in counseling, and the use of technology in counselor education and supervision.

Chet Weld is a licensed professional counselor at Renewal Centers in Tucson, Arizona. He counsels couples and individuals and specializes in faith-based counseling. He earned his master's degree at the University of Arizona in 1977 and his doctorate in counseling psychology at Argosy University in 2006. His primary interest is the integration of psychology with spirituality, and he recently completed research on client expectations of prayer when seeing Christian counselors.

Kelly L. Wester is an assistant professor in the Department of Counseling and Educational Development at the University of North Carolina at Greensboro. She holds a Ph.D. in counseling and human development and M.A. in criminal justice from Kent State University. Her primary research areas deal with self-injurious behaviors; research integrity and evidence-based practices; violent behaviors among youth; gender issues in counseling; and leadership, professional identity, and wellness in counseling.

Ali Wininger is a doctoral student in the counseling program at the University of North Carolina at Greensboro. She was formerly the director of school-based services for Seton Youth Shelters in Virginia Beach, Virginia, where she developed and ran groups for at-risk adolescents as well as doing individual crisis counseling in area schools. She received her master's degree in counseling from Old Dominion University. Her research interests include indigenous/multicultural forms of counseling, adolescents and self-injury, and solution-focused family counseling.